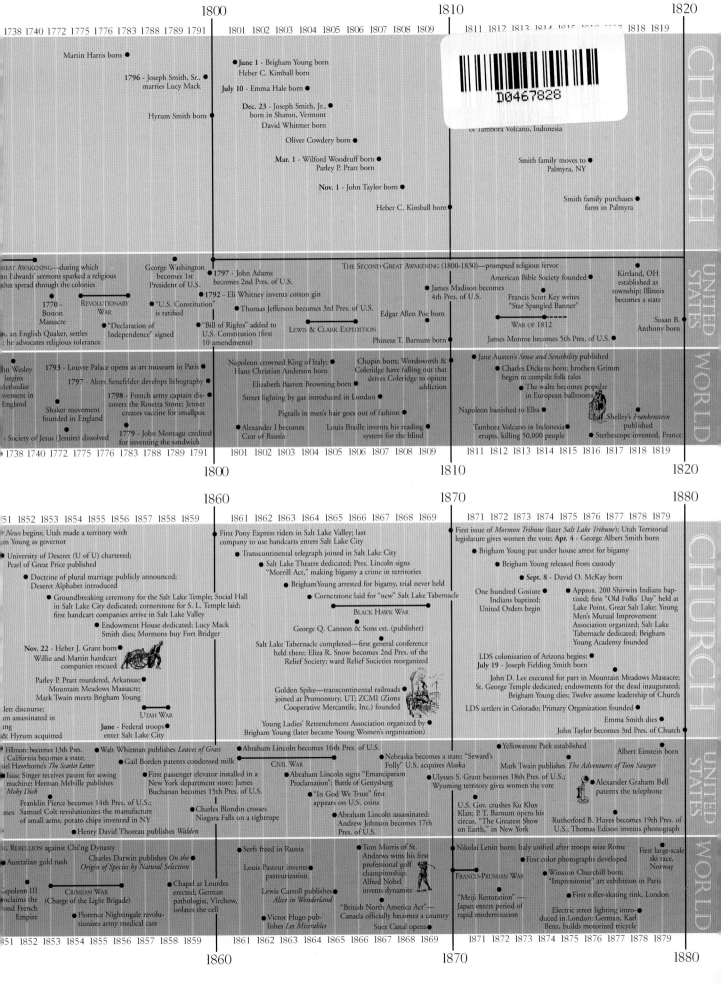

Top panel

Year markers: 1800 · 1810 · 1820

1738 1740 1772 1775 1776 1783 1788 1789 1791 | 1801 1802 1803 1804 1805 1806 1807 1808 1809 | 1811 1812 1813 1814 1815 1816 1817 1818 1819

CHURCH

- Martin Harris born ●
- 1796 - Joseph Smith, Sr., marries Lucy Mack ●
- Hyrum Smith born ●
- ● June 1 - Brigham Young born; Heber C. Kimball born
- **July 10** - Emma Hale born ●
- **Dec. 23** - Joseph Smith, Jr., ● born in Sharon, Vermont; David Whitmer born
- Oliver Cowdery born ●
- **Mar. 1** - Wilford Woodruff born ●; Parley P. Pratt born
- **Nov. 1** - John Taylor born ●
- Heber C. Kimball born ●
- of Tambora Volcano, Indonesia
- Smith family moves to ● Palmyra, NY
- Smith family purchases ● farm in Palmyra

UNITED STATES

- GREAT AWAKENING—during which an Edwards' sermons sparked a religious that spread through the colonies
- George Washington ● becomes 1st President of U.S.
- 1797 - John Adams becomes 2nd Pres. of U.S.
- THE SECOND GREAT AWAKENING (1800-1830)—prompted religious fervor
- American Bible Society founded ●
- Kirtland, OH ● established as township; Illinois becomes a state
- 1770 - Boston Massacre
- REVOLUTIONARY WAR
- ● "U.S. Constitution" is ratified
- 1792 - Eli Whitney invents cotton gin ●
- James Madison becomes ● 4th Pres. of U.S.
- Francis Scott Key writes "Star Spangled Banner"
- n, an English Quaker, settles he advocates religious tolerance
- "Declaration of Independence" signed
- "Bill of Rights" added to ● U.S. Constitution (first 10 amendments)
- Thomas Jefferson becomes 3rd Pres. of U.S. ●
- LEWIS & CLARK EXPEDITION
- Edgar Allen Poe born ●
- WAR OF 1812
- Susan B. Anthony born
- Phineas T. Barnum born ●
- James Monroe becomes 5th Pres. of U.S. ●

WORLD

- hn Wesley begins Methodist vement in England
- 1793 - Louvre Palace opens as art museum in Paris ●
- 1797 - Aloys Senefelder develops lithography ●
- Napoleon crowned King of Italy; ● Hans Christian Anderson born
- Elizabeth Barrett Browning born ●
- Chopin born; Wordsworth & ● Coleridge have falling out that drives Coleridge to opium addiction
- ● Jane Austen's *Sense and Sensibility* published
- ● Charles Dickens born; brothers Grimm begin to compile folk tales
- Shaker movement founded in England
- 1798 - French army captain discovers the Rosetta Stone; Jenner creates vaccine for smallpox ●
- Street lighting by gas introduced in London ●
- ● The waltz becomes popular in European ballrooms
- Pigtails in men's hair goes out of fashion
- Napoleon banished to Elba ●
- Shelley's *Frankenstein* published
- Society of Jesus (Jesuits) dissolved
- 1779 - John Montagu credited for inventing the sandwich
- ● Alexander I becomes Czar of Russia
- Louis Braille invents his reading ● system for the blind
- Tambora Volcano in Indonesia ● erupts, killing 50,000 people
- ● Stethoscope invented, France

1738 1740 1772 1775 1776 1783 1788 1789 1791 | 1801 1802 1803 1804 1805 1806 1807 1808 1809 | 1811 1812 1813 1814 1815 1816 1817 1818 1819

Year markers: 1800 · 1810 · 1820

Bottom panel

Year markers: 1860 · 1870 · 1880

51 1852 1853 1854 1855 1856 1857 1858 1859 | 1861 1862 1863 1864 1865 1866 1867 1868 1869 | 1871 1872 1873 1874 1875 1876 1877 1878 1879

CHURCH

- *News* begins; Utah made a territory with m Young as governor
- ● University of Deseret (U of U) chartered; Pearl of Great Price published
- ● Doctrine of plural marriage publicly announced; Deseret Alphabet introduced
- ● Groundbreaking ceremony for the Salt Lake Temple; Social Hall in Salt Lake City dedicated; cornerstone for S. L. Temple laid; first handcart companies arrive in Salt Lake Valley
- ● Endowment House dedicated; Lucy Mack Smith dies; Mormons buy Fort Bridger
- **Nov. 22** - Heber J. Grant born ●; Willie and Martin handcart companies rescued
- Parley P. Pratt murdered, Arkansas; ● Mountain Meadows Massacre; Mark Twain meets Brigham Young
- lett discourse; m assassinated in ng & Hyrum acquitted
- UTAH WAR
- **June** - Federal troops ● enter Salt Lake City
- First Pony Express riders in Salt Lake Valley; last company to use handcarts enters Salt Lake City
- ● Transcontinental telegraph joined in Salt Lake City
- ● Salt Lake Theatre dedicated; Pres. Lincoln signs "Morrill Act," making bigamy a crime in territories
- ● Brigham Young arrested for bigamy, trial never held
- ● Cornerstone laid for "new" Salt Lake Tabernacle
- BLACK HAWK WAR
- George Q. Cannon & Sons est. (publisher) ●
- Salt Lake Tabernacle completed—first general conference held there; Eliza R. Snow becomes 2nd Pres. of the Relief Society; ward Relief Societies reorganized
- Golden Spike—transcontinental railroads ● joined at Promontory, UT; ZCMI (Zions Cooperative Mercantile, Inc.) founded
- Young Ladies' Retrenchment Association organized by Brigham Young (later became Young Women's organization)
- First issue of *Mormon Tribune* (later *Salt Lake Tribune*); Utah Territorial legislature gives women the vote; **Apr. 4** - George Albert Smith born
- ● Brigham Young put under house arrest for bigamy
- ● Brigham Young released from custody
- ● **Sept. 8** - David O. McKay born
- One hundred Gosiute Indians baptized; United Orders begin
- ● Approx. 200 Shivwits Indians baptized; first "Old Folks' Day" held at Lake Point, Great Salt Lake; Young Men's Mutual Improvement Association organized; Salt Lake Tabernacle dedicated; Brigham Young Academy founded
- LDS colonization of Arizona begins; **July 19** - Joseph Fielding Smith born
- John D. Lee executed for part in Mountain Meadows Massacre; St. George Temple dedicated; endowments for the dead inaugurated; Brigham Young dies; Twelve assume leadership of Church
- LDS settlers in Colorado; Primary Organization founded ●
- Emma Smith dies ●
- John Taylor becomes 3rd Pres. of Church ●

UNITED STATES

- Fillmore becomes 13th Pres.; California becomes a state; iel Hawthorne's *The Scarlet Letter*
- Walt Whitman publishes *Leaves of Grass* ●
- ● Gail Borden patents condensed milk
- ● Abraham Lincoln becomes 16th Pres. of U.S.
- ● Nebraska becomes a state; "Seward's Folly" U.S. acquires Alaska
- ● Yellowstone Park established
- Albert Einstein born ●
- Isaac Singer receives patent for sewing machine; Herman Melville publishes *Moby Dick*
- CIVIL WAR
- First passenger elevator installed in a New York department store; James Buchanan becomes 15th Pres. of U.S.
- Abraham Lincoln signs "Emancipation Proclamation"; Battle of Gettysburg
- Ulysses S. Grant becomes 18th Pres. of U.S.; Wyoming territory gives women the vote
- Mark Twain publishes *The Adventures of Tom Sawyer*
- ● Alexander Graham Bell patents the telephone
- Franklin Pierce becomes 14th Pres. of U.S.; mes Samuel Colt revolutionizes the manufacture of small arms; potato chips invented in NY
- Charles Blondin crosses ● Niagara Falls on a tightrope
- "In God We Trust" first ● appears on U.S. coins
- Abraham Lincoln assassinated; ● Andrew Johnson becomes 17th Pres. of U.S.
- U.S. Gov. crushes Ku Klux Klan; P. T. Barnum opens his circus, "The Greatest Show on Earth," in New York
- Rutherford B. Hayes becomes 19th Pres. of U.S.; Thomas Edison invents phonograph
- ● Henry David Thoreau publishes *Walden*

WORLD

- G REBELLION against Chi'ng Dynasty
- Australian gold rush
- Charles Darwin publishes *On the ● Origin of Species by Natural Selection*
- ● Serfs freed in Russia
- Tom Morris of St. ● Andrews wins his first professional golf championship; Alfred Nobel invents dynamite
- Nikolai Lenin born; Italy unified after troops seize Rome ●
- ● First color photographs developed
- First large-scale ski race, Norway
- apoleon III oclaims the ond French Empire
- CRIMEAN WAR (Charge of the Light Brigade)
- ● Chapel at Lourdes erected; German pathologist, Virchow, isolates the cell
- Louis Pasteur invents pasteurization
- FRANCO-PRUSSIAN WAR
- ● Winston Churchill born; "Impressionist" art exhibition in Paris
- Florence Nightingale revolutionizes army medical care
- Lewis Carroll publishes *Alice in Wonderland*
- "British North America Act"— Canada officially becomes a country
- "Meiji Restoration"— Japan enters period of rapid modernization
- ● First roller-skating rink, London
- ● Victor Hugo publishes *Les Misérables*
- Suez Canal opens ●
- Electric street lighting introduced in London; German, Karl Benz, builds motorized tricycle

51 1852 1853 1854 1855 1856 1857 1858 1859 | 1861 1862 1863 1864 1865 1866 1867 1868 1869 | 1871 1872 1873 1874 1875 1876 1877 1878 1879

Year markers: 1860 · 1870 · 1880

LATTER-DAY

HISTORY

OF THE CHURCH OF JESUS CHRIST
OF LATTER-DAY SAINTS

Cover paintings: *Joseph Smith's First Vision* by Bill Hill, 1978, *Shall We Not Go On In So Great A Cause?* by Clark Kelley Price, 1990, and *Temple Square At Sunset* by Christian Eisele, 1892 all © Intellectual Reserve Inc. Courtesy of the Museum of Church History and Art. Used by permission.

Cover design copyrighted 2000 by Covenant Communications, Inc.
Published by Covenant Communications, Inc.
American Fork, Utah

Printed in Canada
First Printing: November 2000

07 06 05 04 03 02 01 00   10 9 8 7 6 5 4 3 2 1

Library of Congress Cataloging-in-Publication Data

Kelly, Brian, 1940-
Kelly, Petrea, 1942-
     Latter-day history of The Church of Jesus Christ of Latter-day
     Saints / compiled by Brian & Petrea Kelly
          p. cm.
     Includes bibliographical references.
     ISBN 1-57734-737-4
       1. Church of Jesus Christ of Latter-day Saints--History. I. Kelly,
     Petrea. II. Title.

     BX8611 .K38 2000
     289.3'09--dc21   00-050907

LATTER-DAY HISTORY

OF THE CHURCH OF JESUS CHRIST
OF LATTER-DAY SAINTS

compiled by

BRIAN & PETREA
KELLY

Covenant Communications, Inc.

Brian and Petrea Gillespie Kelly live in Highland, Utah. They are the parents of ten children, "all of whom are smarter and better looking than their parents." Brian has worked in various writing and publication assignments for the Church during the last thirty years, and has been recognized both nationally and internationally for his editorial work. Petrea has had articles published in several LDS publications. The Kellys are currently serving a three-year mission assignment in Albuquerque, New Mexico. When they aren't on a mission, and when they have spare time, the Kellys enjoy family activities—one of which is hot-air ballooning. Their other hobbies include gardening, reading, writing, photography, and flying.

TABLE OF

CONTENTS

ACKNOWLEDGMENTS

This book has a rather unusual genesis—most books are written, then recorded for those who prefer to listen to their books rather than read them. This book, however, began as scripts for a set of cassette tapes portraying the history of the Church of Jesus Christ of Latter-day Saints through the writings of the people who participated in that history. We provided some narration to tie it all together and made note of some contemporary activities in the United States and the world. Many listeners requested a printed copy with references so they could study in greater depth. As a result, the editors at Covenant assembled a group of people whose various talents have made this book a reality.

In the original project, Paul Thomas Smith provided a great deal of research, and Janet Thomas assisted with the writing on some of the prophets. In the process of creating this volume, we are again grateful for the research talents of Paul Thomas Smith. We also express our appreciation to Margaret Weber, the art director at Covenant who carefully researched, assembled, and added the wonderful photos; Jessica Warner, who designed the book's cover and created the impressive format and layout of the book; and Shauna Nelson, the managing editor and project coordinator.

While the pictures came from many sources, the primary contributors were William W. Slaughter and April Williamsen of the LDS Church Archives; Bruce Pearson at Visual Resources Library, LDS Church; Bobbie Reynolds, Copyrights and Permission Office, LDS Church; and Russell Winegar at Panorama.

Special thanks to Lew Kofford who started us thinking about the recorded project in the early 1970s, and for his vision in bringing this book to fruition.

Many others have also had a part in bringing this project to completion. We thank each of you.

Brian and Petrea Kelly

INTRODUCTION

True Mormon history begins long before the history of the earth. It started in the Grand Council in heaven, where the Lord revealed his plan to create an earth for his spirit children. Many great and noble individuals were called to fill special missions on this earth. Central to the plan was Jehovah, our Savior, who would give His life for all humankind. Others, including Adam, Abraham, Noah, Enoch, Moses, and Peter were also there in that premortal council. One of these noble and great ones was given the responsibility for the last dispensation of the earth's history, when darkness would cover the earth, and gospel truth would be lost.

Righteous people would hunger and thirst for the word of the Lord, but would not be able to find it. Some, blessed with prophetic vision, knew that a day of light would come again. One of these was Asael Smith, father of Joseph Smith, Sr., who declared, "It has been born in upon my soul that one of my descendants will promulgate a work to revolutionize the world of religious faith" (Joseph Fielding Smith, *Essentials in Church History*, 25). Indeed, his grandson would prepare the earth and its people for the glorious second coming of the Savior, and all things would be restored.

The world stood poised on the brink of a new dispensation. The time was at hand for the Lord's Church to arise and come forth out of the wilderness.

JOSEPH SMITH

Prophet of the Restoration

BIRTH OF A PROPHET

In the year 1805, strong forces were moving the world, but the great and powerful of the earth didn't even notice when, on December 23, a baby was born in a log cabin in Vermont.

Dr. Joseph Adam Dennison, who made his rounds on horseback, delivered the baby boy. He was paid in produce that had been stored for the long winter by the baby's parents, Joseph and Lucy Mack Smith. As the smoke rose from their cabin on Dairy Hill, the Smiths looked out at the pale birch and dark maple trees that covered their hundred-acre farm. In the spring, when the sap rose, the maple trees would produce sweet syrup for their table. Father Joseph had cleared some of the land and planned for next year's crops. He looked forward to the time when his baby boy would grow into a strong son who could help him in the fields. He would give the boy his own name, teach him to fear God, work hard, and speak the truth. God had given Joseph Smith, Sr., much wisdom, but even he did not foresee the child's magnificent future. This child would fulfill Asael Smith's prophecy. One of the noble and great ones from the Council in Heaven was about to begin his mission.

As Joseph grew from baby to boy, his family moved from Vermont to New Hampshire, and four more children joined

JOSEPH SMITH *by William Whitaker.* Joseph served as President from 1832–1844.

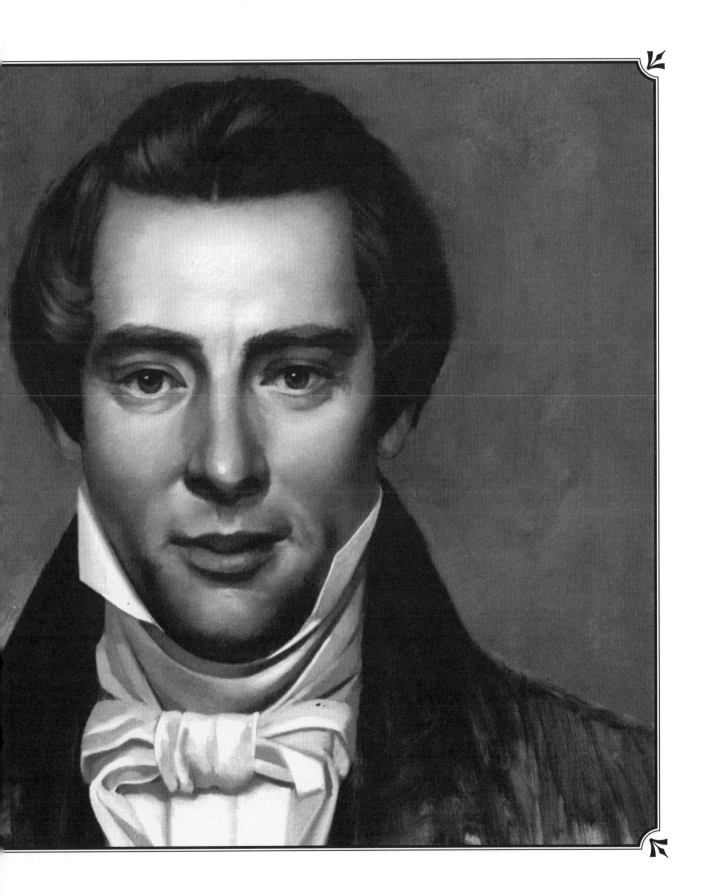

The year 1805 was an important one. Lewis and Clark had reached the west coast of the American continent. Thomas Jefferson was president of the United States. Admiral Nelson had ended Napoleon's bid for naval supremacy in the battle of Trafalgar. The Industrial Revolution had begun in England.

the family. Joseph and his older brothers, Alvin and Hyrum, attended school when they could be spared from their chores. The farm in New Hampshire was producing good harvests, and the family was happy.

TYPHOID COMPLICATIONS

In 1813, a typhoid fever epidemic swept through the Connecticut River Valley. Candles and lanterns burned through the night in hundreds of scattered homes as settlers nursed loved ones through deadly hours of uncertainty. Every day, small silent processions went to lonely graveyards with the bodies of mothers, fathers, and children. Services were short; the sick at home still needed care. During one of these epidemics, all of the Smith children were stricken with the fever. Sophronia was thought to have died, but she recovered after fervent prayers by her parents. Joseph Jr. suffered high fever and other complications, but he and the rest of the children eventually recovered. All seemed well, but a trial was awaiting that would prepare Joseph's character for the future. Joseph's mother, Lucy, wrote:

JOSEPH SMITH MEMORIAL COTTAGE in Sharon, Vermont, commemorates the birthplace of Joseph Smith, Jr.

Joseph, our third son, having recovered from the typhus fever after something like two week's sickness, one day screamed out . . . with a pain in his shoulder, and, in a very short time he appeared to be in such agony that we feared the consequence would prove to be something very serious. We immediately sent for a doctor . . . [who] anointed his shoulder with some bone liniment, but this was of no advantage to him, for the pain continued the same. . . . When two weeks of extreme suffering had elapsed, the attendant physician . . . found that a large fever sore had gathered between his breast and shoulder. He immediately lanced it, upon which it discharged fully a quart of matter.

As soon as the sore had discharged itself the pain shot like lightning (using his own terms) down his side into the marrow of the bone of his leg. . . . My poor boy, at this, was almost in despair, and he cried out "Oh father the pain is so severe, how can I bear it!"

His leg soon began to swell and he continued to suffer the greatest agony for the space of two weeks longer (Lucy Mack Smith, *History of Joseph Smith,* 54).

After three weeks, their physician, Dr. Phinius P. Parkhurst, called in Dr. Stone of Dartmouth Medical School. Twice, incisions were made in Joseph's leg to drain the pus and relieve the pain and swelling. Both times the operation brought relief until the incision healed and the pain again became unbearable.

Dr. Stone called in a group of surgeons headed by Dr. Nathan Smith, the president of the New Hampshire Medical Society, and head of Dartmouth Medical School. Dr. Smith was the world's foremost authority on what was then known as necrosis, or bone death. At the time, the only treatment for this disease was amputation. However, Dr. Smith had pioneered a new treatment that involved removing dead bone by drilling, chipping, and breaking away the diseased area. He was the only person in the country who used this technique. Lucy Smith must have known of this procedure, because she mentioned it to the surgeons.

SMITH HOME IN WEST LEBANON, NEW HAMPSHIRE, where Dr. Nathan Smith performed Joseph Smith's leg operation.

[She] addressed them thus: "Gentlemen, what can you do to save my boy's leg?" They answered, "We can do nothing; we have cut it open to the bone and find it so affected that we consider his leg incurable, and that amputation is absolutely necessary in order to save his life."

This was like a thunderbolt to me. I appealed to the principal surgeon, saying, "Dr. Stone, can you not make another trial? Can you not by cutting around the bone take out the diseased part, and perhaps that which is sound will heal over, and by this means you will save his leg? You will not, you must not, take off his leg until you try once more. I will not consent to let you enter his room until you make me this promise."

After consulting a short time with each other, they agreed to do as I had requested, then, went to see my suffering son. One of the doctors, on approaching his bed, said, "My poor boy, we have come again." "Yes," said Joseph, "I see you have; but you have not come to take off my leg, have you, sir?" "No . . . it is your mother's request that we make one more effort, and that is what we have now come for" (Smith, *History of Joseph Smith*, 56).

IF FATHER WILL HOLD ME, *by Liz Lemon Swindle* portrays young Joseph's painful leg surgery as his father held him in his arms. *oil on canvas*

The principal surgeon, after a short conversation, ordered that Joseph be tied to the bed, but Joseph objected. The doctor insisted that he be restrained, but Joseph resolutely replied: "No, doctor, I will not be bound, for I can bear the operation much better if I have my liberty. . . . I will tell you what I will do—I will have my father sit on the bed and hold me in his arms, and then I will do whatever is necessary in order to have the bone taken out" (Smith, *History of Joseph Smith*, 57). Lucy later recalled:

Looking at me he said, "Mother, I want you to leave the room, for I know you cannot bear to see me suffer so; father can stand it, but you have carried me so much, and watched over me so long, you are almost worn out." Then looking up into my face, his eyes swimming in tears, he continued. "Now, mother, promise me that you will not stay, will you? The Lord will help me, and I shall get through with it." To this request I consented, and getting a number of folded sheets and laying them under his leg, I retired, going several hundred yards from the house, in order to be out of hearing (Smith, *History of Joseph Smith,* 57).

The surgeons commenced operating by boring into the bone of his leg, first on one side of the bone where it was infected, then on the other side, where they broke it off with a pair of forceps or pincers. Lucy continues:

When they broke off the first piece, Joseph screamed out so loudly, that I could not forbear running to him. On my entering the room, he cried out, "Oh, mother, go back, go back; I do not want you to come in—I will try to tough it out, if you will go away."

When the third piece was taken away, I burst into the room again—and oh, my God! what a spectacle for a mother's eye! The wound torn open, the blood still gushing from it, and the bed literally covered with blood. Joseph was pale as a corpse, and large drops of sweat were rolling down his face, whilst upon every feature was depicted the utmost agony!

I was immediately forced from the room, and detained until the operation was completed; but when the act was accomplished, Joseph put upon a clean bed, the room cleared of every appearance of blood, and the instruments which were used in the operation removed, I was permitted again to enter (Smith, *History of Joseph Smith,* 57-58).

FARM THE SMITHS RENTED in Norwich, Vermont. They suffered three crop failures in a row, then moved to Palmyra, New York.

Joseph immediately began to get better, and improved until he soon became strong and healthy. Having passed through a year of sickness and distress, health again returned to the family and they thanked God for helping them through this trial.

Although Joseph recovered, he had to use crutches for three years, and he limped slightly the rest of his life. The sickness left the Smith family financially broken, so in 1813, they moved to Norwich, Vermont, hoping to improve their circumstances. Joseph Smith, Sr., began farming the hillside soil with high hopes.

FAMILY MOVES TO NEW YORK

Thousands of miles away from Vermont, a world event occurred that profoundly affected the Smith family. A volcano in Tambora, Indonesia, erupted, killing 50,000 people and casting tons of ash into the atmosphere.

The volcanic ash, carried by winds high above the earth, reduced sunlight and altered weather throughout the world. In Vermont, it snowed and froze in June. The farmers replanted, but the summer was cold and dry, and very little grew. Farming in Vermont became unprofitable, and the Smiths had to sell their fruit to make up for losses in grain production. Joseph Sr. decided it was time to move his family west. Lucy tells us:

> This was enough; my husband was now altogether decided upon going to New York. . . . Having thus arranged his business, Mr. Smith set out for Palmyra in company with Mr. Howard. After his departure, I and those of the family who were of much size, toiled faithfully, until we considered ourselves prepared to leave at a moment's warning. We shortly received a communication from Mr. Smith, requesting us . . . to take up a journey for Palmyra. . . .
>
> When I again met my husband at Palmyra, we were much reduced—not from indolence, but on account of many reverses of fortune, with which our lives had been rather singularly marked. . . . I was quite happy in once more having the society of my husband, and in throwing myself and the children upon the care and affection of a tender companion and father.
>
> We all now sat down, and counselled together relative to the course which was best of us to adopt in our destitute circumstances, and we came to the conclusion to unite our energies in endeavoring to obtain a piece of land (Smith, *History of Joseph Smith,* 59-64).

Palmyra was located on Mud Creek, about twenty miles south of Lake Ontario. In 1816, it was a small village with a post office, a printing office, and about 1,000 people. However, the Erie Canal was soon to be built, bringing with it the promise of economic progress.

Lucy and the children arrived in Palmyra with only two cents and a few personal belongings to their name. At first, the Smiths lived in a small log cabin on the eastern edge of town. Lucy began painting oil gloss coverings for tables and stands. These sold so well that she was able

WORLD EVENTS

In 1815, Napoleon left Elba and triumphantly returned to France for a hundred days. Austria, Prussia, Britain, and Russia formed an alliance to prevent him from taking over Europe again, and British and Prussian forces defeated Napoleon at Waterloo on June 18. Thus it was an optimistic time. Napoleon had been stopped and exiled. Europe was at peace, and the United States' war with Great Britain had ended (War of 1812). America was growing rapidly, with a population of over seven million. Farmers talked of cheap land to the west, and from time to time families sold out and moved to New York or Pennsylvania to seek new farms and greater opportunities.

NAPOLEON BONAPARTE (1769–1821), Emperor of France, King of Italy

RECONSTRUCTED SMITH LOG CABIN in Palmyra, New York, *(front view in small inset taken in 1998, back view in larger photo)* where the Smith family lived while clearing their farmland and building the frame house. The Smiths were forced to move back into the cabin in 1829 (Hyrum and Jerusha Smith were living there at the time). A slab-sawn room, like the one shown, was added to relieve the cramped quarters. Many significant events of the restoration are associated with this small and humble cabin.

to furnish their house and put food on the table. Joseph, Sr., and his sons Alvin, Hyrum, and Joseph, Jr. worked for various people. Within two years, they had saved enough to make a down payment on 100 wooded acres located on the northwest corner of Manchester Township. The family worked hard cutting down trees, sawing logs, and carving a farm out of the dense forest. Their first year on the land, the family cleared thirty acres for cultivation, constructed a two-room log house with two small sleeping rooms in the attic, and met the payment on the land. Cash was scarce, and making the payments was a constant struggle. Alvin left home to help earn money, and Joseph Sr. opened a shop that was a success with the young men and women of the area who often came to purchase gingerbread pies, boiled eggs, and root beer.

On the fourth of July and other holidays, the Smiths took their goods out into the streets in a homemade handcart. They sold vegetables, hand-made baskets, and birch brooms. The men hired themselves out for common jobs such as gardening, harvesting, welding, brick laying, and barrel making. They also tapped 1,500 maple trees that produced enough sap for the Smiths to boil down 1,000 pounds of syrup. In just a little over two years, the Smith family had gained a farm, a home, furnishings, and friends. Lucy recorded, "We blessed God, with our whole heart, for his mercy which endureth forever" (Smith, *History of Joseph Smith*, 65).

As busy as the family was, Joseph found time for some studies at the local school and owned a few books including *First Lines of Arithmetic, The English Reader,* and *Gospel Sonnets of Spiritual Songs for the Use of Young Scholars.* He also attended sessions of the juvenile debate club.

THE FIRST VISION

A great religious awakening occurred about this time in upstate New York. Religious revival swept so often and burned so hotly through the area that it became known as the "burned over district." Joseph Smith, Jr., stood aloof from much of the emotional fervor, but questions were forming in his heart. He recorded, "Sometime in the second year after our removal to Manchester, there was in the place where we lived an unusual excitement on the subject of religion" (Dean C. Jessee, ed., comp., *The Personal Writings of Joseph Smith,* 197–98). As the various religions contended for converts, bitter feelings arose, with each sect using the scriptures to prove its doctrine and discredit the teachings of others. Joseph recorded:

> In the midst of this war of words and tumult of opinions, I often said to myself: What is to be done? Who of all these parties are right; or, are they all wrong together? If any one of them be right, which is it, and how shall I know it? While I was laboring under the extreme difficulties caused by the contests of these parties of religionists, I was one day reading in the Epistle of James, first chapter and fifth verse, which reads: If any of you lack wisdom, let him ask of God, that giveth to all men liberally, and upbraideth not; and it shall be given him.
>
> Never did any passage of scripture come with more power to the heart of man than this did at this time to mine. It seemed to enter with great force into every feeling of my heart. I reflected on it again and again, knowing that if any person needed wisdom from God, I did. . . .
>
> At length I came to the conclusion that I must either remain in darkness and confusion, or else I must do as James directs. . . . So, in accordance with this, my determination to ask of God, I retired to the woods to make the attempt. It was on the morning of a beautiful, clear day, early in the spring of 1820. It was the first time in my life that I had made such an attempt, for amidst all my anxieties I had never as yet made the attempt to pray vocally.

SCHOOL HOUSE that Joseph attended (above) in Palmyra, New York. Previous to this time, Joseph's parents held school in their home. In Vermont, Joseph attended "common schools" where he learned the three "Rs." *1907*

JOSEPH'S SCHOOL BOOKS. These three textbooks, believed to have been used by Joseph Smith, still exist. They are: *The First Lines of Arithmetic, The English Reader,* and a religious *Reader.* Joseph later gave these books to Richard Bush, a young boy who worked for him on his farm in Nauvoo, Illinois.

SACRED GROVE in Palmyra, New York, where the Father and the Son appeared to fourteen-year-old Joseph Smith in a vision. *Photo taken 1907; identity of boy in photo is unknown.*

After I had retired into the place where I had previously designed to go, having looked around me, and finding myself alone, I kneeled down and began to offer up the desires of my heart to God. I had scarcely done so, when immediately I was seized upon by some power which entirely overcame me, and had such an astonishing influence over me as to bind my tongue so that I could not speak. Thick darkness gathered around me, and it seemed to me for a time as if I were doomed to sudden destruction.

But, exerting all my powers to call upon God to deliver me out of the power of this enemy which had seized upon me, and at the very moment when I was ready to sink into despair and abandon myself to destruction—not to an imaginary ruin, but to the power of some actual being from the unseen world, who had such marvelous power as I have never before felt in any being—just at this moment of great alarm, I saw a pillar of light exactly over my head, above the brightness of the sun, which descended gradually until it fell upon me.

It no sooner appeared than I found myself delivered from the enemy which held me bound. When the light rested upon me I saw two Personages, whose brightness and glory defy all description, standing above me in the air. One of them spake unto me, calling me by name and said, pointing to the other—*This is My Beloved Son. Hear Him!*

My object in going to inquire of the Lord was to know which of all these sects was right, that I might know which to join. No sooner, therefore, did I get possession of myself, so as to be able to speak, than I asked the Personages who stood above me in the light, which of all these sects was right . . . and which I should join.

I was answered that I must join none of them, for they were all wrong; and the Personage who addressed me said that all their creeds were an abomination in his sight; that those professors were all corrupt; that: "they draw near to me with their lips, but their hearts are far from me, they teach for doctrines the commandments of men, having a form of godliness, but they deny the power thereof."

He again forbade me to join with any of them; and many other things did he say unto me, which I cannot write at this time. When I came to myself again, I found myself lying on my back, looking up into heaven. When the light had departed, I had no strength; but soon recovering in some degree, I went home. And as I leaned up to the fireplace, mother inquired what the matter was. I replied, "Never mind, all is well. . . ." It seems as though the adversary was aware, at a very early period of my life, that I was destined to prove a disturber and an annoyer of his kingdom; else why should the powers of darkness combine against me? Why the opposition and persecution that arose against me, almost in my infancy? (Joseph Smith–History 1:10–20).

THE SACRED GROVE is part of an ancient forest where trees grew to a girth of seven feet or more, and soared to heights of one hundred feet. The Church owns this site, and visitors may walk through the grove and enjoy the peaceful spirit that dwells there.

Joseph Smith had gone to God with a question—which church should he join? He had been answered with a glorious vision of the Father and the Son, in

which he was told to join none of them. However, if he thought this glorious manifestation of God's love would be greeted with universal joy, he was soon to learn otherwise. He continues:

Some few days after I had this vision, I happened to be in company with one of the Methodist preachers, who was very active in the before mentioned religious excitement; and, conversing with him on the subject of religion, I took occasion to give him an account of the vision which I had had. I was greatly surprised at his behavior; he treated my communication not only lightly, but with great contempt, saying it was all of the devil, that there were no such things as visions or revelations in these days; that all such things had ceased with the apostles, and that there would never be any more of them.

I soon found, however, that my telling the story had excited a great deal of prejudice against me among professors of religion, and was the cause of great persecution, which continued to increase; and though I was an obscure boy, only between fourteen and fifteen years of age, and my circumstances in life such as to make a boy of no consequence in the world, yet men of high standing would take notice sufficient to excite the public mind against me, and create a bitter persecution; and this was common among all the sects— all united to persecute me. . . .

I have thought since, that I felt much like Paul, when he made his defense before King Agrippa, and related the account of the vision he had when he saw a light, and heard a voice; but still there were but few who believed him; some said he was dishonest, others said he was mad, and he was ridiculed and reviled. But all this did not destroy the reality of his vision. He had seen a vision, he knew he had, and all the persecution under heaven could not make it otherwise; and though they should persecute him unto death, yet he knew, and would know to his latest breath, that he had both seen a light and heard a voice speaking unto him, and all the world could not make him think or believe otherwise.

So it was with me. I had actually seen a light, and in the midst of that light I saw two Personages, and they did in reality speak to me; and though

THE FIRST VISION
by Gary Kapp
God the Father and His Son, Jesus Christ, told Joseph Smith that none of the existing churches were true, and he had been chosen to restore the gospel of Jesus Christ to the earth.
oil on canvas 1998

I was hated and persecuted for saying that I had seen a vision, yet it was true; and while they were persecuting me, reviling me, and speaking all manner of evil against me falsely for so saying, I was led to say in my heart: Why persecute me for telling the truth? . . . Who am I that I can withstand God, or why does the world think to make me deny what I have actually seen? For I had seen a vision; I knew it, and I knew that God knew it, and I could not deny it, neither dared I do it; at least I knew that by so doing I would offend God, and come under condemnation (JS–H 1:21-25).

PERSECUTION

As the persecutions grew, many false stories and rumors circulated about Joseph and the Smith family. Many of these stories depicted the Smiths as lazy and dishonest, but those who knew the family well told a different story. The Smiths' neighbor, Thomas H. Taylor, was once interviewed about the family.

Q: [Were you acquainted with the Smiths, Mr. Taylor?]

A: Yes, I knew them very well. They were very nice men, too. The only trouble was they were ahead of the people; and the people, as in every such case, turned out to abuse them, because they had the manhood to stand for their own convictions. I've seen such work all through life.

Q: What did the Smiths do that the people abuse them so?

A: They did not do anything. Why! these rascals at one time took Joseph Smith and ducked him in the pond that you see over there, just because he preached what he believed, and for nothing else. And if Jesus Christ had been there, they would have done the same to Him. Now I don't believe like he did; but every man has a right to his religious opinions, and to advocate his views, too. If people don't like it, let them come out and meet him on the stand, and show his error. Smith was always ready to exchange views with the best men they had.

Q: Why didn't they like Smith?

A: To tell the truth, there was something about him they could not understand. Some way he knew more than they did, and it made them mad.

Q: But a good many tell terrible stories, about them being rogues, and liars, and such things. How is that?

A: Oh! they were a set of d———d liars. I have had a home here, and been here, except when on business, all my life—ever since I came to this country—and I know these fellows—they make these lies on Smith, because they love a lie better than the truth. I can take you to a great many old settlers here who would substantiate what I say.

Q: Well, that is very kind, Mr. Taylor, and fair; if we have time we'll call around and give you the chance; but we're going first to see these fellows who, so rumor says, know so much against them.

A: All right; but you will find they don't know anything against those men when you put them down to it. They could never sustain anything against Smith (Hyrum L. Andrus & Helen Mae Andrus, *They Knew the Prophet*, 3).

After the First Vision, life did not change much for the Smiths except for the continual harassment of young Joseph. The family worked hard to meet the farm payments and spent long hours trying to earn money and improve their land. Often, the Smith sons took jobs away from home. They were well-known in the neighborhood as hard workers. Joseph's brother, William, recalled:

> Whenever the neighbors wanted a good day's work done they knew where they could get a good hand and they were not particular to take any of the other boys before Joseph either. We cleared sixty acres of the heaviest timber I ever saw. We had a good place. We also had on it from twelve to fifteen hundred sugar trees, and to gather the sap and make sugar molasses from that number of trees was no lazy job. We worked hard to clear our place and the neighbors were a little jealous. If you will figure up how much work it would take to clear sixty acres of heavy timber land, heavier than any here, trees you could not conveniently cut down, you can tell whether we were lazy or not, and Joseph did his share of the work with the rest of the boys (B. H. Roberts, *A Comprehensive History of the Church,* 1:39-40).

But no matter how busy the family was, they always found time for worship in their home. William recounted,

> We always had family prayers since I can remember. I well remember father used to carry his spectacles in his vest pocket, and when we boys saw him feel for his "specs," we knew that was a signal to "get ready for prayers," and if we did not notice it mother would say, "William," or whoever was the negligent one, "get ready for prayers." After the prayer we had a song . . . I remember part of it yet. "Another day has passed and gone, We lay our garments by" (Roberts, *A Comprehensive History of the Church,* 1:34-35).

Now that the family was settled and so much of the farmland had been cleared, Alvin decided it was time for his parents to have a more comfortable home. In the autumn of 1823, the frame was raised and the necessary materials purchased. Observing the work, Alvin dreamed of a better day for his beloved parents. He said, "I am going to have a nice, pleasant room for father and mother to sit in, and everything arranged for their comfort. They shall not work anymore as they have done" (Roberts, *A Comprehensive History of the Church,* 1:32-33).

Angel Moroni

Joseph's vision and calling were never far from his mind, but he had to wait more than three years before he experienced another heavenly manifestation. He recorded:

> During the space of time which intervened between the time I had the vision and the year eighteen hundred and twenty-three . . . I was left to all kinds of temptations; and, mingling with all kinds of society, I frequently fell into many foolish errors, and displayed the weakness of youth, and the foibles

of human nature; which, I am sorry to say, led me into diverse temptations, offensive in the sight of God. In making this confession, no one need suppose me guilty of any great or malignant sins. A disposition to commit such was never in my nature. But I was guilty of levity, and sometimes associated with jovial company, etc., not consistent with that character which ought to be maintained by one who was called of God as I had been. But this will not seem very strange to anyone who recollects my youth, and is acquainted with my native cheery temperament.

In consequence of these things, I often felt condemned for my weakness and imperfections; when, on the evening of the . . . twenty-first of September, after I had retired to my bed for the night, I betook myself to prayer and supplication to Almighty God for forgiveness of all my sins and follies, and also for a manifestation to me, that I might know of my state and standing before him; for I had full confidence in obtaining a divine manifestation, as I previously had one.

While I was thus in the act of calling upon God, I discovered a light appearing in my room, which continued to increase until the room was lighter than at noonday, when immediately a personage appeared at my bedside, standing in the air, for his feet did not touch the floor.

He had on a loose robe of most exquisite whiteness. It was a whiteness beyond anything earthly I had ever seen; nor do I believe that any earthly thing could be made to appear so exceedingly white and brilliant. His hands were naked, and his arms also, a little above the wrist; so, also, were his feet naked, as were his legs, a little above the ankles. His head and neck were also bare. I could discover that he had no other clothing on but this robe, as it was open, so that I could see into his bosom.

Not only was his robe exceedingly white, but his whole person was glorious beyond description, and his countenance truly like lightning. The room was exceedingly light, but not so very bright as immediately around his person. When I first looked upon him, I was afraid; but the fear soon left me.

He called me by name, and said unto me that he was a messenger sent from the presence of God to me, and that his name was Moroni; that God had a work for me to do; and that my name should be had for good and evil among all nations, kindreds, and tongues. . . .

He said that there was a book deposited, written upon gold plates, giving an account of the former inhabitants of this continent, and the source from whence they sprang. He also said that the fulness of the everlasting Gospel was contained in it, as delivered by the Savior to the ancient inhabitants.

Also, that there were two stones in silver bows—and these stones, fastened to a breastplate, constituted what is called the Urim and Thummim—deposited with the plates; and the possession and use of these stones were what constituted "seers" in ancient or former times; and that God had prepared them for the purpose of translating the book.

WORLD EVENTS

America experienced a time of growth after the war with Britain. Shiploads of immigrants arrived daily from the British Isles, and new States joined the Union—Mississippi, Illinois, Missouri, and Maine. There was plenty of land, and prices for farm products were high. The slavery issue troubled the nation when Missouri applied for admission to the Union as a slave-owning state. The Missouri Compromise, however, allowed Maine to join the Union at the same time, as a non-slave state, and averted a split in the nation. Nevertheless, angry talk of secession indicated that the problem was far from solved.

After telling me these things, he commenced quoting the prophecies of the Old Testament. He first quoted part of the third chapter of Malachi; and he quoted also the fourth or last chapter of the same prophecy, though with a little variation from the way it reads in our Bibles. Instead of quoting the first verse as it reads in our books, he quoted it thus:

For behold, the day cometh that shall burn as an oven, and all the proud, yea, and all that do wickedly shall burn as stubble; for they that shall come shall burn them, saith the Lord of Hosts, that it shall leave them neither root nor branch.

And again, he quoted the fifth verse thus: Behold, I will reveal unto you the Priesthood, by the hand of Elijah the prophet, before the coming of the great and dreadful day of the Lord.

He also quoted the next verse differently: *And he shall plant in the hearts of the children the promises made to the fathers, and the hearts of the children shall turn to their fathers. If it were not so, the whole earth would be utterly wasted at his coming.*

In addition to these, he quoted the eleventh chapter of Isaiah, saying that it was about to be fulfilled. He quoted also the third chapter of Acts, twenty-second and twenty-third verses precisely as they stand in our New Testament. He said that that prophet was Christ; but the day had not yet come when "they who would not hear his voice should be cut off from among the people," but soon would come.

He also quoted the second chapter of Joel, from the twenty-eighth verse to the last. He also said that this was not yet fulfilled, but was soon to be. And he further stated that the fullness of the Gentiles was soon to come in. He quoted many other passages of scripture, and offered many explanations which cannot be mentioned here.

Again, he told me, that when I got those plates of which he had spoken—for the time that they should be obtained was not yet fulfilled—I should not show them to any person; neither the breastplate with the Urim and Thummim; only to those whom I should be commanded to show them; if I did, I should be destroyed. While he was conversing with me about the plates, the vision was opened to my mind that I could see the place where the plates were deposited, and that so clearly and distinctly that I knew the place again when I visited it.

After this communication, I saw the light in the room began to gather immediately around the person of him who had been speaking to me, and it continued to do so until the room was again left dark, except just around him; when, instantly I saw, as it were, a conduit open right into heaven, and he ascended until he entirely disappeared, and the room was left as it had been before this heavenly light had made its appearance.

I lay musing on the singularity of the scene, and marveling greatly at what had been told to me by this extraordinary messenger; when, in the midst of my meditation, I suddenly discovered that my room was again beginning to get lighted, and in an instant, as it were, the same heavenly messenger was again by my bedside.

He commenced, and again related the very same things which he had done at the first visit, without the least variation; which having done, he informed me of great judgments which were coming upon the earth, with great desolations by famine, sword, and pestilence; and that these grievous judgments would come on the earth in this generation. Having related these things, he again ascended as he had done before.

By this time, so deep were the impressions made on my mind, that sleep had fled from my eyes, and I lay overwhelmed in astonishment at what I had both seen and heard. But what was my surprise when again I beheld the same messenger at my bedside, and heard him rehearse or repeat over again to me the same things as before; and added a caution to me, telling me that Satan would try to tempt me (in consequence of the indigent circumstances of my father's family), to get the plates for the purpose of getting rich. This he forbade me, saying that I must have no other object in view in getting the plates but to glorify God, and must not be influenced by any other motive than that of building his kingdom; otherwise I could not get them.

After this third visit, he again ascended into heaven as before, and I was again left to ponder on the strangeness of what I had just experienced; when almost immediately after the heavenly messenger had ascended from me a third time, the cock crowed, and I found that day was approaching, so that our interviews must have occupied the whole of that night (JS–H 1:28-47).

THE ANGEL MORONI APPEARS TO JOSEPH SMITH *by Tom Lovell* depicts the nightlong instruction Joseph received from this ancient prophet of God, on September 21, 1823. Moroni spoke of the Lord's judgments, quoted ancient scriptures, and revealed the hiding place of the gold plates.
oil on canvas 1977

Joseph was totally exhausted after the nightlong visit with the heavenly messenger. He got out of bed as usual and went to the fields to work with his father and brothers, but his strength was gone and he could not keep up his normal pace. When his father saw Joseph stumbling through the motions of work, he concluded that he must be sick, and told him to go home and rest. Joseph started for home, but on the way, his strength gave out as he was crossing a fence and he fell to the ground unconscious. The first thing he heard was a voice calling his name. He looked up and saw the angel Moroni, surrounded in glory as the night before. Moroni repeated the things he had told Joseph the night before and commanded him to tell his father about the visions and commandments he had received. Joseph obediently returned to his father and told him everything. Joseph Smith, Sr., did not doubt his son for an instant, saying, "that it was of God, and to go and do as commanded by the messenger" (JS–H 1:50).

And so, walking down the road, Joseph continued a journey he had begun years, even millennia before. From the time he stood as one of the noble and great ones in the Council in Heaven, to his humble birth in a little farmhouse in Vermont, the hand of God had drawn him to a hill, the Hill Cumorah, where a sacred record had lain hidden for centuries. The hill was located about a mile and a half from Joseph's home and was one of the notable landmarks in the area. Joseph had often played there as a boy, and he was familiar with the area. However, this time, as he went to the hill, he went as a prophet of God to keep an appointment with an angel.

THE GOLDEN PLATES

Convenient to the village of Manchester, Ontario County, New York, stands a hill of considerable size, and the most elevated of any in the neighborhood. On the west side of this hill, not far from the top, under a stone of considerable size, lay the plates, deposited in a stone box. This stone was thick and rounding in the middle on the upper side, and thinner towards the edges, so that the middle part of it was visible above the ground, but the edge all around was covered with earth.

THE HILL CUMORAH is situated about a mile and a half south of the Smith's log cabin in Palmyra, NY. Joseph was instructed by the Angel Moroni to return to this place every year on Sept. 22. After four years, Joseph finally received the gold plates, the Urim and Thummim, and a breastplate. *ca. 1907–1912*

Having removed the earth, I obtained a lever, which I got fixed under the edge of the stone, and with a little exertion raised it up. I looked in, and there indeed did I behold the plates, the Urim and Thummim, and the breastplate, as stated by the messenger. The box in which they lay was formed by laying stones together in some kind of cement. In the bottom of the box were laid two stones crossways of the box, and on these stones lay the plates and the other things with them (JS–H 1:51-52).

Western New York, where Joseph Smith lived, produced more wheat than the area could consume, but the recently completed Erie Canal tied the region to New York City, where there was a ready market for all the food the region could produce. The canal was constructed between 1817 and 1825 at a cost of seven million dollars. It reduced travel time between Buffalo and Albany from twenty to eight days. From Albany, the Hudson

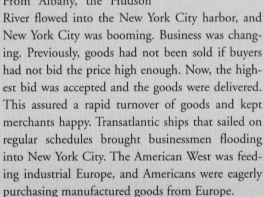

ERIE CANAL LOCKPORT. This canal provided a safe and inexpensive way to transport wheat and other goods to eastern cities.

River flowed into the New York City harbor, and New York City was booming. Business was changing. Previously, goods had not been sold if buyers had not bid the price high enough. Now, the highest bid was accepted and the goods were delivered. This assured a rapid turnover of goods and kept merchants happy. Transatlantic ships that sailed on regular schedules brought businessmen flooding into New York City. The American West was feeding industrial Europe, and Americans were eagerly purchasing manufactured goods from Europe.

While hustle, bustle, and expansion marked the east coast of America, farms and small towns were spreading westward. However, only a handful of trappers, a few Spanish-Mexican missionaries, and several tribes of Indians knew much about the vast area west of the Mississippi River.

That same fall when Joseph Smith walked along the Canandaigua Road toward Cumorah, William H. Ashley and Major Andrew Henry left the ragged frontier town of St. Louis with a group of mountain men, including Jedediah S. Smith, James Bridger, William Sublet, John H. Weber, and Jim Beckworth. These men found a way to cross the Continental Divide by way of a south pass and made their way into present-day Utah, Idaho, Wyoming, and Montana. Occasionally, they had skirmishes with trappers led by Peter Ogden of Britain's Hudson Bay Company, as well as Spanish trappers, including Etienne Provost, and hostile Indians.

In the fall of 1824, Ashley's group of explorers was camped in Cache Valley. The men were speculating about the Bear River, but since none of them knew where the river flowed, twenty-year-old Jim Bridger decided to follow the river downstream in a round reed-bowl boat. He found that the river emptied into a salty body of water that he initially thought might be an arm of the Pacific Ocean. Further exploration, however, revealed it to be a lake.

Joseph tried to remove the plates from the box three times, but was stopped.

"I cried out in the agony of my soul," he said later. "Why can I not obtain them?"

The angel appeared unto me again and said unto me:

"You have not kept the commandments of the Lord which I gave unto you. . . . Therefore, thou wast left unto temptation that thou mightest be acquainted with the power of the adversary. Therefore, repent and call on the Lord [and] thou shalt be forgiven, and in his own due time, thou shalt obtain them."

"For . . . I had been tempted of the adversary, and sought the plates to obtain riches and kept not the commandment that I should have an eye single to the glory of God. Therefore, I was chastened" (Dean C. Jessee, *The Personal Writings of Joseph Smith*, 4-8).

Joseph was filled with the Holy Ghost, the heavens were opened, and the glory of the Lord rested on him.

The angel spoke again, "Look," and as he thus spake, Joseph beheld the 'Prince of Darkness,' surrounded by his innumerable train of associates. It was so fearful a vision, that Joseph ever afterwards found it easier to resist Satan's temptations. After this vision closed, the heavenly messenger said:

All this is shown, the good and the evil, the holy and impure, the glory of God and the power of darkness, that you may know hereafter the two powers and never be influenced or overcome by that wicked one. Behold, whatsoever entices and leads to good and to do good is of God; and whatsoever does not is of that wicked one. . . . you now see why you could not obtain this record; that the commandment of God was strict, and that if ever these sacred things are obtained they must be [obtained] by prayer and faithfulness in obeying the Lord. They are not deposited here for the sake of accumulating gain and wealth for the glory of this world; they were sealed by the prayer of faith; and because of the knowledge which they contain they are of no worth among the children of men, only for their knowledge. On them is contained the fullness of the gospel of Jesus Christ . . . (Roberts, *A Comprehensive History of the Church*, 1:78-79).

The angel Moroni explained to Joseph that ancient American prophets had prepared the plates and had written on them the things they held in greatest reverence. The Lord had promised these prophets that their writings and testimonies would eventually be given to their descendants and the entire world. The angel then gave Joseph a glimpse into the future. Moroni told Joseph:

When it is known that the Lord has shown you these things, the workers of iniquity will seek your overthrow. They will circulate falsehoods to destroy your reputation and also will seek to take your life, but remember this: if you are faithful, and shall hereafter continue to keep the commandments of the Lord, you shall be preserved to bring these things forth. For in due time he will give you a commandment to come and take them. When they are interpreted, the Lord will give the Holy Priesthood to some, and they shall begin to proclaim this gospel and baptize by water, and after that, they shall have power to give the Holy Ghost by the laying on of their hands. Then will persecution rage more and more, for the iniquities of men shall be revealed, and those who are not built upon the rock will seek to overthrow the Church. But it will increase the more opposed, and spread farther and farther, increasing in knowledge till [the members] shall be sanctified, and receive an inheritance where the glory of God will rest upon them. And when this takes place, and all things are prepared, the ten tribes of Israel will be revealed in the north country, whither they have been for a long season; and when this is fulfilled will be brought to pass the saying of the prophet, And the Redeemer shall come to Zion, and unto them that turn from transgression in Jacob, saith the Lord.

But not withstanding the workers of iniquity shall seek your destruction, the arm of the Lord will be extended, and you will be borne off conqueror if you keep all his commandments. Your name shall be known among the nations, for the work which the Lord will perform by your hands shall cause the righteous to rejoice and the wicked to rage. . . . Now, go thy way, remembering what the Lord has done for thee, and be diligent in keeping his commandments and he will deliver thee from temptations and all the arts and devices of the wicked one. Forget not to pray, that thy mind may become strong that . . . thou mayest have power to escape the evil, and obtain these precious things (Orson Pratt, *An Interesting Account of Several Remarkable Visions*, 11-12).

Joseph then recorded that he " was again informed [by the messenger] that the time [for] bringing them [the plates] forth had not yet arrived . . . but he told me that I should come to that place precisely in one year from that time, and that he would there meet with me, and that I should continue to do so until the time should come for obtaining the plates" (Jessee, *The Personal Writings of Joseph Smith*, 206-7).

Joseph returned from the Hill Cumorah filled with wonder. During the days that followed, he received visits from Nephi, Moroni, and other Book of Mormon prophets who instructed him in the gospel. For the family, these were golden days as they learned long lost truths from Joseph while they sat in a circle around the young prophet. His mother later recalled the period after Joseph's visit to the Hill Cumorah.

The ensuing evening, when the family were all together, Joseph made known to them all that he had communicated to his father in the field, and also of his finding the record, as well as what passed between him and the angel while he was at the place where the plates were deposited.

Sitting up late that evening, in order to converse upon these things, together with over-exertion of mind, had much fatigued Joseph; and when Alvin observed it, he said, "Now, brother, let us go to bed, and rise early in the morning, in order to finish our day's work at an hour before sunset, then, if mother will get our suppers early, we will have a fine long evening, and we will all sit down for the purpose of listening to you while you tell us the great things which God has revealed to you." Accordingly, by sunset the next day, we were all seated, and Joseph commenced telling us the great and glorious things which God had manifested to him; but, before proceeding, he charged us not to mention out of the family that which he was about to say to us, as the world was so wicked that when they came to a knowledge of these things, they would try to take our lives . . . After giving us this charge, he proceeded to relate further particulars concerning the work which he was appointed to do, and we received them joyfully. . . . From this time forth, Joseph continued to receive instructions from the Lord, and we continued to get the children together every evening for the purpose of listening while he gave us a relation of the same. I presume our family presented an aspect as singular as any that ever lived upon the face of the earth, all seated in a circle, father, mother, sons and daughters, and giving the most profound attention to a boy, eighteen years of age, who had never read the Bible through in his life.

We were now confirmed in the opinion that God was about to bring to light something . . . that would give us a more perfect knowledge of the plan of salvation and the redemption of the human family. This caused us greatly to rejoice, the sweetest union and happiness pervaded our house, and tranquility reigned in our midst.

During our evening conversations, Joseph would occasionally give us some of the most amusing recitals that could be imagined. He would describe the ancient inhabitants of this continent, their dress, their mode of traveling, and the animals upon which they rode; their cities, their buildings, with every particular; their mode of warfare; and also their religious worship. This he would do with as much ease, seemingly, as if he had spent his whole life among them (Smith, *History of Joseph Smith,* 81-83).

A DEATH IN THE FAMILY

While the Smith family spent their evenings learning from Joseph, their days were busy harvesting crops and working on the new home that Alvin had started for his parents.

RESTORED SMITH FRAME HOUSE. It took the Smith family three years to complete this home. Shortly after they moved in, Russell Stoddard fraudulently obtained the deed to the Smith land. The Smith's were allowed to rent the home for four years. *2000*

When the crops were in and winter was approaching, the Smith family was visited by grief they could hardly bear. Lucy recorded:

> On the 15th of November, 1823, about ten o'clock in the morning, Alvin was taken very sick [and treatment by several different physicians did not help. After a few days of sickness,] he called Hyrum to him and said, "Hyrum, I must die. Now I want to say a few things, which I wish to have you remember. I have done all I could to make our dear parents comfortable. I want you to go on and finish the house and take care of them in their old age, and do not any more let them work hard, as they are now in old age." . . . He called for all the children and exhorted them separately in the same strain as above. But when he came to Joseph, he said, "I am now going to die, the distress which I suffer and the feelings that I have, tell me my time is very short. I want you to be a good boy, and do everything that lies in your power to obtain the Record. Be faithful in receiving instruction, and in keeping every commandment that is given you. Your brother Alvin must leave you; but remember the example which he has set for you; and set the same example for the children that are younger than yourself, and always be kind to your father and mother." . . . Alvin was a youth of singular goodness of disposition—kind and amiable, so that lamentation and mourning filled the whole neighborhood in which he resided (Smith, *History of Joseph Smith,* 86-88).

The winter of sorrow passed, and the sap began to rise in the maple trees. The Smith family busied themselves making syrup, plowing, and planting. They worked hard, finished their new home, and moved from the small log house they had built when they first came to New York. While the men worked in the fields, Lucy and her daughters cooked over a fire, made clothes by hand, did the washing in huge copper kettles, and tended the garden. When September 22 came again, Joseph eagerly went to the Hill Cumorah as instructed by the angel. Lucy recorded:

> Having arrived at the place, and uncovering the plates, he put forth his hand and took them up, but, as he was taking them hence, the unhappy thought darted through his mind that probably there was something else in the box besides the plates, which would be of some pecuniary advantage to him. So . . . he laid them down . . . After covering [the box], he turned round to take the Record again, but behold it was gone. . . .
>
> He kneeled down and asked the Lord why the record had been taken from him; upon which the angel of the Lord appeared to him, and told him that he had not done as he had been commanded, for in a former revelation he had been commanded not to lay the plates down, or put them for a moment out of his hands, until he got into the house and deposited them in a chest or trunk, . . . and, contrary to this, he had laid them down with the view of securing some fancied or imaginary treasure that remained.

In the fall elections of 1824, none of the four candidates for president won a clear majority, and the election fell to the House of Representatives as prescribed by the constitution. John Quincy Adams was elected and inaugurated in January as the sixth president of the United States. Far across the sea, Britain and Russia were at war in Turkey. In South America, Brazil, Bolivia, and Uruguay, all became independent countries. London heard its first performance of Beethoven's Ninth Symphony. James Fennimore Cooper wrote *The Last of the Mohicans*. The great American statesman, Thomas Jefferson, died on July 4, 1826. The new game of baseball was sweeping the country, and became so popular that the first baseball club was organized in Rochester, New York. Big cities like Boston and Berlin enjoyed the luxury of gas-lit streets.

In the moment of excitement, Joseph was overcome by the powers of darkness, and forgot the injunction that was laid upon him.

Having some further conversation with the angel, on this occasion, Joseph was permitted to raise the stone again, when he beheld the plates as he had done before. He immediately reached forth his hand to take them, but instead of getting them, as he had anticipated, he was hurled back upon the ground with great violence. When he recovered, the angel was gone, and he arose and returned to the house, weeping for grief and disappointment (Smith, *History of Joseph Smith,* 83-84).

THE SMITH FAMILY IN PALMYRA

Small towns like Palmyra, New York, experienced little change. There, the sun and seasons dictated the activities of sleigh riding, sugaring, planting and harvesting. Two pleasant years passed for the Smith family—Joseph kept his September 22 appointments with the angel, and Hyrum was married. Work continued on the farm, and the men occasionally still took jobs with neighbors and others to earn cash. Mr. Josiah Stowell hired Joseph to help dig for a silver mine that Mr. Stowell believed had been abandoned by Spanish adventurers. Joseph, however, felt that the project was fruitless, and after a month, he was able to convince Mr. Stowell to stop the search. This job later gave rise to stories that Joseph was a gold digger. Although he found no silver, Joseph did find a treasure—his future wife, Emma Hale. Joseph relates:

During the time that I was thus employed I was put to board with a Mr. Isaac Hale, of [Harmony, Susquehanna County, Pennsylvania.] Twas there that I first saw my wife, (his daughter), Emma Hale. . . . Owing to my still continuing to assert that I had seen a vision, persecution still followed me, and my

MAIN STREET IN PALMYRA, NEW YORK
ca. 1907

wife's father's family was very much opposed to our being married (Jessee, *Personal Writings of Joseph Smith,* 207).

Isaac Hale was a leading member of the community, a successful farmer, and a well-known hunter. He was also a devout Methodist. Emma, his only daughter, was especially dear to him. He had taught her how to ride horses and how to canoe on the river near their home. In addition, she was an accomplished singer and had been trained as a schoolteacher. She was tall, with a dark complexion, dark hair, and dark brown eyes. Joseph, at the age of twenty-one, was over six feet tall. His hair was light brown and his eyes were blue, clear, and calm. They must have made a striking couple. On January 18, 1827, they were married in South Bainbridge, New York, at the home of Squire Tarbell. Years later Emma told her son:

> I was married at South Bainbridge, New York; at the home of Squire Tarbell, by him, when I was in my 22nd or 23rd year. . . . I was visiting at Mr. Stowell who lived in Bainbridge and I saw your father there. I had no intention of marrying when I left home; but during my visit at Mr. Stowell's, your father visited me there. My folks were bitterly opposed to him; and, being importuned by your father, sided by Mr. Stowell, who urged me to marry him, and [preferring to marry him to any other man] I knew, I consented. We went to Squire Tarbell's and were married ("Last Testimony of Emma Smith," Feb., 1879, in possession of the archives of the Reorganized Church of Jesus Christ of Latter-day Saints, Independence, MO).

After their marriage, Joseph and Emma returned to the Smith farm, where Joseph worked for his father. Not long after their marriage, he returned very late from a business trip to Manchester. His family had been very worried. Lucy recounted:

> We always had a peculiar anxiety about [Joseph] whenever he was absent, for it seemed as though something was always taking place to jeopardize his life. . . . He did not get home till the night was far spent. On coming in he threw himself into a chair, apparently much exhausted. My husband did not observe his appearance and immediately exclaimed, "Joseph, why are you so late? Has anything happened to you? We have been much distressed about you these three hours." . . .
> [Joseph] smiled and said in a calm tone, "I have taken the severest chastisement that I have ever had in my life."

EMMA HALE (1804–1879), wife of Joseph Smith and first president of the Relief Society.

JOSEPH SMITH (1805–1844), founded The Church of Jesus Christ of Latter-day Saints.

My husband, supposing that it was from some of the neighbors, was quite angry and observed, "I would like to know what business anybody has to find fault with you!"

Joseph replied, "Stop, father, stop. It was the angel of the Lord. As I passed by the hill of Cumorah, where the plates are, the angel met me and said that I had not been engaged enough in the work of the Lord; that the time had come for the record to be brought forth; and that I must be up and doing and set myself about the things which God had commanded me to do. But, father, give yourself no uneasiness concerning the reprimand which I received, for I now know the course that I am to pursue, so all will be well" (Smith, *History of Joseph Smith,* 100).

On the night September 21, 1827, Joseph and Emma borrowed a wagon from Joseph Knight and left for the Hill Cumorah. Joseph's mother spent the night in worried prayer, afraid that Joseph might again fail to obtain the plates. In Mendon, New York, Heber C. Kimball and his wife Vilate, who had never heard of Joseph Smith, didn't sleep that night either. Heber recorded in his diary:

HILL CUMORAH MONUMENT LIT UP AT NIGHT. The hill was purchased by the Church in 1928. The monument, a forty-foot shaft of granite that stands on the top of the hill, was dedicated by President Heber J. Grant on July 21, 1935. Each year, hundreds of people spend long, hot hours in late June preparing for the largest outdoor pageant in America which is held on this hill in July. Tens of thousands of visitors attend.

I had retired to bed, when John P. Green, . . . who was living within a hundred steps of my house, came and waked me up, calling upon me to come out and behold the scenery in the heavens. I woke up and called my wife and Sister Fanny Young . . . who was living with us, and we went out-of-doors.

It was one of the most beautiful starlight nights, so clear that we could see to pick up a pin. We looked to the eastern horizon, and beheld a white smoke arise toward the heavens; as it ascended, it formed itself into a belt, and made a noise like the sound of the mighty wind, and continued south-west, forming a regular bow dipping in the western horizon. After the bow had formed, it began to widen out and grow clear and transparent, . . . it grew wide enough to contain twelve men abreast.

In this bow an army moved, commencing from the east and marching to the west; they continued marching until they reached the western horizon. They moved in platoons, and walked so close that the rear ranks trod in the steps of their file leaders, until the whole bow was literally crowded with soldiers. We could distinctly see the muskets, bayonets and knapsacks of the men, who wore caps and feathers like those used by the American soldiers in the last war with Britain; and also saw their officers with their swords and equipage, and the clashing and jingling of their implements of war, and could discover the forms and features of the men. The most profound order existed throughout the entire army; when the foremost man stepped, every man stepped at the same time; I could hear the steps. When the front rank reached the western horizon a battle ensued, as we could distinctly hear the report of arms and the rush.

No man could judge of my feelings when I beheld that army of men, as plenty as ever I saw armies of men in the flesh; it seemed as though every hair of my head was alive. This scenery we gazed upon for hours, until it began to disappear.

After I became acquainted with Mormonism, I learned that this took place the same evening that Joseph Smith received the records of the Book of Mormon from the angel Moroni, who had held those records in his possession. My wife, being frightened at what she saw, said, "Father Young, what does all this mean?" "Why it's one of the signs of the coming of the Son of Man," he replied, in a lively, pleased manner (Orson F. Whitney, *The Life of Heber C. Kimball*, 15-17).

In New York, a young man named Brigham Young and his wife Miriam witnessed much the same manifestation. None of these people would realize until years later that this amazing phenomenon had taken place on the same night that Joseph Smith had received the plates. Joseph and Emma spent the entire night on the hill. Emma waited at the bottom while Joseph received instructions from the angel. Joseph recorded:

At length the time arrived for obtaining the plates, the Urim and Thummim, and the breastplate. On the twenty-second day of September, one thousand eight hundred and twenty-seven, having gone as usual at the end of another year to the place where they were deposited, the same heavenly messenger delivered them up to me with this charge: that I should be responsible for them; that if I should let them go carelessly, or through any neglect of mine, I should be cut off; but that if I would use all my endeavors to preserve them, until he, the messenger, should call for them, they should be protected (JS–H 1:59).

When Joseph and Emma turned toward home with the plates and the Urim and Thummim, the sun was rising over the autumn-tinted hills of the late New York summer, symbolic of the new day of gospel knowledge and power that was dawning on the world after a long night in darkness.

Translating the Plates

Joseph Knight was a guest in the Smith home on September 22, 1827. The following morning, he spoke with Joseph Smith. Joseph Knight recorded:

Joseph told me that he had received the plates. He said the sacred records were engraven on plates which had the appearance of gold. Each plate was six inches wide and eight inches long and not quite so thick as common tin. They were filled with engravings and Egyptian characters, and bound together in a volume as the leaves of a book, with three rings running through the whole. The volume was something near six inches in thickness, a part of which was sealed. The characters on the unsealed part were small and beautifully engraved. The whole book exhibited many marks of antiquity in its construction, and much skill in the art of engraving. But he seemed to think more of the glasses, or the urim and thummem [than] he did of the Plates. He said, "I can see anything; they're marvelus" (Jessee, "Joseph Knight's Recollection of Early Mormon History," *Brigham Young University Studies,* vol. 17, Autumn 1976, no. 1, 3).

BOX POSSIBLY USED FOR HOLDING THE GOLD PLATES. Joseph had Hyrum make arrangements with a local carpenter to construct the box. Joseph found work in Macedon to earn enough money to pay the carpenter.

Translating the plates proved to be difficult. When word spread that Joseph Smith had a golden book, the curious came wanting to see the plates. Some even offered to pay to see the record. When Joseph explained that he could not show them to anyone, curiosity turned to hostility and greed, and the plates had to be hidden. At various times, they were hidden in a hollowed-out birch log in the woods, in the Smith home under the hearth, under the floor, in the attic, and out in Father Smith's workshop. They were moved almost daily. Sometimes angels warned Joseph when to move the plates.

I soon found out the reason why I had received such strict charges to keep them safe, and why it was that the messenger had said that when I had done what was required at my hand, he would call for them. For no sooner was it known that I had them, than the most strenuous exertions were used to get them from me. Every stratagem that could be invented was resorted to for that purpose. The persecutions became more bitter and severe than before, and multitudes were on the alert continually to get them from me if possible. . . . The persecution . . . became so intolerable that I was under the necessity of leaving Manchester (JS–H 1:60-61).

Joseph and Emma had no money to travel. One day they happened to meet Martin Harris, a prosperous neighbor who had, on occasion, hired Joseph Smith to help out on his farm. He talked with all the members of the Smith family and became satisfied that Joseph did indeed have the plates. Desiring to assist in the Lord's work, he approached Joseph in Palmyra one day and said to him, "How do you do, Mr. Smith? Here . . . is fifty dollars. I give it to you to do the Lord's work with. No, I give it to the Lord for his own work." Joseph wanted to sign a note for it, but Martin refused (Scot Facer Proctor and Maurine Jensen Proctor, *The Revised and Enhanced History of Joseph Smith By His Mother,* 153).

With this aid from Martin Harris, Joseph and his brother-in-law, Alba Hale, loaded their household goods and belongings on Alba's wagon and hitched up the horses. Joseph, Emma, and Alba, bundled in coats, scarves, hats, and gloves, climbed onto the seat and began the journey south to Harmony, Pennsylvania. They traveled on privately owned toll roads, meandering trails, and cow paths. Since it was winter, the roads and trails were muddy and slippery. At night, they may have stopped at inns, which were little more than private homes with an extra bedroom or two. The trip took two or three days, and at the end of the journey, everyone and everything in the open wagon was no doubt splattered with mud. Stiff from the cold and the wagon's hard seat, Emma must have felt her heart rejoice when she saw her parents' home on the hill by the banks of the Susquehanna River. When she and Joseph moved into a small house just down the hill from her parents, they felt that now, at last, Joseph could begin translating the plates. Joseph recorded: "Immediately after my arrival there I commenced copying the characters off the plates. I copied a considerable number of them, and by means of the Urim and Thummim I translated some of them" (JS–H 1:19).

MARTIN HARRIS LOSES THE 116 PAGES

In February, 1828, Martin Harris visited the Smiths and then traveled to New York City with a copy of some of the characters from the plates and Joseph's translation of these characters. Martin planned to show them to some of the most educated men in the country. Accordingly, he went to Professor Charles Anthon, a well-known scholar of classical studies, at Columbia College. As the author of over thirty books, Anthon was considered the best classicist in America. Martin Harris tells of his interview with the professor:

> I went to the city of New York, and presented the characters which had been translated, with the translation thereof, to Professor Charles Anthon, a gentleman celebrated for his literary attainments. Professor Anthon stated that the translation was correct, more so than any he had before seen translated from the Egyptian. I then showed him those which were not yet translated, and he said that they were Egyptian, Chaldaic, Assyriac, and Arabic; and he said that they were true characters. He gave me a certificate, certifying to the people of Palmyra that they were true characters, and that the translation of such of them as had been translated was also correct. I took the certificate and put it into my pocket, and was just leaving the house, when Mr. Anthon called me back, and asked me how the young man found out that there were gold plates in the place where he found them. I answered that an angel of God had revealed it unto him.
>
> He then said to me, "Let me see that certificate." I accordingly took it out of my pocket and gave it to him, when he took it and tore it to pieces, saying that there was no such thing now as ministering of angels, and that if

MARTIN HARRIS (1783–1875) was a prosperous farmer in the Palmyra area who so firmly believed in Joseph's experience that he mortgaged his land in 1829, and then sold 151 acres in 1831 to pay $3,000 to E.B. Grandin for the publishing of the Book of Mormon. He acted as scribe for the translation of the gold plates until he lost the 116 pages of manuscript. Later, Martin was forgiven by the Lord and was allowed to be one of the Three Witnesses who was shown the gold plates.

I would bring the plates to him he would translate them. I informed him that part of the plates were sealed, and that I was forbidden to bring them. He replied, "I cannot read a sealed book." I left him and went to Dr. Mitchell, who sanctioned what Professor Anthon had said respecting both the characters and the translation (JS–H 1:64-65).

Martin Harris did not realize at the time that this meeting had fulfilled a prophecy made hundreds of years earlier by Isaiah.

And the vision of all is become unto you as the words of a book that is sealed, which men deliver to one that is learned, saying, Read this, I pray thee: and he saith, I cannot; for it is sealed:

And the book is delivered to him that is not learned, saying, Read this, I pray thee: And he saith, I am not learned.

Wherefore the Lord said, Forasmuch as this people draw near me with their mouth, and with their lips do honour me, but have removed their heart far from me, and their fear toward me is taught by the precept of men:

Therefore, behold, I will proceed to do a marvellous work among this people, even a marvellous work and a wonder: for the wisdom of their wise men shall perish, and the understanding of their prudent men shall be hid (Isaiah 29:11-14).

This experience so convinced Martin Harris that the plates did contain the word of God that he left his home and farm, and spent much of the spring of 1828 serving as scribe while Joseph translated the plates. By the middle of June, he had transcribed 116 pages of the translation. Martin's wife disapproved of Joseph and the work he was doing, so Martin requested the privilege of taking the 116 pages to show his wife in Fayette, New York. Joseph asked the Lord, through the Urim and Thummim, if he should allow Martin to take the translation to New York.

I did inquire, and the answer was that he must not. However, he was not satisfied with this answer, and desired that I should inquire again. I did so, and the answer was as before. Still, he could not be contented, but insisted that I should inquire once more. After much solicitation I again inquired of the Lord, and permission was granted him to have the writings on certain conditions; which were, that he show them only to his brother, . . . his own wife, his father and his mother, and a Mrs. Cobb, a sister to his wife. In accordance with this last answer, I required of him that he should bind himself in a covenant to me in a most solemn manner that he would not do otherwise than had been directed. He did so. He bound himself as I required of him, took the writings, and went his way (Smith, *History of the Church*, 1:21).

On June 15, 1828, soon after Martin left with the manuscript, Joseph and Emma's first child was born. They named him Alvin. He lived only a few hours. Emma was very sick, and Joseph, in his grief, hardly had time to think of the manuscript. But, as the days passed, worry and doubt began to grow in his mind. When Emma regained her health, she urged Joseph to travel to Fayette to see what had happened to Martin and the manuscript. Emma's mother came to stay with her while Joseph made the journey. According to Joseph's mother:

Although he [Joseph] was now nearly worn out, sleep fled from his eyes, neither had he any desire for food, for he felt that he had done wrong, and how great his condemnation was he did not know.

Only one passenger was in the stage beside himself: this man observing Joseph's gloomy appearance, inquired the cause of his affliction, and offered to assist him if his services would be acceptable. Joseph thanked him for his kindness, and mentioned that he had been watching some time with a sick wife and child, that the child had died, and that his wife was still very low. . . . Nothing more passed between them upon this subject, until Joseph was about leaving the stage; at which time he remarked, that he still had twenty miles further to travel on foot that night, it being then about ten o'clock. To this the stranger objected, saying, "I have watched you since you first entered the stage, and I know that you have neither slept nor eaten since that time, and you shall not go on foot twenty miles alone this night; for, if you must go, I will be your company."

Joseph . . . thanked the gentleman for his kindness, and, leaving the stage, they proceeded together. When they reached our house it was nearly daylight. The stranger said he was under the necessity of leading Joseph the last four miles by the arm; for nature was too much exhausted to support him any longer. . . .

When Joseph had taken a little nourishment, . . . he requested us to send immediately for Mr. Harris. This we did without delay. And when we had given the stranger his breakfast, we commenced preparing breakfast for the family; and we supposed that Mr. Harris would be there, as soon as it was ready, to eat with us, for he generally came in such haste when he was sent for. At eight o'clock we set the victuals on the table, as we were expecting him every moment. We waited till nine and he came not—till ten, and he was not there—till eleven, still he did not make his appearance. But at half past twelve we saw him walking with a slow and measured tread toward the house, his eyes fixed thoughtfully upon the ground. On coming to the gate, he stopped, instead of passing through, and got upon the fence, and sat there some time with his hat drawn over his eyes. At length he entered the house. Soon after which we sat down to the table, Mr. Harris with the rest. He took up his knife and fork as if he were going to use them, but immediately dropped them. Hyrum, observing this, said, "Martin, why do you not eat; are you sick?" Upon which Mr. Harris pressed his hands upon his temples, and cried out in a tone of deep anguish, "Oh, I have lost my soul!"

Joseph . . . sprang from the table, exclaiming, "Martin, have you lost that manuscript? Have you broken your oath, and brought down condemnation upon my head as well as your own?"

"Yes, it is gone," Martin replied, "and I know not where."

"Oh, my God! Said Joseph . . . All is lost! all is lost! What shall I do? I have sinned. . . . I should have been satisfied with the first answer which I received from the Lord; for he told me that it was not safe to let the writing go out of my possession." He wept and groaned, and walked the floor continually.

At length he told Martin to go back and search again. "No;" said Martin, "it is all in vain; for I have ripped open beds and pillows; and I know it is not there."

"Then must I," said Joseph, "return with such a tale as this? I dare not do it. And how shall I appear before the Lord? Of what rebuke am I not worthy from the angel of the Most High?"

I besought him not to mourn so, for perhaps the Lord would forgive him, after a short season of humiliation and repentance. But what could I do to comfort him, when he saw all the family in the same situation of mind as himself; for sobs and groans, and the most bitter lamentations filled the house. However, Joseph was more distressed than the rest, as he better understood the consequences of disobedience. And he continued pacing back and forth, meantime weeping and grieving, until about sunset, when, by persuasion, he took a little nourishment.

The next morning he set out for home. We parted with heavy hearts, for it now appeared that all which we had so fondly anticipated, and which had been the source of so much secret gratification, had in a moment fled, and fled forever (Smith, *History of Joseph Smith,* 126-29).

WORLD EVENTS

In 1828, a particularly rough political campaign absorbed the nation's attention. John Quincy Adams had never been popular as president. Many of his ideas about a strong central government with weaker states were unpopular with most Americans. Andrew Jackson, on the other hand, was the hero of the many independent-minded men in the nation. His election marked the end of the era of the founding fathers who had been involved in writing the constitution and forming the new nation. The United States was ready to expand, and the common man was the hero. That same year, Turkey acknowledged the independence of Greece, and Mexico abolished slavery.

Joseph suffered the torments of the damned. He found no rest, and could find no peace of conscience. In the bitterness of his soul, he feared to approach the Lord. He returned home to Emma in Harmony, and, for a period of time, the plates and the Urim and Thummim were taken from him. Through this experience, Joseph learned:

The works, and the designs, and the purposes of God cannot be frustrated, neither can they come to naught. . . .

Behold, you should not have feared man more than God. . . .

Behold, thou art Joseph, and thou was chosen to do the work of the Lord, but because of transgression, if thou art not aware, thou wilt fall.

But remember, God is merciful; therefore, repent of that which thou hast done which is contrary to the commandment which I gave you, and thou art . . . again called to the work (D&C 3:1, 7, 9-10).

When Joseph again received the plates, he was given important instructions regarding the 116 pages that he had already translated:

Behold, Satan hath put it into their hearts to alter the words which you have caused to be written, or which you have translated, which have gone out of your hands.

On this wise, the devil has sought to lay a cunning plan, that he may destroy this work.

Verily, I say unto you, that I will not suffer that Satan shall accomplish his evil design in this thing.

Behold, I say unto you, that you shall not translate again those words which have gone forth out of your hands.

And now, verily I say unto you, that an account of those things which you have written, which have gone out of your hands, is engraven upon the plates of Nephi;

Yea, and you remember it was said in those writings that a more particular account was given of these things upon the plates of Nephi.

Behold, there are many things engraven upon the plates of Nephi which do throw greater views upon my gospel; therefore, it is wisdom in me that you should translate this first part of the engraving of Nephi, and send forth this work (D&C 10:10, 12, 14, 30, 38-39, 45).

The Lord, in his wisdom, had Nephi prepare two records of the early years of his people's history. Martin Harris had lost the political history, but the religious history was preserved and is contained in the Book of Mormon as the books of First and Second Nephi, Jacob, Enos, Jarom, and Omni.

Emma Smith and her brother, Rueben Hale, served as scribes for Joseph, but the work was painfully slow since neither of them could work full-time on the project. Joseph prayed for the Lord to send him a scribe and was answered that one would soon be forthcoming. Rain had been falling for days. The sky was dark and forbidding, and the roads were slippery and almost impassable, but Oliver Cowdery was making his way to meet the man people were claiming to be a prophet. To his surprise, Joseph was expecting him when he arrived.

Within a few days, the revelation contained in Section 6 of the Doctrine and Covenants was given to Joseph and Oliver. In the revelation, the Lord told Oliver, "If you desire a further witness, cast your mind upon the night that you cried unto me in your heart, that you might know concerning the truth of these things.

Did I not speak peace to your mind concerning the matter? What greater witness can you have than from God?" (D&C 6:22-23).

Joseph recorded his impressions of Oliver's reaction to this revelation:

> After we had received this revelation, Oliver Cowdery stated to me that after he had gone to my father's to board, and after the family had communicated to him concerning my having the plates, that one night after he had retired to bed he called upon the Lord to know if these things were so, and

OLIVER COWDERY (1806–1850) was a young school teacher who boarded with Joseph's parents. After hearing of Joseph's experience, Oliver went to Harmony to learn the truth of the matter for himself. Within two days of meeting Joseph, he began acting as scribe for the translation of the gold plates. He was one of the Three Witnesses who was shown the gold plates, and later became associate president of the Church. He never wavered in his testimony as one of the Three Witnesses of the gold plates.

the Lord manifested to him that they were true, but he had kept the circumstance entirely secret, and mentioned it to no one; so that after this revelation was given, he knew that the work was true, because no being living knew of the thing alluded to in the revelation but God and himself (Smith, *History of the Church,* 1:35).

The two men worked all day, every day, and the work progressed rapidly. The rain stopped, the sun shone, leaves appeared on the trees and flowers bloomed on the banks of the Susquehanna River. After a time, Oliver requested that he be allowed to translate from the ancient writings. The Lord allowed him to try, but he could not do it even though it had looked easy when Joseph was translating. The Lord told Oliver in a revelation found in Section 9 of the Doctrine and Covenants, why he had failed:

> Behold, you have not understood; you have supposed that I would give it unto you, when you took no thought save it was to ask me.
>
> But . . . I say unto you, that you must study it out in your mind; then you must ask me if it be right, and if it is right I will cause that your bosom shall burn within you; therefore, you shall feel that it is right.
>
> But if it be not right you shall have no such feelings, but you shall have a stupor of thought that shall cause you to forget the thing which is wrong; therefore, you cannot write that which is sacred, save it be given you from me (D&C 9:7-9).

Oliver continued to serve as scribe and later wrote:

> These were days never to be forgotten—to sit under the sound of a voice dictated by the inspiration of heaven, awakened the utmost gratitude of this bosom. Day after day I continued, uninterrupted to write from his mouth, as he translated with the Urim and Thummim, or, as the Nephites would have said, 'Interpreters,' the history or record called the *Book of Mormon* (Roberts, *A Comprehensive History of the Church,* 1:122).

Apparently, after the loss of the 116 pages, Joseph first translated the books of Mosiah, Alma, Helaman, and 3 Nephi. By May, they had reached the section of the Book of Mormon that tells of Christ's visit to the people in America and his commandment that all men should be baptized. Baptism was a controversial subject among the Christians of Joseph's time. Was it necessary? How was it to be done? Who could baptize? At what age should a person be baptized? Joseph and Oliver realized that they knew nothing of the Lord's baptism, but they wanted to obey his commandments

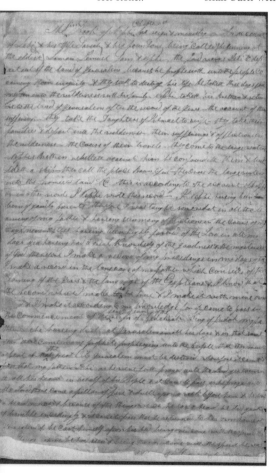

A PAGE OF THE TRANSLATED BOOK OF MORMON MANU-SCRIPT as written in Oliver Cowdery's hand. Martin Harris, Oliver Cowdery, and Emma Smith all served as scribes to Joseph as he translated the characters on the Nephite record using the Urim and Thummim and seer stone..

so they decided they must ask the Lord for direction. They left their desks and went into the woods near the river to pray. Joseph relates:

> While we were thus employed, praying and calling upon the Lord, a messenger from heaven descended in a cloud of light, and having laid his hands upon us, he ordained us saying:
>
> *Upon you my fellow servants, in the name of Messiah, I confer the Priesthood of Aaron, which holds the keys of the ministering of angels, and of the gospel of repentance, and of baptism by immersion for the remission of sins; and this shall never be taken again from the earth until the sons of Levi do offer again an offering unto the Lord in righteousness.*

THE SUSQUEHANNA RIVER, near Harmony, PA. On the banks of this beautiful river, John the Baptist restored the Aaronic Priesthood on May 15, 1829. Peter, James, and John restored the Melchizedek Priesthood later in the spring of 1829. *ca. 1897–1927*

He said this Aaronic Priesthood had not the power of laying on of hands for the gift of the Holy Ghost, but that this should be conferred on us hereafter; and he commanded us to go and be baptized, and gave us directions that I should baptize Oliver Cowdery, and afterwards that he should baptize me.

Accordingly, we went and were baptized. I baptized him first, and afterwards, he baptized me—after which I laid my hands upon his head and ordained him to the Aaronic Priesthood, and afterwards he laid his hands on me and ordained me to the same Priesthood—for so we were commanded.

The messenger who visited us on this occasion and conferred this Priesthood upon us, said that his name was John, the same that is called John the Baptist in the New Testament, and that he acted under the direction of Peter, James and John, who held the keys of the Priesthood of Melchizedek, which Priesthood he said, would in due time be conferred upon us, and that I should be called the first Elder of the Church, and he (Oliver Cowdery) the second. It was on the fifteenth day of May, 1829, that we were ordained under the hand of this messenger, and baptized.

Immediately on our coming up out of the water after we had been baptized, we experienced great and glorious blessings from our Heavenly Father. No sooner had I baptized Oliver Cowdery, than the Holy Ghost fell upon him, and he stood up and prophesied many things which should shortly come to pass. And again, as soon as I had been baptized by him, I also had the spirit of prophecy, when, standing up, I prophesied concerning the rise of this church, and many other things connected with the Church, and this generation of the children of men. We were filled with the Holy Ghost, and rejoiced in the God of our salvation (JS–H 1:68-73).

Oliver also recorded the glorious happenings of that day:

The Lord, who is rich in mercy, and ever willing to answer the consistent prayer of the humble, after we had called upon him in a fervent manner, aside from the abodes of men, condescended to manifest to us his will. On a sudden, as from the midst of eternity, the voice of the Redeemer spake peace to us. While the vail was parted and the angel of God came down clothed with glory, and delivered the anxiously looked for message, and the keys of the gospel of repentance—What joy! what wonder! what amazement! While the world was racked and distracted—while millions were groping as the blind for the wall, and while all men were resting upon uncertainty, as a general mass, our eyes beheld—our ears heard. As in the "blaze of days;" yes, more—above the glitter of the May sunbeam, which then shed its brilliancy over the face of nature! Then his voice, though mild, pierced to the center, and his words, "I am thy fellow-servant," dispelled every fear. We listened—we gazed—we admired! 'Twas the voice of an angel from glory—'twas a message from the Most High! and as we heard we rejoiced, while his love enkindled upon our souls, and we were wrapt in the vision of the Almighty! Where was room for doubt? No where; uncertainty had fled, doubt had sunk, no more to rise, while fiction and deception had fled forever!

But, dear brother . . . think for a moment, what joy filled our hearts, and with what surprise we must have bowed, (for who would not have bowed the knee for such a blessing?) when we received under his hand the holy priesthood as he said; "upon you my fellow servants, in the name of Messiah I confer this priesthood and this authority, which shall remain upon earth, that the sons of Levi may yet offer an offering unto the Lord in righteousness!"

I shall not attempt to paint to you the feelings of this heart, nor the majestic beauty and glory which surrounded us on this occasion; but you will believe me when I say, that earth, nor men, with the eloquence of time, cannot begin to clothe language in as interesting and sublime a manner as this holy personage. No; nor has this earth power to give the joy, to bestow the peace, or comprehend the wisdom which was contained in each sentence as it was delivered by the power of the Holy Spirit! Man may deceive his fellowman, deception may follow deception, and the children of the wicked one may have power to seduce the foolish and untaught, till nought but fiction feeds the many, and the fruit of falsehood carries in its current the giddy to the grave; but one touch with the finger of his love, yes, one ray of glory . . . from the bosom of eternity, strikes it all into insignificance, and blots it forever from the mind! The assurance that we were in the presence of an angel, the certainty that we heard the voice of Jesus, and the truth unsullied as it flowed from a pure personage, dictated by the will of God, is to me past description, and I shall ever look upon this expression of the Savior's goodness with wonder and thanksgiving while I am permitted to tarry, and in those mansions where perfection dwells and sin never comes, I hope to endure in the day which shall never cease! (*Times and Seasons,* 2:201).

THE RESTORATION OF THE MELCHIZEDEK PRIESTHOOD *by Kenneth Riley* depicts Peter, James, and John ordaining Joseph and Oliver to the Melchizedek Priesthood, giving them authority to confer the gift of the Holy Ghost upon those whom they would baptize. *oil on canvas 1965*

Later that spring, the ancient apostles, Peter, James, and John, appeared to Joseph and Oliver and declared that they possessed the keys of the kingdom and the dispensation of the fullness of times. They ordained the two men to the Melchizedek Priesthood, giving them authority to confer the gift of the Holy Ghost upon those whom they would baptize. Within a short time, they baptized Joseph's brothers, Samuel and Hyrum. Joseph recorded:

In various parts of the world during the year of 1829, inventions and discoveries were changing age-old patterns. John Walker's sulfur friction matches made fire portable and easy to make. Many other new conveniences began to separate modern civilization from the previous history of the world. Charles Carol, the richest man in America, constructed the first American railroad to carry freight and passengers. It was named the Baltimore and Ohio. Two important books were published: Audubon's *Birds of North America*, and Webster's *American Dictionary of the English Language*.

Our minds being now enlightened, we began to have the scriptures laid open to our understandings, and the true meaning and intention of their more mysterious passages revealed unto us in a manner which we never could attain to previously, nor ever before had thought of. In the meantime we were forced to keep secret the circumstances of having received the Priesthood and our having been baptized, owing to a spirit of persecution (JS–H 1:74).

THE ORGANIZATION OF THE CHURCH

The citizens of Harmony, Pennsylvania, however, were resistant to new ideas, especially those involving angels and strange writings on gold plates. Their persecutions made it necessary for Joseph Smith to seek another home in which to finish the translation. Oliver wrote to his friend, David Whitmer, in Fayette, New York, and requested that they be allowed to move to his home. David recorded his introduction to the latter-day work:

I first heard of what is now termed Mormonism in the year 1828. I made a business trip to Palmyra, N. Y., and while there stopped with one Oliver Cowdery. A great many people in the neighborhood were talking about the finding of certain golden plates by one Joseph Smith, Jr., a young man of that neighborhood. Cowdery and I, as well as others, talked about the matter, but at that time I paid but little attention to it, supposing it to be only the idle gossip of the neighborhood. Cowdery said he was acquainted with the Smith family, and he believed that there must be some truth in the story of the plates, and that he intended to investigate the matter. . . . After several months Cowdery told me he was going to Harmony, Pa—whither Joseph Smith had gone with the plates on account of [the] persecutions of his neighbors—and see him about the matter. He did go and on his way stopped at my father's house and told me that as soon as he found out anything either truth or untruth he would let me know. After he got there he became acquainted with Joseph Smith, and shortly after, wrote to me telling me that he was convinced that Smith had the records and that he (Smith) had told him that it was the will of heaven that he (Cowdery) should be his scribe to assist in the translation of the plates. . . . Shortly after this Cowdery wrote me another letter in which he gave me a few lines of what they had translated, and he assured me that he knew of a certainty that he had a record of a people that inhabited this continent, and that the plates they were translating from gave a complete history of these people. When Cowdery wrote me these things and told me that he had revealed knowledge concerning the truth of them I showed these letters to my parents, and brothers and sisters. Soon after I received another letter from Cowdery, telling me to come down to Pennsylvania and bring him and Joseph to my father's house, giving me a reason therefore that they had received a commandment from God to that effect (Milton V. Backman, Jr., *Eyewitness Accounts of the Restoration,* 230-31).

David Whitmer said:

> I did not know what to do. I was pressed with my work. I had some twenty acres to plow, so I concluded I would finish plowing and then go. I got up one morning to go to work as usual, and on going to the field, found between 5 and 7 acres of my ground had been plowed during the night. I do not know who did it, but it was done just as I would have done myself, and the plow was left standing in the furrow (Hyrum M. Smith, and Janne M. Sjodahl, *Doctrine and Covenants Commentary,* 73).

The next morning, David went out to spread plaster on his fields, a common way to treat the soil in those times. He had left the plaster in heaps near his father's house, but found that the plaster was gone. He ran to his sister and asked her if she knew what had happened to it.

> . . . Surprised, she said, "Why do you ask me? Was it not all sown yesterday?"
>
> "Not to my knowledge," answered David.
>
> "I'm astonished at that," replied his sister, "for the children came to me in the forenoon, and begged of me to go out and see the men sow plaster in the field, saying, that they never saw anybody sow plaster so fast in their lives. I accordingly went, and saw three men at work in the field, as the children had said, but, supposing that you had hired some help, on account of your hurry, I went immediately into the house, and gave the subject no further attention" (Smith, *History of Joseph Smith,* 136-37).

With his work completed, David left for Pennsylvania and arrived two days later. David relates:

> When I arrived at Harmony, Joseph and Oliver were coming toward me, and met me some distance from the house. Oliver told me that Joseph had informed him when I started from home, where I had stopped the first night, how I read the sign at the tavern, where I stopped the next night, and so forth, and that I would be there that day before dinner. And this was why they'd come out to meet me, all of which was exactly as Joseph had told Oliver, and at which I was greatly astonished (*Millennial Star,* 40:49-50).

Joseph, Oliver, and David left for Fayette the next day in David's wagon. Emma stayed behind on the farm for a few days. David recorded:

> When I was returning to Fayette, with Joseph and Oliver, all of us riding in the wagon, Oliver and I riding on an old fashioned, wooden spring

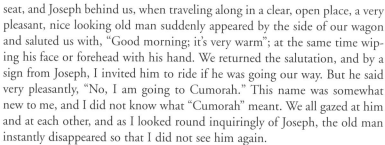

seat, and Joseph behind us, when traveling along in a clear, open place, a very pleasant, nice looking old man suddenly appeared by the side of our wagon and saluted us with, "Good morning; it's very warm"; at the same time wiping his face or forehead with his hand. We returned the salutation, and by a sign from Joseph, I invited him to ride if he was going our way. But he said very pleasantly, "No, I am going to Cumorah." This name was somewhat new to me, and I did not know what "Cumorah" meant. We all gazed at him and at each other, and as I looked round inquiringly of Joseph, the old man instantly disappeared so that I did not see him again.

Sometime after this, my mother was going to milk the cows, when she was met out near the yard by the same old man [judging by her description of him], who said to her, "You have been very faithful and diligent in your labors, but you are tired because of the increase of your toil; it is proper, therefore, that you should receive a witness, that your faith may be strengthened." Thereupon, he showed her the plates. My father and mother had a large family of their own, the addition to it, therefore, of Joseph, his wife Emma, and Oliver, very greatly increased the toil and anxiety of my mother. And although she had never complained she had sometimes felt that her labor was too much, or, at least, she was perhaps beginning to feel so. This circumstance, however, completely removed all such feelings, and nerved her up for her increased responsibilities (Roberts, *A Comprehensive History of the Church,* 1:126-27).

The Whitmers's log home was twenty feet wide by thirty feet long. On the main floor, there was a large room that was used as a kitchen, living room, and sleeping area. A rock fireplace on the west wall dominated the room. Here, Mother Whitmer cooked meals for her daughter, father, four sons, and guests. The fireplace also heated the home and all the water used in the house, burning large piles of wood that were carried into the house daily. The water was carried in buckets to the house from the deep rock-lined well outside. The only other room on the main floor was a small bedroom. Upstairs, there were two more bedrooms. In one of these, Joseph and his scribes worked to complete the translation. While the Whitmers served as scribes, Oliver was hard at work copying the entire manuscript. David Whitmer later described how Joseph translated, and how the Spirit affected the translation.

He was a religious and straightforward man. He had to be; for he was illiterate and he . . . could not translate unless he was humble and possessed the right feelings towards everyone. To illustrate so you can see: One morning when he was getting ready to continue the translation, something went wrong about the house and he was put out about it. Something that Emma, his wife, had done. Oliver and I went upstairs and Joseph came up soon after to continue the translation but he could not do anything. He could not translate a single syllable. He went downstairs, out into the orchard, and made supplication to the Lord; was gone about an hour—came back to the house, and asked Emma's forgiveness and then came upstairs where we were and then the translation went on all right. He could do nothing save he was humble and faithful (Roberts, *A Comprehensive History of the Church,* 1:131).

David continued: "It was a laborious work for the weather was very warm, and the days were long and they [Joseph and Oliver] worked from morning till night. But they were both young and strong and were soon able to complete the work. . . . The translation . . . occupied about one month, that is, from June 1, to July 1, 1829" (Susan Easton Black and Charles D. Tate, Jr., *Joseph Smith, The Prophet, The Man*, 49-50).

THREE WITNESSES

As the translation of the Book of Mormon was nearing completion, Joseph obtained a copyright on the book from R. R. Lansing, the clerk of the North District Court of New York.

In March, the Lord informed Joseph that three individuals would be permitted to see the golden plates. Joseph was told that if Martin Harris would humble himself and acknowledge his mistakes, he would be one of the three. In June, Joseph received a revelation, where the Lord named Oliver Cowdery, David Whitmer and Martin Harris as the men He had chosen to be the witnesses. Joseph sent a message to his parents, requesting that they and Martin Harris come to the Whitmer home as soon as possible.

Lucy Smith wrote that the three of them reached the Whitmer home just as the sun was setting.

> The evening was spent in reading the manuscript . . . and we rejoiced exceedingly.
> The next morning, after . . . reading, singing and praying, Joseph arose from his knees, and approaching Martin Harris with a solemnity that thrills through my veins to this day . . . said, "Martin Harris, you have got to humble yourself before God this day, that you may obtain a forgiveness of your sins. If you do, it is the will of God that you should look upon the plates, in company with Oliver Cowdery and David Whitmer."
> In a few minutes after this, Joseph, Martin, Oliver and David, repaired to a grove, a short distance from the house, where they commenced calling upon the Lord (Smith, *History of Joseph Smith,* 151-52).

Joseph recorded:

. . . Martin Harris, David Whitmer, Oliver Cowdery, and myself, agreed to retire into the woods and try to obtain by fervent and humble prayer, the fulfillment of the promises given in the revelation, that they should have a view of the plates, etc. We accordingly made choice of a piece of woods convenient to Mr. Whitmer's house, to which we retired, and having knelt down, we began to pray in much faith to Almighty God to bestow upon us a realization of these promises. According to previous arrangements, I commenced by vocal prayer to our Heavenly Father, and was followed by each of the rest in succession. We did not, however, obtain any answer or manifestation of the divine favor in our behalf. We again observed the same order of prayer, each calling on and praying fervently to God in rotation, but with the same result as before. Upon this, our second failure, Martin Harris proposed that he should withdraw himself from us, believing, as he expressed himself, that his presence was the cause of our not obtaining what we wished for; he accordingly withdrew from us, and we knelt down again, and had not been many minutes engaged in prayer, when presently we beheld a light above us in the air of exceeding brightness; and, behold, an angel stood before us; in his hands he held the plates. . . . He turned over the leaves one by one, so that we could see them and discover the engravings thereon distinctly. He then addressed himself to David Whitmer, and said, "David, blessed is the Lord, and he that keeps his commandments." When immediately afterwards, we heard a voice from out of the bright light above us, saying, "These plates have been revealed by the power of God, and they have been translated by the power of God. The translation of them which you have seen is correct, and I command you to bear record of what you now see and hear."

I now left David and Oliver, and went in pursuit of Martin Harris, whom I found at a considerable distance fervently engaged in prayer. He soon told me, however, that he had not yet prevailed with the Lord, and earnestly requested me to join him in prayer, that he might also realize the same blessings which we had just received. We accordingly joined in prayer, and ultimately obtained our desires, for before we had yet finished, the same vision was opened to our view . . . whilst at the same moment Martin Harris cried out, apparently in an ecstasy of joy, "Tis enough; mine eyes have beheld!" and jumping up, he shouted hosannah, blessing God and otherwise rejoiced exceedingly (Roberts, *A Comprehensive History of the Church,* 1:137-38).

Lucy records:

When they returned to the house it was between three and four o'clock p.m. Mrs. Whitmer, Mr. Smith and myself, were sitting in a bedroom at the time. On coming in, Joseph threw himself down beside me, and exclaimed, "Father, mother, you do not know how happy I am: the Lord has now caused the plates to be shown to three more besides myself. They have seen an angel, who has testified to them, and they will have to bear witness to the truth of what I have said, for now they know for themselves, that I do not go about to deceive the people, and I feel as if I was relieved of a burden which was almost too heavy for me to bear, and it rejoices my soul, that I am not any

THE THREE WITNESSES, Oliver Cowdery, David Whitmer, and Martin Harris testified to the authenticity of the gold plates from which the record, which is now the Book of Mormon, was translated. Although each of these men were later excommunicated from the Church (Cowdery and Harris returned), none of them denied this testimony. *Lithograph by H.B. Hall & Sons, New York, 1883.*

longer to be entirely alone in the world." Upon this, Martin Harris came in: he seemed almost overcome with joy, and testified boldly to what he had both seen and heard. And so did David, and Oliver, adding that no tongue could express the joy of their hearts, and the greatness of the things which they had both seen and heard (Smith, *History of Joseph Smith,* 152-53).

The written testimony of the three men is contained in the Book of Mormon:

Be it known unto all nations, kindreds, tongues, and people, unto whom this work shall come: That we, through the grace of God the Father, and our Lord Jesus Christ, have seen the plates which contain this record, which is a record of the people of Nephi, and also of the Lamanites, their brethren, and also of the people of Jared, who came from the tower of which hath been spoken. And we also know that they have been translated by the gift and power of God, for his voice hath declared it unto us; wherefore we know of a surety that the work is true. And we also testify that we have seen the engravings which are upon the plates; and they have been shown unto us by the power of God, and not of man. And we declare with words of soberness, that an angel of God came down from heaven, and he brought and laid before our

eyes, that we beheld and saw the plates, and the engravings thereon; and we know that it is by the grace of God the Father, and our Lord Jesus Christ, that we beheld and bear record that these things are true. And it is marvelous in our eyes. Nevertheless, the voice of the Lord commanded us that we should bear record of it; wherefore, to be obedient unto the commandments of God, we bear testimony of these things. And we know that if we are faithful in Christ, we shall rid our garments of the blood of all men, and be found spotless before the judgment-seat of Christ, and shall dwell with him eternally in the heavens. And the honor be to the Father, and to the Son, and to the Holy Ghost, which is one God, Amen.

Oliver Cowdery, David Whitmer, Martin Harris.

EIGHT WITNESSES

A day or two later, eight other men also saw the golden plates. They did not see a heavenly visitor as had the three witnesses, but they did handle the plates and examine them. They also issued a statement that is contained in the Book of Mormon. These eight men were: Christian, Jacob, John, and Peter Whitmer, Jr.—all brothers of David Whitmer; Hyrum Page—a brother-in-law to the Whitmers; Joseph Smith, Sr.; and Hiram and Samuel Smith—Joseph's brothers.

In 1827, when Joseph received the plates from the angel Moroni, he had been instructed to return them to the hill when the translation was completed. After nearly two years of work, trials, and tribulations, the task was completed. Joseph recorded in his journal that he returned the plates to Moroni. Oliver Cowdery, however, recorded more details about returning the plates to the hill. Years later in a stake conference in Farmington, Utah, Brigham Young retold the incident as Oliver had told it to him.

> I believe I will take the liberty to tell you of [a] circumstance that will be as marvelous as anything can be. This is an instant in the life of Oliver Cowdery, but he did not take the liberty of telling such things in meetings as I take. I tell these things to you, and I have a motive for doing so. I want to carry them to the ears of my brothers and sisters, and to the children also, that they may grow to an understanding of some things that seem to be entirely hidden from the human family. Oliver Cowdery went with the prophet Joseph Smith when he deposited these plates. Joseph did not translate all the plates; there was a portion of them sealed which you can learn from the book of Doctrine and Covenants. When Joseph got the plates, the angel instructed him to carry them back to the Hill Cumorah, which he did. Oliver says that when Joseph and Oliver went there, the hill opened and they walked into a cave in which there was a large and spacious room. He says they did not think at that time, whether they had the light of the sun or artificial light, but that it was just as light as day. They laid the plates on a table; it was a large table that stood in the room. Under this table there was a pile of plates as much as two feet high, and there were altogether in this room more plates than probably many wagonloads; they were piled up in the corners and along the walls. . . . The first time they went there, the sword of Laban hung upon the wall. [W]hen they went in again, it had been taken down and laid upon

the table across the gold plates. It was unsheathed, and on it was written these words, "This sword will never be sheathed again, until the kingdoms of this world become the kingdom of our God and his Christ." I tell you this as coming not only from Oliver Cowdery, but others who were familiar with it, and who understood it just as well as we understand coming to this meeting, enjoying the day, and by and by we separate and go away, forgetting most of what is said, but remembering some things. So is it with other circumstances of life. I relate this to you, and I want you to understand it. I take this liberty of referring to those things so that they will not be forgotten and lost (Brigham Young, *Journal of Discourses,* 19:38).

THE PRINTING OF THE BOOK OF MORMON

Mr. Grandin, a printer in Palmyra, New York, agreed to print the Book of Mormon, and Martin Harris promised to pay the $3,000 for the first 5,000 copies of the book. Nevertheless, Mr. Grandin was a bit reluctant to publish the

book because of Joseph's unpopularity, the fear that he would not be paid, and the overwhelming size of the job. In those days, 5,000 copies of a book was a large order, especially since printing was not automated. Each page of type was set by hand, letter by letter. The finished page was then locked together, and ink was spread upon it. Then one paper at a time was pressed on the type to print the page. After the printing was completed, the pages were assembled and then hand sewn to make the finished volume. Joseph left the details of the publication in the hands of Oliver Cowdery and returned to his farm in Harmony, Pennsylvania, giving Oliver these instructions:

THE GRANDIN BUILDING, located on "Exchange Row" in Palmyra, NY, was where the Book of Mormon was first published. The printing office was on the third floor, bindery on the second, and the Palmyra Bookstore was on the ground level. E.B. Grandin agreed to print 5,000 copies of the Book of Mormon, which was a large order at the time. Each page of type was set by hand, letter by letter.

First, that Oliver Cowdery should transcribe the whole. Second, that he should take out one copy at a time to the office, so that if one copy should get destroyed, there would still be a copy remaining. Third, that in going to and from the office, he should always have a guard to attend him, for the purpose of protecting the manuscript. Fourth, that a guard should be kept constantly on the watch, both night and day, about the house to protect the manuscript from malicious persons, who would infest the house for the purpose of destroying the manuscript (Smith, *History of Joseph Smith,* 157).

Evil was never at rest and difficulties continued. Local citizens threatened to boycott the printer, who was sure that 5,000 copies of such a book would never sell, and that he would never get his money. An ex-justice of the peace, Esquire Abner Cole, who used the Grandin presses to print his newspaper, *The Reflector,* began printing excerpts from the Book of Mormon, apparently copying the press sheets on Sunday. Joseph had to threaten legal action for breach of copyright before this nuisance was stopped. All this notoriety did, however, stir interest in the Book of Mormon. The Smiths, Whitmers, and the printer all received many visitors who were interested in the gold Bible. One of these individuals was Solomon Chamberlain, who lived about twenty miles east of Palmyra. He was on his way to Canada when he stayed in the home of a woman who lived only half a mile from the Smiths. She told him about the gold Bible and he wanted to know more. He went to the Smith home and later recalled:

> As I entered the door [and] said, "Peace be to this house," [Hyrum] looked at me as one astonished and said, "I hope it will be peace."
>
> I then said, "Is there anyone here that believes in visions and revelations?" He said, "Yes, we are a visionary house."
>
> I said, "then I will give you one of my pamphlets, which was visionary, and of my own experience."
>
> They then called the people together which consisted of 5 or 6 men who were out at the door. Father Smith was one and some of the Whitmers. They then sat down and read my pamphlet. Hyrum read first, but was so affected, he could not read it. He then gave it to a man, which I learned was Christian Whitmer. He finished reading it. I then opened my mouth and began to preach to them in the words that the angel had made known to me in the vision, that all the churches and denominations on the earth had become corrupt, and [that] no church of God [was] on the earth, but that he would shortly raise up a church that would never be confounded nor brought down, and be like unto the apostolic church. They wondered greatly who had been telling me these things, for, said they, "We have the same things written down in our house, taken from the Gold record that you are preaching to us." I said, "The Lord told me these things a number of years ago." I then said, "If you are a visionary house, I wish you would make known some of your discoveries, for I think I can bear them."
>
> They then made known unto me that they had obtained a gold record and [had] just finished translating it. Now the Lord revealed to me by the gift and power of the Holy Ghost that this was the work I had been looking for. I stayed 2 days and they instructed me in the manuscript from the Book of Mormon.
>
> After I had been there two days, I went with Hyrum and some others to [the] Palmyra printing office where they began to print the Book of Mormon, and as soon as they printed 64 pages, I took them with their leave and pursued my journey to Canada, and I preached all that I knew concerning Mormonism to all, both high and low, rich and poor, and thus you see this was the first, that ever printed Mormonism was preached to this generation. I did not see anyone in traveling 7 or 800 miles that had ever heard of the Gold Bible (so called). I exhorted all people to prepare for the great work of God that was now about to come forth (Milton V. Backman, Jr., *Eyewitness Accounts of the Restoration*, 185-86).

EGBERT BRATT GRANDIN the owner of the printing business that printed the Book of Mormon. He at first refused, but later agreed to print five thousand copies for three thousand dollars, using Martin Harris's farm as collateral.

Another seeker after truth who heard stories about the Book of Mormon was a young man from Boston, Thomas B. Marsh. He reported:

> I called . . . at Lyonstown on a family. . . . on leaving there next morning, the lady enquired if I had heard of the Golden Book found by a youth

named Joseph Smith. I informed her I never heard anything about it . . . she told me I could learn more about it from Martin Harris in Palmyra.

I returned . . . and found Martin Harris at the printing office, in Palmyra, where the first sixteen pages of the Book of Mormon had just been struck off . . . As soon as Martin Harris found out my intentions he took me to the house of Joseph Smith Sen. where Joseph Smith Jun., resided, who could give me any information I might wish. Here I found Oliver Cowdery who gave me all the information concerning the book I desired.

After arriving home and finding my family all well, I showed my wife the sixteen pages of the Book of Mormon which I had obtained, with which she was well pleased, believing it to be the word of God (Dan Vogel, ed. *Early Mormon Documents* 3:347–48).

The Organization of the Church

By the end of March, 1830, the publication of the Book of Mormon was completed. During this period, the Lord had been instructing Joseph on many issues regarding the organization of the Church. The three witnesses to the Book of Mormon—Oliver Cowdery, David Whitmer, and Martin Harris—were instructed to select twelve men who would be ordained as the first twelve apostles in this dispensation. The date of the organization and the name of the Church were revealed, along with essential information about baptism, including the age at which a child should be baptized and the manner of baptism. The Lord clearly outlined the basic organization of the Church and the duties of members and each priesthood office.

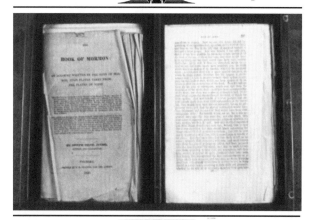

Folded signature pages of the Book of Mormon. John H. Gilbert was the typesetter who received the manuscripts from Hyrum Smith in small installments. Each night, the manuscript was picked up and taken back to the Smith home.

April 6, 1830, was to be the date for the organization of The Church of Jesus Christ.

The rise of the Church of Christ in these last days, being one thousand eight hundred and thirty years since the coming of our Lord and Savior Jesus Christ in the flesh, it being regularly organized and established agreeable to the laws of our country, by the will and commandments of God, in the fourth month, and on the sixth day of the month which is called April (D&C 20:1).

Joseph recalled:

We . . . made known to our brethren that we had received a commandment to organize the Church; and accordingly we met together for that purpose, at the house of Mr. Peter Whitmer, Sen., (being six in number) on Tuesday, the sixth day of April, A.D., one thousand eight hundred and thirty.

Having opened the meeting by solemn prayer to our Heavenly Father, we proceeded, according to previous commandment, to call on our brethren to know whether they accepted us as their teachers in the things of the Kingdom of God, and whether they were satisfied that we should proceed and be organized as a Church according to said commandment which we had received. To these several propositions they consented by a unanimous vote. I then laid my hands upon Oliver Cowdery, and ordained him an Elder of the "Church of Jesus Christ of Latter-day Saints"; after which he ordained me also to the office of an Elder of said Church. We then took bread, blessed it, and brake it with them; also wine, blessed it, and drank it with them. We then laid our hands on each individual member of the Church present, that they might receive the gift of the Holy Ghost, and be confirmed members of the Church of Christ. The Holy Ghost was poured out upon us to a very great degree—some prophesied, whilst we all praised the Lord, and rejoiced exceedingly. . . .

We now proceeded to call out and ordain some others of the brethren to different offices of the Priesthood, according as the spirit manifested unto us: and after a happy time spent in witnessing and feeling for ourselves the powers and blessings of the Holy Ghost, through the grace of God bestowed upon us, we dismissed with the pleasing knowledge that we were now individually members of, and acknowledged of God, "The Church of Jesus of Christ," organized in accordance with commandments and revelations given by Him to ourselves in these last days. . . . Several persons . . . came forward shortly after, and were received into the Church; among the rest, my own father and mother were baptized, to my great joy and consolation; and about the same time, Martin Harris and Orrin Porter Rockwell (Smith, *History of the Church,* 1:74-79).

Only about thirty people attended the meeting in Peter Whitmer's log cabin on April 6, 1830. Although the setting was obscure, the business at hand was of historic significance. The Church of Jesus Christ of Latter-day Saints was to be organized. Six men are listed as the official organizers of the Church: Joseph Smith, Jr., Oliver Cowdery, Hyrum Smith, Peter Whitmer, Jr., Samuel H. Smith, and David Whitmer. However, one of those in attendance was an eleven-year-old boy named David Lewis. He wanted to be baptized, but the Prophet sent him home to discuss it with his parents and get their consent.

WORLD EVENTS

The three major sections of the United States—the North, South, and West—had seemingly irreconcilable differences. The North was becoming increasingly industrialized, and business leaders wanted the government to impose high tariffs on imported goods so that Americans would be forced to buy American manufactured items. The South did not want high tariffs because their main business was agriculture. Much of their cotton was sold to England, and they could buy clothing and furniture from England cheaper than they could buy it from their northern countrymen. The Westerners were mainly interested in land, and they wanted it to remain cheap so they could expand as much as they wished. Each section of the country seemed to feel that its interests took precedence over those of the others. Feelings between the north and south became so bitter that there was talk in South Carolina of nullifying the tariff law. Then, when the Northerners attempted to limit the sale of public lands in the West in order to keep the labor force from migrating, tempers flared. Senator Benton of Missouri claimed that it was a "conflict scheme of injustice, which taxes the south to injure the west, to pauperize the poor of the north" (Richard B. Morris, ed., *Encyclopedia of American History*, 168) in context of the Webster/Haines debate, Jan. 1830.

In 1830, travel was mainly done by horse and buggy, and people thought long and hard about trips of fifteen or twenty miles. The major cities lined the east coast, and only a few hardy explorers had penetrated the forests and deserts west of the Mississippi River. Modern science was in its infancy. Robert Brown had just discovered the cell nucleus in plants. Organic chemistry was just getting started. Chloroform was about to revolutionize surgery. New inventions came forth every year, simplifying and speeding printing, sewing, manufacturing, and transportation.

KNEELING IN
PRAYER AT THE
ORGANIZATION OF
THE CHURCH *by*
William Whitaker
depicts the organiza-
tion of The Church
of Jesus Christ of
Latter-day Saints.
Only about fifty
people were present
at this historic meet-
ing on April 6, 1830
in Peter Whitmer's
log cabin. Six men
are listed as the offi-
cial organizers of the
Church: Joseph
Smith, Jr., Oliver
Cowdery, Hyrum
Smith, Peter
Whitmer, Jr., Samuel
H. Smith, and
David Whitmer.
*charcoal sketch
ca. 1970*

David's parents gave him permission to join, and about twenty-nine days after the Church was organized, on the boy's twelfth birthday, Joseph Smith baptized David in a nearby stream. After the baptism, Joseph tried to persuade him not to go home because a violent thunderstorm had just broken. But the boy had promised his mother that he would return, so Joseph didn't argue the point, promising the boy that the Lord would protect him and get him safely home to his mother. On the way, David became lost, but remembering the prophet's words, he prayed for protection and guidance. He then saw what looked to be a lamp, and followed it to his house.

Several people, including members of the Smith and Whitmer families, were baptized in the days following the organization of the Church. After the organization was completed, Joseph traveled to Colesville, New York. He recorded:

> During this month of April, I went on a visit to the residence of Mr. Joseph Knight, of Colesville, Broom County, New York, with whom and his family I had been for some time acquainted, and whose name I had previously mentioned as having been so kind and thoughtful towards us while translating the Book of Mormon. Mr. Knight and his family were Universalists, but were willing to reason with me upon my religious views,

and were, as usual, friendly and hospitable. We held several meetings in the neighborhood; we had many friends, and some enemies. Our meetings were well attended, and many began to pray fervently to Almighty God, that He would give them wisdom to understand the truth.

Amongst those who attended our meetings regularly, was Newel Knight, son of Joseph Knight. He and I had many serious conversations on the important subject of man's eternal salvation. We had got into the habit of praying much at our meetings, and Newel had said that he would try and take up his cross and pray vocally during meeting; but when we again met together, he rather excused himself. I tried to prevail upon him . . . [but he said] he would wait until he could get into the woods by himself and there he would pray.

Accordingly, he deferred praying until next morning, when he retired into the woods; where . . . he made several attempts to pray, but could scarcely do so, feeling that he had not done his duty, in refusing to pray in the presence of others. He began to feel uneasy, and continued to feel worse both in mind and body, until, upon reaching his own house, his appearance was such as to alarm his wife very much. He requested her to go and bring me to him. I went and found him suffering very much in his mind, and his body acted upon in a very strange manner; his visage and limbs distorted and twisted in every shape and appearance possible to imagine; and finally he was caught up off the floor of the apartment, and tossed about most fearfully.

His situation was soon made known to his neighbors and relatives and in a short time as many as eight or nine grown persons had gotten together to witness this scene. After he had thus suffered for a time, I succeeded in getting hold of him by the hand, when almost immediately he spoke to me, and with great earnestness requested me to cast the devil out of him, saying that he knew he was in him, and that he also knew that I could cast him out.

I replied, "If you know that I can, it shall be done," and then almost unconsciously I rebuked the devil, and commanded him in the name of Jesus Christ to depart from him; when immediately Newel spoke out and said that he saw the devil leave him and vanish from his sight. This was the first miracle which was done in the Church, or by any member of it; and it was done, not by man, nor by the power of man, but it was done by God, and by the power of godliness; therefore, let the honor and the praise, the dominion and the glory, be ascribed to the Father, Son, and Holy Spirit for ever and ever. Amen.

This scene was now entirely changed, for as soon as the devil had departed from our friend his countenance became natural, his distortions of body ceased, and almost immediately the Spirit of the Lord descended upon him, and the visions of eternity were opened to his view. So soon as consciousness returned, his bodily weakness was such that we were obliged to lay him upon his bed, and wait upon him for some time. He afterwards related his experience as follows:

"I now began to feel a most pleasing sensation resting on me, and immediately the visions of heaven were opened to my view. I felt myself attracted upward, and remained for some time enwrapt in contemplation, insomuch that I knew not what was going on in the room. By and by, I felt some weight pressing upon my shoulder and the side of my head, which served to recall me to a sense of my situation. I found that the Spirit of the Lord had actually caught me up off the floor, and that my shoulder and head were pressing against the beams.". . .

During the last week in May, the above-mentioned Newel Knight came to visit us at Fayette, and was baptized by David Whitmer (Smith, *History of the Church,* 1:81-84).

On June 9, 1830, the first conference of the newly restored Church was held in Fayette, New York. It was a spiritual feast as Joseph relates:

Having opened by singing and prayer, we partook together of the emblems of the body and blood of our Lord Jesus Christ. We then proceeded to confirm several who had lately been baptized, after which we called out and ordained several to the various offices of the Priesthood.

Much exhortation and instruction was given, and the Holy Ghost was poured out upon us in a miraculous manner—many of our number prophesied, whilst others had the heavens opened to their view. . . . [Brother Newel Knight] saw heaven opened, and beheld the Lord Jesus Christ, seated at the right hand of the majesty on high, and had it made plain to his understanding that the time would come when he would be admitted into His presence, to enjoy His society for ever and ever. . . . [The] brethren . . . shouted hosannas to God and the Lamb, and rehearsed the glorious things which they had seen and felt, whilst they were yet in the spirit.

Such scenes as these were calculated to inspire our hearts with joy unspeakable, and fill us with awe and reverence for that Almighty Being, by whose grace we had been called (Smith, *History of the Church,* 1:84-85).

PERSECUTION PERSISTS

Four years before, in 1826, Joseph had been in Colesville, where he was working for Josiah Stowell. Apparently he was well-known there, and at least some of the people knew of his visions and the "gold book" he was translating. Now interest ran high when he returned with copies of the book, and he made several trips to the area during the summer of 1830. Joseph always stayed with the Knight family and held meetings with any who were interested. Ministers in Colesville became angry as members of their congregations began to join this new Church, and mobs, led by these ministers, began harassing the Prophet. The night before a baptism, they destroyed a small dam that had been built to create a pond. However, members rebuilt the dam, and Oliver Cowdery baptized thirteen people, including Emma Smith. As evening fell, Saints and friends gathered for a meeting to confirm those who had been baptized that morning. Joseph relates that at that moment,

I was visited by a constable, and arrested by him . . . on the charge of being a disorderly person, of setting the country in an uproar by preaching the Book of Mormon. The constable informed me, soon after I had been arrested, that the plan of those who had got out the warrant was to get me into the hands of the mob, who were now laying in ambush for me; but that he was determined to save me from them, as he had found me to be a different sort of person from what I had been represented to him. I soon found that he had told me the truth in this matter, for not far from Mr. Knight's house, the wagon in which we had set out was surrounded by a mob, who seemed only to await some signal from the constable; but to their great disappointment, he gave the horse the whip and drove me out of their reach.

Whilst driving in great haste one of the wagon wheels came off, which left us once more very nearly surrounded by them, as they had come on in close pursuit. However, we managed to replace the wheel and again left them behind us. He drove on to the town of South Bainbridge, Chenango County, where he lodged me for the time being in an upper room of a tavern; and in order that all might be right with himself and with me also, he slept during the night with his feet against the door, and a loaded musket by his side, whilst I occupied a bed which was in the room; he having declared that if we were interrupted unlawfully, he would fight for me, and defend me as far as it was in his power (Smith, *History of the Church,* 1:88-89).

The following day, a court was convened in the town where Joseph and Emma had been married three years earlier. Joseph Knight had asked two of his neighbors, James Davidson and John Reid, to defend the prophet. Many spectators were present, eager to see Joseph convicted and punished for the crimes they imagined he had committed. Mr. Josiah Stowell, Joseph's former employer, and his two daughters were among the witnesses, but they only proved that Joseph was a man of integrity and honesty. The trial dragged on all day, and finally Joseph was acquitted. However, as soon as he was acquitted, he was served with a warrant from Broome County. Joseph noted:

The constable who served this second warrant upon me had no sooner arrested me than he began to abuse and insult me; and so unfeeling was he with me, that although I had been kept all the day in court without anything to eat since the morning, yet he hurried me off to Broome County, a distance of about fifteen miles, before he allowed me any kind of food whatever. He took me to a tavern, and gathered in a number of men, who used every means to abuse, ridicule and insult me. They spit upon me, pointed their fingers at me saying, "Prophesy, prophesy!" And thus did they imitate those who crucified the Savior of mankind, not knowing what they did.

We were at this time, not far distant from my own house. I wished to be allowed the privilege of spending the night with my wife at my home, offering any wished for security for my appearance; but this was denied me. I applied for something to eat. The constable ordered me some crusts of bread and water. . . . At length we retired to bed. The constable made me lie next to the wall. He then laid himself down by me and put his arm around me, and upon my moving in the least, would clench me fast, fearing that I intended to escape from him, and in this very disagreeable manner did we pass the night (Smith, *History of the Church,* 1:91).

That evening, Joseph Knight was busy arranging for the prophet's defense at the new trial. He talked with John Reid who, with James Davidson, had served as attorneys the day before. Mr. Reid recalled:

> I was again called upon by [the prophet's] friends to defend him against his malignant persecutors, and clear him from the false charges they had preferred against him. I made every reasonable excuse I could, as I was nearly worn out through fatigue and want of sleep; as I had been engaged in lawsuits for two days, and nearly the whole of two nights. But I saw that the persecution was great against him; and here let me say . . . singular as it may seem, while Mr. Knight was pleading with me to go, a peculiar impression or thought struck my mind, that I must go and defend him, for he was the Lord's anointed. I did not know what it meant, but I thought I must go and clear the Lord's anointed. I said I would go, and started with as much faith as the apostles had when they could remove mountains, accompanied by Father Knight, who was like the old patriarchs that followed the ark of God to the city of David (Roberts, *A Comprehensive History of the Church,* 1:210-11).

Joseph recorded,

> Next day I was brought before the magistrate's court . . . and put upon my trial. My former faithful friends and lawyers were again at my side; my former persecutors were arrayed against me (Smith, *History of the Church,* 1:91).

Mr. Reid continued:

> Neither talents nor money were wanting to insure them success. They employed the best lawyer in that county, and introduced twenty or thirty witnesses before dark, but proved nothing. Then they sent out runners and ransacked the hills and vales, grog shops and ditches, and gathered together a company that looked as if they'd come from hell and had been whipped by the soot boy thereof; which they brought forward to testify one after another, but with no better success than before, although they wrung and twisted into every shape, in trying to tell something that would criminate the prisoner. Nothing was proven against him however (Roberts, *A Comprehensive History of the Church,* 1:211-12).

Joseph commented on the day's events:

> In this frivolous and vexatious manner did they proceed for a considerable time, when, finally, Newel Knight was called up and examined by Lawyer Seymour, who had been especially sent for on this occasion . . . and

appeared very anxious and determined that the people should not be deluded by anyone professing the power of godliness, and not "denying the power thereof."

Mr. Knight was sworn, and Mr. Seymour interrogated him as follows:

"Did the prisoner, Joseph Smith, Jun., cast the devil out of you?"

[Newel replied,] "No, sir."

"Why, have not you had the devil cast out of you?"

"Yes, sir."

"And had not Joe Smith some hand in its being done?"

"Yes sir."

"And did not he cast him out of you?"

"No, sir; it was done by the power of God, and Joseph Smith was the instrument in the hands of God, on the occasion. He commanded him to come out of me in the name of Jesus Christ."

"And are you sure that it was the devil?"

"Yes, sir."

"Did you see him after he was cast out of you?"

"Yes, sir! I saw him."

"Pray, what did he look like?"

". . . I believe I need not answer your last question, but I will do it, provided I be allowed to ask you one question first, and you answer me, viz., Do you, Mr. Seymour, understand the things of the spirit?"

"No," answered Mr. Seymour, I do not pretend to such big things."

"Well, then," replied Knight, " it would be of no use to tell you what the devil looked like, for it was a spiritual sight, and spiritually discerned, and of course you would not understand it were I to tell you of it" (Smith, *History of the Church,* 1:92-93).

Joseph continued:

The lawyer dropped his head, whilst the loud laugh of the audience proclaimed his discomfiture. . . .

Mr. Davidson and Mr. Reid followed on my behalf. They held forth in true colors the nature of the prosecution, the malignancy of intention, and the apparent disposition to persecute their client, rather than to afford him justice. . . . And each, in his turn, thanked God that he had been engaged in so good a cause as that of defending a man whose character stood so well to test of such a strict investigation. In fact, these men, although not regular lawyers, were upon this occasion able to put to silence their opponents and convince the court that I was innocent. They spoke like men inspired of God, whilst those who were arrayed against me trembled under the sound of their voices, and quailed before them like criminals before a bar of justice.

The majority of the assembled multitude had now begun to find that nothing could be sustained against me. Even the constable who arrested me, and treated me so badly, now came and apologized to me and asked my forgiveness for his behavior toward me; and so far was he changed, that he informed me that the mob were determined, if the court acquitted me, that they would have me, and rail-ride me, and tar and feather me; and further, that he was willing to favor me and lead me out in safety by a private way.

The court found the charges against me not sustained; I was accordingly acquitted, to the great satisfaction of my friends and vexation of my enemies. . . . Through the instrumentality of my new friend the constable, I was
enabled to escape them and make my way in safety to my wife's sister's house,
where I found my wife awaiting with much anxiety the issue of those ungod-
ly proceedings, and in company with her, I arrived next day in safety at my
own house (Smith, *History of the Church,* 1:93-96).

In spite of the hours Joseph spent preaching, baptizing, solving problems in the
young church, and being harassed by the law, he was also trying to run his farm in

JOSEPH AND EMMA'S
SMALL HOME IN
HARMONY,
PENNSYLVANIA.
The home was locat-
ed on Isaac Hale's
property. During
their stay in this
home, Martin Harris
acted as scribe for
Joseph, then lost the
116-page manu-
script. Joseph and
Emma's first baby
was born and lived
for only a few hours.
Oliver Cowdery
then came here to
act as scribe, and
together, he and
Joseph completed
about 500 pages of
the Book of
Mormon.

Harmony, Pennsylvania. He and Oliver worked together on
the farm in the early part of the summer, but in July, Oliver
traveled to Fayette to stay with the Whitmer family for a time.
He had not been gone long when Joseph received a letter from
him concerning the revelation that is now Section 20 of the
Doctrine and Covenants. Oliver declared that Joseph had
made an error in verse 37, and it should be rewritten according to Oliver's interpretation. Joseph wrote back that it was as
the Lord had revealed it, and not his to change. However, a letter was not sufficient to convince Oliver and the members of
the Whitmer family, who now agreed with him. Joseph had to
travel again from Harmony to Fayette to reason with his
brothers in the gospel and convince them of the truth. Oliver
had often been warned in various revelations to beware of false
pride and ambition; perhaps he felt that his superior education
made him a more qualified spokesman than Joseph was.

In August, Newel Knight and his wife, Sally, traveled to Harmony to visit
Joseph and Emma. Emma and Sally had both been baptized in Colesville on the
day Joseph was arrested, but because his arrest had stopped the meeting, they
had not been confirmed. The two couples decided to hold a sacrament meeting
and confirm the women members of the Church. As Joseph was traveling to
town to buy bread and wine for the sacrament, he was met by a heavenly messenger who gave him the following instructions:

For, behold, I say unto you, that it mattereth not what ye shall eat or
what ye shall drink when ye partake of the sacrament, if it so be that ye do it
with an eye single to my glory—remembering unto the Father my body
which was laid down for you, and my blood which was shed for the remission of your sins.

Wherefore, a commandment I give unto you that you shall not purchase
wine, neither strong drink of your enemies; wherefore, you shall partake of
none except it is made new among you; yea, in this my Father's kingdom
which shall be built up on the earth (D&C 27:2-4).

Joseph returned with this new revelation and they held their sacrament meeting.

The Work Continues

Emma Hale Smith's parents had never accepted Joseph's revelations, but they had tolerated him and had helped the young couple get settled on the farm in Harmony. However, as Joseph's fame spread, the local ministers became increasingly hostile and turned Emma's parents against their son-in-law. Since the Church was growing rapidly in New York, Joseph and Emma decided to move to Fayette. Newel Knight came with his wagon to help them pack up and move again.

Once they were settled, Joseph decided that he needed to return to Colesville to confirm those who had been baptized the previous June. On August 19th, Joseph and Hyrum Smith and John and David Whitmer prepared for the journey. Newel Knight records:

> Knowing it was their duty to visit us, they called upon our Heavenly Father in mighty prayer, that he would grant them an opportunity of meeting us; that he would blind the eyes of their enemies that they might not see, and that on this occasion they might return unmolested. Their prayers were not in vain. A little distance from my house they encountered a large company of men at work upon the public road, among whom were found some of our most bitter enemies, who looked earnestly at the brethren, but not knowing them, the brethren passed on unmolested. That evening the Saints assembled and were confirmed, and partook of the sacrament. We had a happy meeting, having much reason to rejoice in the God of our salvation, and sing hosannas to His holy name ("Newel Knight's Journal," *Scraps of Biography,* 63-64).

The next day Joseph and the others departed unmolested. A few hours later, a mob descended on the Knight home but found that the Mormon Prophet already gone. While all the members of the Church of Jesus Christ were preaching the gospel to friends and relatives on every possible occasion, Samuel H. Smith, the brother of the Prophet, was called, ordained, and set apart to serve as a missionary. His mother Lucy tells of his first missionary journey.

> On the thirtieth of June, Samuel started on a mission, to which he had been set apart by Joseph, and in traveling twenty-five miles, which was his first day's journey, he stopped at a number of places in order to sell his books, but was turned out of doors as soon as he declared his principles. When evening came on, he was faint and almost discouraged, but coming to an inn, which was surrounded with every appearance of plenty, he called to see if the

landlord would buy one of his books. On going in, Samuel inquired of him if he did not wish to purchase a history of the origin of the Indians.

"I do not know," replied the host, "how did you get hold of it?"

"It was translated," rejoined Samuel, "by my brother, from some gold plates that he found buried in the earth."

"You liar!" cried the landlord, "get out of my house—you shan't stay one minute with your books."

Samuel was sick at heart, for this was the fifth time he had been turned out of doors that day. He left the house, and traveled a short distance, and washed his feet in a small brook, as a testimony against the man. He then proceeded five miles further on his journey, and seeing an apple tree a short distance from the road, he concluded to pass the night under it; and here he lay all night upon the cold, damp ground.

In the morning, he arose from his comfortless bed and observing a small cottage at no great distance, he drew near, hoping to get a little refreshment. The only inmate was a widow, who seemed very poor. He asked her for food, relating the story of his former treatment. She prepared him victuals, and, after eating, he explained to her the history of the Book of Mormon. She listened attentively, and believed all that he told her, but, in consequence of her poverty, she was unable to purchase one of the books. He presented her with one, and proceeded to Bloomington, which was eight miles further. Here he stopped at the house of John P. Greene, who was a Methodist preacher, and was at that time about starting on a preaching mission. He, like the others, did not wish to make a purchase of what he considered at that time to be a nonsensical fable, however, he said that he would take a subscription paper, and, if he found anyone on his route who was disposed to purchase, he would take his name, and in two weeks, Samuel might call again, and he would let him know what the prospect was of selling.

After making this arrangement, Samuel left one of his books with him, and returned home. At the time appointed, Samuel started again for the Reverend John P. Greene's in order to learn the success which this gentleman had met with in finding sale[s] for the Book of Mormon. This time, Mr. Smith, and myself accompanied him, and it was our intention to have passed near the tavern, where Samuel was so abusively treated a fortnight previous, but just before we came to the house, a sign of smallpox intercepted us. We turned aside, and meeting a citizen of the place, we inquired of him, to what extent this disease prevailed. He answered, that the tavern keeper, and two of his family had died with it not long since, but he did not know that any one else had caught the disease, and that it

GRAVESTONES OF ISAAC & ELIZABETH HALE, Emma Hale Smith's parents. They were buried at the McKune Cemetery near Harmony, PA. Isaac's marker reads: *"Isaac Hale died Jan. 11, 1839, aged 75 yrs 10 mo. & 10 d's. The body of Isaac Hale, the Hunter, like the cover of an old book, its contents torn out, and stript of its lettering and guilding, lies here food for worms. Yet the work itself shall not be lost for it will, as he believed, appear once more in a new and more beautiful edition, corrected and amended."* Elizabeth's marker reads: *"Elizabeth wife of Isaac Hale died Feb. 16, 1842, aged 75 years 2 mo. & 28 d's."* ca. 1897–1927

was brought into the neighborhood by a traveler, who stopped at the tavern over night. . . .

We arrived at Esquire Beaman's, in Livonia that night. The next morning Samuel took the road to Mr. Greene's, and, finding that he had made no sale of the books, we returned the following day (Smith, *History of Joseph Smith,* 169-70).

Samuel was discouraged with his lack of success on this first missionary journey, but Mr. Greene and his wife both read the copy of the Book of Mormon that he had left with them. They were very impressed and passed it on to other members of their family, including Mrs. Greene's sister and brother-in-law, Miriam and Brigham Young. Brigham, in turn, passed the book along to his brothers and his friend Heber C. Kimball. Lucy tells of another missionary journey:

In the summer after the church was organized, my husband set out, with Don Carlos, to visit his father, Asael Smith. After a tedious journey, they arrived at the house of John Smith, my husband's brother. His wife Clarissa had never before seen my husband, but as soon as he entered, she exclaimed, "There, Mr. Smith. is your brother Joseph."

John, turning suddenly cried out, "Joseph, is this you?"

"It is I," said Joseph; "is my father yet alive? I have come to see him once more, before he dies."

For a particular account of this visit, I shall give my readers an extract from brother John Smith's journal. He writes as follows:

The next morning after Brother Joseph arrived, we set out together for Stockholm to see our father, who was living at that place with our brother Silas. We arrived about dark at the house of my brother Jesse, who was absent with his wife. The children informed us that their parents were with our father, who was supposed to be dying. We hastened without delay to the house of brother Silas, and upon arriving there, were told that father was just recovering from a severe fit, and, as it was not considered advisable to let him or mother know that Joseph was there, we went to spend the night with brother Jesse.

As soon as we were settled, brothers Jesse and Joseph entered into conversation respecting their families. Joseph briefly related the history of his family, the death of Alvin, etc. He then began to speak of the discovery and translation of the Book of Mormon. At this Jesse grew very angry, and exclaimed, "If you say another word about that Book of Mormon, you shall not stay a minute longer in my house, and if I can't get you out any other way, I will hew you down with my broadaxe."

We had always been accustomed to being treated with much harshness by our brother, but he had never carried it to so great an extent before. However, we spent the night with him, and the next morning visited our aged parents. They were overjoyed to see Joseph, for he had been absent from them so long, that they had been fearful of never beholding his face again in the flesh.

After the usual salutations, enquiries, and explanations, the subject of the Book of Mormon was introduced. Father received with gladness that which Joseph communicated; and remarked that he had always expected that something would appear to make known the true Gospel. . . .

After this, Brother Joseph proceeded in conversation, and father seemed to be pleased with every word which he said. But I must confess that I was too pious, at that time, to believe one word of it. . . .

That evening Joseph explained to me the principles of Mormonism, the truth of which I have never since denied. . . .

Before he left me, he requested me to promise him that I would read a Book of Mormon, which he had given me, and even should I not believe it, that I would not condemn it; "for," said he, "if you do not condemn it, you shall have a testimony of its truth." I fulfilled my promise, and thus proved his testimony to be true" (Smith, *History of Joseph Smith,* 172-75).

Father Asael Smith died on October 31, 1830, having lived to see the fulfillment of his prophecy that one of his descendants would revolutionize the religious world.

WORLD EVENTS

In the fall of 1830, Andrew Jackson was halfway through his first term as president of the United States. More people were moving west from the crowded cities on the eastern seaboard. The Erie Canal had been operating for five years, carrying people and supplies from Albany, NY, to Buffalo, NY in a matter of days. The boats went east as well, carrying grain, lumber, and ice to the cities on the coast and ships bound for Europe and India. New York City was already the financial center of the United States. However, stockbrokers no longer did their trading under a tree at 68 Wall Street. Now they plied their trades in an office building. The population of the United States was expanding west. Ohio already had over a million people. Missouri, the westernmost and newest state, became the starting point for trappers and traders who ventured into the Mexican territory, which stretched to the Pacific Ocean.

AN EXPANDING CHURCH

America was becoming larger, more complex and more diverse; and so was The Church of Jesus Christ of Latter-day Saints. Until this time, the story of the Church had been largely the story of Joseph Smith. But this would not be the case anymore. By the fall of 1830, Joseph Smith was well on his way to fulfilling his mission of preparing a people worthy to greet the Savior at His Second Coming. Joseph had seen the Father and the Son, as well as many angels. He had been taught the knowledge of the eternities. He had completed the translation of the Book of Mormon, published it, and, under inspired direction, organized the restored Church of Jesus Christ. A small core of believers had gathered, and many of them were eager to spread the gospel. Each day more converts joined the Church. Some, like Thomas B. Marsh and Solomon Chamberlain, had been converted after reading a few pages of the Book of Mormon manuscript; others, like Newel Knight and some of the citizens of Colesville, New York, had heard Joseph and Oliver preach or had read the complete Book of Mormon. But opposition was growing as well. Already Joseph had been forced to move three or four times. People were beginning to call the believers Mormonites or Mormons because of the Book of Mormon. To the new Saints, however, the future seemed glorious. They knew that the American Indians had a great heritage and they were eager to share that knowledge with them. They also knew that Zion was to be established and that they were to help build it. There was the promise of more revelation, more scriptures, and more knowledge from God. The Church would be fully organized, and they would be part of it. They could not wait to share the gospel with everyone they met.

Samuel Smith, brother to the Prophet, had undertaken the first missionary journey, but had come home discouraged, having left a copy of the Book of Mormon with only a few people. Little did he know that those copies would be read and would help convert many who would become great leaders and missionaries themselves.

NEW CONVERTS

Many were waiting for the gospel but had not yet heard it. Once such person was a stocky young carpenter named Brigham Young who was living in Mendon, New York. He was twenty-nine years old and a member of the Methodist Church. But Brigham expected more from a church than the Methodists could offer.

> I have often prayed, if there is a God in Heaven, save me that I may know all and not be fooled. I saw them get religion all around me—men were rolling and hollering and bawling and thumping, but it had no effect on me—I wanted to know the truth that I might not be fooled.
>
> I read the Bible for myself. When I was told to believe in Jesus Christ, and that was all that was required for salvation, I did not so understand the Bible. I understood from the Bible that when the Lord had a church upon the earth it was a system of ordinances, of laws and regulations to be obeyed, a society presided over and regulated by officers and ministers peculiar to itself, to answer such and such purposes, and bring to pass such and such results. . . . Such a system answering the description given in the Bible I could not find on the earth. . . . When I would ask the ministers of religion . . . if that which is laid down in the New Testament is not the pattern, all the reply I could receive from them was that . . . "these things are done away" (Brigham Young, *Journal of Discourses,* 11:37).

BRIGHAM YOUNG (1801–1877), a stocky young carpenter, was living in Mendon, NY at the time that he first heard the gospel. He was then twenty-nine years old and a member of the Methodist Church. *ca. 1845, Nauvoo, IL*

About this same time, another individual with religious yearnings was living on a farm that he had carved out of the wilderness in northern Ohio. In August 1830, this twenty-three-year-old man, named Parley P. Pratt, sold his farm and home and traveled east, following an inner prompting that he could neither explain nor deny. He planned on visiting his family and friends in New York State, but about halfway through the journey, Parley was impressed that he should make a detour. He soon met a Baptist deacon who told him of a strange new book in his possession. Parley felt a strong desire to read the book, and later recorded:

Next morning I called at his house, where, for the first time, my eyes beheld the BOOK of MORMON—that book of books. . . .

I opened it with eagerness, and read the title page. I then read the testimony of several witnesses in relation to the manner of its being found and translated. After this, I commenced its contents by course. I read all day; eating was a burden, I had no desire for food; sleep was a burden when the night came, for I preferred reading to sleep.

As I read, the spirit of the Lord was upon me, and I knew and comprehended that the book was true, as plainly and manifestly as a man comprehends and knows that he exists. My joy was now full, as it were, and I rejoiced sufficiently to more than pay me for all the sorrows, sacrifices and toils of my life (*Autobiography of Parley P. Pratt,* 20).

Fired with enthusiasm, Parley traveled to Palmyra, where he met Hyrum Smith. After talking most of the night, Parley left the next morning. Before he left, however, Hyrum gave Parley a copy of the Book of Mormon, as Parley did not have one of his own, and had not yet finished reading the book. After walking a while, he sat down by the roadside and read of the Savior's visit to the American continent after His crucifixion. Two days later, Parley returned to Hyrum's home and asked to be baptized. Together, they went to the Whitmer home near Fayette, where Parley met Oliver Cowdery and members of the Whitmer family.

> The 1st of September, 1830, I was baptized by the hand of an Apostle of the Church of Jesus Christ, by the name of Oliver Cowdery. This took place in Seneca Lake, a beautiful and transparent sheet of water in Western New York.
>
> A meeting was held the same evening, and after singing a hymn and prayer, Elder Cowdery and others proceeded to lay their hands upon my head in the name of Jesus, for the gift of the Holy Ghost. After which I was ordained to the office of an Elder in the Church, which included authority to preach, baptize, administer the sacrament, administer the Holy Ghost, by the laying on of hands in the name of Jesus Christ and to take the lead in meetings of worship (*Autobiography of Parley P. Pratt,* 27).

Parley now knew why he had been diverted from his travels, and continued on toward his boyhood home where his wife awaited him. There, in Oswego, New York, he preached the gospel of the restoration to his parents, relatives, friends, and others who would listen. He found that many accepted part of the truth, but only his brother, Orson, believed with all his heart and was baptized.

Second Conference of the Church

The growing Church had some glorious experiences, but its trials and tribulations continued. In Fayette, Joseph was preparing for the second conference of the Church, which was to begin on September 26. Over fifty people had been baptized, and more were joining the Church each week. Although the Church had more enemies than friends, Joseph's most pressing problem came from one of the members. Hiram Page, one of the eight men who had seen and handled the golden plates, said he had a stone that allowed him to receive revelations and instructions for the Church. Newel Knight was with Joseph during this time and recorded:

> About the last of August, 1830, I took my team and wagon to Harmony to move Joseph and his family to Fayette, New York. After arranging my affairs at home, I again set out for Fayette to attend our second conference, which had been appointed to be held at Father Whitmer's, where Joseph then resided. On my arrival I found Brother Joseph in great distress of mind on account of Hiram Page, who had managed to get some dissension of feeling among the brethren by giving revelations concerning the government of the Church and other matters which he claimed to have received through the medium of a stone he possessed. He had quite a roll of papers full of these revelations, and many in the Church were led astray by them. Even Oliver Cowdery and the Whitmer family had

WORLD EVENTS

Far across the sea, in Europe, winds of change were stirring new hopes and ideas in the hearts of the people. A new generation of people was emerging who would be delighted to accept the gospel when missionaries arrived. First, however, would come political change. Since 1815, Austria, Russia, Prussia, and Great Britain had guarded the state of affairs they had created after Napoleon's defeat. By 1830, however, a new middle-class was emerging that was wealthy and educated, but politically powerless. The French king, Charles X, clung to the privileges of royalty and dissolved the Chamber of Deputies when they opposed one of his political appointments. He then limited the liberty of the press and disenfranchised three-fourths of the electors. On July 16, 1830, Paris erupted into open rebellion. For three days, the streets were filled with fighting, and Charles fled to England.

The Chamber of Deputies offered the now vacant throne to Phillipe, Duke of Orleans, and the blue, white and red tricolor replaced the flag of the Bourbons. News that the French had dethroned a king spread like wildfire through Europe. Monarchs trembled on their thrones.

given heed to them, although they were in contradiction to the New Testament and the revelations of these last days. Joseph was perplexed and scarcely knew how to meet this new exigency. That night I occupied the same room that he did, and the greater part of the night was spent in prayer and supplication. After much labor with these brethren, they were convinced of their error and confessed the same, renouncing the revelations as not being of God, but acknowledging that Satan had conspired to overthrow their belief in the true plan of salvation. In consequence of these things, Joseph inquired of the Lord before conference commenced and received a revelation in which the Lord explicitly stated His mind and will concerning the receiving of revelation (Andrus, *They Knew the Prophet,* 13-14).

But, behold, verily, verily, I say unto thee, no one shall be appointed to receive commandments and revelations in this church excepting my servant Joseph Smith, Jun., for he receiveth them even as Moses. . . .

For I have given him the keys of the mysteries, and the revelations which are sealed, until I shall appoint unto them another in his stead. . . .

For all things must be done in order, and by common consent in the church, by the prayer of faith (D&C 28:2, 7, 13).

This revelation was addressed to Oliver Cowdery. Once again, the Lord had to chasten him for pride and his failure to recognize Joseph as the head of the Church. The Lord explained that although Oliver could receive revelation for himself and be inspired as he spoke, his calling did not include giving commandments to the Church.

Newel Knight stated that he was very impressed with the Prophet's handling of this crisis.

During this time we had much of the power of God manifest among us, and it was wonderful to witness the wisdom that Joseph displayed on this occasion, for truly God gave unto him great wisdom and power, and it seems to me that none who saw him administer righteousness under such trying circumstances could doubt that the Lord was with him. He acted not with the wisdom of man, but with the wisdom of God. The Holy Ghost came upon us and filled our hearts with unspeakable joy. Before this memorable conference closed, three other revelations besides the one already mentioned were received from God by our prophet, and we were made to rejoice exceedingly in this goodness (Andrus, *They Knew the Prophet,* 14).

Saints gathered from all over the region to attend the second conference of the Church. Parley Pratt, who had never before met the Prophet, was among the sixty-two attending members. Parley later recorded:

He received me with a hearty welcome, and with that frank and kind manner so universal with him in after years. . . .

President Joseph Smith was in person tall and well built, strong and active, of light complexion, light hair, blue eyes, very little beard, and of an expression peculiar to himself, on which the eye naturally rested with interest, and was never weary of beholding. His countenance was ever mild, affable, beaming with intelligence and benevolence; mingled with a look of interest and an unconscious smile, or cheerfulness, and entirely free from all restraint or affectation of gravity; and there was something connected with this serene and steady penetrating glance of his eye, as if he would penetrate the deepest abyss of the human heart, gaze into eternity, penetrate the heavens, and comprehend all worlds.

He possessed a noble boldness and independence of character; his manner was easy and familiar; his rebuke terrible as the lion; his benevolence unbounded as the ocean; his intelligence universal, and his language abounding in original eloquence peculiar to himself—not polished—not studied—not smoothed and softened by education and refined by art; but flowing forth in its own native simplicity, and profusely abounding in variety of subject and manner. He interested and edified, while, at the same time, he amused and entertained his audience; and none listened to him that were ever weary with his discourse. I have even known him to retain a congregation of willing and anxious listeners for many hours together, in the midst of cold or sunshine, rain or wind, while they were laughing at one moment and weeping the next. Even his most bitter enemies were generally overcome, if he could once get their ears. . . .

In short, in him the characters of a Daniel and a Cyrus were wonderfully blended. The gifts, wisdom and devotion of a Daniel were united with the boldness, courage, temperance, perseverance and generosity of a Cyrus (*Autobiography of Parley P. Pratt,* 31-32).

Joseph Smith recorded that, once contentions and disputes had been resolved, those at the conference experienced a great outpouring of Spirit from the Lord.

At length our conference assembled. The subject of the stone previously mentioned was discussed, and after considerable investigation, Brother Page, as well as the whole Church who were present, renounced the said stone, and all things connected therewith, much to our mutual satisfaction and happiness. We now partook of the Sacrament, confirmed and ordained many, and attended to the great variety of Church business on the first and the two following days of the conference, during which time we had much of the power of God manifested amongst us; the Holy Ghost came upon us, and filled us with joy unspeakable; and peace, and faith, and hope and charity abounded in our midst (Smith, *History of the Church,* 1:115).

MISSIONARY WORK BEGINS

At this time, several of the elders expressed interest in the Lamanites. "The desire being so great, it was agreed that we should inquire of the Lord . . . which we accordingly did, and received the following [revelations]" (Smith, *History of the Church,* 1:118-19). Accordingly, Sections 28, 30, and 32 of the Doctrine and Covenants were received, which called the brethren to preach to the Lamanites.

And now [Oliver], behold, I say unto you that you shall go unto the Lamanites and preach my gospel unto them; and inasmuch as they receive thy teachings thou shalt cause my church to be established among them . . .

And now, behold, I say unto you that it is not revealed, and no man knoweth where the city of Zion shall be built, but it shall be given hereafter. Behold I say unto you it shall be on the borders by the Lamanites. . . .

Behold, I say unto you, Peter [Whitmer], that you shall take your journey with your brother Oliver; for the time has come that it is expedient in me that you shall open your mouth to declare my gospel. . . .

And now concerning my servant Parley P. Pratt, behold, I say unto him that as I live I will that he shall declare my gospel and learn of me, and be meek and lowly of heart. . . .

[And] he shall go with my servants, Oliver Cowdery and Peter Whitmer, Jun., into the wilderness among the Lamanites.

And Ziba Peterson also shall go with them; and I myself will go with them and be in their midst (D&C 28:8-9; 30:5; 32:1-3).

When the conference ended, the women of the Church began at once to help the four missionaries prepare for their travels. Lucy Smith tells of their activities:

As soon as this revelation was received, Emma Smith, and several other sisters, began to make arrangements to furnish those who were set apart for this mission, with the necessary clothing, which was no easy task, as the most of it had to be manufactured out of the raw material.

Emma's health at this time was quite delicate, yet she did not favor herself on this account, but whatever her hands found to do, she did with her might, until so far beyond her strength that she brought upon herself a heavy fit of sickness. . . . And, although her strength was exhausted, still her spirits were the same, which, in fact, was always the case with her, even under the most trying circumstances. I have never seen a woman in my life, who would endure every species of fatigue and hardship, from month to month, and from year to year, with that unflinching courage, zeal and patience, which she has ever done (Smith, *History of Joseph Smith,* 190-91).

The women cut trousers, shirts, and jackets from rough homespun wool, linen, and cotton fabrics, and then sewed clothing for the missionaries. Every pin, needle, and button was used with care, and no thread was wasted. The wool for stockings and sweaters had to be carded, spun on a spinning wheel, and then knit by hand. To make the stockings wear longer, the women added their own long hair to the yarn as they made the heels of the stockings.

In addition to making clothes for the four missionaries, the women also had to prepare daily meals for everyone present. Cooking over the large fireplace in the Whitmer home must have made the room very uncomfortable on sunny September afternoons. Every Monday morning, the laundry was boiled and stirred in large pots and then hung outside to dry. The cows needed to be milked and the chickens fed. But, in spite of all that needed to be done, by October all arrangements had been made, and the men made a covenant with the Lord, which they wrote down and signed before they left.

> Manchester, New York, October 17, 1830.
>
> I Oliver, being commanded by the Lord God, to go forth unto the Lamanites, to proclaim glad tidings of great joy unto them, by presenting unto them the fullness of the Gospel, of the only begotten Son of God; and also, to rear up a pillar as a witness where the temple of God shall be built, in the glorious new Jerusalem; and having certain brothers with me, WHO ARE CALLED OF GOD TO ASSIST ME, whose names are Parley, and Peter and Ziba, do therefore most solemnly covenant with God that I will walk humbly before him, and do this business, and this glorious work according as He shall direct me by the Holy Ghost; ever praying for mine and their prosperity, and deliverance from bonds, and from imprisonment, and whatsoever may befall us, with all patience and faith. Amen. [Signed] Oliver Cowdery (Lyndon W. Cook, *The Revelations of the Prophet Joseph Smith*, 44).

These missionaries were not the only ones called on missions at the conference; Hyrum Smith was called to teach and preside in Colesville, New York. After the conference, he and his family packed up their belongings and moved to Colesville. Shortly after Hyrum left, a man came to his parents' home and demanded payment of a fourteen-dollar debt. The man told Joseph Smith, Sr. that he would be willing forgive the debt if the Smiths would burn all the copies of the Book of Mormon in their home and renounce the whole business. Since they refused to do this, Mr. Smith was arrested and taken to Canandaigua and jailed. Recording his feelings about this humiliating circumstance, he noted:

> I shuddered when I first heard these heavy doors creaking upon their hinges; but then I thought to myself, I was not the first man who had been imprisoned for the truth's sake; and when I should meet Paul in the Paradise of God, I could tell him that I, too, had been in bonds for the Gospel which he had preached. And this has been my only consolation (Smith, *History of Joseph Smith*, 185).

Joseph Smith, Sr., remained in jail for thirty days. While in jail, he taught the gospel to fellow inmates and baptized them after he was released. After this incident, he moved his family to Waterloo, New York, where they had the refreshing experience of being welcomed and befriended by their neighbors.

WORLD EVENTS

While the missionaries were making their way west, another group of men were also making an historic journey. William Sublet traveled from St. Louis to the Rocky Mountains with ten wagons that were each pulled by five mules. This was the first wagon train to the Rockies, and it proved that wagons could cross the Continental Divide and reach the Pacific Ocean. Soon, many more wagon wheels would roll westward as settlers searched for gold, religious freedom, and a better life.

MORE NEW CONVERTS

Oliver Cowdery, Peter Whitmer, Parley Pratt, and Ziba Peterson met with some Lamanites near Buffalo, New York. Because the Lamanites were being forced by the government to move, the elders were not able to preach much; however, the missionaries were able to place two copies of the Book of Mormon. After meeting with the Lamanites, Parley Pratt suggested that the elders stop at his former home in Ohio. He felt that an acquaintance of his, Sidney Rigdon, would be very interested in the news of the restoration, and Parley wanted to share it with him. "At length [we] called on Mr. Rigdon, my former friend and instructor, in the Reformed Baptist Society. He received us cordially and entertained us with hospitality. We soon presented him with a Book of Mormon, and related to him the history of the same. He was much interested, and promised a thorough perusal of the book" (*Autobiography of Parley P. Pratt*, 35).

Rigdon was a careful student of the Bible. He had previously split with several Baptist groups whose views and practices did not correspond with his understanding of the scriptures; but he found that the Campbelites agreed with most of his views. His congregation had built him a church, bought him a farm, and built a home on it because Sidney would not accept money for preaching. He and his family were about to move into the new home when Parley Pratt, Oliver Cowdery, Peter Whitmer, and Ziba Peterson arrived with the Book of Mormon. According to his son, John Rigdon, Sidney was cautious about accepting Parley's word concerning the Book of Mormon.

SIDNEY RIGDON (1793–1876), formerly a Baptist-Campbellite minister, heard about the restoration of the gospel from Parley P. Pratt in 1830 in Mentor, Ohio. After two weeks, Rigdon announced to his congregation that this new church was true. He was baptized by Oliver Cowdery, then immediately immersed himself in missionary work. Sidney experienced revelations with Joseph Smith, served as a counselor in the First Presidency, and was Joseph Smith's spokesman and orator.

My father replied to Parley Pratt, "You need not argue the case with me. I have one bible which I claim to have some knowledge [of] and which I believe to be a revelation of God. But as to this book, I have some doubts. But you can leave it with me when you go away in the morning and I will read it, and when you come again I will tell you what I think about it."

The next morning, they left him the Book of Mormon saying they were going to the town of Kirtland about five miles from there and would be back in about two or three weeks. My father, immediately after the strangers had gone away, commenced to read the book. He got so engaged in it that it was hard for him to quit long enough to eat his meals. He read it both day and night. At last he had read it through and pondered and thought over it.

At length, Pratt and his two companions got back. My father asked them who this Joseph Smith was and how much education he had. They said he was a man about twenty-two years old and had hardly a common school education. My father replied, "If that was all the education he had, he never wrote the book." Pratt told my father that they had converted some people in Kirtland . . . and were a-going to baptize some of them the coming week and would be pleased to have him and his wife come down and see them at the time the baptism took place (John Wickliffe Rigdon, "The Life and Testimony of Sidney Rigdon," ed. Karl Keller, *Dialogue* [Winter 1966], 15-42).

Acceptance of Mormonism would mean the loss of the new home and a complete disruption of life for the Rigdon family, but Sidney and his wife, Phoebe, were both convinced that it was the gospel of Jesus Christ.

Before the baptism, Rigdon felt that he needed to explain to his congregation and friends why he was taking this step. Parley Pratt tells what happened:

> When he had satisfied himself as to the truth of the new message . . . [he] called together a large congregation of his friends, neighbors and brethren, and then addressed them very affectionately for nearly two hours, during most of which time, both himself and nearly all the congregation were melted into tears. He asked forgiveness of everybody who might have had occasion to be offended with any part of his former life; he forgave all who had persecuted or injured him in any manner, and the next morning, himself and wife, were baptized by Elder Oliver Cowdery. I was present, [and] it was a solemn scene, most of the people were greatly affected, they came out of the water overwhelmed in tears (Roberts, *A Comprehensive History of the Church*, 1:226).

PHILO DIBBLE (1806–1895) AND HANNA ANN DEBOIS DIBBLE (1808–1893), early converts to the Church, were sincere and earnest in their quest for the truth. They were quickly converted and baptized.

Rigdon quickly became a leader in the Church. In fact, after he was baptized, he stood in the water and spoke to the crowd for some time. His discourse was so inspiring that several more people came forward and were baptized as he spoke. Many members of his former congregation also joined the Church. The missionaries stayed in the Kirtland area for two to three weeks, teaching and baptizing. Many of those who joined soon became great leaders in the Church. Each conversion was unique, and each changed the person's life forever. Some, like Philo Dibble, accepted the gospel easily:

> I did not feel inclined to make light of such a subject . . .

but thought that if angels had administered to the children of men again I was glad of it; I was afraid, however, it was not true.

The next morning I took my wife . . . and started for Kirtland. . . . on arriving there, we were introduced to Oliver Cowdery, Ziba Peterson, Peter Whitmer, Jr., and Parley P. Pratt. I remained with them all day, and became convinced that they were sincere in their professions. [When Oliver invited those who wished to be baptized to stand, I was one of the five who stood.] When I came out of the water, I knew that I had been born of the water and the spirit, for my mind was illuminated with the Holy Ghost ("Philo Dibble's Narrative," in *Early Scenes in Church History,* 74–76).

Others, like John Murdock, had to struggle to find their answers.

After many years of diligent search and prayer before God, to not only know the truth but also to find a people that lived according to the truth, I found Oliver Cowdery, Parley P. Pratt, Peter Whitmer, and Ziba Peterson, elders of the Church of Latter-day Saints in Kirtland, Ohio, and I being convinced that they not only had the truth, but also the authority to administer the ordinances of the gospel. I therefore was baptized by Elder Pratt and the Spirit of the Lord sensibly attended the ministration and I came out of the water rejoicing and singing praises to God and the Lamb. An impression sensibly rested on my mind that cannot by me be forgotten. This was the third time I had been immersed, but I never before felt the authority of the ordinance, but I felt it this time and felt as though my sins were forgiven. I was confirmed by Elder Cowdery and ordained an elder by the same. I then returned to my family, having been absent four days, carrying with me the Book of Mormon and read it to them and they believed it, for I was filled with the Spirit when I read (Reva Baker Holt, ed., "A Brief Synopsis of the Life of John Murdock," 16).

Orson Hyde greeted the news with skepticism:

I encountered them; but perceiving that they were mostly illiterate men, and at the same time observing some examples of superior wisdom and truth in their teaching, I resolved to read the "golden bible," as it was called. I . . . read a portion of it, but came to the conclusion that it was all fiction. . . . After about three months of careful and prayerful investigation . . . I came to the conclusion that the "Mormons" had more light and a better spirit than their opponents ("History of Orson Hyde [1805-1842]," *Latter-day Saints' Millennial Star,* 26 [1864] 760-61).

Edward Partridge's wife, Lydia recorded her husband's first reaction to the missionaries:

He told them he did not believe what they said, but believed them to be imposters. Oliver Cowdery said he was thankful there was a God in heaven who knew the hearts of all men. After the men were gone my husband sent a man to follow them and get one of their books. After he read it, he said, "I was induced to believe for the reason that I saw the gospel in its plainness as it was taught in the New Testament, and I also knew that none of the sects of the day taught those things." (Richard L. Anderson, "The Impact of the First Preaching in Ohio," *Brigham Young University Studies* [1971] 11:4:474).

However, Edward Partridge refused to be baptized. First, he wanted to meet Joseph Smith.

On Monday, November 22, the missionaries, joined by a new convert, Frederick G. Williams, continued their journey to the frontier and the Lamanites. Parley Pratt summarized their stay in Northern Ohio: "In two or three weeks from our arrival in the neighborhood with the news, we had baptized 127 souls. . . . The disciples were filled with joy and gladness; while rage and lying was abundantly manifested by gainsayers; faith was strong, joy was great, and persecution heavy" (*Autobiography of Parley P. Pratt*, 36).

The size of the Church had tripled in a short time, and many future leaders had been found and gathered from the world. Sidney Rigdon and Frederick G. Williams later became members of the First Presidency with Joseph Smith. Lyman Wight and Orson Hyde became apostles, and Edward Partridge and Newel K. Whitney later became members of the Presiding Bishopric. But all who joined would endure joy, sorrow, triumph, and desolation because of the testimonies they had received.

EDWARD PARTRIDGE (1793–1840) was a prosperous hatter who at first rejected the missionaries. He was then baptized by Joseph Smith in December, 1830. Edward became the first bishop of the Church in 1831. On July 20, 1833 he was tarred and feathered by a Missouri mob intent on driving the Mormons out of Jackson County. He died in Nauvoo, IL.

The local newspaper, the *Painesville Telegraph*, did not let these activities pass unnoticed. Several articles appeared in the paper telling of the arrival of the missionaries, what they taught, and who was baptized. Because Sidney Rigdon was a prominent member of the community, there was an article about his baptism. This type of reporting was common in America. One European visitor wrote, "The influence and circulation of newspapers is great beyond anything known in Europe. In truth, nine-tenths of the population read nothing else. Every village, nay, almost every hamlet, has its press. Newspapers penetrate to every crevice of the nation" (Alexis de Tocqueville, *Democracy in America*, 168).

Most of the papers were weeklies, especially in rural areas. They cost a penny and tended to report the most sensational robberies, thefts, murders, and awful catastrophes. Each paper reported matters of general interest, but also appealed to the prejudices of the special interest groups they represented. Each editor interpreted the news as he saw it, then presented it the way he wanted his readers to see it.

Shortly after the missionaries left Ohio for Missouri, Sidney Rigdon and Edward Partridge traveled to New York to meet the Prophet Joseph, who wrote about the meeting:

> In December Sidney Rigdon came to inquire of the Lord, and with him came Edward Partridge, the latter was a pattern of piety, and one of the Lord's great men. Shortly after the arrival of these two brethren, thus spake the Lord: ". . . Behold, verily, verily, I say unto my servant Sidney, I have looked upon thee and thy works. I have heard thy prayers and prepared thee for a greater work. Thou art blessed, for thou shalt do great things. . . . And a commandment I give unto thee—that thou shalt write for [my servant Joseph]. . . . Tarry with him, and he shall journey with you; forsake him not" (Smith, *History of the Church,* 1:128-31).

The Lord instructed Edward Partridge to be baptized and then declare the gospel abroad. On December 11, the Prophet Joseph baptized him in the Seneca River.

THE YEAR 1831 IN THE CHURCH

The missionaries to the Lamanites spent several days among a tribe of Indians in western Ohio known as the Wyandots. Then they traveled to Cincinnati, where they boarded a steamer bound for St. Louis. However, when they reached the mouth of the Ohio River, the ice was too thick for the boat to proceed. Parley Pratt described the rest of their journey.

> We therefore landed and pursued our journey on foot for two hundred miles, to the neighborhood of St. Louis.
>
> We halted for a few days . . . about twenty miles from St. Louis, on account of a dreadful storm of rain and snow, which lasted for a week or more, during which the snow fell in some places near three feet deep. . . .
>
> In the beginning of 1831 we renewed our journey; and, passing through St. Louis and St. Charles, we travelled on foot for three hundred miles through vast prairies and through trackless wilds of snow—no beaten road; houses few and far between; and the bleak northwest wind always blowing in our faces with a keenness which would almost take the skin off the face. We travelled for whole days, from morning till night, without a house or fire, wading in snow to the knees at every step, and the cold so intense that the snow did not melt on the south side of the houses, even in the mid-day sun, for nearly six weeks. We carried on our backs our changes of clothing, several books, and corn bread and raw pork. We often ate our frozen bread and pork by the way, when the bread would be so frozen that we could not bite or penetrate any part of it but the outside crust.
>
> After much fatigue and some suffering we all arrived in Independence, in the county of Jackson, on the extreme western frontiers of Missouri, and of the United States.

FREDERICK GRANGER WILLIAMS (1787–1842) was a prosperous and respected physician in the Kirtland area before joining the Church in Oct., 1830. He was one of the first high priests of the Church, and second counselor in the initial First Presidency (1833). Frederick was a close friend to Joseph Smith. He played an active role in building the Kirtland Temple, taught at the School of the Prophets, was a member of Zion's Camp, and helped select the revelations to be included in the 1835 edition of the Doctrine and Covenants. *Engraved version of painting by Weber.*

The year 1831 was a troubled one in much of the world. After the French replaced their unpopular king, Charles X, the desire for freedom stirred in Poland, Switzerland, Belgium, and the United States. The Russians ruled the Poles, but when the Poles declared independence, Europe ignored their pleas for help and Czar Nicholas I crushed the revolt. However, the Belgians and Swiss were more successful. With the help of France and Great Britain, Belgium gained independence from the Netherlands and established a separate kingdom. Mass demonstrations in Swiss cities led to an expansion of the right to vote, more liberal legislation, and the principle of popular sovereignty. In America, the Nat Turner slave uprising in Virginia left fifty-seven whites and over one hundred blacks dead.

ENOCH PREACHING *by Gary E. Smith*
After inquiring about the lost books of the Bible, Joseph received the prophecy of Enoch.
gouache on illustration board 1975

This was about fifteen hundred miles from where we had started, and we'd performed most of the journey on foot, through a wilderness country, in the worst season of the year, occupying about four months, during which we'd preached the gospel to tens of thousands of Gentiles and two nations of Indians; baptizing, confirming and organizing many hundreds of people into churches of Latter-day Saints.

This was the first mission performed by Elders of the Church in any of the States west of New York, and we were the first members of the same which were ever on this frontier (*Autobiography of Parley P. Pratt,* 39-40).

The Church of Jesus Christ was now nine months old and had about 200 members in New York and Ohio. Missionaries were bringing new converts to the faith almost daily. In addition to the Book of Mormon, the Lord had revealed many new scriptures and doctrines. After inquiring about the lost books of the Bible, Joseph received the prophecy of Enoch, which contained Enoch's account of a vision he had of the earth from his own time to the Second Coming of the Savior. He saw the flood at the time of Noah, Christ's mortal ministry, and the building of the holy city of Zion in the last days, where the elect would be gathered from the four corners of the earth. Joseph also received revelations that contained practical instructions for the Saints. "Behold, I say unto you [Joseph and Sidney,] that it is not expedient in me that ye should translate any more until ye shall go to the Ohio. And again, a commandment I give unto the church, that it is expedient in me that they should assemble together at the Ohio, against the time that my servant Oliver Cowdery shall return unto them" (D&C 37:1, 3).

This revelation was received in December 1830. Joseph and the others immediately began preparing to leave for Ohio, but first they held a conference early in January in Fayette. Joseph recorded:

The year 1831 opened with a prospect great and glorious for the welfare of the kingdom; for on the 2nd of January, 1831, a conference was held in the town of Fayette, New York, at which the ordinary business of the Church was transacted; and in addition . . . revelation was received. . . . The latter part of January, in company with Brothers Sidney Rigdon and Edward Partridge, I started with my wife for Kirtland, Ohio (Smith, *History of the Church,* 1:140, 145).

KIRTLAND

At this time, Kirtland, Ohio, had a population of about 1,000. The commercial center for the area was the Gilbert and Whitney General Store, which also housed the post office. A gristmill, a few shops, a sawmill, and a hotel added to Kirtland's importance. Several small streams and rivers flowed through the area, which was flat, heavily wooded, and blessed with marvelously rich soil.

Joseph's group arrived in Kirtland on about February 1. When their sleigh stopped in front of the Gilbert and Whitney General Store, Joseph jumped out, quickly walked into the store, extended his hand to one of the owners and exclaimed:

> "Newel K. Whitney! Thou art the man!"
> The man replied, "You have the advantage of me, I could not call you by name as you have me."
> "I am Joseph the Prophet. You've prayed me here, now what do you want of me?" (Joseph Fielding Smith, *Church History and Modern Revelation,* 160).

While in New York, Joseph had seen, in vision, Newel and his wife praying for him to come to Kirtland. Joseph and Emma stayed with the Whitney family for several weeks. Elizabeth Whitney was a kind and gracious hostess, and since Emma was expecting another baby in three months, she was no doubt grateful for the comfort of a nice home.

After his arrival in Kirtland, Joseph was busy establishing guidelines for the Church. He received several revelations in early February that gave the Church long-range direction. During this time, Joseph also received the law of consecration, in which members were instructed to consecrate their property to the Church through the bishop. The bishop would then distribute the goods and property according to members' needs. Edward Partridge served as the first bishop in the Church, and the law of consecration helped him provide for the New York Saints when they arrived the following spring. The law also helped many converts who came from all parts of the world as the Church grew. This revelation, now known as Section 42 of the Doctrine and Covenants, also contains counsel on righteousness and clean living.

NEWEL K. WHITNEY STORE in Kirtland, Ohio, was the commercial center for the area. The store sold general merchandise. It also housed the post office. Joseph saw, in a vision, Newel and his wife praying for him to come to Kirtland. Joseph arrived about Feb. 1 and went straight into the store and introduced himself to Mr. Whitney. This was the beginning of a close friendship between the two men. Joseph and Emma stayed at the Whitney's home for awhile, and Joseph received many revelations at the Whitney Store (Word of Wisdom and United Order). He also worked on the Bible translation and held sessions of the School of the Prophets here. *ca. 1897–1927*

Missionary Efforts Among the Lamanites

While Joseph was strengthening the Church in Ohio, the missionaries to the Lamanites had reached Independence, Missouri. Independence was a small, rugged frontier town. Beyond it, to the west, were several Indian tribes that had been moved to the area by the United States government. Peter Whitmer and Ziba Peterson worked as tailors, while Oliver Cowdery, Parley Pratt and Frederick Williams met with the leader of the Indians, Chief Anderson. Parley described their meeting:

> [We] were soon introduced to an aged and venerable looking man, who had long stood at the head of the Delawares. . . .
>
> He was seated on a sofa of furs, skins and blankets, before a fire in the center of his lodge; which was a comfortable cabin, consisting of two large rooms.
>
> His wives were neatly dressed, partly in calicos and partly in skins; and wore a vast amount of silver ornaments. As we entered his cabin he took us by the hand with a hearty welcome, and then motioned us to be seated on a pleasant seat of blankets, or robes. His wives, at his bidding, set before us a tin pan full of beans and corn boiled together, which proved to be good eating; although the three of us made use alternately of the same wooden spoon.
>
> [The next day] some forty men collected around us . . . who, after shaking us by the hand, were seated in silence; and in a grave and dignified manner awaited the announcement of what we had to offer. . . . Elder Cowdery then commenced as follows:
>
> "Aged Chief and Venerable Council of the Delaware nation; we are glad of this opportunity to address you as our red brethren and friends. We have travelled a long distance from towards the raising sun to bring you glad news; we have traveled the wilderness, crossed the deep and wide rivers, and waded in the deep snows, and in the face of the storms of winter, to communicate to you great knowledge which has lately come to our ears and hearts; and which will do the red man good as well as the pale face.

INDEPENDENCE,
MISSOURI
ca. 1897–1927

Once the red men were many; they occupied the country from sea to sea—from the rising to the setting sun; the whole land was theirs; the Great Spirit gave it to them, and no pale faces dwelt among them. But now they are few in numbers; their possessions are small, and the pale faces are many.

Thousands of moons ago, when the red men's forefathers dwelt in peace and possessed this whole land . . . the Great Spirit talked with them, and revealed His law and His will, and much knowledge to their wise men and prophets. This they wrote in a Book; together with their history, and the things which should befall their children in the latter days. This Book was written on plates of gold, and handed down from father to son for many ages and generations.

It was then that the people prospered, and were strong and mighty; they cultivated the earth; built buildings and cities, and abounded in all good things, as the pale faces now do. But they became wicked; they killed one another and shed much blood; they killed their prophets and wise men, and sought to destroy the Book. The Great Spirit became angry, and would speak to them no more; they had no more good and wise dreams; no more visions; no more angels sent among them by the Great Spirit; and the Lord commanded Mormon and Moroni, their last wise men and prophets, to hide the Book in the earth, that it might be preserved in safety, and be found and made known in the latter day to the pale faces who should possess the land; that they might again make it known to the red man; in order to restore them to the knowledge of the will of the Great Spirit and to His favor. And if the red man would then receive this Book and learn the things written in it, and do according thereunto, they should cease to fight and kill one another; [and] should become one people; cultivate the earth in peace, in common with the pale faces, who were willing to believe and obey the same Book, and be good men and live in peace.

Then should the red men become great, and have plenty to eat and good clothes to wear, and should be in favor with the Great Spirit and be his children, while he would be their Great Father, and talk with them, and raise up prophets and wise and good men amongst them again, who should teach them many things. This book, which contained these things, was hid in the earth by Moroni, in a hill called by him, Cumorah, which hill is now in the State of New York, near the village of Palmyra, in Ontario County.

In that neighborhood there lived a young man named Joseph Smith, who prayed to the Great Spirit much, in order that he might know the truth; and the Great Spirit sent an angel to him, and told him where this book was hid by Moroni; and commanded him to go and get it. He accordingly went to the place, and dug in the earth, and found the Book written on golden plates.

But it was written in the language of the forefathers of the red man; therefore this young man, being a pale face, could not understand it; but the angel told him and showed him, and gave him knowledge of the language, and how to interpret the Book. So he interpreted it into the language of the pale faces, and wrote it on paper, and caused it to be printed, and published thousands of copies among them; and sent us to the red man to bring some copies of it to them, and to tell them this news. So we have now come from him, and here is a copy of the Book, which we now present to our red friend, the chief of the Delawares, and which we hope he will cause to be read and known among his tribe; it will do them good."

We then presented him with a Book of Mormon.

There was a pause in the council, and some conversation in their own tongue, after which the chief made the following reply:

"We feel truly thankful to our white friends who have come so far, and been at such pains to tell us good news, and especially this new news concerning the Book of our forefathers; it makes us glad in here [in our hearts]. . . . It is now winter, we are new settlers in this place; the snow is deep, our cattle and horses are dying, our wigwams are poor; we have much to do in the spring—to build houses, and fence and make farms; but we will build a council house, and meet together, and you shall read to us and teach us more concerning the Book of our fathers and the will of the Great Spirit."

. . . We continued for several days to instruct the old chief and many of his tribe. The interest became more and more intense on their part, from day to day, until at length nearly the whole tribe began to feel a spirit of inquiry and excitement on the subject.

We found several among them who could read, and to them we gave copies of the Book, explaining to them that it was the book of their forefathers.

Some began to rejoice exceedingly, and took great pains to tell the news to others, in their own language (*Autobiography of Parley P. Pratt,* 41-44).

The interest the Indians expressed in the missionaries' message inevitably came to the attention of other preachers and ministers, who complained to the Indian agents. The Mormons were soon ordered out of Indian country as disturbers of the peace. Parley recorded:

We accordingly departed from the Indian country, and came over the line, and commenced laboring in Jackson County, Missouri, among the whites. We were well received, and listened to by many and some were baptized and added to the Church.

Thus ended our first Indian Mission, in which we had preached the gospel in its fullness, and distributed the record of their forefathers among three tribes: . . . the Catteraugus Indians, near Buffalo, N.Y., the Wyandots of Ohio, and the Delawares west of Missouri.

We trust that at some future day, when the servants of God go forth in power to the remnant of Joseph, some precious seed will be found growing in their hearts, which was sewn by us in that early day. . . .

THE CHURCH MOVES TO OHIO, SPRING 1831
Parley continued:

Elders Cowdery, Whitmer, Peterson, myself, and F. G. Williams, who accompanied us from Kirtland, now assembled in Independence, Jackson County, Missouri, and came to the conclusion that one of our number had better return to the Church in Ohio, and perhaps to headquarters in New York, in order to communicate with the Presidency, report ourselves, pay a visit to the numerous churches we had organized on our outward journey, and also to procure more books.

For this laborious enterprise I was selected by the voice of my four brethren. I accordingly took leave of them, and of our friends in the country, and started on foot.

In nine days, I arrived in St. Louis, [a] distance of three hundred miles. It was now the latter part of February; the snow had disappeared, the rivers were breaking up, and the whole country inundated as it were with mud and water. I spent a few days with a friend in the country . . . and then took a steamer in St. Louis bound for Cincinnati, where I landed in safety after a passage of one week. From Cincinnati I travelled on foot to Strongville,

WORLD EVENTS

An industrial revolution was taking place in England in the 1820s and 30s that would eventually sweep the rest of Europe and America. Watt's steam engine provided the power to run Compton's Mule, a machine that allowed one worker to produce as much cloth as 200 hand spinners. It was no longer efficient for workers to spin and weave at home. Instead, factories were built to house the new machines. Towns grew around the factories, and

CHILDREN WORKING IN FACTORIES in England during the Industrial Revolution were subjected to cruel and often inhuman working conditions.

rows of tiny houses huddled together spewing coal smoke from their fireplaces. The factories belched even more smoke, and a fine black dust settled everywhere.

English families moved from the rural areas to these factory towns by the thousands. But they soon found that their lives were even more miserable than before, as men, women, and children began to work in the factories. In fact, many employers preferred women and children because they could be paid less. The workday varied from ten to eighteen hours, with no breaks. Orphan children were virtual slaves of the mill owners and were chained to their machines during the day and locked up at night so they could not run away. Children were also

employed in the coal mines because they were small and quick. Many of them did not live to see adulthood.

In America, the factory system also took hold. In Rhode Island, Massachusetts, and New Hampshire, huge textile mills were built to make cloth. "Lowell girls" worked in many of the mills. These single girls, between the ages of eighteen and twenty-two, lived in company housing and worked from five in the morning until late in the evening. In their spare time, the girls were lectured on religion and obedience. While some factories provided the girls with educational opportunities, many times the girls were practically slaves. They exhausted their youth, and were sent home to die when they could no longer work. They were called "Lowell girls" because Francis Lowell, co-owner of most of the mills, came up with the idea.

The men, women, and children who worked in the factories and mills endured the same dismal conditions as their counterparts in Great Britain. They had no political rights, and never had enough to eat. Their churches were full of pageantry and ritual, but offered very little comfort and hope. They longed for fresh air, good food, truth, wisdom, and a brighter day.

Ohio, forty miles from Kirtland. This last walk consisted of some two hundred and fifty miles, over very bad, muddy road; and for some days I had found myself much fatigued, and quite out of health. Hearing of some brethren in Strongville, I determined to inquire them out, and try their hospitality to a sick and weary stranger. . . .

I accordingly approached the house of an old gentleman by the name of Coltrin, about sundown, and inquired if they could entertain a weary stranger who had no money. The old gentleman cast his eyes upon me and beheld a weary, weather-beaten traveller; soiled with the toil of a long journey; besmeared with mud, eyes inflamed with pain, long beard, and a visage lengthened by sickness and extreme fatigue. After a moment's hesitation he bade me welcome, and invited me into his house. . . .

The next morning I found myself unable to rise from my bed, being severely attacked with the measles.

I came near dying, and was confined for one or two weeks among them, being scarcely able to raise my head. I was watched over night and day, and had all the care that a man could have in his father's house.

As I recovered in part, being still very weak, I was provided with a horse on which I arrived at Kirtland. Hundreds of the saints now crowded around to welcome me, and to inquire after my brethren whom I had left in Missouri.

Here also I again met President Joseph Smith, who had, during our absence, come up from the state of New York.

I found the churches in Ohio had increased to more than a thousand members, and those in New York to several hundred.

I also heard from my wife, from whom I had been absent about six months. The news was that the whole Church in the State of New York, including herself (for she had joined during my absence), was about to remove to Ohio in the opening spring. I, therefore, was advised to proceed no further eastward, but to await their arrival (*Autobiography of Parley P. Pratt,* 44-47).

THE WORK ROLLS ON

Shortly after Joseph arrived in Ohio, he wrote to Martin Harris who was still in New York, "I send you this to inform you that it is necessary for you to come here as soon as you can. . . . You will also bring . . . all the books [meaning, undoubtedly, the Book of Mormon], as the work here is breaking forth on the East, West, North, and South. You will also inform the elders who are there in New York State that all of them who can be spared should come without delay . . . and this by the commandment of the Lord . . . as he has a great work for them all in this our imheritance" (Pearson H. Corbett, *Hyrum Smith, Patriarch*, 80).

Joseph also wrote in a similar vein to other members of the Church in New York, including his brother Hyrum. "Safe arrival—busy regulating the church here. Disciples numerous—devil has made attempts to overcome. Serious job but the Lord is with us; have overcome and all things regular. Work breaking forth on right and left—good call for Elders here . . ." (Corbett, *Hyrum Smith, Patriarch*, 81).

Complying with these instructions, members in New York sold their farms, gathered their belongings, and prepared to depart for the relative wilderness of Ohio. Martin Harris sold his farm, and paid $3,000 to the printer of the Book of Mormon.

Most of the Saints traveled together. The Colesville Saints traveled in one group, while other groups came from Fayette, Waterloo, and other places. Hyrum Smith and his father traveled overland before the ice broke, but the rest waited for the waterways to become passable. Lucy Smith led her children and a group of friends and neighbors. She recorded:

> We hired a boat of a certain Methodist preacher, and appointed a time to meet at our house, for the purpose of setting off together; and when we were thus collected, we numbered eighty souls. The people of the surrounding country came and bade us farewell, invoking the blessings of heaven upon our heads. . . .
>
> Soon after this, we were pushed off and under fine headway [on the Erie Canal].
>
> I then called the brethren and sisters together, and reminded them that we were traveling by the commandment of the Lord, as much as Father Lehi was, when he left Jerusalem; and, if faithful, we had the same reasons to expect the blessings of God. . . . We then seated ourselves and sang a hymn. The captain was so delighted with the music, that he called to the mate, saying, "Do, come here, and steer the boat; for I must hear that singing."

MARTIN HARRIS FARMLAND IN PALMYRA, NY. Martin sold his wheat farm of 151 acres in compliance with the instructions from Joseph that the Church was moving to Kirtland, OH. *ca. 1907*

...

... The music sounded beautifully upon the water, and had a salutary effect upon every heart, filling our souls with love and gratitude to God, for his manifold goodness towards us. . . .

On getting about half way to Buffalo, the canal broke. This gave rise to much murmuring and discontentment, which was expressed in terms like the following:

"Well, the canal is broke now, and here we are, and here we are likely to be, for we can go no farther. We have left our homes, and here we have no means of getting a living, consequently we shall have to starve."

"No, no," said I, "you will not starve, brethren, not anything of that sort; only do be patient and stop your murmuring. I have no doubt that the hand of the Lord is over us for good; perhaps it is best for us to be here a short time. . . ."

"Well, well," returned the sisters, "I suppose you know best; but it does seem as if it would have been better for us to have stayed where we were, for there we could sit in our rocking chairs, and take as much comfort as we pleased, but here we are tired out, and have no place to rest ourselves" (Smith, *History of Joseph Smith,* 195-98).

LUCY MACK SMITH (1775–1855) married Joseph Smith, Sr., in 1796. They had nine children who grew to adulthood: Alvin (1798–1823), Hyrum (1800–1844), Sophronia (1803–*unknown*), Joseph, Jr. (1805–1844), Samuel (1808–1844), William (1811–1894), Catherine (1812–1900), Don Carlos (1816–1841), Lucy (1821–1882).

Lucy was a religious woman, and believed her son, Joseph, when he told her of his vision in the Sacred Grove. She firmly supported him through many hardships and persecutions. Lucy died on May 14, 1856, in Nauvoo, IL. *ca. 1832–1918*

While waiting for the repairs to be made, some of the brethren organized a meeting and preached to about 100 people. The next day, the Saints were able to continue their journey and arrived in Buffalo only five days after leaving Waterloo. In Buffalo, they met the Colesville Saints and another group led by Thomas B. Marsh, but none of them could proceed because ice still blocked Lake Erie. Some felt that they should keep the fact that they were Mormons a secret, for they feared mob action against them. But Lucy and her group continued with their hymn singing and prayers. Lucy also found lodging for the women and children of her group who were ill, and then sought out a Captain Blake who had formerly worked for her brother. Blake arranged deck passage on his boat and told her to stand by for departure as soon as the ice broke. Lucy continues:

Turning to our own company, I said, "Now, brethren and sisters, if you will all of you raise your desires to heaven, that the ice may be broken up, and we be set at liberty, as sure as the Lord lives, it will be done." At that instant, a noise was heard like bursting thunder. The captain cried, "Every man to his post." The ice parted, leaving barely a passage for the boat, and so narrow that as the boat passed through, the buckets of the waterwheel were torn off with a crash, which, joined with the words of command from the captain, the hoarse answering of the sailors, the noise of the ice, and the cries and confusion of the spectators, presented a scene truly terrible. We had barely passed through the avenue when the ice closed together again, and the Colesville brethren were left in Buffalo, unable to follow us.

As we were leaving the harbor, one of the bystanders exclaimed, "There goes the Mormon company! That boat is sunk in the water nine inches deeper than ever it was before, and, mark it, she will sink—there is nothing surer." In fact, they were so sure of it that they went straight to the office and had it published that we were sunk, so that when we arrived at Fairport we read in the paper the news of our own death (Smith, *History of Joseph Smith,* 204-5).

Although many were plagued with seasickness, they eventually crossed Lake Erie and reached Fairport, Ohio, where Lucy's sons Samuel and Joseph met them. From there, they traveled in wagons to Kirtland.

Lucy rejoiced, "Here I met my beloved husband and great was our joy. Many . . . can imagine with what feelings I recite such scenes as that which followed the reunion of our family; but let it pass—imagination must supply the ellipses" (Smith, *History of Joseph Smith*, 207).

JOSEPH AND EMMA'S TWIN BABIES

On April 30, 1831, tiny cries of newborn babes, Thaddeus and Louisa, were heard in the Smith home. The cries, however, were weak. Soon both infants were still and dead. Not far away, John Murdock's wife also gave birth to twins, Joseph and Julia. There, the cries were strong and hunger great, but their mother passed quickly into death. John looked at his other three children, then wrapped the babies in blankets and took them to Emma. Finally, Emma was able to use the little clothes she had painstakingly prepared. Finally, the cradles were full. The blue eyes opened, and young mouths searched for food. Emma's tears were dried, and her heart was comforted.

The fact that Joseph and Emma's first three children had died shortly after birth was due to the level of medical care in America in those times. Doctors were usually not involved with childbirth, which was left to midwives or neighboring women. Doctors, who *may* have attended medical school, performed amputations and bleedings, and administered strong medicines like arsenic and strychnine. Tuberculosis, diphtheria, cholera, typhus, and yellow fever were incurable, and thousands died from these diseases every year.

AN OUTPOURING OF KNOWLEDGE AND BLESSINGS

In the spring of 1831, as the snows melted, and the crocus lifted their gold blossoms out of the snow and mud, the Lord poured knowledge and power upon the heads of His chosen people. Joseph Smith received nearly a dozen recorded revelations between the February day he arrived in Kirtland and the following June. These revelations, which are found in Sections 41-51 of the Doctrine and Covenants, cover the organization of the Church and instructions for missionaries. The office of bishop was established, and the duties of other officers in the priesthood were detailed.

Much was revealed concerning the condition of the world in the last days and the glorious Second Coming of the Savior. The Saints were urged to share with the poor, live the law of consecration, and avoid evil. They were also taught that only the Prophet could receive revelation for the Church.

A conference was called for June, and the Saints were promised that the location of Zion would be revealed. But, in the meantime, Kirtland was to be the gathering place.

That spring, Parley Pratt had been sent on a mission to the Shakers in the Cleveland area. As he was returning, he visited several branches of the Church and found some strange practices. He recorded:

> As I went forth among the different branches, some very strange spiritual operations were manifested, which were disgusting, rather than edifying. Some persons would swoon away, and make unseemly gestures, and be drawn or disfigured in their countenances. . . . Others would seem to have visions and revelations, which were not edifying, and which were not congenial to the doctrine and spirit of the gospel. In short, a false and lying spirit seemed to be creeping into the Church.
>
> All of these things were new and strange to me. . . .
>
> Feeling our weakness and inexperience, and lest we should err in judgment concerning these spiritual phenomena, myself, John Murdock, and several other Elders, went to Joseph Smith, and asked him to inquire of the Lord concerning these spirits or manifestations.

VALLEY ROAD TO
KIRTLAND TEMPLE
The Kirtland Ohio
Temple is on the
horizon to the right.
1907

Brother Pratt gives us some interesting details about how the Prophet received revelation, noting the following:

> After we had joined in prayer in his translating room, he dictated in our presence [a] revelation. . . . Each sentence was uttered slowly and very distinctly, and with a pause between each, sufficiently long for it to be recorded, by an ordinary writer, in long hand.
>
> This was the manner in which all his written revelations were dictated and written. There was never any hesitation, reviewing, or reading back, in order to keep the run of the subject; neither did any of these communications undergo revisions, interlinings, or correction. As [the Prophet] dictated them so they stood, so far as I have witnessed; and I was present to witness the dictation of several communications of several pages each (*Autobiography of Parley P. Pratt,* 48).

The revelation received at this time, Section 50 of the Doctrine and Covenants, revealed that there are false spirits deceiving the world. It further revealed how these false spirits may be detected and gave the Saints assurance that the Good Shepherd was watching over his flock.

As usual, when there was great progress in the Church, there was also great opposition. Foolish errors crept in among the members, and the Lord said, "Satan hath sought to deceive you, that he might overthrow you" (D&C 50:3).

In addition, the usual roster of enemies outside the Church continued their taunts, persecutions, lies, and other devices to try to destroy God's work. False newspaper stories were common. The *Painesville Telegraph* led the attack with comments like:

> The whole gang of these deluded mortals, except a few hypocrites, are profound believers in witchcraft, ghosts, goblins, &c. From the best information we can obtain, the work has entirely stopped in this country, and some who have been the most ardent are beginning to have misgivings on the subject. Martin Harris, the head man here as it respects property, left here a few days ago on a sojourn to your country, having received a special command thither forthwith. Cowdery has been heard of far up the Missouri, pretending to have great success in his mission; but as ignorant as too many of the people are, it is hardly possible that so clumsy an imposition can spread to any considerable extent (Dan Vogel, ed., *Early Mormon Documents,* 3:9-10).

After Joseph Smith settled in Kirtland, the papers kept close track of his actions and statements, often ridiculing, misquoting, and editorializing to prove that the Mormons were at least crazy, if not downright evil.

Oliver Cowdery, Ziba Peterson, Peter Whitmer, and Dr. Frederick G. Williams were still in Missouri teaching both Indians and whites. They frequently wrote to Joseph Smith to report their progress and sent their letters with travelers, or by way of the newly formed U.S. postal system. In one letter, Oliver wrote:

Our Dearly Beloved Brethren; I have nothing particular to write as concerning the Lamanites; because of a short journey which I have just returned from, and in consequence of which I have not written to you since the 16th of last month. Brother Ziba Peterson and myself went into the county east, which is Lafayette, about forty miles; and, in the name of Jesus, we called on the people to repent, many of whom are, I believe, earnestly searching for truth, and if sincerely, I pray they may find that precious treasure, for it seems to be wholly fallen in the streets, and equity cannot enter.

The letter we received from you informed us that the opposition was great against you. Now, our beloved brethren, we verily believe that we also can rejoice that we are counted worthy to suffer shame for His name; for almost the whole country, consisting of Universalists, Atheists, Deists, Presbyterians, Methodists, Baptists, and other professed Christians, priests and people; with all the devils from the infernal pit are united, and foaming out their own shame [against us]. God forbid that I should bring a railing accusation against them, for vengeance belongeth to Him who is able to repay; and herein, brethren, we confide.

I am lately informed of another tribe of Lamanites, who have abundance of flocks of the best kinds of sheep and cattle; and they manufacture blankets of superior quality. The tribe is very numerous; they live three hundred miles west of Santa Fe, and are called Navahoes. Why I mention this tribe is

because I feel under obligations to communicate to my brethren, any information concerning the Lamanites that I meet with in my labors and travels; believing, as I do, that much is expected from me in the cause of our Lord; and doubting not that I am daily remembered before the throne of the Most High by all mine brethren, as well by those who have not seen my face in the flesh as by those who have.

We begin to expect our brother Parley P. Pratt soon; we have heard from him only when he was at St. Louis. We are all well, bless the Lord; and preach the gospel we will, if earth and hell oppose our way—for we dwell in the midst of scorpions—and in Jesus we trust. Grace be with you all. Amen. Oliver Cowdery (Smith, *History of the Church*, 1:181-82).

THE FOURTH CONFERENCE OF THE CHURCH

Members gathered in Kirtland on the 3rd of June 1831, for the fourth conference of The Church of Jesus Christ of Latter-day Saints. Two thousand members attended the several days of meetings and received instruction from the Prophet and revelation from the Lord. For the first time in this dispensation, several men were

JOHN WHITMER (1802–1878) was one of the Eight Witnesses who saw and handled the gold plates. He never denied this experience, nor his testimony of their sacred validity, even though he left the Church, was excommunicated, and even joined the mobs in persecuting the Saints. *ca. 1860s*

ordained to the office of high priest in the Melchizedek Priesthood. John Whitmer, the newly appointed Church historian, kept a record of the conference:

> Joseph Smith, Jun., prophesied . . . that the man of sin would be revealed. While the Lord poured out His Spirit upon His servants, the devil took a notion to make known his power. He bound Harvey Whitlock and John Murdock so they could not speak, and others were affected but the Lord showed to Joseph, the seer, the design of the thing: he commanded the devil in the name of Christ, and he departed to our joy and comfort. . . . The spirit of the Lord fell upon Joseph in an unusual manner, and he prophesied that John the Revelator was then among the Ten Tribes of Israel who had been led away by Shalmaneser, king of Assyria, to prepare them for their return from their long dispersion, to again possess the land of their fathers. He prophesied many more things that I have not written. After he had prophesied, he laid his hands upon Lyman Wight and ordained him to the High Priesthood, [i.e., ordained him a High Priest] after the holy order of God. And the spirit fell upon Lyman, and he prophesied concerning the coming of Christ. . . . He said the coming of the Savior should be like the sun rising in the east, and will cover the whole earth. So with the coming of the Son of Man; yea, He will appear in His brightness and consume all [the wicked] before Him; and the hills will be laid low, and the valleys be exalted, and the crooked be made straight, and the rough smooth. And some of my brethren shall suffer martyrdom for the sake of the religion of Jesus Christ, and seal their testimony of Jesus with their blood. He saw the heavens opened and the Son of Man sitting on the right hand of the Father, making intercession for his brethren, the Saints. He said that God would work a work in these last days that tongue cannot express and the mind is not capable to conceive. The glory of the Lord shone around (Smith, *History of the Church,* 1:175-176, nn. 2, 4).

Joseph Smith felt that the conference had been successful and beneficial for the members. He summarized, "It was clearly evident that the Lord gave us power in proportion to the work to be done, and strength according to the race set before us, and grace to help as our needs required. Great harmony prevailed; several were ordained; faith was strengthened; and humility, so necessary for the blessing of God to follow prayer, characterized the Saints" (Smith, *History of the Church,* 1:176-77).

The final revelation of the conference called many of the brethren on missions. The missionaries were to travel to Missouri by different routes, preaching as they went, and were to meet on the borders of the lands of the Lamanites, where Oliver Cowdery, Peter Whitmer, Ziba Peterson, and Frederick G.

WORLD EVENTS

Travel was still difficult in the early 1830s, especially on the frontier. However, improvements were coming. In January 1830, a train pulled out of Baltimore station, beginning the operations of the Baltimore and Ohio Railroad Company. There was no puffing, no whistle, and no clanging bell. A horse pulled the train. By August, however, a new kind of power had been developed—a steam locomotive called *Tom Thumb.* In an attempt to convince the skeptics, the steam-powered *Tom Thumb* raced a horse on a nine-mile course. The *Tom Thumb* never once had the lead. It sprang a leak in the boiler and didn't even finish the race. Spectators enjoyed it immensely and were convinced that horses were superior to steam engines.

In the year 1831, on a farm in Virginia, twenty-two-year-old Cyrus McCormick was putting the finishing touches on a new invention. The mechanical reaper became the world's greatest weapon against hunger. The reaper was a two-wheeled horse-drawn chariot that had a vibrating cutting blade, a reel to bring the grain within its reach, and a platform to receive the falling grain. It was so noisy that men had to walk alongside to calm the frightened horses. Within a few years, however, the machine was harvesting thousands of acres, especially after steam engines replaced the horses. McCormick soon moved west with his new machine and helped turn the mid-west into America's breadbasket.

Williams were still laboring. Once they all had gathered in that place, the Lord promised to reveal the location of the city of Zion, the New Jerusalem.

The members from Colesville, New York, who had settled briefly in Thompson, Ohio, were instructed to move to Missouri. Newel Knight led this little colony of about sixty people as they hastily prepared for another 1,000-mile journey.

ON TO MISSOURI

Two weeks after the conference, Joseph Smith and his brethren embarked on the western mission. He wrote:

On the 19th of June, in company with Sidney Rigdon, Martin Harris, Edward Partridge, William W. Phelps, Joseph Coe, Algernon S. Gilbert and his wife, I started from Kirtland, Ohio, for the land of Missouri, agreeable to the commandment before received, wherein it was promised that if we were faithful, the land of our inheritance, even the place for the city of the New Jerusalem, should be revealed. We went by wagon, canal boats, and stages to Cincinnati. . . . We left Cincinnati in a steamer, and landed at Louisville, Kentucky, where we were detained three days in waiting for a steamer to convey us to St. Louis. At St. Louis, myself, Brothers Harris, Phelps, Partridge and Coe, went by land on foot to Independence, Jackson County, Missouri, where we arrived about the middle of July, and the rest of the company came by water a few days later. . . .

The meeting of our brethren, who had long awaited our arrival, was a glorious one, and moistened with many tears. It seemed good and pleasant for brethren to meet together in unity. But our reflections were many, coming as we had from a highly cultivated state of society in the east, and standing now upon the confines or western limits of the United States, and looking at the vast wilderness of those that sat in darkness; how natural it was to observe the degradation, leanness of intellect, ferocity, and jealousy of a people that were nearly a century behind the times, and to feel for those who roam about without the benefit of civilization, refinement, or religion; yea, and exclaim in the language of the Prophets: "When will the wilderness blossom as the rose? When will Zion be built up in her glory, and where will Thy temple stand, unto which all nations shall come in the last days?" (Smith, *History of the Church,* 1:188-89).

The town of Independence stood on the banks of the Missouri River, the last outpost on the western edge of the United States. From there, traders carried fabrics, clothing, cutlery, and other goods to the Mexican settlements along the Santa Fe Trail. They returned with horses, and gold and silver coins.

The ones who survived the four-month trip made profits of two to three hundred percent. Fur traders came to Independence from the northwest with their bundles of beaver, otter, and muskrat pelts, and bison, bear, and deer skins that they sold to buy weapons, ammunition, and traps. Though only four years old, Independence already boasted twenty general stores, blacksmiths, wagon shops, hotels, and saloons. The new brick courthouse was the pride of the town. It was two stories high, had twelve windows, a tall square spire, and a chimney in each corner.

While the Missouri River provided commerce, two other rivers—the Big Blue and Little Blue—gave their names to the fertile area. When Washington Irving visited the region, he commented that the soil was rich, and the forests more beautiful than anything he had ever seen. But most of the area's inhabitants were not interested in farming. They were buffalo hunters, fur traders, trappers, merchants, muleskinners, teamsters, and government agents. There were also a few missionaries and ministers who hoped to reclaim the souls of the rough and wild populous from certain damnation.

LOCATION OF ZION REVEALED

On July 20, 1831, Joseph received the promised revelation naming the location of Zion.

> Hearken, O ye elders of my church, saith the Lord your God, who have assembled yourselves together, according to my commandments, in this land, which is the land of Missouri, which is the land which I have appointed and concentrated for the gathering of the saints.
>
> Wherefore, this is the land of promise, and the place for the city of Zion.
>
> And thus saith the Lord your God, if you will receive wisdom here is wisdom. Behold, the place which is now called Independence is the center place; and a spot for the temple is lying westward, upon a lot which is not far from the courthouse.
>
> Wherefore, it is wisdom that the land should be purchased by the saints, and also every tract lying westward, even unto the line running directly between Jew and Gentile (D&C 57:1-4).

Joseph recalled:

> The first Sabbath after our arrival in Jackson County, Brother W. W. Phelps preached to a western audience over the boundary of the United States, wherein were present specimens of all the families of the earth; Shem, Ham, and Japheth: several of the Lamanites or Indians—representative of Shem; quite a respectable number of negroes—descendants of Ham; and the balance was made up of citizens of the surrounding country, and fully represented themselves as pioneers of the West (Smith, *History of the Church*, 190-91).

The following week, the sixty members from Colesville, New York, arrived in Independence, Missouri. Newel Knight's aged and sick mother, Polly, was part of the group. "[My mother] would not consent to stop traveling. . . . Her greatest desire was to set her feet upon the land of Zion, and have her body interred in that land. I went on shore and bought lumber to make a coffin, [in] case she should die before we arrived at our place of destination—so fast did she fail. But the Lord gave her the desire of her heart, and she lived to stand upon that land (Smith, *History of the Church*, 1:199 n. 1). She arrived in Zion near the end of July, and died on August 6.

The Saints purchased land to build a settlement, and on August 2, they met with Joseph. He recorded:

I assisted the Colesville branch of the Church to lay the first log, for a house, as [the] foundation of Zion in Kaw township, twelve miles west of Independence. The log was carried and placed by twelve men, in honor of the twelve tribes of Israel. At the same time, through prayer, the land of Zion was consecrated and dedicated by Elder Sidney Rigdon for the gathering of the saints. . . . [Sidney asked those present]:

"Do you receive this land of your inheritance with thankful hearts from the Lord?"

Answer from all: "We do."

"Do you pledge yourselves to keep the law of God in this land, which you never have kept in your own lands?"

"We do."

"Do you pledge yourselves to see that others of your brethren who shall come hither, do keep the laws of God?"

"We do." . . .

"I now pronounce this land consecrated and dedicated unto the Lord for a possession and inheritance for the Saints, and for all the faithful servants of the Lord to the remotest ages of time. In the name of Jesus Christ, having authority from Him. Amen" (Smith, *History of the Church*, 1:196, n. 2).

Joseph continued:

It was a season of joy . . . and afforded a glimpse of the future, which time will yet unfold to the satisfaction of the faithful. . . . On the third day of August, I proceeded to dedicate the spot for the Temple, a little west of Independence, and there were also present Sidney Rigdon, Edward Partridge, W. W. Phelps, Oliver Cowdery, Martin Harris, and Joseph Coe.

The 87th Psalm was read:—His foundation is in the holy mountains.

The Lord loveth the gates of Zion more than all the dwellings of Jacob.

Glorious things are spoken of thee, O city of God. Selah.

I will make mention of Rahab and Babylon to them that know me: behold Philistia, and Tyre, with Ethiopia; this man was born there.

And of Zion it shall be said, This and that man was born in her; and the Highest Himself shall establish her. The Lord shall count when he writeth up the people, that this man was born there. Selah.

As well the singers as the players on instruments shall be there: all my springs are in thee." The scene was solemn and impressive (Smith, *History of the Church,* 1:196, 198-99).

THE LAND OF ZION

Now that they knew this to be the land of Zion, the brethren wanted to share their joy with the members in Ohio and elsewhere. Joseph and Sidney prepared a description of the area as it appeared to them, that summer of 1831. Joseph recorded:

The country is unlike the timbered states of the East. As far as the eye can reach the beautiful rolling prairies lay spread out like a sea of meadows; and are decorated with a growth of flowers so glorious and grand as to exceed description. . . . Only on the water courses is this timber to be found. There are strips from one to three miles in width, and following faithfully the meanderings of the streams, it grows in luxuriant forests. The forests are a mixture of oak, hickory, black walnut, elm, ash, cherry, honey locust, mulberry, coffee bean, hack berry, boxelder, and bass wood; with the addition of cottonwood, butterwood, pecan, and soft and hard maple upon the bottoms. The shrubbery is beautiful, and consists in part of plums, grapes, crab apple, and persimmons.

The soil is rich and fertile; from three to ten feet deep. . . . It yields in abundance, wheat, corn, sweet potatoes, cotton and many other common agricultural products. Horses, cattle and hogs, though of an inferior breed, are tolerably plentiful and seem nearly to raise themselves by grazing in the vast prairie range in summer, and feeding upon the bottoms in winter. The wild game is less plentiful of course where man has commenced the cultivation of the soil, than in the wild prairies. Buffalo, elk, deer, bear, wolves, beaver and many smaller animals here roam at pleasure. Turkeys, geese, swans, ducks, yea a variety of the feathered tribe, are among the rich abundance that grace the delightful regions of this goodly land—the heritage of the children of God (Smith, *History of the Church,* 1:196-97).

Sidney noted:

The season is mild and delightful nearly three quarters of the year, and as the land of Zion, situated about equal distances from the Atlantic and Pacific oceans, as well as from the Alleghany and Rocky Mountains—it bids fair—when the curse is taken from the land—to become one of the most blessed places on the globe. The winters are milder than the Atlantic states of the same parallel of latitude, and the weather is more agreeable; so that were the virtues of the inhabitants only equal to the blessings of the Lord which He permits to crown the industry of those inhabitants, there would be a measure of good things of life, for the benefit of the Saints, full, pressed down, and running over even an hundred-fold. The disadvantages here, as in all new countries, are self evident—lack of mills and schools; together with the natural privations and inconveniences which the hand of industry, the refinement of society, and the polish of science, overcome (Smith, *History of the Church,* 1:197-98).

And Joseph continued:

But all these impediments vanish when it is recollected what the Prophets have said concerning Zion in the last days; how the glory of Lebanon is to come upon her; the fir tree, the pine tree, and the box tree together, to beautify the place of His sanctuary, that he may make the place of His feet glorious. Where for brass, He will bring gold; and for iron, He will bring silver; and for wood, brass; and for stones, iron; and where the feast of fat things will be given to the just; yea, when the splendor of the Lord is brought to our consideration for the good of His people, the calculations of man and the vain glory of the world vanish, and we exclaim "Out of Zion the perfection of beauty, God hath shined" (Smith, *History of the Church,*1:198).

BLESSINGS AND PERSECUTIONS

When Joseph Smith and ten elders boarded canoes and started down the Missouri River toward St. Louis, Newel Knight and the rest of the Saints began creating a community in the wilderness of western Missouri. Newel Knight wrote about their adventure:

The time now passed in our common labors, in building houses, plowing, sowing grain, and all other labor necessary to build up a new country. We were not accustomed to a frontier life, so things around us seemed new and strange and the work we had to do was of a different nature to that which had been done in the East. Yet we took hold with cheerful hearts, and with a determination to do our best, and with all diligence went to work to secure food and prepare for the coming winter ("Newel Knight's Journal," *Scraps of Biography,* 72).

Parley, Orson Pratt, and others had left Kirtland on missions in June. Their work in Ohio, Illinois, and Indiana was so successful that they did not reach Missouri until September. They were disappointed to

WORLD EVENTS

On July 4, 1831, while the nation was celebrating its fifty-fifth birthday, James Monroe, the fifth president of the United States, died in New York City. He had fought in the Revolutionary War, and served as ambassador to France. He negotiated the Louisiana Purchase, which more than doubled the size of the United States. During his time in office, Florida was purchased from Spain, and the Missouri Compromise had temporarily averted Civil War. His Monroe Doctrine had also closed the Americas to colonization by European powers.

That summer, politics were heating up for the 1832 national elections. A third party, the Anti-Masons, was trying to win votes. Originally organized to protest the secrecy and alleged anti-democratic views of the Masons, the party had started in New York State and spread to several other states. The Anti-Masonic party even had its own newspapers. William W. Phelps edited one of the papers until he joined the Church and moved to Kirtland in 1831. However, the party had a difficult time finding candidates to represent them because most of the leading men at that time were Masons. Nonetheless, the party's idea of having an open political nominating convention, rather than a closed-door caucus, was an idea that later caught on with the other political parties and is still used today.

find that the other brethren had already left, but were content with the knowledge that they had converted many, and that they now stood in the land of Zion. Upon his arrival, Parley became very ill and could not return to Ohio, so he spent the winter with the Colesville Saints, noting that:

> The winter was cold, and for some time about ten families lived in one log cabin, which was open and unfinished, while the frozen ground served for a floor. Our food consisted of beef and a little bread made of corn, which had been grated into coarse meal by rubbing the ears on a tin grater. This was rather an inconvenient way of living for a sick person; but it was for the gospel's sake, and all were very cheerful and happy.
>
> We enjoyed many happy seasons in our prayer and other meetings, and the Spirit of the Lord was poured out upon us, and even on the little children, insomuch that many of eight, ten, or twelve years of age spake, and prayed, and prophesied in our meetings and in our family worship. There was a spirit of peace and union and love and good will manifested in this little Church in the wilderness, the memory of which will be ever dear to my heart (*Autobiography of Parley P. Pratt,* 56).

Three days into their journey down the Missouri River, Joseph and his companions camped at McIlwaine's Bend. Brother Phelps, in an open vision, by daylight, saw the destroyer and his most horrible power ride upon the face of the waters. Others heard a noise, but did not see the vision.

The next morning, after prayers, Joseph received this explanation from the Lord:

> It is not needful for this whole company of mine elders to be moving swiftly upon the waters, whilst the inhabitants on either side are perishing in unbelief.
>
> Nevertheless, I suffered it that ye might bear record; behold, there are many dangers upon the waters, and more especially hereafter;
>
> For I, the Lord, have decreed in mine anger many destructions upon the waters; yea, and especially upon these waters.
>
> Nevertheless, all flesh is in mine hand, and he that is faithful among you shall not perish by the waters. . . .
>
> Behold, I, the Lord, in the beginning blessed the waters; but in the last days, by the mouth of my servant John, I cursed the waters. Wherefore, the days will come that no flesh shall be safe upon the waters (D&C 61:3-6, 14-15).

Accordingly, the rest of the trip was made by land. By the end of August, Joseph was back in Kirtland. He, Emma, and the four-month-old twins then

ORSON PRATT (1811–1881) the younger brother of Parley P. Pratt, was baptized by Parley two weeks after Parley himself was baptized. Orson was one of the original Quorum of the Twelve, and later became the leader of the European Mission. He and Erastus Snow were the first Saints to enter the Salt Lake Valley. Orson was known as a mathematician, editor, writer, and pioneer.

moved to Hiram, Ohio, about thirty miles southeast of Kirtland, where they lived with the John Johnson family. There, too, the blessings of God were more than matched by persecution from the adversary.

ENEMIES FROM WITHOUT

The *Painesville Telegraph* had printed hostile stories about the Mormons ever since the missionaries had arrived in the area.

Editor E.D. Howe kept his readers informed about the Mormons:

> The members of the church are not permitted to question the infallibility of Joe Smith or anything he may say as being a commandment of God. All members who dared question or express doubts concerning these messages, Howe claimed, were immediately expelled as heretics (Backman, Jr., *The Heavens Resound,* 57).

During that fall of 1831, another voice was heard in the hostile press. Ezra Booth, who had accompanied the Prophet and others on the western mission, and taken part in laying the foundations of Zion and the dedication of the temple site, became hostile toward the Church. After he left the Church, he wrote nine letters to the newspaper "exposing" Mormonism. Joseph explained:

> About this time Ezra Booth came out as an apostate. He came into the Church upon seeing a person healed of an infirmity. . . . He had been a Methodist priest for some time previous to his embracing the fulness of the Gospel . . . and upon his admission into the Church he was ordained an Elder. . . . He went up to Missouri as a companion of Elder Morley; but when he actually learned that faith, humility, patience, and tribulation go before blessing[s], and that God brings low before He exalts; that instead of the "Savior's granting him power to smite men and make them believe," (as he said he wanted God to do in his own case)—when he found he must become all things to all men, that he might peradventure save some; and that, too, by all diligence, by perils by sea and land, as was the case in the days of Jesus—then he was disappointed. . . . He turned away, and . . . became an apostate, and wrote a series of letters, which, by their coloring, falsity, and vain calculations to overthrow the work of the Lord, exposed his weakness, wickedness and folly, and left him a monument of his own shame, for the world to wonder at (Smith, *History of the Church,* 1:215–16).

Considering the narrow points of view of the various newspapers at that time, it was natural for the Church to desire a voice of its own so that it could publish news and information for Church members who were scattered throughout at least a half dozen states. So W. W. Phelps was sent to Cincinnati

THE EVENING AND THE MORNING STAR NEWSPAPER was created so that the brethren could publish news and information for Church members who were scattered throughout at least a half dozen states. W. W. Phelps was sent to Cincinnati to buy a press and some type, and then he traveled to Independence, Missouri where he began publishing this newspaper. Shortly thereafter, they used the press to print 3,000 copies of the revelation that is now D&C 1. *June issue, 1832*

1

THE EVENING AND THE MORNING STAR.

Vol. I. Independence, Mo. June, 1832. **No. 1.**

Revelations.

THE ARTICLES AND COVENANTS OF THE CHURCH OF CHRIST.

THE rise of the Church of Christ in these last days, being one thousand eight hundred and thirty years since the coming of our Lord and Savior Jesus Christ, in the flesh; it being regularly organized and established agreeable to the laws of our country, by the will and commandments of God in the fourth month and on the sixth day of the month, which is called April: Which commandments were given to Joseph, who was called of God and ordained an Apostle of Jesus Christ, an Elder of this Church; and also to Oliver, who was called of God an Apostle of Jesus Christ, an Elder of this Church, and ordained under his hand; and this according to the grace of our Lord and Savior Jesus Christ to whom be all glory both now and forever. Amen.

to buy a press and some type. From there, he traveled to Missouri where he began publishing a monthly paper, the *Evening and Morning Star*. During the early part of the fall of 1831, Joseph and Sidney Rigdon were translating the Bible, but after a special conference on November 1, they were commanded to publish the commandments that had been received up to that time. Thus, they turned their efforts to publishing these revelations.

The Lord revealed His preface to the Book of Commandments, now Section 1 of the Doctrine and Covenants, and the appendix, now Section 133. Oliver Cowdery carried the revelations to Independence, where W. W. Phelps, having set up the press, started to print 3,000 copies.

Enemies from Within

At a conference of members in Hiram, Ohio, in November 1831, there was a new challenge to Joseph's authority. Some of the brethren believed that some-one with more learning could write the revelations from God better. The Lord promptly issued a challenge in another revelation, Section 67 of the Doctrine and Covenants:

> Your eyes have been upon my servant Joseph Smith, Jun., and his language you have known, and his imperfec-tions you have known; and you have sought in your hearts knowledge that you might express beyond his language. . . .
>
> Now, seek ye out of the Book of Commandments, even the least that is among them, and appoint him that is the most wise among you; Or, if there be any among you that shall make one like unto it, then ye are justified in say-ing that ye do not know that they are true.
>
> But if ye cannot make one like unto it, ye are under condemnation if ye do not bear record that they are true (D&C 67:5-8).

Joseph recorded:

> After the foregoing was received, William E. McLellin, as the wisest man, in his own estimation, having more learning than sense, endeavored to write a commandment like unto one of the least of the Lord's, but failed; it was an awful responsibility to write in the name of the Lord. The Elders and all present that witnessed this vain attempt of a man to imitate the language of Jesus Christ, renewed their faith in the fulness of the Gospel, and in the truth of the commandments and revelations which the Lord had given to the Church through my instrumentality; and the Elders signified a will-ingness to bear testimony of their truth to all the world (Smith, *History of the Church, 1:225*).

WORLD EVENTS

That fall, 1831, in England, a young man was preparing for a jour-ney that would provide him with his life's work and would shape the way people viewed their world. As a poor student, he was warned by his father that he would be a disgrace to himself and all his family. He entered medical school but failed because he preferred fishing, riding, hunting, shooting, and collecting marine animals to long hours in lecture halls and libraries filled with dusty volumes. At the age of twenty-two, Charles Darwin sailed as a naturalist on board the *H. M. S. Beagle* to study the coasts of Patagonia, Chile, Peru, and the Pacific Islands.

THE FIRST BISHOP

Edward Partridge, the first bishop of the Church, was called to live and preside in Independence, Missouri. When Newel K. Whitney was called by revelation to be the bishop of the Kirtland area, he responded:

> "I cannot see a bishop in myself, Brother Joseph; but if you say it's the Lord's will, I'll try."
>
> Joseph replied, "You need not take my word alone, go and ask the Father for yourself."
>
> Newel did this, and in the silence of the night, he received these words, "Thy strength is in me." So he accepted the call and became the Bishop of Kirtland, Ohio (B. H. Roberts, *Outlines of Ecclesiastic History*, 348–49).

CONFERENCE OF THE CHURCH AND NEW REVELATIONS

On January 25, 1832, conference was held in Amherst, Ohio. Here, for the first time, Joseph Smith was sustained and ordained as President of the High Priesthood. After the conference, Joseph returned to the task of translating the Bible. He noted:

> From sundry revelations which had been received, it was apparent that many important points touching the salvation of man had been taken from the Bible, or lost before it was compiled. It appeared self-evident from what truths were left, that if God rewarded every one according to the deeds done in the body the term "Heaven," as intended for the Saints' eternal home must include more kingdoms that one. Accordingly, on the 16th of February, 1832, while translating St. John's Gospel, myself and Elder Rigdon saw [a] vision (Smith, *History of the Church,* 1:245).

This was a glorious vision of the degrees of glory, found in Section 76 of the Doctrine and Covenants. Several other priesthood holders were present at the Johnson home in Hiram, Ohio. Among them was Philo Dibble who recorded:

> I saw the glory and felt the power, but did not see the vision. . . .
>
> Joseph would, at intervals, say: "What do I see?" . . . Then he would relate what he had seen or what he was looking at. Then Sidney replied, "I see the same." Presently Sidney would say "what do I see?" and would repeat what he had seen or was seeing, and Joseph would reply, "I see the same."
>
> This manner of conversation was repeated at short intervals to the end of the vision, and during the whole time not a word was spoken by another person. Not a sound nor motion [was] made by anyone but Joseph and Sidney, and it seemed to me that they never moved a joint or limb during the time I was there, which I think was over an hour, and to the end of the vision.

WILLIAM E. MCLELLIN (1806–1883). An early convert to the Church, and an ordained Apostle, McLellin later became disaffected and challenged the Prophet's "ability" to write revelations. When given the opportunity to do better than Joseph at this task, he failed miserably. Joseph characterized him as "having more learning than sense." McLellin apostatized and joined the mob in Far West, ousting women and children from their homes and looting freely.
ca. 1840

Andrew Jackson's first term as president was plagued with some lingering issues. One involved the tariff. For many years, the United States had imposed a steep tariff on imported goods. This protected the northeastern manufacturers but was very unpopular in the southern states where, without the tariff, goods could have been purchased cheaper from Europe than from Boston. The so-called Tariff of Abominations, adopted in 1828, was especially unpopular. In December 1831, Andrew Jackson recommended to Congress that the tariff gradually be reduced. The new bill, however, did not go far enough to satisfy the south, and South Carolina decided to take action. Their legislature declared the tariffs null and void, and ordered that the tariffs could not be enforced within the state. They also threatened that if the Federal Government attempted to force the state to comply, South Carolina would secede from the Union. Jackson's reply to the threat was plain, and he boldly stated that one state assuming the power to annul a law of the United States was in direct contradiction to the Constitution, and was wholly destructive to its principles and objectives. The debate raged all through 1832, but there seemed to be no solution.

Another major issue was the Second Bank of the United States in Philadelphia. As the central bank of the nation, it regulated the money supply and the expansion of credit. Many people wanted it destroyed, including Andrew Jackson, who thought it was too powerful. A small war brewed in Washington and Philadelphia over this issue, but the solution had to wait until the election of 1832.

Joseph sat firmly and calmly all the time in the midst of a magnificent glory, but Sidney sat limp and pale, apparently as limber as a rag. Observing [this], Joseph remarked, smilingly, "Sidney is not as used to it as I am" (Jack M. Lyon, Linda Ririe Gundry, and Jay A. Parry, *Best-Loved Stories of the LDS People*, 206-7).

Joseph Smith stated:

Nothing could be more pleasing to the Saints . . . than the light which burst upon the world through [that] vision. Every law, every commandment, every promise, every truth, and every point touching the destiny of man, from Genesis to Revelation, where the purity of the scriptures remains unsullied by the folly of men, go to show the perfection of the theory [of different degrees of glory in the future life], and witnesses the fact that that document is a transcript from the records of the eternal world, the sublimity of the ideas; the purity of the language; the scope for action; the continued duration for completion, in order that the heirs of salvation may confess the Lord and bow the knee; the rewards for faithfulness, and the punishments for sins, are so much beyond the narrow-mindedness of men, that every honest man is constrained to exclaim: "It came from God" (Smith, *History of the Church*, 1:252-53).

In the following weeks, five more sections of the Doctrine and Covenants were received, Sections 77 through 81. These revelations explained the Revelation of St. John, provided more information about the law of consecration, and called several men on missions. But again, in the midst of all this glory and power, there was hate, jealousy, and bitterness.

PERSECUTION AND APOSTASY CONTINUES

Some joined Ezra Booth in apostasy. The Prophet chastised Olfstead Johnson for rebellion, so he and his brothers Eli, Edward, and John, Jr., left the Church, charging that Joseph was trying to rob them of their inheritance and take their father's property. Simonds Ryder, who had joined the Church after witnessing a miracle, became disaffected when he received a letter signed by Joseph and Sidney that had his name spelled Rider rather than Ryder. He later became the leader of a group determined to drive Joseph Smith from Hiram, Ohio. Simonds claimed:

> Several converts were made, and their success seemed to indicate an immediate triumph in Hiram. But when they went to Missouri . . . they left their papers behind. This gave their new converts an opportunity to become acquainted with the internal arrangements of their church, which revealed to them the horrid fact that a plot was laid to take their property from them . . . and place it under the control of Joseph Smith the prophet. This was too much for the Hiramites, and they left the Mormonites faster than they had ever joined them. . . . Some, who had been the dupes of this deception, determined not to let it pass with impunity; and, accordingly, a company was formed of citizens from Shalersville, Garrettsville, and Hiram, in March 1832, and proceeded to headquarters in the darkness of the night, and took Smith and Rigdon from their beds, and tarred and feathered them both (Parkin, *Conflict at Kirtland,* 254).

Joseph recalled the incident:

> On the 24th of March, the twins before mentioned, which had been sick of the measles for some time, caused us to be broken of our rest in taking care of them, especially my wife. In the evening I told her she had better retire to rest with one of the children, and I would watch with the sicker child. In the night she told me I had better lie down on the trundle bed, and I did so, and was soon after awakened by her screaming murder, when I found myself going out of the door, in the hands of about a dozen men; some of whose hands were in my hair, and some had hold of my shirt, drawers and limbs. . . . I made a desperate struggle, as I was forced out to extricate myself, but only cleared one leg, with which I made a pass at one man, and he fell on the door steps. I was immediately overpowered again; and they swore . . . they would kill me if I did not be still, which quieted me. . . . They then seized me by the throat and held on till I lost my breath. After I came to, as they passed along with me, about thirty rods from the house, I saw Elder Rigdon stretched out on the ground, whither they had dragged him by his heels. I supposed he was dead. I began to plead with them, saying, "You will have mercy and spare my life, I hope." To which they replied, "g—d—ye, call on yer God for help, we'll show ye no mercy." . . . Then they turned to the right, and went about thirty rods further . . . into the meadow . . . when a group of mobbers collected a little way off, and said, "Simonds, Simonds, come here;" . . . They held a council, and as I could

occasionally overhear a word, I supposed it was to know whether or not it was best to kill me. They returned after a while, when I learned that they had concluded not to kill me, but to beat and scratch me well, and tear off my shirt and drawers and leave me naked. One cried, "Simonds, Simonds, where's the tar bucket?" "I don't know," answered one, "where 'tis, Eli left it." They ran back and fetched the bucket of tar, when one exclaimed with an oath, "Let us tar up his mouth;" and they tried to force the tar-paddle into my mouth; I twisted my head around, so they could not . . . They then tried to force a vial into my mouth, and broke it in my teeth. All my clothes were torn off me except my shirt collar; and one man fell on me and scratched my body with his nails like a mad cat, and then muttered out, ". . . That's the way the Holy Ghost falls on folks!"

Then they left me, and I attempted to rise, but fell again; I pulled the tar away from my lips, so that I could breathe more freely, and after a while I began to recover, and raised myself up, whereupon I saw two lights. I made my way towards one of them, and found it was Father Johnson's. When I came to the door, I was naked, and the tar made me look as if I were covered with blood, and when my wife saw me she thought I was all crushed to pieces, and fainted. During the affray abroad, the sisters of the neighborhood had collected at my room. I called for a blanket, they threw me one and shut the door; I wrapped it around me and went in. . . .

My friends spent the night in scraping and removing the tar, and washing and cleansing my body; so that by morning I was ready to be clothed again. This being the Sabbath morning, the people assembled for meeting at the usual hour of worship, and among them came also the mobbers: . . . Simonds Ryder, a . . . leader of the mob . . . and Felatiah Allen, Esq., who gave the mob a barrel of whiskey to raise their spirits [and many others]. With my flesh all scarified and defaced, I preached to the congregation as usual, and in the afternoon of the same day baptized three individuals (Smith, *History of the Church,* 1:261-64).

JOSEPH SMITH
PREACHING
by Mike Malm
Joseph Smith, Jr.
preached to a group
of people gathered at
the John Johnson
farm in Hiram,
Ohio, in March
1832—the morning
after he was severely
beaten, tarred, and
feathered.
oil on canvas 1997

THE HARVEST OF SOULS, 1832

Joseph Smith quickly recovered from the dreadful experience of being tarred and feathered that March night. The chipped tooth he received in the struggle caused a slight speech problem, but Sidney Rigdon did not fare so well. Joseph reported:

The next morning I went to see Elder Rigdon, and found him crazy, and his head highly inflamed, for they had dragged him by his heels, and those, too, so high from the ground that he could not raise his head from the rough, frozen surface, which lacerated it exceedingly; and when he saw me he called to his wife to bring him his razor. She asked him what he wanted of it; and he replied, to kill me. Sister Rigdon left the room, and he asked me to bring his razor; I asked him what he wanted of it, and he replied he wanted to kill his wife; and he continued delirious some days. . . . Elder Rigdon removed to Kirtland with his family—then sick with the measles—the following Wednesday; and, on account of the mob, he went to Chardon on Saturday, March 31st (Smith, *History of the Church,* 1:265).

These two leaders of the Church were not the only victims of the mob. Joseph reports: "During the mobbing one of the twins [Joseph S. Murdock] contracted a severe cold, continued to grow worse until Friday, and then died" (Smith, *History of the Church,* 1:265). For the fourth time, Joseph and Emma deposited a tiny body in the ground. Their first-born son, Alvin, lay buried in Harmony, Pennsylvania, near Emma's parents. The twins, Thadeus and Louisa, were buried in Kirtland, Ohio. Now, little Joseph was placed in a grave in Hiram, Ohio. Joseph and Emma stayed with the Johnson family for a few days, but mobsters continued to molest and menace the home.

JOHN JOHNSON FARM in Hiram, Ohio, where Joseph and Emma Smith lived from 1831–32. *ca. 1900*

The law of consecration was the doctrine that seems to have fired the mobsters to action. Many of the mobsters were former Church members who felt that the Prophet was trying to rob them of their inheritance. They justified their actions as a defense of private property. Other factors behind the mobbing included Joseph's claim that the Bible contained many errors, the peoples' fear that Hiram might become headquarters for the Church, their misunderstandings of Mormon doctrines, and simple jealousy.

FIRST PRESIDENCY ESTABLISHED

After the journey from Ohio, Joseph found the brethren in Missouri generally enjoying good health and faith, and extremely glad to see him again. Joseph recorded:

On the 26th, I called a general council of the Church, and was acknowledged as the President of the High Priesthood, according to a previous ordination at a conference of High Priests, Elders and members, held at Amherst, Ohio, on the 25th of January, 1832. The right hand of fellowship was given to me by the Bishop, Edward Partridge, in behalf of the Church. The scene was solemn, impressive, and delightful. . . . On the 27th, we transacted . . . considerable business for the salvation of the Saints, who were settling among a ferocious set of mobbers, like lambs among wolves. It was my endeavor to so organize the Church, that the brethren might eventually be independent of every incumbrance beneath the celestial kingdom, by bonds and covenants of mutual friendship, and mutual love (Smith, *History of the Church,* 1:267-69).

This action made Joseph the presiding officer of the Church. His counselors were Sidney Rigdon, and Jesse Goss; but Goss did not prove valiant in the faith and was soon excommunicated; Frederick G. Williams was appointed counselor in his place. A native of Connecticut, Williams was forty-five years old. He owned a farm near Kirtland, but was also a doctor, and was practicing medicine when Parley Pratt, Oliver Cowdery, Ziba Peterson, and Peter Whitmer preached the gospel to him. He accepted it at once and accompanied the missionaries to Missouri on their mission to the Lamanites. His diligence and faithfulness qualified him to serve with the Prophet as a member of the First Presidency.

Several important events occurred at the conference in Missouri. First, the Saints decided to publish the hymns that Emma Smith had collected. And second, Kirtland was appointed by revelation to be the first stake of Zion. Missouri would be the center place, increasing in beauty and holiness, and her borders were to be enlarged, while all around her, the stakes (like the stakes that support a tent) were to be strengthened so that Zion could arise and put on her beautiful garments.

One of the actions taken to strengthen the Church against enemies was the organization of the United Firm, which consisted of two general stores: the Gilbert Whitney and Company store in Independence, and the Newel K. Whitney and Company store in Kirtland. This allowed the Saints to buy goods at their own stores rather than from their enemies. The stores also served as clearing houses for those who contributed to the Church, and those who needed assistance.

While Joseph counseled with the Saints in Missouri, dozens of missionaries were laboring in various parts of the United States. Some of these missionaries reaped baptisms from seeds that had been sown by the very first missionaries. Joseph Smith, Sr., and his son Don Carlos had traveled to share the good news with family members living in Potsdam, New York, shortly after the Church was organized in 1830. Young Joseph's grandparents received the news with joy, and some of his other relatives were also interested in the gospel. Joseph, Sr., left a copy of the Book of Mormon with his brother John so he could study it and decide whether it was true. A year or so later, Elders Joseph H. Wakefield and Solomon Humphries arrived in Potsdam. They baptized several members of the Smith family, including three of the Prophet's uncles, an aunt, his grandmother, and a fifteen-year-old cousin, George A. Smith. George had studied many religions, and had been sealed up to damnation nine times by a congregational minister with whom he had had the audacity to disagree. A wealthy Presbyterian was so impressed with the boy that he offered him seven years free schooling if he would not become a Mormon. However, George did not accept the man's offer. He had found the answers to his prayers and questions in the gospel of Jesus Christ. Very soon after his baptism he traveled to Kirtland to meet his cousin, the Prophet, and participate in the growth of the Church. In Mendon, New York, two of the missionaries found a group of people who had already read the Book of Mormon.

Samuel H. Smith had been rather discouraged after his first mission in 1830, but the copies of the Book of Mormon he left with John P. Green and Phineas Young had not been sitting idle on the shelf. Phineas read the book and then gave it to his father, John Young, who proclaimed it the greatest work he had ever seen. Then sister Fanny Young read a copy and passed it on to her brother Brigham, his wife Miriam, and other family members. Their friends, the Greenes and the Kimballs, also read the book. When the missionaries arrived, they found a whole branch of the Church just waiting for baptism.

Brigham later wrote of the struggles, questions, and answers he encountered in the two-year process of his conversion.

> Upon the first opportunity I read the Book of Mormon, and then sought to become acquainted with the people who professed to believe it. . . . I watched to see whether good common sense was manifest; and, if they had that, I wanted them to present it in accordance with the Scriptures.

EMMA'S HYMNS *by Liz Lemon Swindle* The Lord instructed Emma to "make a selection of sacred hymns. . . . For my soul delighteth in the song of the heart; yea, the song of the righteous is a prayer unto me" (D&C 25:11–12). In this same section of the Doctrine and Covenants, the Lord indicated his love for Emma, calling her an "elect lady." *oil on canvas*

I could not have more honestly and earnestly have prepared myself to go into eternity, than I did to come into this Church; and when I had ripened everything in my mind, I drank it in, and not till then (Young, *Journal of Discourses,* 8:38).

It was nearly a year after he first saw the Book of Mormon until Brigham met a member of the Church. He was converted by reading the doctrines contained in the book, but he was not about to join the Church until he had evaluated whether the members taught and lived the way their scriptures indicated they should. "When I saw a man without eloquence, or talents for public speaking, who could only say, 'I know . . . that the Book of Mormon is true, that Joseph Smith is a Prophet of the Lord,' the Holy Ghost proceeding from that individual illuminated my understanding, and light, glory, and immortality were before me. . . . I was encircled by them, filled by them, and I knew for myself that the testimony of the man was true" (Young, *Journal of Discourses* 1:90).

BRIGHAM YOUNG MILLSTREAM located in Mendon, NY, where Brigham Young and Heber C. Kimball were baptized.

Still, Brigham waited and studied more. He and his friend Heber Kimball attended several meetings of the Mormon branch in Columbia, Pennsylvania, and when Brigham was fully converted, he traveled to Canada to share this new knowledge with his brother Joseph.

April 14th, 1832, I was baptized by Eleazer Miller, who confirmed me at the water's edge. We returned home, about two miles, the weather being cold and snowy; and before my clothes were dry on my back he laid his hands on me and ordained me an elder, at which I marvelled. According to the words of the Savior, I felt a humble, childlike spirit, witnessing unto me that my sins were forgiven (*Manuscript History of Brigham Young*).

Brigham's good friend, Heber C. Kimball, had also been seeking truths for several years and was baptized that same month. Even before his baptism, he had many glorious experiences with the Spirit. In Mendon, New York, he had seen a marvelous vision of the armies marching across the heavens on that September night, five years earlier, when Joseph Smith was on the hill Cumorah, receiving the gold plates from the Angel Moroni. While he was investigating the Church, Kimball had another remarkable experience:

On one occasion, Father John Young, Brigham Young, Joseph Young and myself had come together to get up some wood for Phineas H. Young. While we were thus engaged we were pondering upon these things which had been told us by the Elders, and upon the saints gathering to Zion, when the glory of God shone upon us, and we saw the gathering of the saints to Zion, and the glory that would rest upon them; and many more things connected with that great event, such as the sufferings and the persecutions that would come upon the people of God, and the calamities and judgments that would come upon the people of the world.

These things caused such great joy to spring up in our bosoms, that we were hardly able to contain ourselves, and we did shout aloud, "Hosannah to God and the Lamb" (Whitney, *Life of Heber C. Kimball*, 19).

Meanwhile, Joseph and the other brethren were concluding their visit to Missouri. Joseph noted, "Before we left Independence, Elder Rigdon preached two most powerful discourses, which so far as outward appearance was concerned, gave great satisfaction to the people" (Smith, *History of the Church*, 1:270-71).

While the Saints may have enjoyed the sermons, the nonmember residents of Independence were not favorably impressed. The Reverend Benton Pixley recorded his account of the Rigdon speech.

> [He said] the Epistles are not and were not given for our instruction, but for the instruction of a people of another age and country, far removed from ours, of different habits and manners, and needing different teaching; and that it is altogether inconsistent for us to take the Epistles written for that people, of that age of the world, as containing suitable instruction for this people at that age of the world. The Gospels too, we are given by them to understand, are so mutilated and altered as to convey little of the instruction which they should convey. Hence we are told a new revelation is to be sought—is to be expected, indeed is coming forthwith (William Mulder and A. Russell Martensen, eds., *Among the Mormons*).

HEBER CHASE KIMBALL (1810–1868) was baptized on June 15, 1832 with his wife, Vilate. Heber and Brigham were close friends, and Vilate was Brigham's niece. Faithful and loyal to the Church and its leaders, this tall, powerful man was a devoted missionary, Apostle, and counselor to President Brigham Young. He was well loved for his delightful sense of humor. *ca. 1853*

The brethren's return trip to Kirtland was not without incident, as Joseph recorded:

> [We went] by stage to St. Louis, from thence to Vincennes, Indiana; and from thence to New Albany, near the falls of the Ohio River. Before we arrived at the latter place, the horses became frightened, and while going at full speed Bishop Whitney attempted to jump out of the coach, but having his coat fast, caught his foot in the wheel, and had his leg and foot broken in several places; at the same time I jumped out unhurt. We put up at Mr.

The missionaries were reaping a glorious harvest of souls, but another reaper was stocking the earth with a more grim purpose. Cholera, a dreaded disease of the intestinal tract that can cause death in as little as six hours, was being spread from seaport to seaport, and threatened to cover the whole earth. The epidemic had started in India in 1826. By 1832, it was called a pandemic because it was so widespread. No one knew it at the time, but the cholera germ flourishes in unsanitary conditions, and since none of the cities had pure water supplies, or adequate waste disposal systems, the disease spread rapidly through drinking water.

Porter's public house, in Greenville, for four weeks, while Elder Rigdon went directly forward to Kirtland. . . . One day when I arose from the dinner table, I walked directly to the door and commenced vomiting most profusely. I raised large quantities of blood and poisonous matter, and so great were the muscular contortions of my system, that my jaw in a few moments was dislocated. This I succeeded in replacing with my own hands, and made my way to Brother Whitney (who was on the bed), as speedily as possible; he laid his hands on me and administered to me in the name of the Lord, and I was healed in an instant. . . . Brother Whitney had not had his foot moved from the bed for nearly four weeks, when I went into his room, after a walk in the grove, and told him if he would agree to start for home in the morning, we would take a wagon to the river, about four miles, and there would be a ferry-boat in waiting which would take us quickly across, where we would find a hack which would take us directly to the landing, where we should find a boat, in waiting, and we would be going up the river before ten o'clock, and have a prosperous journey home. He took courage and told me he would go. We started next morning and found everything as I had told him, for we were passing rapidly up the river before ten o'clock, and landing at Wellsville, took the stage coach to Chardon, from thence in a wagon to Kirtland, where we arrived some time in June (Smith, *History of the Church*, 1:271-72).

ST. LOUIS, MISSOURI

St. Louis was the most important city in Missouri, and the brethren often passed through as they traveled between Kirtland and Independence. Located on the west bank of the Mississippi River, just below the mouth of the Missouri, St. Louis was in a perfect location to command western trade. The city had been established in 1764 by French fur traders and named for King Louis IX of France. It had grown quickly. From its ports, steamboats transported men and supplies out to beaver country and carried back tons of pelts. From 1815 until 1830, the brown pelts that passed through the musty waterfront warehouses brought $3,750,000 into St. Louis. The waterfront was lined with grog shops where trappers, river men, ex-soldiers, and drifters met to drink, gamble, boast, and fight.

Above the levy stood the magnificent homes of those who had made fortunes in the fur trade. These members of high society read at least one of the three city newspapers, attended plays and parties, and even bought books. Four hairdressers teased ladies' locks into elaborate chignons in back, and stiff ringlets around the face. Dressmakers created elegant dresses that had an abundance of lace about the neckline, long skirts with at least three ruffles, and enormous sleeves. Milliners designed dainty bonnets of lace and silk to frame the face and protect it from the harsh rays of the sun.

The gentlemen settled their differences in a gentlemanly fashion. They took their grievances, by rowboat, to the local field of honor, Bloody Island. There they would pace off their positions, raise their pistols, and coolly fire. This left at least seven prominent citizens dead between 1810 and 1831. Like most cities of the time, the streets were muddy ditches and public services were nonexistent. Still, it must have been exciting for the brethren to visit the bustling city.

Once back in Kirtland, Ohio, Joseph and Sidney Rigdon resumed work on revising the Bible. Some of the missionaries returned from their fields of labor, and it was thrilling for the Prophet to hear accounts of their success in teaching and baptizing. In October, Joseph made a quick journey to Albany, New York, and Boston with Bishop Whitney to buy supplies for the store. He returned on November 6, immediately after the birth of his son, Joseph Smith III, the first of his and Emma's children to survive. Two days later, he greeted some visitors. Brigham Young and his two little girls had moved in with the Kimball family. Brigham and Heber had a great desire to meet Joseph Smith, as recorded by Brigham:

> In September, 1832, Brother Heber C. Kimball took his horse and wagon, Brother Joseph Young and myself accompanying him, and started for Kirtland to see the Prophet. We visited many friends on the way, and some branches of the church. We exhorted them and prayed with them, and I spoke in tongues. Some pronounced it genuine and from the Lord, and others pronounced it of the devil. We proceeded to Kirtland and stopped at John P. Greene's, who had just arrived there with his family. We rested a few minutes, took some refreshments and started to see the Prophet. We went to his father's house and learned that he was in the woods chopping. We immediately repaired to the woods, where we found the Prophet, and two or three of his brothers, chopping and hauling wood. Here my joy was full at the privilege of shaking the hand of the Prophet of God, and receiving the sure testimony, by the spirit of prophecy, that he was all that any man could believe him to be as a true Prophet. He was happy to see us and bid us welcome. We soon returned to his house, he accompanying us.
>
> In the evening a few of the brethren came in, and we conversed upon the things of the kingdom. He called upon me to pray; in my prayer I spoke in tongues. As soon as we arose from our knees, the brethren flocked around him, and asked his opinion concerning the gift of tongues that was upon me. He told them it was the pure Adamic language. Some said to him they expected he would condemn the gift Brother Brigham had, but he said, "No, it is of God, and the time will come when Brigham Young will preside over

BRIGHAM YOUNG spent many months studying the Book of Mormon, comparing it to the Bible, and carefully pondering the new doctrines. He was baptized on April 14, 1832, by Eleazer Miller, and proved to be a stalwart in the kingdom. *ca. 1851–52*

this church." The latter part of this conversation was in my absence (Roberts, *A Comprehensive History of the Church*, 1:287, n. 18).

Although just a little more than two years had passed since the Church of Jesus Christ had been organized in Fayette, New York, much had transpired. Joseph was no longer a lone voice telling of the restoration of the gospel. Many had joined the Church and accepted him as a prophet. There were strong men and women standing behind him now, over 1,000 of them, waiting for his leadership. These Saints were ready to give their all for the advancement of the kingdom, willing to leave home and family to serve missions, and willing to move to strange new lands and build homes, cities, and temples. However, the Church had strong enemies too. Old settlers in Missouri and disaffected former members of the Church were not above mobbing, tarring and feathering, burning homes, beating men, and tormenting women to drive the Mormons from their midst. There were weak members within the Church too. Selfishness, laziness, and envy all kept the Saints from becoming saintly.

SETTLING IN MISSOURI

Joseph Smith celebrated his twenty-seventh birthday on December 23, 1832. Less than thirteen years had passed since

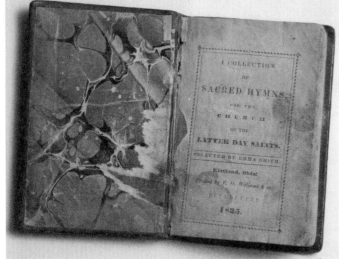

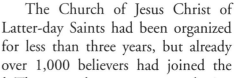

that spring day when he knelt in prayer in a grove of trees to ask the Lord which of the many churches he should join. His answer had come in a marvelous vision of the Father and the Son. Then, there had been visits from the angel Moroni, and the work of translating the golden plates into the Book of Mormon. In the beginning, only Joseph's family had believed him, then some friends, and then a few strangers.

The Church of Jesus Christ of Latter-day Saints had been organized for less than three years, but already over 1,000 believers had joined the restored kingdom of God. These members were now gathering in Independence, Missouri, to help build the holy city of Zion. Missionaries carried the Book of Mormon and the restored gospel to the Lamanites, and anyone else in America who would listen. In Kirtland, Ohio, Joseph and his friend Sidney Rigdon were working on a revised version of the Bible. Their questions led to new revelations, including a glorious vision of the degrees of glory. The Church-owned press in Missouri published a book of rev-

FIRST HYMNAL of the Church containing the hymns Emma Smith selected under the Lord's direction.

elations and commandments; a Church newspaper, the *Evening and Morning Star*; and a new hymn book.

The work was progressing rapidly, but Satan had not given up. Since that day in the Sacred Grove, when the forces of darkness had bound and almost consumed him, Joseph knew he would face many obstacles while trying to do the Lord's work. There had been persecutions, and former friends had turned against him. He had been arrested on false charges, harassed in court, and tarred and feathered.

However, Joseph and Emma now had a son, Joseph III, who, at two months of age, was strong and healthy. Their adopted daughter, Julia, was nearly two years old. Spiritual gifts were being poured out on the Saints, and it was a time of happiness. On Christmas Day, Joseph wrote about some of the troubles in the world:

> Appearances of troubles among the nations became more visible this season than they had previously been since the Church began her journey out of the wilderness. The ravages of the cholera were frightful in almost all the large cities on the globe . . . while the United States, amid all her pomp and greatness, was threatened with immediate dissolution. The people of South Carolina, in convention assembled (in November), passed ordinances, declaring their state a free and independent nation; and appointed Thursday, the 31st day of January, 1833, as a day of humiliation and prayer, to implore Almighty God to vouchsafe His blessings, and restore liberty and happiness within their borders. President Jackson issued his proclamation against this rebellion, called out a force sufficient to quell it, and implored the blessings of God to assist the nation to extricate itself from the horrors of the approaching and solemn crisis (Smith, *History of the Church*, 1:301).

While musing on the problems the United States was facing, Joseph received a revelation that was hardly comforting.

> Verily, thus saith the Lord concerning the wars that will shortly come to pass, beginning at the rebellion of South Carolina, which will eventually terminate in the death and misery of many souls;
>
> And the time will come that war will be poured out upon all nations, beginning at this place.

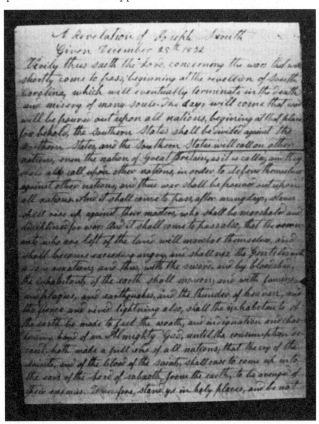

For behold, the Southern States shall be divided against the Northern States and the Southern States will call on other nations, even the nation of Great Britain, as it is called, and they shall also call upon other nations, in order to defend themselves against other nations; and then war shall be poured out upon all nations.

And it shall come to pass, after many days, slaves shall rise up against their masters, who shall be marshaled and disciplined for war. . . .

And thus, with the sword and by bloodshed the inhabitants of the earth shall mourn; and with famine, and plague, and earthquake, and the thunder of heaven, and the fierce and vivid lightning also, shall the inhabitants of the earth be made to feel the wrath, and indignation, and chastening hand of an Almighty God, until the consumption decreed hath made a full end of all nations. . . . Wherefore, stand ye in holy places, and be not moved, until the day of the Lord come (D&C 87:1-4, 6, 8).

Joseph gave copies of this revelation to friends and referred to it in correspondence. In a letter to N. E. Seaton, a newspaper editor in Rochester, New York, Joseph boldly stated:

And now I am prepared to say by the authority of Jesus Christ, that not many years shall pass away before the United States shall present such a scene of bloodshed as has not a parallel in the history of our nation; pestilence, hail, famine, and earthquake will sweep the wicked of this generation from off the face of the land, to open and prepare the way for the return of the lost tribes of Israel from the north country (Smith, *History of the Church*, 1:315-16).

WORLD EVENTS

In November of 1832, voters flocked to the polls to elect Andrew Jackson and his running mate, Martin Van Buren. Jackson considered his overwhelming victory a mandate to continue his war against the Second Bank of the United States in Philadelphia. Jackson withdrew all government funds from the bank and deposited the money in various state banks. This destroyed the power that the Central Bank had over the banking system and was greeted with joy by New Yorkers who resented Philadelphia's role as the financial capital of the nation. Bankers who wanted freedom from regulation, and small businessmen who opposed special privileges and monopolies also applauded the move.

On December 27, Joseph received the revelation that is now found in Section 88 of the Doctrine and Covenants when a group of the brethren met together to seek instruction and guidance. Frederick G. Williams, clerk of the council, kept the minutes and recorded the following:

A conference of high priests assembled in the translating room in Kirtland, Ohio, commenced by prayer, then brother Joseph arose and said to receive revelation and the blessings of heaven it was necessary to have our minds on God, and exercise faith, and become of one heart, and of one mind. Accordingly, we all bowed down before the Lord, after which, each one arose and spoke in his turn, his feelings and determination to keep the commandments of God. And then proceeded to receive the revelation (Cook, *The Revelations of the Prophet Joseph Smith*, 186-87).

The revelation provided information about the last days, the judgment of the world, and a promise of blessings to the righteous. It also contained a commandment for the Saints to build a temple at Kirtland, and to establish a school of the prophets. Samuel Smith wrote in his journal:

"Soon after we returned, some of the Elders assembled together & the word of the Lord was given through Joseph & the Lord declared that those Elders who were the first labourers in this vineyard should assemble themselves together to . . . establish a school, and appoint a teacher among them, and get learning by study and by faith, get a knowledge of countries, languages, and so forth" (Cook, *The Revelations of the Prophet Joseph Smith*, 318).

An extract from the minutes follows:

Opened with prayer by the President [Joseph Smith] and after much speaking praying and singing, all done in Tongues proceded to washing hands faces feet in the name of the Lord . . . each one washing his own after which the president girded himself with a towel and again washed the feet of all the Elders wiping them with the towel . . . The President said after he had washed the feet of the Elders, as I have done so do ye wash ye therefore one anothers feet pronouncing at the same time through the power of the Holy Ghost that the Elders were all clean from the blood of this generation but that those among them who should sin wilfully after they were thus cleansed and sealed up unto eternal life should be given over unto the buffetings of Satan ubntil the day of redemption. Having continued all day in fasting & prayer before the Lord at the close they partook of the Lord's supper (Cook, *The Revelations of the Prophet Joseph Smith,* 186).

The members who had been called to settle in Missouri were busy building homes and developing farms. Emily Coburn, a sister-in-law to Newel Knight, wrote:

Cabins were built and prepared for families as fast as time, money and labor could accomplish the work; and our homes in this new country presented a prosperous appearance—almost equal to paradise itself—and our peace and happiness as we flattered ourselves, were not in a great degree deficient to that of our first parents in the garden of Eden, as no labor or painstaking was spared in the cultivation of flowers and shrubbery, of a choice selection . . . (Emily M. Austin, *Mormonism; or Life Among the Mormons*, 67).

The Latter-day Saints were different than most of their Missouri neighbors. Many of the Mormons were from the northeastern part of the United States. They were accustomed to nice homes, trade, commerce, and education. Levi Hancock, who traveled through Missouri as a missionary observed:

The houses were so scattered that we could not do any better than to preach by the firesides. We were treated well sometimes, and sometimes not so friendly. We traveled slowly and continued to preach to the people whenever we got a chance. The people we met were good livers, if they had a mind to be, but the way they managed was more like beasts than like humans. They had dogs and horses and cows and pigs and chickens in abundance around the house, and in the house, and mixed together. In the cold weather, doors were opened night and day, snow flying and the wind blowing through. The cracks were not chinked; they used rags for beds, grounds for floors. The children were ragged and dirty. They had corn pudding dodger to eat, with a little bacon and sassafras tea (partially quoted in John L. Fowles, "Missouri and the Redemption of Zion: A Setting for Conflict," eds. Arnold K. Garr and Clark V. Johnson, 159).

The small-town mentality of an uneducated, frontier society welcomed rumors of the Mormon intrusion as an exciting, yet fearful diversion to an otherwise placid, rural existence. [Richmond, Missouri, circulated more fear-

SETTLING MISSOURI
by C.C.A. Christensen
oil on canvas
ca. 1870

ful premonitions of the Mormons than most towns, because] Mormon settlers were believed to be the source of trouble and violence in nearby communities. Rumors of hundreds of armed Mormon converts preparing to
destroy Richmond were quickly embraced by gullible citizens. As slanderous
hearsay spread, then escalated, attempts to establish truth were dismissed by
townsfolk, who accepted only the extreme speculations that aligned with
their prejudice (Susan Easton Black, "The Evils of Rumor," 119).

The Mormons sought to overcome the hardships of frontier life by cooperation. This practice of looking after one another, however, did not endear the
Mormons to their nonmember neighbors, who regarded them as clannish, thus
raising further unfounded suspicions.

Nevertheless, the Mormons banded together, established their own stores,
built their own schools, and attempted to live the law of consecration by helping the poor. They also preached, and sought converts among the Indians and
the white members of the community. This, of course, did not please the ministers of the area. When Joseph and some of the brethren visited in the spring of
1832, Sidney Rigdon preached to the Saints, and met with the angry ministers.
Reverend Pixley was the leader of the hostile clergy of whom Newel K. Whitney
observed, "His talk was of the bitterest kind, and his speeches perfectly inflammatory, and he appeared to have influence among the people, to carry them
with him in his hellish designs" (Roberts, *A Comprehensive History of the Church,*
1: ch. 26, n. 6).

Besides preaching his anti-Mormon sentiments locally, the reverend wrote
letters to the eastern press claiming to be an authority on the Mormons and
their beliefs. Pixley wrote:

> Sir—Dwelling as I do among a people called Mormonites, and on the
> very land which they sometimes call Mount Zion . . . and where, at no dis-
> tant period, they expect the reappearing of the Lord Jesus to live and reign
> with them on earth, a thousand years—I have thought perhaps it might be a
> part of duty, to inform those who may feel interested in relation to this
> subject, that although there have been four or five hundred Mormonites in
> all . . . arrived at this place, yet there is no appearance here different from that
> of other wicked places. The people eat, and drink, and some get drunk, suf-
> fer pain and disease, live and die like other people, the Mormons themselves
> not excepted . . . and several of them have died, yet none have been raised
> from the dead. . . . They tell indeed of working miracles . . . These things,
> however, are not seen to be done, but only said to be done. People, therefore,
> who set their faces for the Mount Zion of the West (which, by the by is on a
> site of ground not much elevated) must calculate on being disappointed, if
> they . . . expect much above what is common in any new country of the West.
> . . . Their best prerequisite for the reception of their expected Saviour, it
> would seem . . . is their poverty.
>
> They profess to hold frequent converse with angels; some go . . . as far
> as the third heaven, and converse with the Lord Jesus face to face. . . . They

profess to know where the Ark of the Covenant, Aaron's rod, the pot of Manna, &c. now remain hid. Their possessions here are small, very small, compared with their numbers. . . .

The idea of equality is held forth; but time will show that some take deeds of property in their own names . . . Under these circumstances, it takes no prophetic eye to foresee that there will soon be a murmuring. . . . Indeed, there already begins to be some feeling, and some defection arising from this subject. There is much reason to believe they cannot hold together long (as quoted in William Mulder and A. Russell Mortensen, eds., *Among the Mormons,* 73-74).

The Reverend Pixley's letters did contain some truth. Some of the members of the Church had bought property in their own names instead of consecrating it to the Church, and this caused dissension and ill feeling among the Church members.

Any member who wanted to come to Missouri was supposed receive a recommend from his bishop or branch president and be accepted by the bishop in Zion before moving. However, some ignored this procedure and just showed up, expecting to receive a plot of land. This put a great strain on the resources of the Church. Seven high priests—Oliver Cowdery, John Whitmer, William W. Phelps, Edward Partridge, Isaac Morley, John Corrill, and Sidney Gilbert—had been called to administer affairs in Zion, but some members set up their own branches and refused to follow these brethren's counsel.

After Joseph's brief visit in the spring of 1832, some members were bitter because Joseph did not stay with them. He was concerned about dissensions among the Saints who were supposed to build the New Jerusalem. After this visit he wrote: "The Saints . . . were settling among a ferocious set of mobbers, like lambs among wolves. It was my endeavor to so organize the Church, that the brethren might eventually be independent of every incumbrance beneath the celestial kingdom, by bonds and covenants of mutual friendship, and mutual love" (Smith, *History of the Church,* 1:269).

Some of the Saints, however, continued in their disobedience. Elder Newel Knight recorded in his journal:

Brother Joseph from time to time sent copies of revelations to me for the benefit of the branch over which I presided. . . . On reading one of these revelations to the branch, my aunt . . . arose and contradicted the revelation. She went to such a length that I felt constrained to rebuke her by the authority of the Priesthood. At this she was angry, and from that time sought to influence all who would listen to her. The result was a division of feeling in the branch. . . . Sister Peck at length began to feel the weight of what she had done, but she could not recall it. She seemed racked with great torment, her mind found no rest, until a burning fever brought her to a sick bed. . . . At last, she sent for P. P. Pratt, Lyman Wight, and myself, we laid our hands upon her and administered to her, after which she looked up in despair and said she hoped I would deliver her from the awful state she was in. Her whole frame was racked with intense anguish while her mind seemed almost in despair. . . . I felt impressed to call the branch together that evening. . . .

When the meeting had been opened as usual, I arose, not knowing what to do or what to say. After requesting the prayers and the united faith of all present, the Spirit of the Lord came upon me, so that I was able to make plain the cause of Sister Peck's illness—that she had risen up in opposition to the Priesthood, which had been placed over that branch of the Church, and contradicted the revelations of God, and that by the sympathies shown her, a division of feeling had gained advantage over them, until Sister Peck had fallen completely under the power of Satan, and could not extricate herself. I told the brethren and sisters, if they would repent of what they had done, and renew their covenants with one another and with the Lord, and uphold the authorities . . . and also the revelations . . . it would be all right with Sister Peck, for this would break the bands of Satan and make us free. . . .

[They] all came forward and agreed to do so. I then went to Sister Peck, and in the name of Jesus Christ, and by virtue of the Holy Priesthood, commanded the evil powers to depart from her, and blessed her with peace and strength, both body and mind. . . . Early the next morning I called to see her, she stretched out her hand as soon as she saw me, and said, "O, Brother Newel, forgive me! I did not believe one word you said last night, but when I awoke this morning, I found I was not in hell." Her rejoicings were very great, and union again prevailed with us, and we all felt we had learned a lesson that would be of lasting benefit to us ("Newel Knight Journal," *Scraps of Biography*, 73-75).

In letters to Church leaders in Missouri, the prophet reprimanded the Saints for not living the way they should:

Our hearts are greatly grieved at the spirit which is breathed . . . the very spirit which is wasting the strength of Zion like a pestilence; and if it is not detected and driven from you, it will ripen Zion for the threatened judgments of God. Remember God sees the secret springs of human action, and knows the hearts of all living. . . .

If Zion will not purify herself, so as to be approved of in all things, in His sight, He will seek another people; for His work will go on until Israel is gathered, and they who will not hear His voice, must expect to feel His wrath. Let me say unto you, seek to purify yourselves . . . lest the Lord's anger be kindled to fierceness. Repent, repent, is the voice of God to Zion (Smith, *History of the Church*, 1:316-17).

The Evening and the Morning Star, written and published by William W. Phelps, was another source of conflict between the Saints and their neighbors. The paper was the Church's voice to its members and the world at large, but even though it was the only newspaper in the region, it did not carry much local, national, or worldwide news. Instead, as Phelps proclaimed in the first issue: "As this paper is devoted to the great concerns of eternal things and the gathering of the Saints, it will leave politics, the gainsayers of the world, and many other matters, for their proper channels, endeavoring by all means to set an example

The most important issue for the United States government in 1833 was the problem with South Carolina, which had adopted an ordinance nullifying the tariffs of 1828 and 1832, and threatening to secede from the Union if Washington forced the issue. In February, the Senate passed the Force Bill, which gave the president power to use the army and navy against South Carolina if necessary. In the meantime, Henry Clay introduced a new tariff bill that would gradually reduce the tariffs over a nine-year period. President Jackson signed the bill, and crisis, for the moment, was averted.

The year 1833 abounded in good literature. Browning, Dickens, Balzak, Lamb, and Longfellow all published great works. The most popular literature of the day, however, was the autobiography of Davy Crockett.

before the world, which, when followed, will lead our fellow-men to the gates of glory, where the wicked cease from troubling, and where the weary will find rest" (Smith, *History of the Church*, 1:275).

Members and leaders of other religious denominations found the material distasteful.

Joseph Smith was not entirely happy with the newspaper either. He warned Phelps, "We wish you to render the Star as interesting as possible, by setting forth the rise, progress, and faith of the church, as well as the doctrine; for if you do not render it more interesting . . . it will fall, and the church will suffer a great loss thereby" (Roberts, *A Comprehensive History of the Church*, 1:286-87).

Although the Church was prospering in Kirtland, there was great concern about the state of affairs in Jackson County, Missouri. Letters from the Missouri Saints were bitter, accusative, and filled with complaints. On January 14, 1833, twelve high priests appointed Orson Hyde and Hyrum Smith to write a letter to the bishop, his council, and the inhabitants of Zion. Orson wrote:

Brother Joseph, and certain others, have written to you on this all-important subject, but you have never been apprised of these things by the united voice of the conference of . . . High Priests. . . .

We therefore, Orson and Hyrum, the committee appointed by said conference to write this epistle . . . now take up our pen to address you in the name of the conference, relying upon the arm of the Great Head of the Church. . . .

At the time Joseph, Sidney, and Newel left Zion, all matters of hardness and misunderstanding were settled and buried (as they supposed), and you gave them the hand of fellowship; but, afterwards, you brought up all these things again, in a censorious spirit, accusing Brother Joseph . . . of seeking after monarchial power and authority. . . . We are sensible that this is not the thing Brother Joseph is seeking after, but to magnify the high office and calling whereunto he has been called . . . by the command of God, and the united voice of this Church. . . .

We are aware that Brother Gilbert is doing much, and has a multitude of business on hand; but let him . . . do his business in the spirit of the Lord, and then the Lord will bless him, otherwise the frown of the Lord will remain upon him. There is . . . an uneasiness in Brother Gilbert, and a fearfulness that God will not provide for His Saints in these last days, and these fears lead him on to covetousness. This ought not so to be; but let him do just as the Lord has commanded him, and then the Lord will open His coffers, and his wants will be liberally supplied. . . .

Brother Phelps' letter . . . is also received and carefully read, and it betrays a lightness of spirit that ill becomes a man placed in the important and responsible station that he is placed in. . . . We want to see a spirit in Zion, by which the Lord will build it up; that is the plain, solemn, and pure spirit of Christ. Brother Phelps requested in his last letter that Brother Joseph should come to Zion; but we say that Brother Joseph will not settle in Zion until she repent, and purify herself, and abide by the new covenant. . . .

The cause of God seems to be rapidly advancing in the eastern country; the gifts are beginning to break forth so as to astonish the world, and even believers marvel at the power and goodness of God. Thanks be rendered to His holy name for what He is doing. We are your unworthy brethren in the Lord, and may the Lord help us all to do His will, that we may at last be saved in His kingdom. Orson Hyde, Hyrum Smith (Smith, *History of the Church*, 1:318-21).

That winter was a time of great blessing for the Saints in Kirtland. Joseph Smith recorded:

The winter [1832-1833] was spent in translating the Scriptures; in the School of the Prophets; and sitting in conferences. I had many glorious seasons of refreshing. The gifts which follow them that believe and obey the Gospel . . . began to be poured out amongst us, as in ancient days;—for as we . . . were assembled in conference, on the 22nd day of January, I spoke to the conference in another tongue, and was followed in the same gift by Brother Zebedee Coltrin, and he by Brother William Smith, after which the Lord poured out His Spirit in a miraculous manner, until all the Elders spake in tongues, and several members, both male and female, exercised the same gift. . . . Praises were sung to God and the Lamb; speaking and praying, all in tongues, occupied the conference until a late hour at night, so rejoiced were we at the return of these long absent blessings.

On the 23rd of January, we again assembled in conference; when, after much speaking, singing, praying, and praising God, all in tongues, we proceeded to the washing of feet . . . as commanded of the Lord. Each Elder washed his own feet first, after which I girded myself with a towel and washed the feet of all of them, wiping them with the towel with which I was girded. Among the number, my father presented himself, but before I washed his feet, I asked of him a father's blessing, which he granted by laying his hands upon my head, in the name of Jesus Christ, and declaring that I should continue in the Priest's office, until Christ comes. At the close of the scene, Brother Frederick G. Williams, being moved upon by

ZEBEDEE COLTRIN (1804–1887) was a member of the Presidency of the First Quorum of the Seventy, 1835–1837.

the Holy Ghost, washed my feet in token of his fixed determination to be with me in suffering, or in journeying, in life or in death, and to be continually on my right hand; in which I accepted him in the name of the Lord.

I then said to the Elders, As I have done so do ye; wash ye, therefore, one another's feet; and by the power of the Holy Ghost I pronounced them all clean from the blood of this generation; but if any of them should sin wilfully after they were thus cleansed, and sealed up unto eternal life, they should be given over unto the buffetings of Satan until the day of redemption. Having continued all day in fasting and prayer, and ordinances, we closed by partaking of the Lord's supper. I blessed the bread and wine in the name of the Lord, when we all ate and drank, and were filled; then we sang a hymn, and the meeting was adjourned (Smith, *History of the Church*, 1:322-24).

After visiting with Joseph Smith in September 1832, Brigham Young returned to his two little daughters in Mendon, New York. He arranged for them to stay with Sister Vilate Kimball, and then left on a mission. He reported:

In company with my brother Joseph, I started for Kingston, Upper Canada, on foot, in the month of December, the most of the way through snow and mud from one to two feet deep.

In crossing from Gravelly Point to Kingston, on the ice which had frozen the night previous, the ice was very thin and bent under our feet, so that in places the water was half shoe deep, and we had to separate from each other, the ice not being capable of holding us. We travelled about six miles on the ice, arrived at Kingston, and found a friend. . . . We commenced preaching and bearing our testimony to the people. . . . Proceeding to West Loboro, we baptized about 45 souls. . . . In the month of February, 1833, we started for home, crossing from Kingston on the ice, just before it broke up (*Manuscript History of Brigham Young*).

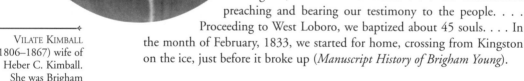

VILATE KIMBALL (1806–1867) wife of Heber C. Kimball. She was Brigham Young's niece, and helped care for Brigham's two little daughters when his first wife died.

WORD OF WISDOM REVEALED

In February 1833, Joseph and some other brethren in Kirtland were meeting in the School of the Prophets when Joseph received an important revelation—Section 89 of the Doctrine and Covenants, also known as the Word of Wisdom. Many years later, in 1868, Brigham Young, speaking in a conference, told what brought forth this revelation:

I think I am as well acquainted with the circumstances which led to the giving of the Word of Wisdom as any man in the Church, although I was not present at the time to witness them. The first school of the prophets was held in a small room, situated over the prophet Joseph's kitchen, in a house which belonged to Bishop Whitney, and which was attached to his store, which store might probably be about fifteen feet square. In the rear of this building was a kitchen, probably ten by fourteen feet, containing rooms and pantries. Over this kitchen was situated the room in which the prophet received revelations and in which he instructed his brethren. . . . When they assembled together in this room, after breakfast, the first [thing] they did was to light their pipes, and while smoking, talk about the great things of the kingdom, and spit all over the room, and as soon as the pipe was out of their mouths, a large chew of tobacco would then be taken. Often when the

prophet entered the room to give the school instructions he would find himself in a cloud of tobacco smoke. This, and the complaints of his wife at having to clean so filthy a floor, made the Prophet think upon the matter, and he inquired of the Lord relating to the conduct of the Elders in using tobacco, and the revelation known as the Word of Wisdom, was the result of his inquiry. . . .

So we see that almost the very first teachings the first Elders of this Church

THE SCHOOL OF THE PROPHETS was located in the room above the kitchen in Bishop Newel K. Whitney's store in Kirtland, OH. The Lord instructed Joseph to establish this school to prepare members to preach the gospel and to get learning in all the disciplines. Here Joseph Smith gave the seven formal "Lectures on Faith." Top photo shows the doorway into the room. Bottom photo shows the room itself. *ca. 1977*

received were as to what to eat, what to drink, and how to order their natural lives, that they might be united temporally as well as spiritually. This is the great purpose which God has in view in sending to the world . . . the gospel of life and salvation. It will teach us how to deal, how to act in all things, and how to live with each other to become one in the Lord (Young, *Journal of Discourses*, 12:158).

Line upon line, Church doctrines were being revealed, and step by step, the Church was being established. One of these steps was the organization of the First Presidency on March 18, 1833. Joseph Smith recorded:

I laid my hands on Brothers Sidney and Frederick, and ordained them to take part with me in holding the keys of this last kingdom, and to assist in the Presidency of the High Priesthood, as my Counselors; after which I exhorted the brethren to faithfulness and diligence in keeping the commandments of God, and gave much instruction for the benefit of the Saints, with a promise that the pure in heart should see a heavenly vision; and after remaining a short time in secret prayer, the promise was verified; for many present had the eyes of their understandings opened by the Spirit of God, so as to behold many things. . . . Many of the brethren saw a heavenly vision of the Savior, and concourses of angels, and many other things, of which each has a record of what he saw (Smith, *History of the Church*, 1:334).

GATHERING CLOUDS IN MISSOURI

The Saints' second winter in Independence, Missouri, was coming to a close. They now had homes, farms, and gardens. They had their own stores and mills, and their children attended school. They gathered on Sundays and often on weekdays to pray, sing, preach, and worship. As the snow melted, and the Missouri hillsides began to turn green, the Saints gathered to celebrate the organization of the Church. Newel K. Knight wrote: "On the 6th of April, 1833, the Church met together at the ferry on Big Blue river to celebrate the Church's birthday. This was the first celebration of the kind and the Saints felt their privilege and enjoyed themselves in the worship of their Heavenly Father, and praised His holy name. The brethren returned to their homes, renewed in spirit, and rejoicing in heart" ("Newel Knight Journal," *Scraps of Biography*, 75).

Joseph Smith also recorded an account of the celebration, but he contrasted the joy and peace of the Saints with conditions in the rest of the world.

It was an early spring, and the leaves and blossoms enlivened and gratified the soul of man like a glimpse of Paradise. The day was spent in a very agreeable manner, in giving and receiving knowledge which appertained to this last kingdom—it being just 1800 years since the Savior laid down His life that men might have everlasting life, and only three years since the Church had come out of the wilderness, preparatory for the last dispensation. The Saints had great reason to rejoice (Smith, *History of the Church*, 1:337).

While the Saints in Missouri had glorious plans for the future, some of their neighbors had misgivings about Zion being built in their midst. They feared and resented the Mormons, and their ministers did their best to keep these fears and resentments alive. Reverend Finis Ewing of the Presbyterian Church declared, "Mormons are the common enemy of mankind, and ought to be destroyed" (Smith, *History of the Church,* 1:392). There had been some harassment ever since the first Saints arrived in Missouri, but in April of 1833, the detractors began to organize themselves.

Shortly after the celebration that commemorated the organization of the Church, Newel Knight wrote:

WORLD EVENTS

While the Saints were rejoicing in the celebration of the organization of the Church, news reached the United States that famine had caused the deaths of 30,000 people in the Cape Verde Islands. A series of sixteen earthquakes shook the West Indian Islands, and Turkey and Egypt were at war. But most disastrous were the reports that the Asiatic cholera was still spreading in Europe. In fifteen years, this disease had claimed about sixty million lives.

> Such peace and happiness were not however, to continue long without an interruption from our enemies, for when the Saints rejoice, the devil is mad, and his children and his servants partake of his spirit. . . . Before this month had closed, a most dreadful and diabolical spirit of persecution manifested itself all around us. An immense mob collected together expressing the determination to drive us from our homes, for they would not allow the "Mormons" to live in their midst.
>
> On hearing this news, a number of the brethren met together and prayed to God to overrule the wicked designs of the mob meeting, that they might not have power to agree upon their plans, or to execute their wicked threats. They broke up in a regular row, and for a time all was well. As might be expected, this caused considerable uneasiness among us, and it required great wisdom and care on our part to keep the Saints quiet, and to keep them at their labors ("Newel Knight Journal," *Scraps of Biography,* 75).

During the early part of 1833, Joseph Smith received several revelations. However, the subject of revelation continued to trouble some members of the Church. Joseph stated in a letter to Jared Carter:

> I will inform you that it is contrary to the economy of God for any member of the Church, or any one, to receive instructions for those in authority, higher than themselves; therefore you will see the impropriety of giving heed to them; but if any person have a vision or a visitation from a heavenly messenger, it must be for his own benefit and instruction; for the fundamental principles, government, and doctrine of the Church are vested in the keys of the kingdom. . . .
>
> And again we never inquire at the hand of God for special revelation only in case of their being no previous revelation to suit the case; and that in a council of High Priests.
>
> . . . It is a great thing to inquire at the hands of God, or to come into His presence; and we feel fearful to approach Him on subjects that are of lit-

tle or no consequence, to satisfy the queries of individuals, especially about things the knowledge of which men ought to obtain in all sincerity, before God, for themselves, in humility by the prayer of faith. . . . I speak these things not by way of reproach, but by way of instruction (Smith, *History of the Church*, 1:338-39).

When Joseph received instructions to build a temple in Kirtland, Ohio, a building committee was appointed and a letter was sent to all the branches requesting donations. As usual, however, problems arose. Joseph recorded: "June 3rd, a conference of High Priests convened in the translating room in Kirtland. The first case presented was that of 'Doctor' Philastus Hurlburt, who was accused of un-Christian conduct with women, while on a mission to the east. On investigation it was decided that his commission be taken from him, and that he be no longer a member of the Church of Christ" (Smith, *History of the Church,* 1:352).

In that same meeting, Joseph also recorded that progress was being made toward beginning construction of the temple.

> The next matter before the conference was to ascertain what should be the dimensions or size of the house, that is to be built for a house of worship and for the School of the Prophets. I had received a revelation on the size of the house in which the word of the Lord was that it should be fifty-five feet wide, and sixty-five feet long, in the inner court. The conference appointed Joseph Smith, Jun., Sidney Rigdon and Frederick G. Williams, to obtain a draft or construction of the inner court of the house (Smith, *History of the Church,* 1:352).

Only two days later, on June 5, construction began. "June 5—George A. Smith hauled the first load of stone for the Temple, and Hyrum Smith and Reynolds Cahoon commenced digging the trench for the walls of the Lord's house, and finished the same with their own hands" (Smith, *History of the Church, 1:353*).

THE CITY OF ZION

In June, Joseph sent the Missouri Saints instructions for building the city of Zion. In the past, cities just grew around a natural port, a mill, or some other favorable site. No one had thought to plan a city before it was built, and zoning was nonexistent. However, Joseph's practical ideas made for beautiful cities. Joseph wrote:

> The plat contains one mile square; all the squares in the plat contain ten acres each, being forty rods square. . . . Each lot is four perches in front and twenty back, making one half of an acre in each lot. . . . The . . . squares in the

WORLD EVENTS

The unknown regions of the world held great interest for hardy explorers. In 1833, Sir John Ross completed his second expedition to the Arctic, and Alex Burns had explored one of the world's most remote mountain ranges—the Hindu Kush in Central Asia. Scientists explored new uses for electricity, and, about this time, Samuel Morse began working on a way to communicate using electricity.

middle are for public buildings . . . [The] first is for temples for the use of the presidency. [It is to contain 12 temples.]

The whole plot is supposed to contain from fifteen to twenty thousand people: you will therefore see that it will require twenty-four buildings to supply them with houses of worship, schools, etc. . . .

South of the plot . . . is to be laid off for barns, stables, etc., for the use of the city; so that no barns or stables will be in the city among the houses. . . . On the north and south are to be laid off the farms for the agriculturists . . . and it cannot be laid off without going too great a distance from the city, there must also be some laid off on the east and west.

When this square is thus laid off and supplied, lay off another in the same way, and so fill up in the world in these last days; and let every man live in the city, for this is the city of Zion. All the streets are of one width, being eight perches wide. . . . No one lot, in this city, is to contain more than one house, and that to be built twenty-five feet back from the street, leaving a small yard in front, to be planted in a grove, according to the taste of the builder; the rest of the lot for gardens; all the houses are to be built of brick and stone (Smith, *History of the Church*, 1:357-59).

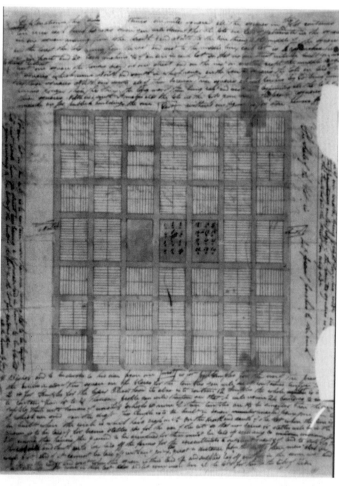

JOSEPH SMITH'S PLAT MAP OF THE CITY OF ZION, NEW JERUSALEM The city was to be one mile square, with provisions for other cities to be laid out as the population expanded. The city blocks would each cover ten acres, with generous provisions for homes, spacious yards, schools, businesses, and temples. Livestock were to be kept on farms outside the city limits.

Joseph also sent instructions for a temple in Zion that was actually to be twelve temples. Individual temples were designated for the presidency of the High Priesthood, the different priesthood quorums, and for other purposes. The Saints were instructed to begin with the temple for the presidency.

A description of the house of the Lord, which is to be built first in Zion: The house of the Lord for the Presidency, is eighty-seven feet long, and sixty feet wide. . . .

The pulpit in the west end of the house is to be occupied by the High Priesthood.

. . . The pulpit in the east end of the house is to be occupied by the Lesser Priesthood. . . . The pulpits are to be finished with panel work, in the best workmanlike manner; and the building to be constructed of stone and brick of the best quality. Observe particularly that as there are pulpits at each

end of the house, the backs of the congregation must be to one of them, and they will want occasionally to change. In order for this the house must have pews . . . and in the pews let the seats be loose, that they may slip from one side of the pew to the other, so as to face either pulpit, as the occasion may require.

The side view represents five windows in each story. . . .

Make your house fourteen feet high between the floors. . . . Let the foundation of the house be of stone. . . . On the top of the foundation . . . let there be two rows of hewn stone, and then commence the brick-work on the hewn stone. The entire height of the house is to be twenty-eight feet. . . . The end view represents five windows of the same size as those at the side, the middle window excepted, which is to be the same, with the addition of side lights. . . . The doors are to be five feet wide, and nine feet high, and to be on the east end of the house. . . . The roof of the house is to have one fourth pitch, the door to have Gothic top, the same as the windows. . . . A belfry is to be in the east end, and a bell of very large size (Smith, *History of the Church,* 1:359-62).

TROUBLING TIMES

However, trouble was on the horizon. For Church members who were considering moving to Missouri, the *Evening and Morning Star* published an article to inform them about Missouri's laws concerning blacks. After quoting the laws, the article concluded, "Slaves are real estate in this and other states, and wisdom would dictate great care among the branches of the Church of Christ on this subject" (Smith, *History of the Church,* 1:378).

The article stirred up such furor, that a special edition was printed on July 16, seeking to clarify the Church's position on the issue. But the explanation only aroused more mistrust. Reverend Pixley wrote a tract entitled, "Beware of False Prophets," which he distributed house to house in order to stir up anger against the Church. Newel Knight, who was living in Independence, recorded:

> While peaceful pursuits characterized the doings of the Saints, the mobocratic spirit of our enemies was but slumbering for a short time. . . . In July it again burst forth. The sectarian priests and missionaries around us were among the first to come out both secretly and openly against us. Among the more active of these was a Mr. Pixley, who did not content himself in slandering us to the people of Jackson Co., but also wrote to eastern papers, telling horrible lies about us. . . . Nor did he confine his actions to the white settlers, but tried to stir up the Indians against us, and used every means in his power to accomplish his purposes. . . . The public mind became so excited that on the 20th of July a meeting was called and largely attended by not only the rabble of the county, but also by men holding official positions. . . . It was stated, among other imaginary evils, that we were poor, and . . . did not possess much of this world's goods, which was, apparently, a crime in their estimation. We were also accused of believing in the gifts and blessings of the ancient gospel. . . . It was resolved that no Mormon shall in future move and settle in this county; that those now here shall give a definite pledge of their intention to move out of the county within a reasonable time; that the editor of the Star be required forthwith to close his office and discontinue the business of printing in this county. . . .
>
> These resolutions were . . . unanimously adopted. It was thereupon agreed that a committee of twelve be appointed forthwith to wait on the Mormon leaders, and see that the foregoing requisitions be strictly complied with by them.
>
> After an adjournment of two hours, the meeting again convened, and the committee of twelve reported that they had called on Mr. Phelps, the editor of the Star, Edward Partridge, the Bishop of the sect, and Mr. Gilbert, the keeper of the Lord's storehouse, and some others, and that they declined giving any direct answers to the requisitions made of them, and wished an unreasonable time for consultation, not only with their brethren here, but in Ohio.
>
> Whereupon it was unanimously resolved by the meeting that the Star printing office should be razed to the ground, and the type and press secured. Which resolution was, with the utmost order, and the least noise and disturbance possible, forthwith carried into execution. . . . No blood was spilled, nor any blows inflicted. The meeting then adjourned until the 23rd . . . ("Newel Knight Journal," *Scraps of Biography,* 76).

PERSECUTIONS INCREASE

Fifteen-year-old Mary Rollins Lightner, and her sister Caroline, witnessed the destruction of the press and the printing office. Mary noted:

The mob was tearing down the printing office, a two-story building, driving Brother Phelps' family out of the lower part of the house. [The mob] brought out some large sheets of paper, saying, "Here are the Mormon Commandments." My sister [Caroline], 12 years old (I was then 14) and myself were in a corner of a fence watching them. When they spoke about them being the commandments, I was determined to have some of them. So while their backs were turned, prying out the gable end of the house, we ran and gathered up all we could carry in our arms. As we turned away, two of the mob got down off the house and called on us to stop, but we ran as fast as we could, through a gap in the fence into a large corn field, and the two men after us. We ran a long way in the field, laid the papers on the ground, then laid down on top of them. The corn was very high and thick. They hunted all around us, but did not see us. After we were satisfied they had given up the search, we tried to find our way out of the field. The corn was so tall we thought we were lost. On looking up we saw some trees that had been girdled to kill them. We . . . came to an old log stable, which looked like it had not been used for years. Sister Phelps and family were there, carrying in brush and piling it up at one side of the stable to make their beds on. She asked us what we had. We told her. . . . She took them . . . Oliver Cowdery bound them in small books and gave me one (*Deseret Evening News,* Feb. 20, 1904, 24. As quoted in *Best Loved Stories of the LDS People,* 191-92).

SAVING THE BOOK OF COMMANDMENTS *by Clark Kelley Price* depicts the destruction of the press and printing office in W. W. Phelps's home. The mob was inflamed over an article printed in *The Evening and the Morning Star* regarding slavery.

THE BOOK OF COMMANDMENTS later became the Doctrine and Covenants. Two young girls grabbed as many pages as they could and hid from the mob in a cornfield.

However, the destruction of the press and printing house did not satisfy the mob. A few days later they met and prepared a document that declared:

We, the undersigned, citizens of Jackson County, believing that an important crisis is at hand, as regards our civil society, in consequence of a pretended religious sect of people that have settled, and are still settling in our county, styling themselves "Mormons," and intending, as we do, to rid our society, "peaceably if we can, forcibly if we must," . . . deemed it expedient, and of the highest importance, to form ourselves into a company for the better and easier accomplishment of our purpose. . . .

It is more than two years since the first of these fanatics, or knaves, (for one or the other they undoubtedly are) made their first appearance amongst us, and pretended . . . to hold personal communication and converse face to face with the Most High God; to receive communications and revelations direct from heaven; to heal the sick by laying on hands; and . . . to perform all the wonder-working miracles wrought by the inspired Apostles and Prophets of old. . . .

We have every reason to fear that . . . they were of the very dregs of that society from which they came, lazy, idle, and vicious. . . . They brought into our country little or no property with them. . . . More than a year since, it was ascertained that they had been tampering with our slaves, and endeavoring to sow dissensions and raise seditions amongst them. In a late number of the *Star*, published in Independence by the leaders of the sect, there is an article inviting free negroes and mulattoes from other states to become "Mormons," and remove and settle among us. . . . They declare openly that their God has given them this county of land, and that sooner or later they must and will have possession of our lands for an inheritance; and, in fine . . . we believe it a duty we owe to ourselves, our wives, and children, to the cause of public morals, to remove them from among us (Smith, *History of the Church*, 1:374-76).

The local justice of the peace, the judge, the constable, the county clerk, the Indian agent, an attorney, the postmaster, and some merchants and other citizens signed the document. They demanded that the Saints leave the area by January 1834 and that no more Mormons be allowed to move into the town. To ensure that the members didn't forget and try to prolong their stay, the mobbers kept up a steady harassment. Newel Knight documented the trials many of the Saints faced, as well as their attempts to seek justice:

DANIEL DUNKLIN was the Governor of Missouri when the Saints were driven from their homes. He professed sympathy for their cause, but did little to enforce or ensure protection or redress.

It was decided to petition Governor Dunklin for redress and protection, and Brothers Orson Hyde and W. W. Phelps were sent to Jefferson city for that purpose, bearing a document setting forth our grievances, and giving details of the shameful proceedings of July.

The governor received these brethren courteously, but gave them no answer. . . . He stated that he desired to maintain law and order in the state, and was willing to do anything in his power to assist in the protection of the Saints. He subsequently wrote:

"No citizen, nor number of citizens, have a right to take the redress of their grievances, whether real or *imaginary* into their own hands; such conduct strikes at the very existence of society, and subverts the foundation on which it is based.

"Obtain a warrant, let it be placed in the hands of the proper officer, and the experiment will be treated whether laws can be peaceably executed or not. In the event that they cannot be, and that fact is officially notified to me, my duty will require me to take such steps as will enforce a faithful execution of them."

This communication comforted the hearts of the brethren, for they felt they were not entirely left in the hands of the ruthless mob, but that they would be protected in their rights. They renewed their labors and felt to rejoice before their Heavenly Father.

In the meantime, the brethren in Independence retained four lawyers from Clay Co., named Wood, Reese, Doniphan, and Atchinson, with a fee of one thousand dollars. As soon as the mob heard of this they became very much enraged. They disregarded the compact and assembled together vowing vengeance on all the "Mormons," being determined that we should leave forthwith. From the 31st of October, until the 4th of November, there was one continual scene of outrages of the most hideous kind. The mob collected in different parts of the county and attacked the Saints in most of their settlements, houses were unroofed, others were pulled down, leaving women and children, and even the sick and the dying exposed to the inclemency of the weather. Men were caught and whipped or clubbed until they were bruised from head to foot, and some were left upon the ground for dead. The most horrid threats and implications were uttered against us, and women and children were told, with cursings, that unless they left the country immediately, they should be killed. The brethren had to get together to protect themselves, and they went from place to place to assist those who were threatened. ("Newel Knight Journal," *Scraps of Biography*, 79-80).

Philo Dibble, who was living in the Whitmer settlement, west of Independence, wrote:

In the fall of 1833, a sectarian preacher by the name of M'Coy came to the Whitmer settlement where I was living to buy up all the guns he could, representing that he wanted them for the Indians. We suspected no trouble, and quite a number of us sold our guns to him. The sequel of his action was, however, soon apparent to us, for rumors soon reached us of mobs assembling and threats being made to drive us from the County.

When the mob first began to gather and threaten us, I was selected to go to another County and buy powder and lead. The brethren gave me the privilege of choosing a man to go with me. I took with me a man by the name of John Poorman. We thought we were good for four of the mob. We went to the town of Liberty, Clay County, and purchased the ammunition, and returned safely.

Soon after I returned[,] a mob of about one hundred and fifty came upon us in the dead hour of night, tore down a number of our houses and whipped and abused several of our brethren. I was aroused from my sleep by the noise caused by the falling houses, and had barely time to escape to the woods with my wife and two children when they reached my house, and proceeded to break in the door and tear the roof off. I was some distance away from where the whipping occurred, but I heard the blows of heavy ox goads upon the backs of my brethren distinctly. The mob also swore that they would tear down our grist mill, which was situated at the Colesville branch, about three miles from the settlement, and lest they should really do so, and as it was the only means we had of getting our grain ground, we were counseled to gather there and defend it. We accordingly proceeded there the next morning. The following night two men came into our camp, pretending they wanted to hire some men to work for them. Brother Parley ordered them to be taken prisoners, when one of them struck him a glancing blow on the head with his gun, inflicting a severe wound. We then disarmed them and kept them as prisoners until morning, when we gave them back their arms and let them go.

The next day we heard firing down in the Whitmer settlement, and seventeen of our brethren volunteered to go down and see what it meant. When these seventeen men arrived at the Whitmer settlement, the mob came against them and took some prisoners ("Early Scenes in Church History," *Four Faith-Promoting Classics*, 82-83).

The day after the attack, Parley Pratt left with Thomas B. Marsh for Lexington to tell the circuit judge about the persecutions. The two men made the forty-mile trip on horseback, taking back roads to avoid being seen by their enemies. The circuit judge refused to give them a warrant, but instead advised them to fight and kill the outlaws. Parley wrote:

Having been without sleep for the three previous nights, and much of the time drenched with rain, this, together with the severe wound I had received, caused me to feel much exhausted. No sooner had sleep enfolded me in her kind embrace than a vision opened before me.

I was in Jackson County; heard the sound of the firearms, and saw the killed and wounded lying in their blood. . . .

Next morning we pursued our journey homeward with feelings of anxiety indescribable. Ever officer of the peace had abandoned us to our fate; and it seemed as if there was no alternative but for men, women and children to be exterminated. As we rode on, ruminating upon these things, a man met us from Independence, who told us there was a battle raging when he left; and how it terminated he knew not.

This only heightened our feelings of anxiety and suspense. We were every instant drawing near to the spot where we might find our friends alive and victorious, or dead, or perhaps in bondage, in the hands of a worse than savage enemy.

On coming within four miles of Independence, we ventured to inquire the distance at a certain house; this we did in order to pass as strangers, and also, in hopes to learn some news; the man seemed frightened, and inquired where we were from. We replied, from Lexington. Said he, "Have you heard what has happened?" We replied, "That we had heard there was some difficulty, but of all the participants we had not been informed." "Why," said he, "the Mormons have riz, and have killed six men."

We then passed on, and as soon as we were out of sight, we left the road and took into the woods (*Autobiography of Parley P. Pratt*, 79-80).

On November 4, in Christian Whitmer's cornfield near Independence, fifty or sixty mobbers confronted about thirty of the brethren. The members of the mob appeared excited by the destruction and misery they were causing and seemed to welcome the chance to shed the blood of the Mormons. Philo Dibble fought along with the other brethren and recorded:

We all responded and met the mob in battle, in which I was wounded with an ounce ball and two buck shot, all entering my body just at the right side of my naval. The mob [was] finally routed, and the brethren chased them a mile away. Several others of the brethren were also shot, and one, named Barber, was mortally wounded. After the battle was over, some of the brethren went to administer to him, but he objected to their praying that he might live, and asked them if they could not see the angels present. He said the room was full of them, and his greatest anxiety was for his friends to see what he saw, until he breathed his last, which occurred at three o'clock in the morning.

A young lawyer named Bazill, who came into Independence and wanted to make himself conspicuous, joined the mob, and swore he would wade in blood up to his chin.

He was shot with two balls through his head, and never spoke. There was another man, whose name I fail to remember, that lived on the Big Blue, who made a similar boast. He was also taken at his word. His chin was shot off, or so badly fractured by a ball that he was forced to have it amputated, but lived and recovered, though he was a horrible sight afterwards.

After the battle I took my gun and powder horn and started for home. When I got about half way I became faint and thirsty. I wanted to stop at Brother Whitmer's to lay down. The house, however, was full of women and children, and they were so frightened that they objected to my entering, as the mob had threatened that wherever they found a wounded man they would kill men, women and children.

I continued on and arrived home, or rather at a house in the field where the mob had not torn down, which was near my own home. There I found my wife and two children and a number of other women who had assembled. I told them I was shot and wanted to lay down.

They got me on the bed . . . and my wife went out to see if she could find any of the brethren. In searching for them she got lost in the woods and was gone two hours, but learned that all the brethren had gone to the Colesville branch, three miles distant, taking all the wounded with them save myself.

The next morning I was taken farther off from the road, that I might be concealed from the mob. I bled inwardly until my body was filled with blood, and remained in this condition until the next day at five p.m. I was then examined by a surgeon who was in the Black Hawk war, who said that he had seen a great many men wounded, but never saw one wounded as I was that ever lived. He pronounced me a dead man.

David Whitmer, however, sent me word that I should live and not die, but I could see no possible chance to recover. After the surgeon had left me, Brother Newel Knight came to see me, and sat down on the side of my bed. He laid his right hand on my head, but never spoke. I felt the Spirit resting upon me at the crown of my head before his hand ever touched me, and I knew immediately that I was going to be healed. It seemed to form like a ring under the skin, and followed down my body. When the ring came to the wound, another ring formed around the first bullet hole, also the second and third. Then a ring formed on each shoulder and on each hip, and followed down to the ends of my fingers and toes and left me. I immediately arose and discharged three quarts of blood or more, with some piece of my clothes that had been driven into my body by the bullets. I then dressed myself and went out doors. . . . From that time not a drop of blood came from me, and I never afterwards felt the slightest pain or inconvenience for my wounds, except that I was somewhat weak from the loss of blood.

The next day I walked around the field, and the day following I mounted a horse and rode eight miles, and went three miles on foot. . . .

The night of the battle, the mob took all my household furniture, and after my recovery I crossed the river to Clay County, leaving behind me a drove of hogs, three cows and all of my crop, which I never recovered ("Early Scenes in Church History," 83-85).

On November 5, the day after the battle, Lieutenant Governor Lilburn W. Boggs called out the militia to protect the Mormons. However, one of the leaders of the mob, Colonel Pitcher, was chosen to lead the militia, and some of the troops in the militia also had been members of the mob. Colonel Pitcher demanded that the Saints turn over all their weapons, assuring them that the mobbers would also give up their weapons.

When Parley Pratt and Brother Marsh arrived in Independence, they found the battle over, the brethren without weapons, and the women and children fleeing from the mob.

EXPULSION FROM JACKSON COUNTY, WINTER 1833–34

When Parley Pratt returned to Independence and found that the mob had been fighting with the Mormons, his first concern was for his family. He recorded:

My horse being weary I started on foot, and walked through the wilderness in darkness; avoiding the road lest I should fall into the hands of the enemy.

I arrived home about the middle of the night, and furnishing my wife with a horse, we made our escape in safety.

When night again overtook us we were on the bank of the Missouri River, which divided between Jackson and Clay Counties. Here we camped for the night, as we could not use the ferry till morning. Next morning we crossed the river, and formed an encampment amid the cottonwoods on its bank.

While we thus made our escape, companies of ruffians were ranging the country in every direction; bursting into houses without fear, knowing that the people were disarmed; frightening women and children, and threatening to kill them if they did not flee immediately. . . .

On Tuesday and Wednesday nights, the 5th and 6th of November, women and children fled in every direction. One party of about one hundred and fifty fled to the prairie, where they wandered for several days, mostly without food; and nothing but the open firmament for their shelter. Other parties fled towards the Missouri River. During the dispersion of women and children, parties were hunting the men, firing upon some, tying up and whipping others. . . .

Thursday, November 7. The shore began to be lined on both sides of the ferry with men, women and children; goods, wagons, boxes, provisions, etc., while the ferry was constantly employed; and when night again closed upon us, the cottonwood bottom had much the appearance of a camp meeting. Hundreds of people were seen in every direction, some in tents and some in the open air around their fires, while the rain descended in torrents. Husbands were enquiring for their wives, and wives for their husbands; parents for children, and children for parents. . . .

Next day our company still increased, and we were principally engaged in felling cottonwood trees and directing them into small cabins. The next night being clear, we began to enjoy some degree of comfort.

About two o'clock the next morning [November 13th] we were called up by the cry of signs in the heavens. We arose, and to our great astonishment all the firmaments seemed enveloped in splendid fireworks, as if every star in the broad expanse had been hurled from its course, and sent lawless through the wilds of ether. Thousands of bright meteors were shooting through space in every direction, with long trains of light following in their course. This lasted for several hours, and was only closed by the dawn of the rising sun. Every heart was filled with joy at this majestic display of signs and wonders (*Autobiography of Parley P. Pratt*, 81-83).

The Pratt family home was one of over 200 burned by the mob. Everything that had been left behind was either plundered or destroyed by the Saints' enemies while the members fled into neighboring counties. They were welcomed in Clay County, but in Van Buren and Lafayette Counties they were forced to move on.

Algernon Sidney Gilbert, Isaac Morley, John Corrill, and William McLellin were arrested, charged with assault and battery, and taken directly to court. However, spectators in the courtroom were shouting, threatening the prisoners, and firing guns. The trial was forced to adjourn when all the lights were shot out. The men were kept in prison overnight and released the next morning, but it was a harrowing experience for the brethren who were among the most respectable and law-abiding citizens in the area. Brother McLellin recorded:

Two large men stepped up to me, and each clenched an arm, and thus gallanted me to the most horrid, soul harrowing, lonesome place into which my feet ever entered, before or since. What! to be locked, chained, and barred, within a little room only twelve feet square!! And that too, where mobbers and murderers had dwelt, and there forced to remain during a dark, lonesome night . . . without any certainty as to the future. Oh thou uneasy uncertainty! Thou horror-fed moment of prison life!!! Surrounded by scores of beings "who feared not God, nor regarded the rights of man." The roar of musketry and the yells of more than heathen savages continually saluted our ears. The darkness of the night added to the fury of the scene. The next hour, yea, the next moment, an infuriated mob, so hateful were, may have entered heated with spirits more infertile than wine and put us to torture, yea, a dismal death. Sleep, that composer and soother of troubles, fled entirely from our eyes. I paced the narrow contracted cell to and fro, while thousands of reflections filed through my anxious mind. My fellow prisoners could give me no consolation, for they too were in entire uncertainty as to our fate.

One thought, however, kept our hearts from sinking. It occasionally visited my mind during that long night, as a bee would its hive, "I am innocent of their charge—I am suffering for Christ's and truth's sake, and I shall get my reward either in life or at the resurrection of the just."

In the early twilight of the morning, the jailer, and several others entered the dismal abode. Now sirs, if you will agree to remove from the county forthwith, we will release you without trial. The agreement was made, we were released from jail, and fled from the town (*Ensign of Liberty* [January 1848], 62).

It seems that no one was spared the cruelty of the mob. Newel Knight recorded:

I must not omit to mention one act of cruelty, which, if possible, seems to surpass all others. In one of the settlements were four families of very old men, infirm and very poor. They seemed to think that they would not be molested and so remained behind, but no sooner did the mob learn of it, than they went to their houses, broke their windows and doors, and hurled great stones into their rooms endangering their lives; thus were these poor old men, and their families, driven before the ruthless mob in mid-winter. These men had served in the Revolutionary war, and Brother Jones [one of the four] had been one of General Washington's body guard, but this availed them nothing, for they were of the hated people (Roberts, *A Comprehensive History of the Church*, 1:344).

THE FIRST PRESIDENCY

Joseph Smith and Sidney Rigdon had been on a mission to Canada during the month of October. When they returned on November 4, Joseph recorded some impressions about his counselors:

Brother Sidney is a man whom I love, but he is not capable of that pure and steadfast love . . . that should characterize a President of the Church of Christ. This, with some other little things, such as selfishness and independence of mind . . . are his faults. But not withstanding these things, he is a very great and good man; a man of great power of words, and can gain the friendship of his hearers very quickly. He is a man whom God will uphold, if he will continue faithful to his calling. . . .

Brother Frederick G. Williams is one of those men in whom I place the greatest confidence and trust, for I have found him ever full of love and brotherly kindness. He is not a man of many words, but is ever winning, because of his constant mind. . . . He is perfectly honest and upright, and seeks with all his heart to magnify his Presidency in the Church of Christ, but fails in many instances, in consequence of a want of confidence in himself. . . . Blessed be Brother Frederick, for he shall never want a friend, and his generation after him shall flourish. The Lord hath appointed him an inheritance in Zion (Smith, *History of the Church*, 1:443-44).

The Saints React

Gradually, the Saints in Kirtland began to hear about the events in Missouri. On November 25, Orson Hyde and John Gould arrived in Kirtland and provided firsthand accounts of what they had seen. Joseph promptly wrote a letter to Bishop Partridge asking for details. The prophet also counseled:

> It is not the will of the Lord for you to sell your lands in Zion. . . . Every exertion should be made to maintain the cause you have espoused, and to contribute to the necessities of one another, as much as possible. . . . Remember not to murmur at the dealings of God with His creatures. . . .
>
> We know not what we shall be called to pass through before Zion is delivered and established; therefore, we have great need to live near to God, and always to be in strict obedience to His commandments. . . . You will recollect that the Lord has said, that Zion should not be removed out of her place; therefore the land should not be sold . . . until the Lord in His wisdom shall open a way for your return . . . if you can purchase a tract of land in Clay County for present emergencies, it is right you should do so, if you can do it, and not sell your land in Jackson County (Smith, *History of the Church*, 1:450-51).

A few days later Joseph received a revelation, Section 101 of the Doctrine and Covenants, in which the Lord explained why this calamity had been allowed to befall the Saints in Zion.

> I, the Lord, have suffered the affliction to come upon them, wherewith they have been afflicted, in consequence of their transgressions. . . .
>
> Therefore, they must needs be chastened and tried, even as Abraham, who was commanded to offer up his only son.
>
> For all those who will not endure chastening, but deny me, cannot be sanctified. . . . There were jarrings, and contentions, and envyings, and strifes, and lustful and covetous desires among them; therefore by these things they polluted their inheritances.
>
> . . . [L]et your hearts be comforted concerning Zion; or all flesh is in mine hands; be still and know that I am God.
>
> Zion shall not be moved out of her place, notwithstanding her children have scattered. They that remain, and are pure in heart, shall return, and come to their inheritances, they and their children, with songs of everlasting joy, to build up the waste places of Zion (D&C 101:2, 4-6, 16-18).

When winter came, the Saints in Clay County were living in tents, rough log houses, vacant slave cabins, and anything they could find. Day-to-day life was difficult. Elder Phelps wrote in a letter to Joseph Smith:

> The condition of the scattered Saints is lamentable, and affords a gloomy prospect. . . . We are in Clay, Ray, Lafayette, Jackson, Van Buren, and other counties, and cannot hear from one another oftener than we do from you. I know it was right that we should be driven out of the land of Zion, that the

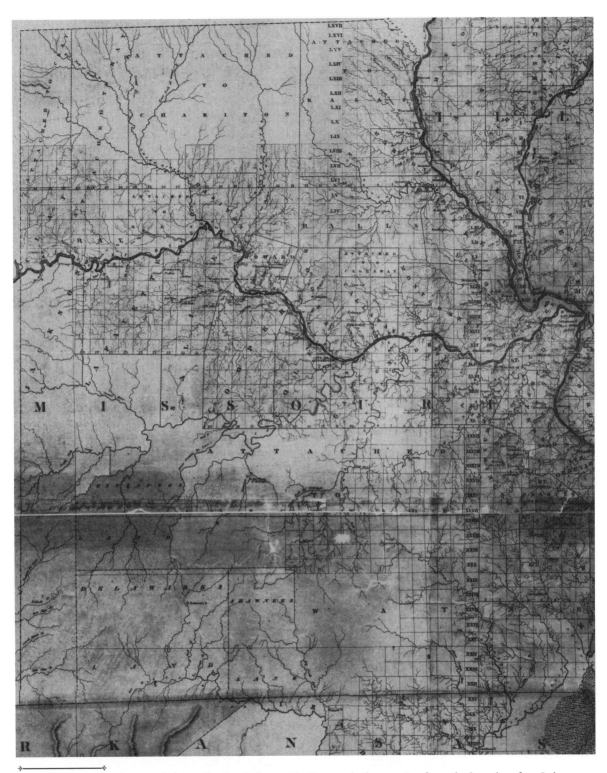

MISSOURI COUNTIES. The Saints fled into Clay, Ray, Lafayette, Van Buren and other counties after mobs drove them from Jackson County. Clay County residents welcomed the Saints, but Lafayette and Van Buren Counties forced the Saints to move on. *Partial map of the states of Missouri, Illinois, and territory of Arkansas by E. Brown and E. Barcroft. ca. 1827*

rebellious might be sent away. But, brethren, if the Lord will, I should like to know what the honest in heart shall do? Our clothes are worn out; we want the necessaries of life (Smith, *History of the Church,* 1:457).

In spite of the general gloom, Brother Phelps was inspired to write a hymn that became a favorite among Church members. "Now let us rejoice in the day of salvation. No longer as strangers on earth need we roam. Good tidings are sounding for us and each nation, And shortly the hour of redemption will come" (*Hymns of the Church of Jesus Christ of Latter-day Saints,* 3).

Following Joseph Smith's instructions in seeking to find a peaceful and legal way of regaining their homes and property, the Saints wrote letters to Governor Daniel Dunklin. The attorney general promised to help the Saints return to their homes, and the local judge offered to hold a court of inquiry in Jackson County as soon as possible. However, since the Saints were scattered in several counties, had little money to hire legal aid, and could not safely enter Jackson County, the offer did not help much. The brave few who did venture back soon found that the mob's hatred had not cooled. Ira Willis, who crossed the river back into Jackson County in search of a lost cow, received a savage beating.

Solomon Chamberlain, one of the first to join the Church in Palmyra, New York, and one of the first Missouri settlers, obtained a rifle, three pistols, a broadsword, and six daggers, then dressed himself in a full suit of buckskin and a wolf skin cap. Calling himself "Old Buckskin," he returned to Jackson County to execute vengeance on God's enemies. He apparently attracted a bit of attention and was soon taken prisoner. However, the mob, after drinking all night, simply damned him and told him to get out of their way.

Finding the people of Van Buren County unsympathetic to their plight, some of the Saints decided to return to their homes near Independence. Mrs. Abigail Lyman Leonard tells of her experience:

> Soon after our arrival in the old deserted place . . . [at] about eleven o'clock at night, while we were comfortably seated around a blazing fire, built in an old-fashioned Dutch fireplace . . . some one on going out discovered a crowd of men at a little distance from the house, on the hill. This alarmed the children, who ran out, leaving the door open. In a moment or two five armed men pushed their way into the house and presented their guns to my husband's breast, and demanded, "Are you a Mormon?" My husband replied: "I profess to belong to the Church of Christ." They then asked him if he had any arms, and on being told that he had not, one of them said: "Now, d—n you, walk out doors!" My husband was standing up, and did not move.
>
> Seeing that he would not go, one of them laid down his gun, clutched a chair, and dealt a fierce blow at my husband's head; but fortunately the chair struck a beam overhead, which turned and partially stopped the force of the blow, and it fell upon the side of his head and shoulders with too little force to bring him down, yet enough to smash the chair in pieces upon the hearth. The fiend then caught up another chair, with which he succeeded in knock-

ing my husband down beneath the stair-way. They then struck him several blows with a chairpost, upon the head, cutting four long gashes in his scalp. The infuriated men then took him by the feet and dragged him from the room. They raised him to his feet, and one of them, grasping a large boulder, hurled it with full force at his head; but he dropped his head enough to let the stone pass over, and it went against the house like a cannon ball. Several of them threw him into the air, and brought him [down], with all their might, at full length upon the ground. When he fell, one of them sprang upon his breast, and stamping with all his might, broke two of his ribs.

They then turned him upon his side, and with a chair-post dealt him many severe blows upon the thigh. . . . Next they tore off his coat and shirt, and proceeded to whip him with their gun-sticks. I had been by my husband during this whole affray, and one of the mob seeing me, cried out, "Take that woman in the house, or she will overpower every devil of you." Four of them presented their guns to my breast, and jumping off the ground with rage, uttering the most tremendous oaths, they commanded me to go into the house. This order I did not obey, but hastened to my husband's assistance, taking stick after stick from them, till I must have thrown away twenty.

By this time, my husband felt that he could hold out no longer, and raising his hands toward heaven, asking the Lord to receive his spirit, he fell to the ground, helpless. Every hand was stayed, and I asked a sister who was in the house to assist me to carry him in doors.

We carried him in, and after washing his face and making him as comfortable as possible, I went forth into the mob, and reasoned with them, telling them that my husband had never harmed one of them, nor raised his arm in defence against them. They then went calmly away, but the next day circulated a report that they had killed one Mormon.

After the mob had gone, I sent for the elder, and he, with two or three of the brethren, came and administered to my husband, and he was instantly healed. The gashes on his face grew together without leaving a scar, and he went to bed comfortable. In the morning I combed the coagulated blood out of his hair, and he was so well that he went with me to meeting that same day (Edward W. Tullidge, *Women of Mormondom*, 165–66).

THE WORK PROGRESSES

Even though the Church of Jesus Christ was plagued with persecution, and the Saints were driven from their homes in the middle of winter, the work of the Lord continued to progress. Leaving their families, missionaries were called to seek out the honest in heart. Most of the missionaries worked in the northeastern part of the United States and Canada. Many people had not yet heard the glad tidings, and some were eagerly waiting. Wilford Woodruff was twenty-six years old, unmarried, and living in Richland, New York, with his brother, Azmon, and his wife, Elizabeth. Wilford, who had been seeking the truth for many years, wrote:

At an early age, my mind began to be exercised upon religious subjects, but I had never made a profession of religion until 1830 when I was twenty-three years of age. I did not then join any church for the reason that I could not find a . . . church that had for its doctrine, faith, and practices those principles, ordinances, and gifts which constituted the gospel of Jesus Christ as taught by Him and His apostles. Neither did I find anywhere the manifestations of the Holy Ghost. . . . When I conversed with the ministers . . . they would always tell me that prophets, apostles, revelations, healings, etc., were given to establish Jesus Christ and His doctrine, but that they have ever since been done away with, because [they were] no longer needed in the Church and Kingdom of God. Such a declaration I never could and never would believe. . . .

From the study of the Bible I found that the principle of cause and effect was the same in all ages, and that the divine promises made were to all generations. At the same time, I found no changes in the gospel in the days of Christ and the apostles, or that there would be any change in the plan of salvation in the last days (Matthias F. Cowley, *Wilford Woodruff: History of His Life and Labors*, 14-15).

WILFORD WOODRUFF was one of those who were eagerly awaiting the truth of the restored gospel. His conversion was the beginning of a life of sacred service. *ca. 1850s*

Early in his life, Wilford Woodruff had an experience that prepared him to receive the gospel. He recorded:

In the days of my youth I was taught by an aged man named Robert Mason, who lived in Sainsbury, Connecticut. By many he was called a prophet; to my knowledge, many of his prophecies had been fulfilled. The sick were healed by him through the laying on of hands in the name of Jesus Christ, and devils were cast out. . . .

Father Mason did not claim that he had any authority to officiate in the ordinances of the gospel, nor did he believe that such authority existed on the earth. He did believe, however, that it was the privilege of any man who had faith in God to fast and pray for the healing of the sick by the laying on of hands. He believed it his right and the right of every honest-hearted man or woman to receive light and knowledge. . . .

The last time I ever saw him he related to me the following vision which he had in his field in open day: "I was carried away in a vision and found myself in the midst of a vast orchard of fruit trees. I became hungry and wandered through this vast orchard searching for fruit to eat, but I found none. While I stood in amazement at finding no fruit in the midst of so many trees, they began to fall to the ground as if torn up by a whirlwind. They continued to fall until there was not a tree standing in the whole orchard. I immediately saw thereafter shoots springing up from the roots and forming themselves into young and beautiful trees. These budded, blossomed, and brought forth fruit which ripened and was the most beautiful to look upon of anything my eyes have ever beheld. I stretched forth my hand and plucked some of the fruit. I gazed upon it with delight; but when I was about to eat of it, the vision closed and I did not taste the fruit.

"At the close of the vision I bowed down in humble prayer and asked the Lord to show me the meaning of the vision. Then the voice of the Lord came to me saying: "Son of man, thou hast sought me diligently to know the truth concerning my Church and Kingdom among men. This is to show you that my Church is not organized among men in the generation to which you belong; but in the days of your children the Church and Kingdom of God shall be made manifest with all the gifts and the blessings enjoyed by the Saints in past ages. You shall live to be made acquainted with it, but shall not partake of its blessings before you depart from this life. You will be blessed of the Lord after death because you followed the dictation of my Spirit in this life" (Cowley, *Wilford Woodruff: History of His Life and Labors*, 15-17).

Wilford continues:

When Father Mason had finished relating the vision and its interpretation, he said, calling me by my Christian name: "Wilford, I shall never partake of this fruit in the flesh, but you will and you will become a conspicuous actor in the new kingdom." He then turned and left. . . . These were the last words he ever spoke to me upon the earth. To me this was a very striking circumstance. . . . On this occasion he said he felt impelled by the Spirit of the Lord to relate it to me. The vision was given to him about the year 1800. He related it to me in 1830. . . . I had given myself up to the reading of the Scriptures and to earnest prayer before God day and night as far as I could. . . . I had pleaded with the Lord many hours in the forest, among the rocks, and in the fields, and in the mill—often at midnight for light and truth and for His Spirit to guide me in the way of salvation. My prayers were answered and many things were revealed to me. My mind was open to the truth so that I was fully satisfied that I should live to see the Church of Christ established upon the earth and to see a people raised up who would keep the commandments of the Lord (Cowley, *Wilford Woodruff: History of His Life and Labors*, 17-18).

ZERA PULSIPHER (1789–1872) was one of the missionaries whose inspired preaching led to the conversion of Wilford Woodruff. *ca. 1840*

On December 29, 1833, two missionaries from the Church of Jesus Christ, Zera Pulsipher and Elijah Cheney, called at the home of Azmon Woodruff, where Wilford was living, but the two brothers were not at home. Azmon's wife, knowing that her husband and brother-in-law would be interested in the new religion, found out where the missionaries would be preaching. When the men returned, she told them about the missionaries and the meeting that was to be held that evening in the local schoolhouse. Wilford recorded his response to the news:

Upon my arrival home my sister-in-law informed me of the meeting. I immediately turned out my horses and started for the schoolhouse without waiting for supper. On my way I prayed most sincerely that the Lord would give me His spirit, and that if these men were the servants of God I might know it, and that my heart might be prepared to receive the divine message they had to deliver.

When I reached the place of meeting, they found the house already packed. My brother Azmon was there before I arrived. He was equally eager to hear what these men had to say. I crowded my way through the assembly and seated myself upon one of the writing desks where I could see and hear everything that took place.

Elder Pulsipher opened with prayer. He knelt down and asked the Lord in the name of Jesus Christ for what he wanted. His manner of prayer and the influence which went with it impressed me greatly. The spirit of the Lord rested upon me and bore witness that he was a servant of God. After singing, he preached to the people for an hour and a half. The spirit of God rested mightily upon him and he bore a strong testimony of the divine authenticity of the Book of Mormon and of the mission of the Prophet Joseph Smith. I believed all that he said. The spirit bore witness of its truth. Elder Cheney then arose and added his testimony to the truth of the words of Elder Pulsipher.

Liberty was then given by the elders to any one in the congregation to arise and speak for or against what they had heard as they might choose. Almost instantly I found myself upon my feet. The spirit of the Lord urged me to bear testimony to the truth of the message delivered by these elders. I exhorted my neighbors and friends not to oppose these men; for they were the true servants of God. They had preached to us that night the pure gospel of Jesus Christ. When I sat down, my brother Azmon arose and bore a similar testimony. He was followed by several others (Cowley, *Wilford Woodruff: History of His Life and Labors*, 33).

LYMAN WIGHT (1796–1858) ordained John Corrill and Isaac Morley as counselors to Bishop Partridge; he saw the Savior in vision and prophesied with great power. He later apostatized and left the Church.
ca. 1850

Wilford started reading the Book of Mormon, and the Spirit confirmed that what he was reading was of God. Two days later, on December 31, Zera Pulsipher baptized Wilford Woodruff. Wilford recorded, "The snow was about three feet deep, the day was cold, and the water was mixed with ice and snow, yet I did not feel the cold" (Backman, *The Heavens Resound*, 129).

That evening, Wilford and his brother were confirmed members of the Church. A few days later, Elder Pulsipher organized the Saints in Richmond into a branch and ordained Wilford to the office of a teacher in the Aaronic Priesthood.

On January 1, 1834, Bishop Edward Partridge presided over a conference in Clay County, Missouri. Many Saints who recently had been driven from Jackson County attended the conference. At the conference the members organized themselves so they could help one another survive the winter. They also decided to send two men to Kirtland to get advice from Joseph Smith on whether they should start a new settlement, move to another place, or attempt to return to Jackson County. Lyman Wight and Parley Pratt volunteered to go to Ohio, even though it would be a great hardship for both men and their families. Parley recorded:

I was at this time entirely destitute of proper clothing for the journey; and I had neither horse, saddle, bridle, money nor provisions to take with me; or to leave with my wife, who lay sick and helpless most of the time. . . .

Nearly all had been robbed and plundered, and all were poor. As we had to start without delay, I almost trembled at the undertaking; it seemed to be all but an impossibility; but "to him that believeth all things are possible." I started out of my house . . . I hardly knew which way to go, but I found myself in the house of brother John Lowry, and was intending to ask him for money; but as I entered his miserable cottage in the swamp . . . I found him sick in bed with a heavy fever, and two or three others of his family down with the same complaint, on different beds in the same room. He was vomiting severely, and was hardly sensible of my presence. I thought to myself, "well, this is a poor place to come for money, and yet I must have it; I know of no one else that has got it; what shall I do?" I sat a little while. . . . At length another Elder happened in; at that instant, faith sprung up in my heart . . . I said to the Elder that came in: "Brother, I am glad you have come; these people must be healed, for I want some money of them, and must have it."

We laid our hands on them and rebuked the disease; brother Lowry rose up well; I did my errand, and readily obtained all I asked. This provided in part for my family's sustenance while I should leave them. I went a little further into the woods of the Missouri bottoms, and came to a camp of some brethren, by the name of Higbee, who owned some horses; they saw me coming, and, moved by the Spirit, one of them said to the other, "there comes brother Parley; he's in want of a horse for his journey—I must let him have old Dick;" this being the name of the best horse he had.

"Yes," said I, "brother, you have guessed right; but what will I do for a saddle?"

"Well," says the other, "I believe I'll have to let you have mine." I blessed them and went on my way rejoicing.

I next called on Algernon Sidney Gilbert . . . then sojourning in the village of Liberty—his store in Jackson County having been broken up, and his goods plundered and destroyed by the mob.

"Well," says he, "brother Parley, you certainly look too shabby to start a journey; you must have a new suit; I have got some remnants left that will make you a coat," etc.

A neighboring tailoress and two or three other sisters happened to be present [and] exclaimed, "Yes, brother Gilbert, you find the stuff and we'll make it up for him." This arranged, I now lacked only a cloak; this was also furnished by Brother Gilbert.

Brother Wight was also prospered in a similar manner in his preparations. Thus faith and the blessings of God had cleared up our way to accomplish what seemed impossible (*Autobiography of Parley P. Pratt*, 87-88).

JOHN LOWRY (1799–1867) was healed of a heavy fever by Parley P. Pratt and generously contributed monies for Elder Pratt's mission to Ohio. *ca. 1840*

In an amazingly short time, the necessary preparations were made and the men set out for Ohio on January 12. Those who stayed behind continued to press their legal claims for justice, and on February 24, 1834, a grand jury met to investigate the troubles in Missouri. William Phelps, John Corrill, Edward Partridge, and others were subpoenaed to appear before the court in Jackson County. A contingent of soldiers from Clay County escorted the men to within a mile of Independence, where the men waited in a vacant cabin while attorneys for the two sides met. By mid-morning the attorneys had decided that public excitement was too high for the court to meet safely.

While there, Brother Phelps brought charges against Samuel Lucas and others for the destruction of the printing press and the loss of his home. Edward Partridge also charged Mr. Lucas and five others with assault. When the case came up, the court ruled that Mr. Phelps's home did not belong to him, and that the press had been simply moved to another location. Since no damage was done, the defendants were found not guilty.

As for those who had beat, tarred, and feathered Bishop Partridge, the defendants shamelessly claimed to have done their dastardly deeds in self-defense. The court then ruled that they were not guilty.

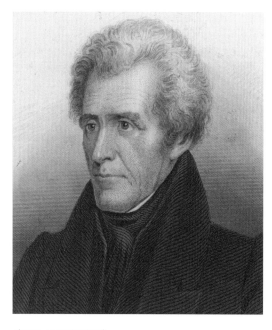

Because the Mormons could not receive justice in Jackson County, the brethren returned to Clay County and appealed to the governor. Governor Dunklin ordered that Colonel Pitcher be arrested and tried for disarming the Mormons and leaving them to the mercy of the mob. When the trial was held, Pitcher was ordered to return the weapons to the Mormons, but since the guns had all disappeared into the hands of the mobbers, they were never returned.

Governor Dunklin offered to help the Saints return to their homes, but he did not feel he had the authority to keep an armed force stationed in Jackson County to ensure the Mormons' safety. He urged the Saints to take their cause to President Andrew Jackson. Accordingly, the members drafted a petition with 114 signatures and sent it to the president. The Saints explained their situation:

Between one and two thousand of the people called "Mormons" [have] been driven by force of arms from the county of Jackson . . . , being compelled to leave their highly cultivated fields . . . on account of our belief in direct revelation from God . . . according to the Holy Scriptures. We know that such illegal violence has not been inflicted upon any sect or community of people by the citizens of the United States since the Declaration of Independence. That this is a religious persecution is notorious throughout our country; for while the officers of the county, both civil and military, were accomplices in these unparalleled outrages, engaged in the destruction of the printing office, dwelling houses, etc., . . . our numbers being greatly inferior to the enemy were unable to stand in self-defense (Smith, *History of the Church*, 1:484).

While waiting for President Jackson to respond to their petition, the Saints began building temporary homes, planting crops, and trying to regain some measure of comfort. Although the Church had grown both in number and in knowledge of the will of the Lord, the dream of building the city of Zion had, for now, been frustrated. Nevertheless, work on the temple in Kirtland was progressing, and strong new converts were joining the Church. Although the Saints wondered when they would be allowed to return to Jackson County, they felt that even if their appeals to the government failed, the Lord would open up a way for them to resume building Zion.

GATHERING ZION'S CAMP, SPRING 1834

In the United States of America—"the land of the free"—mobs had driven honest, God-fearing people from their homes and farms, had stolen or destroyed their animals, and had burned their crops and homes because their beliefs were different than those of their neighbors.

The Saints had built homes, started farms, stores, schools, and even a newspaper, but their dream had faded. No one had expected such violence and hate from the citizens of Jackson County that November of 1833. Driven like cattle by their neighbors' guns, whips, firebrands, and clubs, the Saints crossed the Missouri River into Clay County, where the citizens were sympathetic and helpful for the most part. Still, the Saints wondered: Did the Lord want them to abandon their dream of building the New Jerusalem? Would the other members of the Church come to their aid? Could the government of the United States restore their property to them?

In Kirtland, Ohio, a new press was purchased to replace the one destroyed by the Missouri mob. In December it was assembled and ready to begin printing. Oliver Cowdery served as editor. Of Oliver, Joseph said:

> Blessed of the Lord is Brother Oliver, nevertheless there are two evils in him that he must needs forsake, or he cannot altogether escape the buffetings of the adversary. If he forsake these evils he shall be forgiven, and shall be made like unto the bow which the Lord hath set in the heavens; he shall be a sign and an ensign unto the nations. Behold, he is blessed of the Lord for his constancy and steadfastness in the work of the Lord; wherefore, he shall be blessed in his generation . . . and he shall be helped out of many troubles; and if he keep the commandments, and hearken unto the counsel of the Lord, his rest shall be glorious (Smith, *History of the Church*, 1:465).

Joseph did not elaborate on the evils that affected Oliver's relationship with the Lord and the Church, but apparently, Joseph did not feel he could totally depend on his old friend.

Regarding the faithfulness of his own mother and father, Joseph commented:

> Her soul is ever filled with benevolence and philanthropy. . . . And blessed is my father, for the hand of the Lord shall be over him, for he shall see the affliction of his children pass away. . . .

Joseph went on to pronounce the following blessings upon each of the members of his family.

> Blessed of the Lord is my brother Hyrum, for the integrity of his heart; he shall be girt about with truth, and faithfulness shall be the strength of his loins: from generation to generation he shall be a shaft in the hands of his God to execute judgment upon his enemies . . . and when he is in trouble and great tribulation hath come upon him, he shall remember the God of Jacob; and He will shield him from the power of Satan. . . .
>
> Blessed of the Lord is my brother Samuel, because the Lord shall say unto him, Samuel, Samuel; therefore he shall be made a teacher in the house of the Lord, and the Lord shall mature his mind in judgment. . . .
>
> Brother William is as the fierce lion . . . in the pride of his heart, he will neglect the more weighty matters until his soul is bowed down in sorrow; and then he shall return and call on the name of his God, and shall find forgiveness, and shall wax valiant (Smith, *History of the Church*, 1:465-66).

Another valiant servant was Brigham Young, who recorded:

> In the month of September, in conformity to the counsel of the Prophet, I made preparations to gather up to Kirtland, and engaged a passage for myself and two children. . . . We arrived in Kirtland in safety, travelling by land, where I tarried all winter, and had the privilege of listening to the teachings of the Prophet and enjoying the society of the Saints, working hard at my former trade. In the fall of 1833, many of the brethren had gathered to Kirtland, and not finding suitable employment, and having some difficulty in getting their pay after they had labored, several went off to Willoughby, Painesville and Cleveland. I told them I had gathered to Kirtland because I was so directed by the Prophet of God, and I was not going away to Willoughby, Painesville, Cleveland, nor anywhere else to build up the Gentiles, but I was going to stay here and seek the things that pertained to the kingdom of God by listening to the teachings of his servants, and I should work for my brethren and trust in God and them that I would be paid. I labored for Brother Cahoon and finished his house, and although he did not know he could pay me when I commenced, before I finished he had paid me in full. I then went to work for Father

John Smith and others, who paid me, and sustained myself in Kirtland, and when the brethren who had gone out to work for the Gentiles returned, I had means, though some of them were scant (*Manuscript History of Brigham Young*).

FIRST HIGH COUNCIL ORGANIZED

In February 1834, Joseph was inspired to organize the first high council of the Church, as part of the Kirtland Stake. At that time, the First Presidency of the Church, Joseph Smith, Sidney Rigdon, and Frederick G. Williams, was also the presidency of the Kirtland Stake, so this first high council was responsible for the Church as a whole. Joseph explained that this was the restoration of another part of the ancient Church. He recorded:

Jerusalem was the seat of the church council in ancient days. The apostle Peter was the President of the council, and held the keys of the Kingdom of God on earth. No man is capable of judging a matter in council, unless his own heart is pure. In ancient days, councils were conducted with such strict propriety that no one was allowed to whisper, be weary, leave the room, or get uneasy in the least, until the voice of the Lord was obtained (*Kirtland Council Minute Book,* 30).

HYRUM SMITH'S
KIRTLAND HOME
ca. 1897–1927

Section 102 of the Doctrine and Covenants records that this first high council was organized on February 17, 1834.

The high council was appointed by revelation for the purpose of settling important difficulties which might arise in the church, which could not be settled by the church, or the Bishops council, to the satisfaction of the parties. . . . [The council consisted of:] 1, Oliver Cowdery; 2, Joseph Coe; 3, Samuel H. Smith; 4, Luke Johnson; 5, John S. Carter; 6, Silvester Smith; 7, John Johnson; 8, Orson Hyde; 9, Jared Carter; 10, Joseph Smith, Sr.; 11, John Smith; 12, Martin Harris (D&C 102:2, 34).

Joseph Smith laid his hands upon each of the twelve members of the high council and ordained them to their calling. He also called Oliver Cowdery, Joseph Smith, Sr., and Hyrum Smith as assistants to the presidency, to help them in their duties.

Brigham Young, who had been widowed since September of 1832, found a new wife, and was married in Kirtland. He noted, "In February, 1834, I married Mary Ann Angel, who took charge of my children, kept my house, and labored faithfully for the interest of my family and the kingdom" (*Manuscript History of Brigham Young*).

Meanwhile, Parley Pratt and Lyman Wight arrived in Kirtland from Clay County, Missouri, on February 22. On Sunday, February 23, they preached to the Saints who met in the Methodist church. On Monday they reported to the presidency and high council that in the three months since they had been expelled from Jackson County, there had been no progress in returning the Saints to their homes. They recounted the lack of justice they had received from the government and told of the sufferings and hardships the Saints were enduring.

Joseph sought guidance from the Lord and received the revelation contained in Section 103 of the Doctrine and Covenants.

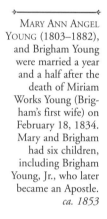

MARY ANN ANGEL YOUNG (1803–1882), and Brigham Young were married a year and a half after the death of Miriam Works Young (Brigham's first wife) on February 18, 1834. Mary and Brigham had six children, including Brigham Young, Jr., who later became an Apostle.
ca. 1853

Behold, I will give unto you a revelation and commandment, that you may know how to act in the discharge of your duties concerning the salvation and redemption of your brethren, who have been scattered on the land of Zion. . . . .

Therefore let my servant Joseph Smith, Jun., say unto the strength of my house, my young men and the middle aged—Gather yourselves together unto the land of Zion.

And let all the churches send up wise men with their moneys, and purchase lands even as I have commanded them. . . .

It is my will that my servant Parley P. Pratt and my servant Lyman Wight should not return to the land of their brethren, until they have obtained companies to go up unto the land of Zion, by tens, or by twenties, or by fifties, or by an hundred, until they have obtained to the number of five hundred of the strength of my house.

Behold this is my will . . . but men do not always do my will.

Therefore, if you cannot obtain five hundred, seek diligently that peradventure you may obtain three hundred. And if ye cannot obtain three hundred, seek diligently that peradventure ye may obtain one hundred. . . .

Ye shall not go up unto the land of Zion until you have obtained a hundred of the strength of my house, to go up with you unto the land of Zion (D&C 103:1, 22-23, 30-34).

Joseph Smith promptly announced his intention of going to Zion, and thirty or forty of the brethren volunteered to accompany him. Many of the brethren were called to seek volunteers from the members of the Church in Ohio, Indiana, Michigan, and the eastern states so that the 500 men the Lord had called for would be available. Although their purpose was to find volunteers among the members of the Church, the brethren still preached and baptized at every opportunity. Parley Pratt recorded:

We visited Freedom, Catteraugus County, N.Y.; tarried over Sunday, and preached several discourses, to which the people listened with great interest; we were kindly and hospitably entertained among them. We baptized a young man named Herman Hyde; his parents were Presbyterians, and his mother, on account of the strength of her traditions, thought that we were wrong, and told me afterwards that she would much rather have followed him to an earthly grave than to have seen him baptized.

Soon afterwards, however, herself, her husband, and the rest of the family, with some thirty or forty others, were all baptized and organized into a branch of the Church—called the Freedom Branch—from which nucleus the light spread and souls were gathered into the fold in the regions round. Thus mightily grew the word of God (*Autobiography of Parley P. Pratt*, 89).

GATHERING MONEY

Joseph was trying to gather money and goods to help the Missouri Saints, but money was also needed to continue the work on the temple in Kirtland. Joseph Holbrook recorded in his journal that:

"Orson Hyde and Orson Pratt from Kirtland visited the Branch and informed us that there was a revelation for the brethren to take a journey to the land of Zion. I put down my name. Chandler Holbrook and Otis Shumway making three in all and to be in Kirtland the first day of May for to go to the land of Zion with our brethren who should assemble there (*History of Joseph Holbrook, 1806-1805*).

Joseph Smith recorded that in a meeting in Avon, New York: "It was voted . . . that Fathers Bosley and Nickerson, Elder McWithey and Brother Roger Orton, should exert themselves to obtain two thousand dollars for the present relief of Kirtland. They all agreed to do what they could to obtain it, firmly believing it could be accomplished by the first of April" (Smith, *History of the Church*, 2:44).

In Richland, New York, Parley Pratt and Harry Brown informed Wilford Woodruff of the call for young and able-bodied men to go to Kirtland to participate in Zion's Camp. Wilford promptly settled his business affairs and said good-bye to his family. Joseph recorded that money trickled in.

After the lecture, I requested the brethren and sisters to contribute all the money they could for the deliverance of Zion; and received twenty-nine dollars and sixty-nine cents. . . . I attended conference and had a glorious time. Some few volunteered to go to Zion, and others donated sixty-six dollars and thirty-seven cents for the benefit of the scattered brethren in Zion. . . . I received, by letters from friends in the East, and of the brethren in Kirtland, the sum of two hundred and fifty-one dollars and sixty cents (Smith, *History of the Church*, 2:50, 52, 61).

And so, throughout the month of April, men and money were gathered. However, by May 1, only a few more than 100 men had assembled to partici-

pate in Zion's Camp. Although far short of the goal, it was a start. On Sunday, May 4, Joseph preached to the brethren and promised that if they would live as they should, keep the commandments of the Lord, and not murmur against the Lord and his servants, they would all return safely to their families. Still, it was not easy for men to leave their homes and embark on such an adventure. Heber C. Kimball recorded: "We started on the 5th of May, (1834) and truly this was a solemn morning to me. I took leave of my wife and children and friends, not knowing whether I would see them again in the flesh, as myself and brethren were threatened both in that country and in Missouri by enemies, that they would destroy us and exterminate us from the land" (Whitney, *Life of Heber C. Kimball*, 40).

THE WESTERN MARCH, SUMMER 1834

Andrew Jackson redefined the office of president of the United States. While previous presidents had followed the lead of Congress, Jackson had vetoed twelve acts of Congress during his two terms. In contrast, all of the presidents before him combined had only used the veto nine times. Jackson made the Executive Office the center of government, and he became a symbol of what the people wanted—democracy, simplicity, and national power. Nevertheless, President Jackson had no desire to involve himself in the situation with the Mormons in Missouri. Lewis Cass, of the War Department, answered the Saints in a letter dated May 2, 1834.

> The President has referred to this department . . . the letter addressed to him by yourselves . . . requesting his interposition in order to protect your persons and property.

In answer, I am instructed to inform you, that the offenses of which you complain, are violations of the laws of the state of Missouri, and not of the laws of the United States. . . .

The President cannot call out a military force to aid in the execution of the state laws, until the proper requisition is made upon him by the constituted authorities (Smith, *History of the Church*, 1:493).

ZION'S CAMP

The men of Zion's Camp were mostly young. Nearly all of the 130 men were elders, priests, teachers, or deacons; Sidney Rigdon, Oliver Cowdery, and the older men stayed in Kirtland to continue work on the temple. The men of Zion's Camp took twenty baggage wagons filled with supplies for themselves, and clothing and provisions for the Saints in Missouri. Since there was no room in the wagons, the volunteers walked. By May 7, the group was assembled near New Portage, Ohio, about forty miles south of Kirtland. Here, more men joined the group and Joseph organized the men for the journey. Joseph wrote:

> Through the remainder of this day I continued to organize the company, appoint such other officers as were required, and gave such instructions as were necessary for the discipline, order, comfort and safety of all concerned. I divided the whole band into companies of twelve, leaving each company to elect its own captain, who assigned each man in his respective company his post and duty, generally in the following order: Two cooks, two firemen, two tent men, two watermen, one runner, two wagoners and horsemen, and one commissary. We purchased flour, . . . baked our own bread, and cooked our own food, generally, which was good, though sometimes scanty; and sometimes we had johnny-cake or corndodger instead of flour bread. Every night before retiring to rest, at the sound of the trumpet, we bowed before the Lord in the several tents, and presented our thank-offerings with prayer and supplication; and at the sound of the morning trumpet, about four o'clock, every man was again on his knees before the Lord, imploring His blessing for the day (Smith, *History of the Church*, 2:64-65).

Wilford Woodruff, who had been a member of the Church for less than six months, and who had met the Prophet only a week before setting out on Zion's Camp, later recorded:

> When the members of Zion's Camp were called, many of us had never beheld each other's faces; we were strangers to each other and many had never seen the prophet. . . . We gained an experience that we never could have gained in any other way. We had the privilege of beholding the face of the prophet, and we had the privilege of travelling a thousand miles with him, and seeing the workings of the Spirit of God with him, and the revelations of Jesus Christ unto him, and the fulfilment of those revelations (Young, *Journal of Discourses*, 13:158).

While the Kirtland group was being organized, a group of fourteen men and boys, led by Hyrum Smith and Lyman Wight, was setting out from Pontiac, Michigan, with the intention of joining the main group before it reached Jackson County, Missouri.

Zion's Camp moved on. The men traveled until they reached Richfield, Ohio, on Sunday, August 8, 1834. Here they stopped to worship, receive the sacrament, and hear a sermon by Sylvester Smith. Oliver Cowdery wrote a circular to the Church on May 10 that explained the intentions of Zion's Camp.

> It is no doubt known to you, that a large number of our brethren have lately gone out for the deliverance of the afflicted Saints, who have been dispossessed of their lands and homes by a lawless band of men. . . .
>
> When these brethren have arrived in the vicinity . . . they will wait for our brethren who have been driven out, to inform the governor of that state, that they are ready to go back to their lands. The governor is bound to call out the militia and take them back, and has informed our brethren of his readiness to do so previous to this time. When orders arrive from the Governor to the military commanding officer, in that vicinity to guard our brethren back, then it is expected that all will march over, the former residents as well as those now on the way. . . . The company . . . will be sufficiently strong in the strength of the Lord to maintain the ground, after the militia have been discharged, should those wicked men be desperate enough to come upon them (Stanley R. Gunn, *Oliver Cowdery: Second Elder and Scribe*, 112-13).

One of the members of Zion's Camp was fifteen-year-old George A. Smith. He kept the record of their travels and recorded the first signs of discord among the brethren:

> On Wednesday, 14th [of May 1834] we had been unable to obtain sufficient baking and cooking utensils, and as our commissary had been disappointed in getting a supply of bread . . . we began to be straitened for the staff of life. Men were sent on to Bellefontaine to have a supply baked by the time we should arrive, and although every measure practicable had been taken, Sylvester Smith murmured against the Prophet because the Camp was not supplied with bread. . . . On the sixteenth he recorded: During the day being very much fatigued with carrying my musket I put it into the baggage wagon, which was customary, and when I arrived at camp in the evening my gun could not be found. This circumstance was exceedingly mortifying to me and many of the brethren accused me of carelessness, and ridiculed me about losing my gun. Jenkins Salsibury took the most pleasure in ridiculing me for my carelessness. I afterwards learned . . . that my gun was pawned for whisky by one of our company, and have always believed that Jenkins Salisbury, who was very fond of the good creature, disposed of it, in that way (George A. Smith, "My Journal," *The Instructor*, 81 [1946], 78, 95).

This large group of men passing through the countryside aroused much curiosity and interest. However, on several occasions, their numbers seemed multiplied, which discouraged would-be troublemakers. Wilford Woodruff recorded:

> We were followed by spies hundreds of miles to find out the object of our mission. We had some boys in the camp. George A. Smith was among the youngest. When they could get him alone they would question him, thinking that he looked green enough for them to get what they wanted out of him. The following questions were frequently put and answered:
>
> [Q:] "My boy, where are you from?"
> George: "From the East."
> [Q:] "Where are you going?"
> George: "To the West."
> [Q:] "What for?"
> George: "To see where we can get land cheapest and best."
> [Q:] "Who leads the camp?"
> George: "Sometimes one, sometimes another."
> [Q:] "What name?"
> George: "Captain Wallace, Major Bruce, Orson Hyde, James Allred, etc." (Smith, *History of the Church*, 2:67).

Joseph Smith also kept a record of their travels:

> The 17th of May we crossed the state line of Ohio, and encamped for the Sabbath just within the limits of Indiana, having traveled about forty miles that day. Our feet were very sore and blistered, our stockings wet with blood, the weather being very warm. At night a spy attempted to get into our camp, but was prevented by our guard. We had our sentinels posted every night, on account of spies who were continually striving to harass us, steal our horses, etc.
>
> This evening there was a difficulty between some of the brethren and Sylvester Smith, on occasion of which I was called to decide in the matter. Finding a rebellious spirit in Sylvester Smith, and to some extent in others, I told them they would meet with misfortunes, difficulties and hindrances, and said, "and you will know it before you leave this place," exhorting them to humble themselves before the Lord and become united, that they might not be scourged. A very singular occurrence took place that night and the next day, concerning our teams. On Sunday morning, when we arose, we found almost every horse in the camp so badly foundered that we could scarcely lead them a few rods to the water. The brethren then deeply realized the effects of discord. When I learned the fact, I exclaimed to the brethren, that for a witness that God overruled and had His eye upon them, all those who would humble themselves before the Lord should know that the hand of God was in this misfortune, and their horses should be restored to health immediately; and by twelve o'clock the same day the horses were as nimble as ever, with the exception of one of Sylvester Smith's, which soon afterwards died. . . .

About this time the Saints in Clay County, Missouri, established an armory, where they commenced manufacturing swords, dirks, pistols, stocking rifles, and repairing arms in general for their own defense against mob violence; many arms were purchased; for the leading men in Clay County rendered every facility in their power, in order, as they said, "to help the 'Mormons' settle their own difficulties, and pay the Jackson mob in their own way" (Smith, *History of the Church*, 2:68-69).

Zion's Camp marched across Indiana and, on May 24, crossed the state line into Illinois. Hyrum Smith and Lyman Wight's group was, at this time, in Tazewell County, Illinois, camped near the home of Joseph Rich, where they held a meeting and preached. A non-Mormon, Hosea Stout, who attended the meeting, recorded: "The effect of their preaching was powerful on me and when I considered that they were going up to Zion to fight for their lost inheritance under the special direction of God it was all that I could do to refrain from going. James and I let them have one yoke of oxen" (Wayne Stout, *Hosea Stout, Utah's Pioneer Statesman*, 33-34).

The main group, under Joseph Smith, continued to be harassed by spies and troublemakers. Joseph wrote: "Notwithstanding our enemies were continually breathing threats of violence, we did not fear, neither did we hesitate to prosecute our journey, for God was with us . . . and the faith of our little band was unwavering. We know that angels were our companions, for we saw them" (Smith, *History of the Church*, 2:73).

This was the first time most of the men had seen the great American prairie. The ground was so flat that distances were deceptive. Some of the brethren set out in pursuit of deer that appeared very close, only to discover that they were miles away. The water on the prairie was also different. It was full of little animals called "wigglers," which had to be strained out of the drinking water.

Joseph taught the members of the camp at every opportunity. He recorded:

> In pitching my tent, we found three massasaugas or prairie rattlesnakes, which the brethren were about to kill, but I said, "Let them alone—don't hurt them! How will the serpent ever lose his venom, while the servants of God possess the same disposition, and continue to war upon it? Men must become harmless, before the brute creation; and when men lose their vicious dispositions and cease to destroy the animal race, the lion and the lamb can dwell together, and the sucking child can play with the serpent in safety." The brethren took the serpents carefully on sticks and carried them across the creek. I exhorted the brethren not to kill a serpent, bird, or animal of any kind during our journey unless it became necessary in order to preserve ourselves from hunger (Smith, *History of the Church*, 2:71-72).

Every day except Sunday, the camp marched westward across Illinois. George A. Smith recorded how various members handled the hardships and trials of the camp.

The prophet Joseph took a full share of the fatigues of the entire journey. In addition to the care of presiding over it, he walked most of the time, and had a full proportion of blistered, bloody, and sore feet, which was the natural result of walking for twenty-five to forty miles a day, in a hot season of the year. But during the entire trip he never uttered a murmur or complaint. While most of the men in the camp complained to him of sore toes, blistered feet, long drives, scanty supply and provisions, poor quality of bread, bad corndodger, frozen butter, strong honey, maggoty bacon and cheese, etc., even a dog could not bark at some men without their murmuring at Joseph. If they had to camp with bad water, it would nearly cause a rebellion, yet we were the Camp of Zion, and many of us were prayerless, thoughtless, careless, heedless, foolish or devilish, and yet we did not know it. Joseph had to bear with us, and tutor us, his children (*Memoirs of George A. Smith*, 25).

Early in June the men reached the Illinois River, and Heber Kimball recorded an interesting experience:

On Tuesday, the 3rd, several of us went up with the Prophet to the top of a mound on the bank of the Illinois River, which was several hundred feet above the river, and from the summit we had a pleasant view of the surrounding country. We could overlook the tops of the trees and the meadow or prairie on each side of the river as far as our eyes could extend, which was one of the most pleasant scenes I ever beheld. On the top of this mound there was the appearance of three altars, which had been built of stone, one above the other, according to the ancient order, and the ground was strewn with human bones. This caused in us very peculiar feelings, to see the bones of our fellow creatures scattered in this manner—fellow creatures who had been slain in ages past. We felt prompted to dig down into the mound, and sending for a shovel and hoe, we proceeded to move away the earth. At about one foot in depth we discovered the skeleton of a man, almost entire, and between two of his ribs we found an Indian arrow, which had evidently been the cause of his death. . . .

The same day we pursued our journey. While on our way we felt anxious to know who the person was who had been killed by that arrow. It was made known to Joseph that he had been an officer who fell in battle, in the last destruction among the Lamanites, and his name was Zelph. This caused us to rejoice much, to think that God was so mindful of us as to show these things to His servant. Brother Joseph had enquired of the Lord and it was made known to him in a vision (Whitney, *Life of Heber C. Kimball*, 46-47).

Joseph Smith adds a few more details about the warrior Zelph:

The visions of the past being opened to my understanding by the Spirit of the Almighty, I discovered that the person whose skeleton was before us was a white Lamanite, a large, thick-set man, and a man of God. His name was Zelph. He was a warrior and a chieftain under the great prophet Onandagus, who was known from the Hill Cumorah, or eastern sea to the

Rocky Mountains. The curse was taken from Zelph, or, at least in part—one of his thighbones was broken by a stone flung from a sling, while in battle, years before his death. He was killed in battle by the arrow found among his ribs, during the last great struggle of the Lamanites and Nephites (Smith, *History of the Church*, 2:79-80).

Heber C. Kimball recorded another prophecy Joseph Smith made that same day.

> While we were refreshing ourselves and teams, about the middle of the day, Brother Joseph got up in a wagon and said he would deliver a prophecy. After giving the brethren much good advice, he exhorted them to faithfulness and humility, and said the Lord had told him that there would be a scourge come upon the camp in consequence of the fractious and unruly spirits that appeared among them, and they would die like sheep with the rot; still if they would repent and humble themselves before the Lord, the scourge in a great measure might be turned away, "but, as the Lord lives, this camp will suffer for giving way to their unruly temper" (Whitney, *Life of Heber C. Kimball*, 47-48).

END OF THE CAMP, SUMMER 1834

On June 4, Zion's Camp reached the Mississippi River, which marked the boundary between Illinois and Missouri. Because the river was more than a mile wide at this point, it was necessary for the men to use a ferryboat to cross the great river.

After crossing, the group traveled to the Salt River where some members had settled. They camped there for a few days and were joined by the group from Michigan. Zion's Camp now numbered 205 volunteers.

While at Salt River, the brethren practiced with their weapons, drilled, marched, and caught up on personal matters. Heber C. Kimball decided to do his laundry.

> My first attempt at washing my clothes took place at Salt River. My shirts being extremely dirty, I put them into a kettle of water and boiled them for about two hours, having observed that women who washed boiled their clothes. . . . I then took them and washed them, endeavoring to imitate a woman washing as near as I could. I rubbed the clothes with my knuckles instead of the palm of my hand, and rubbed the skin off so that my hands were very sore for several days. My attempts were vain in trying to get the dirt out of the clothes. I wondered at this considerably, and scolded and fretted because I could not get the dirt out, and finally gave it up, and wrung them and hung them out to

WORLD EVENTS

Abraham Lincoln was elected to the Illinois legislature in 1834. At the age of twenty-five, he had worked as rail-splitter, boatman, storekeeper, post-master, and surveyor. He was a member of the Whig party, and wanted a powerful central government to encourage business, develop natural resources, and make internal improvements. He was elected President of the United States in 1860, issued the Emancipation Proclamation in 1863, and was assassinated in 1865.

ABRAHAM LINCOLN (1809–1865) *by Dale Kilbourn*

dry. Having no flat-irons to iron them, I took them to Sisters Holbrook and Ripley to get them ironed. When they saw them they said I had not washed my clothes. I told them I had done my best, and although I had boiled them two hours before washing, and had washed them so faithfully that I had taken the skin off my knuckles, still I had not been successful in getting the dirt out. They laughed heartily, and informed me that by boiling before washing I had boiled the dirt into them (Whitney, *Life of Heber C. Kimball*, 50).

Joseph sent Orson Hyde and Parley P. Pratt to Jefferson City to request that Governor Dunklin fulfill his pledge and restore the Saints to their land in Jackson County. Zion's Camp left the Salt River on June 12. Meanwhile, Parley Pratt had met with Governor Dunklin.

We had an interview with the Governor, who readily acknowledged the justice of the demand, but frankly told us he dare not attempt the execution of the laws in that respect, for fear of deluging the whole country in civil war and bloodshed. He advised us to relinquish our rights, for the sake of peace, and to sell our lands from which we had been driven. . . . We retired, saying to ourselves: "That poor coward ought, in duty, to resign; he owes this, morally at least, in justice to his oath of office" (*Autobiography of Parley P. Pratt*, 94).

In the meantime, rumors were flying in Jackson County. John Corrill recorded: "[The mob] repaired to the different ferries on the river, to guard them, and I have been credibly informed that they have since continued to guard the river . . . from one end of Jackson County to the other. And for fear that we would return and enjoy our dwellings again, they set fire to and burned them down, and then raised a report that the 'Mormons' went over and burnt their houses" (Smith, *History of the Church*, 2:92, n.8).

About 150 Mormon homes were destroyed, and weapons were distributed to the anti-Mormon residents of Jackson County. Some families left the county, either because they did not share the violent hatred for the Mormons, or because they feared being caught in the middle of a battle.

On Sunday, June 15, Elders Pratt and Hyde returned to Zion's Camp and reported their visit with Governor Dunklin. Joseph and some of the other brethren met with them in a solitary grove and were very disappointed to learn of the Governor's response. The Saints were surprised at the Governor's stance since, just days before his meeting with Pratt and Hyde, he had written in a letter to Colonel J. Thornton stating, "A more clear and indisputable right does not exist, than that of the Mormon people, who were expelled from their homes in Jackson County, to return and live on their lands" (Smith, *History of the Church*, 2:85).

However, when the time came, Dunklin feared that war would erupt if he helped the Mormons return to their homes. So he did nothing.

The following day, Judge Wylan tried to seek a compromise. He called a meeting at the Liberty Courthouse in Clay County, where a group of Jackson County citizens presented a proposal. They proposed that either they would buy the Mormon land at double the assessed value, if the Mormons would promise never to return, or that the Mormons could buy all of their enemies' land at double the assessed value, and they would leave the country. The Mormons promised to respond in a week. They also promised that they would not initiate any hostilities in the meantime.

Zion's Camp was located on the bank of the Grand River. After the meeting in Liberty, James Campbell, one of the residents of Jackson County, decided to return to Jackson, raise an army, and go out and meet Joseph Smith and Zion's Camp. Campbell vowed, "The eagles and turkey buzzards shall eat my flesh if I do not fix Joe Smith and his army so that their skins will not hold shucks, before two days are passed" (Smith, *History of the Church,* 2:99).

Joseph Smith recorded Campbell's fate:

> They went to the ferry and undertook to cross the Missouri River after dusk, and the angel of God saw fit to sink the boat about the middle of the river, and seven out of the twelve that attempted to cross, were drowned. Thus, suddenly and justly, went they to their own place. Campbell was among the missing. He floated down the river some four or five miles, and lodged upon a pile of drift wood, where the eagles, buzzards, ravens, crows, and wild animals ate his flesh from his bones, to fulfill his own words (Smith, *History of the Church*, 2:99).

Each day, Zion's Camp drew closer to Jackson County and danger. There were constant rumors that mobbers were about to attack the camp. Occasionally, armed men would ride into camp, make threats, and then ride away. Although the Saints tried to move as fast as possible, they were plagued with wagon problems and other inconveniences. On Thursday evening, they made camp on an elevated piece of land between the Little Fishing and Big Fishing Rivers. Heber C. Kimball recorded:

> Just as we halted and were making preparations for the night, five men rode into camp and told us we should see hell before morning, and such horrible oaths as came from their lips I never heard before. They told us that sixty men were coming from Richmond, who had sworn to destroy us, also seventy more were coming from Clay County, to assist in our destruction. These men were black with passion, and armed with guns, and the whole country was in a rage against us, and nothing but the power of God could save us. All this time the weather was pleasant. Soon after these men left us we discovered a small black cloud rising in the west, and not more than twenty minutes passed away before it began to rain and hail; but we had very little hail in our camp. All around us the hail was heavy; some of

the hailstones, or rather lumps of ice, were large as hens' eggs. The thunder rolled with awful majesty, and the red lightnings flashed through the horizon, making it so light that I could see to pick up a pin almost any time through the night. The earth quaked and trembled, and there being no cessation it seemed as though the Almighty had issued forth His mandate of vengeance. The wind was so terrible that many of our tents were blown down. We were not able to hold them up; but there being an old meeting house close at hand, many of us fled there to secure ourselves from the storm. Many trees were blown down, and others were twisted and wrung like a withe. The mob came to the river two miles from us, but the river had risen to that height that they were obliged to stop without crossing over. The hail fell so heavily upon them that it beat holes in their hats, and in some instances even broke the stocks off their guns; their horses, being frightened, fled, leaving the riders on the ground. Their powder was wet, and it was evident that the Almighty fought in our defense. This night the river raised forty feet.

In the morning I went to the river in company with Brother Joseph Smith, Hyrum Smith, Brigham Young and others, as we had it in contemplation to proceed that morning to Liberty, Clay County; but we could not continue our journey as there was no way to cross the river. It was then overflowing its banks. . . . Previous to this rain falling, it was no more than ankle deep. . . .

The next day, when we moved into the country we saw that the hail had destroyed the crops, and we saw that it had come in some directions within a mile and in other directions within a half mile of our camp. . . . The ground was literally covered with branches of the trees which had been cut off by the hail (Whitney, *Life of Heber C. Kimball*, 52-54).

Zion's Camp traveled five miles and then camped again. Here, Colonel Sconce and two other men from Ray County visited them. Joseph related:

[They] came to see us, desiring to know what our intentions were; "for," said he, "I see that there is an Almighty power that protects this people, for I started from Richmond . . . with a company of armed men, having a fixed determination to destroy you, but was kept back by the storm, and was not able to reach you." When he entered our camp he was seized with such a trembling that he was obliged to sit down to compose himself. . . . I . . . gave a relation of the sufferings of the Saints in Jackson County, and also our persecutions generally, and what we had suffered by our enemies for our religion; and that we had come one thousand miles to assist our brethren, to bring them clothing, etc., and to reinstate them upon their own lands; and that we had no intention to molest or injure any people, but only to administer to the wants of our afflicted friends; and that the evil reports circulated about us were false, and got up by our enemies to procure our destruction. When I had closed a lengthy speech, the spirit of which melted them into compassion, they arose and offered me their hands, and said they would use their influence to allay the excitement which everywhere prevailed against us (Smith, *History of the Church*, 2:105-6).

CHOLERA

Then cholera broke out in the camp. Joseph Hancock, who had become ill during the storm was the first victim. Joseph called the camp together and told them that the cholera was the sickness he had prophesied would come upon them due to their rebelliousness and disobedience. On Sunday, June 22, Joseph received a revelation from the Lord explaining His will regarding the city of Zion in Jackson County.

> . . . Were it not for the transgressions of my people, speaking concerning the church and not individuals, they might have been redeemed even now.
>
> But behold, they have not learned to be obedient . . . but are full of all manner of evil. . . .
>
> And are not united according to the union required by the law of the celestial kingdom; And Zion cannot be built up unless it is by the principles of the law of the celestial kingdom; otherwise I cannot receive her unto myself. . . .
>
> Therefore, in consequence of the transgressions of my people, it is expedient in me that mine elders should wait for a little season for the redemption of Zion—That they themselves may be prepared, and that my people will be taught more perfectly, and have experience, and know more perfectly concerning their duty, and the things which I require at their hands. . . .
>
> For behold, I do not require at their hands to fight the battles of Zion; for, as I said in a former commandment . . . I will fight your battles (D&C 105:2-5, 9-10, 14).

In this revelation, Section 105 in the Doctrine and Covenants, the Lord commanded the Saints to retain title to their land in Jackson County and instructed them to buy more land when they were able. Some members of Zion's Camp were counseled to settle in Missouri, but they were warned not to reveal the Lord's plans to their nonbelieving neighbors. The Lord promised the Saints that they would one day possess Zion, "but first let my army become very great, and let it be sanctified before me, that it may become fair as the sun, and clear as the moon, and that her banners may be terrible unto all nations;

That the kingdoms of this world may be constrained to acknowledge that the kingdom of Zion is in very deed the kingdom of our God and his Christ" (D&C 105:31-32).

George A. Smith recorded in his journal that after this revelation was received, several men apostatized because they were not allowed to fight against the Missourians.

When the time came for the Mormons to reply to the compromise proposals, Bishop Partridge and others met with Joseph to discuss the situation. The Saints wanted to buy their neighbors' land, but they could not raise the money since they had been driven from their homes and all of their possessions had been stolen or destroyed.

A counterproposal was drafted and signed by Joseph Smith and others, offering to buy out those who felt they could not live with the Mormons in Jackson County. Payment was to be made in one year, and the value of the land was to be determined by twelve disinterested men, six from each group. On Monday, June 23, Zion's Camp was within five miles of Liberty, but they were asked not to enter the city in order to prevent possible problems with local residents. Accordingly, they camped near Sidney Gilbert's home on the banks of Rush Creek.

A council of high priests assembled, and some of the men, including Edward Partridge, William Phelps, Isaac Morley, John Corrill, John, Peter, Christian and David Whitmer, Newel Knight, Parley Pratt, and Simeon Carter were called to go to Kirtland to be endowed in the new temple. Sidney Gilbert was one of those called, but he said that he could not do it. The next day, the cholera broke out all over the camp. Joseph recorded:

> Our ears were saluted with cries and moanings, and lamentations on every hand; even those on guard fell to the earth with their guns in their hands, so sudden and powerful was the attack of this terrible disease. At the commencement, I attempted to lay on hands for their recovery, but I quickly learned by painful experience, that when the great Jehovah decrees destruction on any people, and makes known His determination, man must not attempt to stay His hand. The moment I attempted to rebuke the disease I was attacked, and had I not desisted in my attempt to save the life of a brother, I would have sacrificed my own (Smith, *History of the Church*, 2:114).

Immersing the victim in cold water was thought to cure the disease, so some members of Zion's Camp climbed into the creek for relief. In all, sixty-eight Saints were struck with the disease and fourteen died, including John Carter, Seth Hancock, Sidney Gilbert, Jesse Smith, Eber Wilcox, and Betsy Parish.

To help prevent the spread of the disease, the members of Zion's Camp were dispersed among Church members in the area. The epidemic lasted four long days. All who were not sick worked to care for those who were. Finally, Joseph called the brethren together and told them that if they would keep the Lord's commandments, and obey the Prophet's counsel, the plague would be stayed. The brethren covenanted with uplifted hands, and the disease was stopped.

On July 3, Joseph Smith authorized Lyman Wight to discharge the members of Zion's Camp. That same day, Joseph also organized a high council like the one in Kirtland. David Whitmer was called to serve as president of the second stake in the Church, with William W. Phelps and John Whitmer as counselors. The members of the high council were Christian Whitmer, Newel Knight, Lyman Wight, Calvin Bebee, William E. McLellin, Solomon Hancock,

Thomas B. Marsh, Simeon Carter, Parley P. Pratt, Orson Pratt, John Murdock, and Levi Jackman.

RESULTS OF ZION'S CAMP, WINTER 1834–35

While camped in Missouri, Wilford Woodruff wrote to an old friend:

> When I arrived, at my journey's end, I took the first opportunity and I wrote a long letter to Father Mason, and I told him I had found the church of Christ that he had told me about. I told him about its organization and the coming forth of the Book of Mormon; that the Church had Prophets, Apostles, and all the gifts and blessings in it, and that the true fruit of the kingdom and church of Christ were manifest among the Saints as the Lord had shown him in the vision. He received my letter and read it over many times, and handled it as he had handled the fruit in the vision; but he was very aged, and soon died. He did not live to see any Elder to administer the ordinances of the gospel unto him.
>
> The first opportunity I had, after the doctrine of baptism for the dead was revealed, I went forth and was baptized for him. He was a good man and a true prophet, for his prophecies have been fulfilled (Wilford Woodruff, "Leaves from My Journal," 8).

Some felt that Zion's Camp was a failure because the Saints in Jackson County had not been returned to their homes. However, the men had brought much-needed supplies to the members, and perhaps more importantly, the camp served to unite the Saints together in a brotherhood. Most of the men in Zion's Camp had only been members of the Church for a short time, and many had never met the Prophet before this time. The experience shared by these New Englanders, New Yorkers, Ohioans, frontiersmen, craftsmen, and farmers united them in more than faith alone. Joseph Young, the father of Brigham Young, related:

> Brother Joseph Smith said to Brother Brigham and Brother Joseph, "If you will go with me in the camp to Missouri, and keep my counsel, I promise you, in the name of the Almighty, that I will lead you there and back again, and not a hair of your head shall be harmed." We followed the prophet to Missouri, and kept his counsel, every jot and tittle, and we were preserved according to the prophet's words. The men of that camp were a band of brethren. Joseph the prophet led us to Zion, not as a haughty chieftain, not as an arrogant man, but a man filled with the Holy Ghost, and oh how kind and modest he was when he led us, but, how determined and resolute in carrying out the will of the Lord (*Manuscript History of Brigham Young*, 8).

One man who especially benefitted from participating in Zion's Camp and studying under Joseph Smith was Brigham Young. The things he learned would help him lead the Church through future trials. Just as he had done during his first months in Kirtland, Brigham Young had closely observed his camp leader, taking mental notes on how an expedition might be led. This knowledge proved valuable when he later organized the Saints to travel to the Salt Lake Valley.

Joseph Smith left Missouri on July 9 with his brother Hyrum, Frederick G. Williams, and several others. On the way, he stopped in Richmond, Missouri to visit the newspaper editor who had printed a story claiming that "Joe Smith, the Mormon leader" had been wounded in a battle with the mob, and had died three days later as a result of those wounds. Even with the living evidence to the contrary standing in his office, the editor had difficulty believing that Joe Smith was not dead.

JOSEPH RETURNS TO KIRTLAND

When Joseph Smith returned to his family and the Saints in Kirtland, he found gossip, rumors, and accusations spreading out of control. The first man from Zion's Camp to reach Kirtland was Roger Orton. He had left Missouri during the cholera epidemic and had reported that everyone was dying, which greatly alarmed those who were waiting for their fathers and husbands. Some felt the whole undertaking had been a failure. Others regretted that there had been no fighting. Sylvester Smith was especially outspoken against the Prophet. He called Joseph a tyrant, a pope, a king, a usurper, an abuser of men, an angel, and a false prophet who prophesied lies in the name of the Lord and took consecrated monies. The Kirtland high council met to discuss these charges and found Joseph innocent. Sylvester later apologized.

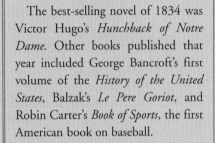

Joseph wrote the brethren in Missouri, told them the news from Kirtland, reviewed the things he had taught them before he left, and urged them to continue to petition the governor and president for the right to return to their land. He also advised them to:

> [U]se every effort . . . to gather . . . and locate themselves, to be in readiness to move into Jackson County in two years from the eleventh of September next, which is the appointed time for the redemption of Zion . . . if the church with one united effort perform their duties. . . . Let not this be noised abroad; let every heart beat in silence, and every mouth be shut. . . . We have a great work to do, and but little time to do it in; and if we do not exert ourselves to the utmost in gathering up the strength of the Lord's house . . . there remaineth a scourge for the Church, even that they shall be driven from city to city, and but few shall remain to receive an inheritance (Smith, *History of the Church*, 2:145-46).

The Saints in Missouri continued rebuilding their lives in Clay County. Bishop Partridge's daughter, Emily, recorded how her family lived:

The Saints found homes as best they could, searching out and making habitable all the old shanties and hovels that could be found, endeavoring to keep as near together as possible. Father and Elder John Corrill procured an old log cabin that had been used for a stable, and cleaned it up as best they could and moved their families in. There were one large room and a lean-to, but that was not of much use as the floor was nearly all torn up, and the rats and rattlesnakes were too thick for comfort. There was a large fireplace in the one habitable room, and blankets were hung up a few feet back from the fire, and the two families, 15 or 16 in number, were gathered inside of those blankets to keep from freezing, for the weather was extremely cold. So cold that the ink would freeze in the pen as father sat writing close to the fire (*Women's Exponent*, 15 Feb. 1885, 138).

Since they didn't own much land in Clay County, most of the Mormons were forced to work as day laborers. Typical wages were fifty cents a day, and were earned by cutting wood, quarrying stone, making bricks, working in mills, or building homes for the wealthy. The women spun cloth or did laundry. Soon after the Saints arrived, a large slaughterhouse was built, and many found jobs slaughtering hogs and packing meat for shipping. Joseph Knight built a gristmill; and some of the men taught school. Many of the young women, including Eliza Partridge, taught in small home schools. Eliza wrote: "It was no uncommon thing in those days for our Mormon girls to go out among the Missourians and teach their children for a small remuneration. I received but thirty dollars and my board while I was gone" (Hyrum L. Andrus, *Doctrines of the Kingdom*, 343).

An experienced schoolteacher might earn thirty-five dollars a month. Corn was twenty cents a bushel and wheat forty cents. Seventy-five pounds of flour could be purchased for one dollar and seventy-five cents; and pork was two dollars and fifty cents per hundredweight. The Mormons gained a reputation for thrift and industry. A non-Mormon named Thorp wrote:

> The Mormons, in the main, were industrious, good workers, and gave general satisfaction to their employers, and could live on less than any people I ever knew. Their women could fix a good palatable meal out of that which a gentile's wife would not know how to commence to get one half a dinner or breakfast. They had the knack of economizing, which was a great help to their men, as they had mostly to earn their bread and butter by day work (Joseph Thorp, *Early Days in the West*, March 1924, 2–4).

WORLD EVENTS

An invention that received little attention in 1834 would later change the world. An English mathematician named Charles Babbage, frustrated by the inaccuracies of mathematical tables, invented a machine that would rapidly and accurately calculate complex mathematical functions. He called it an analytical engine. The machine required thousands of wheels, levers, and belts, was as big as a football field, and needed half a dozen steam locomotives to power it. The analytical engine was never built, but the theories behind it led to the modern computer.

As soon as they were able to do so, the Saints began to buy land and establish their own farms and businesses in Clay County.

Joseph Smith spent the late summer and fall quarrying rock for the Kirtland temple, attending to Church business and taking short missionary journeys. In Pontiac, Michigan, Edward Stevenson saw the prophet preach for the first time. Edward later recorded:

> I first saw Joseph Smith at Pontiac, Michigan, in 1834, when he visited the Pontiac Branch. The meetings were crowded. The Prophet stood at a table for a pulpit. Before he got through, he was in the midst of the congregation with uplifted hand. His countenance seemed to assume a heavenly whiteness. He testified with great power concerning the visit of the Father and the Son, and the conversation he had with them. Never before did I feel such power. . . .
>
> During the Prophet's visit, he came to our house. My heart swelled with love as I selected and presented him with some of our choice apples (Andrus, *They Knew the Prophet,* 85-86).

In the meantime, work continued on the temple in Kirtland. Heber C. Kimball recorded some of the sacrifices his family made:

> Our women were engaged in knitting and spinning, in order to clothe those who were laboring at the building. And the Lord only knows the scenes of poverty, and tribulation and distress, which we all passed through to accomplish it. My wife would toil all summer. She took 100 pounds of wool to spin on shares which, with the assistance of a girl, she spun, in order to furnish clothing for those engaged in building the temple. And although she had the privilege of keeping half the quantity of wool for herself, as her recompense for her labor, she did not reserve even so much as would make a pair of stockings. She spun and wove and got the cloth dressed and cut and made up into garments, and gave them to the laborers. Almost all the sisters in Kirtland, labored in knitting, sewing, spinning, etc, for the same purpose, while we went up to Missouri.
>
> After we returned from our journey to the West, the whole Church united in this great undertaking, and every man lent a helping hand. Those who had not teams went to work in the stone quarry and prepare the stones. . . . The prophet, being our foreman, would put on his tow frock, and tow pantaloons, and go into the quarry. The Presidency, High Priests, and Elders, all alike, assisting. Those who had teams assisted in drawing the stone to the house (Whitney, *Life of Heber C. Kimball,* 67-68).

The new semester of the School of the Prophets, the new building for the printing office and many other matters occupied Joseph's days. He recorded, "No month ever found me more busily engaged than November; but, as my life consisted of activity and unyielding exertions, I made this my rule: *When the Lord commands, do it*" (Smith, *History of the Church,* 2:170).

In December, Joseph and Emma received their patriarchal blessings from Joseph Smith, Sr., the Church Patriarch. Joseph's blessing reviewed and reinforced promises made to him by various heavenly messengers. Emma's blessing contained the following:

> Emma, thou art blessed of the Lord, for thy faithfulness and truth, thou shalt be blessed with thy husband, and rejoice in the glory which shall come upon him. Thy soul has been afflicted because of the wickedness of men in seeking the destruction of thy companion, and thy whole soul has been drawn out in prayer for his deliverance; rejoice, for the Lord thy God has heard thy supplications. Thou hast grieved for the hardness of the hearts of thy father's house, and thou hast longed for their salvation. The Lord will have respect to thy cries, and by his judgments will cause some of them to see their folly and repent of their sins; but it will be by affliction that they will be saved. Thou shalt see many days, yea the Lord will spare thee till thou art satisfied, for thou shalt see thy Redeemer. Thy heart shalt rejoice in the great work of the Lord, and no one shall take thy rejoicing from thee. Thou shalt ever remember the great condescension of thy God in permitting thee to accompany my son when the angel delivered the record of the Nephites to his care. Thou hast seen much sorrow because the Lord has taken from thee three of thy children. In this thou art not to be blamed, for he knows thy pure desires to raise up a family, that the name of my son might be blessed. And now, behold, I say unto thee, that thus sayeth the Lord, if thou will believe, thou shalt yet be blessed in this thing and thou shalt bring forth other children to the joy and satisfaction of thy soul, and to the rejoicing of thy friends. Thou shalt be blessed with understanding, and the power to instruct thy sex, teach thy family righteousness, and thy little ones the way of life, the holy angels shall watch over thee and thou shalt be saved in the kingdom of God (Emma Hale Smith, patriarchal blessing, given by Patriarch Joseph Smith, Sr., 9 December, 1834, Kirtland Ohio, Patriarchal Blessing Book #1, LDS Archives).

Early in 1835, Brigham and Joseph Young visited with Joseph Smith one Sunday afternoon. Brigham recorded:

> When Zion's Camp went to Missouri in 1834, there were no apostles or seventies in the Church. After we'd returned, my brother, Joseph Young, and myself had been singing after preaching in a meeting. Brother Joseph Smith said, "Come, go down to my house with me."
> We went and sang to him a long time, and talked with him. He then opened the subject of the Twelve and Seventies for the first time I ever thought of it (Andrus, *They Knew the Prophet*, 35).

Joseph Young recorded part of what the Prophet told them:

> On the 8th day of February, in the year of our Lord 1835, the Prophet Joseph Smith called Elders Brigham and Joseph Young to the chamber of his residence in Kirtland, Ohio, it being the Sabbath day. . . . He proceeded to

relate a vision . . . of the state and condition of those men who died in Zion's Camp, in Missouri. He said, "Brethren, I have seen those men who died of the cholera in our camp; and the Lord knows if I get a mansion as bright as theirs, I ask no more." At this revelation he wept, and for a time he could not speak. He said to[Brigham], "I wish you to notify all the brethren living in the branches, within a reasonable distance from this place, to meet at a general conference on Saturday next. I shall then and there appoint twelve Special Witnesses, to open the door of the Gospel to foreign nations, and you . . . will be one of them." He then proceeded to enlarge upon the duties of their calling. . . . He then turned to Elder Joseph Young with quite an earnestness, as though the vision of his mind was extended still further, and addressing him, said, "Brother Joseph, the Lord has made you President of the Seventies." . . . It was a strange saying, "The Lord has made you President of the Seventies," as though it had already taken place, and it caused these brethren to marvel (Smith, *History of the Church*, 2:181 n.).

APOSTLES AND SEVENTIES

The meeting was called and the brethren assembled. Joseph introduced the business, which was to appoint twelve apostles and the seventies. He lectured on the duties of the men who would hold these offices, and asked the congregation if they would be satisfied to have the Spirit of the Lord dictate the choice of the elders to be apostles. All present agreed that the Lord should choose the men, and the meeting proceeded. They sang a hymn and then adjourned the meeting for an hour. When they met again, Oliver Cowdery, David Whitmer, and Martin Harris, the Three Witnesses to the Book of Mormon, prayed and were blessed by the First Presidency. They then named the first twelve apostles of this dispensation.

The men were: Lyman E. Johnson, Brigham Young, Heber C. Kimball, Orson Hyde, David W. Patton, Lucas Johnson, William E. McLellin, John F. Boynton, Orson Pratt, William Smith, Thomas B. Marsh, and Parley P. Pratt. Most of these men were ordained to their calling later that day by the Three Witnesses. Parley and Orson Pratt, and Thomas B. Marsh, however, were away on missions, and were ordained when they returned from the mission field.

Heber C. Kimball recorded his feelings when this calling came to him:

> It was far from my expectation of being one of the number, as heretofore I had known nothing about it, not having the privilege of seeing the revelations, as they were not printed. . . . We were severally called in to the Stand, and there received our ordinations, under the hands of Oliver Cowdery, David Whitmer, and Martin Harris. These brethren ordained us to the apostleship, and predicted many things which should come to pass, that we should have power to heal the sick, cast out devils, raise the dead, give sight to the blind, have power to remove mountains, and all things should be subject to us through the name of Jesus Christ, and angels should minister unto us, and many more things too numerous to mention (*Times and Seasons*, 6:868).

Revelations and Scriptures, 1835

In the historic meeting where the twelve apostles were named, Oliver Cowdery delivered a general charge to the new apostles, telling them that before the Church was organized in 1830:

> The Lord gave us a revelation that, in process of time, there should be twelve men chosen to preach His Gospel, to Jew and Gentile. Our minds have been on a constant stretch, to find who these twelve were; when the time should come we could not tell; but we sought the Lord by fasting and prayer to have our lives prolonged to see this day, to see you. . . . You will have difficulties by reason of your visiting all the nations of the world. You will need wisdom in a tenfold proportion to what you have ever had; you will have to combat the prejudices of all nations. Should you in the least degree come short of your duty, great shall be your condemnation, for the greater the calling, the greater the transgression. I therefore warn you to cultivate great humility. . . .
>
> It is necessary that you receive a testimony from heaven for yourselves; so that you can bear testimony to the truth of the Book of Mormon, and that you have seen the face of God. . . . Never cease striving until you have seen God face to face. Strengthen your faith; cast off your doubts, your sins, and all your unbelief; and nothing can prevent you from coming to God. Your ordination is not full and complete till God has laid His hand upon you (Smith, *History of the Church*, 2:194-96).

Joseph Smith instructed the apostles always to keep a record of their meetings. He said that he had learned the importance of record keeping through sad experience, for he had neglected to keep notes of all the decisions, items of doctrine, and other matters in the early days of his ministry. On February 28, the members of the Church met again, and the members of the First Quorum of Seventy were selected. The seven presidents were: Hazen Aldrich, Joseph Young, Levi W. Hancock, Leonard Rich, Zebedee Coltrin, Lyman Sherman, and Silvester Smith. All of these men had been members of Zion's Camp. Of these men, Joseph Smith said:

> Brethren, some of you are angry with me, because you did not fight in Missouri; but let me tell you, God did not want you to fight. He could not organize his kingdom with twelve men to open the gospel door to the nations of the earth, and with seventy men under their direction to follow in their tracks, unless he took them from a body of men who had offered their lives, and who had made as great a sacrifice as did Abraham. Now, the Lord has got his twelve and his seventy (Roberts, *A Comprehensive History of the Church*, 1:377-78).

Thomas B. Marsh became the first President of the Quorum of the Twelve. This decision was made on the basis of age. He was the oldest. The rest of the brethren were then assigned their positions in the quorum according to their ages. Later, seniority in the quorum became based on date of ordination, rather than physical age. On March 28, 1835, the new quorum of apostles met with the First Presidency of the Church. The twelve were soon called on various missions to begin their task of carrying the gospel to the world. The men, overwhelmed by the size of the work before them, and by their own feelings of inadequacy, sought a revelation from the Lord.

The revelation they received is contained in Section 107 of the Doctrine and Covenants and is subtitled "The Revelation on Priesthood."

> There are, in the church, two priesthoods, namely, the Melchizedek and Aaronic . . . . The Melchizedek Priesthood holds the right of presidency, and has power and authority over all the offices in the church in all ages of the world, to administer in spiritual things. . . . The second priesthood is called the Priesthood of Aaron. . . . It is an appendage to the greater, or the Melchizedek Priesthood, and has power in administering outward ordinances. . . . The twelve traveling councilors are called to be the Twelve Apostles, or special witnesses of the name of Christ in all the world—thus differing from other officers in the church in the duties of their calling. . . . The Seventy are also called to preach the gospel, and to be especial witnesses unto the Gentiles and in all the world. The decisions of these quorums, or either of them, are to be made in all righteousness, in holiness, and lowliness of heart, meekness, and long suffering, and in faith, and virtue and knowledge, temperance, patience, godliness, brotherly kindness and charity. . . . It is the duty of the Twelve, also, to ordain and set in order all the other officers of the church, . . . And again the duty of the President of the office of the High Priesthood is to preside over the whole church, and to be like unto Moses. . . . yea, to be a seer, a revelator, a translator, and a prophet, having all the gifts of God, which he bestows upon the head of the church (D&C 107:1, 8, 13-14, 23, 25, 30, 58, 91-92).

This revelation tells the duties and privileges of the offices in the priesthood, and outlines some of the history of the priesthood upon the earth. It concludes with this challenge:

> Wherefore, now let every man learn his duty, and to act in the office in which he is appointed, in all diligence.
> He that is slothful shall not be counted worthy to stand, and he that learns not his duty, and shows himself not approved shall not be counted worthy to stand. Even so. Amen (D&C 107:99-100).

Having been ordained, taught, and prepared, the new apostles set forth on their missions to the world on May 4, 1835. As in ancient times, they traveled two by two without purse or scrip. They were called to the eastern United States and Canada. While they were gone, Elders John Whitmer and W. W. Phelps, two of the leaders of the Church in Missouri, arrived in Kirtland. Brother Whitmer was appointed to be the new editor of the Church newspaper, the

In New York City, the *New York Herald* was started in a cellar in 1835. James Gordon Bennett, the paper's publisher, editor, and salesman, produced the four-page penny paper. The paper was unique for the time because it did not support any political party or interest group, but instead, tried to report all the news. Although Bennett wanted to startle his readers more than inform them, he pioneered modern reporting techniques, and his paper was soon a commercial success.

Hans Christian Anderson published his first stories, including *Tinderbox* and *The Princess and the Pea*. German poet and liberal social critic, Heinrich Heine published a critical history of Germany's religion and philosophy. The German government, however, fearing social reform, banned his works.

PEARL OF GREAT PRICE FACSIMILE NO. 2 from the Book of Abraham representing, among other important concepts, the creation and the Godhead.

Messenger and Advocate. Brother Phelps, meanwhile, moved in with Joseph Smith's family, and helped compile and edit the Book of Commandments.

Work on the temple slowed as men attended the School of the Prophets and went on missions, but progress continued.

THE WRITINGS OF ABRAHAM AND JOSEPH

Visitors frequently came to Kirtland to meet the prophet. However, one visitor during that summer of 1835 brought items of special interest to the Church. Joseph notes that:

On the 3rd of July, Michael H. Chandler came to Kirtland to exhibit some Egyptian mummies. There were four human figures, together with some two or more rolls of papyrus, covered with hieroglyphic figures and devices. As Mr. Chandler had been told I could translate them, he brought me some of the characters, and I gave him the interpretation. . . . Soon after this, some of the Saints at Kirtland purchased the mummies and papyrus, . . . and with W. W. Phelps, and Oliver Cowdery as scribes, I commenced the translation of some of the characters or hieroglyphics, and much to our joy, found that one of the rolls contained the writings of Abraham, another the writings of Joseph of Egypt. . . . Truly we can say, the Lord is beginning to reveal the abundance of peace and truth (Smith, *History of the Church*, 2:235-36).

Oliver Cowdery wrote to a friend about the history of the mummies.

Upon the subject of the Egyptian records, or rather the writings of Abraham and Joseph . . . I may say a few words. This record is beautifully written in papyrus with black, and a small part, red ink or paint, in perfect preservation. The characters are such as you find upon the coffins of mummies, hieroglyphics and etc. with many characters or letters exactly like the present, though perhaps not quite so square. . . .

These records were obtained from one of the Catacombs in Egypt, near the place where once stood the renowned City of Thebes, by the Celebrated French Traveller, Antonio Sebolo. . . .

[Eleven of the mummies were removed.] He made a will of the whole to Mr. Michael H. Chandler, then in Philadelphia, Pa., his nephew. . . . Mr. Chandler paid the duties upon his mummies and took possession of the same. Up to this time they had not been taken out of the coffins or the coffins opened.

On opening the coffins he discovered that in connection with two of the bodies were something rolled up with the same kind of linen, saturated with the same bitumen, which when examined proved to be two rolls of papyrus. . . .

The language in which this record is written is very comprehensive, and many of the hieroglyphics exceedingly striking.

The evidence is apparent upon the fact, that they were written by persons acquainted with the history of the Creation, the fall of man, and more or less of the correct ideas . . . of the Deity.

The representation of the Godhead—three—yet in one, is curiously drawn to give simply, though impressively, the writers' views of that exalted personage (Gunn, *Oliver Cowdery, Second Elder and Scribe*, 235-38).

The body of scripture was growing. The revelations Joseph Smith had received were compiled and made available to all the members of the Church. In August 1835, Church members voted to accept these revelations as scripture and to call them the Doctrine and Covenants.

SKETCH OF THE GUIDE TO JOSEPH SMITH PAPYRI Papyrus included with Egyptian mummies in the Chandler exhibit. Joseph was able to translate the hieroglyphics and found that they contained the writings of Abraham, and Joseph of Egypt.

An earlier attempt to print some of the revelations had failed when the press was taken by the mob and the printing plates destroyed. However, this new book, in addition to the revelations, included a series of lectures that had been delivered at the School of the Prophets, called the *Lectures on Faith*. It also included two articles written by Oliver Cowdery on government and marriage. Since these lectures and articles were not considered scripture, they were not included in later editions.

Many people were now learning about and accepting the gospel. Miss Eliza Roxey Snow knew about the Mormons; her mother and sister had joined the Church when the missionaries first came to Ohio, but it was not until 1835 that she embraced the gospel. Shortly after her baptism, Eliza recorded:

As I was reflecting on the wonderful events transpiring around me, I felt an indescribable, tangible sensation . . . commencing at my head and enveloping my person and passing off at my feet, producing inexpressible happiness. Immediately following, I saw a beautiful candle with an unusual long, bright blaze, directly over my feet. I sought to know the interpretation, and received the following: "The lamp of intelligence shall be lighted over your path" (Janet Peterson and LaRene Gaunt, *Elect Ladies*, 26).

After her baptism, Eliza lived with Joseph and Emma Smith and taught school. She was anxious for her brother, Lorenzo, to share the joy she had found, so she urged him to join her in Kirtland and study Hebrew with the brethren. He was attending Oberlin College and wanted to graduate and become a great military leader. Lorenzo had seen Joseph and heard him preach in 1831, in Hiram, Ohio. But at the age of 17, he was not very interested in religious matters. At Oberlin, he was exposed to various religious denominations, but was not impressed. He wrote to his sister, Eliza, "If there is nothing better than is to be found here in Oberlin College, goodbye to all religions" (Eliza R. Snow, *Biography and Family Record of Lorenzo Snow*, 5).

In the autumn of 1835, he left Oberlin and moved to Kirtland to study Hebrew. By then, the apostles had returned from their missions and the School of the Prophets had resumed. Joshua Seixas was teaching Hebrew. The temple walls had been finished, and they sparkled from the special plaster that had been made with crushed glassware. The roof was completed, and the masons were putting the finishing coat of plaster on the interior.

GLORIOUS VISIONS

December was peaceful for the Smith family in Kirtland that year. They lived in what formerly had been the Gilbert and Whitney general store. Julia was now almost five years old, and little Joseph had recently celebrated his third birthday. Joseph and Emma also rejoiced in the knowledge that another baby would be born next June.

The winter was cold, and the snow was about a foot deep. Joseph's daily diary indicates how he spent the winter.

> *Sunday, 20.*—At home all day. Took solid comfort with my family. Had many serious reflections. . . .
>
> *Monday, 21.*—At home. Continued my studies. O may God give me learning, even language; and endow me with qualifications to magnify His name while I live. . . .
>
> *Tuesday, 22.*—Spent this day endeavoring to treasure up knowledge for the benefit of my calling.
>
> *Wednesday 23.*—In the forenoon, at home, studying the Greek language. And also waited upon the brethren who came in, and exhibited to them the papyrus. . . .

Friday 25.—Enjoyed myself at home with my family, all day, it being Christmas, the only time I have had this privilege so satisfactorily for a long period.

Sunday 27.—At the usual hour, attending meeting at the school house. President Cowdery delivered a very able and interesting discourse.

In the afternoon, Brother Hyrum Smith and Bishop Partridge delivered each a short and interesting lecture, after which the sacrament was administered (Smith, *History of the Church*, 2:344-45).

That December, the first Church hymn books were printed. The hymns included standard Christian favorites, as well as compositions by Church members like W. W. Phelps, and Parley Pratt. The hymns were printed without music, and were sung to familiar melodies that may have differed in each congregation.

On January 21, 1836, Joseph Smith and many leading authorities of the Church held a very spiritual meeting. As they participated in the ordinances of the priesthood, a marvelous vision was opened to Joseph:

> The heavens were opened upon us, and I beheld the celestial kingdom of God, and the glory thereof, whether in the body or out I cannot tell.
>
> I saw the transcendent beauty of the gate through which the heirs of that kingdom will enter, which was like unto circling flames of fire;
>
> Also the blazing of throne of God, whereon was seated the Father and the Son.
>
> I saw the beautiful streets of that kingdom, which had the appearance of being paved with gold. I saw fathers Adam, and Abraham; and my father and mother; and my brother Alvin, that has long since slept.
>
> And I marveled how it was that he had obtained an inheritance in that kingdom, seeing that he had departed this life before the Lord had set his hand to gather Israel the second time, and had not been baptized for the remission of sins.
>
> Thus came the voice of the Lord unto me, saying: "All who have died without a knowledge of this gospel, who would have received it if they had been permitted to tarry, shall be heirs of the celestial kingdom of God.
>
> Also, "All that shall die henceforth without a knowledge of it, who would have received it with all their hearts, shall be heirs of that kingdom;
>
> For I, the Lord, will judge all men according to their works, according to the desire of their hearts."

WORLD EVENTS

The United States was fighting its second war against the Seminole Indians of Florida. After the first war, the Seminoles had been assigned a reservation north of Lake Okeechobee, but soon, the whites wanted the reservation land too. The Indians, under Chief Osceola, hid their families in the Everglades and fought the American troops. About 2,000 United States soldiers were killed in this tiny war that cost about $50,000,000 and lasted until Chief Osceola died in 1842.

Signs of a coming conflict in Mexico also began to appear. The Mexican colony of Texas was beginning to resist Santa Anna's oppressive government; and in 1835, Texans declared their freedom from Mexico and formed a provisional government.

About this time, a new weapon was patented that made it easier for men to kill one another. Samuel Colt developed the single-barreled, six-shot revolver.

In England, William Henry Fox Talbot took a photograph of Lacock Abby, in Wiltshire. It was the first photograph ever taken using a new process called calotype that produced a negative that could be used to create numerous prints.

However, the most spectacular event in 1835 was the appearance of a strange, glowing visitor in the night sky—Halley's comet. As the comet streaked across the sky, a baby was born. The baby, Samuel L. Clemens, would later write *Tom Sawyer* and *Huckleberry Finn*, and would be known to the world as Mark Twain. When the comet reappeared seventy-five years later, this great writer was called home to his Maker.

And I also beheld that all children who die before they arrive at the years of accountability are saved in the celestial kingdom of heaven (D&C 137:1–10).

Joseph also saw visions of the Twelve Apostles. Heber C. Kimball recorded:

> During this time many great and marvelous visions were seen, one of which I will mention which Joseph the Prophet had concerning the Twelve. His anxiety was and had been very great for their welfare, when the following vision was manifested to him, as near as I can recollect.
>
> He saw the Twelve going forth, and they appeared to be in a far distant land. After some time, they unexpectantly met together, apparently in great tribulation, their clothes all ragged, and their knees and feet sore. They formed into a circle, and all stood with their eyes fixed upon the ground. The Savior appeared and stood in their midst and wept over them . . . but they did not discover Him. He (Joseph) saw until they had accomplished their work, and arrived at the gate of the celestial city; there, Father Adam stood and opened the gate to them, and as they entered, he embraced them one by one and kissed them. He then led them to the throne of God, and then the Savior embraced each one of them and kissed them, and crowned each one of them in the presence of God. The impression this vision left on Brother Joseph's mind was so acute [in] nature, that he could never refrain from weeping while rehearsing it (Whitney, *Life of Heber C. Kimball*, 93-94).

Joseph also saw two of his brethren serving as missionaries in strange circumstances, and recorded:

> I also beheld Elder McLellin in the south, standing upon a hill, surrounded by a vast multitude, preaching to them, and a lame man standing before him supported by his crutches; he threw them down at his word and leaped as a hart, by the mighty power of God. Also, I saw Elder Brigham Young standing in a strange land, in the far south and west, in a desert place, upon a rock in the midst of about a dozen men of color, who appeared hostile. He was preaching to them in their own tongue, and the angel of God standing above his head, with a drawn sword in his hand, protecting him, but he did not see it (Smith, *History of the Church*, 2:381).

DEDICATING THE TEMPLE, SPRING 1836

Since June of 1833, the temple had been the major focus of the Church in Kirtland. Truman Angel was in the temple one day when Frederick G. Williams, a member of the First Presidency, visited. In a letter to John Taylor in 1885, Truman wrote:

> F. G. Williams came into the Temple about the time the main hall 1st floor was ready for dedication. He was asked, how does the house look to you? He answered that it looked to him like the model he had seen. He said President Joseph Smith, Sidney Rigdon and himself were called to come

before the Lord and the model was shown to them. He said the vision of the Temple was thus shown them and he could not see the difference between it and the House as built (Karl Ricks Anderson, *Joseph Smith's Kirtland: Eyewitness Accounts*, 157).

The building cost about $60,000. This was a very large sum for the struggling young Church. Members contributed some of the money, but Joseph Smith was forced to go into debt to finance most of the construction. Eliza Snow joined the Church shortly before the building was completed. She commented:

> With very little capital, except brain bone and sinew, combined with unwavering trust in God, men women and even children worked with their might. While the brethren labored in their departments, the sisters were actively engaged in boarding and clothing workman, not otherwise provided for. All living as abstemiously as possible, so that every cent might be appropriated to the grand object, while their energies were stimulated by the prospect of participating in the blessing of the house built by the direction of the Most High and accepted by him (Roberts, *A Comprehensive History of the Church*, 1:390, n. 45).

The Lord had promised that the Saints would be endowed with power from on high in the temple. Joseph was in the temple when he saw the vision of the celestial kingdom, and visions of the future of the Twelve Apostles. In March, preparations began for the temple dedication. Special meetings were held, and everyone who had worked on the temple received a blessing from the prophet. Benjamin F. Johnson, a faithful member of the Church, attended these meetings:

WORLD EVENTS

As the Saints worked to finish the temple, American history was being made. Texas had declared independence from Mexico and had set up its own government. Mexico, of course, tried to end the rebellion and bring Texas back under its control. Mexican troops attacked a small garrison at a fort called the Alamo on February 23. The men at the Alamo fought valiantly, but after eleven days, on March 6, all 187 men in the fort were dead, including Davy Crockett and Jim Bowie. However, on April 21, the Mexican forces were defeated and Texas became an independent republic.

> Previous to the dedication of the Temple, on the 27th of March, 1836, all who had labored upon it were called together, and in the public congregation received their blessings under the hands of the First Presidency. I felt a great joy in these prophetic words that filled and thrilled me. Yet all the time I was thinking that these blessings would only be for those who had labored with their hands upon the Temple. As I had not myself worked on it, not being strong enough for such labor, I felt that I would not receive any blessing and it grieved me exceedingly. On the last day of blessings, I was standing by the door in the crowded congregation. How I did yearn for a blessing! As the last blessing was given, the Prophet earnestly looked towards the door where I was standing and said to his brother Hyrum, "Go and see if there is not one more yet to be blessed."
>
> Brother Hyrum came to the door and put his hand upon my shoulder and asked me if I had not worked upon the Temple.

I said, "No sir," but it seemed like passing a sentence upon my fondest hopes.

He then asked me if I had done nothing towards it.

I then thought of a new gun I had earned and given as a donation, and of the brick I had helped to make. I said, "I did give often."

"I thought there was a blessing for you," he said; and he almost carried me to the stand.

The Prophet blessed me with a conformation of all his father had sealed upon me in my patriarchal blessing, and many more also. I felt then that the Lord had respect for my great desire (Andrus, *They Knew the Prophet*, 101-2).

The temple resembled a New England meetinghouse but had some rather unique features. Eliza Snow recorded her description of the temple:

There was a peculiarity in the arrangement of the inner court which made it more than ordinarily impressive—so much so, that a sense of sacred awe seemed to rest upon all who entered. . . . Four pulpits stood one above another, in the center of the building, from north to south, both on the east and west ends; those on the west for the presiding officers of the Melchizedek Priesthood, and those on the east for the Aaronic: and each of the pulpits was separated by curtains of white painted canvas, which were let down and drawn up at pleasure. In front of each of these two rows of pulpits was a sacrament table for the administration of that sacred ordinance. In each corner of the court was an elevated pew for the singers, the choir being distributed into four compartments. In addition to the pulpit curtains, were others, intersecting at right angles, which divided the main ground-floor wall into four equal sections, giving to each, one half of one set of pulpits (B. H. Roberts, *Outlines of Ecclesiastical History*, 387-88).

The pulpits were lavishly carved, and the interior was finished with all the skill and care the Saints possessed. Brigham Young left the School of the Prophets and personally supervised the final painting. On the morning of March 27, a very large crowd gathered at the temple doors. George A. Smith recorded:

When the temple was completed there was a great manifestation of power. The brethren gathered together to its dedication. We considered it a very large building. Some nine hundred and sixty could be seated, and there would still be room for a few to stand. . . . The elders from every part of the country had come together . . . to the dedication. The congregation was so large that we could not all get in; and when the house was full, then, of course, the doors were closed, and no more admitted. This caused Elder Frazier Eaton, who had paid seven hundred dollars towards the building of the house, to apostatize, because he did not get there early enough to the meeting. When the dedication prayer was read by Joseph, it was read from a

printed copy. This is a great trial of faith to many. "How can it be that the prophet should read a prayer?" What an awful trial it was, for the Prophet to read a prayer. The service of the dedication being over, it was repeated again on the next day to accommodate those who had not been able to get in on the first day. . . .

On the first day of the dedication, President Frederick G. Williams . . . bore testimony that the Savior dressed in his vesture without seam, came into the stand and accepted of the dedication of the house. . . . That evening there was a collection of Elders, Priests, Teachers, and Deacons, etc., amounting to four hundred and sixteen gathered in the house; there were great manifesta-

THE KIRTLAND OHIO TEMPLE was dedicated March 27, 1836, by the Prophet Joseph Smith. It was an occasion of many marvelous spiritual manifestations. *1907*

tions of power, such as speaking in tongues, seeing visions, administration of angels. Many individuals bore testimony that they saw angels, ... and there came a shock on the house like the sound of a mighty rushing wind and almost every man in the house arose, and hundreds of them were speaking in tongues, prophecying or declaring visions, almost with one voice (Young, *Journal of Discourses*, 11:9-10).

Heber C. Kimball also recorded the events of that day:

At the dedication an address was delivered by Elder Rigdon. . . . He spoke two hours and a half. The tenure of his discourse went to show the toils, sufferings, privations, and hardships, the brethren and sisters had to endure while building this house, and compared it with the sufferings of the Saints in the days of the Savior. After the address, the voice of the assembly was taken in reference to receiving and upholding the several presidents of the different quorums in their standing. The vote was unanimously in the affirmative in every instance. A hymn was sung, and then we had an interesting address from President Joseph Smith, and closed with a dedication prayer written by the prophet.

During the ceremonies of the dedication, an angel appeared and sat near President Joseph Smith Sen., and Frederick G. Williams, so that they had a fair view of his person. He was a very tall personage, black eyes, white hair, and stoop shouldered; his garment was whole, extending near his ankles; on his feet he had sandals. He was sent as a messenger to accept of the dedication (Whitney, *Life of Heber C. Kimball*, 90-91).

Joseph Smith read the dedicatory prayer that he had written for the occasion. The prayer is now contained in the Doctrine and Covenants as Section 109.

Thanks be to thy name, O Lord God of Israel.

Thou who hast commanded thy servants to build a house to thy name in this place [Kirtland].

And now thou beholdest, O Lord, that thy servants have done according to thy commandment.

And now we ask thee, Holy Father, in the name of Jesus Christ . . . to accept of this house. . . .

For thou knowest that we have done this work through great tribulation; and out of our poverty we have given of our substance to build a house to thy name, that the Son of Man might have a place to manifest himself to his people. . . .

Put upon thy servants the testimony of the covenant, that when they go out and proclaim thy word they may seal up the law, and prepare the hearts of thy saints for all those judgments thou art about to send, in thy wrath, upon the inhabitants of the earth, because of their transgressions, that thy people may not faint in the day of trouble.

Have mercy, O Lord, upon all the nations of the earth. . . .

Remember the kings, the princes, the nobles, and the great ones of the earth, and all people . . . all the poor, the needy, and afflicted ones of the earth. . . .

We ask thee to have mercy upon the children of Jacob, that Jerusalem, from this hour, may begin to be redeemed;

And the yolk of bondage may begin to be broken off from the house of David;

And the children of Judah may begin to return to the lands which thou didst give to Abraham, their father. . . .

Remember all thy church, O Lord, with all their families . . . with all their sick and afflicted ones, with all the poor and meek of the earth; that the kingdom which thou hast set up without hands, may become a great mountain, and fill the whole earth;

That thy church may come forth out of the wilderness of darkness, and shine forth fair as the moon, clear as the sun, and terrible as an army with banners;

And be adorned as a bride for that day when thou shalt unveil the heavens, and cause the mountains to flow down at thy presence, and the valleys to be exalted, the rough places made smooth; that thy glory may fill the earth.

That when the trump shall sound for the dead, we shall be caught up in the cloud to meet thee, that we may be ever with the Lord;

That our garments may be pure, that we may be clothed upon with robes of righteousness, with palms in our hands, and crowns of glory upon our heads, and reap eternal joy for all our sufferings (D&C 109:1-5, 38, 54, 62-64, 72-76).

W. W. Phelps composed a new hymn for the dedication. "The Spirit of God Like a Fire is Burning" expressed the Saints' great joy for the restoration of the gospel. It concluded with a chorus of exultation, where the Saints join with the angels to shout, "Hosanna, Hosanna to God and the Lamb." The hymn was sung after the dedicatory prayer, and has often been sung at temple dedications since that time.

Another feature of this, and subsequent temple dedications, was the Hosanna Shout. Eliza Snow recorded:

A singular incident in connection with the shout may be discredited by some, but it is verily true. A notice had been circulated that children in arms would not be permitted at the dedication of the temple. A sister who had come a long distance with her babe, six weeks old, having on her arrival heard the above requisition went to the patriarch, Joseph Smith, Sr., in great distress, saying that she knew no one with whom she could leave her infant; and to be deprived of the privilege of attending the dedication seemed more than she could endure. The ever generous and kind-hearted father volunteered to take the responsibility on himself, and told her to take her child, at the same time, giving the mother a promise that her babe should make no disturbance; and the promise was verified. But when the congregation shouted hosanna, that babe joined in the shout. As marvelous as that incident may appear to many, it is not more so than other occurrences on that occasion (Tullidge, *Women of Mormondom*, 94-95).

The evening after the dedication, a priesthood meeting was held in the temple. Harrison Burgess, one of those present, recorded:

> I was in a meeting in the upper part of the Kirtland Temple, with about one hundred of the high priests, seventies and elders. The Saints felt to shout "Hosanna," and the Spirit of God rested upon me in mighty power. I beheld the room lighted up with a peculiar light, such as I have never seen before, soft and clear, and the room looked to me as though it had neither roof nor floor to the building. I beheld Joseph and Hyrum Smith and Roger Orton, enveloped in the light.
>
> Joseph exclaimed aloud, "I behold the Saviour, the Son of God." Hyrum: "I behold the angels of heaven."
>
> Brother Orton exclaimed, "I behold the chariots of Israel."
>
> All those who were in the room felt this power of God to [the] degree that many prophesied, and the power of God was made manifest, the remembrance of which I shall never forget while I live upon the earth (Andrus, *They Knew the Prophet*, 52).

Joseph also recorded some of the events of this meeting.

> I met with the quorums in the evening and instructed them respecting the ordinance of washing of feet . . . and gave them instructions in relation to the spirit of prophecy, and called upon the congregation to speak. . . . "Do not quench the spirit, for the first one that opens his mouth shall receive the spirit of prophecy."
>
> Brother George A. Smith arose and began to prophesy, when a noise was heard like the sound of a rushing mighty wind, which filled the Temple, and all the congregation simultaneously arose, being moved upon by an invisible power; many began to speak in tongues and prophesy; others saw glorious visions; and I beheld the Temple was filled with angels, which fact I declared to the congregation. The people of the neighborhood came running together hearing an unusual sound within, and seeing a bright light, like a pillar of fire resting upon the temple, and we were astonished at what was taking place. This continued until the meeting closed at eleven p.m. (Smith, *History of the Church*, 2:428).

HEAVENLY VISITORS

The spiritual feast continued through the following week as the dedication services were repeated for those who had not been able to get into the building for the first session. The following Sunday, on April 3, Thomas B. Marsh and David W. Patten spoke in the regular Sunday services. After assisting in the passing of the sacrament, Joseph retired to the pulpit and, with Oliver Cowdery, bowed in solemn prayer. Joseph recorded:

> The veil was taken from our minds, and the eyes of our understanding were opened.
>
> We saw the Lord standing upon the breastwork of the pulpit, before us; and under his feet was a paved work of pure gold, in color like amber.

His eyes were as a flame of fire; the hair of his head was white like the pure snow; his countenance shown above the brightness of the sun; and his voice was as the sound of the rushing of great waters, even the voice of Jehovah, saying,

"I am the first and the last; I am he who liveth, I am he who was slain; I am your advocate with the Father.

Behold, your sins are forgiven you; you are clean before me; therefore, lift up your heads and rejoice.

Let the hearts of your brethren rejoice, and let the hearts of all my people rejoice, who have with their might, built this house to my name.

For behold, I have accepted this house, and my name shall be here; and I will manifest myself to my people in mercy in this house.

JESUS CHRIST APPEARING TO JOSEPH SMITH AND OLIVER COWDERY IN THE KIRTLAND TEMPLE *by Gary E. Smith*
This painting depicts the appearance of the Savior in the Kirtland Temple on April 3, 1836. Other heavenly visitors also appeared—Moses, Elias, and Elijah.
oil on canvas 1980

Yea, I will appear unto my servants, and speak unto them with my own voice, if my people will keep my commandments, and do not pollute this holy house.

Yea the hearts of thousands and tens of thousands shall greatly rejoice in consequence of the blessings which shall be poured out, and the endowment which my servants have been endowed in this house.

And the fame of this house shall spread to foreign lands; and this is the beginning of the blessing which shall be poured out on the heads of my people. Even so. Amen" (D&C 110:1-10).

After this marvelous vision, the great prophets of the Old Testament appeared to Joseph and Oliver bringing keys that could finally be restored now that a temple had been prepared and dedicated. Joseph recorded:

. . . The heavens were again opened unto us; and Moses appeared before us, and committed unto us the keys of the gathering of Israel from the four parts of the earth, and the leading of the ten tribes from the land of the north.

After this, Elias appeared, and committed the dispensation of the gospel of Abraham, saying that in us and our seed all generations after us should be blessed.

After this vision had closed, another great and glorious vision burst upon us; for Elijah the prophet, who was taken to heaven without tasting death, stood before us, and said:

"Behold, the time has fully come, which was spoken of by the mouth of Malachi," testifying that he [Elijah] "should be sent, before the great and dreadful day of the Lord come—to turn the hearts of the fathers to the children, and the children to the fathers, lest the whole earth be smitten with a curse—

Therefore, the keys of this dispensation are committed into your hands; and by this ye may know that the great and dreadful day of the Lord is near, even at the doors" (D&C 110:11-16).

It is interesting to note that this vision occurred on April 3, during the Jewish Passover when Jews set an extra place at their tables and leave their doors open in expectation of Elijah's return.

❖❖

April of 1835 was a high point in the history of the Church of Jesus Christ. The Savior himself had accepted the temple, and many had seen visions, receiving a powerful witness of the work. Even though the building of Zion had been postponed, the Saints now felt they would have the strength to be righteous enough to succeed. Zion's Camp, the calling of the Twelve Apostles and the seventy, the publication of the Doctrine and Covenants, and the dedication of the Kirtland Temple all had served to unite the Saints. If they could continue to grow in number and in unity, they would come forth out of the wilderness and shine forth "fair as the moon, clear as the sun, and terrible as an army with banners."

❖❖

When the Kirtland Temple was dedicated in April of 1836, The Church of Jesus Christ of Latter-day Saints had approximately 2,000 members. In addition to presiding over the Church, Joseph was busy translating the papyri he had acquired the previous year from Michael Chandler. He also made frequent missionary journeys, provided for his family, and taught, counseled, blessed, encouraged, chastised, and nurtured members of the Church. In May of 1836, he was reunited with his grandmother.

May 17.—I went in company with my brother Hyrum, in a carriage to Fairport, and brought home my grandmother, Mary Smith, aged ninety-three years. . . . She had come five hundred miles to see her children. . . . She was much pleased at being introduced to her greatgrand-children, and expressed much pleasure and gratification on seeing me.

My grandfather, Asael Smith, long ago predicted that there would be a prophet raised up in his family, and my grandmother was fully satisfied that it was fulfilled in me.

On May 27, after a few days visit with her children, which she enjoyed extremely well, my grandmother fell asleep without sickness, pain or regret. She breathed her last about sunset, and was buried in the burial ground near the Temple. . . . She had buried one daughter, two sons and her husband, . . . and left five sons and three daughters still living (Smith, *History of the Church,* 2:442-43).

A MISSION FOR PARLEY

Since joining the Church, Elder Parley Pratt had spent most of his time traveling and preaching. In the spring of 1836, the members of the Quorum of the Twelve were preparing to leave on missions, but Parley was deep in debt and thought it might be best to stay home, work, pay off his debts, and care for his sick wife. He wrote:

> I had retired to my rest one evening . . . and was pondering my future course, when there came a knock at the door. . . . Elder Heber C. Kimball and others entered my house, and being filled with the spirit of prophecy, they blessed me and my wife, and prophesied as follows.
>
> "Brother Parley, thy wife shall be healed from this hour, and shall bear a son, and his name shall be Parley. . . . Arise, therefore and go forth in the ministry, nothing doubting. Take no thoughts for your debts, nor the necessaries of life, for the Lord will supply you with abundant means. . . .
>
> Thou shalt go to upper Canada, even to the city of Toronto . . . and there thou shalt find a people prepared for the fulness of the gospel . . . and from the things growing out of this mission, shall the fulness of the gospel spread into England. . . ."
>
> This prophecy was the more marvelous, because being married near ten years, we had never had any children; and for near six years my wife had been consumptive, and had been considered incurable. However, we called to mind the faith of Abraham of old . . . . and we took courage.
>
> I now began in earnest to prepare for the mission and in a few days all was ready. I took an affectionate leave of my wife, mother and friends, and started for Canada (*Autobiography of Parley P. Pratt,* 110).

Parley's faith was put to the test when he was on the shore of Lake Ontario.

> [I] entered Hamilton, a flourishing town at the head of Lake Ontario; but my place of destination was Toronto, around on the north side of the lake. If I went by land I would have a circuitous route, muddy and tedious to go on foot. The lake had just opened, and steamers had commenced plying between the two places; two dollars would convey me to Toronto in a few hours, and save some days of laborious walking; but I was an entire stranger in Hamilton . . . and money I had none. . . . I retired to a secret place in a

forest and prayed to the Lord for money to enable me to cross the lake. I then entered Hamilton and commenced to chat with some of the people. I had not tarried many minutes before I was accosted by a stranger, who inquired my name and where I was going. He also asked me if I did not want some money. . . . [and] gave me ten dollars and a letter of introduction to John Taylor, of Toronto, where I arrived the same evening (*Autobiography of Parley P. Pratt*, 113-14).

Elder Pratt combed the city of Toronto trying to arrange for a place to preach, but no one would let him use a church, public hall, or courthouse. He knew that he must preach in this town, but there seemed to be no way.

. . . I had exhausted my influence and power without effect. I now repaired to a pine grove just out of the town, and kneeling down, called on the Lord. . . .

I then arose and . . . going to the house of John Taylor, had placed my hand on my baggage to depart from [the] place . . . when a few inquiries on the part of Mr. Taylor caused a few moments' delay, during which a lady by the name of Walton entered the house, and, being an acquaintance of Mrs. Taylor's, was soon engaged in conversation with her in an adjoining room. I overheard the following:

"Mrs. Walton, I'm glad to see you; there is a gentleman here from the United States who says the Lord sent him to this city to preach the gospel. He has applied in vain to the various authorities for opportunity to fulfill his mission, and is now about to leave the place. He may be a man of God; I am sorry to have him depart."

"Indeed!" said the lady, well, I now understand the feelings and spirit which brought me to your house at this time. I've been busy over the wash tub and too weary to take a walk; but I felt impressed to walk out. I then thought I would make a call on my sister, the other side of town; but passing your door, the spirit bade me to go in; but I said to myself I'll go in when I return; but the spirit said: go in now. I accordingly came in, and I'm thankful that I did so. Tell the stranger that he is welcome to my house. I am a widow, but I have a spare room and bed, and food in plenty. He shall have a home at my house, and two large rooms to preach in just when he pleases. . . . I [will] go and gather my relatives and friends to come in this very evening and hear him talk; for I feel by the Spirit that he is a man sent by the Lord with a message which will do us good."

The evening found me quietly seated at her house, in the midst of a large number of listeners. . . .

"Well, Mrs. Walton, I will frankly relate to you and your friends the particulars of my message and the nature of my commission. A young man in the State of New York, whose name is Joseph Smith, was visited by an angel of God [and] was enabled to obtain an ancient record, written by men of old on the American continent, and containing the history, prophecies and gospel in plainness as revealed to them by Jesus and his messengers. This same Joseph Smith and others were also commissioned by the angels . . . and ordained to the apostleship; with authority to organize the Church . . . and cause the full, plain gospel to be preached in all the world.

By these apostles, . . . I have been ordained as an Apostle, and sent forth . . . to minister the baptism of repentance for the remission of sins, in the name of Jesus Christ; and to administer the gift of the Holy Ghost, to heal the sick, to comfort the mourner, [and] bind up the broken in heart. . . .

I was also directed to this city by the Spirit of the Lord with a promise that I should find a people here prepared to receive the gospel. . . ."

"Well, Mr. Pratt, this is precisely the message we were waiting for; we believe your words and are desirous to be baptized" (*Autobiography of Parley P. Pratt,* 114-17).

With that beginning, Elder Pratt preached and soon baptized several new members, including John Taylor, his wife, Lenora Cannon Taylor, Joseph Fielding and his two sisters, Mary and Mercy.

After ministering in and about Toronto for about two months I found it necessary to return home. . . . I accordingly gave out word in a meeting . . . that I should take [a] boat for home next morning. Now all this time I had asked no man for money, nor had I explained my circumstances. However, on shaking hands at the close of the next meeting, several bankbills were secretly shaken into my hands, amounting in all to several hundred dollars. . . . I thanked the Lord God of Israel for the fulfillment of the first instalment of Brother Kimball's prophecy, and went on my way rejoicing. On my arrival in Kirtland I was enabled to meet my most urgent debts. . . . I found my wife had been healed of her seven years' illness. . . . After a pleasant visit with the Saints, I took my wife with me and returned again to Toronto, in June 1836 (*Autobiography of Parley P. Pratt,* 128-29).

In Kirtland, a future Church leader was studying the Book of Mormon and the Church of Jesus Christ. He was Lorenzo Snow.

I was baptized by Elder John Boynton, then one of the Twelve Apostles, June, 1836, in Kirtland, Ohio. . . .

Some two or three weeks after I was baptized, one day while engaged in my studies, I began to reflect upon the fact that I had not obtained a knowledge of the truth of the work . . . and I began to feel very uneasy. I laid aside my books, left the house and wandered around through the fields under the oppressive influence of a gloomy, disconsolate spirit, while an indescribable cloud of darkness seemed to envelop me. I had been accustomed, at the close of the day, to retire for secret prayer, to a grove a short distance from my lodgings, but at this time, I felt no inclination to do so. The spirit of prayer had departed and the heavens seemed like brass over my head. At length, realiz-

JOHN TAYLOR (1808–1887) Born in Milnthorpe, England, John moved to Canada in 1832 and was baptized in 1836. He was with the Prophet and Hyrum when they were killed at Carthage. Though he was wounded at that time, he lived to serve as a faithful Apostle, then as the third President of the Church.

ing that the usual time had come for secret prayer, I concluded I would not forgo my evening service, and as a matter of formality, knelt as I was in the habit of doing, and in my accustomed retired place, but not feeling as I was wont to feel.

I had no sooner opened my lips in an effort to pray, than I heard a sound, just above my head, like the rustling of silken robes and immediately the Spirit of God descended upon me, completely enveloping my whole person, filling me, from the crown of my head to the soles of my feet, and O, the joy and happiness I felt!! No language can describe the almost instantaneous transition from a dense cloud of mental and spiritual darkness into a refulgence of light and knowledge, as it was at that time imparted to my understanding. I then received a perfect knowledge that God lives, that Jesus Christ is the Son of God, and of the restoration of the holy Priesthood and the fullness of the Gospel. It was a complete baptism—a tangible immersion in the heavenly principle element, the Holy Ghost; and even more real and physical in its effects upon every part of my system than the immersion by water. . . .

I cannot tell how long I remained in the full flow of the blissful enjoyment and divine enlightenment, but it was several minutes before the celestial element which filled and surrounded me began gradually to withdraw. On arising from my kneeling posture, with my heart swelling with gratitude to God, beyond the power of expression, I felt—I knew that He had conferred on me what only an omnipotent being can confer (Snow, *Biography and Family Record of Lorenzo Snow*, 7-8).

LORENZO SNOW (1814–1901) was baptized in June, 1836, and served missions to England, Italy, and Switzerland. He became the fifth President of the Church on Sept. 13, 1898. His efforts to rescue the Church from financial ruin proved successful and he is remembered for his efforts to exhort the Saints to pay their tithing.

When the Saints in Missouri were driven from their homes in Jackson County, they believed that they would only be in Clay County for a short time. However, more than a year passed and the Saints still had not been able to return to Zion. Hostility against the Saints began to appear again, and on July 29, 1836, local citizens held a meeting and produced a resolution.

It is apparent to every reflecting mind that a crisis has arisen in this country. . . . At this moment, the clouds of civil war are rolling up their fearful masses. . . . This painful state of things has been produced mainly by the rapid and increasing emigration of that people commonly called Mormons. . . .

They came to our county . . . friendless and penniless . . . their destitute and miserable condition . . . excited the deep sympathies of the philanthropic and hospitable citizens of this county. . . . They always declared that they looked [upon this county] as a temporary asylum; and that, whenever . . . citizens of this county should request it, they would promptly leave us in peace as they found us.

That period has now arrived. . . . Their rapid emigration, their large purchases, . . . the remarks of the ignorant and imprudent portion of them, that this country is destined by heaven to be theirs are received . . . by a large portion of this community, as strong and convincing proofs that they intend to make this county their permanent home, the centre and general rendezvous of their people.

These are some of the reasons why these people have become objects of the deepest hatred and detestation to many of our citizens. They are eastern men, whose manners, habits, customs, and even dialect, are essentially different from our own. They are non-slaveholders, and opposed to slavery. . . . They are charged . . . with keeping up a constant communication with our Indian tribes on our frontiers, with declaring . . . that the Indians are part of God's chosen people. . . . We do not vouch for the correctness of these statements; but whether they are true or false, their effect has been the same in exciting our community. . . .

We urge the Mormons to use every means to put an immediate stop to the emigration of their people to this county. We earnestly urge them to seek some other abiding place (Smith, *History of the Church*, 2:449-50).

Mormon leaders denied interfering with the slaveholders and Indians, but they prepared the Saints for another move so that bloodshed could be avoided. The Saints again appealed to Governor Dunklin, but although he expressed his personal sympathy, he decided that "public sentiment may become paramount law; and when one man or society of men becomes so obnoxious to that sentiment as to determine the people to be rid of him or them, it is useless to run counter to it. All I can say to you is that in this Republic, the *vox populi* is the *vox dei*" (Smith, *History of the Church*, 2:462).

Individuals friendly toward the Mormons began working in the state legislature to create a new county in the sparsely settled northern part of Missouri. Church leaders also evaluated the area for possible settlement. However, since the area was believed to be uninhabitable, it was determined that the new Mormon county should be created near Shoal Creek and the Grand River. A new county, named Caldwell, was soon created, but the new governor, Lilburn W. Boggs, insisted that a non-Mormon county also be created. This county was called Davis and was located north of Caldwell. Since Davis County included part of the land that had been set aside for Caldwell County, the Saints had less land than they had expected, but they set to work, and began settling their first town in the new area—Far West.

Late in July 1836, Joseph and Hyrum Smith, Sidney Rigdon, and Oliver Cowdery traveled to Salem, Massachusetts. Ebenezer Robinson explained one of the purposes of the trip.

A brother in the Church by the name of Burgess had come to Kirtland and stated that a large amount of money had been secreted in the cellar of a certain house in Salem, Massachusetts, which had belonged to a widow and he thought he was the only person now living who had knowledge of it or the location of the house. Four of the leading men of the Church had been to Salem, Massachusetts in search of this hidden treasure spoken of by Brother Burgess, that is Joseph Smith, Jr., Hyrum Smith, Sidney Rigdon, and Oliver Cowdery. They left home on the 25th of July and returned in September. Brother Burgess met them in Salem, evidently according to appointment. But time had wrought such a change that he could not for certain point out the house and soon left. They, however, found a house which they felt was the right one and hired it. Well, it's needless to say they failed to find that treasure (Ebenezer Robinson, "Items of Personal History of the Editor," in *The Return*, 104-5).

Since the Church was deeply in debt, Brother Burgess's story of treasure was intriguing. The temple, the printing office, and the Whitney store had depleted cash reserves and required the brethren to borrow money. The rapid growth of the Church, the poverty of many members, as well as the time the men spent on Church business had all contributed to the financial problems. The Church did own large tracts of land, but these could not be converted easily into cash.

The brethren had not been in Salem long when they received a revelation, now Section 111 in the Doctrine and Covenants.

> I, the Lord your God, am not displeased with your coming this journey, notwithstanding your follies.
>
> I have much treasure in this city for you, for the benefit of Zion, and many people in this city, whom I will gather out in due time. . . .
>
> Concern not yourselves about your debts, for I will give you power to pay them . . . for there are more treasures than one for you in this city (D&C 111:1-2, 5, 10).

This prophecy may have been at least partly fulfilled in 1841 when Erastus Snow baptized over 100 people in Salem. However, while Joseph and the others were in Salem, they preached and transacted Church business before returning to Kirtland in September. Money problems continued to plague the Saints, so they decided to band together and form a bank of their own. This was a common practice in the western United States at that time. Joseph recorded:

On the 2nd of November, the brethren at Kirtland drew up certain articles of agreement, preparatory to the organization of a banking institution to be called the "Kirtland Safety Society." President Oliver Cowdery was delegated to Philadelphia to procure plates for the institution; and Elder Orson Hyde to repair to Columbus with a petition to the legislature of Ohio, for an act of incorporation (Smith, *History of the Church*, 2:467-68).

Unfortunately, Elder Hyde presented the petition to a newly elected legislature that was refusing all new bank charters. When the charter for the Kirtland Safety Society was rejected, Oliver Cowdery returned to Kirtland. Instead of creating a bank, the Saints decided to organize a joint stock company; and the Kirtland Safety Society Anti-Banking Company was created. About $20,000 in gold coin and paper securities were acquired through the sale of stock in the company, and the anti-bank printed notes that began to circulate in January 1837. Now, citizens of Kirtland could borrow against their land, obtain the notes, and buy goods and services at local stores. In 1829 there were 329 state banks. By 1837, there were 788. Each bank printed its own money and issued credit on its own terms.

WILLARD RICHARDS (1804–1854) WITH WIFE, JENNETTA (1817–1845), & SON, HEBER JOHN. Jennetta Richards was the first person baptized in England on July 31, 1837. She married Willard in England on Sept. 24, 1838. Two months after this image was made, she fell ill and passed away. She was buried in the southwest corner of her garden in Nauvoo, but in 1868 her remains were brought to Salt Lake City for reburial. *Daguerreotype made in Nauvoo, IL, Mar. 26, 1845.*

WILLARD RICHARDS

As the year ended, another future Church leader was baptized. Brigham Young recorded:

> In October, my cousins Levi and Willard Richards, arrived in Kirtland. Willard, having read the Book of Mormon, came to inquire further concerning the work of God. I invited him to make his home at my house, which he did, and investigated thoroughly the principles and doctrines set forth by the Prophet and elders of the Church. December 31st, he requested baptism at my hands, which ordinance I administered to him in the presence of Elder Heber C. Kimball and others, who had spent the afternoon in cutting the ice to prepare for the ceremony (*Manuscript History of Brigham Young*).

As the new year opened, Parley Pratt was completing his mission in Canada.

> The truth had now triumphed in Canada, as was predicted on my head. . . . Several branches of the Church had been organized, and Elders had been ordained to take care of the flocks and to continue the work. I took an affectionate leave of my friends in that country, and, with my wife, returned home. Where I had labored, the Lord had opened the hearts of the Saints suf-

ficiently to pay up my debts, as had been predicted; and at the turn of the season, less than a twelvemonth from the date of brother Kimball's prophecy, my wife bore me a son, and we called his name Parley. He was born early in the morning of March 25th, 1837. . . .

My dear wife had now lived to accomplish her destiny; and when the child was dressed and she looked upon it and embraced it, she ceased to live in the flesh. . . . A few days previous to her death, she had a vision . . . that she should have the privilege of departing from this world of sorrow and pain, and of going to the Paradise of rest as soon as she had fulfilled the prophecy in relation to the promised son. . . . She was overwhelmed with a joy and peace indescribable.

She was buried in the churchyard near the Temple in Kirtland, Ohio. My grief, and sorrow, and loneliness I shall not attempt to describe (*Autobiography of Parley P. Pratt*, 140-42).

CEMETERY NEAR
KIRTLAND TEMPLE
Burial place of Parley
P. Pratt's wife.
1907

The Kirtland Safety Society was also having problems. Its founders had hoped that it would solve the financial problems of the Church, but without a state charter, the notes were only good among the members of the Society. As the notes began to circulate at less than face value, some began to complain. Eliza Snow wrote:

A spirit of speculation had crept into the hearts of some of the Twelve, and nearly, if not every quorum, was more or less infected. Most of the Saints were poor, and now prosperity was dawning upon them—the Temple was completed, and in it they had been recipients of marvelous blessings, and many who had been humble and faithful to the performance of every duty—ready to go and come at every call of the Priesthood, were getting haughty in their spirits, and lifted up in the pride of their hearts. As the Saints drank in the love and spirit of the world, the Spirit of the Lord withdrew from their hearts, and they were filled with pride and hatred toward those who maintained their integrity. They linked themselves together in an opposing party—pretended that they constituted the Church, and claimed that the Temple belonged to them (Smith, *History of the Church*, 2: 487-88 n. 4).

While Joseph was on a mission in Michigan, a meeting was held in the temple. Brigham Young recorded:

The spirit of speculation, disaffection, and apostasy imbibed by many of the Twelve, which ran through all the quorums of the Church, prevailed so extensively that it was difficult for any to see clearly the path to pursue.

On a certain occasion, several of the Twelve, the witnesses to the Book of Mormon, and others of the Authorities of the Church, held a council in the upper room of the Kirtland Temple. The question before them was to ascertain how the Prophet Joseph could be deposed, and David Whitmer appointed President of the Church. Father John Smith, Brother Heber C. Kimball and others were present who were opposed to such measures. I rose up, and in a plain and forcible manner told them that Joseph was a Prophet, and I knew it and that they might rail and slander him as much as they pleased, they could not destroy the appointment of the Prophet of God, they could only destroy their own authority, cut the thread that bound them to the Prophet of God and sink themselves to hell. Many were highly enraged at my decided opposition to their measures, and Jacob Bump, an old pugilist was so exasperated that he could not be still. Some of the brethren near him put their hands on him, and requested him to be quiet, but he writhed and twisted his arms and body saying, 'How can I keep my hands off that man?' I told him if he thought it would give him any relief, he might lay them on. This meeting was broken up without the apostates being able to unite on decided measures of opposition. This was a crisis when earth and hell seemed leagued to overthrow the Prophet and the Church of God. The knees of many of the strongest men of the Church faltered.

During the siege of darkness I stood close by Joseph and with all the wisdom and power God bestowed upon me, put forth my utmost energies to sustain the servant of God and unite the quorums of the Church (*Manuscript History of Brigham Young*).

Economics, confusion, and jealousy all contributed to problems in Kirtland. Pride and arrogance infected the high council, the seventies, and even the Quorum of the Twelve. Parley Pratt was one of the strong men of the Church who faltered.

About this time . . . there were jarrings and discords in the Church at Kirtland, and many fell away and became enemies and apostates. There were also envyings, lyings, strifes and divisions, which caused much trouble and sorrow . . . and at one time, I also was overcome by the same spirit in a great measure, and it seemed as if the very powers of darkness which war against the Saints were let loose upon me. But the Lord knew my faith, my zeal, my integrity of purpose, and he gave me the victory.

I went to Brother Joseph Smith in tears, and with a broken heart and contrite spirit, confessed wherein in I had erred in spirit, murmured, or done or

WORLD EVENTS

A new president of the United States had been elected and took office in January 1837. Martin Van Buren, the Democratic candidate, was elected by a narrow margin, and he stepped into a tangle of economic problems. The country was plunging into a recession that he had not caused and could not prevent.

PRESIDENT MARTIN VAN BUREN (1782–1862)

said amiss. He frankly forgave me, prayed for me and blessed me. Thus, by experience, I learned more fully to discern and to contrast the two spirits and to resist the one and cleave to the other (*Autobiography of Parley P. Pratt*, 144).

While in this spirit of doubt and confusion, Parley met with his friend and recent convert, John Taylor. After Elder Pratt had voiced his concerns, Brother Taylor replied:

> I am surprised to hear you speak so, Brother Parley. Before you left Canada you bore a strong testimony to Joseph Smith being a Prophet of God, and to the truth of the work he has inaugurated; and you said you knew these things by revelation, and the gift of the Holy Ghost. You gave to me a strict charge to the effect that though you or an angel from heaven was to declare anything else I was not to believe it. Now Brother Parley, it is not a man that I am following, but the Lord. . . . If the work was true six months ago, it is true today; if Joseph was then a prophet, he is now a prophet (B. H. Roberts, *The Life of John Taylor*, 40).

Joseph Smith recorded in July of 1837:

> Some time previous to this I resigned my office in the "Kirtland Safety Society," disposed of my interest therein, and withdrew from the institution; being fully aware, after so long an experiment, that no institution of the kind, established upon just and righteous principles for a blessing not only to the Church but the whole nation, would be suffered to continue its operations in such an age of darkness, speculation and wickedness. Almost all the banks throughout the country, one after the other, have suspended specie payment, and gold and silver have risen in value in direct ratio with the depreciation of paper currency. The great pressure of the money market is felt in England as well as America, and bread stuffs are everywhere high. The season has been cool, wet and backward (Smith, *History of the Church*, 2:497).

Joseph Smith noted how the desire for quick wealth affected the spiritual welfare of Church members.

At this time the spirit of speculation in lands and property of all kinds, which was so prevalent throughout the whole nation, was taking deep root in the Church. As the fruits of this spirit, evil surmisings, fault-finding, disunion, dissension, and apostasy followed in quick succession . . . it seemed as though all the powers of earth and hell were combining their influence in an especial manner to overthrow the Church at once, and make a final end. Other institutions refused the Kirtland Safety Society's notes. The enemy abroad and apostates in our midst united in their schemes; flour and provisions were turned towards other

WORLD EVENTS

The financial panic of 1837 was caused by many complex and interrelated factors. President Jackson required that federal land had to be paid for in silver or gold, which ended the credit boom in the western United States and caused property prices to fall. Many states had started huge improvement projects, turnpikes, canals, and railroads with borrowed money; when they could not pay back their loans, the banks failed.

markets and many became disaffected towards me, as though I were the sole cause of those very evils I was most strenuously striving against and which were actually brought upon us by the brethren not giving heed to my counsel (Smith, *History of the Church*, 2:487-88).

Joseph Smith struggled to unify the Church members.

> No quorum in the Church was entirely exempt from the influence of false spirits. . . . . Even some of the Twelve were so far lost . . . as to begin to take sides, secretly, with the enemy. In this state of things . . . God revealed to me that something new must be done for the salvation of His Church. And on or about the first of June, 1837, Heber C. Kimball, one of the Twelve, was set apart by the spirit of prophecy and revelation, prayer and laying on of hands, of the First Presidency, to preside over a mission to England, to be the first foreign mission of the Church of Christ in the last days (Smith, *History of the Church*, 2:488-89).

TAKING THE GOSPEL TO GREAT BRITAIN

Elder Kimball received his call from the Prophet. He recorded:

> On Sunday, the 4th day of June, 1837, the Prophet Joseph came to me, while I was seated in . . . the Temple in Kirtland, and whispering to me, said, "Brother Heber, the Spirit of the Lord has whispered to me 'Let my servant Heber go to England and proclaim my gospel and open the door of salvation to that nation'" (Whitney, *Life of Heber C. Kimball*, 103).

Brother Kimball was overcome by feelings of inadequacy and asked if Brigham Young could accompany him, but the Prophet said he had other work for Brigham. Heber then resolved: "The moment I understood the will of my Heavenly Father, I felt the determination to go at all hazards, believing He would support me and endow me with every qualification that I needed, and although my family was dear to me and I should leave them almost destitute, I felt that the cause of truth outweighed every other consideration" (Whitney, *Life of Heber C. Kimball*, 104).

However, Heber was soon given a companion. Joseph Smith related: "While we were ordaining him, Orson Hyde, another of the Twelve, came in, and upon listening to what was passing, his heart melted within him. . . . he acknowledged all his faults, asked forgiveness, and offered to accompany President Kimball on his mission to England. His offer was accepted and he was set apart for that purpose" (Smith, *History of the Church,* 2:489-90).

Two more missionaries, Willard Richards and Joseph Fielding, were soon added to the group. On the morning of June 13, Elder Robert B. Thompson stopped at the Kimball home. He had been called on a mission to Canada and was going to travel part of the way with the missionaries to England. He wrote:

> The door being partly open, I entered and felt struck with the sight which presented itself to my view. I would have retired, thinking that I was intruding, but I felt riveted to the spot. The father was pouring out his soul to [God] that He would grant him a prosperous voyage across the mighty ocean, and make him useful . . . and that He . . . would supply the wants of his wife and little ones. He then, like the patriarchs, and by virtue of his office, laid his hands upon their heads individually, leaving a father's blessing upon them. . . . While thus engaged his voice was almost lost in the sobs of those around. . . . His emotions were great, and he was obliged to stop at intervals, while the big tears rolled down his cheeks. . . . My heart was not stout enough to refrain; in spite of myself, I wept, and mingled my tears with theirs. At the same time I felt thankful that I had the privilege of contemplating such a scene. I realized that nothing could induce that man to tear himself from so affectionate a family group, from his partner and children who were so dear to him—nothing but a sense of duty and a love to God and attachment to his cause (Whitney, *Life of Heber C. Kimball*, 108-9).

The missionaries crossed Lake Erie to Buffalo, and then traveled to New York City. There they met John Goodson, Isaac Russell, and John Snyder, who had come from Canada to participate in the mission to England. The men crossed the Atlantic aboard the ship *Garrick*, and arrived in Liverpool on July 20, 1837. After a few days, the missionaries felt inspired to go to Preston where they began their missionary labors. The day the elders entered Preston, a general election was being held for members of Parliament. Heber recorded:

> I never witnessed anything like it in my life. Bands of music playing. Flags flying in all directions. Thousands of men, women and children parading the streets, decked with ribbons characteristic of the politics of the several candidates. . . . One of the flags was unrolled before us, nearly over our heads . . . having on it the following motto: "Truth Will Prevail," in large gilt letters. It being so very seasonable, and the sentiment being so very appropriate to us in our situation, we cried aloud, "Amen! Thanks be to God, Truth Will Prevail" (Whitney, *Life of Heber C. Kimball*, 121-22).

The missionaries in Preston contacted Joseph Fielding's brother, James, who was a pastor. He allowed the missionaries to preach in his chapel, but when he found that his congregation was accepting the new doctrine, he became hostile and shut his doors against them. However, many people had become interested in the message of the missionaries so they started preaching in private homes. Before long, a group of converts was ready for baptism. Elder Kimball wrote:

Saturday evening it was agreed that I should go forward and baptize, the next morning, in the River Ribble, which runs through Preston. . . . The next morning I witnessed a scene of satanic power and influence which I shall never forget. About daybreak, Elder Isaac Russell . . . came up to where Elder Hyde and myself were sleeping, and called out "Brother Kimball, I want you should get up and pray for me that I may be delivered from the evil spirits that are tormenting me to such a degree that I feel I cannot live long unless I obtain relief."

I immediately arose. . . . Elder Hyde threw his feet out, and sat up on the bed, and we laid our hands on him, I being mouth, and prayed that the Lord would have mercy on him, and rebuked the devil.

While thus engaged, I was struck with great force by some invisible power, and fell senseless to the floor. The first thing I recollected was being supported by Elders Hyde and Richards, who were praying for me. . . . My agony was so great I could not endure it, and I arose, bowed my knees and prayed. I then arose and sat up on the bed, when a vision was opened to our minds, and we could distinctly see the evil spirits, who foamed and gnashed their teeth at us. Space appeared before us, and we saw the devils coming in legions, with their leaders who came within a few feet of us. They came towards us like armies rushing to battle. They appeared to be men of full stature, possessing every form and feature of men in the flesh, who were angry and desperate; and I shall never forget the vindictive malignancy depicted on their countenances as they looked me in the eye; and any attempt to paint the scene . . . or portray their malice and enmity, would be vain. I perspired exceedingly. . . . I felt excessive pain, and was in the greatest distress for some time. I cannot even look back on the scene without feelings of horror; yet by it I learned the power of the adversary, his enmity against the servants of God, and got some understanding of the invisible world. We distinctly heard those spirits talk and express their wrath and hellish designs against us. However, the Lord delivered us from them and blessed us exceedingly that day (Whitney, *Life of Heber C. Kimball*, 129-31).

At ten A.M. the morning of Sunday, July 30, the elders and nine converts met beside the Ribble River. Several thousand spectators who had lined the river viewed George D. Watt's baptism, the first baptism in England in this dispensation. A few days later, Jennetta Richards was baptized and then confirmed by Elder Kimball. She was the first person confirmed in England. The missionaries then spread out into other towns in Northern England and continued to preach, baptize, and establish branches of the Church.

In the fall of 1837, missionaries were working in England, Wilford Woodruff was preaching in Connecticut, George A. Smith was laboring in the southern states, and Lorenzo Snow was seeking converts in Ohio. Hyrum Smith was in Far West, Missouri, and John Taylor was presiding over the mission in Canada. Through the work of these men, the Church was growing stronger every day. However, in Kirtland, the spirit of dissension still raged. The Kirtland Safety Society had failed, and many of the Saints lost large sums of money. Joseph Smith was approximately $100,000 in debt.

Those who felt that Zion's Camp had been a failure saw the losses at the Kirtland Safety Society as further proof that Joseph was a fallen prophet. Thomas Marsh, the President of the Quorum of the Twelve, was also offended because Heber C. Kimball had been sent on the first foreign mission. Marsh felt that, as President of the Quorum, he should have been sent instead of Elder Kimball. William Smith, one of the apostles, was frequently angry with Joseph and others in the quorum. Other rebellious leaders included Luke and Lyman Johnson, John Boynton, John Whitmer, Martin Harris, William W. Phelps and Frederick G. Williams. However, Brigham Young and Heber Kimball, probably the least prominent of the apostles at this point in history, remained humble and obedient.

Joseph continued his work in spite of the dissention. In the summer of 1837 he went on a short mission to Canada. There, he found that Sampson Avard had set himself as the head of the Church in that area. However, when Joseph arrived, Avard acknowledged his mistakes and repented.

Two members of their stake presidency—John Whitmer and W. W. Phelps—had bought large tracts of land in Caldwell County with Church money, registering the land in their own names and planning to make a profit when they resold it to Church members. They were reprimanded and forgiven after the men repented of their mistake. Joseph recorded:

> I returned to Kirtland on or about the 10th of December. During my absence in Missouri Warren Parrish, John F. Boynton, Luke S. Johnson, Joseph Coe, and some others united together for the overthrow of the Church. Soon after my return this dissenting band openly and publicly renounced the Church of Christ of Latter-day Saints and claimed themselves to be the old standard, . . . set me at naught, and the whole Church, denouncing us as heretics. . . . The work began to spread in England with great rapidity. . . . And on Christmas Day, December 25th, Elders Kimball and Hyde, and Joseph Fielding . . . assembled in the "cock pit," with about three hundred saints. . . . This was the first public conference of the Church in England, and at this conference the Word of Wisdom was first publicly taught in that country (Smith, *History of the Church*, 2:528-29).

This was a period in U.S. history characterized by a spirit of violence toward anyone whose ideas were considered "different." Elijah Lovejoy, an abolitionist and newspaper editor, set up shop in St. Louis, Missouri. When he refused to moderate the tone of his editorials that called for an end to slavery, he was threatened with mob violence. He moved his paper across the Mississippi River to Alton, Illinois, but his press was attacked and destroyed on several occasions. Finally, on November 7, 1837, he was killed by a mob while defending his building.

As the Saints in Kirtland became more numerous and increasingly active in local politics, those hostile to the Mormons, including ministers of other churches, and newspaper editors, stepped up their activities against the Church. Most disagreements stemmed from the fact that in 1837, Latter-day Saints held sixty-five percent of the town offices and tended to be Democrats, while most of their neighbors were Whigs.

FLIGHT TO FAR WEST

By December, the apostates and enemies of the Church had become so powerful and violent that those who supported the Prophet Joseph were in danger. Brigham Young fled Kirtland on December 22, leaving his wife and young family, including one-month-old twins. Joseph recorded:

> January 1838—A new year dawned upon the Church in Kirtland in all the bitterness of the spirit of apostate mobocracy; which continued to rage and grow hotter and hotter, until Elder Rigdon and myself were obliged to flee from its deadly influence. . . . On the evening of the 12th of January, about ten o'clock, we left Kirtland, on horseback, to escape mob violence, which was about to burst upon us. . . . At eight o'clock on the morning of the 13th, arrived in Norton Township. . . . Here we tarried about 36 hours when our families arrived; and on the 16th we pursued our journey with our families in covered wagons toward the city of Far West, in Missouri (Smith, *History of the Church*, 3:1).

It took three months to travel to Far West, and the Smiths arrived in mid-March. They had lived above the general store in Kirtland for almost four years. Now they were homeless, and dependent on the charity of the members in Far West. The Smith family included Joseph and Emma; Julia, their adopted seven-year-old daughter; five-year-old Joseph; and eighteen-month-old Frederick. Emma also was expecting another baby in June.

With their leaders gone, the rest of the Church members soon left Kirtland and traveled to Missouri. One small group, which included Eliza R. Snow's family, left early in the spring. Eliza recorded: "Towards the end of April 1838, our father left Kirtland with twenty-one souls in company. . . . We started with horse and ox teams. . . . Our journey from Kirtland to Far West was rendered tedious in consequence of rainy weather. We arrived in Far West on the sixteenth of July with my brother very sick in bed" (Snow, *Biography and Family Record of Lorenzo Snow*, 24-25).

Lorenzo, Eliza's brother, had gotten sick during the journey and was unable to go on. The family stayed with Sidney Rigdon's family while Lorenzo was nursed back to health. Meanwhile, Lorenzo's father continued on to Adam-ondi-Ahman where he purchased a plantation with a double log house. Eventually, the family settled down on this plantation to help build Zion.

The Smith family, which consisted of Joseph Sr., Lucy, Don Carlos, William, Catherine, and Sophronia and their families, were traveling to Far West. Lucy recorded:

> Sometimes we lay in our tents, through driving storms; and at other times we were traveling on foot through marshes and quagmires. Once . . .

we lay all night exposed to the rain . . . when I arose in the morning, I found that my clothes were perfectly saturated with the rain. However, I could not mend the matter by a change of dress, for the rain was still falling rapidly, and I wore my clothes in this situation, three days; in consequence of which I took a severe cold, so that when we arrived at the Mississippi [River], I was unable to walk or sit up. After crossing this river, we stopped at a . . . hut, a most unlovely place, yet the best shelter we could find. This hut was the birthplace of Catharine's son Alvin (Smith, *History of Joseph Smith*, 251-52).

Don Carlos's wife, Agnes, gave birth to a child just two weeks before they began the trip. Although it was a miserable journey, the group eventually reached Far West and moved into a one-room log house.

The faithful members of the Seventy, who were still in Kirtland, met in the temple and organized Kirtland Camp, which was patterned after Zion's Camp, and all who agreed to obey the rules and help one another were allowed to join. Five hundred and fifteen people with their livestock, wagons, tents, and possessions assembled on July 6 to begin the journey. Parts of Kirtland were left desolate, and most homes near the temple were abandoned. Only a few Mormon families remained behind.

The Kirtland Camp followed the same route as Zion's Camp—southwest through Ohio, west across Indiana and Illinois, then across northern Missouri to Far West. The members of Kirtland Camp arrived in Far West on October 1. They had traveled 866 miles and suffered sickness, persecution, death, sorrow, and hunger. They also buried fourteen children and one adult along the trail.

As the Ohio Saints were traveling that summer of 1838, the Church members in Missouri were passing through trials of their own. Joseph recorded: "When I had arrived within one hundred and twenty miles of Far West, the brethren met me with teams and money to help me forward. . . .On the 14th of March, as we were about entering Far West, many of the brethren came out to meet us. . . . We were immediately received under the hospitable roof of brother George W. Harris, who treated us with all possible kindness" (Smith, *History of the Church,* 3:8).

A month before Joseph arrived, the high council had met to consider charges against William W. Phelps and John and David Whitmer of the stake presidency. Thomas B. Marsh kept a record of the meeting.

> Elder George M. Hinckle . . . spoke many things against them, setting forth in a plain and energetic manner the iniquity of Elders Phelps and Whitmer in using the monies which were loaned to the Church. Also David Whitmer's wrong-doing in persisting in the use of tea, coffee, and tobacco. Elder Lyman Wight stated that he considered all other accusations of minor importance compared to brothers Phelps and Whitmer selling their lands in Jackson County. He said that . . . they had flatly denied the faith in so doing (Smith, *History of the Church*, 3:4).

The high council and then the members of the Church in Missouri voted in favor of excommunicating the stake presidency. Two of the apostles, Thomas B. Marsh and David Patton, were appointed to preside over the stake until the prophet arrived and ratified their action.

In early April, the high council met to consider charges against Oliver Cowdery. He was accused of persecuting the brethren, trying to destroy the character of Joseph Smith, and leaving the Church and his callings to practice law against the Church. Because he was not repentant, he was excommunicated. The next day, David Whitmer was excommunicated for not observing the Word of Wisdom, separating himself from the Church, siding with dissenters, and neglecting his callings. The faithful Saints feared that these apostates would stir up the nonmembers in persecution against them.

Since Martin Harris had already been excommunicated, all of the Three Witnesses to the Book of Mormon had now left the Church. Three of the Eight Witnesses also separated themselves from the Saints during this period—Jacob Whitmer, John Whitmer, and Hiram Page. However, Joseph Smith, Sr., Hyrum Smith, and Samuel Smith were still true to the faith. Unfortunately, two of the Eight Witnesses, Peter and Christian Whitmer, had already died by this time.

In mid-June, Sidney Rigdon delivered a powerful sermon based on the scripture, "Ye are the salt of the earth." It contained thinly veiled warnings that the Saints would not allow the dissenters to cause trouble. Some members took the sermon a step further and circulated a notice that warned Oliver Cowdery, the Whitmers, and others to leave Missouri at once or face physical violence. Of course, the leaders of the Church did not approve this document. It was signed by Sampson Avard who, a few months earlier, had tried to set himself up as the head of the Church in Canada.

In England, Heber Kimball was preparing to go home.

> April 9—My mind reverted back to the time when I first arrived in that country, and the peculiar feelings that possessed me when I traveled from Liverpool to Preston eight months before. Then I was a stranger in a strange land. . . . I now had hundreds of brethren to whom I was united with bonds most endearing and sacred (Whitney, *Life of Heber C. Kimball*, 194).

Elder Joseph Fielding was appointed president of the mission in England with Willard Richards and William Clayton as counselors. Elders Kimball and Hyde then boarded the *Garrick* and headed for home. They reached Kirtland in late May and quickly arranged their affairs and moved to Missouri with the rest of the Church.

WILLIAM CLAYTON (1814–1879) was a valuable servant in the Lord's work. William arrived in Nauvoo in December of 1840. He served as the Prophet's private secretary, and was also the Temple Recorder and City Treasurer. He wrote the beloved hymn "Come, Come Ye Saints" as a tribute for the birth of his son. *ca. 1840*

In Missouri, Joseph continued to receive revelations. Section 115 gave the official name of the Church: "For thus shall my church be called in the last days, even The Church of Jesus Christ of Latter-day Saints. Verily I say unto you all: Arise and shine forth, that thy light may be a standard for the nations" (D&C 115:4-5).

Parley P. Pratt remarried in May 1838. His new wife was Marianne Frost Sterns, who was the widow of Nathan Sterns. She had a four-year-old daughter. The family soon moved to Far West, Missouri, where Parley began to build a home and farm. He recorded that the Independence Day celebration in Far West was a grand affair.

> On the 4th of July, 1838, thousands of the citizens who belonged to the Church of the Saints, assembled at the city of Far West . . . in order to celebrate our nation's birth. We erected a tall standard, on which was hoisted our national colors, the stars and stripes, and the bold eagle of American liberty. Under its waving folds we laid the corner stone of a Temple of God, and dedicated the land and ourselves and families to Him who preserved us in all our troubles. An address was then delivered by S. Rigdon, in which was portrayed in lively colors the oppression which we had suffered at the hands of our enemies (*Autobiography of Parley P. Pratt*, 149).

Sidney Rigdon's speech was the Saints' declaration of independence from mob violence. He declared:

> We take God and all the holy angels to witness, this day, that we warn all men, in the name of Jesus Christ to come on us no more for ever, for from this hour we will bear it no more. . . . that mob that comes on us to disturb us, it shall be between us and them a war of extermination. We will never be the aggressors . . . but shall stand for our own until death. . . . We this day, then, proclaim ourselves free with a purpose and determination that never can be broken. No, never! No, never! No, never! (Roberts, *A Comprehensive History of the Church*, 1:441).

Even though Caldwell County had been established so the Mormons could live in Missouri in peace, the Saints were never free from threats of violence. As more Saints streamed into northern Missouri, the old tensions grew.

About this time, Sampson Avard and others organized a secret society called the Danites whose purpose was to defend the Church against dissenters and mobs. Avard claimed that the First Presidency directed him, but this was not true. After going beyond merely defending the Church, the Danites became an embarrassment and source of problems.

However, in spite of the threat of mob violence, the Mormons in Missouri lived their lives with vigor and enthusiasm. Families bought land, built homes and farms, and settled down. Here, they thought they would be able to accomplish their dream of building Zion. In May, Joseph explored the area.

> I left Far West, in company with Sidney Rigdon, Thomas B. Marsh, David W. Patten, Bishop Partridge, . . . and many others, for the purpose of visiting the north country, and laying off a stake of Zion . . . laying claim to lands to facilitate the gathering of the Saints, and for the benefit of the poor. We passed through a beautiful country the greater part of which is prairie, and thickly covered with grass and weeds, among which is plenty of game such as deer, turkey, and prairie hen. We crossed Grand River at the mouth of Honey Creek and Nelson's Ferry. Grand River is a large, beautiful, deep, and rapid stream. We pursued our course up the river, mostly through timber, for about eighteen miles when we arrived at Colonel Lyman Wight's home. He lives at the foot of Tower Hill (a name I gave the place in consequence of the remains of an old Nephite altar or tower that stood there). . . . In the afternoon, I went up the river about half a mile . . . for the purpose of selecting and laying claim to a city plan in Daviess County . . . which the brethren called "Spring Hill," but by the mouth of the Lord it was named Adam-ondi-Ahman, because, said He, it is the place where Adam shall come to visit his people, or the Ancient of Days shall sit as spoken of by Daniel the Prophet. In the evening . . . a council of the brethren voted unanimously to secure the land on Grand River, and between this and Far West (Smith, *History of the Church*, 3:34-36).

They explored and surveyed the area for several weeks and found several promising town sites. Joseph returned home on June 1, and the following day Emma had another son, Alexander Hale Smith.

By late June, enough families had settled in the new town of Adam-ondi-Ahman that Joseph traveled there to organize a stake. John Smith was called as stake president with Reynolds Cahoon and Lyman Wight as counselors; Vincent Knight was called as bishop, and a high council was organized.

On July 8, 1838, Joseph Smith received several revelations. Some directed specific individuals to dispose of their property in Kirtland and come to Zion, and others dealt with tithing and other issues. "Verily, thus saith the Lord, I require all their surplus property to be into the hands of the bishop of my church in Zion.

And after that, those who have thus been tithed shall pay one-tenth of all their interest annually and this shall be a standing law unto them forever . . ." (D&C 119:1, 4).

Section 118 of the Doctrine and Covenants was given in response to prayers regarding the Twelve.

WORLD EVENTS

Probably the most festive event of 1838 took place in London, England. People flocked to the city to see their young queen as she rode in the state coach to Westminster Abbey for her coronation. She was crowned with much pomp and ceremony. However, the old crown was too heavy for young Victoria, so a new crown, complete with diamonds, pearls, sapphires, and a great ruby, known as the Black Princess Ruby, was made for her.

Europe and America seemed to be getting closer every year. In 1838 it took only fifteen days to cross the Atlantic by steamship. The *New York Herald* newspaper implemented a new idea—foreign correspondents in various European capitals.

> Let the Twelve be organized . . . And next spring let them depart to go over the great waters, and there promulgate my gospel:
>
> Let them take leave of my saints in the city of Far West on the twenty-sixth day of April next, on the building-spot of my house, saith the Lord.
>
> Let my servant John Taylor and also my servant John E. Page, and also my servant Wilford Woodruff, and also my servant Willard Richards, be appointed to fill the places of those who have fallen, and be officially notified of their appointment (D&C 118:1, 4-6).

The newly appointed apostles were informed of their new callings, but it was some time before they could meet together, since Willard Richards was in England and some of the brethren were in different parts of the United States and Canada.

August 6 was Election Day in the town of Gallatin. William Penniston, a leader of the anti-Mormon mob in Clay County, arrived early, stood on a barrel, and began to address the crowd of voters. Joseph Smith recorded:

> [He] harangued the electors for the purpose of exciting them against the "Mormons," saying "the Mormon leaders are a set of horse thieves, liars, counterfeiters." He further stated that the members of the church were dupes . . . they would steal . . . and if they suffered the "Mormons" to vote, the people would soon lose their suffrage. . . . Richard, called Dick Welding, the mob bully just drunk enough for the occasion, . . . attempted to strike Brown, who gradually retreated, parrying the blow with his umbrella. . . . Parry Durphy sought to suppress the difficulty by holding Welding's arm, when five or six of the mobbers seized Durfey and commenced beating him with clubs, boards, and crying, "Kill him, kill him," when a general scuffle commenced with fists and clubs, the mobbers being about ten to one of the brethren. . . . During about five minutes it was one succession of knock downs, when the mob dispersed to get fire arms. . . . The brethren not having arms, thought it wisdom to return to their farms, collect their families, and hide them in a thicket of hazel bush which they did, and stood guard around them through the night, while the women and children lay on the ground in the rain (Smith, *History of the Church*, 3:56-58).

The next morning in Far West, Joseph heard that two or three of the brethren had been killed, that they had been prevented from voting, and that a mob was determined to drive the Saints from Daviess County. He started at once for Gallatin with fifteen or twenty armed men, and was relieved to find out that no one had been killed.

The following day, Joseph and an escort rode to the home of Adam Black, the justice of the peace in Daviess County, to ask his support in keeping peace. Mr. Black signed a statement promising that he would not join with the mobbers, but as soon as Joseph left the county, he issued an affidavit stating that Joseph had threatened him with death if he did not sign the statement of peace. He further stated that Joseph was leading five hundred armed men about the county taking vengeance and driving old settlers from their homes.

A warrant was issued for the arrest of Joseph Smith and Lyman Wight, and Governor Boggs ordered that the militia be ready to act in the case of either an Indian or Mormon rebellion.

Small acts of violence continued to plague the Saints, especially those in Daviess County. In spite of this, the Saints continued to improve their land and establish new towns. The Kirtland Camp arrived in September and began settling in Adam-ondi-Ahman. However, rumors and threats of danger prompted about half of the camp to stop in Illinois rather than venture into Missouri.

The most intense persecution shifted from Daviess to Carroll County and the little settlement of DeWitt. By early October, mobbers had surrounded the Saints in that town. A message was sent to the governor asking for help, but he replied that the quarrel was between the Mormons and the mob and that they should fight it out themselves.

At a quarterly conference held at Far West on October 6, several men were called on missions, and vacancies in various quorums were filled. Elder John Taylor, who had recently arrived from Canada, addressed the conference.

A circuit court judge ordered a militia to protect the Saints in DeWitt, but most of the militia disobeyed orders and joined the mob. Joseph, who was in DeWitt at the time, recorded:

> General Parks informed us that . . . he would be obliged to draw them off . . . for fear they would join the mob; consequently he could offer us no assistance. . . . We had now no hopes whatever of successfully resisting the mob, who kept constantly increasing; our provisions were entirely exhausted, and we were worn out by continually standing on guard. . . . Some of the brethren perished from starvation. . . . The Saints finally, through necessity, had to comply and leave the place . . . gathering as many wagons as could be got ready, which was about seventy, with a remnant of the property they had been able to save . . . they left DeWitt and started for Caldwell County on the afternoon of Thursday, October 11, 1838. . . . [T]he whole banditi started for Daviess County, taking with them their cannon. . . . On my arrival in Caldwell, I was informed . . . that a company of mobbers, eight hundred strong, were marching toward a settlement of our people in Daviess County. The brethren assembled on the public square of Far West and informed a company of about one hundred who took a line of march for Adam-ondi-Ahman. . . . [T]his company were militia of the county of Caldwell acting under Lieutenant Colonel George M. Hinkle agreeable to the order of General Doniphan. The special object of this march was to protect Adam-ondi-Ahman (Smith, *History of the Church*, 3:158-63).

The mob burned some outlying homes and drove off livestock, but the mobbers dispersed when the Mormons organized themselves. Some of mob-

GOVERNOR LILBURN WILLIAMS BOGGS (1796–1860). He was the governor of Missouri who signed the "Extermination Order" on Oct. 27, 1838, which forced the Mormons out of Missouri. This act earned him one of the most infamous names in Mormon history. When he issued this order, Boggs stated *"The Mormons must be treated as enemies, and must be exterminated or driven from the state, if necessary, for the public peace."* ca. 1830s

bers, however, returned to their log cabins, removed their possessions, set fire to their own homes and then reported to the authorities that the Mormons had attacked them.

Several months prior to this incident, Joseph Smith had counseled the Saints to gather in the cities. However, many Saints had not followed the Prophet's advice and now were lucky to have escaped with their lives. Far West became packed with Saints who had gathered in the town for protection. Both sides in the conflict sent letters and documents to the authorities, claiming innocence and protesting the evils of the other side. Then Elder Thomas B. Marsh, the President of the Quorum of the Twelve, apostatized, and went to Richmond. One of Marsh's first actions was to make an affidavit stating:

> They have among them a company, considered true Mormons, called the Danites, who have taken an oath to support the heads of the church in all things that they say or do, whether right or wrong. . . . [I]f the people of Clay and Ray made any movement against them, this destroying company were to burn Liberty and Richmond. . . . It is believed by every true Mormon, that Smith's prophecies are superior to the laws of the land. I have heard the prophet say that he would yet tread down his enemies, and walk over their dead bodies; and if he was not let alone, he would be a second Mohammed to this generation, and that he would make it one gore of blood from the Rocky Mountains to the Atlantic Ocean (Smith, *History of the Church*, 3:167 n.).

Orson Hyde, who also was angry with the Prophet, left Far West. Regarding Marsh's statement he commented: "The most of the statements in the foregoing disclosure I know to be true; the remainder I believe to be true" (Smith, *History of the Church,* 3:167 n.).

John Taylor later remarked:

In 1838, the best-selling books were Charles Dickens' *Oliver Twist* and *Nicholas Nickleby*. John James Audubon published the last volume in his series, *The Birds of America*. Berlioz, Chopin, and Wagner were composing music, and the Swedish nightingale, Jennie Lind, made her debut in Stockholm.

> [I]t is to be hoped, for the sake of the true brethren, that some things were added by our enemies that they did not assert, but enough was said to make this default and apostasy very terrible. . . . I was in Far West at the time . . . and was mixed up with all prominent Church affairs . . . and I know these things are not true. I have heard a good deal about Danites, but I never heard of them among the Latter-day Saints (Smith, *History of the Church*, 3:168 n.).

MOB VIOLENCE ESCALATES

In Missouri, the governor's mailbox was filled with false statements about terrible atrocities committed by the Mormons. Small bands of mobbers continued to prey upon outlying homesteads, and on October 24, a group of thirty or forty men under a Captain Bogart took Nathan Pinkham, William Seeley, and Addison Green prisoner. When the brethren in Far West were informed of the situation, they organized a group of men to follow Bogart and free the prisoners. James and Drusilla Hendricks lived nearby. Mrs. Hendricks gave the following account of their experiences and the events of that night:

> We all gave up our land and agreed to go to Caldwell County. We were to be let alone there, so we were glad to do so and not be mixed up with the mobbers. . . . We soon selected a place, built a cabin, and cut hay, for we had but little time to prepare for winter. We . . . began to live as we supposed the Saints would live. . . . On March 23, 1838, my fifth child was born and we called his name Joseph Smith Hendricks. The summer passed until August without any trouble . . . . Our trouble began over the election. . . . This scene of things continued until October 24, 1838, when the mob gathered on the south of us and sent out word that they would burn everything they came to and that they already had two of our brethren as prisoners and the prairies were black with smoke.
>
> We had no chance of taking care of our vegetables, so my husband said that we had better make the cabbage into kraut, so we went to work and finished it at ten o'clock that night. He asked if I would go with him to get a stone to weight the kraut. I walked behind him and watched his form, for he always stood erect. The thought came to me that I might never see him so straight and erect again. I couldn't tell my feelings if I should try, but I said nothing. We had prayer and went to bed and fell asleep. I dreamed that something had befallen him and I was gathering him in my arms when Bro. [Charles] C. Rich called at the door for him. . . . They had word that the mob was on Crooked River ten miles south of us . . . and was doing damage. I got up and lit a fire . . . while he brought his horse to the door. I got his overcoat and put his pistols in the pockets. Then got his sword and belted it on him. He bid me goodnight and got on his horse, and I took his gun from the rack and handed it to him and said, "Don't get shot in the back." I had got used to his going, so went to bed and went to sleep (Kenneth W. Godfrey, Audrey M. Godfrey, Jill Mulvay Derr, *Women's Voices*, 87–90).

Heber Kimball also recorded some of the events of the battle at Crooked River:

> A company of sixty or seventy persons immediately volunteered in Far West to watch [the mob's] movements, and if necessary, repel their attacks. They chose Elder Patten for their leader, and commenced their march about midnight, and came up to the mob at the dawn of October 25. As the brethren were marching quietly along the road near the top of the hill, they were fired upon. When young O'Bannion reeled out of the ranks, and fell mortally wounded. Captain Patten ordered his men to charge the mob . . . on the creek below. It was yet so dark that little could be seen, looking to the west; but the mob could see Captain Patten and his men in the dawning light, when they fired a broadside and three or four of the brethren fell. Captain Patten ordered the fire returned. . . . . The mob were soon put to

flight and crossed the river at the ford. One of the mob fired from behind a tree and shot Captain Patten, who instantly fell mortally wounded, the ball having pierced his abdomen (Whitney, *Life of Heber C. Kimball*, 212-13).

After her husband left for Crooked River, Drusilla Hendricks went back to bed.

I was aroused from my sleep suddenly, and I thought the yard was full of men and they were shooting. I was on my feet before I knew what I was doing. I went to the window but all was still. . . . I ventured to open the door. It was getting light enough, so I could see very little. I went out and around the house and found there was no one there. Then I was worse scared than ever. . . . I got the children up and walked the floor and watched the road. I tried to work but could not. I tried to keep still but could not. I went to the loom to try and weave. . . . I could not weave at all, but had not sat there but a few moments when I saw Mr. T. Snider (he did not belong to the church, but a good man) get off his horse at the gate. I saw him wipe his eyes. I knew that he was crying. He came to the door and said, "Mr. Hendricks wishes you to come to him." I asked where. He said, "To the widow Metcalfs." . . . There was a woman in the house that I had taken care of for weeks. I told her to do the best she could with the children, and I mounted the horse behind Mr. Snyder. We had four miles to ride. . . . I went into the house. Sister [Ann] Patten had just reached the bed where her husband [David Patten] lay and I heard him say, "Ann, don't weep. I have kept the faith and my work is done." My husband lay within three feet of Brother Patten, and I spoke to him. He could speak but could not move any-more than if he were dead. I tried to get him to move his feet but he could not.

My husband was shot in the neck where it cut off all feeling to his body. It is of no use for me to try and tell how I felt, for that is impossible, but I could not have shed a tear if all had been dead before me. I went to work to try and get my husband warm. I rubbed and steamed him.

One of the brethren told me how he fell, for he was close to him. After he had fallen, one of the brethren asked him which side he was on (for it was not yet light enough to see) and all the answer he made was the watchword "God and Liberty." On hearing this, it melted me to tears and I felt better . . . . We stayed here until almost night when one of our neighbors . . . came with a wagon and bed in it and took us to Far West (Godfrey et al., *Women's Voices*, 90–92).

THE BATTLE OF
CROOKED RIVER
by C.C.A. Christensen
Seven men under
Captain David Patten
were wounded, three
of whom lost their
lives.

Through priesthood blessings, Brother Hendricks regained some mobility but remained an invalid. The following March, Sister Hendricks moved her family to Quincy, Illinois. Her husband broke out in sores, and the family was out of food. She reflected:

The conflict began in my mind. . . . "Your folks told you your husband would be killed, and are you not sorry you did not listen to them?" I said, "no, I am not. I did what was right. If I die, I am glad I was baptized for the remission of my sins, for I have an answer of a good conscience." But after that, a third person spoke. It was a still, small voice, this time saying, "Hold on, the Lord will provide." I said I would for I would trust in Him and not grumble (Godfrey, *Women's Voices*, 95–96).

Lorenzo Snow was on a mission in Kentucky when the troubles broke out in Missouri. When he learned that the Saints had been expelled from Missouri, he traveled to Ohio and later joined the main body of Saints in Illinois. Eliza and the rest of the Snow family, however, had experienced the Missouri persecutions. Eliza recorded:

A spirit of mobocracy was boldly manifested by leading citizens in the county opposing the Latter-day Saints . . . preventing their vote. . . . also by the laying an embargo on all of the flouring mills in that section, and preventing our people from obtaining breadstuff. Our father had an abundance of wheat, but could get no grinding. In this dilemma we had to resort to graters, made by perforating tin pails and stovepipes, on which we grated corn for bread material. . . . [O]ur grated corn meal, when cooked by the usual process of bread making, was not quite so solid as lead, but bore a more than satisfactory resemblance to it. "Necessity, the mother of invention," prompted experimenting, and we set our wits to work to make our meal not only [edible], but palatable. . . . We had a fine crop of Missouri pumpkins. . . . These we stewed and when boiling hot, stirred it into our grated meal, which, when seasoned with salt and nicely baked—well buttered or in milk, was really very delicious; the main thing was to get enough, especially after the mob had driven in the scattered settlers, by which the number of our family was increased to twenty-five (Snow, *Biography and Family Record of Lorenzo Snow*, 42).

On Saturday, October 27, the Saints were attending the funeral of Apostle Patten, who had been killed in the battle at Crooked River, when Governor Boggs issued an order calling for the extermination of the Mormons.

> I have received . . . information which changes the whole face of things, and places the Mormons in the attitude of open and avowed defiance of the laws, and of having made open war upon the people of this state. . . . The Mormons must be treated as enemies and must be exterminated or driven from the state. . . . Their outrages are beyond all description (Smith, *History of the Church*, 3:175).

HAUN'S MILL MASSACRE

The mobbers found out about the extermination order and attacked a small Mormon settlement at Haun's Mill. Joseph Young had recently arrived in Haun's Mill, and was enjoying a tranquil afternoon with his family. Mr. Young recorded:

> The banks of Shoal Creek on either side teemed with children sporting and playing, while their mothers were engaged in domestic employments and their fathers employed in guarding the mills and other property, while others engaged in gathering in their crops for their winter consumption. The weather was very pleasant, the sun shone clear, all was tranquil. . . . It was about four o'clock, while sitting in my cabin with my babe in my arms, and my wife standing by my side, the door being open, I cast my eyes on the opposite bank of Shoal Creek and saw a large company of armed men, on horses, directing their course towards the mills with all possible speed. . . . At this moment, David Evans, seeing the superiority of their numbers (there being two hundred and forty of them, according to their own account), swung his hat, and cried for peace. This not being heeded, they continued to advance, and their leader, Mr. Nehemiah Comstock, fired a gun, which was followed by a solemn pause of ten or twelve seconds, when, all at once, they discharged about one hundred rifles, aiming at a blacksmith shop into which our friends had fled for safety; and charged up to the shop, the cracks of which between the logs were sufficiently large to enable them to aim directly at the bodies who had there fled for refuge. . . . There were several families tented in the rear of the shop, whose lives were exposed, and amidst a shower of bullets fled to the woods in different directions. . . . [F]inding myself in the uttermost danger, the bullets having reached the house where I was living, I committed my family to the protection of heaven, and leaving the house on the opposite side, I took a path which led up the hill, following in the trail of three of my brethren that had fled from the shop. . . . I secreted myself in a thicket of bushes where I lay until eight o'clock in the evening, at which time I heard a female voice calling my name in an under tone, telling me that the mob had gone and there was no danger. I . . . went to the house of Benjamin Lewis, where I found my family . . . in safety, and two of my friends mortally wounded, one of whom died before morning. . . . After daylight appeared, some four or five men, who with myself, had escaped with our lives . . . repaired . . . to the mills, to learn the condition of our friends, whose fate we had but too truly anticipated. . . . We immediately prepared and carried them

to the place of internment. The last office of kindness due to the remains of departed friends, was not attended with the customary ceremonies or decency, for we were in jeopardy, every moment expecting to be fired upon by the mob. . . . The place of burying was a vault in the ground formerly intended for a well, into which we threw the bodies of our friends. The number killed and mortally wounded in this wanton slaughter was eighteen or nineteen. To finish their work of destruction, this band of murderers . . . proceeded to rob the houses, wagons, and tents of bedding and clothing; drove off horses and wagons . . . and even stripped the clothing from the bodies of the slain. According to their own account, they fired . . . upwards of sixteen hundred shots at a little company of men, about thirty in number (Smith, *History of the Church*, 3:184-86).

Warren and Amanda Smith and their children were among the Saints who were moving from Kirtland to Missouri in the fall of 1838. They reached Haun's Mill the afternoon of October 30, and decided to stop for the night. Amanda recorded:

A little before sunset a mob of three hundred came upon us. The men hallooed for the women and children to run for the woods; and they ran into an old blacksmith's shop, for they feared, if we all ran together, they would rush upon us and kill the women and children. The mob fired before we had time to start from our camp. Our men took off their hats and swung them and cried "quarters" until they were shot. The mob paid no attention to their cries nor entreaties. . . . I took my little girls, my boy I could not find, and started for the woods. The mob encircled us on all sides but the brook. I ran down the bank, across the mill-pond on a plank, up the hill into the bushes. The bullets whistled around me all the way like hail, and cut down the bushes on all sides of us. One girl was wounded by my side, and fell over a log, and her clothes hung across the log; and they shot at them, expecting they were hitting her; and our people afterwards cut out of that log twenty bullets.

I sat down and witnessed the dreadful scene. When they had done firing, they began to howl and one would have thought that all the infernos had come from the lower regions. They plundered the principal part of our goods, took our horses and wagons, and ran off howling like demons.

I came down to view the awful sight. Oh horrible! My husband, and one son ten years old, lay lifeless upon the ground, and one son seven years old, wounded very badly. The ground was covered with the dead.

It was sunset; nothing but horror and distress; the dogs filled with rage, howling over their dead masters; the cattle caught the scent of the innocent blood, and bellowed; a dozen helpless widows, thirty or forty fatherless children, crying and moaning for the loss of their fathers and husbands; the groans of the wounded and dying were enough to have melted the heart of anything but a Missouri mob.

There were no men or not enough to bury the dead; so they were thrown into a dry well and covered with dirt. The next day the mob came back. They told us we must leave the state forthwith, or be killed. It was cold weather, and they had our teams and clothes, our husbands were dead or wounded. I told them they might kill me and my children, and welcome.

AMANDA BARNES SMITH (1809–1886) Amanda's oldest son, Willard, was the first person to go into the blacksmith shop after the massacre. His father and brother had been killed, and his little brother Alma lay badly wounded. Amanda, through direct answer to prayer and divine guidance, was able to nurse her little Alma back to health.
ca. 1840

I now leave it with this honorable government [the United States] to say what my damages may be, or what they would be willing to see their wives and children slaughtered for, as I have seen my husband, son and others.

I lost in property to the mob—fifty dollars, damage of horses and time . . . one gun . . . in short, my all. Whole damages are more than the state of Missouri is worth (Smith, *History of the Church*, 3:324–25).

TREACHERY IN FAR WEST

The day of the Haun's Mill massacre, the Saints in Far West learned about the governor's extermination order. Joseph Smith recorded:

On the 30th of October a large company of armed soldiers were seen approaching Far West. They came up near to the town . . . and encamped for the night. We were informed that they were militia, ordered out by the governor for the purpose of stopping our proceedings, it having been represented to his excellency . . . that we were the aggressors and had committed outrages in Daviess County (Smith, *History of the Church*, 3:187–88).

The Saints spent the night building a fortification of wagons and timber while the women gathered their valuables and prepared to flee. The men were outnumbered by their enemies five to one. Joseph continued:

About eight o'clock a flag of truce was sent from the enemy, which was met by several of our people, and it was hoped that matters would be satisfactorily arranged after the officers had heard a true statement of all the circumstances. Colonel Hinkle went to meet the flag. . . . The enemy was reinforced by about fifteen hundred men today. . . . Towards evening I was waited upon by Colonel Hinkle, who stated that the officers of the militia desired to have an interview with me and some others, hoping that the difficulties might be settled without having occasion to carry into effect the exterminating orders which they had received from the governor. I immediately complied with the request, and in company with Elders Sidney Rigdon and Parley P. Pratt, Colonel Wight and George W. Robinson, went in to the camp of the militia. But judge my surprise, when . . . we were taken as prisoners of war, and treated with the utmost contempt (Smith, *History of the Church*, 3:187-88).

Parley Pratt recorded what happened when he rode out to what he thought would be a council with the militia's officers:

As we approached the camp of the enemy General Lucas rode out to meet us with a guard of several hundred men.

The haughty general rode up, and, without speaking to us, instantly ordered his guards to surround us. They did so very abruptly, and we were marched into camp surrounded by thousands of savage looking beings, many of whom were dressed and painted like Indian warriors. These all set up a constant yell like so many bloodhounds let loose upon their prey. . . . If the vision of the infernal regions could suddenly open to the mind, with thousand of malicious fiends, all clamoring, exulting, deriding, blaspheming, mocking, railing, raging and foaming like a troubled sea, then could some idea be formed of the hell which we had entered.

In the camp we were placed under a strong guard and were without shelter during the night . . . in the midst of a great rain (*Autobiography of Parley P. Pratt*, 159-60).

AMASA LYMAN (1813–1877) joined the Church in 1832, and walked a distance of seven hundred miles to meet the Prophet in Hiram, Ohio.

The next morning Hyrum Smith and Amasa Lyman were taken prisoner. The militia's officers held a court and sentenced all the prisoners to be shot. Samuel Lucas, the commanding officer, ordered:

To Brigadier General Doniphan. Sir:—You will take Joseph Smith and the other prisoners into the public square of Far West, and shoot them at 9 o'clock tomorrow morning. Signed, Samuel D. Lucas, Major General commanding.

[General Doniphan, however, replied:]

It is cold-blooded murder. I will not obey your order. My brigade shall march for Liberty tomorrow morning at 8 o'clock; and if you execute these men, I will hold you responsible before an earthly tribunal, so help me God. Signed, A. W. Doniphan, Brigadier-General (Smith, *History of the Church*, 3:190–91 n. 2).

The mob, now called "the governor's troops," entered Far West and plundered and ransacked the town. They forced the men to sign away their property and violated the women. Another eighty men were taken prisoner and brought to the public square. Joseph recorded:

> We, after much entreaty, were suffered to see our families, being attended all the while by a strong guard. I found my wife and children in tears. . . . When I entered my house, they clung to my garments, their eyes streaming with tears, while mingled emotions of joy and sorrow were manifested in their countenances. . . . Who can realize the feelings which I experienced at that time, to be thus torn from my companion, and leave her surrounded with monsters in the shape of men, and my children, too, not knowing how their wants would be supplied; while I was to be taken far from them in order that my enemies might destroy me when they thought proper to do so (Smith, *History of the Church*, 3:193).

Parley Pratt said good-bye to his family:

> I went to my house, being guarded by two or three soldiers; the cold rain was pouring down without, and on entering my little cottage, there lay my wife sick of a fever. . . . At her breast was our son Nathan, an infant of three months, and by her side a little girl of five years. On the foot of the same bed lay a woman in travail, who had been driven from her home in the night. . . my wife burst into tears; I spoke a few words of comfort, telling her to try to live for my sake and the children's; and expressing a hope that we should meet again though years might separate us. She promised to try to live. I then embraced and kissed the little babies and departed.
>
> As I returned from my house towards the troops in the square, I halted . . . at the door of Hyrum Smith, and heard the sobs and groans of his wife, at his parting words. She was then near confinement and needed more than ever the comfort and consolation of a husband's presence. As we returned to the wagon we saw Sidney Rigdon taking leave of his wife and daughters. . . . In the wagon sat Joseph Smith, while his aged father and venerable mother came up overwhelmed with tears, and took each of the prisoners by the hand with a silence of grief too great for utterance. . . . Orders were given and we moved slowly away, under the conduct of General Wilson and his whole brigade (*Autobiography of Parley P. Pratt*, 162-63).

The mob's leaders took great pride in their prisoners and fought to see who would have the honor of displaying them before the public. General Wilson, who had been part of the Jackson County mob, declared:

GENERAL ALEXANDER WILLIAM DONIPHAN (1808–1887), Missouri Militia. General Doniphan refused to execute Joseph Smith and others, and wrote to his superiors, *"It is cold-blooded murder. I will not obey your order . . ."* Doniphan, a lawyer, later served in the Missouri state legislature, fought in the Mexican War, was a delegate in 1861 to help avoid the drift toward civil war, and briefly served in the Civil War as a Union major general in the in the Missouri State Guard. *Engraved by Charles B. Hall*

"It was repeatedly insinuated, by the other officers and troops that we should hang you prisoners on the first tree we came to on the way to Independence. But I'll be d——d if anybody shall hurt you. We just intend to exhibit you in Independence. Let the people look at you and see what a d——n set of fine fellows you are. And more particularly, to keep you from that old bigot of a General Clark" (Smith, *History of the Church*, 3:200 n. 2).

On their way to Jackson County, the Prophet comforted Parley Pratt:

"As we arose and commenced our march on the morning of November 3, Joseph Smith spoke to me and the other prisoners, in a low, but cheerful and confidential tone; said he: "Be of good cheer, brethren; the word of the Lord came to me last night that our lives should be given us, and that whatever we may suffer during this captivity, not one of our lives should be taken" (*Autobiography of Parley P. Pratt,* 164).

When they reached Jackson County, many people gathered to see the prisoners. After a few days, the men were delivered to General Clark in Richmond. It was here that the Saints found out the details of the treaty that George Hinkle had agreed to in their behalf. General Clark informed the Saints:

It now befalls upon you to fulfill the treaty that you have entered into, the leading items of which I shall now lay before you. The first requires that your leading men be given up to be tried according to law; this you have already complied with. The second is, that you deliver up your arms; this has been attended to. The third stipulation is, that you sign over your properties to defray the expenses of the war; this you have also done. Another article yet remains for you to comply with, and that is, that you leave the state forthwith. . . . The orders of the governor to me were, that you should be exterminated, and not allowed to remain in the state, and had not your leaders been given up, the terms of the treaty complied with, before this, you and your families would have been destroyed and your houses in ashes. There is a discretionary power vested in my hands which I shall exercise in your favor for a season; for this lenity you are indebted to my clemency. I do not say that you shall go now, but you must not think of staying here another season. . . . As for your leaders, do not once think—do not imagine for a moment—do not let it enter your mind that they will be delivered, or that you will see their faces again, for their fate is fixed. Their die is cast, their fate is sealed. . . . I would advise you to scatter abroad, and never again organize yourselves. . . . You have always been the aggressors—you have brought upon yourselves these difficulties (Smith, *History of the Church*, 3:202-4).

DIGNITY AND MAJESTY

About sixty brethren were held in Richmond while General Clark and others tried to figure out how to legally try and convict civilians in a military court-martial for crimes they did not commit. Joseph and six other men were kept under tight security and were even chained together. Parley Pratt wrote:

In one of those tedious nights we had lain as if in sleep till the hour of midnight had passed, and our ears and hearts had been pained, while we had listened for hours to the obscene jests, the horrid oaths, the dreadful blasphemies and filthy language of our guards, . . . as they recounted to each other their deeds of rapine, murder, robbery, etc., which they had committed among the "Mormons" while at Far West and vicinity. They even boasted of defiling by force wives, daughters and virgins and of shooting or dashing out the brains of men, women and children.

I had listened till I became disgusted, shocked, horrified, and so filled with the spirit of indignant justice . . . but had said nothing to Joseph, or anyone else, although I lay next to him and knew he was awake. On a sudden, he arose to his feet and spoke in a voice of thunder, or as the roaring lion, uttering as near as I can recollect, the following words:

"Silence, ye fiends of the infernal pit. In the name of Jesus Christ I rebuke you, and command you to be still; I will not live another minute and hear such language. Cease such talk, or you or I die this instant!"

He ceased to speak. He stood erect in terrible majesty. Chained and without a weapon, calm, unruffled and dignified as an angel, he looked upon the quailing guards, . . . whose knees smote together, and who, shrinking into a corner, or crouching at his feet, begged his pardon, and remained quiet till the change of guards.

I have seen the ministers of justice, clothed in magisterial robes, and criminals arraigned before them, while life was suspended on a breath, in the courts of England; I have witnessed a Congress in solemn session to give laws to nations; I have tried to conceive of kings, of royal courts, of thrones and crowns; and of emperors assembled to dedicate the fate of kingdoms; but dignity and majesty have I seen but once, as it stood in chains, at midnight, in a dungeon in an obscure village of Missouri (*Autobiography of Parley P. Pratt*, 179–80).

Joseph and some of the other prisoners were moved to Liberty Jail in Clay County, while Parley Pratt and a few others remained in the Richmond Jail. Joseph noted that the prisoners enjoyed few comforts: "We were sometimes visited by our friends . . . but frequently we were not suffered to have that privilege. Our food was of the coarsest kind, and served up in a manner which was disgusting.

MAJESTY IN CHAINS *by Liz Lemon Swindle* depicts Joseph Smith as he rebuked the foul-mouthed and blasphemous prison guards in a Richmond, Missouri jail. *oil on canvas*

Thus, in a land of liberty, in the town of Liberty, Clay County, Missouri, my fellow prisoners and I in chains and dungeons, saw the close of 1838" (Smith, *History of the Church,* 3:244).

However, not all of the apostles had been arrested. Heber C. Kimball wrote:

> I have no doubt that I would also have been taken a prisoner, for every means was adopted by Hinkle to have me taken, but he could not remember me. The mob had not become acquainted with Brother Brigham, as he lives three or four miles from the city on Mill Creek; and I had not been there over three weeks when the mobbing commenced.
>
> The murders, house-burnings, robberies, rapes, drivings, whippings, imprisonments, and other sufferings and cruelties inflicted upon the people of God . . . have only in part been laid before the world (Whitney, *Life of Heber C. Kimball,* 222–23).

In Far West, Brigham and Heber secretly met with the brethren who had not been killed or arrested and reorganized the high council. On December 19 they ordained John Taylor and John E. Page as apostles. These brethren previously had been called to the Quorum of the Twelve by revelation and approved by the members of the Church, but the ordinations had not been performed. Soon after the new year began, Joseph sent the Saints a letter of instruction from

Liberty Jail, reminding them of the revelation that called the Twelve on missions. He also informed the brethren:

> It will be necessary for you to get the Twelve together, ordain such as have not been ordained . . . and proceed to regulate the Elders as the Lord may give you wisdom. We nominate George A. Smith and Lyman Sherman to take the places of Orson Hyde and Thomas B. Marsh.
>
> Brethren, fear not, but be strong in the Lord and in the power of His might . . . neither think it strange concerning the fiery trials with which we are tried . . . for so the wicked persecuted the prophets which were before us.
>
> Brethren, pray for us, and cease not till our deliverance comes, which we hope may come. Brethren, we remain yours in hope of eternal life. Signed Joseph Smith, Jr., Sidney Rigdon, Hyrum Smith. N.B. Appoint the oldest of those of the Twelve, who were first appointed, to be president of your quorum (Whitney, *Life of Heber C. Kimball*, 238).

A COVENANT OF COMPASSION

In accordance with these instructions, Brigham Young became President of the Quorum of the Twelve Apostles.

In February, Brigham Young left Far West with his wife, children, and Heber Kimball's family. Heber, because he was unknown to the enemies of the Church, stayed behind to visit the prisoners, deliver petitions to the state legislature, and try to obtain the release of the Prophet and the others.

During January of 1839, while the Prophet was in prison, Brigham Young and the other Apostles prepared to help the Saints leave the state. Government investigations and actions were postponed for so long that the members lost hope that they would ever regain their land and be allowed to stay in Missouri.

Elias Smith served as secretary in a meeting held in Far West. He recorded:

> Resolved: That it is the opinion of this meeting that an exertion should be made to ascertain how much can be obtained from the individuals of [the Church], and that it is the duty of those who have, to assist those who have not, and that thereby we may, as far as possible, within and of ourselves, comply with the demands of the Executive. . . . On the motion of Brigham Young, it was resolved that we this day enter into a covenant to stand by and assist each other to the utmost of our abilities in removing from this state and that we will never desert the poor who are worthy, till they shall be out of the reach of the exterminating order (Smith, *History of the Church*, 3:250).

More than 200 members signed the covenant. Some of the brethren helped gather members of the Church who still lived outside Far West. Others collected food and equipment. The families of the prisoners were moved first, and on February 6, Stephen Markham helped Emma Smith and her four little children leave the area. They walked 150 miles across Missouri toward Illinois. Under her skirts, Emma carried two cotton bags filled with Joseph's papers, including his inspired revisions of the Bible. They crossed the frozen Mississippi River on

February 15 and waited in Quincy, Illinois, for Joseph to be freed from jail. Joseph Smith recorded that during the month of February:

> At a meeting of The Church of Jesus Christ of Latter-day Saints, held in the town of Quincy . . . Elder John P. Greene . . . stated that a liberal offer had been made . . . of about twenty thousand acres, lying between the Mississippi and Des Moines rivers at two dollars per acre, to be paid in twenty annual installments, without interest. . . . Bishop Partridge thought it was not expedient . . . to collect together but thought it better to scatter into different parts.
>
> *February 14th*—The persecution was so bitter against Elder Brigham Young and his life was so diligently sought for that he was compelled to flee and he left Far West for Illinois. My father and mother started this day for Quincy with an ox team.
>
> *February 25th*—At a meeting of the Democratic Association, held this evening at Quincy, Adams County, Illinois, Mr. Lindsay introduced a resolution setting forth that the people called "Latter-day Saints" were many of them in a situation requiring the aid of the citizens of Quincy, and recommending that measures be adopted for their relief. . . . After we were cast into prison, we heard nothing but threatenings, that if any judge or jury . . . should clear any of us, we should never get out of the state alive. This soon determined our course, and that was to escape out of their hands as soon as we could, and by any means we could. After we had been some length of time in prison, we demanded a habeas corpus . . . which with some considerable reluctance, was granted. After the investigation, Sidney Rigdon was released . . . he was let out of jail secretly in the night . . . . pursued by a body of armed men. . . . [I]t was through the direction of a kind Providence that he escaped out of their hands, and safely arrived in Quincy, Illinois (Smith, *History of the Church*, 3:260-64).

OF ONE HEART— EMMA CROSSING THE ICE, *by Liz Lemon Swindle* Emma and her children crossing the frozen Mississippi River on their way to Illinois to await Joseph's release from Liberty jail. *oil on canvas*

RESPITE IN ILLINOIS

The Saints were treated kindly in Illinois. The Democratic Association of Quincy met with Church leaders, and instructed the townspeople to help the Latter-day Saints. The citizens of Quincy opened their homes and helped the Saints obtain food and other supplies. In the meantime, a man named Isaac Galland heard of the Saints' plight and suggested that the members gather in the area of Commerce, north of Quincy.

Meanwhile, Brigham Young, John Taylor, and the other apostles helped the Saints settle in Illinois. Eleven men were called to stay in Far West to supervise the Saints' exodus, help the poor, distribute goods and food, and arrange for wagons and teams.

From prison, Joseph wrote letters to his family, friends, and the Church. In a letter to Emma, he wrote:

> It is now about five months and six days since I have been under the grimace, of a guard night and day, and within the walls, grates and squeaking iron doors, of a lonesome, dark, dirty prison. . . . I think of you and the children continually. . . . I want you should not let those little fellows, forget me, tell them Father loves them with a perfect love, and he is doing all he can to get away from the mob to come to them, do teach them all you can, that they may have good minds, be tender and kind to them. . . . Tell them Father says they must be good children and mind their mother. My dear Emma there is great responsibility resting upon you, in preserving yourself in honor and sobriety, before them and teaching them right things, to form their young and tender minds, that they begin in right paths, and not get contaminated when young by seeing ungodly examples (Jessee, *The Personal Writings of Joseph Smith*, 425).

Probably the most important letter that Joseph wrote from prison was sent on March 25. It contained counsel to the Church, and recounted powerful yet poignant revelations he had received. Parts of this letter now make up Sections 121, 122, and 123 of the Doctrine and Covenants.

Of One Heart— Liberty Jail *by Liz Lemon Swindle* depicts the Prophet's loneliness and longing as he pleads with the Lord for comfort and reassurance.

oil on canvas

> My son, peace be unto thy soul; thine adversity and thine afflictions shall be but a small moment; And then, if thou endure it well, God shall exalt thee on high.
>
> How long can rolling waters remain impure? What power shall stay the heavens? As well might man stretch forth his puny arm to stop the Missouri River in its decreed course, or to turn it upstream, as to hinder the Almighty from pouring down knowledge from heaven upon the heads of the Latter-day Saints. Behold, there are many called, but few are chosen. And why are they not chosen? Because their hearts are set so much upon the things of this world, and aspire to the honors of men, that they do not learn this one lesson—That the rights of the priesthood are inseparably connected with the powers of heaven, and that the powers of Heaven cannot be controlled nor handled only upon the principles of righteousness.
>
> . . . Know thou my son, that all these things shall give thee experience and shall be for thy good (D&C 121:7-8, 33-36; 122:7).

In early April, a group of men met with Captain Bogart—one of the leaders of the mob—to discuss expelling the remaining Mormons from Missouri. John Whitmer and Theodore Turley were in the room. Joseph Smith recorded that at this meeting:

> Eight men . . . presented the paper containing the revelation of July 8, 1838 . . . directing the Twelve to take leave of the saints in Far West on the building site of the Lord's house on the 26th of April, to go to the isles of the sea, and then asked him to read it.
>
> Turley said, "Gentlemen, I am well acquainted with it."
>
> Bogart then replied, "Then you as a rational man will give up Joseph Smith's being a prophet and an inspired man? He and the Twelve are now scattered all over creation; let them come here if they dare; if they do, they will be murdered. As that revelation cannot be fulfilled, you will now give up your faith."
>
> "In the name of God, that revelation will be fulfilled," replied Turley.
>
> Bogart continued, "If they come, they will get murdered; they dare not come to take their leave here . . . you had better do as John Corrill has done; he's going to publish a book called Mormonism Fairly Delineated; he is a sensible man, and you had better assist him."
>
> "I now call upon you, John Whitmer: you say Corrill is a moral and a good man; do you believe him when he says the Book of Mormon is true, or

when he says it is not true? . . . All I know is that you have published to the world that an angel did present those plates to Joseph Smith."

To this, John Whitmer responded, "I handled those plates. There were fine engravings on both sides. I handled them. . . . They were shown to me by a supernatural power" (Smith, *History of the Church*, 3:306-7).

On April 6, the prisoners were finally released from Liberty Jail. Joseph Smith recorded: "Judge King evidently fearing a change of venue, or some movement on our part to escape . . . (and most probably expecting that we would be murdered on the way) hurried myself and fellow prisoners off to Daviess County under a guard of about ten" (Smith, *History of the Church*, 3:308).

Liberty Jail had been a miserable place. The building was twenty-two feet square and had double walls. The outer walls were made of stone and the inner walls were made of oak logs. Between these walls was a one-foot space that had been filled with loose rocks. Inside the jail were two rooms about fourteen feet square. The ceilings were so low that a man Joseph's size could not stand up straight. The upper room had two small barred windows and contained beds made of rough-hewn logs that were covered with straw. The food was so bad it sometimes made the men sick. Five months of imprisonment and inactivity took a toll on the prisoners' strength. Joseph recorded:

> *Monday, April 8th*—After a tedious journey—for our long confinement had enfeebled our bodily powers—we arrived in Daviess County where we were delivered into the hands of William Morgan, Sheriff.
>
> *Tuesday, April 9th*—Our trial commenced before a drunken grand jury. Austin A. King presiding Judge was drunk as the jury for they were all drunk together. Brother Markham arriving among us this afternoon, brought us a written copy of a statute which had passed the legislature, giving us the privilege of a change of venue on our own affidavit.
>
> *Wednesday, April 10th*—The day was spent in the examination of witnesses before the grand jury. Doctor Sampson Avard was one of the witnesses. Brother Markham was not permitted to give his testimony.
>
> *Thursday, April 11th*—The grand jury brought in a bill for murder, treason, burglary, arson, larceny, theft, and stealing against Lyman Wight, Alexander McRae, Caleb Baldwin, Hyrum Smith and myself (Smith, *History of the Church*, 3:309-15).

Peter H. Burnett was one of Joseph's attorneys during the trial in Daviess County. He wrote the following description of the Prophet:

> Joseph Smith, Jr. was at least six feet high, well formed, and weighed about one hundred and eighty pounds. His appearance was not prepossessing and his conversational powers were but ordinary. You could tell at a glance that his education was very limited. He was an awkward but vehement speaker. In conversation, he was slow and used too many words to express his

ideas and would not generally go directly to a point. But with all these draw-backs, he was much more than an ordinary man. He possessed the most indomitable perseverance, was a good judge of men and deemed himself born to command and he did command. His views were so strange and striking and his manner was so earnest, and apparently so candid, that you could not but be interested. And there was a kind, a familiar look about him that pleased you. He had the capacity for discussing a subject in different aspects and for proposing many original views, even on ordinary matters. He had great influence over others. As evidence of this, I will state that on Thursday, just before I left to return to Liberty, I saw him out among the crowd, conversing freely with every one, and seeming to be perfectly at ease. In the short space of five days he had managed so to mollify his enemies that he could go unprotected among them without the slightest danger. Among the Mormons he had much greater influence than Sidney Rigdon. The latter was a man of superior education, an eloquent speaker, of fine appearance and dignified manners; but he did not possess that native intellect of Smith and lacked his determined will (Peter H. Burnett, *Recollections and Opinions of an Old Pioneer*, 66-67).

Joseph and the others obtained a change of venue and left for Boone County on the morning of April 15 under strong guard. Hyrum Smith later recorded:

A mittimus was made out by Judge Birch, without date, name, or place. They [the court officials at Gallatin, Daviess County] fitted us out with a two-horse wagon, and horses and four men, besides the sheriff, to be our guard. We . . . went as far as Di-Ahman that evening and stayed till morning. There we bought two horses of the guard, and paid for one of them in clothing, which we had with us; and for the other we gave our note. We went down that day as far as Judge Morin's. There we stayed until the next morning, when we . . . traveled on the road about twenty miles. There we bought a jug of whiskey, with which we treated the company; and while there the sheriff showed us the mittimus before referred to, without date or signature, and said that Judge Birch told him never to carry us to Boone County and never to show the mittimus; and, said he, I shall take a good drink of grog and go to bed and you may do as you have a mind to do. Three others of the guard drank freely of whiskey . . . and they also went to bed, and were soon asleep, and the other guard went along with us, and helped to saddle the horses. Two of us mounted the horses, and the other three started on foot, and we took our change of venue for the state of Illinois, and in the course of nine or ten days arrived safe at Quincy, . . . where we found our families in a state of poverty, although in good health (Smith, *History of the Church*, 3:423).

The Saints who were still in Far West faced increasing mob violence. Ten to fifteen thousand Saints had left Missouri and abandoned everything they owned, including farms, homes, businesses, and livestock. By April 20, the town was almost deserted.

When Heber C. Kimball found out that Joseph and the others were no longer in jail, he returned to the Far West area to wait for Brigham Young and the other apostles. He recorded:

> I kept myself concealed in the woods, and passed round the country, notifying the brethren and sisters to be on hand at the appointed time for the laying of the cornerstone.
>
> *April 25*—This night, which was beautiful, clear moonlight, Elders Brigham Young, Orson Pratt, John E. Page, John Taylor, Wilford Woodruff, George A. Smith, and Altheus Cutler, arrived from Quincy, Illinois, and rode into the public square early on the morning of the 26th. All seemed still as death.
>
> *April 26*—We held a conference at the house of brother Samuel Clark, cut off 31 persons from the church and then proceeded to the building spot of the Lord's house, where, after singing, we recommended laying the foundation, agreeably to the revelation given July 8, 1838, by rolling a stone, upwards of a ton weight, upon or near the southeast corner.
>
> In company with Brother Brigham Young, we ordained Wilford Woodruff and George A. Smith (who had been previously nominated by the First Presidency, accepted by the Twelve, and acknowledged by the Church at Quincy) members of the quorum of the Twelve Apostles; and Darwin Chase and Norman Shearer (who were liberated from Richmond prison on the 24th, Seventies. They sat on the southeast cornerstone while we ordained them.
>
> The Twelve then individually called upon the Lord in prayer, kneeling on the cornerstone; after which, "Adam-ondi-Ahman" was sung.
>
> The brethren wandered among our deserted houses, many of which were in ruins.
>
> We went to Father Clarke's, breakfasted, and before sunrise departed. I accompanied my brethren, riding thirty miles that day. We continued our journey to Quincy, where I found my family well and in good spirits, on the 2nd of May (Whitney, *Life of Heber C. Kimball*, 252-53).

A few Saints attended this last meeting of the Twelve in Far West. Joseph's records state that after the meeting:

> As the Saints were passing away from the meeting, Brother Turley said to Elders Page and Woodruff, "Stop a bit, while I bid Isaac Russell goodbye"; and knocking at the door, called Brother Russell. His wife answered, "Come in, it is Brother Turley." Russell replied, "It is not; he left here two weeks ago"; and appeared quite alarmed.; but on finding it was Brother Turley, asked him to sit down; but the latter replied, "I cannot, I shall lose my company." "Who is your company?" enquired Russell. "The Twelve." "The Twelve?" "Yes, don't you know that this is the ttwenty-sixth and the day the Twelve were to take leave of their friends on the foundation of the Lord's house to go to the islands of the sea? The revelation is now fulfilled, and I am going with them." Russell was speechless and Turley bid him farewell. The brethren immediately returned to Quincy, taking with them the families from Tenny's Grove (Smith, *History of the Church*, 3:399-40).

STARTING OVER IN NAUVOO

The Church of Jesus Christ of Latter-day Saints was nine years old that spring of 1839. The families who had lived in Missouri were now homeless and dependent on the charity of others. But they were hopeful. The Prophet and other leaders were alive, and plans were being made for a new city and a new start. In May of 1839, a general conference was held near Quincy, Illinois. Joseph Smith recorded some of the matters of business taken up in that meeting.

> That George A. Smith be acknowledged as one of the Twelve Apostles. That Elders Orson Hyde and William Smith be allowed the privilege of appearing personally before the next general conference . . . to give an account of their conduct. . . . That the conference do sanction the mission intended for the Twelve to Europe, and that they will do all in their power to enable them to go. That the next general conference be held on the first Saturday in October next (Smith, *History of the Church*, 3:345).

The Saints chose to build their new town in an area north of Quincy. Joseph bought a farm with a house on it and moved his young family to a site on the banks of the Mississippi River. "Friday, May 10, 1839—I arrived with my family at the White purchase and took up my residence in a small log house on the bank of the river, about one mile south of Commerce City, hoping that I and my friends may here find a resting place for a little season at least" (Smith, *History of the Church,* 3:349).

Joseph had selected an area along the banks of the Mississippi River as the Saints' new home. Two cities were to be built, the city on the east side of the river was to be called Nauvoo the Beautiful, and the city on the west side of the river was to be called Zarahemla. Joseph began to buy land in the area and encouraged the Saints to do the same. Philo Dibble related the circumstances of one land purchase:

> When Joseph first came to Nauvoo, then called Commerce, a Mr. White living there preferred to sell him his farm for two thousand and five hundred dollars. Five hundred dollars of the amount to be paid down, and the balance one year from that time. Joseph and the brethren were talking about this offer when some of them said, "We can't buy it, for we lack the money."
>
> Joseph took out his purse, and emptying out its contents, offered a half dollar to one of the brethren, which he declined accepting, but Joseph urged him to take it, and then gave each of the other brethren a similar amount, which left him without any. Addressing the brethren he said: "Now you all have money, and I have none; but the time will come when I will have money and you will have none!"
>
> He then said to Bishop Knight, "You go back and buy the farm!" The bargain was closed and the obligations drawn up, but how the money was going to be raised neither Brother Knight nor the other brethren could see.

The next morning Joseph and several of the brethren went down to Mr. White's to sign the agreement and make the first payment on the land. A table was brought out with the papers upon it, and Joseph signed them, moved back from the table and sat with his head down, as if in thought for a moment. Just then a man drove up in a carriage and asked if Mr. Smith was there. Joseph hearing it, got up and went to the door.

The man said, "Good morning, Mr. Smith; I am on a speculation today. I want to buy some land, and I thought I would come and see you."

Joseph then pointed around where his land lay, but the man said, "I can't go with you today to see the land. Do you want any money this morning?"

Joseph replied he would like some, and when the stranger asked how much, he told him five hundred dollars.

The man walked into the house with Joseph, emptied a small sack of gold on the table, and counted out that amount. He then handed to Joseph another one hundred dollars saying, "Mr. Smith, I make you a present of this."

After this transpired, Joseph laughed at the brethren and said: "You trusted in money; but I trusted in God. Now I have money and you have none" (Andrus, *They Knew the Prophet*, 71-72).

Wilford Woodruff recorded how his family lived when they first came to the Nauvoo area:

In company with Brother Brigham Young and our families, I left Quincy on the 15th of May, arriving in Commerce on the 18th. After an interview with Joseph, we crossed the river at Montrose, Iowa. President Brigham Young and myself, with our families, occupied one room about fourteen feet square. Finally Brother Young obtained another room and moved into it; then Brother Orson Pratt and family moved into the same room with myself and family. . . . It was a very sickly time; Joseph had given up his home in Commerce to the sick, and had a tent pitched in his dooryard and was living in that himself. The large number of saints who had been driven out of Missouri were flocking into Commerce, but had no homes to go to, and were living in wagons, in tents and on the ground; many, therefore, were sick through the exposure to which they were subjected. Brother Joseph had waited on them until he was worn out and nearly sick himself (Cowley, *Wilford Woodruff: History of His Life and Labors*, 103-4).

At this point, only four Mormons remained in the state of Missouri—Parley P. Pratt, King Follett, Morris Phelps, and Luman Gibbs. The prisoners had learned that Joseph and the others were now safe in Illinois, and when summer came, they decided to attempt an escape. On July 4, they made a flag from a shirt, wrote "Liberty" on it in large red letters and hung it from their prison window. That evening when the guards brought dinner, the prisoners were ready. Elder Pratt recorded:

No sooner was the key turned than the door was seized by Mr. Follett with both hands. . . . He soon opened a passage, which was in the same instant filled by Mr. Phelps, and followed by myself and Mr. Follett. The old jailer strolled across the way, and stretched out his arms . . . but all to no purpose. One or two leaps brought us to the bottom of the stairs, carrying the old gentleman with us headlong, helter skelter. . . . The jailer's wife . . . not only assisted in the scuffle, but cried out so loud that the town was soon alarmed. We found ourselves in the open air in front of the prison and in full view of the citizens who had already commenced to rally, while Mr. Phelps and the jailer still clinched fast hold of each other like two mastiffs. However, in another instant he cleared himself, and we were all three scampering off through the fields towards the thicket.

By this time the town was all in motion. . . . The streets on both sides of the fields where we were running were soon thronged with soldiers in uniform, mounted riflemen, footmen . . . boys, dogs, etc., all running, rushing, screaming, swearing, shouting, bawling and looking, while clouds of dust rose behind them. . . . But we kept our course for the thickets, our toes barely touching the ground, while we seemed to leap with the fleetness of a deer. . . . Our friends who had stood waiting in the thickets . . . sprang forward to the edge of the fields and ran back again to the horses as if the using of their own limbs would serve to add nimbleness to those of the prisoners. . . . "Fly quickly, they are upon you!"

"Which way shall we go?"

" Where you can. Fly, fly, I say, instantly." These words were exchanged with the quickness of thought while we were mounting and reining our horses; in another instant we were all separated from each other (*Autobiography of Parley P. Pratt*, 215-17).

Parley Pratt soon found his escape blocked by a man with a rifle. But wheeling his horse and dashing off in another direction, he escaped into a thick forest. After hiding in the forest for a few hours, he tied up his horse and fell asleep. When he awoke, he found that his horse had run away so he continued his journey on foot. It was over 100 miles to the Illinois state line.

King Follett soon was recaptured, but Elder Phelps escaped by riding hard and pretending to be part of the mob. He rode all the way to the ferry, and soon was with family and friends in Illinois.

Orson Pratt, Mrs. Phelps, and Brother Clark, who had assisted with the escape, managed to avoid the mob and make their way back to Illinois. Parley Pratt arrived in Illinois five days after the escape. He was tired and sick from his long and difficult journey, but he was free. He noted:

Being once more at liberty and in the enjoyment of the society of family and friends, I spent a few days in rest and refreshment. . . . After a few days . . . we moved to Nauvoo, a new town, about fifty miles above Quincy [where] I met Brother Joseph Smith, from whom I had been separated since the close of the mock trial in Richmond the year previous. Neither of us could refrain from tears as we embraced each other once more as free men.

. . . He blessed me with a warmth of sympathy and brotherly kindness which I shall never forget. Here also I met with Hyrum Smith and many others of my fellow prisoners. . . . Father and Mother Smith were also overwhelmed with tears of joy and congratulation; they wept like children as they took me by the hand; but, O, how different from the tears of bitter sorrow which was pouring down their cheeks as they gave us the parting hand in Far West (*Autobiography of Parley P. Pratt*, 253-54).

MIRACULOUS HEALINGS

The Saints in Nauvoo were busy draining swamps, clearing trees, building cabins, planting crops, and building a new town. Soon, however, a sickness, probably malaria, struck many of the people. Joseph and Emma opened their home to the sick, but they soon became ill themselves. Wilford Woodruff recorded that on July 22:

> . . . while I was living in this cabin . . . we experienced, with the Prophet Joseph Smith, a day of God's power. . . . On the morning of the 22nd of July, 1839, he arose, reflecting upon the situation of the Saints of God in their persecutions and afflictions. He called upon the Lord in prayer, the power of God rested upon him mightily, and as Jesus healed all the sick around Him in His day, so Joseph, the Prophet of God, healed all around on this occasion. He healed all in his house and dooryard; then, in the company with Sidney Rigdon and several of the Twelve, went among the sick lying on the bank of the river, where he commanded them in a loud voice, in the name of Jesus Christ, to rise up and be made whole, and they were all healed. When he had healed all on the east side of the river that were sick, he and his companions crossed the Mississippi River in a ferry-boat to the west side, where we were, at Montrose. The first house they went into was President Brigham Young's. He was sick on his bed at the time. The Prophet went into his house and healed him, and they all came out together. As they were passing by my door, Brother Joseph said: "Brother Woodruff, follow me." They crossed the public square and entered Brother Fordham's house. Brother Fordham had been dying for an hour, and we expected each minute would be his last. I felt the spirit of God that was overpowering His Prophet. When we entered the house, Brother Joseph walked up to Brother Fordham and took him by the right hand, his left hand holding his head. He saw that Brother Fordham's eyes were glazed, and that he was speechless and unconscious. After taking his hand, he looked down into the dying man's face and said: "Brother Fordham, do you not know me?" At first there was no reply, but we could all see the effect of the spirit of God resting on the afflicted man. Joseph again spoke, "Elijah, do you not know me?"

With a low whisper, Brother Fordham answered, "Yes."

The Prophet then said, "Have you not faith to be healed?"

The answer, which was a little plainer than before, was "I am afraid it is too late. If you had come sooner I think I might have been." He had the appearance of a man waking from sleep. It was the sleep of death.

Joseph then said, "Do you believe that Jesus is the Christ?"

"I do, Brother Joseph," was the reply.

Then the Prophet of God spoke with a loud voice, as in the majesty of Jehovah: "Elijah, I command you, in the name of Jesus of Nazareth, to arise and be made whole." The words of the Prophet were not like the words of a man, but like the voice of God. It seemed to me that the house shook on its foundation. Elijah Fordham leaped from his bed like a man raised from the dead. A healthy color came to his face and life was manifested in every act. His feet had been done up in Indian meal poultices; he kicked these off his feet, scattered the contents, then called for his clothes and put them on. He asked for a bowl of bread and milk, and ate it. He then put on his hat and followed us into the street, to visit others who were sick. . . . Among the number present were Joseph and Hyrum Smith, Sidney Rigdon, Brigham Young, Heber C. Kimball, George A. Smith, Parley P. Pratt, Orson Pratt, and Wilford Woodruff.

As soon as we left Brother Fordham's house, we went into the house of Brother Joseph B. Noble, who was very low. When we entered the house, Brother Joseph took Brother Noble by the hand, and commanded him, in the name of Jesus Christ, to arise and be made whole. He did arise, and was healed immediately. The case of Brother Noble was the last one of healing upon that day. It was the greatest day for the manifestation of the power of God through the gift of healing since the organization of the Church. When we left Brother Noble's, the Prophet Joseph, with those who had accompanied him from the other side, went to the bank of the river to return home.

While waiting for the ferry-boat, a man of the world, knowing of the miracles which had been performed, came to Joseph and asked him if he would not go and heal twin children of his, about five months old, who were both lying sick nigh unto death. The Prophet said he could not go; but . . . said he would send some one to heal them; and he turned to me and said, "You go with the man and heal his children." He took a red silk handkerchief out of his pocket, gave it to me, told me to wipe their faces with the handkerchief when I administered to them, and they should be healed . He also said to me: "As long as you will keep that handkerchief, it shall remain a league between you and me." I went with the man, did as the Prophet commanded me, and the children were healed. I have possession of the handkerchief unto this day (Cowley, *Wilford Woodruff: History of His Life and Labors*, 104-6).

MISSIONS TO GREAT BRITAIN

The Twelve Apostles had been called on a mission to Great Britain. However, due to the persecutions, their departure had been delayed. Now, the members of the Quorum of the Twelve were trying to settle their families in Nauvoo. They built cabins, made the necessary preparations, and then set out on their missions. Wilford Woodruff was among the first to leave:

Inasmuch as the devil had been thwarted in a measure by the Twelve going to Far West and returning without harm, it seemed as though the destroyer was determined to make some other attempt upon us to hinder us from performing our missions; for as soon as any one of the Apostles began to prepare for starting he was smitten with chills and fever, or sickness of some kind. Nearly all of the quorum of the Twelve or their families began to be sick, so it still required the exercise of a good deal of faith and perseverance to start off on a mission.

Early upon the morning of the 8th of August, I arose from my bed of sickness, laid my hands upon the head of my sick wife, Phoebe, and blessed her. I then departed from the embrace of my companion, and left her almost without food or the necessaries of life. She suffered from my departure with the fortitude that becomes a saint.

Elder John Taylor was going with me; we were the first two of the quorum . . . who started upon that mission. Brother Taylor was about the only man . . . who was not sick.

Soon a brother came along with a wagon, and took us in. . . . We came to Parley P. Pratt. . . . He was hewing a log preparatory to building a cabin. He said: "Brother Woodruff, I have no money, but I have an empty purse, which I will give you." . . . We went a few rods further and met Brother Heber C. Kimball, also hewing a log. He said, "As Parley has given you a purse, I have got a dollar I will give you to put in it." He gave me both a dollar and a blessing. . . . During the day I rode . . . over a very rough road in the bottom of a wagon, shaking with the ague, and suffering very much (Cowley, *Wilford Woodruff: History of His Life and Labors,* 108-10).

Even Brother Taylor, whose health had seemed good, did not escape the sickness. He fainted on August 28, but journeyed on. He continued to grow worse, and finally was forced to stop in Indiana for several weeks. Brothers Woodruff and Coltrin continued on without him even though they themselves were not entirely well. In December they all met in New York City. Elder Pratt recorded:

On the 29th of August, 1839, I took leave of my friends in Nauvoo and started for a foreign land. I was accompanied by my wife and three children . . . and Elders Orson Pratt and Hyrum Clark. We journeyed in our own private carriage, drawn by two horses. Our route lay through the wild . . . countries of Illinois, Indiana and Michigan, for about five hundred and eighty miles to Detroit . . . [where] we sold our horses and carriage, . . . and took passage on a steamboat down Lake Erie to Buffalo—distance three hundred miles. . . . We took the Erie Canal and railroad to Albany—distance three hundred and fifty miles. Thence to New York by steamer down the Hudson River—distance one hundred and fifty miles. Here we arrived in safety after a journey of about one thousand and four hundred miles. We found the church in New York strong in the faith, and rejoicing in the truth. . . . In this city I resided with my family some six months, during which I preached . . . and also superintended the printing and publishing of several of our books (*Autobiography of Parley P. Pratt,* 257-59).

Before leaving on his mission, Brigham Young took every opportunity to learn from the Prophet Joseph. He wrote: "Brother Joseph taught many important and glorious principles calculated to benefit and bless . . . unfolding keys of knowledge whereby to detect Satan and preserve us in the favor of God" (*Manuscript History of Brigham Young*).

Brigham and his family had the fever, and Sister Young had recently given birth to a new baby. Nevertheless, Brigham left for his mission as planned.

> *September 14, 1839*—I started from Montrose on my mission to England. My health was so poor I was unable to go thirty rods to the river without assistance.
>
> After I'd crossed the river I got Israel Barlow to carry me on his horse, behind him, to Heber C. Kimball's, where I remained sick till the 18th. I left my wife sick with a babe only ten days old, and all of my children sick and unable to wait upon each other (*Manuscript History of Brigham Young*).

Brigham's wife recovered enough to join her husband at the Kimball home and see him off. Heber Kimball wrote:

> *September 18.* . . . our trunks were put into the wagon by some brethren; I went to my bed and shook hands with my wife who was then shaking with the chill, having two children lying sick by her side; I embraced her and my children, and bade them farewell.
>
> It was with difficulty we got into the wagon, and started down the hill about ten rods; it appeared to me as though my very inmost parts would melt within me at leaving my family in such a condition, as it were almost within the arms of death. I felt as though I could not endure it. I asked the teamster to stop, and said to Brother Brigham, "This is pretty tough, isn't it? Let's rise up and give them a cheer." We arose and swinging our hats three times over our heads shouted, "Hurrah! Hurrah for Israel." Vilate, hearing the noise, arose from her bed and came to the door. She had a smile on her face. Vilate and Mary Ann Young cried out to us, "Goodbye, God bless you." We returned the compliment, and then told the driver to go ahead. After this I felt a spirit of joy and gratitude having had the satisfaction of seeing my wife standing upon her feet, instead of leaving her in bed, knowing well that I should not see them again for two or three years (Whitney, *Life of Heber C. Kimball*, 265-66).

The brethren were sick and totally dependent upon the Lord and the good-will of others. Sometimes they were helped in mysterious and marvelous ways. Brigham Young recorded:

> While in Pleasant Garden we obtained some money, so that, with the five dollars we previously had, amounted to $13.50. When we got into the stage, we did not expect to be able to ride but a short distance. We rode as far as Indianapolis, paid our passages, and found we had sufficient means to take our passages for Richmond, Ia.
>
> When we arrived at this place we found we had means to take us to Dayton, to which place we proceeded. . . . We expected to stop here and

preach until we got means to pursue our journey. I went to my trunk to get money to pay my bill and found that we had suf-ficient to pay our passages to Columbus. . . .

When I paid my bill I found I had sufficient to pay our passages to Wooster. . . . When we arrived there I went to my trunk again to get money to pay our bill, and found sufficient to pay our passages to Cleveland. . . . We proceeded to Kirtland . . . where we found a good many friends and brethren who were glad to see us. I had a York schilling left; and on looking over our expens-es I found we had paid out over $87.00 out of the $13.50 we had at Pleasant Garden.

We . . . picked up what money we could gather, which was insufficient to convey us to New York. There was not a healthy man among us, and some more fitted for a hospital than a journey (*Manuscript History of Brigham Young*).

BRIGHAM'S TRUNK in which he kept the monies he and Heber C. Kimball had collected for their mission travels. In a miraculous manner, there was always enough money for their expenses, even though the funds they gathered had been very meager.

Brigham Young and some of the elders boarded a steamboat to cross Lake Erie. During the journey, a severe wind arose in the night. He wrote: "I went upon deck and felt impressed in spirit to pray to the Father in the name of Jesus for a forgiveness of my sins, and then I felt to command the winds to cease and let us go safe on our journey. The winds abated and I felt to give glory and honor and praise to that God who rules all things" (*Manuscript History of Brigham Young*).

Brigham Young and the others reached New York City on January 31, 1840. They had been traveling for three and a half months. Elders Taylor and Woodruff had sailed for England in December, but the rest of the brethren had to stay in New York and raise money for their passage.

A TRIP TO WASHINGTON, D.C.

Meanwhile, Joseph Smith, Sidney Rigdon, Elias Higby, and Orrin Porter Rockwell were on their way to Washington, D.C. They were carrying documents and petitions to present to the Congress of the United States to prove the injustices the Saints had suffered in Missouri.

During the journey, President Rigdon became so ill that he and Porter Rockwell stopped in Columbus, Ohio, while Joseph and Elias Higby continued on to Washington by stagecoach. Travel in those times could be quite exciting. Joseph recorded one such incident:

While on the mountains some distance from Washington, our coach-man stepped into a public house to take his grog, when the horses took fright and ran down the hill at full speed. I persuaded my fellow travelers to be quiet and retain their seats, but had to hold one woman to prevent her from throwing her infant out of the coach . . . opening the door, I secured my hold on the side of the coach the best way I could, and succeeded in placing myself in the coachman's seat, and reining up the horses, after they had run some two or three miles, and neither coach, horses, or passengers received any injury. My course was spoken of in the highest terms of commendation, as being one of the most daring and heroic deeds, and no language could express the gratitude of the passengers, when they found themselves safe, and the horses quiet. . . . but on inquiring my name, to mention as the author of their safety, and finding it to be Joseph Smith, the "Mormon Prophet," as they called me, I heard no more of their praise, gratitude, or reward (Smith, *History of the Church*, 4:23-24).

They arrived in Washington on November 28, 1839, and set about their business the next day. Joseph recorded their activities in a letter to his brother Hyrum and the Saints in Nauvoo:

On Friday morning 29th, we proceeded to the house of the President. We found a very large and splendid palace, surrounded with a splendid enclosure, decorated with all the fineries and elegancies of this world. We went to the door and requested to see the President. We were immediately introduced into an upper apartment, where we met the President, and were introduced into his parlor, where we presented him with our letters of introduction. As soon as he had read one of them, he looked upon us with a kind of half frown and said, "What can I do? I can do nothing for you! If I do anything I shall come in contact with the whole state of Missouri."

But we were not to be intimidated; and demanded a hearing, and constitutional rights. Before we left him he . . . observed that he felt to sympathize with us, on account of our sufferings.

We have spent the remainder of our time in hunting up the representatives in order to get our case brought before the House. For a general thing there is but little solidarity and honorable deportment among those who are sent here to represent the people; but a great deal of pomposity and show (Smith, *History of the Church*, 4:40).

After a couple of weeks in Washington, Joseph left the political business to Judge Higby while he took a train to Philadelphia to preach the gospel and meet with Saints. In Philadelphia, he met with Orson and Parley Pratt. Parley recorded:

He taught me many great and glorious principles concerning God and the heavenly order of eternity. It was at this time that I received from him the first idea of eternal family organization. It was Joseph Smith who taught me how to prize the endearing relationships of father and mother, husband and wife; of brother and sister, son and daughter. It was from him that I learned that the wife of my bosom might be secured to me for time and all eternity; and that the refined sympathies and affections which endeared us to each other emanated from the fountain of divine eternal love. It was from him that

I learned that we might cultivate these affections, and grow and increase in the same to all eternity. . . . I had loved before, but I knew not why. But now I loved—with a pureness—and intensity of elevated, exalted feeling, which would lift my soul from the transitory things of this groveling sphere and expand it as the ocean. . . . I could now love with the spirit and with the understanding also. Yet at the same time, my dearly beloved brother, Joseph Smith, had barely touched a single key; had merely lifted a corner of the veil and given me a single glance into eternity (*Autobiography of Parley P. Pratt*, 259–60).

Joseph returned to Washington and met again with President Van Buren who stated, "Gentlemen, your cause is just, but I can do nothing for you. If I take up for you, I shall lose the vote of Missouri" (Smith, *History of the Church*, 4:80). Joseph then concluded:

His whole course went to show that he was an office-seeker; that self-aggrandizement was his ruling passion, and that justice and righteousness were no part of his composition. I found him such a man as I could not conscientiously support at the head of our noble Republic. I also had an interview with Mr. John C. Calhoun, whose conduct towards me very ill became his station. I became satisfied that there was little use for me to tarry (Smith, *History of the Church*, 4:80).

Before he left Washington, Joseph preached a few sermons. Matthew S. Davis, a member of Congress attended one of these sermons and wrote to his wife:

My dear Mary—I went last evening to hear "Joe Smith," the celebrated Mormon, expound his doctrine. He is not an educated man: but he is a plain, sensible, strong-minded man. Everything he says, is said in a manner to leave an impression that he is sincere. There is no levity, no fanaticism, no want of dignity in his deportment. He is apparently from forty to forty-five years of age, rather above the middle stature, and what you ladies would call a very good looking man. He is by profession a farmer, but he is evidently well read.

Throughout his whole address, he displayed strongly a spirit of charity and forbearance. . . . I have changed my opinion of the Mormons. They are an injured and much-abused people (Smith, *History of the Church*, 4:78-79).

Unfortunately, the Mormons' requests for help never made it out of the Senate Judiciary Committee. Joseph left for home in early February. Judge Higby stayed a few weeks longer, but finally concluded:

[T]he decision is against us, or in other words unfavorable. . . they believe redress can only be had in Missouri, the courts and the legislature. . . . I feel now that we have made our last appeal to all earthly tribunals; that we should now put our whole trust in the God of Abraham, Isaac, and Jacob. We have a right now which we could not heretofore so fully claim—that is, of asking God for redress and redemption, as they have been refused us by man (Smith, *History of the Church*, 4:88).

In March of 1840, the Prophet was back in Nauvoo supervising the city's development. Meanwhile, Brigham Young and the other apostles in New York had finally raised enough money to pay for their passage to England. Brigham recorded:

> We engaged our passages for Liverpool on board the Patrick Henry and paid $18.00 each for a steerage passage, furnished our own provisions and bedding, and paid the cook $1.00 each for cooking. Brother H. C. Kimball and myself occupied a lower berth, Brother Parley and Orson Pratt, the one over us. Brother George A. Smith and R. Headlock an upper berth at their feet. Two Englishmen occupied the berth below. The brethren in New York furnished us with ample supply of provisions by donation. The sisters made us ticks and filled them with straw for our beds and filled some bags with straw for our pillows (*Manuscript History of Brigham Young*).

In December, when Wilford Woodruff and John Taylor had arrived in England, they met with Willard Richards. The brethren decided that John Taylor and Joseph Fielding should labor in Liverpool, while Elder William Clayton was to serve in Manchester, and Elder Theodore Turley was to work in Birmingham. Wilford Woodruff was called to serve in the Staffordshire Potteries, and later recorded:

JOHN BENBOW (1800–1874) was a wealthy farmer in Herefordshire, England. He and his wife belonged to a devout group—United Brethren—who were seeking the truth. The spirit directed Wilford Woodruff to the Benbow's farm where he preached to large gatherings. At the end of thirty days, Wilford had baptized two hundred and five people. *ca. 1840*

> I labored in the Staffordshire Potteries . . . from the 22nd of January until the 2nd of March, preaching every night in the week and two or three times on the Sabbath. I baptized, confirmed and blessed many, and we had a good open field for labor. . . . March 1, 1840 was my birthday; I was thirty-three years of age. It being Sunday, I preached twice during the day to a large assembly in the city hall, in the town of Hanley . . . and while singing . . . the spirit of the Lord rested upon me and the voice of God said to me, "This is the last meeting that you will hold with this people for many days." I was astonished at this as I had many appointments. . . . In the morning I went in secret before the Lord, and asked him what was His will concerning me. The answer I received was that I should go to the south; for the Lord had a great work for me to perform there, as many souls were waiting for His word. On the 3rd of March I took coach and rode . . . then walked a number of miles to Mr. John Benbow's hill farm, . . . Herefordshire. I found Mr. Benbow to be a wealthy farmer. . . . He and his wife received me with glad hearts and thanksgiving. . . . I also rejoiced greatly at the news Mr. Benbow gave me, that there was a company of men and women—over six hundred in number— who had broken off from the Wesleyan Methodists, and had taken the name of United Brethren. . . . [They] were searching for light and

truth, but had gone as far as they could, and were calling upon the Lord continually to open the way before them and send them light and knowledge, that they might know the true way to be saved. When I heard these things I could clearly see why the Lord had commanded me . . . to go south (Cowley, *Wilford Woodruff: History of His Life and Labors,* 115-17).

The following evening, on March 5, Elder Woodruff preached his first sermon in the home of John Benbow.

> I also preached at the same place on the following evening, and baptized six persons, including Mr. John Benbow, his wife and four preachers of the United Brethren. I spent most of the following day in clearing out a pool of water and preparing it for baptizing, as I saw that many would receive that ordinance. I afterwards baptized six hundred persons in that pool of water (Cowley, *Wilford Woodruff: History of His Life and Labors,* 117).

Before long, the local rector became alarmed because only fifteen people were attending his meetings. He decided to take action. Brother Woodruff records:

> When I arose to speak . . . a man entered the door and informed me that he was a constable, and had been sent by the rector of the parish with a warrant to arrest me. I asked him, "For what crime?" and he said, "For preaching to the people." I told him that I, as well as the rector, had a license for preaching . . . and that if he would take a chair I would wait upon him after meeting. . . . For an hour and a quarter I preached the first principles of the everlasting gospel. The power of God rested upon me, the spirit filled the house, and the people were convinced. At the close of the meeting I opened the door for baptism, and several offered themselves. Among the number were four preachers and the constable. . . . The constable went to the rector and told him that if he wanted Mr. Woodruff taken for preaching the gospel, he must go over himself and serve the writ; for he had heard him preach the only true gospel sermon he had ever listened to in his life. The rector did not know what to make of it, so he sent two clerks of the Church of England as spies, to attend our meeting, and find out what we did preach. They both were pricked in their hearts, received the word of the Lord gladly, and were baptized. The rector became alarmed, and did not venture to send anybody else (Cowley, *Wilford Woodruff: History of His Life and Labors,* 117-18).

On April 6, the ship *Patrick Henry* docked in Liverpool with Brigham Young, Heber C. Kimball, Parley and Orson Pratt, and George A. Smith on board. A few days later, John Taylor, Wilford Woodruff, and other elders gathered in Preston to hold a conference. Nearly two thousand members from thirty-three branches attended the meetings. Willard Richards was ordained an apostle, and Brigham Young was sustained as President of the Quorum of the Twelve. The Saints decided to publish a hymnbook and a monthly periodical called *The Millennial Star*. They also decided to obtain copyrights so the Book

of Mormon and Doctrine and Covenants could be printed locally. The brethren also decided to issue recommends to the members who wanted to emigrate to America.

Following the conference, the elders spread out across the country to preach the gospel and baptize the converted. Parley Pratt was appointed to edit and publish *The Millennial Star.* He moved to Manchester to begin his work, and the first issue of the *Star* appeared in May. On its cover was a new hymn Parley had written especially for this occasion: "The Morning Breaks, the Shadows Flee."

THE MILLENNIAL STAR was first issued monthly and contained twenty-four pages. Later, it became a weekly paper and continued as such for many years. Its purpose was to enlighten and enrich the Saints' understanding.

✦✦

Between April of 1840 and April of 1841, the missionaries carried the gospel to Scotland, Ireland, Wales, and many cities in England. They organized branches, ordained local priesthood leaders, healed the sick, traveled countless miles, and sent many Saints to America. At the time, eight of the apostles were serving in Great Britain.

Meanwhile, Orson Hyde was sent on a very special mission. He was to dedicate the Holy Land for the return of the Jews. On his way to Jerusalem in the spring of 1841, he met with his eight brothers in England.

Life was hard for the missionaries' wives and families who stayed in Nauvoo. The families of the missionaries were dependent upon the charity of the Church while their husbands were away, but the Church was poor and times were hard for everyone. Illness and deprivation were prevalent, and many families saw loved ones die. But new life came into the city when the first group of converts from Great Britain arrived that summer. By early June, about 250 homes had been built in and around Nauvoo. Meanwhile, the brethren in Britain sent word that more missionaries were needed in that part of the world. Several members of the Quorum of Seventy were called, including Lorenzo Snow. Lorenzo wrote:

Early in the spring of 1840, I was appointed to a mission in England,
and I started on or about the twentieth of May. I here record a circumstance

which occurred a short time previous—one which has been riveted on my memory, never to be erased, so extraordinary was the manifestation. At the time, I was at the house of Elder H. G. Sherwood; he was endeavoring to explain the parable of our Savior, when speaking of the husbandman who hired servants and sent them forth at different hours of the day to labor in His vineyard.

While attentively listening to his explanation, the spirit of the Lord rested mightily upon me—the eyes of my understanding were opened, and I saw as clear as the sun at noonday, with wonder and astonishment, the path way of God and man. I formed the following couplet which expresses the revelation as it was shown to me. "As man now is, God once was: As God now is, man may be" (Snow, *Biography and Family Record of Lorenzo Snow*, 46).

In July of 1840, John C. Bennett, a prominent citizen of the state of Illinois, wrote to Joseph Smith offering to help create a city for the Saints, and expressing his desire to be baptized. In Joseph's reply, he described the site he had chosen for the city:

> Our principal location is at this place, Nauvoo, (formerly Commerce), which is beautifully situated on the banks of the Mississippi, immediately above the lower rapids, and is probably the best and most beautiful site for a city on the river. It has a gradual ascent from the river nearly a mile, then a fine level and fertile prairie . . . but like all other places on the river, is sickly in summer. The number of inhabitants is nearly three thousand, and is fast increasing. If we are suffered to remain, there is every prospect of its becoming one of the largest cities on the river. . . . It is our intention to commence the erection of some public buildings next spring. I desire all the Saints as well as all lovers of truth and correct principles, to come to this place as fast as possible. . . . Let all that will, come, and partake of the poverty of Nauvoo freely (Smith, *History of the Church*, 4:177-78).

WORLD EVENTS

England in 1840 was a pretty grim place for the majority of the working-class people. Most lived in poor conditions and worked long hours in factories and mines for low wages. Prices were high, and most workers had no hope of raising their standard of living.

In the fall of 1840, Joseph and the Church suffered a great personal loss. Joseph records:

> Monday, [September] 14—My father, Joseph Smith, Sen., Patriarch of the whole Church of Jesus Christ of Latter-day Saints, died at Nauvoo. . . . He was the first person who received my testimony after I had seen the angel, and exhorted me to be faithful and diligent to the message I had received. He was baptized April 6th, 1830. . . . The exposures he suffered brought on consumption, of which he died, aged sixty-nine years. He was six feet, two inches high, was very straight, and remarkably well proportioned. He was very strong and active. . . . He was one of the most benevolent of men; opening his house to all who were destitute (Smith, *History of the Church*, 4:189-91).

Before he died, Father Smith gave blessings to the various members of his family. To his wife:

> Mother, do you not know, that you are the mother of as great a family as ever lived upon the earth? The world loves its own, but it does not love us. It hates us because we are not of the world; therefore, all its malice is poured out upon us, and they seek to take away our lives. When I look upon my children, and realize that although they were raised up to do the Lord's work, yet they must pass through scenes of trouble and affliction as long as they live upon the earth; and I dread to leave them surrounded by enemies (Smith, *History of Joseph Smith*, 308-9).

ELECTIONS

In the 1840 elections, the Mormons generally voted for the Whig candidates because both Governor Boggs and President Van Buren were Democrats. William Henry Harrison, an easy-going and apparently pliable member of the Whig party, won the election and became President of the United States. That fall, Governor Boggs of Missouri demanded that Governor Carlin of Illinois return Joseph Smith, Sidney Rigdon, Parley Pratt, and others to Missouri.

In the meantime, during the October conference, the Church voted to begin work on a new temple. Joseph also taught the Saints about the priesthood and the doctrine of baptizing for the dead. By December, John C. Bennett had pushed the Nauvoo charter through the state legislature. The charter provided for the organization of the city, the formation of the Nauvoo Legion, and the establishment of the University of Nauvoo.

On January 19, 1841, the Prophet Joseph received an important revelation that is now found in Section 124 of the Doctrine and Covenants.

> Verily, thus saith the Lord unto you my servant Joseph Smith . . . to make a solemn proclamation of my gospel . . . to all the kings of the world, to the four corners thereof, to the honorable president-elect, and the high-minded governors of the nation in which you live, and to all the nations of the earth scattered abroad.
>
> Let it be written in the spirit of meekness and by the power of the Holy Ghost. . . . Build a house for boarding, a house that strangers may come from afar to lodge therein; therefore, let it be a good house, worthy of all acceptation, that the weary traveler may find health and safety while he shall contemplate the word of the Lord . . . and build a house to my name for the most high to dwell therein.
>
> For there is not a place found on earth that he may come to and restore again that which was lost unto you, or which he hath taken away, even the fullness of the priesthood.
>
> For a baptismal font there is not upon the earth, that they, my saints, may be baptized for those who are dead.
>
> For I design to reveal unto my church things which have been kept hid from before the foundation of the world, things that pertain to the dispensation of the fulness of times (D&C 124:1, 3-4, 23, 27-29, 40).

In this same revelation, Hyrum Smith was released as a member of the First Presidency and William Law was selected to take his place. Hyrum was then called to be the Church Patriarch. He was also given all the keys and gifts, priesthood, and blessings that had formerly been given to Oliver Cowdery. "And from this time forth I appoint unto him that he may be a prophet, and a seer, and a revelator unto my church, as well as my servant, Joseph; that he may act in concert also with my servant Joseph" (D&C 124:94-95).

In February, elections were held in Nauvoo. John C. Bennett was elected Mayor, and Joseph and Hyrum Smith and Sidney Rigdon were elected to positions on the city council.

THE NAUVOO TEMPLE

Work began on the temple on March 1, and by April 6, the eleventh anniversary of the organization of the Church, the basement had been dug and the foundation walls were high enough for the cornerstone to be laid. Joseph recorded some of the festivities of that day:

> At an early hour the several companies comprising the "Nauvoo Legion" . . . assembled. At half-past seven o'clock a.m., the fire of artillery announced the arrival of Brigadier-Generals Law and Don Carlos Smith . . . at 8:00, Major General Bennett was conducted to his post. At half-past nine o'clock

JOSEPH MUSTERING THE NAUVOO LEGION *by C. C. A. Christensen* This was a unit of the Illinois state militia, and every male between the ages of eighteen and forty-five, regardless of religious affiliation, was required to enlist. Joseph Smith was a Lieutenant General in the Nauvoo Legion.

a.m., Lieutenant-General Smith, with his guard, staff and field officers arrived at the ground, and were presented with a beautiful silk national flag by the ladies of Nauvoo. . . . At twelve noon, the procession arrived upon the Temple ground. . . . President Sidney Rigdon then addressed the assembly. The architects . . . by the direction of the First Presidency, lowered the first (the southeast corner)stone to its place, and [I] pronounced the benediction as follows: "This principal cornerstone in representation of the First Presidency, is now duly laid in honor of the Great God; and may it there remain until the whole fabric is completed; and may the same be accomplished speedily; that the saints may have a place to worship God, and the Son of Man have where to lay His head" (Smith, *History of the Church*, 4:326-29).

The stake presidency then laid the southwest cornerstone. The high council laid the cornerstone in the northwest corner and the bishops then laid the northeast cornerstone. After this, the band played and the choir sang. Joseph summarized: "In conclusion, we will say we never witnessed a more imposing spectacle. . . . Such a multitude of people moving in harmony, in friendship, in dignity, told in a voice not easily misunderstood, that they were a people of intelligence, and virtue and order; in short, that they were Saints; and that the God of love, purity and light, was their God . . . and that they were blessed and happy" (Smith, *History of the Church*, 4:331).

While the Saints in Nauvoo were laying the cornerstones for the temple, many of the Saints in Great Britain attended a conference to celebrate the eleventh anniversary of the organization of the Church. Wilford Woodruff recorded:

On the 6th of April, 1841, the General Conference of the British Mission was held in Carpenter's Hall, Manchester, at which there were present nine of the quorum of the Twelve; namely, President Brigham Young, Heber C. Kimball, Orson Hyde, Parley P. Pratt, Orson Pratt, Willard Richards, Wilford Woodruff, John Taylor, and George A. Smith. The total membership of the British mission at that time was represented as 5,814, and 800 besides had emigrated to America. . . . At this conference the Twelve blessed and set apart Orson Hyde for his mission to Jerusalem. This was the first time and the only time in this dispensation that the Twelve Apostles sat in conference as a quorum in a foreign land (Cowley, *Wilford Woodruff: History of His Life and Labors*, 144).

Elder Hyde began his ministry to the Jews by writing a letter to Dr. Solomon Hirschell, president of the Jewish community in London. Rabbi Hirschell had broken his leg and was unable to receive visitors. After recounting the story of his vision in March, 1840, Elder Hyde wrote:

Aware that I have written very plainly upon these points, that have come within my notice, you believe me, sir, when I assure you, that my pen is pointed with friendship, and dipped in the fountain of love and goodwill toward your nation. The thoughts which it records have proceeded from a heart grateful to the Almighty, that the time has arrived when the day star of your freedom already begins to dispel the dark and gloomy clouds which have separated you from the favor of your God (Howard H. Barron, *Orson Hyde: Missionary, Apostle, Colonizer*, 119).

Back in Nauvoo, general conference continued for several days following the laying of the temple cornerstones. John C. Bennett was called as a temporary assistant to the First Presidency because Sidney Rigdon was ill, and Lyman Wight was called as an apostle to replace David W. Patten who had been killed in Missouri.

Finally, the time came for most of the apostles to return home to their families in Nauvoo. Brigham Young, looking back on a very successful year, recorded:

> It truly seemed a miracle to look upon the contrast between our landing and departing from Liverpool. We landed in the Spring of 1840, as strangers in a strange land and penniless. But through the mercy of God we have gained many friends, established churches in almost every noted town and city in the Kingdom of Great Britain, baptized between seven and eight thousand, printed 5,000 Books of Mormon, 3,000 hymn books, 2,500 volumes of *The Millennial Star* and 50,000 tracts, and emigrated to Zion 1,000 souls, established a permanent shipping agency, which will be a great blessing to the saints, and have left sown in the hearts of many thousands the seeds of eternal truth, which shall bring forth fruit to the honor and glory of God, and yet we have lacked nothing to eat, drink or wear: in all these things I acknowledge the hand of God (Roberts, *A Comprehensive History of the Church*, 2:86).

Some of the apostles headed straight for Nauvoo when they reached New York. Others visited relatives and attended to business. Phoebe Woodruff met her husband in New York and they visited family members in the area. One night, Wilford had a remarkable dream that he later related.

> Over fifty years ago while in Boston, I dreamed that the saints migrated to the Rocky Mountains, built a temple and dedicated it. At that dedicatory services Elders were set apart to go among the Gentile nations to bind the law and seal the testimony. That when after our arrival here the question was discussed as to what materials should be used in the temple building, some suggesting brick and others

WORLD EVENTS

The most popular books in the early 1840s were James Fennimore Cooper's *The Pathfinder* and Charles Dickens's *The Old Curiosity Shop*; Robert Browning, James Russell Lowell, and Henry Wadsworth Longfellow were writing poetry; and Edgar Allen Poe's first detective story was published. The British humor periodical *Punch* appeared. Audiences in Leipzig heard the first performance of Schumann's First Symphony while others listened to works by Wagner and Mendelssohn. Adolph Sachs, a Belgian, invented a new instrument called the saxophone; and a dance from Czechoslovakia—the polka—was all the rage in Europe and America. An important advance in agriculture was made when a German chemist discovered the fundamentals of artificial fertilizer. In America, President William Henry Harrison died of pleurisy after only one month in office. This was the first time a U.S. president had died in office, and John Tyler, the vice-president, became president, as provided in the Constitution.

adobe. I made the remark that it would never be built of anything else than cut granite (Wilford Woodruff, Salt Lake 18th Ward Chapel. L. John Nuttall Papers, Letter Press Book #4, 285, 7 October 1891).

THE NAUVOO YEARS

As Joseph became known in the state of Illinois, he tried to meet with leading officials and talk with them about the Church's goals and problems.

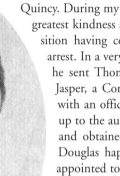

THOMAS CARLIN, governor of Illinois from Dec. 7, 1838 to Dec. 8, 1842. He treated the Prophet with kindness and respect to his face, but later betrayed him to his enemies.

Friday, [June] 4—I called on Governor Carlin, at his residence in Quincy. During my visit with the Governor, I was treated with the greatest kindness and respect; nothing was said about any requisition having come from the Governor of Missouri for my arrest. In a very few hours after I left the Governor's residence he sent Thomas King, Sheriff of Adams County, Thomas Jasper, a Constable of Quincy and some others as a posse with an officer from Missouri, to arrest me and deliver me up to the authorities of Missouri. . . . I returned to Quincy and obtained a writ of habeas corpus. Judge Stephen A. Douglas happening to come to Quincy that evening, he appointed to give a hearing on the writ on the Tuesday following, in Monmouth, Warren County, where the court would then commence a regular term. . . . A young lawyer from Missouri volunteered to plead against me; he tried his utmost to convict me but was so high with liquor, and chewed so much tobacco, that he often called for cold water. Before he had spoken many minutes, he turned sick, requested to be excused by the court, and went out of the court house puking all the way down stairs. As the Illinoisans call the Missouri people "pukes," this circumstance caused considerable amusement to the members of the bar. During his plea, his language was so outrageous that the judge was twice under the necessity of ordering him to be silent.

Mr. O. H. Browning then commenced his pleadings . . . which were powerful; and when he gave a recitation of what he himself had seen at Quincy and on the banks of the Mississippi river when the saints were . . . exterminated from Missouri, when he tracked the persecuted women and children by their bloody footmarks in the snow, they were so affecting that the spectators were often dissolved in tears. Judge Douglas himself and most of the officers also wept (Smith, *History of the Church*, 4:364-69).

The court decided to free Joseph and not return him to Missouri. This prompted Joseph to remark: "Thus have I been once more delivered from the fangs of my cruel persecutors for which I thank God my Heavenly Father" (Smith, *History of the Church*, 4:370-71).

While Elder Orson Hyde was in London, he wrote to Joseph Smith about his travels and plans for the future:

I was sorry that Elder Page had been so tardy in his movements. . . . Most gladly would I have hailed him as a companion to the oriental continent; but my hopes of that are fled. I shall go alone or find some other person. . . . I have written a book to publish in the German language setting forth our doctrine and principles in as clear and concise a manner as I possibly could. . . . It is very hard times in England. Thousands have nothing to do, and are literally starving. Trade of all sorts is at the lowest ebb. Very cold and dry. No harvest unless rain come[s] soon. You will discover that the greater part of the English brethren have always worked under masters; and they have not so much notion of planning and shifting for themselves . . . as the Americans. . . . They are a very industrious people whenever they can get employment. . . . I have just received a note from Dr. S. Herschel, President Rabbi of the Hebrew community of this country, in reply to a very polite note which I sent him, requesting the indulgence of a personal interview. But in consequence of a very severe accident . . . he is confined to his room, and unable to grant the asked indulgence.

I have addressed to him a communication upon the subject of my mission. . . . "[T]he daystar of your freedom already begins to dispel the dark and gloomy clouds which have separated you from the favor of your God. . . . Now therefore, O ye children of the covenant, repent of all your backslidings, and begin, as in days of old, to turn to the Lord your God. Arise! arise! and go out from among the Gentiles; for destruction is coming from the North to lay their cities waste. Jerusalem is thy home. There the God of Abraham will deliver thee. There the bending heavens shall reveal the long-looked-for Messiah in fleecy clouds of light and glory" (Smith, *History of the Church*, 4:373-78).

When Heber Kimball returned to Nauvoo after his mission to the British Isles, he recorded:

We landed in Nauvoo on the 1st of July, and when we struck the dock I think there were about three hundred Saints there to meet us, and a greater manifestation of love and gladness I never saw before. President Smith was the first one that caught us by the hand. . . . When we got sight of Nauvoo we were surprised to see what improvements had been made since we left home. . . . There were not more than thirty buildings in the city when we left about two years ago, but at this time there are twelve hundred, and hundreds of others in progress. . . . I never knew the Church in so good a state as at the present time; they feel well and in good spirits, and filled with love and kindness. Most of our English brethren have got themselves places and houses built for them, and many of them say they never felt better in their lives and have no desire to return to their native land, for they have houses and land of their own, what they never before were in possession of (Whitney, *Life of Heber C. Kimball*, 313-15).

Joseph Smith's journal reveals some of the events in Nauvoo during that summer of 1841.

Sunday, July 25—Elder George A. Smith married Bathsheba W. Bigler. Don Carlos Smith performed the ceremony, which was the last official act of his life, he being very feeble at the time.

Sunday, August 1—All the Quorum of the Twelve Apostles who were expected here this season, with the exception of Willard Richards and Wilford Woodruff, have arrived. We have listened to the accounts which they give of their success, and the prosperity of the work of the Lord in Great Britain with pleasure. . . . Perhaps no men ever undertook such an important mission under such peculiarly distressing and unpropitious circumstances. . . . They truly went forth weeping, bearing precious seed, but have "returned with rejoicing, bearing their sheaths with them."

Saturday, August 7—My youngest brother, Don Carlos Smith, died this morning in the 26th year of his age.

Tuesday, August 10—I spent the day in council with Brigham Young, Heber C. Kimball, John Taylor, Orson Pratt, and George A. Smith. . . . I directed them to send missionaries to New Orleans, South Carolina, Massachusetts, Maryland, and Washington, D.C. I also requested the Twelve to take the burden of the business of the Church in Nauvoo. The department of English literature and mathematics, of the University of the City of Nauvoo, is in operation under the tuition of Professor Orson Pratt.

Sunday, August 15—My infant son, Don Carlos, died aged 14 months 2 days (Smith, *History of the Church*, 4:389-402).

On August 16, 1841, a special conference was held in Nauvoo. Elias Smith, the clerk of the conference recorded: "President Joseph Smith said that the time had come when the Twelve should be called upon to stand in their place next to the First Presidency" (Smith, *History of the Church*, 4:403).

Meanwhile, Orson Hyde reported on his visit to the Holy Land.

I have been at Cairo, on the Nile, because I could not get a passage direct. Syria is in a dreadful state—a war of extermination is going on between the Druses and Catholics. It is no uncommon thing to find persons in the streets without heads. I have seen Jerusalem precisely according to the vision which I had. I saw no one with me in the vision; and although Elder Page was appointed to accompany me there, yet I found myself there alone. . . . On Sunday morning, October 24, a good while before day, I arose from sleep, and went out of the city as soon as the gates were opened, crossed the brook Kedron, and went up on the Mount of Olives, and there, in solemn silence, with pen, ink, and paper, just as I saw in the vision, offered up the following prayer:

"Grant . . . O Lord, in the name of Thy well-beloved Son, Jesus Christ, to remove the barrenness and sterility of this land, and let springs of living water break forth to water its thirsty soil. . . . Let the land become abundantly fruitful when possessed by its rightful heirs. Let thy great kindness conquer and subdue the unbelief of thy people. Incline them to gather in upon this land according to thy word, let the large ships of the nations bring them from the distant isles and let kings become their nursing fathers and queens with motherly fondness wipe the tear of sorrow from their eye and all the glory and honor will we ascribe unto God and the lamb forever and ever. Amen."

On the top of Mount Olives I erected a pile of stones as a witness according to ancient custom. On what was anciently called Mount Zion, where their temple stood, I erected another. . . . I am now about to go on board a fine ship for Trieste, and from thence I intend to proceed to Regensburg and there publish our faith in the German language (Smith, *History of the Church*, 4:455-59).

BAPTISMAL FONT

At the October conference, Joseph Smith announced that baptisms for the dead would now be performed only in the temple. This encouraged the Saints to work harder to complete the building, and by November 8, the baptismal font in the new temple was completed and dedicated so the baptisms for the dead could resume. Joseph described the font:

> The baptismal font is situated in the center of the basement room. . . . It is constructed of pine timber; and put together of staves tongued and grooved, oval shaped, sixteen feet long and twelve feet wide. . . . [T]he moulding of the cap and base are formed of beautiful carved work in antique style.
>
> The font stands upon twelve oxen, four on each side, and two at each end, their heads, shoulders, and fore legs projecting out from under the font; they are carved out of pine plank, glued together, and copied after the most

SILVER BROTHERS IRON WORKS in Salt Lake City, Utah, made the oxen that were used on the baptismal font in the Salt Lake Temple. *ca. 1892*

beautiful five-year-old steer that could be found in the country, and they are an excellent striking likeness of the original; the horns were formed after the most perfect horn that could be procured. The oxen and ornamental mouldings . . . were carved by Elder Elisha Fordham . . . which occupied eight months of time (Smith, *History of the Church*, 4:446).

A few days later, the Prophet noted, "I spent the day in counsel with the Twelve Apostles at the house of President Young. I told the brethren that the Book of Mormon was the most correct of any book on earth and the keystone of our religion and a man could get nearer to God by abiding its precepts than by any other book" (Smith, *History of the Church*, 4:461).

In January 1842, Joseph opened the "Red Brick Store" in Nauvoo. Above the store were large rooms where the leaders of the Church and the community often met. Emma worked long and hard helping Joseph unload wagons full of supplies for the store. She stocked the shelves and helped run the store. On February 6 she gave birth to a son who did not live.

RED BRICK STORE in Nauvoo, IL. Joseph Smith opened this store on Jan. 5, 1842. This building also served as Church and city administrative offices, and was used by various committees for meetings (Church and civic). It was on the second floor of this store that Joseph Smith "assisted in the organization" of the Relief Society on March 17, 1842. *ca. 1885*

Early in March, the Book of Abraham was published in the *Times And Seasons*. The Book of Abraham was a translation of the papyrus scrolls that Joseph had obtained in Kirtland, Ohio. Persecution and imprisonment had kept him from translating the document, but the work had finally been completed. This Book of Abraham is now found in the Pearl of Great Price. Another important piece of literature was also published in March 1842. Mr. John Wentworth, editor of the *Chicago Democrat*, had asked Joseph for a brief history of the Church and a statement of its beliefs. The letter contained the first published account of the prophet's early spiritual experiences and concluded with thirteen statements of belief that are now known as the Articles of Faith.

PLURAL MARRIAGE

It is not known when the doctrine of plural marriage was first revealed to Joseph. Some sources indicate that he had mentioned it as early as 1831, but it wasn't until 1841 that he began to teach others about the doctrine. Eliza R. Snow, one of his plural wives, told of Joseph's reluctance to begin the practice:

TINY HANDS *by Liz Lemon Swindle* depicts the sorrow of Joseph and Emma when their infant son, Joseph Murdock Smith, died.

oil on canvas

> The Prophet Joseph . . . described the mental ordeal he experienced in overcoming the repugnance of his feelings, the natural result of the force of education and social custom, relative to the introduction of plural marriage. He knew the voice of God—he knew the commandment of the Almighty to him was to go forward—to set the example and establish Celestial plural marriage. He knew that he had not only his own prejudices and prepossessions to combat and to overcome, but those of the whole Christian world stared him in the face; but God, who is above all, had given the commandment and He must be obeyed. Yet the Prophet hesitated and deferred from time to time, until an angel of God stood by him with a drawn sword, and told him that, unless he moved forward and established plural marriage, his Priesthood would be taken from him and he should be destroyed (Snow, *Biography and Family Record of Lorenzo Snow*, 69-70).

Heber C. Kimball was among the first to be told of the principle of plural marriage. His daughter, Helen, recorded:

> My mother often told me that she could not doubt the plural order of marriage was of God, for the Lord revealed it to her in an answer to prayer.
> In Nauvoo, shortly after his return from England, my father, among others of his brethren, was taught the plural wife doctrine, and was told by

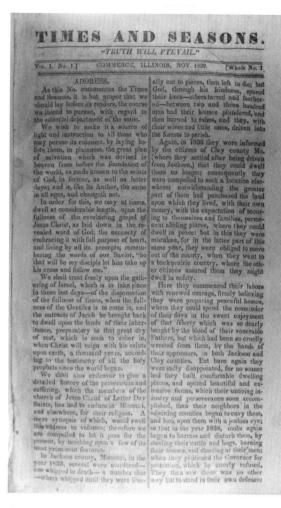

TIMES AND SEASONS
Don Carlos Smith
originally published
this as a private news-
paper in partnership
with Ebenezer
Robinson. After the
death of Don Carlos,
Robinson's publishing
policies were not
in accordance with
the Twelve. They
subsequently bought
Robinson's paper and
printing business, and
Joseph Smith was
listed as editor and
publisher. John Taylor
and Wilford Wood-
ruff also played key
roles in editing and
publishing this paper.

Joseph, the Prophet, three times, to go and take a certain woman as his wife; but not till he commanded him in the name of the Lord did he obey. At the same time Joseph told him not to divulge this secret, not even to my mother, for fear that she would not receive it.

My father realized the situation fully, and the love and reverence he bore for the Prophet was so great that he would sooner have laid down his life than have betrayed him. This was one of the greatest tests of his faith he had ever experienced. The thought of deceiving the kind and faithful wife of his youth, whom he loved with all his heart, and who with him had borne so patiently their separations, and all the trials and sacrifices they had been called to endure, was more than he felt able to bear.

The woman he was commanded to take was an English lady named Sarah Noon. She had been married and was the mother of two little girls, but left her husband on account of his drunken and dissolute habits. Father was told to take her as his wife and provide for her and her children, and he did so.

My mother had noticed a change in his manner and appearance, and when she inquired the cause, he tried to evade her questions. . . . He became sick in body, but his mental wretchedness was too great to allow of his retiring, and he would walk the floor till nearly morning.

The anguish of their hearts was indescribable, and when she found it was useless to beseech him longer, she retired to her room and bowed before the Lord and poured out her soul in prayer. . . . My father's heart was raised at the same time in supplication. While pleading as one would plead for life, the vision of her mind was opened, and, as darkness flees before the morning sun, so did her sorrow . . . vanish away.

Before her was illustrated the order of the celestial marriage, in all its beauty and glory, together with the great exaltation and honor it would confer upon her . . . if she would accept it and stand in her place by her husband's side. She also saw the woman he had taken to wife, and contemplated with joy the vast and boundless love and union which this order would bring about, as well as the increase of her husband's kingdoms.

With a countenance beaming with joy, for she was filled with the spirit of God, she returned to my father, saying: "Heber, what you kept from me the Lord has [shown] me."

She covenanted to stand by him and honor the principle, which covenant she faithfully kept. . . . She gave my father many wives, and they also found in my mother a faithful friend (Whitney, *Life of Heber C. Kimball*, 325–28).

THE MASONS

During this period, most men in America, including many in the Church, were members of the Masonic fraternity. Joseph records:

> *Tuesday, March 15*—I officiated as grand chaplain at the installation of the Nauvoo Lodge of Free Masons, at the grove near the temple. Grand Master Jonas, of Columbus being present, a large number of people assembled on the occasion. The day was exceedingly fine; all things were done in order, and universal satisfaction was manifested. In the evening I received the first degree in Free Masonry in the Nauvoo Lodge, assembled in my general business office (Smith, *History of the Church*, 4:550-51).

Heber Kimball informed Parley Pratt in England that "there was near 200 been made Masons. . . . All of the Twelve Apostles had become members except Orson Pratt. There is a similarity of Priesthood in Masonry. Brother Joseph said Masonry was taken from Priesthood but has become degenerated. But many things are perfect" (Stanley B. Kimball, *Heber C. Kimball: Mormon Patriarch and Pioneer*, 85).

The Grand Master of the Free Masons who came to Nauvoo to establish a Masonry lodge wrote a letter to the editor of the *Advocate* in Columbus, Ohio:

> Having recently had occasion to visit the city of Nauvoo, I cannot permit the opportunity to pass without expressing the agreeable disappointment that awaited me there. I had supposed . . . that I should witness an impoverished, ignorant and bigoted population, completely priest-ridden and tyrannized over by Joseph Smith, the great prophet of these people.
>
> On the contrary, to my surprise, I saw a people apparently happy, prosperous and intelligent. . . . I saw no idleness, no intemperance, no noise, no riot—all appeared to be contented, with no desire to trouble themselves with anything except their own affairs.
>
> During my stay of three days, I became well acquainted with their principal men, and more particularly with their Prophet, the celebrated "Old Joe Smith." I found him hospitable, polite, well informed and liberal. . . . Of course on the subject of religion, we widely differed, but he appeared to be quite as willing to permit me to enjoy my right of opinion, as I think we ought to let the Mormons enjoy theirs.
>
> From all I saw and heard, I am led to believe that, before many years, the city of Nauvoo will be the largest and most beautiful city of the west, provided the Mormons are unmolested in the peaceable enjoyment of their rights and privileges (Smith, *History of the Church*, 4:565-66).

THE ORGANIZATION OF THE RELIEF SOCIETY

Everyone in Nauvoo helped build the temple. The men donated time, materials, and money, while the women made

SARAH MELISSA GRANGER KIMBALL HOME, Nauvoo, IL. This is where the women met to discuss the organization of a Ladies' Society.

clothing and fixed meals. Sarah Melissa Granger Kimball, the wife of Hyrum Kimball, wrote:

> In the summer of 1843, a Miss Cook was seamstress for me. The subject of combining our efforts for assisting the temple hands came up in conversation. She desired to help, but had no means to furnish. I told her I would furnish material if she would make some shirts for the workmen. It was then suggested that some of our neighbors might wish to combine means and effort with ours, and we decided to invite a few to come and consult with us on the subject of forming a Ladies' Society. The neighboring sisters met in my parlor and decided to organize. I was delegated to call on Sister Eliza R. Snow and ask her to write a constitution and by-laws, and submit them to President Smith prior to our next meeting. When she read them to him, he replied that the constitution and by-laws were the best he had ever seen.

"But," he said, "this is not what you want. Tell the sisters their offering is accepted of the Lord, and he has something better for them than a written constitution. I invite them all to meet with me and a few of the brethren next Thursday afternoon, and I will organize the women under the priesthood after the pattern of the priesthood." He further said, "The church was never perfectly organized until the women were thus organized" (Andrus, *They Knew the Prophet*, 131).

ORGANIZATION OF THE RELIEF SOCIETY *by Nadine Barton* depicts the sisters meeting with the Prophet to be organized officially as a Relief Society. *oil on canvas 1986*

Joseph Smith, John Taylor, and Willard Richards presided at the first meeting, which was attended by eighteen women. After opening the meeting with the hymn "The Spirit of God Like a Fire Is Burning," Joseph told the women that their society was to help the brethren do good works, look after the needs of the poor, and strengthen the morals and virtues of the community. Emma Smith was elected the first president of the new female Relief Society at Nauvoo.

She selected Sarah M. Cleveland and Elizabeth Ann Whitney as her counselors. A week later, Eliza R. Snow was called as secretary, and Elvira Cole became treasurer. The Prophet spoke again at their second meeting:

> This is a charitable society, and according to your natures; it is natural for females to have feelings of charity. . . . You are now placed in a situation in which you can act according to these sympathies which God has planted in your bosoms.
>
> If you live up to your privileges, the angels cannot be restrained from being your associates. . . . I now turn the key in your behalf in the name of the Lord, and this Society shall rejoice, and knowledge and intelligence shall flow down from this time henceforth (Smith, *History of the Church*, 4:605-7).

The Relief Society grew quickly from this small start. By the end of the first year, there were 1,189 members. The women met weekly during the spring, summer, and fall. Eventually, the group became so large that they had to meet in the grove where Sunday services were held.

＋＜

QUEEN VICTORIA (1819–1901) Victoria was crowned Queen in 1837. Elder Lorenzo Snow presented her and His Royal Highness, Prince Albert, with two copies of the Book of Mormon. *1853*

As 1842 drew to a close, Lorenzo Snow was finishing up his mission in Great Britain. However, one important task remained. Eliza Snow wrote: "Before leaving London, Elder Lorenzo Snow presented to her Majesty Queen Victoria and his Royal Highness Prince Albert, two neatly bound copies of the Book of Mormon which had been donated by President Brigham Young and left in the care of Elder Snow for that purpose" (Smith, *History of the Church*, 6:181).

In the meantime, Joseph Smith was sharing important gospel truths with some of the priesthood holders in Nauvoo.

> I spent the day in the upper part of the store . . . in council with General James Adams, Patriarch Hyrum Smith, Bishops Newel K. Whitney and George Miller, and President Brigham Young and Elders Heber C. Kimball and Willard Richards, instructing them in the principles and order of the priesthood, attending to washings, anointings, endowments and the communication of keys pertaining to the Aaronic Priesthood, and so on to the highest

order of the Melchizedek Priesthood, setting forth the order pertaining to the Ancient of Days, and all those plans and principles by which any one is enabled to secure the fullness of those blessings which have been prepared for the Church of the First Born, and come up and abide in the presence of the Eloheim in the eternal worlds. In this council was instituted the ancient order of things for the first time in these last days. And the communications I made to this council were of things spiritual and to be received only by the spiritual minded: and there was nothing made known to these men but what will be made known to all the saints of the last days so soon as they are prepared to receive, and a proper place is prepared to communicate them . . . therefore, let the saints be diligent in building the temple (Smith, *History of the Church*, 5:1-2).

TROUBLE IN MISSOURI

But trouble was brewing again in Missouri. Joseph read in the *Quincy Quake* newspaper:

> The Assassination of ex-Governor Boggs of Missouri—Lilburn W. Boggs, late governor of Missouri, was assassinated at his residence in Independence, Missouri, by an unknown hand, on the 6th instant. He was sitting in a room by himself, when some person discharged a pistol loaded with buckshot, through an adjoining window, three of the shots took effect in his head, one of which penetrated the brain. . . . Footprints were found beneath the window, and the pistol which gave the fatal shot. The governor was alive on the seventh, but no hopes are entertained for his recovery. . . . There are several rumors in circulation in regard to the horrid affair; one of which throws the crime upon the Mormons (Smith, *History of the Church*, 5:14-15).

However, Boggs did not die from his wounds. Joseph denied any involvement in the assassination attempt, but a warrant was issued for the arrest of Joseph Smith and Porter Rockwell. When Lorenzo Snow returned to Nauvoo, Joseph had a private meeting with him.

> At the interview on the banks of the Mississippi, in which the Prophet Joseph explained the doctrine of Celestial Marriage, I felt very humble, and in my simplicity besought him earnestly to correct me and set me right if, at any time, he should see me indulging any principle or practice that might tend to lead astray, into forbidden paths; to which he replied, "Brother Lorenzo, the principles of honesty and integrity are founded within you, and you will never be guilty of any serious error or wrong, to lead you from the path of duty. The Lord will open your way to receive and obey the law of Celestial Marriage." During the conversation, I remarked to the Prophet I thought he appeared to have been endowed with great additional power during my mission in England. He said it was true; the Lord had bestowed on him additional divine power (Snow, *Biography and Family Record of Lorenzo Snow*, 70).

In anticipation of renewed persecution, the Prophet had been looking ahead to a time when the Saints would leave Nauvoo.

> *Saturday, August 6*—Passed over the river to Montrose, Iowa. . . . I prophesied that the saints would continue to suffer much affliction and would be driven to the Rocky Mountains, many would apostatize, others would be put to death by our persecutors or lose their lives in consequence of exposure or disease, and some of you will live to go and assist in making settlements and build cities and see the saints become a mighty people in the midst of the Rocky Mountains (Smith, *History of the Church*, 5:85).

On August 8, the Prophet again was arrested:

> This forenoon I was arrested by the Deputy Sheriff of Adams County . . . on a warrant issued by Governor Carlin, founded on a requisition from Governor Reynolds of Missouri, upon the affidavit of ex-Governor Boggs, complaining of the said Smith as "being an accessory before the fact, to an assault with intent to kill made by one Orrin P. Rockwell on Lilburn W. Boggs," on the night of the sixth of May, 1842. Brother Rockwell was arrested at the same time as principal. . . . The municipal court issued a writ of habeas corpus, . . . these officers left . . . and returned to Governor Carlin for further instructions and myself and Rockwell went about our business (Smith, *History of the Church*, 5:86-87).

After this arrest, Joseph realized that if he were arrested again, Governor Carlin would send him back to Missouri. Knowing that he would never leave Missouri alive, Joseph went into hiding for the rest of the summer and fall.

In December, Thomas Ford was inaugurated as the new governor of Illinois in December. Ford was from northern Illinois and was neither for nor against the Mormons. Soon after his inauguration, Joseph sent a delegation to find out his views on extraditing the Prophet to Missouri. Believing that Ford could be trusted, Joseph came out of hiding. Following the new governor's advice, Joseph allowed himself to be tried in Springfield. The judge concluded:

> The affidavit is insufficient . . . because . . . it charges no crime committed in the state of Missouri. The affidavit simply says that [Mr. Boggs] believes that Smith was accessory before the fact to the intended murder. . . . It is not said who shot him, or that the person was unknown. . . . Let an order be entered that Smith be discharged from his arrest (Smith, *History of the Church*, 5:230-31).

LIFE IN NAUVOO

In spite of occasional problems, life in Nauvoo was pleasant. There were large farms outside the city, but most homes had both a vegetable garden and a flower garden. Construction was the town's major industry, but in addition to the sawmills and brickyards, the Saints made matches, rope, gloves, bonnets, pottery, jewelry, combs, and spinning wheels. There were tailors, weavers, cobblers, bakers, and wagon makers. The children attended public schools, and university classes were held in homes and public buildings. A drama company or a lecturer occasionally would come to town, but most entertainment was homemade.

Many young people lived in Nauvoo, and they were very much like children everywhere. Joseph recorded:

> In the latter part of January 1843, a number of young people assembled at the house of Elder H. C. Kimball, who warned them against the various temptations to which youth is exposed. . . . Another meeting was held the ensuing week. . . . Elder Kimball delivered addresses, exhorting the young people to study the scriptures, . . . also to keep good company and to keep pure and unspotted from the world.
>
> I addressed the young people . . . expressing my gratitude to Elder Kimball for having commenced this glorious work which would be the means of doing a great deal of good, and said the gratitude of all good men and of the youth would follow him through life. . . . I advised them to organize themselves into a society for the relief of the poor, and recommended to them a poor lame English brother (Maudsley) who wanted a house built. I advised them . . . to collect funds for this purpose, and perform this charitable act as soon as the weather permitted.
>
> William Cutler was chosen president and Marcellus L. Bates, clerk. Andrew Cahoon, Claudius V. Spencer and Stephen Perry were appointed to draft a constitution for the society.
>
> The next meeting was addressed by Elders Brigham Young, Heber C. Kimball and Jedediah M. Grant, whose instructions were listened to with breathless attention (Smith, *History of the Church*, 5:320-22).

The city of Nauvoo held elections in February of 1843. Joseph Smith was elected mayor. Now, with this official civic calling, Joseph informed the members that, "a Prophet is a Prophet only when he is acting as such" (Smith, *History of the Church,* 5:265).

Porter Rockwell had been hiding in Philadelphia but decided to return to Nauvoo. Almost as soon as he got off the steamboat in St. Louis, he was recognized, arrested, and charged with the attempted murder of Lilburn W. Boggs.

Meanwhile, Joseph began to have doubts about Sidney Rigdon, his counselor in the First Presidency. Disheartened, he wrote, "Of the Twelve Apostles chosen in Kirtland, and ordained under the hands of Oliver Cowdery, David Whitmer and myself, there have been but two but what have lifted their heel against me. Namely, Brigham Young and Heber C. Kimball" (Smith, *History of the Church*, 5:412).

ORRIN PORTER ROCKWELL (1813–1878), was Joseph Smith's body guard. He was baptized on April 6, 1830, and kept his hair long because the Prophet promised him he would be protected as long as he did so. He was arrested in 1842 and falsely charged with the attempted murder of Governor Boggs. After Joseph's death, Porter moved west with the Saints.

Nine men received their endowments in May of 1842. However, it was more than a year before more endowments were performed. Joseph's wife, Emma, had refused to believe the doctrine of plural marriage. When she finally accepted it, she received her temple endowments in May of 1843. The wives of the men who had previously received their endowments were now endowed, with Emma officiating for the women. For the first time in this dispensation, couples were then sealed for eternity. These first temple ceremonies usually took place in the upper rooms of the Red Brick Store.

Elizabeth Ann Whitney was one of the select few who participated in temple ordinances during that spring and summer of 1843. She later wrote, "The Prophet said that the angel who committed the ordinances to him said that he was only to reveal them to such persons as were pure, full of integrity to the truth, and worthy to be entrusted with divine messages, . . . that to spread them abroad would only be like casting pearls before swine, and that the most profound secrecy must be maintained" (Carol Cornwall Madsen, *In Their Own Words*, 201).

When life in Nauvoo became settled, a new emphasis was placed on missionary work. Most of the Twelve Apostles were sent on summer missions to the eastern states to preach and raise money for the temple and the Nauvoo House. Several other missionaries were also called. Jacob Zundell and Frederick Moeser were called to Germany; Dan Jones was called to Wales; James Sloan was called to Ireland; and Addison Pratt, Noah Rogers, Benjamin F. Guard, and Knowlton F. Hanks were called to the Pacific Islands.

ELIZABETH ANN SMITH WHITNEY (1800–1882), was one of the select few who participated in temple ordinances in Nauvoo during the summer of 1843.

BRITISH SAINTS

Many members in Nauvoo had come from England in the past two years. Elder Pratt recorded the experiences of a typical group of Saints who left their homeland for a new life.

In the month of September, 1841, . . . our chartered ship, the Tyree, sailed with two hundred and seven passengers on the morning of the 21st of September. They weighed anchor about ten o'clock, and hoisted sail before a fair wind; moving away under the flag of liberty—the American stars and stripes.

The emigrants were all on deck, and in good spirits; and as our little boat came off with three hearty cheers, they were singing their favorite hymn: "How firm a foundation ye saints of the Lord, Is laid for your faith in his excellent word!" The last lines which we heard as their voices were lost in the distance were as follows: "When through the deep waters I call thee to go,

The rivers of sorrow shall not thee o'erflow." Hats and handkerchiefs were still waving in view as the last token of farewell. Soon all was a dim speck upon the ocean; a few moments more and they vanished from view in the wide expanse and were lost in the distance. May God speed them onward in their course, and land them safely in their destined port (*Autobiography of Parley P. Pratt*, 315-16).

When the English Saints reached Nauvoo, three to six months later, they were absorbed quickly into society. With the help of other Church members, they found work, bought property, built homes, and became part of the community. The wide-open spaces of Illinois must have seemed quite different to those who had come from the dark, cramped mining and milling towns of Northern England.

When Parley Pratt returned home from England in the autumn of 1843, he left 10,000 members under the direction of Thomas Ward, Lorenzo Snow, and Hyrum Clark. After a long and miserable journey, he was delighted to see Nauvoo. A short time later, he wrote an interesting letter to a friend in England.

Provisions are cheaper than ever; Indian corn is twenty cents per bushel; wheat, forty cents; flour $3.50 per barrel; oats 15 cents per bushel; pork and beef, from 2 to 3 cents per lb.; butter, ten cents; sugar, 5 cents; chickens, 8 cents each. Cows from 8 to 10 and 12 dollars per head; good horses, from 25 to 50 dollars; land from 1¼ to 4 dollars per acre. . . . Brother William Smith, Joseph's brother, is a member of the legislature of Illinois. . . .They have introduced two bills for the purpose of taking away all our Nauvoo charters for they have both been lost without becoming a law, and the charters still stand good. . . . The fact is, it grieves the enemies of the saints very much to see them enjoying political privileges in common with others, and every exertion is made to hinder the progress of a people and of principles which they consider as already becoming too formidable to be easily trampled under foot (*Autobiography of Parley P. Pratt*, 286-87).

POLITICAL DILEMMAS

On May 18, 1843, Joseph Smith and several elders of the Church dined with one of the most famous judges in the state of Illinois—Stephen A. Douglas. He asked about the history of the persecutions of the Church in Missouri and was very sympathetic. Joseph told him, "Judge, you will aspire to the presidency of the United States and if you ever turn your hand against me or the Latter-day Saints, you will feel the weight of the hand of the Almighty upon you and you will live to see and know that I have testified the truth to you for the conversation of this day will stick to you through life" (Smith, *History of the Church*, 5:394).

On June 23, 1843, Joseph Smith was arrested while visiting relatives over 100 miles from Nauvoo. The arresting officers, Sheriff Joseph H. Reynolds of Jackson County, Missouri, and Constable Harmon T. Wilson of Carthage,

Illinois, waved pistols and threatened to kill the Prophet and Stephen Markham. It was more of a kidnapping than an arrest. The men refused Joseph's request for legal counsel and hurried him off to the town of Dixon. However, the citizens of Dixon became so enraged at the treatment Joseph was receiving that Reynolds, realizing that he would have to fight off the whole town, allowed Joseph to consult with an attorney.

In the meantime, Stephen Markham swore out writs against Reynolds and Wilson for threatening his life and that of Joseph. Soon, the two lawmen found themselves in the custody of the constable at Dixon. Cyrus Walker, a well-known criminal lawyer and politician who was running for Congress, offered to defend Joseph, hoping that it would get him the Mormon vote.

The closest judge was out of town so they all headed for Quincy, a journey of several days. When word of these events reached Nauvoo, many of Joseph's friends from the Nauvoo Legion rode out to join their leader and make sure he was not harmed.

Surrounded by a growing number of Mormons, Reynolds became rather nervous knowing that the Saints had ample reason to hate him from their experiences in Missouri. Since Nauvoo was closer than Quincy, it was decided to hold the court there. As the group approached Nauvoo, thousands of people turned out to greet the Prophet. He recorded:

> I was a prisoner in the hands of Reynolds, the agent of Missouri, and Wilson, his assistant. They were prisoners in the hands of Sheriff Campbell, who had delivered the whole of us into the hands of Colonel Markham, guarded by my friends, so that none of us could escape.
>
> When the company from the city came up, I . . . got out of the buggy; and, after embracing Emma and my brother Hyrum . . . I mounted my favorite horse, Old Charlie, when the band struck up "Hail Columbia" and proceeded to march slowly towards the city, Emma riding by my side into town. The carriages having formed a line, the company with me followed next, and the citizens fell in the rear. . . . The streets were generally lined on both sides with the brethren and sisters (Smith, *History of the Church*, 5:459).

The municipal court of Nauvoo freed Joseph from the arrest warrant, thus overturning the warrant issued by the governor. Reynolds and Wilson left Nauvoo for Carthage, threatening to raise a mob to come and take Joseph by force.

When the state elections were held in August, Joseph voted for Cyrus Walker, who had defended him during the last trial. However, he told the Saints, "Brother Hyrum tells me this morning that he has had a testimony to the effect that it would be better for the people to vote for Hodge, and I never knew Hyrum to say he ever had a revelation and it failed" (Pearson H. Corbett, *Hyrum Smith, Patriarch*, 306).

Hodge and the Democrats won—the Whigs were furious, and distrust of Mormon political power grew. On September 6, 1843, a meeting was held in

Carthage, Illinois. The resolution that was adopted was all too familiar to the Saints.

> A certain class of people have obtruded themselves upon us, calling themselves Mormons, or Latter-day Saints, and under the sacred garb of Christianity, assumed . . . that they the more easily, under such a cloak, perpetrate the most lawless and diabolical deeds that have ever, in any age of the world, disgraced the human species. . . . [We] find them yielding implicit obedience to the ostensible founder of this sect, who is a pretended prophet . . . and under this Heaven-daring assumption claiming to set aside . . . all those moral and religious institutions which have been established by the Bible . . . and at the same time entertaining the most absolute contempt for the laws of man. . . .
>
> We pledge ourselves in the most solemn manner to resist all wrongs which may be hereafter attempted to be imposed on this community by the Mormons . . . peaceably, if we can, but forcibly, if we must (Smith, *History of the Church*, 6:4-6).

However, this time the Saints were determined to use their political power to protect themselves. Joseph recorded, "We agreed to write a letter to the five candidates for the Presidency of the United States, to inquire what their feelings were towards us as a people, and what their course of action would be in relation to the cruelty and oppression that we have suffered from the state of Missouri, if they were elected" (Smith, *History of the Church,* 6:63).

><

In August of 1843, Joseph's family moved from their log homestead into a lovely and spacious home. The many rooms, however, were an inconvenience for Emma who always seemed to have a houseful of the sick, the poor, and the homeless. In addition, at least two of Joseph's plural wives lived with them. Emma's attitude toward polygamy alternated between acceptance and fierce opposition, and the strain of dealing with this emotional struggle took its toll on both Joseph and Emma. Throughout the summer, each recorded many days of illness.

In July, Joseph wrote down the revelation on the new and everlasting covenant—now Section 132 of the Doctrine and Covenants. Some reports indicate that Emma was so angry when she saw the revelation that she burned it. But other copies had been made and it had already been read to the high council of the Nauvoo Stake.

Problems with Sidney Rigdon continued to plague the Prophet. The conference report indicates that:

> President Joseph Smith addressed the conference. . . . He stated his dissatisfaction with Elder Sidney Rigdon as a Counselor, not having received any material benefit from his labors or counsels since their escape from

Missouri. Several complaints were then brought forward in reference to his management in the post office; a supposed correspondence in connection with John C. Bennett, with ex-governor Carlin, and with the Missourians, of a treacherous character; also his leaguing with dishonest persons in endeavoring to defraud the innocent (Smith, *History of the Church*, 6:47).

Rigdon spoke in his own defense and was so eloquent that when Joseph called for the members to release Rigdon as a counselor in the First Presidency, they refused. Joseph then said, "I have thrown him off my shoulders, and you have again put him on me. You may carry him, but I will not" (Smith, *History of the Church,* 6:49).

PORTER ROCKWELL RETURNS TO NAUVOO

On Christmas Day, the Mansion House was the scene of one of the biggest events of the Nauvoo social season.

> Monday, December 25—a large party supped at my house, and spent the evening in music, dancing, etc., in a most cheerful and friendly manner. During the festivities a man with his hair long and falling over his shoulders, and apparently drunk, came in and acted like a Missourian. I requested the

captain of the police to put him out of doors. A scuffle ensued, and I had an opportunity to look him full in the face, when, to my great surprise and joy untold, I discovered it was my long-tried, warm, but cruelly persecuted friend, Orrin Porter Rockwell, just arrived from nearly a year's imprisonment, without conviction, in Missouri. The following is his statement:

"I was on my way from New Jersey to Nauvoo; and while at St. Louis, on the 4th of March, 1843, was arrested by a Mr. Fox, on oath of Elias Parker, who swore I was the O. P. Rockwell advertised in the papers as having attempted to assassinate Lilburn W. Boggs.

Was about four days going to Independence. . . . A large crowd gathered around. Some were for hanging me at once. . . . In two or three days, underwent a sham trial. . . . Fox was the main witness, and he swore falsely.

The magistrate committed me to prison for my safe preservation, as he was afraid the people would kill me; but he could find no crime against me.

My mother found where I was and she came to see me and brought me $100 whereby I was enabled to fee Mr. Doniphan for his services as counsel. The time of my trial being continually delayed, I began to be uneasy. [Eventually] I was tried for breaking Independence jail. . . . the jury brought in a verdict of a five minutes' imprisonment in the county jail; but I was kept there four or five hours, during which time several attempts were made to get up some other charge against me. . . . I traveled in the fields by the side of the road . . . with all of the skin off my feet.

The third day I walked till noon, and then hired a man to carry me the remainder of the day for seventy-five cents.

I then continued my journey about thirty miles, where I rested three days to recruit my feet. I was then carried twenty-five miles on horseback and walked the same day twenty-five miles" (Smith, *History of the Church*, 6:134-42).

Rockwell had traveled for several days and finally crossed the river to Nauvoo in a small boat. In Missouri, Rockwell had learned that at least one of Joseph's close friends was corresponding with his enemies. He passed the information on to the Prophet.

A few days later in a public speech, the Prophet declared, "My life is more in danger from some little dough-head of a fool in this city than from all my numerous and inveterate enemies abroad. I am exposed to far greater danger from traitors among ourselves than from enemies without . . . *and we have a Judas in our midst*" (Smith, *History of the Church*, 6:152).

This statement caused a lot of soul-searching, especially among those in high positions of the Church who had not accepted plural marriage. A great deal of confusion followed. William Law complained that the police were harassing him, and one evening when some people built a fire near William Marks's home, he thought they were threatening his life. Joseph mused:

What can be the matter with these men? Is it that the wicked flee when no man pursueth, that hit pigeons always flutter, that drowning men clutch at straws, or that Presidents Law and Marks are absolute traitors to the Church, that my remarks could produce such an excitement in their minds.

Can it be possible that the traitor whom Porter Rockwell reports to me as being in correspondence with my Missouri enemies is one of my quorum? (Smith, *History of the Church*, 6:170).

Political matters were also concerning the Prophet. In January of 1844, it appeared that the candidates for president would be Martin Van Buren and Henry Clay. Joseph recorded:

Monday, January 29, 1844—At ten a.m. the Twelve Apostles, together with brother Hyrum and John P. Greene, met at the mayor's office, to take into consideration the proper course for this people to pursue in relation to the coming Presidential election. The candidates for the office of President . . . are Martin Van Buren and Henry Clay. It is morally impossible for this people, in justice to themselves, to vote for the re-election of President Van Buren.

As to Clay, his sentiments and cool contempt of the people's rights are manifested in his reply—"You had better go to Oregon for redress," which would prohibit any true lover of our constitutional privileges from supporting him at the ballot-box.

It was therefore moved by Willard Richards and voted unanimously—that we will have an independent electoral ticket, and that Joseph Smith be a candidate for the next Presidency (Smith, *History of the Church*, 6:187-88).

GENERAL JOSEPH SMITH FOR U.S. PRESIDENT BUTTON On January 31, 1844, Joseph announced that he would be a candidate for the U.S. Presidency. He was killed less than six months later.

The idea of moving to the Oregon territories was not entirely new. President Smith had been thinking about this possibility for at least a year. Eliza Snow records, "On the 20th of February 1844, the Prophet Joseph Smith instructed the Twelve Apostles to send a delegation and make explorations in Oregon and California, and seek a good location to which we can remove after the Temple is completed, and "where we can build a city in a day and have a government of our own" (Snow, *Biography and Family Record of Lorenzo Snow*, 76).

JOSEPH'S PROFOUND TEACHINGS

Joseph Smith was the mayor of the largest city in Illinois and a candidate for president of the United States. He and the Saints had built a beautiful city from a swamp, and the temple was nearing completion. However, the doctrines that were being taught were more important than any of these achievements. In April 1844, Joseph spoke at the funeral of King Follett.

There are but a very few beings in the world who understand rightly the character of God. . . . God himself was once as we are now, and is an exalted man, and sits enthroned in yonder heavens! It is the first principle of the gospel to know for a certainty the character of God and to know that we may converse with him as one man converses with another, that he was once a man like us. Yea, that God himself, the father of us all, dwelt on an earth the same as Jesus Christ himself did.

In the beginning, the head of the Gods called a council of the Gods; and they came together and concocted a plan to create the world and people it. . . . Now the word create . . . does not mean to create out of nothing; it means to organize. . . . The intelligence of spirits had no beginning, neither will it have an end. . . . Intelligence is eternal and exists upon a self-existent principle. It is a spirit from age to age and there is no creation about it. All the minds and spirits that God ever sent into the world are susceptible of enlargement.

The first principles of man are self-existent with God. God himself, finding he was in the midst of spirits and glory, because he was more intelligent, saw proper to institute laws whereby the rest could have a privilege to advance like himself.

The greatest responsibility in this world that God has laid upon us is to seek after our dead . . . it is necessary that the sealing power should be in our hands to seal our children and our dead for the fullness of the dispensation of times—a dispensation to meet the promises made by Jesus Christ before the foundation of the world for the salvation of man.

You mourners have occasion to rejoice, speaking of the death of Elder King Follett; for your husband and father is gone to wait until the resurrection of the dead . . . for at the resurrection your friend will rise in perfect felicity and go to celestial glory. . . . I have a father, brothers, children, and friends

NAUVOO, IL. Joseph Smith and the Saints built a beautiful city from a swamp, and their crowning achievement was the construction of the Nauvoo Temple (seen in the distance on the horizon).

who have gone to the world of spirits. They are only absent for a moment. They are in the spirit, and we shall soon meet again.

You don't know me; you never knew my heart. No man knows my history. I cannot tell it: I shall never undertake it. . . . If I had not experienced what I have, I would not have believed it myself (Smith, *History of the Church*, 6:303-17).

No one on earth could speak with more power and authority about the nature of God and the meaning of life than Joseph Smith did that spring morning. The Church had experienced both growth and adversity during the fourteen years since it had been organized in a small log cabin in New York. There were now over 25,000 members and the organization of the Church seemed complete. The Quorums of the First Presidency, Twelve Apostles, and Seventy were functioning. There were stakes, high councils, wards and bishoprics, quorums of elders, priests, teachers, and deacons; the women were organized in the Relief Society. The Saints had built a city, and the temple was nearly complete. But as usual, the Saints' success engendered hate, distrust, disloyalty, and fear. Some felt that the government and economic policies of the Church and Nauvoo were un-American since there was no separation of church and state. The practice of polygamy also caused concern.

The day after the conference, Joseph gave a brief but important talk where he answered questions the Saints had been asking since the spring of 1830. Where is Zion? How shall we build it? Joseph instructed:

You know very well that the Lord has led this church by revelation. I have another revelation in relation to economy in the church—a great, grand, and glorious revelation.

I will give you the first principles. You know there has been great discussion in relation to Zion—where it is, and where the gathering of the dispensation is and which I am now going to tell you. The prophets have spoken and written upon it; but I will make a proclamation that will cover a broader ground. The whole of America is Zion itself, from North to South.

The declaration this morning is, that as soon as the Temple and baptismal font are prepared, we calculate to give the Elders of Israel their washings and anointings, and attend to those last and more impressive ordinances without which we cannot obtain celestial thrones. But there must be a holy place prepared for that purpose.

I have received instructions from the Lord that from henceforth wherever the Elders of Israel shall build up churches and branches unto the Lord throughout the States, there shall be a stake of Zion. It is a glorious proclamation, and I reserved it to the last, and designed it to be understood that this work shall commence after the washings, anointings and endowments have been performed here.

I would teach it more fully—the spirit is willing but the flesh is weak. God is not willing to let me gratify you; but I must teach the Elders, and they should teach you (Smith, *History of the Church*, 6:318-20).

It was essential for the temple to be completed and for the Saints to receive their endowments before Zion could be built. And Zion was to be greater than anyone had dreamed.

After Joseph's talk, Brigham Young spoke at the conference, saying, "It was a perfect sweepstakes when the Prophet called North and South America Zion. Let us go to and build the temple with all our might, that we may build up the kingdom. . . . It is a perfect knock-down to the devil's kingdom. There is not a faithful elder who cannot, if he is humble and diligent, build up the Church. . . . We will build up churches and establish Zion and her stakes" (Smith, *History of the Church,* 6:321-22).

A short time later, Joseph Smith met with the Quorum of the Twelve. Wilford Woodruff recorded:

> The last speech that Joseph Smith ever made to the quorum of the apostles was in a building in Nauvoo, and it was such a speech as I never heard from mortal man before or since. He was clothed upon with the spirit and power of God. His face was clear as amber; the room was filled as with consuming fire. Said he:
>
> "You Apostles of the Lamb of God have been chosen to carry out the purposes of the Lord on Earth. Now, I have received, as the Prophet, Seer and Revelator, standing at the head of this dispensation, every key, every ordinance, every principle and every priesthood that belongs to the last dispensation and fullness of times. And I have sealed all these things upon your heads" (George Reynolds and Janne M. Sjodahl, *Commentary on the Book of Mormon,* 1:425).

CONSIDERATIONS FOR MOVING WEST

Orson Hyde was sent to Washington, D.C., to propose to Congress and President Tyler that the Church be hired to provide security on the western frontier. Congress and the president, however, were hesitant to approve the Saints' request for fear of angering the British and the Mexicans. Still, the trip was a success. In a letter in May of 1844, Orson wrote:

> It is the opinion here among the politicians that it will be extremely difficult to have any bill pass in relation to the encouragement of emigration to Oregon. . . . But all concur in the opinion that we are authorized already.
>
> In case of a removal to that country, Nauvoo is the place of general rendezvous. Our course from thence would be westward through Iowa bearing a little north until we came to the Missouri river . . . thence up the north fork of the Platte to the mouth of the Sweetwater river . . . and thence up said Sweetwater river to the South Pass of the Rocky Mountains . . . about eleven hundred miles from Nauvoo.
>
> Judge Douglas has given me a map of Oregon, and also a report on an exploration of the country lying between the Missouri River and the Rocky Mountains . . . by Lieut. J. C. Freemont, of the Corps of Topographical Engineers. . . . The people are so eager for it here that they have even stolen it

out of the library. . . . The book is a most valuable document to anyone contemplating a journey to Oregon (Smith, *History of the Church*, 6:374-75).

At this time, the West had been only partially explored. Thomas H. Benton, a Senator from Missouri, was the leading proponent of the theory of manifest destiny. He believed that the United States should stretch from the Atlantic to the Pacific Oceans. Using his influence in Washington, he arranged to have his son-in-law, John C. Fremont, appointed to conduct a topographical survey of the central Rockies, especially the South Pass. Fremont's party left in June of 1842. Kit Carson served as guide, and Charles Preuss served as the official topographer.

Fremont's romantic descriptions of the West stirred the American imagination. His information about camping sites, water holes, and necessary supplies was invaluable to those who later settled the new land.

JOSEPH NOMINATED FOR PRESIDENT

In May, a national political convention was held in Nauvoo. Joseph Smith was nominated to run for president and Sidney Rigdon was chosen as the vice-presidential candidate. Joseph's political platform advocated a powerful central government that would be able to intervene in individual states if the rights of individuals were being violated. He also advocated a national bank and the abolition of slavery. He called for the annexation of Texas and Oregon, and suggested reducing the size of Congress. Within a few weeks, numerous Church leaders left Nauvoo to campaign in different parts of the country. Sidney Rigdon moved to Pennsylvania to establish residency and run his campaign. Shortly after this, the Prophet's journal records:

Friday, June 7, 1844—The first and only number of the *Nauvoo Expositor* was published, edited by Sylvester Emmons.

Monday, June 10, 1844—I was in the City Council . . . investigating the merits of the Nauvoo Expositor, and also the conduct of the Laws, Higbees, Fosters, and others, who have formed a conspiracy for the purpose of destroying my life, and scattering the saints.

The council passed an ordinance declaring the Nauvoo Expositor a nuisance, and also issued an order to me to abate the said nuisance. I immediately ordered the Marshall to destroy it without delay. About 8 p.m., the Marshall returned and reported that he had removed the press, type, printed-paper and thrown the fix-

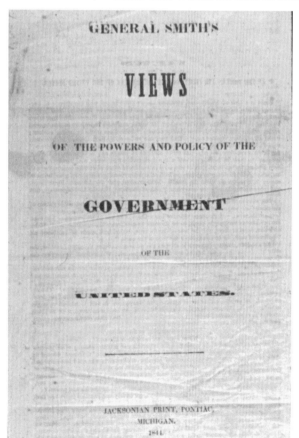

GENERAL SMITH'S VIEWS FOR PRESIDENTIAL ELECTION The Prophet's platform advocated a powerful central government that would protect individual rights. He also advocated the abolition of slavery.

tures into the street, and destroyed them. This was done because of the libelous and slanderous character of the paper, its avowed intention being to destroy the municipality and drive the saints from the city (Smith, *History of the Church*, 6:432-33).

The prospectus of the *Nauvoo Expositor* declared: "The publishers therefore deem it a sacred duty . . . to advocate through the columns of the Expositor *the unconditional repeal of the Nauvoo City charter* . . . to advocate unmitigated *disobedience to political revelations*, and to censure and decry gross moral imperfections wherever found . . . to oppose with uncompromising hostility any union of church and state" (Smith, *History of the Church*, 6:443-44).

George Laub, a member of the city council, wrote, "Brother Joseph told us that God showed to him in an open vision in daylight that if he did not destroy that printing press (Nauvoo Expositor) that it would cause the blood of saints to flow in the streets. . . . I write what I know and seen and heard for myself" (Laub, George, "Diary of George Laub").

Joseph's political aspirations greatly concerned his enemies. Also, Nauvoo's policies, which had forced taverns and houses of ill repute out of business, added to the hostility. Fearing that the paper would stir up the Church's many enemies and result in mob violence against the city, the city council sanctioned the destruction of the press.

On Wednesday morning, Joseph was arrested. He and members of the city council were charged with committing a riot. A trial, presided over by Daniel H. Wells, who at that time was not a member of the Church, did not satisfy the Saints' enemies. The citizens of Carthage armed themselves, and anti-Mormon feelings rose. Joseph declared martial law in Nauvoo so the Saints could be ready in case they were attacked. Letters were sent to Governor Ford, President Tyler, and various judges. The Twelve Apostles were called home. Governor Ford came to Carthage and requested that Joseph send someone to tell the Mormon side of the story, and John Taylor, Willard Richards, and Dr. J. M. Bernhisel were sent with a stack of documents and affidavits. Elder Taylor recorded:

GOVERNOR THOMAS FORD (1800–1850), governor of Illinois, often appeared to be sympathetic to the Mormons' plight, but in reality he was a weak-willed man who succumbed to public pressure. After the deaths of Joseph and Hyrum, he wrote a most unsympathetic letter to W. W. Phelps.

> After waiting the Governor's pleasure for some time, we had an audience—but such an audience. He was surrounded by some of the vilest and most unprincipled men in creation.
>
> We then in brief related an outline of the difficulties, and the course we had pursued from the commencement of the troubles up to the present, and, handing him the documents, respectfully submitted the whole. During our conversation and explanations with the Governor we were frequently, rudely and impudently contradicted by the fellows he had around him.
>
> He opened and read a number of the documents himself and as he proceeded he was frequently interrupted by "That's a lie . . . that's an infernal falsehood . . . that's a blasted lie!" etc.

NAUVOO EXPOSITOR. This slanderous newspaper published only one issue. It accused the Prophet and the Saints of unsavory politics and practices, and advocated the repeal of the Nauvoo Charter. Joseph ordered the press to be destroyed without delay.

At the termination of our interview . . . the Governor informed us that he would prepare a written communication for Gen. Smith, which he desired us to wait for. We were kept waiting for this instrument some five or six hours (Smith, *History of the Church*, 6:543-44).

The governor demanded that Joseph come to Carthage. Joseph considered going to Washington to present the matter to President Tyler. Abraham C. Hodge who was with Joseph that evening of Saturday, June 22, recorded:

Joseph said, "Brethren, here is a letter from the Governor." . . . After it was read through, Joseph remarked, "There is no mercy—no mercy here." Hyrum said, "No; just as sure as we fall into their hands we are dead men." . . . All at once Joseph's countenance brightened up and he said, "The way is open. It is clear to my mind what to do. All they want is Hyrum and myself; then tell everybody to go about their business, and not to collect in groups, but to scatter about. There is no doubt they will come here and search for us. Let them search; they will not harm you in person or property, and not even a hair of your head. We will cross the river tonight, and go away to the West" (Smith, *History of the Church*, 6:545-46).

MARTYRDOM AT CARTHAGE

Joseph and Hyrum crossed the river and prepared to go west. The next day a posse arrived in town to search for Joseph and his brother. That afternoon, Porter Rockwell delivered a letter to Joseph from his wife. Emma asked him to

THE PROPHET REIGNED HIS HORSE; JUST ONE LAST LOOK AT FAIR NAUVOO *by Harold Hopkinson* depicts Joseph Smith's last look at the city of Nauvoo before he was taken to Carthage. He poignantly remarked that "This is the loveliest place and the best people under the heavens." *oil on canvas 1979*

CARTHAGE JAIL, IL
Joseph and Hyrum
Smith were murdered
here on June 27,
1844, by a mob of
rogue Illinois state
militia members. John
Taylor and Willard
Richards were with
the Prophet and his
brother during the
assassination. The
Smiths were supposed
to be under Governor
Thomas Ford's guar-
antee of safety.
Richards's short note
to Nauvoo reads, ". . .
*Our guard was forced,
as we believe, by a
band of Missourians
from 100 to 200 . . ."*
ca. 1885

return and give himself up. Some of the Saints even accused the Prophet of cow-
ardice for leaving the people alone.

After reading the letter, Joseph said, "If my life is of no value to my friends,
it is of none to myself. . . . Brother Hyrum, you are the oldest, what shall we
do?"

Hyrum said, "Let us go back and give ourselves up, and see the thing out."

Joseph said, "If you go back I will go with you, but we shall be butchered"
(Smith, *History of the Church,* 6:549).

Joseph returned to Nauvoo, and after spending Sunday night with his family, he set out for Carthage. Willard Richards, who accompanied the Prophet to
Carthage, wrote:

> Joseph paused when they got to the Temple, and looked with admira-
> tion first on that and then on the city, and remarked, "This is the loveliest
> place and the best people under the heavens; little do they know the trials
> that await them." . . . Four miles west of Carthage . . . they met Captain
> Dunn with a company of about 60 mounted militia. Joseph said [to his com-

panions], "Do not be alarmed, brethren, for they cannot do more to you than the enemies of truth did to the ancient Saints—they can only kill the body. *. . . I am going like a lamb to the slaughter, but I am calm as a summer's morning. I have a conscience void of offense toward God and toward all men. If they take my life I shall die an innocent man, and my blood shall cry from the ground for vengeance, and it shall be said of me 'he was murdered in cold blood'"* (Smith, *History of the Church*, 6:554-55).

At first, Joseph and the others stayed in a boarding house in Carthage, but after a few days they were arrested and placed in prison without a hearing. When the governor and his troops left town on the afternoon of Thursday, June 27, the prisoners knew the end was near. Joseph asked John Taylor to sing a popular song, "A Poor Wayfaring Man of Grief." Willard Richards wrote that a few minutes after five p.m.:

There was a little rustling at the outer door of the jail, and a cry of surrender, and also a discharge of three or four firearms. . . . The mob encircled the building, and some of them rushed by the guard up the flight of stairs, burst open the door, and began the work of death, while others fired in through the open windows.

Hyrum was retreating back in front of the door . . . when a ball struck him in the left side of the nose, and he fell on his back on the floor saying, "I am a dead man!" As he fell on the floor, another ball from the outside entered his left side . . . another ball from the door grazed his breast, and entered his head by the throat; subsequently a fourth ball entered his left leg.

Joseph reached round the door casing and discharged his six shooter into the passage, some barrels missing fire. Elder Taylor . . . attempted to jump out of the window, where a ball fired from within struck him on his left thigh, hitting the bone. . . . He fell on the window sill, when a ball fired from the outside struck his watch in his vest pocket, and threw him back into the room.

After he fell into the room he was hit by two more balls. . . . He rolled under the bed. . . . One ball struck him on the left hip, which tore the flesh in a shocking manner.

Joseph, seeing there was no safety in the room, turned calmly from the door, dropped his pistol on the floor, and sprang into the window, when two balls pierced him from the door and one entered his right breast from with-

JOHN TAYLOR'S POCKET WATCH
John Taylor's plan to leap out the jail's east window was thwarted by a bullet that caused him to fall on the windowsill, then by another bullet from outside that struck his pocket watch. The bullet's force was deflected and Elder Taylor's life was saved. *1898*

out and he fell outward into the hands of his murderers, exclaiming, "Oh, Lord, my God!"

At this instant the cry was raised, "He's leaped the window!" and the mob on the stairs and in the entry ran out.

I reached my head out of the window, and watched some seconds to see if there were any signs of life. . . . Being fully satisfied that he was dead . . . I rushed toward the prison door. . . . Mr. Taylor called out, "Take me." I . . . caught Mr. Taylor under my arm and rushed by the stairs into the dungeon, stretched him on the floor and covered him with a bed in such a manner as not likely to be perceived.

I said to Mr Taylor, "This is a hard case to lay you on the floor, but if your wounds are not fatal, I want you to live to tell the story." A company of the mob again rushed up the stairs, but finding only the dead body of Hyrum, they were again descending the stairs, when a loud cry was heard, "The Mormons are coming!" which caused the whole band of murderers to flee precipitately to the woods (Smith, *History of the Church*, 6:617-21).

ONLY GRIEF

When Governor Ford heard that Joseph and Hyrum Smith had been murdered, he feared a Mormon uprising and warned the citizens of Carthage to flee. But there was no uprising, only grief. Lucy Mack Smith, the mother of the two martyrs, wrote:

After the corpses were washed and dressed in their burial clothes, we were allowed to see them. I had for a long time braced every nerve, roused every energy of my soul, and called upon God to strengthen me, but when I entered the room and saw my murdered sons extended both at once before my eyes and heard the sobs and groans of my family . . . it was too much; I sank back, crying to the Lord in the agony of my soul, "My God, my God, why hast thou forsaken this family!" A voice replied, "I have taken them to myself that they might have rest." . . . Oh! at that moment how my mind flew through every scene of sorrow and distress which we had passed, together, in which they had shown the innocence and sympathy which filled their guileless hearts. As I looked at their peaceful, smiling countenances, I seemed almost to hear them say, "Mother, weep not for us, we have overcome the world by love; we carried to them the gospel that their souls might be saved; they slew us for our testimony, and thus placed us beyond their power; their ascendancy is for a moment, ours is an eternal triumph" (Smith, *History of Joseph Smith*, 324-25).

DEATH MASKS OF JOSEPH AND HYRUM SMITH

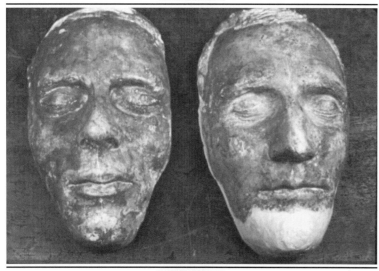

Thousands of Saints filed through the Mansion House to view the bodies of their slain leaders. The bodies secretly were buried in the basement of the Nauvoo House to keep them from being desecrated by the mob. At the public funeral, the coffins, which had been filled with sandbags, were buried near the temple, and an uneasy peace settled upon Nauvoo.

Josiah Quincy, a former mayor of Boston who had visited Joseph a few months before he was killed, wrote:

JOSIAH QUINCY (1802–1882) former mayor of Boston, Massachusettes, visited Joseph a few months before he was martyred. *ca. 1840*

> It is by no means improbable that some future textbook for the use of generations yet unborn will contain a question like this: What historical American of the nineteenth century has exerted the most powerful influence upon the destinies of his countrymen? And it is by no means impossible that the answer to that interrogatory may be thus written: Joseph Smith, the Mormon Prophet. And the reply, as absurd as it doubtless seems to most men now living, may be an obvious commonplace to their descendants. . . . Fanatic, imposter, charlatan, he may have been; but these hard names furnish no solution to the problem he presents to us.
>
> Born in the lowest ranks of poverty, without book-learning, and with the homeliest of all human names, he had made himself at the age of thirty-nine a power upon earth. His influence, whether for good or for evil, is potent today, and the end is not yet. If the reader does not know just what to make of Joseph Smith, I cannot help him out of the difficulty. I myself stand helpless before the puzzle (Roberts, *A Comprehensive History of the Church*, 2:349-50).

John Taylor's sentiments are preserved in Section 135 of the Doctrine and Covenants.

> Joseph Smith, the Prophet and Seer of the Lord, has done more, save Jesus only, for the salvation of men in this world, than any other man that ever lived in it. In the short space of twenty years, he has brought forth the Book of Mormon, which he translated by the gift and power of God, and has been the means of publishing it on two continents; has sent the fullness of the everlasting gospel which it contained, to the four quarters of the earth; has brought forth the revelations and commandments which compose this book of Doctrine and Covenants, and many other wise documents and instructions for the benefit of the children of men; gathered many thousands of the Latter-day Saints, founded a great city, and left fame and a name that cannot be slain. He lived great, and he died great in the eyes of God and his people; and like most of the Lord's anointed in ancient times, has sealed his mission and his works with his own blood; and so has his brother Hyrum. In life they were not divided, and in death they were not separated! (D&C 135:3).

A QUESTION OF LEADERSHIP

Most of the Apostles were away from Nauvoo at the time of the murders; however, several of them recorded feeling despair and grief on the day the Prophet was killed. Brigham Young, sitting in a railroad depot in Boston, was overcome by a heavy depression of spirit. Several weeks later, he heard about the martyrdom. Brigham later wrote: "The first thing I thought of was whether Joseph had taken the keys of the kingdom with him from the earth. Brother Orson Pratt sat on my left. We were leaning back in our chairs. Bringing my hand down on my knee I said, 'The keys of the kingdom are right here with the church'" (Tullidge, *The Life of Brigham Young*, 106).

JOSEPH'S GRAVE SITE OVERLOOKING THE MISSISSIPPI RIVER Joseph and Hyrum's bodies were secretly buried in the basement of the Nauvoo House to keep them from being desecrated by the mob.

On July 18, Elder Woodruff recorded in his journal: "President Brigham Young arrived in the city of Boston, also Elders Orson Hyde, Heber C. Kimball and Orson Pratt. We met together in council, and agreed to counsel the elders and brethren having families at Nauvoo, to return immediately to them" (Smith, *History of the Church*, 7:197).

On Saturday, August 3, Sidney Rigdon arrived in Nauvoo from Pittsburgh. He was invited to meet with the members of the Twelve, but failed to keep his appointment. The next morning he preached to the Saints. Willard Richards recorded:

> He related a vision which he said the Lord had shown him concerning the situation of the church, and said there must be a guardian appointed to build the church up to Joseph.
>
> He said he was the identical man that the ancient prophets had sung about, wrote and rejoiced over.
>
> Elder William Marks, president of the stake, gave public notice (at the request of Elder Rigdon) that there would be a special meeting of the church on Thursday, the 8th inst., for the purpose of choosing a guardian (President and trustee) (Smith, *History of the Church*, 7:224-25).

Three days later, Brigham Young and Wilford Woodruff arrived in Nauvoo. Elder Woodruff recorded in his journal: "We . . . were welcomed with joy by all the citizens we met . . . . and [I] truly felt to rejoice, to once more meet with my wife, children and friends. . . . When we landed in the city a deep gloom seemed to rest over the city of Nauvoo, which we never experienced before" (Smith, *History of the Church*, 7:228).

The next day, at a meeting of the apostles, high council, and high priests, Sidney Rigdon repeated his claim to be the guardian of the Church. Brigham Young replied:

> I do not care who leads the church . . . but one thing I must know, and that is what God says about it. I have the keys and the means to obtaining the mind of God on the subject. . . . Joseph conferred upon our heads all the keys and powers belonging to the Apostleship which he himself held before he was taken away, and no man or set of men can get between Joseph and the Twelve in this world or the world to come.
>
> How often has Joseph said to the Twelve, "I have laid the foundation and you must build thereon, for upon your shoulders the kingdom rests" (Smith, *History of the Church*, 7:230).

The following day, the Saints met to hear Sidney Rigdon and members of the Twelve discuss who should lead the Church. Seven of the apostles, including Brigham Young, who was senior member and President of the Quorum, Heber C. Kimball, Parley P. Pratt, Orson Pratt, Willard Richards, Wilford Woodruff, and George A. Smith were present. John Taylor was recovering from the injuries he had received in Carthage, and Orson Hyde, John E. Page, William Smith, and Lyman Wight had not yet returned to Nauvoo. Elder Rigdon spoke in the morning, and Brigham Young addressed the congregation in the afternoon.

> There has been much said about President Rigdon being President of the Church, and leading the people. . . . Brother Rigdon has come 1,600 miles to tell you what he wants to do for you. If the people want President Rigdon to lead them they may have him; but I say unto you that the Quorum of the Twelve have the keys of the kingdom of God in all the world.
>
> The Twelve are appointed by the finger of God. Here is Brigham. Have his knees ever faltered? Have his lips ever quivered? Here is Heber and the rest of the Twelve, an independent body who have the keys of the Priesthood—the keys of the kingdom of God to deliver to all the world: this is true, so help me God. They stand next to Joseph, and are the First Presidency of the Church.
>
> You cannot fill the office of a prophet, seer and revelator: God must do this.
>
> Again, perhaps some think that our beloved Brother Rigdon would not be honored, would not be looked to as a friend: but if he does right and remains faithful, he will not act against our counsel nor we against his, but act together, and we shall be as one.
>
> You cannot appoint a prophet; but if you let the Twelve remain and act in their place, the keys of the kingdom are with them and they can manage the affairs of the church and direct all things aright (Smith, *History of the Church*, 7:233-35).

As Brigham was speaking, many of those present witnessed a marvelous transformation. "For this humble follower of Christ was clothed with the very appearance, the very voice and manners of the martyred Prophet. The people, thousands of them, bore witness to this event then and in after years (Susa Gates, *The Life Story of Brigham Young*, 44).

When the vote was called for, the congregation supported the proposition that the Twelve Apostles should assume leadership of the Church. Brigham's first official act was to call for the Saints to hasten their work on the temple.

Joseph Smith, the first Prophet of the Church of Jesus Christ of Latter-day Saints was gone. The Saints' enemies thought that the Church would die along with him, but the Quorum of Twelve Apostles still had the keys and power necessary to continue God's work, and the Church kept growing.

BRIGHAM YOUNG AT A COUNCIL MEETING IN AN UPPER ROOM OF THE NAUVOO TEMPLE *by Dale Kilbourn* Brigham Young spoke to the congregation of Saints, many of whom witnessed a marvelous transformation. Brigham "was clothed with the . . . appearance . . . voice and manners of the martyred Prophet." The congregation sustained his proposition that the Twelve should lead the Church.
oil on canvas 1960

BRIGHAM
YOUNG

Lion of the Lord

Brigham Young was born in Vermont on June 1, 1801. He was the ninth child in a strict, Puritan, New England family. The family was very poor, and Brigham's mother was ill much of the time. As a youth, Brigham attended only eleven days of formal schooling. He later said:

> Brother Heber and I never went to school until we got into Mormonism. That was the first of our schooling. We never had the opportunity of letters in our youth, but we had the privilege of picking up brush, chopping down trees, rolling logs and working amongst the roots, and of getting our shins, feet and toes bruised. I learned how to make bread, wash the dishes, milk the cows and make butter; and can beat most of the women in this community at housekeeping. Those are about all the advantages I gained in my youth. I know how to economize, for my father had to do it (Young, *Journal of Discourses*, 5:97).

Brigham's mother died when he was fourteen years old, and he became a carpenter's apprentice. He was very good at his work and soon had his own business. Brigham married Miriam Works in October 1824, built a house in Mendon, New York, and practiced his trade. With his friend, Heber Kimball, he investigated the various churches, seeking one that taught the doctrines found in the Bible.

BRIGHAM YOUNG served as President from 1847–1877.

Miriam soon had two little daughters, but she had been diagnosed with consumption. Brigham worked as a carpenter, tended his wife, and did the housework. In the fall of 1831, he heard the gospel of the restoration from Alpheus Gifford and Elial Strong. After a thorough investigation of the Church and its members, Brigham and Miriam were baptized in the spring of 1832; Miriam died a few months later. Brigham was thirty-one years old. After his wife's death, Brigham Young devoted his life to The Church of Jesus Christ of Latter-day Saints. He traveled thousands of miles as a missionary, suffered through persecution, studied diligently at the feet of Joseph, and developed new talents.

In Kirtland, he married Mary Ann Angel, a marvelous woman who took care of his two children, bore many children of her own, sent Brigham on missions, accepted hardships, and stood beside her husband for the rest of her life. Brigham's daughter, Clarissa, described her father:

> Let me give you some idea of my father. No child ever loved, revered, and cherished a father more than I did mine. . . . He had the affection and tenderness of a woman for his family and friends. He was good to look at, and I fail to recall an instance when he was not immaculate in person and dress. He had well-shaped hands and feet, a clear white skin, and blue eyes—the kind that radiate love and tenderness—and a mouth that was firm, commanding the respect of all with whom he came in contact. Few could resist the wonderful personality that made him so beloved of his people. He was of medium height, rather large, with beautiful light brown curly hair, a high brow that was broad and intelligent, a long, straight nose, and a chin that denoted character and firmness (Clarissa Young Spencer, *Brigham Young at Home*, 16-17).

When Brigham became leader of the Church, his primary concern was to complete the temple so that the people could be endowed before leaving Nauvoo. He was certain that the Saints would be forced to leave, but he hoped they would have enough time to prepare. Brigham said, "We want to build the Temple in this place, if we have to do it as the Jews built the walls of the temple in Jerusalem, with a sword in one hand and the trowel in another" (Smith, *History of the Church*, 7:256).

At the October conference, the entire Quorum of the Twelve was sustained as the First Presidency of the Church. Eighty-five men were sent to preside over the various missions in the United States, and Wilford Woodruff was sent to England to preside over the European Mission. In November, Emma Smith gave birth to Joseph's last child, David Hyrum Smith.

WIDOWED EMMA SMITH (1804–1879) WITH DAVID HYRUM SMITH (1844–1904), David was born on November 17, 1844, five months after his father, Joseph Smith, Jr., was martyred. Emma married Lewis Bidamon in December, 1847. David grew up in Nauvoo and was a member of the Reorganized Church of Jesus Christ of Latter-day Saints. He was known by many as an intelligent man with a good sense of humor. In 1877, however, he was institutionalized in an asylum in Elgin, IL, for "developing insanity," and remained there until he died. *ca. 1845*

THE MOVE WEST

Early in 1845, the leaders of the Church began to discuss Joseph Smith's idea of moving the entire Church west. They began to study a copy of Fremont's book about the Rocky Mountains. In June, Brigham Young wrote to Wilford Woodruff in England:

> The capstone of the Temple was laid by the Twelve on Saturday morning the 24th of May. . . . The frame work of the roof is on the building. . . . The new stone front is mostly cut.
>
> Nauvoo, or, more properly, the "City of Joseph," looks like a paradise. All the lots and land, which have heretofore been vacant and unoccupied, were enclosed in the spring, and planted with grain and vegetables, which makes it look more like a garden of gardens than a city. . . . Hundreds of acres of prairie land have also been enclosed, and are now under good cultivation, blooming with corn, wheat, potatoes, and other necessaries of life (Smith, *History of the Church*, 7:430-31).

More than a year had passed since the Prophet Joseph had been murdered when the Saints' enemies started burning outlying farms. Brigham wrote to some of the persecutors:

> We have commenced making arrangements to remove from the country previous to the recent disturbances. One thousand families, including the Twelve, the high council, the trustees and general authorities of the church, are fully determined to remove in the spring. The church as a body desire to remove with us and will if sales can be affected so as to raise the necessary means. We have some hundreds of farms and some two thousand houses for sale in this city and county (Whitney, *Life of Heber C. Kimball*, 349).

Brigham recorded:

> Every hundred have established one or more wagon shops; wheelwrights, carpenters and cabinetmakers are nearly all foremen wagon makers and many are at work in every part of the town preparing timber for making wagons. The timber is cut and brought into the city green; hub, spoke and felloe timber boiled in salt and water, and other parts kiln dried; shops are established at the Nauvoo House, Masonic Hall, and Arsenal, nearly every shop in town is employed in making wagons.
>
> Teams are sent to all parts of the county to purchase iron; blacksmiths are at work night and day and all hands are busily engaged getting ready for our departure westward as soon as possible (Smith, *History of the Church*, 7:536).

In October, the finished parts of the temple were dedicated and ordinance work began. Through the winter, Brigham Young practically lived at the tem-

NAUVOO TEMPLE SUNSTONE. The exterior of the Nauvoo Temple was decorated with sunstones and starstones. Joseph saw these features in a vision before the temple was constructed.

THE NAUVOO TEMPLE. The temple's main entrance faced west, and its edifice was 128 feet long, 88 feet wide, and 65 feet high. Its spire rose 165 feet from the ground. It was made of light gray limestone and was built at an estimated cost of $750,000.

ple. He recorded that he slept only four hours a day and spent the rest of the time administering temple ordinances to the worthy Saints, and studying maps and explorers' accounts of the west. Gradually his mind turned toward an area west of the Rocky Mountains. The Saints had planned to leave Nauvoo in April of 1846, but the exodus began in February as pressure from the Saints' enemies increased.

Susa Young, one of Brigham's daughters, wrote that "each family of five persons was expected to have one good wagon, three yoke of cattle, two cows, three sheep, one thousand pounds of flour, twenty pounds of sugar, one rifle and ammunition, a tent and poles, from ten to twenty pounds of seeds, twenty-five to one hundred pounds of farming tools, bedding and cooking utensils" (Gates, *The Life Story of Brigham Young*, 52).

In addition, Brigham Young took vegetable and flower seeds, slips and cuttings, and tools and implements of every kind. He also took some of the Nauvoo Temple furnishings, including the bell.

The first wagons to leave Nauvoo were ferried across the Mississippi River. However, late in February, the river froze and the Saints were able to drive their wagons across the ice. This sudden cold snap hastened the Saints' departure, but wasn't very comfortable for camping. Eliza Snow recorded:

> I crossed the Mississippi River on the 12th of February. . . . We camped near the bank of the river, in a small grove. We were poorly prepared for the journey before us, especially at this season of the year. A heavy snowstorm occurred, after which the weather turned intensely cold, and caused considerable suffering. My brother had two wagons and a small tent, one cow and a scant supply of provisions and clothing, and yet was much better off than some of our neighbors in our general encampment. As applicable to the circumstances, I here insert a poem which I wrote in camp:
>
> > *Lo, a mighty host of Jacob, tented on the western shore*
> > *Of the noble Mississippi they had crossed to cross no more.*
> > *At the last day-dawn of winter, Bound with frost and wrapped in snow;*
> > *Hark, the cry is "Onward, onward! Camp of Israel, rise and go."*
> > *All at once is life and motion, trunks and beds and baggage fly;*
> > *Oxen yoked, and horses harnessed, Tents rolled up and passing by:*
> > *Soon the carriage wheels are moving, Onward to a woodland dell,*
> > *Where at sunset all are quartered, Camp of Israel, all is well.*
> > *Where is Freedom? Where is Justice?*
> > *Both have from this nation fled; And the blood of martyred Prophets*
> > *Must be answered on its head.*
> > *Therefore, to your tents, oh Jacob! Like our father Abra'm dwell;*
> > *God will execute his Purpose—*
> > *Camp of Israel, all is well.*
> > (Snow, *Biography and Family Record of Lorenzo Snow*, 85-88).

The struggling Saints felt a strong kinship with the children of Israel who had fled from Egypt. They, too, were leaving for a promised land. They, too, had a Moses to lead them—Brigham Young—who followed the pattern established by Moses and organized the Saints into groups of tens and hundreds. He also reminded them often that they needed to be righteous to succeed.

The Saints camped at Sugar Creek, nine miles from Nauvoo. On February 24, the thermometer there registered twelve degrees below zero. The following week, 500 wagons left Sugar Creek and headed west. Travel was slow. When the weather got warmer and the rains came, the Saints struggled through the thick Iowa mud. Brigham Young, Jr., wrote:

> Traveling through the swamps and bogs of Iowa was slow and painful in the extreme. For miles and miles the wagons labored heavily over corduroy road, or rather a bridge made of logs lashed together with tough willows. This terrible swamp was full of danger and difficulty. Here and there were swell or moors with a little sod over the seas of water and mud below. If one wagon got across a swell in safety no other would dare follow in its tracks, for they would have sunk out of sight. Each wagon straddled the tracks of the last, and even then the wheels would sink through the twelve-inch sod into the muddy lake below, and sometimes hours would be consumed in traversing a quarter of a mile (Gates, *The Life Story of Brigham Young*, 62).

As the Saints struggled on, one of the Church's most famous and favorite hymns was composed. William Clayton, scribe for Brigham Young, was a member of the lead party. When he received word that his wife, Diantha, who was still in Nauvoo, had given birth to a healthy baby boy, he wrote new, inspiring words to a tune he often had sung in England.

> Come, come ye Saints, no toil nor labor fear,
> But with joy wend your way.
> Though hard to you this journey may appear,
> Grace shall be as your day.
> 'Tis better far for us to strive our useless cares from us to drive,
> Do this and joy, your hearts will swell.
> All is well, all is well
> (*Hymns of the Church of Jesus Christ of Latter-day Saints*, 30).

Parley Pratt kept a record of the trek across Iowa:

> Arriving at a place on a branch of Grand River we encamped for a while, having travelled much in the midst of great and continued rains, mud and mire. Here we enclosed and planted a public farm of many hundred acres and commenced settlement, for the good of some who were to tarry and of those who should follow us from Nauvoo. We called the place "Garden Grove." It is in Iowa, perhaps one hundred and fifty miles from Nauvoo. After assisting to fence this farm and build some log houses, I was dispatched ahead by the Presidency with a small company to try to find another location. I now steered through the vast and fertile prairies and groves without a tract or anything but a compass to guide me—the country being entirely wild and without inhabitants. . . . After journeying thus for several days, and while lying encamped on a small stream which we had bridged, I took my horse and rode ahead some three miles in search of one of the main forks of Grand River. . . . I came suddenly to some round and sloping hills, grassy and crowned with beautiful groves of timber; while alternate open groves and forests seemed blended in all the beauty and harmony of an English park. While beneath and beyond, on the west, rolled a main branch of Grand River. . . . Being pleased and excited at the beauty before me, I cried out, "this is Mount Pisgah." . . . In a few days, [the President and council] arrived and formed a general encampment here, and enclosed another farm of several thousand acres. This became a town and resting place for the Saints for years. . . . In July we arrived at the Missouri River, near Council Bluffs. There we

encamped for several weeks; opened a trade with upper Missouri, exchanging wagons, horses, harness and various articles of furniture, cash, etc., for provisions, oxen, cows, etc. In the meantime we built a ferry boat, fixed landings, made dugways, etc., and commenced ferrying over the Missouri. The ferry ran night and day for a long time and still could not complete the crossing of the camps till late in the season (*Autobiography of Parley P. Pratt*, 307-8).

THE MIGRATION CONTINUES

All through the spring and summer, wagons rolled out of Nauvoo and across Iowa. Towns sprung up quickly at Garden Grove, Mount Pisgah, and on the banks of the Missouri River. Those first to arrive planted crops to be harvested by those who came later. Each settlement was carefully organized along priesthood lines and there were strict rules governing behavior. It took Brigham Young's lead party almost four months to cross Iowa. When he reached the Missouri River, he received the news about the war between the United States and Mexico.

THE MORMON BATTALION

Now at war with Mexico, the United States government proposed that the Mormons provide a battalion of men to help defend the country. Many Church members responded with dismay. Was the government trying to rob them of their able-bodied men and boys to thwart their progress?

THE MORMON BATTALION *by George M. Ottinger* The U.S. government asked the Mormons for a battalion of men to help defend the country, now at war with Mexico. The money earned by the 500 volunteers helped their families and the Church, and proved the Mormons were loyal citizens. *oil on canvas 1880*

Brigham Young, however, responded, "I propose that 500 volunteers be mustered, and I will do my best to see that all their families are brought forward, so far as my influence can be extended, and to feed them when I have anything to eat myself . . . This is the first offer we have ever had from the government to benefit us" (Preston Nibley, *Brigham Young, The Man and His Work*, 77).

By manning the battalion, over 500 Saints were able to travel west at government expense. Additionally, the soldiers' wages helped their families and the Church. It also gave the Saints a chance to prove that they were loyal citizens of the United States in spite of all that had transpired against them. Brigham Young promised the recruits that no blood would be shed if they lived the gospel and were righteous. Still, in spite of the benefits, there were great personal sacrifices.

Drusilla Hendricks' husband had been badly wounded by the mob in Missouri and still could not walk without help. She had supported the family through the years in Nauvoo, and had now brought them across Iowa. Her oldest son, William, was finally old enough to be of some help, but he was also old enough to join the Battalion. Drusilla did not want him to go.

> I got ready to get breakfast, and when I stepped up on the wagon tongue to get my flour, I was asked by the . . . spirit . . . if I did not want the greatest glory and I answered with my natural voice, "Yes, I did."
>
> "Then how can you get it without making the greatest sacrifices," said the voice.
>
> I answered, "Lord, what lack I yet?"
>
> "Let your son go in the Battalion," said the voice.
>
> I said, "It is too late. They are to be marched off in this morning." That spirit then left me with the heartache. I got breakfast and called the girls and their Father to come to the tent for prayers. William came wet with dew from the grass and we sat down around the board and my husband commenced asking the blessing on our food, when Thomas Williams came shouting at the top of his voice, saying, "Turn out men, Turn out for we do not wish to press you but we lack some men yet in the Battalion." William raised his eyes and looked me in the face. I knew then that he would go as well as I know now that he has been. I went to milk the cows. I thought the cows would be shelter for me and I knelt down and I told the Lord if He wanted my child to take him, only spare his life. . . . I felt it was all I could do. Then the voice answered me, saying, "It shall be done unto you as it was unto Abraham when he offered Isaac on the alter." I don't know whether I milked or not, for I felt the Lord had spoken to me (Carol Cornwall Madsen, *Journey to Zion*, 35–36).

When the 541 men of the Mormon Battalion left Winter Quarters with over a hundred women and children, plans to move the rest of the Saints further west were put on hold. Instead, the Saints prepared to make the coming winter as comfortable as possible. Those who had been through Zion's Camp and the expulsions from Kirtland and Missouri knew how to live in the wilderness. They knew the value of preparation and cooperation, but many of the Saints had joined the Church during the Nauvoo years. The English Saints had been mostly city dwellers and had no experience living in the wilderness. Brigham traveled from camp to camp teaching, instructing, exhorting, and preparing the people for the coming winter and their trek across the plains and mountains the following spring.

PREPARING FOR THE JOURNEY

In the meantime, the Saints continued to pour out of Nauvoo and on to the Iowa prairie until Garden Grove, Mount Pisgah, and Winter Quarters were bustling cities. The men harvested the wild grass and the crops that the first company of pioneers had planted that spring. The men built houses for their families, and corrals and shelters for their animals. Sometimes, they traveled to nearby settlements to work and earn money. The women cared for their families, taught their children, preserved food for the winter, and tried to make their primitive homes as comfortable as possible.

Even though most of the Saints had left Nauvoo, the fury of the mob was unleashed against the few who had been too sick, old, or poor to join the exodus. Over 600 Saints were forced by the mob to leave Nauvoo. They huddled on the western shore of the Mississippi River until Brigham Young sent them food and assistance. On October 9, flocks of quail settled all around them. The birds were so tame that the Saints were able to catch them with their bare hands. Like the children of Israel, God had provided for them, and the Saints had their first good meal in a long time.

Brigham Young presided over the camp at Winter Quarters, and other members of the Quorum of the Twelve presided over the settlements at Garden Grove and Mount Pisgah. Lorenzo Snow indicated that in spite of the discomforts and inconveniences, the Saints still knew how to enjoy themselves.

During the long winter months, I sought to keep up the spirits and courage of the Saints in Pisgah, not only by inaugurating meetings for religious worship

POTTER'S SLOUGH NEAR MONTROSE. As they fled from Nauvoo, the "refugee" Saints huddled on the western shore of the Mississippi River. The Lord sent flocks of tame quail, and the Saints could catch them and eat them— their first good meal in a long time. *1907*

NAUVOO, ILLINOIS. TEMPLE ON THE HILL *ca. 1846*

and exercises, but also . . . encouraging proper amusements of various kinds. . . . As a sample, I will attempt a description of one, which I improvised for the entertainment of as many as I could reasonably crowd together in my humble family mansion, which was a one-story edifice about fifteen by thirty, constructed of logs, with a dirt roof and ground floor, displaying at one end a chimney of modest height, made of turf cut from the bosom of Mother Earth. Expressly for the occasion we carpeted the floor with a thin coating of clean straw and draped the walls with white sheets drawn from our featherless beds.

How to light our hall suitably for the coming event was a consideration of no small moment, and one which levied a generous contribution on our ingenuity. But we succeeded. From the pit where they were buried, we selected the largest and fairest turnips—scooped out the interior and fixed short candles in them, placing them at intervals around the walls, suspending others from the ceiling above, which was formed of earth and cane. These lights imparted a very peaceable, quiet, Quakerlike influence, and the light reflected through those turnips rinds imparted a very picturesque appearance.

The hours were enlivened, and happily passed, as we served up a dish of succotash, composed of short speeches, full of life and sentiment, spiced with enthusiasm, appropriate songs, recitations, toasts, conundrums, exhortations, etc., etc. At the close, all seemed perfectly satisfied, and withdrew, feeling as happy as though they were not homeless (Snow, *Biography and Family Record of Lorenzo Snow*, 91-92).

But life at Pisgah was not all fun and festivity. Lorenzo wrote:

In Pisgah, Charlotte gave birth to a daughter (my first-born) which we named Lenora, after my eldest sister. Also, Adaline gave birth to a daughter, named Rosetta, after my mother.

Little Lenora was taken sick and died, and with deep sorrow we bore her remains to their silent resting place, to be left alone, far from her father and the mother who gave her birth. Sarah Ann also gave birth to a daughter, named after my sister and her mother, Eliza Sarah.

Before the spring opened and grass grew sufficient to sustain our stock, we were under the necessity of felling trees, to feed our animals upon the buds and twigs, to keep them alive.

In the latter part of winter, my only cow sickened and died, a loss which we seriously felt. She had been a great help to us on our journey, by supplying us with milk—was remarkably domesticated, kind and gentle. . . . People familiar with the circumstances of the Saints at that time would readily pardon my family for shedding a few tears on the occasion (Snow, *Biography and Family Record of Lorenzo Snow*, 93).

Meanwhile, in Winter Quarters, Brigham frequently met with the brethren to plan and organize the companies for the coming trek to the Rocky Mountains. On Thursday, January 14, they met at Heber C. Kimball's home and sought to know the will of the Lord. The minutes of the meeting record that:

President Young commenced to give the word and will of God concerning the immigration of the saints and those who journey with them. At four-thirty p.m., the council adjourned. At seven, the Twelve met at Elder Benson's. President Young continued to dictate the will and word of the Lord. Friday, January 15, the Twelve Apostles met at Ezra T. Benson's. It was decided that the word and will of the Lord should be laid before the councils of the church (Municipal High Council Minutes of Winter Quarters).

WINTER QUARTERS
by C.C.A. Christensen depicts a wagon train moving out of Winter Quarters, Nebraska, in the spring of 1847. *oil on canvas ca. 1870s*

This revelation, detailing how the pioneers were to be organized, is now contained in Section 136 of the Doctrine and Covenants.

Let all the people of The Church of Jesus Christ of Latter-day Saints . . . be organized into companies with a covenant and promise to keep all the commandments and statutes of the Lord our God.

Let each company bear an equal proportion . . . in taking the poor, the widows, the fatherless, and the families of those who have gone into the army.

. . . And if ye do this with a pure heart, in all faithfulness, ye shall be blessed.

Go thy way and do as I have told you, and fear not thine enemies; for they shall not have power to stop my work.

Zion shall be redeemed in mine own due time.

My people must be tried in all things, that they may be prepared to receive the glory that I have for them, even the glory of Zion.

Thy brethren have rejected you and your testimony, even the nation that has driven you out; And now comes the day of their calamity, even the days of sorrow . . . and their sorrow shall be great unless they speedily repent. For they killed the prophets . . . . and they have shed innocent blood, which crieth from the ground against them.

Now, therefore, hearken, O ye people of my church . . . be diligent in keeping all my commandments, lest judgments come upon you, and your faith fail you, and your enemies triumph over you (D&C 136:2, 8, 11, 17-18, 31, 34-36, 41-42).

By spring, the vanguard company of the Camp of Israel was ready to head west. Brigham Young had seen the Saints' destination in vision, and spirits were high. This first group left Winter Quarters on April 7. Susa Young wrote:

The whole company consisted of one hundred and forty-three men, three women and two children—148 souls. They had seventy-two wagons, ninety-three horses, fifty-two mules, sixty-six oxen and nineteen cows besides seventeen dogs and some chickens. They carried a cannon to overawe the Indians. There were blacksmiths, mechanics, farmers and builders, so that the band was ready not only to fight its way through, but also to construct homes; and when they should reach a place which God should designate as their journey's end, they were prepared to colonise, settle and build up the country, and to till the earth (Gates, *The Life Story of Brigham Young*, 84).

BREAKING A NEW TRAIL

Rather than follow the established trail on the south side of the Platte River, the Mormons broke a new trail on the north side. Orson Pratt was assigned to calculate the distance traveled each day. Since they had no measuring devices, they fastened a chain around a wheel. William Clayton was then given the job of counting the number of revolutions the wheel made each day. Driven by boredom, he invented an odometer.

By June 1—Brigham Young's 46th birthday—this first group of pioneers reached Fort Laramie. They stopped for a few days and were joined by some

FORT LARAMIE, WYOMING

members of the Mormon Battalion and a group of Saints from Mississippi. After they left Fort Laramie, the Saints met several people who knew a great deal about the Rocky Mountains and the west. Moses Harris told stories of arid and treeless valleys and encouraged the Saints to continue on to California. Jim Bridger, who had discovered the Great Salt Lake in 1824, told Brigham, "Mr. Young, I would give a thousand dollars if I knew an ear of corn could be ripened in the Great Basin (John A. Widtsoe, *Discourses of Brigham Young*, 81).

Miles Goodyear had spent the winter in Weber Valley. He also told of meager results from his attempts at farming. At Green River, Wyoming, the group met Sam Brannon who earlier had taken a shipload of Saints from the east coast around South America to California. He had established a settlement near San Francisco and now had come to meet Brigham and escort him to California's rich farmlands and mild climate. In spite of all of this, Brigham Young moved on toward the Salt Lake Valley. To those who questioned him about their exact destination he would only reply, "I shall know the place when I see it" (Gates, *The Life Story of Brigham Young*, 96).

In order to cross the Rocky Mountains, the pioneers had to build roads. The work was difficult and slow. Also, Brigham Young and several others became ill with Mountain Fever. Orson Pratt and a few others went on ahead to build roads while the sick lagged behind. On July 21, Erastus Snow brought the advance party a message from Brigham Young. Erastus reported that Brigham was somewhat better, but still weak. Brigham instructed the advance party to head north when they entered the valley until they came to a stream. Here, they were instructed to camp and begin at once to plow and plant the seeds they had carried from Winter Quarters.

Erastus Snow asked, "If the ground is as hard and sterile as reported how can we put our plows in?"

Brigham replied, "Throw up a dam and let the water soak the land. Then it will soften up so you can plow it" (Gates, *The Life Story of Brigham Young*, 98).

Later that day, Orson Pratt and Erastus Snow caught their first glimpse of the valley and the lake. Brother Pratt recorded, "We could not refrain from a shout of joy which almost involuntarily escaped from our lips the moment this grand and lovely scenery was within our view" (Roberts, *A Comprehensive History of the Church*, 3:216).

Levi Jackman helped build the first road into Emigration Canyon. He recorded in his journal:

JIM BRIDGER (1804–1881), Mountain man, trapper, and explorer, Jim Bridger is usually credited with being the first to see the Salt Lake. He had serious doubts about crops maturing in the Valley.

BRIGHAM YOUNG'S
FIRST VIEW OF THE
SALT LAKE VALLEY
by John Hafen
President Young
rode into the Salt
Lake Valley in
Wilford Woodruff's
carriage. Brigham
had been ill with
fever for several days
and was still weak.
He recognized the
valley from visions
he had seen.
etching

Tuesday, 20th of July, 1847—We left [Canyon Creek] this morning and struck up a ravine. Our journey for a number of days had been rather gloomy. The mountains on both sides have been so high and the ravines so cracked that we could see but a short distance and it looked as though we were shut up in a [gulch] without any chance for escape. . . . After we got to the top of the hill, we had a long steep hill to go down. This is what is now called the Big Mountain. We came this day about seven miles.

Wednesday [the] 21st—We soon left the ravine and went up a steep hill about half a mile up. This is now called the Little Mountain.

From the top of this hill, like Moses on Pisgah's top, we could see a part of the Salt Lake Valley, our long anticipated home. We did truly rejoice at the sight. . . .

Thursday, July 22, 1847—Our move was slow. . . . It took us till four p.m. to fix the road and go about four miles. We had to pass through a canyon that was full of timber mostly of small maple and the bluffs came almost together at the bottom. And when we finally got through, it seemed like bursting from the confines of prison walls into the beauties of a world of pleasure and freedom.

We now had entered the valley and our vision could extend far and wide. We were filled with joy and rejoicing and thanksgiving. We could see to the west about thirty miles distant to Salt Lake, stretching itself northwest to a distance unknown to us. And the valley extending far to the north and south. No timber was to be seen only in the mountains. We went on west about two miles and camped on a creek with plenty of grass and some brush for fire.

Friday, July 23rd—We went a short distance north to a small grove on a little stream and camped. Brother Orson called the camp together and dedicated this country to the Lord. We then commenced plowing to put in a little early corn, buckwheat, potatoes, peas, beans, etc. ("A Short Sketch of the Life of Levi Jackman," typescript, Special Collections, Harold B. Lee Library, Brigham Young University).

Two days later, Wilford Woodruff recorded:

On the twenty-fourth I drove my carriage, with President Young lying on a bed in it, into the open valley, the rest of the company following. When we came out of the canyon, into full view of the valley, I turned the side of my carriage around, open to the west, and President Young arose from his bed and took a survey of the country. While gazing on the scene before us, he was enwrapped in vision for several minutes. He had seen the valley before in vision, and upon the occasion he saw the future glory of Zion and Israel, as they would be, planted in the valleys of the mountains. When the vision had passed, he said, . . . "This is the right place. Drive on" (Nibley, *Brigham Young, The Man and His Work,* 98-99).

Four days after their arrival, on July 28, Brigham Young and a number of brethren walked northward from the temporary camp to a spot midway between the north and south forks of a stream of water known as City Creek. Placing his cane in the ground, Brigham exclaimed, "Here we will build the temple of our God." Elder Woodruff then drove a stake into the small hole made by Brigham's cane point. That evening a council meeting was held and the

city was planned. It was decided that the city would be laid out in blocks with 132-foot-wide streets and 20-foot-wide sidewalks. Four blocks were set aside in various parts of the city for public parks and recreation grounds, but the temple block was to be the heart of the new city that was to be called the City of the Great Salt Lake.

ELLEN SAUNDERS KIMBALL. HARRIET DECKER YOUNG. CLARA DECKER YOUNG.

© AUG-1919 FLORA B. HORNE.

FIRST UTAH PIONEER WOMEN, 1847.

Three women were part of the first group to enter the Salt Lake Valley. They were Harriet Wheeler Young, the wife of Lorenzo Young; Clara Decker Young, a wife of Brigham Young; and Ellen Saunders Kimball, a wife of Heber C. Kimball.

Harriet was not pleased with her new home. "Weak and weary as I am," she said, "I would rather go a thousand miles farther than remain in such a forsaken place as this" (Gates, *The Life Story of Brigham Young,* 101).

To most people, Brigham Young's ability to lead the Saints across the plains to the Salt Lake Valley was clear evidence of his genius, but Brigham didn't see it that way. "I do not wish men to understand that I had anything to do with our being moved here. That was the providence of the Almighty; it was the power of God that wrought out salvation for this people, I never could have devised such a plan" (Widtsoe, *Discourses of Brigham Young,* 480).

As more Saints arrived, Brigham started building a home for his wife, Clara Decker Young. By August, there were over 400 settlers in the Salt Lake Valley. They built a fort by attaching their homes and forming a rectangle. The east side of the fort was built of logs, and the other sides were made from adobe. Brigham Young insisted on windows for ventilation, and on the careful disposal of waste.

FIRST UTAH PIONEER WOMEN Three women were part of the first group to enter the Salt Lake Valley in 1847. They were Ellen Saunders Kimball (1824–1871), a wife of Heber C. Kimball; Harriet Page Wheeler Decker Young (1803–1871), the wife of Lorenzo Young; and Clarissa Caroline Decker Young (1828–1889), a wife of Brigham Young. *Engraving by H.B. Hall & Sons.*

Clara wrote, "We were the first to move into the fort; our house had a door and a wooden window, which through the day was taken out for light, and nailed in again at night. There was a port-hole at the east end of the fort which could be opened and closed at pleasure. We had adobe chimneys and a fireplace in the corner with a clay hearth" (Gates, *The Life Story of Brigham Young*, 108).

JOHN SMITH was the Prophet Joseph's uncle who supervised the building of houses at Garden Grove.

In August, Brigham and several of the other men left the valley to return to Winter Quarters. They planned to spend the winter at Winter Quarters and then lead the rest of the Saints to the valley the following spring. John Smith, a cousin to the Prophet Joseph, was appointed to preside in Salt Lake during their absence. On the way back across the plains, Brigham's group met five or six more companies of Saints who were making their way to the Salt Lake Valley. When these companies arrived, the city's population grew to over 2,000. Eliza R. Snow was in one of these later companies and wrote:

> I stayed with Clara Decker Young who came with the Pioneers. She was living in a log-house about eighteen feet square, which constituted a portion of the east side of the fort. . . . . This hut, like most of those built the first year, was roofed with willows and earth, the roof having but little pitch, the first comers having adopted the idea that the valley was subject to little if any rain, and our roofs were nearly flat. We suffered no inconvenience from this fact until about the middle of March, when a long storm of snow, sleet and rain occurred, and for several days the sun did not make its appearance. The roof of our dwelling was covered deeper with earth than the adjoining ones, consequently it did not leak so soon, and some of my neighbors huddled in for shelter; but one evening, when several were sitting around, the water commenced dripping in one place, and then in another. They dodged it for a while, but it increased so rapidly that they finally concluded they might as well go to their own wet houses. After they'd gone I spread my umbrella over my head and shoulders as I ensconced myself in bed, the lower part of which, not shielded by the umbrella, was wet enough before morning. The earth overhead was thoroughly saturated, and after it commenced to drip the storm was much worse indoors than out (Gates, *The Life Story of Brigham Young*, 114).

The pioneers were blessed with a rather mild first winter, but they were over 1,000 miles from the nearest store. Meals were made from whatever food the Saints had been able to carry with them. They had been able to harvest some food from the crops that had been planted in late July, but wild game and wild plants made up most of their diet. Because supplies were scarce, animal skins were frequently used for clothing, and people often went barefoot or wore moccasins.

Brigham Young reached Winter Quarters on the last day of October. He spent the winter refining the organization of the Church and the pioneer companies. Orson Hyde told of an important meeting that took place that winter.

[T]he Twelve Apostles met at Hyde Park, Pottawattamie County, Iowa. . . . We were in prayer and council, communing together, and what took place on that occasion? The voice of God came from on high, and spake to the Council. Every latent feeling was aroused, and every heart melted. What did it say unto us? "Let my servant, Brigham, step forth and receive the full power of the presiding Priesthood in my Church and Kingdom." This was the voice of the Almighty unto us at Council Bluffs. . . . It has been said by some that Brigham was appointed by the people, and not by the voice of God. I do not know that this testimony has often, if ever, been given . . . but I am one that was present on that occasion, and did hear and feel the voice from heaven and we were filled with the power of God (Roy W. Doxey, *Latter-day Prophets and the Doctrine and Covenants*, 4:26-27).

MORMON PIONEERS ON THE PLAINS Pioneers gathered in front of their wagons. *Taken near South Pass, Wyoming, 1866*

WAGONS CROSSING THE PLATTE RIVER *ca. 1865–1868*

BRIGHAM YOUNG SUSTAINED

In a conference at Kanesville on Dec. 27, 1847, this revelation was presented to the Saints. Brigham Young was sustained as President of the Church, with Heber C. Kimball and Willard Richards as his counselors. John Smith was called as Church Patriarch.

During the following year's general conference at Winter Quarters on April 6, 1848, this action was confirmed. Oliver Cowdery attended this conference and bore his testimony. He was joyfully readmitted to the Church and was rebaptized on November 12, 1848. He planned to go west with the

Saints, but was in poor health. He later died on March 3, 1850, in the home of David Whitmer.

CRICKETS AND SEAGULLS

Early in the spring of 1848, Brigham Young again headed west. Meanwhile, the Saints in the Salt Lake Valley were faced with an unexpected problem. John R. Young recorded the following:

MIRACLE OF THE GULLS
by Minerva Teichert

As the summer crept on, and the scant harvest drew nigh, the fight with the crickets commenced. Oh, how we fought and prayed and battled against the myriads of black, loathsome insects that flowed down like a flood of filthy water from the mountainside. And we should surely have been inundated, and swept into oblivion, save for the merciful Father's sending of the blessed sea gulls to our deliverance.

The first I knew of the gulls, I heard a sharp cry. Upon looking up, I beheld what appeared like a vast flock of pigeons coming from the northwest. It was about three o'clock in the afternoon. My brother Franklin and I were trying to save an acre of wheat of father's. . . . The wheat was just beginning to turn yellow. The crickets would climb the stalk, bite off the head then come down and eat it. To prevent this, my brother and I each took an end of a long rope, stretched it full length, then walked through the grain holding the ropes so as to hit the heads, and thus knock the crickets off. From sunrise till sunset we kept at this labor; for as darkness came the crickets sought shelter, but with the rising of the sun they commenced their ravages again.

I have been asked how numerous were the gulls? There must have been thousands of them. Their coming was like a great cloud; and when they passed between us and the sun, a shadow covered the field. I could see the gulls setting for more than a mile around us. They were very tame, coming within four or five yards of us.

At first we thought that they, also, were after the wheat, and this added to our terror; but we soon discovered that they devoured only the crickets. Needless to say, we quit drawing the rope, and let our gentle visitors have full possession of the field. As I remember it, the gulls came every morning for about three weeks, when their mission was apparently ended, and they ceased coming. The precious crops were saved (Gates, *The Life Story of Brigham Young*, 117-18).

By September, Salt Lake City's population had increased to 5,000 people. But life was still difficult. George A. Smith wrote:

For the next three years we were reduced to considerable straits for food. Fast meetings were held, and contributions constantly made for those who had no provisions. Every head of a family was issued rations to those dependent upon him, for fear this supply of provisions should fall short. Raw hides, wools, rabbits, thistle roots, Sego roots, and everything that could be thought of that would preserve life were resorted to. There were a few deaths by eating poisonous roots (Gates, *The Life Story of Brigham Young*, 123-24).

OTHER CHALLENGES

One of the most challenging problems the pioneers faced was learning to farm in a desert climate. Since there was no rain for months at a time, they developed the first irrigation system in modern America. The lack of manufactured goods was another problem. However, the Saints built their own factories and found or produced all the raw materials necessary to make clothing, furniture, tools, machinery, utensils, cooking pots, and other necessities. In the fall of 1848, Heber C. Kimball predicted that within two years, goods would be cheaper and more plentiful in Salt Lake City than in St. Louis or New York.

The Indians were another problem. The Salt Lake Valley may have appeared empty to the first pioneers, but it was home to several bands of wandering Indian tribes. Brigham Young counseled the Saints to feed the Indians and not fight with them. But there were occasional problems that often were caused by non-Mormons who were passing through the territory.

Brigham Young had always intended the new settlement to be part of the United States, and the Stars and Stripes were unfurled within days of the pioneers' first arrival in the valley. In 1849 a convention was held in Salt Lake City. Those assembled drafted a constitution and called the area the State of Deseret. The new government was similar to that of the United States except that everyone—man, woman, Indian, black, or white—was allowed to vote. Brigham Young was elected governor, and a year later, the United States admitted part of the State of Deseret into the Union as a territory. The new territory was named Utah after the Ute Indians who inhabited the region. Brigham Young was retained as governor, but political appointees from the east were sent to fill other government offices. The historian, George Bancroft, wrote:

The year 1848 was also an important year in world history. France, Austria, Italy and Prussia were torn by revolution as the people tried to throw off oppressive monarchs. British settlers arrived in New Zealand. While in Brussels, Karl Marx and Frederick Engels published a small book called *The Communist Manifesto*.

BAPTISM OF SHIVWITS INDIANS. Daniel D. McArthur baptizing Shivwits Indians in a stream near St. George, Utah. Augustus P. Hardy is shown standing on the banks. *March 1875*

> The authorities were kindly received by the saints; and had they been men of ability and discretion, content to discharge their duty without interfering with the social and religious peculiarities of the people, all would have been well; but such was not their character or policy, Judge Brocchus espe-

INDIANS IN FRONT
OF ZCMI. The
Native American
Indians in Utah
roamed freely in
comparison to
everywhere else in
the west.
1869

cially was a vain and ambitious man, full of self-importance, fond of intrigue, corrupt, revengeful, hypocritical (Gates, *The Life Story of Brigham Young*, 166).

GOLD FEVER

The isolation the Saints had hoped for did not last long. Gold was discovered in California, and word of the discovery soon spread across the country.

In 1849, gold seekers began streaming across the country. Salt Lake City was halfway between St. Louis and California and became a popular stopping point. Elder Kimball had been correct; goods poured into the city and prices fell. Of course, the travelers brought other things as well—drunkenness, profanity, immorality, and gold fever. Brigham Young warned:

> Some have asked me about going. I have told them that God has appointed this place for the gathering of his Saints, and you will do better right here than you will by going to the gold mines. Those who stop here and are faithful to God and his people will make more money and get richer than you that run after the gold of this world; and I promise you in the name of

the Lord that many of you that go, thinking you will get rich and come back, will wish you had never gone away. . . . Here is the place God has appointed for his people (Nibley, *Brigham Young, The Man and His Work,* 127).

SETTLING DESERET

Very few of the Saints succumbed to gold fever. Most stayed and prospered where they were. In the meantime, Brigham Young sent pioneers out to settle new towns in the vast territory of Deseret, which included all of present-day Utah and parts of Colorado, Wyoming, Idaho, New Mexico, Arizona, Nevada, California, and Oregon. During the first two years, the Saints spread only as far as Utah and Weber Valleys, but soon settlements dotted Deseret. Salt Lake City became a beautiful city with fine homes and gardens. The cities and towns of Provo, Ogden, Manti, Fillmore, Moab, Logan, Brigham City, and Genoa; and Las Vegas, Nevada; and San Bernardino, California, also began to flourish.

In addition to the pioneers' efforts to make the desert blossom, they continued their missionary work. Thousands of converts from Britain and Northern Europe were ready and eager to join the Saints in Deseret, but many of them were very poor. At conference in September, 1849, Brigham Young suggested establishing a fund so these poor emigrants could travel to Zion. The Saints donated what they could to the Perpetual Emigrating Fund, and many new converts were able to make the journey. In all, over 17,000 Saints emigrated from Europe between 1840 and 1854. When they arrived in Salt Lake, these emigrants were trained in new skills so they could help themselves and others. Susa Young wrote:

A bureau was organised called the "Public Works." The project began with the establishment of a series of shops of divers trades inside the Temple grounds. There was a carpenter shop, machine shop, paint shop, and many others,

each presided over by a capable leader. . . . Branch establishments were also set up in other sections of the country.

It was easy to supply work as the Temple and Tabernacle were in course of construction, as were also the Council House, the Social Hall, the Salt Lake City Theatre and many other public buildings. In addition, there were the building of bridges and the digging of canals and the erection of forts. The "Public Works" became a general clearing house for all who were seeking work. As soon as the workers became accustomed to American ways and conditions they branched out for themselves and established businesses of their own (Gates, *The Life Story of Brigham Young*, 211).

Brigham Young continued to work on his own farms and homes in spite of the heavy load he carried as President of the Church and governor of the territory. One day, Jedediah M. Grant came to seek counsel, and found Brother Brigham working on his roof.

He yelled up to the Prophet, "Brother Brigham, I want to ask you about an important matter."

Brigham responded, "Well, wait until this evening and come into my council room."

But brother Grant persisted, "Now, Brother Brigham, don't you think it is time you quit pounding nails and spending your time like this? We have many carpenters but only one Governor and one President of the Church. The people need you more than they need a good carpenter" (Gates, *The Life Story of Brigham Young*, 212).

Brigham dropped his hammer and nails and came down off the roof. After that, he rarely spent his time doing manual labor, but instead, attended to the affairs of the Church and state.

One of the first structures built in Salt Lake City was a bowery for general meetings. It was

EMBARKATION OF THE SAINTS FROM LIVERPOOL
by Ken Baxter
Brigham Young suggested that the Saints establish a fund so poor emigrants could travel to Zion. It was called the Perpetual Emigration Fund.

COUNCIL HOUSE
ca. 1865–1868

SOCIAL HALL, Salt
Lake City. The hall
was dedicated
January, 1853, and
was used for social
and cultural gather-
ings. In 1922, the
building was razed.
View of the city
looking east from
Main Street, show-
ing E.T. Benson
home, Social Hall,
and other dwellings.
ca. 1858

open to the elements and could only be used in the summer, so in 1851, the Saints started building a tabernacle. The building was made of adobe, was 126 feet long and 64 feet wide, and had a roof of native white pine shingles. It could seat 2500 people. The first meeting held in the new building was the April 1852 General Conference. Brigham Young spoke at the meeting.

> Four years ago, when the brethren came into this valley, Brother George A. Smith delivered his first lecture upon the cannon, for there were no houses wherein the people could assemble. . . . The first large place we had to meet was the Bowery. We felt comfortable in it, and I felt as thankful for it as I ever did for anything in my life; but as quick as the falling weather came, it drove the Saints away. . . . Now we have a convenient room, the best hall I ever saw in my life. . . . I trust we shall renew our strength, meet here to pray and to praise the Lord, and partake of the sacrament, until our feelings are perfectly pure (Nibley, *Brigham Young, The Man and His Work*, 177-78).

At a conference held in August of 1852, 107 men were called on missions to the United States, Canada, Great Britain, Germany, Denmark, Norway, South Africa, Australia, China, Siam, Hindustan, British Ghana, and the Sandwich Islands.

THE TEMPLE

On February 14, 1853, a large group of Saints gathered on temple block to hear Brigham Young make an important announcement. President Young called the congregation to order and said:

> The Lord wished us to gather to this place. He wished us to cultivate the earth and make these valleys like the Garden of Eden, and to build a temple as soon as circumstances would permit. Seven years ago tomorrow, about eleven o'clock, I crossed the Mississippi River with my brethren, not knowing at that time whither we were going, but firmly believing that the Lord

HANDCART MISSION-
ARIES OF 1855. Taken
at a meeting of the mis-
sionaries in England to
discuss the plan of
sending emigrants from
the Missouri River to
the Salt Lake Valley in
handcart trains. *Top row
(l to r):* Edmund Ellsworth,
Joseph A. Young, William
H. Kimball, George D.
Grant, James Ferguson,
James A. Little, Philemon
Merrill. *Middle row:*
Edmund Bunker,
Chauncey Webb, Franklin
D. Richards, Daniel
Spencer, Dan Jones,
Edward Martin. *Bottom
row:* James Bond, Spicer
Crandall, W. Dunbar,
James Ross, Daniel
McArthur.

had in reserve for us a good place in the mountains, and that he would lead us directly to it. It was but seven years since we left Nauvoo, and we are now ready to build another Temple (Young, *Journal of Discourses*, 1:277).

After speaking, Brigham Young took a spade and broke ground for the Salt Lake Temple. The following April, the cornerstones were laid. Brigham said:

> I scarcely ever say much about revelations, or visions, but suffice it to say, five years ago last July I was here, and saw in the spirit the temple not ten feet from where we have laid the chief cornerstone. I have not inquired what kind of temple we should build. Why? Because it was represented before me. I have never looked upon that ground, but the vision of it was there. Wait until it is done. I will say however, that it will have six towers instead of one. Now I do not want any of you to apostatize because it will have six towers, to begin with, and Joseph only built one. . . . The time will come when there will be one in the centre of temples . . . and on the top, groves and fish ponds but we shall not see them here at present (Widtsoe, *Discourses of Brigham Young*, 410).

INDIAN TROUBLES

In 1853, the Indians under Chief Walker became increasingly hostile and made several raids on outlying farms and settlements. President Young encouraged the people to build forts for protection. Finally, after several months of hostilities, Brigham Young and Chief Walker met near Nephi. At first, Walker refused to talk with the Prophet, but after Brigham blessed and healed the chief's sick daughter, he relented and agreed to return the animals he and his men had stolen.

SALT LAKE TEMPLE
SITE DEDICATION AND
GROUNDBREAKING,
Salt Lake City, Utah.
Feb. 14, 1853

WILLARD RICHARDS

In March 1854, Willard Richards died. At the time of his death, he was serving as Second Counselor in the First Presidency. Since his baptism in December of 1835, Willard had been exceptionally valiant in the Lord's work. He had served as a missionary in England, had been Joseph Smith's trusted secretary, and was in Carthage Jail with Joseph and Hyrum when they were martyred. His careful journals and records have blessed the entire Church.

WILLARD RICHARDS, a devoted servant of the Lord. He had a close bond of friendship with Joseph Smith.

UTAH TERRITORIAL CAPITOL BUILDING IN FILLMORE, UTAH
ca. 1890

GOVERNOR YOUNG

In the early days of the territory, Fillmore was the area's political capital, and Brigham Young often traveled there to transact government business. Brigham's four-year term as governor was due to expire in 1854, so President Franklin Pierce sent Lieutenant Colonel Edward J. Steptoe with about 200 men to evaluate conditions in the Utah territory. Steptoe had been offered the governorship, but after spending time among the Saints, he wrote to President Pierce:

Whereas Governor Brigham Young possesses the entire confidence of the people of this territory, without distinction of party or sect; and from personal acquaintance . . . we find him to be a firm supporter of the Constitution and laws of the United States, and a tried pillar of republican institutions . . . and whereas, his reappointment would better subserve the territorial interest than the appointment of any other man . . . possess[ing] in an eminent degree every qualification to the discharge of his official duties and unquestioned integrity and ability, that he is the most suitable person that can be selected for that office.

We therefore take great pleasure in recommending him to your favorable consideration and do honestly request his reappointment as governor and superintendent of Indian affairs for this territory (Roberts, *A Comprehensive History of the Church*, 4:183-84).

HANDCARTS

After an exceptionally cold and severe winter, drought and grasshoppers plagued the Saints in 1855. Again, the pioneers faced hunger and suffering. Brigham Young rationed his family to a half pound of wheat per day. The drought and severe winter killed over half of the Church's oxen and cattle. In addition, the wagons and other equipment that had been traveling back and forth across the plains were about worn out. And yet many still wanted to come to Zion. In September, 1855, Brigham wrote to Franklin D. Richards in Liverpool:

I've been thinking how we would operate another year. We cannot afford to purchase wagons and teams as in times past. I am consequently thrown back upon my old plan to make handcarts, and let the emigration foot it. They can come just as quick, if not quicker, and much cheaper. They will only need ninety days rations from the time of their leaving the Missouri River, and as settlements extend up the Platte, not that much. The carts can be made without a particle of iron, with wheels hooped, made strong and light, and one or two of them will bring all they will need upon the plains (*Millennial Star*, vol. 17, 813).

HANDCART COMPANY FACING BLIZZARD near Devil's Gate, Wyoming.

MORMONS PASSING THROUGH IOWA ON THEIR WAY TO UTAH FROM ILLINOIS.

HANDCART
COMPANIES PASS
THROUGH IOWA
The Mormon Saints
pulling handcarts
received catcalls and
ridicule as they
passed through Iowa.

That summer, over 1,300 English Saints pulled handcarts across the plains. The first three companies were as successful as Brigham Young had imagined. But two companies, the Willie and Martin Companies, left too late in the season and became trapped in snow and freezing weather in the mountains. As conference convened on October 5, Brigham Young spoke:

I will now give this people the subject and the text for . . . the conference. It is this: . . . many of our brethren and sisters are on the plains with handcarts, and probably many of them are now seven hundred miles from this place, and they must be brought here; we must send assistance to them. The text will be, "to get them here." . . .

I shall call upon the Bishops this day. I shall not wait until tomorrow, nor until the next day, for 60 good mule teams and 12 or 15 wagons. . . . Also, 12 tons of flour, and 40 good teamsters. I will tell you that all your faith, religion, and profession of reli-

WORLD EVENTS

In the 1850s, the United States moved closer to Civil War as Kansas became a battlefield between free and slave states. The Crimean War ended early in 1856 when Alexander II, the new Czar of Russia, accepted terms set by England, France, and Turkey. Walt Whitman published *Leaves of Grass*, and Longfellow wrote "The Song of Hiawatha." Charlotte Bronte died; and the first iron steamer of the Kennard line crossed the Atlantic in just nine and one-half days. The Scottish explorer and missionary, David Livingstone, discovered Victoria Falls on the Zambezi River deep in the interior of Africa.

gion will never save one soul of you in the Celestial Kingdom of God, unless you carry out just such principles as I am now teaching you. Go and bring in those people now on the plains (LeRoy R. and Ann W. Hafen, *Handcarts to Zion*, 120-21).

Within two days, wagons were on their way loaded with food, clothing, and bedding donated by the Saints. However, about 200 of the handcart pioneers died before they could be rescued. President Young said:

> There is not a person, who knows anything about the counsel of the First Presidency concerning the immigration but what knows that we have recommended it to start in season . . . hereafter I am going to lay an injunction and place a penalty, to be suffered by any elder or elders who will start the immigration . . . after a given time, and the penalty shall be, that they shall be severed from the Church, for I will not have such late starts again (Nibley, *Brigham Young, The Man and His Work*, 262).

EDWARD MARTIN FAMILY Edward Martin (1818–1882) served in the Mormon Battalion, and was the captain of the Martin Handcart Company of 1856. He became a photographer in Salt Lake City. *ca. 1870*

THE LION HOUSE,
WHITE HOUSE, AND
BEEHIVE HOUSE *(l to r)*
were homes of
Brigham Young.
ca. 1865

SUSA AMELIA YOUNG
GATES (1856–1933),
one of Brigham's
daughters. She was
the first child born in
the Lion house.

BRIGHAM'S HOMES

In 1856, Brigham Young completed his third home in the territory. His first permanent home was called the White House and was the home of Mary Ann Angel Young and her large family. The Beehive House was Brigham's official residence and contained his offices. It was also the home of Lucy Decker Young and her family. The Lion House was home for the rest of his families. It contained storerooms, kitchens, a washroom, and a schoolroom for the children. On the main floor were sitting rooms and a large front parlor. The upper floor had twenty rooms. Susa Young Gates, one of Brigham's daughters, wrote of her life in this remarkable family:

> The Lion House was the loved home of as healthy and happy a family of mothers and children as ever dwelt beneath a roof. On this I speak with knowledge . . . for I was the first child born under its unique roof . . . my mother moving into her sitting-room suite as the boards were being nailed on the floors and just in time for my own birth.
> Dear, great-hearted Aunt Zina was the gentle priestess who presided over most of the beds of birth and death,

sickness and pain. She, together with Aunt Clara, my own mother, and splendid Aunt Eliza R. Snow, were the various nurses and authorities on all the ills humanity is heir to.

Food and meal-times in the Lion House were necessarily exact as to time and measured as to servings. Plenty of milk, vegetables, and fruit, but careful helpings of meat and desserts.

One of the very best cooks and managers was "Aunt Twiss," and she was in charge of the kitchen staff in the Lion House. She had no children and she loved her work.

The custom of evening prayer-time in the Lion House was as fixed as the stars. About seven o'clock the rhythmic sound of the prayer-bell was heard . . . and the flying feet of children, the quiet coming of his lady wives filled the halls with clatter and soon every chair was taken.

A hymn or two was joyously sung . . . then came the quiet prayer of gratitude and adoration; of appeal for each loved one and for all the world; for the work of the Lord . . . and for protection from evil and accident. . . . Father often remained to talk over the events of the day with such of his wives as cared to remain, and some of the older children.

Lights were pretty generally out at 10 o'clock, and we were all up by seven or half-past seven in the morning.

BRIGHAM YOUNG AND HIS DAUGHTERS MONTAGE, portrays Brigham (center) and twenty-nine of Brigham's daughters. *Top row:* Maria Dougall, Fanny Thakher, Alice Clawson, Elizabeth Ellisworth, Vilate Decker, Luna Thakher, Mary Ann Craxall, Ella ? *Second row:* Emmie Crosby, Myra Rossiter, Jeanette Easton, Emily Clawson, Zina Card, Eudora Hagan. *Third row:* Phebe Beatie, Eva Dans, Nabbie Clawson, Susa Gates, Josephine Young. *Bottom row:* Marinda Conrad, Louise Ferguson, Ruth Henly, Andelle Harrison, Fannie Clayton, Talula Wood, Clarissa Spencer, Mariam Harly, and Mabel Sanborn.

The Sabbath was strictly observed.

It is generally understood that my father had nineteen wives; but of that number, some were widows and wives in name only, to whom father gave a home. Of his wives, sixteen bore him children, six of them having but one child. The rest of them had children varying from two to ten. He had fifty-six living children, ten of them dying in infancy. There were twenty-six sons and thirty daughters.

I was born and reared in the Lion House. In all my life in that beloved home I never heard my father speak an unkind or irritable word to one of his wives. I never heard a quarrel between my father's wives.

The world knows Brigham Young as a statesman and coloniser; but to his children he was an ideal father. Kind to a fault, tender, thoughtful, just and firm. He spoke but once, and none were so daring as to disobey. . . . None of us feared him, all of us adored him (Gates, *The Life Story of Brigham Young*, 326–35).

Another daughter, Clarissa, adds her impressions of her father:

On the day of my birth, July 23, 1860, a company of saints had made the customary trip to Brighton, and they had no sooner reached their destination than word was brought to Father that my mother had taken ill. To the great disappointment of his people, who felt that no gathering of any sort was complete without their leader, he turned around and went immediately back to the city in order to be with Mother during her ordeal. As I was his fifty-first child, the birth of a baby was far from being a novelty in the family, but his consideration for each of his wives, or any other member of his family was such that he would willingly forego any pleasure of his own if he could be of comfort or assistance to them (Clarissa Young Spencer, *Brigham Young at Home*, 15-16).

JOHNSON'S ARMY

A number of government officials had lived in Utah since it became a territory. Most got along well with the people, but a few were extremely unpopular and incompetent. Some of these made inflammatory and untrue statements about conditions in the territory when they returned to the east. Judge Drummond spoke of all the male members of the Church taking an oath to resist the laws of the country. He even went so far as to say that Brigham Young sanctioned the destruction of Supreme Court records.

Such ill-founded reports aroused bitter anti-Mormon feelings, and some officials in Washington were sure that the Saints were in open rebellion. James Buchanan, a Democrat from Pennsylvania was elected president in 1856. He decided it was time to deal with the charges against the residents of the territory of Utah. However, the action President Buchanan took stunned both the Mormons and the nation.

As the Saints were celebrating the tenth anniversary of their arrival in the Salt Lake Valley on July 24, 1857, Abraham O. Smoot, Judson Stoddard, and Orrin Porter Rockwell rode into town. Smoot and Judson had ridden from the states in only twenty days to deliver an important message to President Young. An army of the United States, with 2,500 men, was on its way to Utah. Also, a new governor, Alfred Cumming, had been appointed and was traveling with the army. On Sunday, Brigham mentioned the approaching army in his speech:

> Woe, woe to that man who comes here to unlawfully meddle with me and this people. If they kill me it is all right; but they will not until the time comes, and I think I shall die a natural death. Would it not make any man or community angry to endure and reflect upon the abuse our enemies have heaped upon us, and are still striving to pour out upon God's people? (Nibley, *Brigham Young, The Man and His Work*, 289).

ABRAHAM OWEN SMOOT (1815–1895), was the head of a company of 139 people who arrived in the Salt Lake Valley in 1847. (left)

ORRIN PORTER ROCKWELL rode in with news that a U.S. army was on its way to Utah.(right)

ALFRED CUMMING (1802–1873) was appointed governor of Utah Territory from 1858–1861.

An army representative arrived in Salt Lake on September 8, 1857, to purchase food and supplies for the troops that were coming to invade Utah and wipe out the Mormons. Brigham Young told him that the Saints would not sell supplies to the army and further stated:

> We do not want to fight the United States. . . . We are supporters of the Constitution of the United States, and we love that Constitution, and respect the laws of the United States. . . . If the government persists in sending an army to destroy us, in the name of the Lord we shall conquer them. If they dare to force the issue, I shall not hold the Indians by the wrist any longer; they shall go ahead and do as they please; . . . you may tell the government to stop all emigration across this continent, for the Indians will kill all who attempt it; and if

PONY EXPRESS GATE
AT FORT BRIDGER,
WYOMING. Fort
Bridger was burned as
part of a resistance
strategy against the
approaching army.

an army succeeds in penetrating this valley, tell the government to see that it has forage and provisions in store, for they will find here only a charred and barren waste (Nibley, *Brigham Young, the Man and His Work*, 296-97).

Daniel H. Wells and the brethren under his command gathered in Echo Canyon to resist the approaching army. They burned Fort Bridger and then Fort Supply. Wells's orders were:

> Use every exertion to stampede their animals and set fire to their trains. Burn the whole country before them, and on their flanks. Keep them from sleeping by night surprises; blockade the road by felling trees or destroying the river fords where you can. . . . Keep your men concealed as much as possible, and guard against surprises [but] take no life (Roberts, *A Comprehensive History of the Church*, 4:279-80).

In February, Colonel Thomas L. Kane arrived from California to help the Saints negotiate with the Federal Government. Brigham Young welcomed him warmly, and the two spent hours deciding what action to take. Colonel

Kane met with Governor Cummings and assured him that the Saints would accept him as their governor.

While Kane was meeting with Governor Cummings, the Saints evacuated Salt Lake City. Brigham Young and his family moved to Provo, but Brigham returned to Salt Lake to greet the new governor and assure him that the government records had not been destroyed. When Cummings found that he had been able to assume his post without the aid of the army, he sent a message to the General Johnson that the army was no longer needed. President Buchanan sent a peace commission to the Mormons, but insisted that the troops stay in the valley. Brigham Young replied:

> I thank President Buchanan for forgiving me, but I can't really tell what I have done. I know one thing, and that is, that the people called "Mormons" are a lawful and loyal people and ever have been. . . . What has the United States Government permitted mobs to do to us? . . . We have been plundered and whipped, our houses burned, our fathers, mothers, brothers, sisters, and children butchered and murdered by the score. We have been driven from our homes time and time again.
>
> Do not send your armed mobs into our midst.
>
> Now let me say to you, Peace Commissioners, we are willing that the troops should come into our country, but not to stay in our cities. They may pass through [it] if needs be, but you must not quarter them nearer than forty miles to any city (Gates, *The Life Story of Brigham Young*, 189-90).

PARLEY P. PRATT

The Church received more disturbing news that year. Parley P. Pratt was murdered in Arkansas. Parley had served as a missionary in Canada, Great Britain, the Pacific Islands, South America, and the United States. He also wrote numerous books and tracts and edited several Church publications. In addition, Parley wrote a number of hymns, including "The Morning Breaks, The Shadows Flee," "An Angel from on High," and "Jesus, Once of Humble Birth." He had shared a prison cell with the Prophet Joseph in Missouri and had endured much persecution for the gospel's sake. John Taylor wrote of Parley:

COLONEL THOMAS L. KANE helped negotiate with the Federal Government when Johnson's Army arrived in the Salt Lake Valley.

GENERAL ALBERT SIDNEY JOHNSON (1803–1862) led the army to the Valley. *ca. 1860*

THE CELEBRATION OF LINCOLN'S INAUGURAL AT THE BEEHIVE HOUSE, 1861 on South Temple street, Salt Lake City, included a military and civil procession a mile in length, artillery firing, speeches, and fireworks. *Ken Baxter oil on canvas 1978*

In 1856, George Bernard Shaw and Sigmund Freud were born. The English cast Big Ben, the thirteen-and-a-half-ton bell that hangs in the British Houses of Parliament. Workers began constructing the Suez Canal, and the first British Open Golf Championship was held. In 1860, Abraham Lincoln was elected president of the United States. Lincoln had been fairly friendly to the Saints when he was in the Illinois Legislature, and shortly after he took office, Brigham Young sent Thomas Stenhouse to determine what the president's policy would be toward the Latter-day Saints. Lincoln responded:

Stenhouse, when I was a boy on the farm in Illinois there was a great deal of timber on the farms which we had to clear away. Occasionally, we would come to a log which had fallen down. It was too hard to split, too wet to burn, and too heavy to move, so we plowed around it. That's what I intend to do with the Mormons. You go back and tell Brigham Young that if he will let me alone, I will let him alone (Nibley, *Brigham Young, The Man and His Work*, 369).

He possessed a comprehensive mind, coupled with a sound judgment. He manifested an indomitable fortitude under the most trying circumstances, and in adversity and trials, as well as in prosperity, . . . [he] was indeed a true Latter-day Saint, an honorable Apostle, a good and kind husband, an affectionate father, a true friend, and an honest man. He has gone—but has left a name and a fame that will live throughout time and burst forth in eternity; and in the morning of the first resurrection . . . I expect to meet Brother Parley in the resurrection of the just (*Autobiography of Parley P. Pratt*, xvii- xviii).

CIVIL WAR

In 1861, telegraph lines were stretched across the continent to Utah. Brigham Young sent the first message: "Utah has not seceded, but is firm for the Constitution and laws of our once happy country" (Nibley, *Brigham Young, The Man and His Work*, 369).

After Lincoln was elected, South Carolina seceded from the Union. Mississippi, Florida, Alabama, Georgia, Louisiana, and Texas soon followed. On February 4, 1861, delegates met in Montgomery, Alabama and formed the Confederate States of America. After the Southerners attacked the Union-held Fort Sumpter in Charleston Harbor, compromise became impossible. Soon, the border states of Virginia, Tennessee, and North Carolina had joined the Confederacy, and by April 1861, the Civil War had begun. The troops at Camp Floyd in Utah were ordered back east to fight in the new war.

William Clayton, in a letter to George Q. Cannon, commented, "Today commences the sale of all the government property at Camp Floyd, by auction—buildings, grain, hay and everything except arms and ammunition, soldiers' clothing, wagons and teams. They will move away for the states within two weeks and thus ends the great Buchanan Utah Expedition, costing the government millions and accomplishing [comparatively] nothing" (Nibley, *Brigham Young, The Man and His Work*, 374).

SOLDIERS AT CAMP FLOYD located southwest of Fairfield, Utah. *ca. 1858*

About a year later, government troops were again stationed near Salt Lake City. A group of 750 volunteers from California, under the command of Colonel Connor, were marching east to help the Union cause when they were ordered to stop in Salt Lake to guard the Overland Trail and the telegraph lines. Both the troops and the Saints protested, but the Secretary of War ordered that the troops stay. Instead of using Camp Floyd, these soldiers built a camp north of Salt Lake City that they called Fort Douglas.

Salt Lake City was growing rapidly and several important buildings were constructed in the 1860s. The building that most surprised visitors to Salt Lake City was the theater. Clarissa Young explained:

It was not strange that Father should have made this great effort to construct a theatre, for he never felt that his responsibilities to his people ended with his spiritual leadership. People were always
amazed when they saw, for the first time, this wonderful
theatre, built in the days when materials had to be
hauled across a thousand miles of country by ox teams
and   wagons.
. . . Father realized that this people, being almost
completely shut off from contacts with the outside
world, must themselves provide the means for their
cultural uplift and entertainment. . . . Years after the
theatre was built he said: "If I were placed on a cannibal

island and given a task of civilizing its people, I would straightway build a theatre for the purpose" (Spencer, *Brigham Young at Home*, 146-47, 168).

When the army left in 1861, work resumed on the Salt Lake Temple. Because the temple would take many years to complete, the Endowment House had been built on Temple Square in 1854 so that some of the temple ordinances could be performed.

Most of the Saints were not directly affected by the Civil War, but travel and trade were disrupted, and manufactured goods became scarce in the territory. Brigham Young said, "At no distant period, merchandising and imported goods will cease in this territory. . . . I feel like urging upon the people the necessity of preparing to grow and manufacture that which they consume" (Nibley, *Brigham Young, The Man and His Work*, 377).

The Saints attempted to become self-sufficient. The cotton mission was established in the south, and iron and other necessities began to be produced. In the summer of 1863, a miner found gold in Bingham Canyon. However, the ore was generally low grade and difficult to mine. Also, the citizens of Utah were not about to close their businesses and drop their plows in the fields to go hunting for gold. Brigham Young told them:

> It is a fearful deception that all the world labors under, and many of this people, too, . . . that gold is wealth. On the bare report that gold was discovered in these west mountains, men left their thrashing machines, and their horses at large to eat up and trample down and destroy the precious bounties of the earth. They at once sacrificed all at the glittering shrine at the popular idol, declaring they were now going to be rich, and would raise wheat no more. Should this feeling become universal on the discovery of gold mines in our immediate vicinity, nakedness, starvation, utter destitution and annihilation would be the inevitable lot of this people.
>
> Can you not see that gold and silver rank among the things that we are the least in want of? We want an abundance of wheat and fine flour, of wine and oil, and of every choice fruit . . . we want silk, wool, cotton, flax . . . we want vegetables of various kinds . . . we want the coal and iron that are con-

SALT LAKE ENDOWMENT HOUSE was located on northwest corner of Temple Square from 1855 to 1889, at which time it was razed by order of President Wilford Woodruff. Sacred ordinances were performed here while the Saints were building the temple.

MAIN STREET, SALT LAKE CITY was the location of the telegraph office, and Hooper, Eldredge & Co. Dry Goods & Grocery store. *ca. 1861–1864*

THE SALT LAKE
TABERNACLE UNDER
CONSTRUCTION. East
end of the Tabernacle,
with the interior filled
with scaffolding. *1866*

THE SALT LAKE
TABERNACLE.
Construction began
in 1863, and was
completed in 1867.

cealed in these ancient mountains, the lumber from our sawmills, and the rock from our quarries. . . . Gold and silver serve as mere tinsel to give the finishing touch to all this greatness (Roberts, *A Comprehensive History of the Church*, 5:68).

THE TABERNACLE

In 1865, one the most distinctive features of the Salt Lake City skyline began to take shape. Clarissa Young wrote:

THE SALT LAKE TABERNACLE UNDER CONSTRUCTION. East end of the Tabernacle, with the interior filled with scaffolding. *1866*

THE SALT LAKE TABERNACLE. Construction began in 1863, and was completed in 1867.

Father conceived the idea for the great elliptical, dome-shaped tabernacle in rather an interesting manner. A convert by the name of Henry Grow arrived in the city from Philadelphia. . . . Father sent him to both the Weber and Jordan Rivers to build bridges over these streams.

After the completion of these bridges, Father complimented Brother Grow very highly on the splendid workmanship which he had displayed, and in a conversation between them one day said, "Henry, I am desirous of constructing a building for our people . . . and I have been wondering what plan we should use, for I have built many buildings and no two alike, and I am anxious that this should be different to anything else. . . . Henry, I had an egg for breakfast this morning, cooked hard, and in lieu of chopping it through the center, I cut in through it end-wise and set it on tooth-picks. I was strongly impressed that we might use this plan for the building" (Spencer, *Brigham Young at Home*, 271-72).

Susa Young Gates described the finished building:

The work began September 1, 1865, and religious services were held there in 1867. The great elliptical roof, finished dream of Brigham Young, rests upon forty-four sandstone piers, three feet thick and twenty feet high. The great building is 250 feet long by 150 feet wide and 80 feet in height. Wooden pegs and thongs of rawhide were used in place of nails, which were not to be had at that time and place.

The crowning feature is the magnificent organ, built by a gifted convert from Australia, Joseph Ridges. It was built necessarily of native material. . . . It rises in splendor of design back of the pulpits, filling the west end of the building and flanked by the choir seats with spaces for three or four hundred singers.

The great building, with its huge unsupported roof seats 8,000 people comfortably. . . . Some modern improvements . . . have been added; but the building remains substantially as Brigham Young planned it and as his associates and friends built it. If he were asked, however, "Who was the architect, the designer of the Tabernacle and the Temple?" he would answer at once and with solemn intonation, as he always did: "God is the Supreme Architect. We owe all our inspiration, our love of beauty and the knowledge of how to express our views to the Father in Heaven who gives to His children what they ask for and what they need (Gates, *The Life Story of Brigham Young*, 228–29).

THE TRANSCONTINENTAL RAILROAD

When the Civil War ended, the government decided to build a transcontinental railroad. Brigham Young welcomed the idea and contracted work from the Union Pacific. In a letter to his son, John W., who was on a mission in England, he wrote:

Traveling to the States now is not what it was before the railroad had been pushed so far this way. The time spent in staging is much shortened, lessening the fatigue and the duration of the journey. . . . It will be sure to help us, and be advantageous to the Zion of our God, though the wicked are contemplating terrible things respecting us as soon as they can finish the railroad. . . .

Improvements will progress, railroads and telegraph lines and cables will be built and stretched; but instead of these things acting as an aid to our enemies, they will increase our facilities and accelerate the progress of the work of the Lord (Dean C. Jessee, *Letters of Brigham Young to His Sons*, 105).

Clarissa Young wrote:

Father had hoped that the overland railroad would pass directly through Salt Lake City and was very much disappointed when it became definitely known that the route was to be through Ogden, nearly forty miles to the north. However, he was not one to waste time mourning over lost advantages, and long before the completion of the Union Pacific, he made plans to build another railroad connecting the capital city of Utah with the main line.

The Utah Central Railroad Company was organized in March, 1869, with Father as president. . . . Father advanced all the money for the prelimi-

RAILROAD CONSTRUCTION. View of the trestle over Weber River and railroad Tunnel No. 3 in Weber Canyon. The railroad enabled Saints to come to Utah more quickly and comfortably than in wagon train companies. *ca. 1869*

nary surveys for the first two years, paying the engineers and furnishing all the supplies, and none of it was paid back until after all the work was completed (Spencer, *Brigham Young at Home*, 241).

REORGANIZATION OF THE RELIEF SOCIETY

In 1867, Brigham Young reorganized the Relief Society, which had not functioned since the pioneers had left Nauvoo. Eliza R. Snow was called as general president. Brigham stated:

> We believe that women are useful, not only to sweep houses, wash dishes, make beds, and raise babies, but that they should stand behind the counter, study law or physic, or become good bookkeepers and be about to do the business in any counting house, and all this to enlarge their sphere of usefulness for the benefit of society at large (Widtsoe, *Discourses of Brigham Young*, 216).

Susa Young Gates, one of the leaders in the Relief Society, wrote of the many activities they embraced.

> The work of the Relief Society is first for the uplift of woman and the home; it is also charitable in its application. Representatives of the Society visit all the families of the saints in their . . . districts monthly, as well as those of strangers, visitors, or any who may be in need. They ascertain spiritual and temporal needs, collect monthly charitable donations, give food or needed supplies to poor families, arrange for help if there is sickness—they are themselves often the nurses for the poor; they assist if death invades a house, they mourn with the mourners, they comfort and bless all with whom they come in contact. As a result there were no orphan asylums, no poorhouses, amongst the Latter-day Saints. The aged and infirm, the orphan and helpless little ones were taken care of by relatives, friends or by opened homes of the members.
>
> Under the wise leadership of Sister Snow many other remarkable outgrowths developed from the Society itself. Suffrage societies were organised; ward Relief Society halls were built, the gleaning and saving of grain was instituted and granaries were built. Women's Co-operative stores were established and a Woman's exchange was opened in Salt Lake City. Nurse classes were organised; women physicians were sent east to study their profession; a woman's hospital was instituted, and women were encouraged to act upon school boards and take a vital part in civic life (Gates, *The Life Story of Brigham Young*, 299-301).

THE MUTUAL IMPROVEMENT ASSOCIATION

In 1869, Brigham Young decided that the younger women needed an organization of their own. He told his daughters:

> All Israel are looking to my family and watching the example set by my wives and children. For this reason I desire to organise my own family first into a society for the promotion of habits of order, thrift, industry, and char- ity; and above all things I desire them to retrench from their extravagance in dress, in eating and even in speech. . . . I am weary of the manner in which our women seek to outdo each other in all the foolish fash- ions of the world.
>
> I want you to set your own fashions. Let your apparel be neat and comely, and the workmanship of your hands. I have long had it in my mind to organize the young ladies of Zion into an association so that they might assist the older members of the Church, their fathers and mothers, in propagating, teaching, and practicing the principles I have been so long teaching. . . . I wish our girls to obtain a knowledge of the Gospel for themselves (Gates, *The Life Story of Brigham Young*, 305).

Eliza R. Snow and Mary Isabella Horn were called to organize Retrenchment Societies for the youth of the Church. These later became known as the Mutual Improvement Association. In 1866, George Q. Cannon began publishing a Sunday School periodical called the *Juvenile Instructor*.

DEATH OF HEBER C. KIMBALL

On June 22, 1868, Brigham Young's oldest and dearest friend, Heber C. Kimball, passed away. They had become friends in Mendon, New York, and had studied religion together. They had read the Book of Mormon, heard the gospel, and had even been baptized on the same day. They had been chosen and set apart as apostles, and had labored and suffered together through the experiences at Kirtland, Far West, Nauvoo, and the Salt Lake Valley. Heber had also been Brigham's counselor in the First Presidency for twenty years. At Heber's funeral, Brigham said:

> I will relate to you my feelings concerning the departure of Brother Kimball. He was a man of as much integrity, I presume, as any man who ever lived on the earth. I have been personally acquainted with him forty-three years and I can testify that he has been a man of truth, a man of benevolence, a man that was to be trusted. . . . He has fallen asleep for a certain purpose—to be pre- pared for a glorious resurrection. . . . What can we say to one another? Live as he has lived; be as faithful as he has been; be as full of good works as his life has manifested to us (Whitney, *The Life of Heber C. Kimball*, 495-97).

Elder George A. Smith was chosen to replace Heber C. Kimball as a counselor in the First Presidency. At this time, Church membership was about 100,000. Nine stakes had been organized in the territory, and hundreds of missionaries were out preaching the gospel.

Brigham Young traveled extensively among the various settlements. In his later years, he usually spent the winter in St. George, and visited the towns between there and Salt Lake on the way. He also usually traveled north at least once a year. A correspondent to *The Deseret News,* Salt Lake City's major newspaper, commented:

> It would be difficult to place too high an estimate upon the value of these visits of President Young to the various settlements. The people have local officers, whose counsels and instructions are sound and reliable; but a visit from the Presidency and Twelve is refreshing to the officers and people. They

GEORGE A. SMITH (1817–1875) was one of the speakers on the first Sunday in the Valley. *ca. 1860s*

DESERET NEWS BUILDING Looking north towards the tithing office. *ca. 1868*

partake of the spirit which prevails at headquarters, and can better keep pace with their brethren who reside there. Without these visits, the people might become narrowed up in their feelings and sectional.

In the early days of our residence here, when President Young and his brethren visited the settlements, they had to go prepared to camp out . . . now all this is changed. The settlements are close together. . . . A still greater change awaits us ere long. It is not too much to expect that in a few years hence we will have a line of rails laid from one end of the territory to the other, and if President Young wishes to attend a conference at St. George, he can step into the cars on Saturday morning, and be there by evening (Nibley, *Brigham Young, The Man and His Work*, 440-41).

DIGNITARIES AT PROMONTORY POINT, not far from Brigham City, Utah. At this place, the Union Pacific and Central Pacific Railroads were joined.
May 10, 1869

In May of 1869, the transcontinental railroad was finally finished. Two trains filled with dignitaries met in Utah at Promontory, not far from Brigham City. The last rails were laid, and a polished laurel tie was placed under the last joint. Four specially forged spikes, two gold, one silver, and one a composite of gold, silver, and iron, were dropped into predrilled holes. When the last spike was driven, the telegraph operator sent a message.

PROMONTORY SUMMIT, UTAH, MAY 10TH, 1869. THE LAST RAIL IS LAID, THE LAST SPIKE DRIVEN STOP THE PACIFIC RAILROAD IS COMPLETED STOP THE POINT OF JUNCTION IS 1,086 MILES WEST OF THE MISSOURI RIVER AND 600 MILES EAST OF SACRAMENTO CITY STOP LELAND STANFORD, CENTRAL PACIFIC RAILROAD, T C DURRANT, SIDNEY DILLON, JOHN DUFF, UNION PACIFIC RAILROAD (Nibley, *Brigham Young, The Man and His Work*, 448).

Brigham Young was visiting the southern settlements at the time and did not attend the ceremonies. However, a meeting to honor the occasion was held in the Tabernacle in Salt Lake. A few days later, Brigham Young returned and work soon began on a branch line from Ogden to Salt Lake City.

RETURN OF MARTIN HARRIS

On August 30, 1870, an elderly man arrived by train in Salt Lake City. Martin Harris, one of the original Three Witnesses to the Book of Mormon, had been away from the Church for thirty-two years, but Edward Stephenson had met Brother Harris while serving a mission back east. Elder Stephenson wrote:

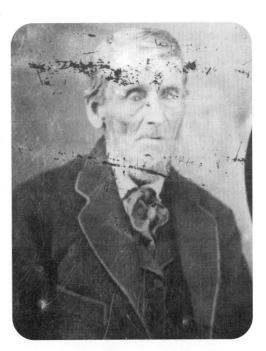

> He took from under his arm a copy of the Book of Mormon, the first edition, I believe, and bore a faithful testimony. . . . After my arrival in Utah in 1870, I was inspired to write Martin Harris, and soon received a reply that the Spirit of God, for the first time, prompted him to go to Utah. President Brigham Young . . . requested me to get up a subscription and emigrate Martin to Utah, he subscribing twenty-five dollars for that purpose. Having raised the subscription to about two hundred dollars, I took railroad cars for Ohio. . . . On the 29th of August we arrived in Ogden, and on the following day in Salt Lake City (Nibley, *Brigham Young, The Man and His Work*, 463–64).

Brigham Young invited Brother Harris to speak in October conference. Martin said:

MARTIN HARRIS (1783–1875) arrived in Salt Lake City by train in 1870. He had been away from the Church for 32 yrs., but had returned and was rebaptised. He lived the rest of his life in Cache County. *ca. 1875*

> I had the honor of being the scribe for the Prophet Joseph Smith in translating a portion of the Book of Mormon, but through my carelessness and through my want of foresight, the manuscript that I had written was lost, and never regained, and I justly received censure and reprimand from the Prophet Joseph Smith. Now I have returned to the bosom of the Church with the hope and prayer in my heart that I may again be admitted a member (Nibley, *Brigham Young, The Man and His Work*, 464).

Brother Harris was rebaptised and lived the rest of his life in Cache County.

ULYSSES SIMPSON GRANT was the last general of the Union forces in the Civil War. He was elected President of the U.S. in 1868, then reelected in 1872. *ca. 1860–1870*

PHINEAS T. BARNUM opened "The Greatest Show on Earth." *ca. 1840*

THE ST. GEORGE TEMPLE

Increasing persecution by the government of the United States was one of the reasons the leaders of the Church decided to begin building another temple, even though the Salt Lake Temple was not finished. Congress had passed an anti-bigamy law in 1862, and the government was trying to force the Church to abandon the practice of polygamy. Interference from the government caused work on the temple in Salt Lake City to slow to a standstill, so Brigham Young sent the workers south where they could build another temple far from the government officials. Erastus Snow recorded:

> It was revealed here in St. George to the Prophet Brigham Young that there should be variations made in the temples to be built. This was given unto the Prophet Brigham in answer to his question, "Oh, Lord, show unto Thy servants if we shall build temples after the same pattern." The answer came, "Do you all build your houses out after the same pattern? Do you, after increasing your families, build after the same pattern used when your family is small? So shall the growth of the knowledge of the principles of the Gospel among my people cause diversity in the pattern of the temples" (Lauritz G. Petersen, "The Kirtland Temple," *Brigham Young University Studies* 1972, vol. 12, no. 4, 400).

When the site for the St. George Temple was dedicated on November 9, 1871, Susa Young wrote that "workmen were brought down from the north and organized into groups as masons, carpenters, road-builders, loggers, quarrymen and as plasterers and painters" (Gates, *The Life Story of Brigham Young*, 235-36).

President Brigham Young presided at the dedication of the St. George Temple on April 6, 1871. This was the first temple to be completed in Utah, even though the Saints began construction on the Salt Lake Temple first.

BRIGHAM YOUNG ARRESTED

Brigham Young was seventy years old when the United States Marshal arrested him, on October 2, 1871, on charges of polygamy. He appeared before Judge

McKean and posted a $5,000 bail. Three months later, he again appeared before Judge McKean. This time, he was charged with murder based on the testimony of Bill Hickman, who claimed that Brigham Young had ordered the death of Richard Yates in Echo Canyon in 1857. Judge McKean refused to set bail and ordered that President Young be held a prisoner in his own home under the guard of the United States Marshal until a trial could take place. Weeks and months dragged by, and the case still had not come to trial. However, on April 15, 1872, the United States Supreme Court ruled that all the juries Judge McKean had drawn in the past year had been illegal, and the case against the Prophet was dropped.

CONSTRUCTION ON THE ST. GEORGE TEMPLE. The site was selected in 1871 by Brigham Young, and was dedicated in 1877. View of the temple being stuccoed. Standing on parapet are Aaron McDonald, Robert McQuarrie (saw in hand) and George Laub (wearing apron). *Feb. 28, 1876*

THE UNITED ORDER

The United States was suffering from a depression. Utah was not greatly affected, but Brigham Young encouraged the Saints to be as independent as possible so they would not be pulled into economic disaster. He encouraged the members of the Church to work together, to cooperate and become self-sufficient. To accomplish this, he instituted the United Order in 1874. He explained:

> I want you to be united. If we should build up and organize a community, we would have to do it on the principle of oneness. . . . A city of one hundred thousand or a million people could be united into a perfect family,

and they could work together. We now want to organize the Latter-day Saints, every man, woman and child among them who has a desire to be organized into this holy order, the Order of Enoch. This order is the order of heaven, the family of heaven on earth. It is the children of our Father here upon the earth organized into one body or family to operate together (Widtsoe, *Discourses of Brigham Young*, 285).

In practice, there were at least four different types of United Order. In Brigham City, a system of cooperatively owned and run businesses functioned very successfully under the direction of John Taylor. In St. George, the members received wages for their labors, and at the end of the season, they divided profits equally. In the larger cities, like Salt Lake, Ogden, and Provo, each ward owned a business, specialized farm, or factory, and exchanged goods with each other. In Orderville, the members did not hold any private property at all, but held everything in common. All of these orders were eventually abandoned.

WORLD EVENTS

In Paris, the impressionist painters Monet, Renoir, Pissarro, Degas, and others held their first exhibition. The gunsmith firm of E. Remington and Sons began to manufacture typewriters, and Jules Verne wrote *Around the World in 80 Days*.

BRIGHAM CITY COOPERATIVE BOOT, SHOE, HARNESS & HAT DEPT. This was a part of a system of cooperatively owned and operated businesses, which were run under the direction of John Taylor. It was a type of United Order.

A Tireless Leader

As he grew older, Brigham Young suffered from arthritis and other ailments. In 1873, he called five additional counselors to the First Presidency: Lorenzo Snow, Brigham Young, Jr., Albert Carrington, John W. Young, and George Q. Cannon. He resigned from many of the businesses he had supervised, and simplified his life. In answer to an inquiry from the editor of the *New York Herald*, Brigham Young reviewed some of his accomplishments.

Brigham Young at age seventy-five.
June 1, 1876

The result of my labors for the last 26 years, briefly summed up, are: The peopling of this Territory by the Latter-day Saints of about 100,000 souls; the founding of over 200 cities, towns and villages inhabited by our people, which extend to Idaho in the north, Wyoming in the east, Nevada in the west, and Arizona in the south, and the establishment of schools, factories, mills and other institutions calculated to improve and benefit our community.

All my transactions and labors have been carried on in accordance with my calling as a servant of God. I know no difference between spiritual and temporal labors. God has seen fit to bless me with means, and as a faithful steward, I use them to benefit my fellow men—to promote their happiness in this world in preparing them for the great hereafter.

My whole life is devoted to the Almighty's service, and while I regret that my mission is not better understood by the world, the time will come when I will be understood, and I leave to futurity the judgment of my labors and their result as they shall become manifest (Nibley, *Brigham Young, The Man and His Work*, 491–92).

BRIGHAM YOUNG, JR.
(1836–1903)
(left) *ca. 1863–1900*

ALBERT CARRINGTON
(1813–1889)
(center) *ca. 1872–1885*

JOHN W. YOUNG
(right)
ca. 1860–1870

These were three of the five men who were called by Brigham Young as additional counselors to the First Presidency.

Brigham Young was not content just to be a spiritual leader to his people. He helped them colonize the wilderness. He stressed the importance of education. Even when the pioneers were living in tents in Winter Quarters, or crossing the plains in wagons, he had encouraged mothers to continue to teach their children. When they became settled, he established a private school for his family, and encouraged each ward to have a school. The University of Deseret was organized in 1850; and in 1875, he organized a school in Provo called Brigham Young Academy. Brigham instructed Karl G. Maeser, the principal and teacher of the school: "Brother Maeser, whatever you teach, even the multiplication tables, do it with the Spirit of the Lord" (Gates, *The Life Story of Brigham Young*, 292).

On August 27, 1876, the Academy opened with 26 students. President Young also established the LDS University of Salt Lake City, which later become the LDS Business College. On July 24, 1877, he deeded 96 acres in Cache

Valley for the Brigham Young College in Logan, which functioned until 1926. Brigham said, "Education is the power to think clearly, the power to act well in the world's work, and the power to appreciate life" (Gates, *The Life Story of Brigham Young*, 292).

Families were a frequent subject in Brigham Young's sermons. He stressed the roles of parents and the importance of teaching the gospel in the home.

> It is for the husband to learn how to gather around his family the comforts of life, how to control his passions and temper, and how to command the respect, not only of his family but of all his brethren, sisters, and friends. It is the calling of the wife and mother to know what to do with everything that is brought into the house, laboring to make her home desirable to her husband and children, making herself an Eve in the midst of a little paradise of her own creating, securing her husband's love and confidence, and tying her offspring to herself , with a love that is stronger than death, for an everlasting inheritance.
>
> Let the husband make an improvement upon his kitchen and pantry and upon his bedrooms for the benefit of his family, and improve his gardens, walks, etc., beautifying your habitations and their surroundings, making pavements and planting shade trees (Widtsoe, *Discourses of Brigham Young*, 198).

BRIGHAM YOUNG ACADEMY, LEWIS BUILDING. Large group of students in front of the Lewis Building. *ca. 1880*

One of Brigham Young's most important projects was temple building. Work on the temples continued in spite of poverty, persecution, and problems with procuring materials. The St. George temple was completed in 1877 and was dedicated as part of April conference that year. Susa Young Gates, who was living in St. George, wrote:

> The temple is 141 feet long and 93 feet wide. The walls are built of sandstone painted white, which measure 84 feet from the ground to the top of the parapets and the tower is 135 high. The beautiful, massive-buttressed white

THE ST. GEORGE TEMPLE was the first temple completed in Utah. The first temple endowments for the dead were performed here. *ca. 1877*

Temple crowns the Valley's gorgeous-coloured green, black-red beauty. It was built by free-will offerings and by appropriates from the tithings of the people. The total cost of the completed building was considerable more than $500,000.00.

In April, 1877, the Temple was formally dedicated by the Leaders in solemn conclave. The services and ceremonies revealed to the Prophet and taught by him in Nauvoo to Brigham Young were fully expounded to all good men and sisters ministering in the new Temple. . . . He urged the people . . . to search out their genealogies, to prepare their records, to go forth vicariously in the waters of baptism, thus releasing the spirits of their beloved ancestors from their prison houses behind the veil (Gates, *The Life Story of Brigham Young*, 236).

On the way back to Salt Lake City, Brigham stopped in Manti to dedicate a temple site. Years later, a citizen of Manti reported:

THE MANTI TEMPLE under construction. Brigham Young chose the site on June 25, 1875. The temple was dedicated by Wilford Woodruff on May 17, 1888. It was the third temple completed in Utah. *September 16, 1884*

Manti Temple,

In an early day when President Young and party were making the location of the settlement here, President Heber C. Kimball prophesied that the day would come when the temple would be built on this hill. Some disbelieved and doubted the possibility of even making a settlement here. Brother Kimball said, "Well, it will be so, and more than that, the rock will be quarried from that hill to build it with, and some of that stone from that quarry will be taken to help complete the Salt Lake Temple." . . . Early on the morning of April 25th, 1877, President Brigham Young asked Brother Warren S. Snow to go with him to the Temple hill. Brother Snow says: "We two were alone: President Young took me to the spot where the Temple was to stand; we went to the southeast corner, and President Young said: "Here is the spot where the prophet Moroni stood and dedicated this piece of land for a Temple site" (Whitney, *Life of Heber C. Kimball*, 435–36)

Then on May 18, 1877, Brigham Young traveled to Logan and dedicated another temple site. During that year, the Prophet reorganized stakes and replaced leaders as he traveled throughout the territory. He encouraged the various priesthood quorums to organize as explained in the Doctrine and Covenants, and suggested that the Aaronic Priesthood should be given to some of the youth. In the October conference of that same year, George Q. Cannon commented on President Young's reorganization of the Church:

I do not believe myself that President Young could have felt as happy, as I know he does feel, had he left the church in the condition it was in when he commenced his labors last spring. I am convinced that it has added greatly to his satisfaction; it has been a fitting consummation to the labors of his long life that he should be spared to organize the church throughout these valleys in the manner in which it is now organized (Young, *Journal of Discourses*, 19:232).

THE DEATH OF A PROPHET

In August of 1877, Brigham became very ill. His daughter, Zina, wrote:

When he was placed on the bed in front of the window, he seemed to partially revive, and opening his eyes, he gazed upward, exclaiming, "Joseph! Joseph! Joseph!" and the divine look in his face seemed to indicate that he was communicating with his beloved friend, Joseph Smith, the Prophet. This name was the last word he uttered. As we saw his life ebbing rapidly, we all knelt down around the bed and Uncle Joseph offered a fervent prayer to God that his going should be in peace and not in distress. I knelt where I had a full view of his countenance, and in the middle of the prayer I was impelled to open my eyes, and father's face was radiant with an inward glory. It seemed a cloud of light surrounded him (Leonard J. Arrington, *Brigham Young: American Moses*, 199).

At his funeral, his friend and counselor, George Q. Cannon, said:

He had been the brain, the eye, the ear, the mouth and hand for the entire Church of Jesus Christ of Latter-day Saints. From the greatest details connected with the organization of this Church, down to the smallest minutiae connected with the work, he has left the impress of his great mind. From the organization of the Church, and the construction of Temples . . . the creation of a . . . Territorial government, down to the small matter of directing the shape of these seats upon which we sit this day; upon all these things, as well as upon all the settlements of the Territory, the impress of his genius is apparent. . . . He had that power, that wonderful faculty, which God gave him, and with which he was inspired (Nibley, *Brigham Young, The Man and His Work*, 534).

Brigham Young took a small group of beleaguered Saints, who were threatened with extermination, and led them into the wilderness. The Saints were tested, tried, and strengthened, and under Brigham Young's leadership, they prospered and grew strong. The Church was one step nearer to the prophecy in the Doctrine and Covenants: "In this the beginning of the rising up and the coming forth of my church out of the wilderness—clear as the moon, and fair as the sun, and terrible as an army with banners" (D&C 5:14).

BRIGHAM YOUNG'S GRAVE SITE in Salt Lake City on 1st Avenue between State Street and "A" Street. *ca. 1905*

BRIGHAM YOUNG'S GRAVE.

Brigham Young made many friends during his life. Sir Richard Burton, the British explorer and author, visited Salt Lake City and wrote a book about his impressions called *City of the Saints.* Of Brigham Young, he wrote:

> His manner is at once affable and impressive, simple and courteous; his want of pretension contrasts favorably with certain pseudo-prophets that I have seen. . . . He shows no signs of dogmatism, bigotry, or fanaticism, and never once entered—with me at least—upon the subject of religion. He impresses a stranger with a certain sense of power; his followers are, of course, wholly fascinated by his superior strength of brain. He assumes no airs of extra sanctimoniousness, and has the plain, simple manners of honesty. His followers deem him an angel of light, his foes a goblin damned; he is, I presume, neither one nor the other (Roberts, *A Comprehensive History of the Church*, 4:536–37).

Some claimed that Brigham Young had not received revelations like Joseph Smith. But Orson Hyde stated:

WORLD EVENTS

When Brigham Young died, Queen Victoria had been proclaimed Empress of India, Thomas Edison invented the phonograph, and the very first lawn tennis championship was played at Wimbledon.

> Some persons say that Brigham does not give revelations as did Joseph Smith. But let me tell you, that Brigham's voice has been the voice of God from the time he was chosen to preside, and even before. Who that has heard him speak, or that has read his testimonies or that is acquainted with his instructions, does not know that God is with him? . . . He possesses skill, wisdom, and power that trouble wise men and rulers. (Young, *Journal of Discourses*, vol. 8).

Brigham said of himself, "I never professed to be Brother Joseph, but Brother Brigham, trying to do good to this people. I am no better, nor any more important than another man who is trying to do good" (Widtsoe, *Discourses of Brigham Young*, 460).

Brigham Young was an intensely practical man with an eternal view. He taught the Saints:

> I have Zion in my view constantly. We are not going to wait for angels, or for Enoch and his company to come and build up Zion, but we are going to build it. We will raise our wheat, build our houses, fence our farms, plant our vineyards and orchards, and produce everything that will make our bodies comfortable and happy, and in this manner, we intend to build up Zion on the earth and purify it and cleanse it from all pollutions. Let there be an hallowed influence go from us over all things over which we have any power; over the soil we cultivate, over the houses we build, and over everything we possess; and if we cease to hold fellowship with that which is corrupt and establish the Zion of God in our hearts, in our own houses, in our cities, and throughout our country, we shall ultimately overcome the earth (Widtsoe, *Discourses of Brigham Young*, 443).

JOHN
TAYLOR
"The Kingdom of God or Nothing"

After Brigham's death, there were no questions about who would lead the Church. The duties of the First Presidency were placed with the Council of the Twelve, and the question of seniority among the Twelve had been clarified. John Taylor, the senior member or the quorum was made presiding officer over the Church. Speaking at Brigham young's funeral, John Taylor offered words of comfort and encouragement to the Saints:

> Today is a solemn day for Israel. We have before us the body of the man who has led us for the last thirty-three years. Thirty-three years ago, I was with and witnessed the departure of our first president Joseph Smith. President Young, after leading the Church and buffeting the trials and persecutions to which the Church has ever been subject, has at length in these valleys of the mountains, after having accomplished the object of his life and done the work, lain down to sleep in the midst of a loving and affectionate family and surrounded by faithful and tried friends. As has been said, his name and his fame are known among all people and a knowledge of these events has spread to the uttermost bounds of the everlasting hills. The work we are engaged in is not the work of man. Joseph Smith did not originate it, neither did Brigham Young nor the twelve nor any mor-

JOHN TAYLOR served as President from 1880–1887. *ca. 1881–1883*

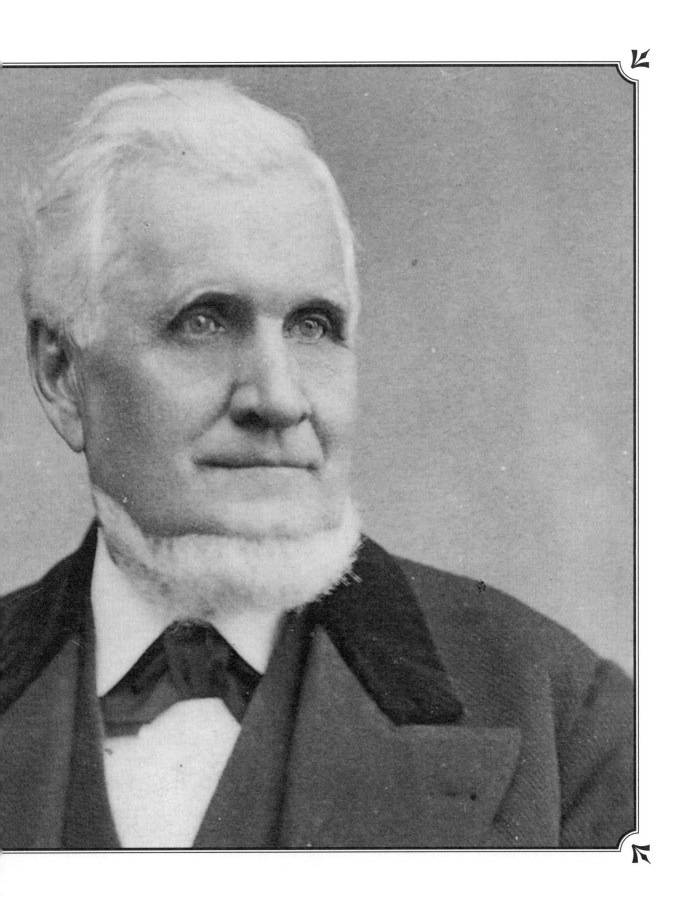

tal man. It emanated from God. He is its author, his eye over us, he is watching every movement and every transaction that transpires now, and that has transpired ever since the commencement, and will continue so to do. He will guide the ship to the latter end and while we mourn a good and great man dead, I see thousands of staunch and faithful ones around me and before me who are for Israel, for God and His kingdom, men who are desirous to see His will done on earth, as angels do it in heaven (Roberts, *A Comprehensive History of the Church*, 5:516-517).

Although John Taylor became the presiding officer of the Church after Brigham Young died, he wasn't officially named President of the Church for three years. Born in the Lake District of England, President Taylor was seventeen years old when he was made a preacher in the Methodist Church. One day while walking with a companion, he suddenly stopped and remarked, "I have a strong impression on my mind, that I have to go to America to preach the gospel!" (Roberts, *The Life of John Taylor*, 28).

John immigrated to Canada in 1832. During the journey, the ship he was sailing on encountered severe storms. While the captain was afraid that the ship would be lost, John was not. Recalling that experience he said, "I went on deck at midnight and amidst the raging elements felt as calm as though I was sitting in a parlor at home. I believed I should reach America and perform my work" (Roberts, *The Life of John Taylor*, 28-29).

LEONORA CANNON TAYLOR (1796–1868) was John Taylor's first wife.

In Toronto, John contacted the Methodists in the area and began preaching. During this time, he met and married Lenora Cannon. When he told her of the revelation he had had in his youth about preaching in America, she asked, "Are you not now preaching the gospel in America?" But John responded, "This is not the work; it is something of more importance" (Roberts, *The Life of John Taylor*, 30).

Knowing that something was lacking, John Taylor fasted and prayed for the kingdom of God to be made known to him. Then, one day, the Taylors met Parley P. Pratt, who told them about the restored gospel. They accepted the message of truth and were baptized on May 9, 1836. The following year, John Taylor left Canada for Kirtland to fill a vacancy in the Quorum of the Twelve. John then left to serve a two-year mission in England, and shortly after his return, the Prophet Joseph revealed the principle of plural marriage to the apostles. John had a difficult time accepting this principle. He said, "I had always entertained strict ideas of virtue, and I felt as a married man that this was to me, outside of this principle, an appalling thing to do. . . . Hence, nothing but a knowledge of God, and the revelations of God, and the truth of them, could have induced me to embrace such a principle" (Roberts, *The Life of John Taylor*, 100).

John Taylor was in Carthage Jail with the Prophet Joseph, Hyrum Smith, and Willard Richards when the mob killed Joseph and Hyrum. John was shot in the chest, but his pocket watch stopped what probably would have been a fatal shot. He was wounded five times during the attack, but rolled under the bed and escaped further harm. Although seriously wounded, he recovered with few ill effects. Elder Taylor wrote a lament for the Prophet Joseph and Hyrum in a hymn:

> Oh, give me back my Prophet dear and Patriarch. Oh give them back to Saints of Latter-days to cheer and lead them in the gospel track. But, oh, they're gone from my embrace, from earthly scenes their spirits fled. Two of the best of Adam's race now lie entombed among the dead (John Taylor, *The Gospel Kingdom*, ed. G. Homer Durham, 385-86).

John Taylor and his family made the trek to Utah in 1847. Two years later, he was called on a mission to France. He supervised the translation of the Book of Mormon into French, and then went to Germany to have it translated into German. He spent two years in New York City editing a newspaper called *The Mormon*, which was published to tell the truth about Mormonism and defend it against accusations. The ambitious enterprise stood proudly between two big New York dailies, *The New York Herald* and *The New York Tribune*. Brigham Young said of the newspaper, "It is probably one of the strongest edited papers that is now published" (Roberts, *The Life of John Taylor*, 271).

When he returned to Utah, John continued to write and publish. His best-known work is *Mediation and Atonement, a Treatise on the Role of the Savior in the Salvation of Man*. He also served as superintendent of public schools. President Taylor was able to continue some of the projects Brigham Young had started; however, Brigham Young Academy began to have financial problems that threatened to close the school. Zina Young Williams, Brigham Young's daughter and Dean of Women, decided to take matters into her own hands.

THE MORMON NEWSPAPER in New York City that John Taylor edited. Its purpose was to tell the truth about Mormonism and defend it against accusations.

JOHN TAYLOR was the third President of the Church. He served 48½ years as a General Authority.

I went to Salt Lake with a special mission upon my mind. After earnest prayer, I decided something must be done. President Taylor sent for me when he found I was there, and invited me to join his family in the old Gardo House where he then resided. After a pleasant hour with the family, he took me to his private library, and said he had something of importance to tell me. While there I felt impressed to relieve my mind upon the subject that had so distressed us all with regard to the finances of the school . . . He took my hand in a fatherly way and said:

"My dear child, I have something of importance to tell you that I know will make you happy. I have been visited by your father. He came to me in the silence of the night, clothed in brightness, and with a face beaming with love and confidence, told me things of great importance, and among others, that the school being taught by Brother Maeser was accepted in the heavens and was a part of the great plan of life and salvation, that Church schools should be fostered for the good of Zion's children, and there was a bright future in store for the preparing of the children of the covenant for future usefulness in the kingdom of God, and that Christ, Himself, was directing and had a care over this school" (Zina Young Williams Card, "Short Reminiscent Sketches of Karl G. Maeser," unpublished typescript, Special Collections, Harold B. Lee Library, Brigham Young University, 3-4).

Just as the financial problems were being solved, the school building burned down. Classes were moved to a warehouse, and work began on new buildings. During the eight years that the new Academy was under construction, Karl Maeser and his children would visit the site of the future campus. His daughter, Eva, recalled:

We used to go every Sunday morning that the weather would permit to the foundation of the building. There weren't even sidewalks. At that time it was outside of Provo. I didn't even remember when the cornerstones were laid, but all I can remember is that the mortar and rocks were breaking away from the foundation and my father would point to the different rooms and he would say: "This will be the office. This will be the reading room."

I looked up and said, "But, Father, it will never be finished. The foundation is crumbling away, even the rocks are falling." He had a cane which had belonged to Brigham Young which he always carried and it had a dog's head on the end. I remember how my father stood up and put that cane in the ground and said, pointing to Temple Hill: "No, my child. This will be finished and many more and on that hill, for I have seen it" (Alma P. Burton, "Karl G. Maeser, Mormon Educator," MS Thesis, Brigham Young University, 1950).

BRIGHAM YOUNG ACADEMY FACULTY. (l to r) Willard Done, James E. Talmage, Joseph Nelson, Karl G. Maeser (principal), Jennie Tanner, Benjamin Cluff, Jr., and Joseph B. Keeler. Karl Maeser (1828–1901) is known as the "father of Brigham Young University." He joined the Church in Germany in 1855. Brigham Young assigned him to organize the Brigham Young Academy in April, 1876. *ca. 1885*

BRIGHAM YOUNG ACADEMY

Although Brigham Young Academy suffered financial difficulties for several years, the school's longevity was no longer in doubt.

THE PRIMARY ORGANIZATION

One significant Church program had an interesting start. One hot summer day in 1878, a casual visit led to the establishment of the Primary. Eliza R. Snow, Emmeline B. Wells and several other sisters were returning from a Relief Society

conference in Farmington, Utah. While waiting for a train, the women stopped at the home of Aurelia Spencer Rogers. During the visit, the conversation turned to children, especially the rough and sometimes careless manners of the young boys. Aurelia Rogers asked her guests, "What will our girls do for good husbands, if this state of things continues? Could there not be an organization for little boys, and have them trained to make better men?" (Richard S. Van Wagoner and Steven C. Walker, *A Book of Mormons*, 256).

Eliza R. Snow approached President Taylor about a new program for children and received his approval. She next wrote to Aurelia: "I feel assured that the inspiration of heaven is directing you, and that a great and very important movement is being inaugurated for the future of Zion (Jill Mulvay Derr, Janath Russell Cannon, and Maureen Ursenbach Beecher, *Women of Covenant*, 119).

As Aurelia began organizing the first Primary meeting, she felt that the girls should be included as well. While pondering over what needed to be done, she received a personal assurance of her work.

FIRST PRIMARY PRESIDENCY. Aurelia Read Spencer Rogers (1834–1922) was the first Primary President, and her counselors were Matilda Morehouse W. Barrett and Lillie Tucket Freeze. Aurelia was concerned that young children should receive appropriate spiritual training. The first Primary was held on August 25, 1878.

> I seemed to be carried away in the spirit, or at least I experienced a feeling of untold happiness which lasted three days and nights. During that time nothing could worry or irritate me; if my little ones were fretful or the work went wrong, I had patience, could control in kindness, and manage my household affairs easily. This was a testimony to me that what was being done was of God (Derr, Cannon, and Beecher, *Women of Covenant*, 119).

Aurelia and her counselors visited every house in the ward and recorded the names and ages of each child—224 of them. On Sunday, August 25, 1878, Aurelia stood on the steps of the meetinghouse in Farmington, Utah, and watched as the children arrived for that first historic meeting.

Eliza R. Snow helped wards throughout the west organize and start their own Primary programs. The association grew as dedicated leaders devoted themselves to teaching the children.

In October of 1880, the First Presidency was reorganized and John Taylor was sustained as the third President of the Church, with George Q. Cannon and Joseph

F. Smith as counselors. President Taylor, well-known for his meticulous grooming, stood tall and straight in his black coat, white shirt, and well-polished boots. One of his sons had the job of making his father's boots shine like a mirror each day.

Well respected by his colleagues and the leadership of the Church, John Taylor was the subject of a revelation given to Wilford Woodruff in January of 1880.

> Again, hear ye the word of the Lord, oh, ye mine apostles, whom I have chosen in these last

FARMINGTON CHAPEL, UTAH where the first Primary was held. *1900*

JOHN TAYLOR'S FIRST PRESIDENCY. George Q. Cannon, President John Taylor, and Joseph F. Smith. *ca. 1880*

THE ASSEMBLY HALL was completed and used for the first time in April, 1880, the fiftieth anniversary of the organization of the Church.
ca. 1895

days to bear record of my name and to lead my people Israel until the coming of the Son of Man. I the Lord have raised up unto you my servant John Taylor to preside over you and to be a law giver unto my Church. He has mingled his blood with that of the martyred prophets. Nevertheless, while I have taken my servants Joseph and Hyrum Smith unto myself, I have preserved my servant John Taylor for a wise purpose in me (Wilford Woodruff Journal, 26 January 1880, undated entry following the summary of 1880).

FIFTIETH ANNIVERSARY OF THE CHURCH

The Church passed a monumental milestone and prepared to celebrate its fiftieth anniversary. The Assembly Hall on Temple Square had been built and was used for the first time during the April 1880 conference. John Taylor spoke:

I am happy to have the privilege of meeting with the Saints in this new hall. . . . On the 6th day of April the Church will have been organized fifty years. On the fiftieth year, in former times, among the ancients, they had what was termed a year of jubilee. Slaves were liberated. People who were in debt were forgiven their indebtedness. . . . We have had in operation for quite a length of time, what is known as the "Perpetual Emigration Fund Company," and a great many of you that are present have contributed to that Fund. And as it is a jubilee year . . . it occurred to me that we ought to do something . . . to relieve those that are oppressed with debt, to assist those that are needy, to break the yoke off those that may feel themselves crowded upon, and to make it a time of general rejoicing. . . . We have contemplated to release one-half of the indebtedness of those who are indebted to the P.E. Fund (John Taylor, General Conference, 4 and 7 April, 1880).

A vote was taken at the 1880 October conference, and the Pearl of Great Price was formally accepted as scripture. Also, the Doctrine and Covenants, which had been divided into chapters and verses, was recanonized. The Church now had four Standard Works of scripture.

The walls of the Salt Lake Temple rose sixty-five feet above the ground, but it would be years before the tem-

SALT LAKE TEMPLE UNDER CONSTRUCTION. View of Temple Square from the southeast, showing the temple under construction, the Tabernacle, Assembly Hall. Charles R. Savage's photograph gallery and the Council House are shown in the foreground. *ca. 1883*

ple would be finished. However, the temples in Logan and Manti were almost complete. The Logan Temple was ready for dedication in the spring of 1884. Heber J. Grant, with his wife and baby daughter, accompanied President Taylor to the dedicatory services.

President Taylor directed the temple recorder to note the following:

> The Lord is well pleased and has accepted this house and our labors in its dedication, also the labors of the people in its building and beautifying, and whatever the Saints may feel to place into it, to ornament and embellish, will also be acceptable. I feel to bless you my brethren here present, in the name of Israel's God, and you and your families shall be blest, and God will raise you up and lift you on high. I feel like shouting hallelujah. Hallelujah, glory to God ("Diary of John Nuttall," entry for Thursday, 22 May 1884. Special Collections, Harold B. Lee Library, Brigham Young University).

CONFLICT BETWEEN THE FEDERAL GOVERNMENT AND THE CHURCH

As the Saints established a viable community in the west, powerful groups in the east sought to strengthen federal control over the territory. In 1862, Congress passed an act that prohibited polygamy and disincorporated the

Church. The act attacked not only polygamy, but also the Saints' economic well-being and political rights. The law was deemed unconstitutional, but twenty years later, Congress passed the Edmunds Act, named for Senator George R. Edmunds of Vermont. This act attempted to eliminate the Mormon Church as a power in Utah. It declared all political offices in the territory vacant and sought to fill them with federal appointees. The Edmunds Act imposed heavy penalties for practicing polygamy, and declared that cohabitation with a polygamist wife was a misdemeanor, punishable by a fine, imprisonment, or both.

In April conference President Taylor said: "Let us treat it the same as we did this morning in coming through the snow storm—put up our coat collars and wait till the storms subsides. . . . While the storm lasts it is useless to reason with the world; when it subsides, we can talk to them" (Francis M. Gibbons, *Dynamic Disciples: Prophets of God*, 79).

JOHN TAYLOR
ca. 1870–1887

When the brethren met, they discussed how they would respond to the Edmunds Act and how their chances for statehood would be affected. The Church, which was simply following a commandment of the Lord, felt that the practice of polygamy would cease when the Lord commanded that it should be stopped. President Taylor commented on the conflict between the Federal Government and the Church.

When the Constitution of the United States was framed and adopted, those high contracting parties did positively agree that they would not interfere with religious affairs. Now, if our marital relations are not religious, what is? This ordinance of marriage was a direct revelation to us through Joseph Smith, the Prophet. You may not know it, but I know that this is a revelation from God and a command to his people, and therefore it is my religion. I do not believe that the Supreme Court of the

United States has any right to interfere with my religious views, and in doing it they are violating their most sacred obligations (Joseph Fielding Smith, *Essentials of Church* History, 577).

When President Taylor visited the Saints in Colorado, New Mexico, and Arizona in 1874 and 1875, so many members of the Church were being arrested and jailed that he advised them to seek refuge in Mexico. In a letter to a stake president in an Arizona stake, President Taylor and George Q. Cannon said, "Better for parts of families to remove and go where they can live in peace than to be hauled to jail and incarcerated in the territory with thieves and murderers and other vile characters" (Thomas Cottam Romney, *The Mormon Colonies in Mexico*, 52).

By the end of 1885, hundreds of Church members fled to the Mexican State of Chihuahua, where they founded the settlements of Colonia Juarez, Colonia Dublan, and Colonia Diaz. The following year, President Taylor advised Charles

Ora Card to seek a place of refuge for persecuted members of the Cache Valley Stake in Logan, Utah. President Card led a group of members north to Alberta and settled what later became known as Cardston.

Although warrants had been issued for the arrest of members of the First Presidency, President Taylor returned to Salt Lake City and addressed the Saints on Sunday, February 1, 1885. In this, his last public sermon, he advised the members not to retaliate against federal officials.

> [Let there be] no breaking of heads, no bloodshed, rendering evil for evil. Let us try to cultivate the spirit of the gospel and adhere to the principles of truth. While other men are seeking to trample the Constitution under foot, we will try to maintain it. I will tell you what you will see by and by. You will see trouble! *trouble!* TROUBLE enough in these United States. And as I have said before, I say *today—I tell you in the name of God, WOE! to them that fight against Zion, for God will fight against them* (Roberts, *The Life of John Taylor*, 383-84).

COLONIA JUAREZ, Chihuahua, Mexico
ca. 1900

MEXICAN COLONIES
Porter and his family in Pacheco, Mexico, with the Pacheco School in background.
ca. 1887–1894

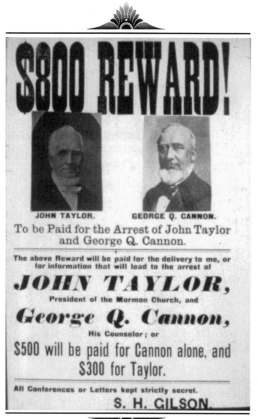

WANTED POSTER for John Taylor and George Q. Cannon for polygamy. $500 offered for Cannon, and $300 for Taylor. Historians suppose that the lower reward for Taylor was for one of two reasons: either they were trying to insult Taylor, or it was because Cannon was a wealthy man.

After this last public appearance, President Taylor and his counselors went into hiding. President Joseph F. Smith went to Hawaii. President Cannon, whom the authorities wanted because of his profound influence on Church members, seldom spent two nights in the same place. The arrests and persecution crippled every type of commercial trade and industry. Anyone who professed a belief in the Church was disenfranchised, and not allowed to vote or serve in public office. On June 11, 1886, the U.S. Marshal and his aides forced their way into the Gardo House and searched the building from cellar to garret. They did not find President Taylor because he was hiding in a specially built closet on the top floor. At one point, the marshals stood within one foot of him.

President Taylor remained in hiding for over two years. He managed Church affairs through letters and with the aid of messengers. In a letter to the Church membership dated July 24, 1885, President Taylor wrote:

> Although we have changed our office from time to time, we have been able to perform our duties with the exception of public addresses as much as when at home. How long it shall be the good pleasure of our God, our Heavenly Father, that we shall continue in our present condition, mattereth not. We hope always to be resigned to His providences and to accept at His hands all that it may be His good pleasure to call us to endure, whether prosperity or adversity, freedom or imprisonment, life or death ("Religious Persecutions: Address to the Saints," *Millennial Star* 47: 529-32).

However, the raids and persecutions against the Church members took its toll. As President Taylor's health began to fail, letters were sent to the Quorum of the Twelve. President Smith and President Cannon met at the Prophet's side. This was the first time the First Presidency had been together in more than two and a half years. John Taylor passed away at 7:55 P.M. on Monday, July 25, 1887:

> . . . in Kaysville, Utah, with Sister Taylor at his bedside. His body was removed to the Gardo House on the night of July 26, and in the early morning of the 29, the day of his funeral, the family assembled to pay their last respects to this beloved prophet before he was taken to the Tabernacle, where for four and one-half hours over 25,000 people filed by and gazed in sadness upon the countenance of this noble man of God they had learned to trust and love as their distinguished servant, friend and leader (Roberts, *The Life of John Taylor*, 499).

This was a time of sadness and hardship for the Saints—President John Taylor had died, Church property had been confiscated, female suffrage in the Utah Territory had been abolished, political rights had been taken away, and the Church had been disincorporated. Nighttime raids by law officers terrified the Saints, but the Church members remained firm in their resolve to live according to their beliefs.

After President Taylor's death, Wilford Woodruff became the new leader of the Church.

GARDO HOUSE, on South Temple street in Salt Lake City, was built as an official residence for Church presidents. *ca. 1890*

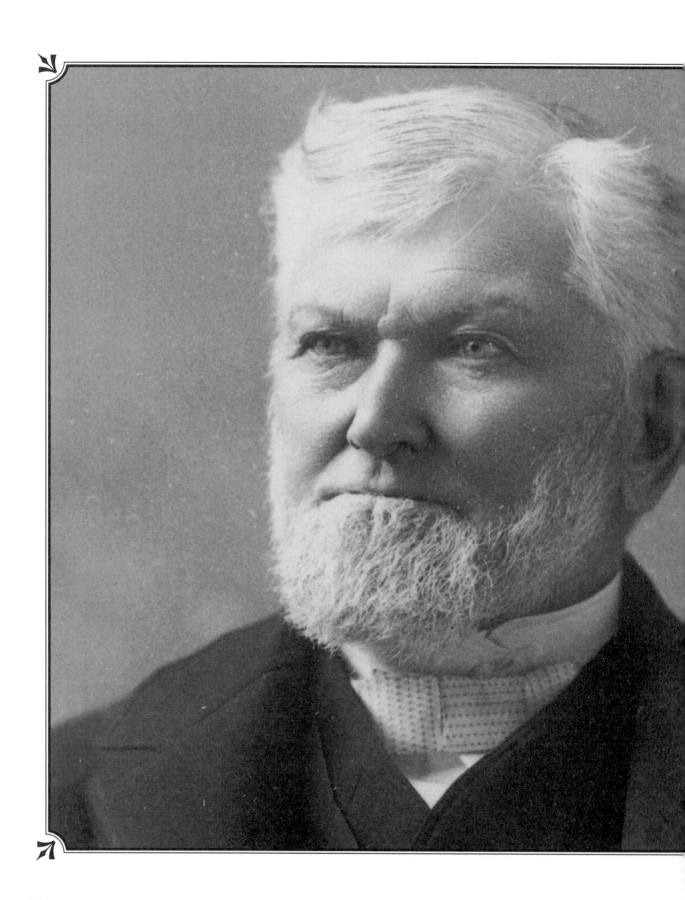

WILFORD

WOODRUFF

Wilford the Faithful

The Perpetual Emigration Fund Company had aided many Saints who traveled to the United States. However, the courts had dissolved the company and filed suit against it and the Church. President Woodruff had to deal with this and other pressing financial matters when he became the Prophet.

Wilford Woodruff had been a scribe to both Joseph Smith and Brigham Young. He was a respected leader of the Church and known for his work as a missionary and historian. Wilford Woodruff's own accounts of his forefathers indicated that he came from a hardy and long-lived people. He said, "My grandfather, Josiah Woodruff, lived nearly one hundred years. He possessed an iron constitution and performed a great deal of manual work up to the time of his death" (Cowley, *Wilford Woodruff: History of His Life and Labors*, 3-4).

Wilford was the third son of Aphek and Beulah Woodruff. His mother died of spotted fever when he was only fifteen months old. Aphek worked as a miller and taught Wilford the trade.

In many ways, it was a miracle that Wilford survived to grow to manhood. As a child, he experienced a series of accidents, but he seemed to have an unseen guardian protecting him from death or permanent injury. Wilford summarized his accident-prone childhood in his diary.

WILFORD WOODRUFF served as President from 1889–1898.

When three years of age, I fell into a caldron of scalding water and although instantly rescued, I was badly burned. . . . One Saturday evening with my brothers, Azmon and Thompson, while playing in the chamber of my father's house, contrary to his instructions, I made a misstep and fell to the bottom of the stairs, breaking one of my arms in the fall. . . . My father owned a number of horned cattle, among which was a surly bull. One evening I was feeding pumpkins to the cattle, and the bull leaving his own, took the pumpkin I had given to a cow which I called mine. I was incensed at the selfishness of this male beast, and promptly picked up the pumpkin he had left, to give it to the cow. No sooner had I got in my arms than the bull came plunging toward me with great fury. I ran down the hill with all my might, the bull at my heels. My father, seeing the danger I was in, called to me to throw down the pumpkin, but (forgetting to be obedient) I held on, and as the bull was approaching me with the fierceness of a tiger, I made a misstep and fell flat. . . . The pumpkin rolled out of my arms, the bull leaped over me, ran his horns into the pumpkin and tore it to pieces. Undoubtedly he would have done the same thing to me if I had not fallen to the ground. . . . During the same year . . . I fell from a porch across some timber, and broke my other arm.

Not many months passed [when] in company with several other boys, I went to the saw mill and got upon the headlock of the carriage to ride. . . . Before I was aware of it my leg was caught between the headlock and the fender post and broken in two (Cowley, *Wilford Woodruff: History of His Life and Labors*, 5-6).

In addition to broken limbs, Wilford was almost suffocated when a load of hay fell on him. On another occasion, he almost drowned, but was pulled to safety and revived. He nearly froze to death in a blinding snowstorm when he stopped in the shelter of a tree and fell asleep; he severely cut his foot with an axe, and was bitten by a mad dog that was in the last stages of rabies. At age seventeen, he had yet another serious accident. He recorded:

I was riding a very ill-tempered horse, which . . . suddenly leaped from the road and ran down the steepest part of the hill, going at full speed amid the thickest of the rocks . . . until he struck a rock nearly breast high, which threw him to the earth. I went over his head, landing squarely upon my feet almost one rod in front of the horse. Alighting upon my feet was probably the means of saving my life; for if I had struck the ground upon any other part of my body, it probably would have killed me instantly. As it was, one of my legs was broken in two places and both my ankles put out of place in a shocking manner (Cowley, *Wilford Woodruff: History of His Life and Labors*, 8–9).

Wilford's accident problems plagued him even on the day he became a member of the Church. He said, "The day that I was baptized into the Church of Jesus Christ of Latter-day Saints—December 31, 1833—my horse, with newly calked shoes, kicked the hat off my head. If he had struck two inches lower, doubtless he would have killed me instantly" (Cowley, *Wilford Woodruff: History of His Life and Labors*, 9).

Moments later, this horse was yoked with another and hitched to a sled made of loose boards. Wilford, standing on the boards, was thrown forward and became caught under the sled. The frightened horses ran down a hill and Wilford was dragged under the sled behind them. Luckily, the road was smooth and Wilford escaped serious injury.

Although Wilford was interested in religion, he had not joined a church because he had not been able to find one that taught the doctrines, principles, ordinances, and gifts of the gospel that Jesus Christ and his apostles had taught. Ministers told Wilford that prophets, apostles, revelations, and healings had been done away with and were no longer needed. Wilford, however, could not accept this. One day, an aged man named Robert Mason, who lived in a neighboring town, told Wilford that he would be involved in the restoration of the true gospel of Christ. Wilford recorded their discussion.

> Father Mason did not claim that he had any authority to officiate in the ordinances of the gospel, nor did he believe that such authority existed on the earth. . . . He believed it his right and the right of every honest-hearted man or woman to receive light and knowledge, visions, and revelations by the prayer of faith.
>
> The last time I ever saw him he related to me the following vision which he had in his field in open day:
>
> I was carried away in a vision and found myself in the midst of a vast orchard of fruit trees. I became hungry and wandered through this vast orchard searching for fruit to eat, but I found none. . . . [The trees] began to fall to the ground as if torn up by a whirlwind. They continued to fall until there was not a tree standing in the whole orchard. I immediately saw three aftershoots springing up from the roots and forming themselves into young and beautiful trees. These budded, blossomed, and brought forth fruit which ripened. . . . I stretched forth my hand and plucked some of the fruit. I gazed upon it with delight but when I was about to eat of it, the vision closed and I did not taste the fruit. . . .
>
> I bowed down in humble prayer and asked the Lord to show me the meaning of the vision. Then the voice of the Lord came to me saying: . . . "This is to show you that my church is not organized among men in the generation to which you belong. But in the days of your children the Church and the Kingdom of God shall be made manifest with all the gifts and the blessings enjoyed by the Saints in past ages. You shall live to be made acquainted with it, but shall not partake of its blessings before you depart this life."
>
> When Father Mason had finished relating the vision and its interpretation, he said, calling me by my Christian name:

"Wilford, I shall never partake of this fruit in the flesh, but you will and you will become a conspicuous actor in the new kingdom."

He then turned and left me. These were the last words he ever spoke to me upon the earth.

The vision was given to him about the year 1800. He related it to me in 1830. . . . Three years later when I was baptized into the Church . . . I wrote him a long letter in which I informed him that I had found the true gospel with all its blessings. . . .

He received my letter with great joy and had it read over to him many times. . . . He was very aged and soon died without having the privilege of receiving the ordinances of the gospel. . . .

The first opportunity I had after the truth of baptism for the dead was revealed, I went forth and was baptized for him in the temple font at Nauvoo (Cowley, *Wilford Woodruff: History of His Life and Labors*, 16-18).

The spring after his baptism, Wilford moved to Kirtland to be with the Saints and the prophet. Wilford spent ten of his first fifteen years in the Church preaching the gospel in Canada, England, and the Southern United States. He had been a member only a year when he began to have an overwhelming desire to tell others about the gospel. Wilford recorded that he went to a secluded spot to pray.

Before I arose from my knees, the Spirit of the Lord rested upon me and bore witness that my prayer was heard and should be answered upon my head. I arose very happy and walked through thick woods . . . into an open road. As I entered the roadway, I met Judge Elias Higby. Brother Higby was a high priest and very faithful man. . . . I had associated with him daily, but never mentioned to him my desire to preach the gospel. To my surprise, as soon as I approached him, he said:

"Brother Wilford, the Spirit of the Lord tells me that you should be ordained to go and preach the gospel" (Cowley, *Wilford Woodruff: History of His Life and Labors*, 46- 47).

A few days later, Wilford Woodruff was ordained a priest and sent to preach the gospel in Arkansas and Tennessee. He later served missions in the Eastern States, the Canadian Fox Islands and Great Britain. In England, Elder Woodruff met with great success. He relates an experience that happened when he had been preaching north of Birmingham:

> March 1, 1840 was my birthday. I was thirty-three years of age. It being Sunday, I preached twice during the day to a large assembly in the city hall . . . and administered the Sacrament to the Saints. In the evening I again met with a large assembly of the Saints and strangers and while singing the first hymn, the Spirit of the Lord rested upon me and . . . said to me, "This is the last meeting that you will hold with this people for many days." I was astonished at this, as I had many appointments in that district.
>
> In the morning I went in secret before the Lord, and asked Him what was His will concerning me. The answer I received was that I should go to the south; for the Lord had a great work for me to perform there (Cowley, *Wilford Woodruff: History of His Life and Labors*, 116).

A recent convert, William Benbow, suggested that Elder Woodruff visit his brother at Hill Farm in Herefordshire. The brother, John Benbow, and his wife, Jane, received the gospel with glad hearts. They belonged to a congregation of about 600 members that had broken off from the Methodist Church and was searching for the true gospel of Christ. Elder Woodruff said: "When I heard these things I could clearly see why the Lord had commanded me . . . to leave that place of labor and go to the south for in Herefordshire there was a great harvest-field for gathering many saints into the Kingdom of God" (Cowley, *Wilford Woodruff: History of His Life and Labors*, 117).

With the exception of one individual, the entire congregation was converted to the Church.

PHOEBE CARTER WOODRUFF, wife of Wilford Woodruff and staunch defender of plural marriage. *ca. 1840*

✦✦

In 1837, when Wilford was thirty years old, he married Phoebe Carter in Kirtland, Ohio. Wilford built a home in Nauvoo, but sold it when the Saints moved west. When the first pioneer company was organized, Wilford was appointed as captain of the first ten wagons— a significant honor. During his first trek across the plains, Wilford's family stayed in Winter Quarters. His unique fishing skills helped him provide the company with fresh fish during their journey. He had learned about fly-fishing during one of us missions to England, and found that this method of fishing was very successful in America. Wilford wrote about the first time he tried his dry flies in America.

> The brethren caught several brook trout which was the first I had seen since I left England, and as we were to spend the next day at the Fort, I calculated on a day of fishing. As soon as I had my breakfast next morning, I rigged up my fishing rod that I had brought with me from Liverpool, fixed my reel line and artificial fly, and went to one of the brooks close by to try my luck.
>
> The men at the Fort said that there were but few trout in the streams, and a good many of the brethren were already at the creek with their rods trying their skill, baiting with fresh meat and grasshoppers, but no one was catching any.
>
> I threw my fly into the water, and it being the first time that I had ever tried the artificial fly in America or ever saw it tried, I watched it as it floated upon the water with as much interest as Franklin did his kite when he was experimenting in drawing lightning from the sky; and as he received great joy when he saw the electricity descend on his kite string, so was I highly gratified when I saw the nimble trout dart at my fly hook, and run away with the line.
>
> I fished two or three hours during the morning and evening and caught twelve in all. One-half of them would weigh three-fourths of a pound each, while all the rest of the camp did not catch three pounds in all, which was taken as proof that the artificial fly is far the best to fish with (Cowley, *Wilford Woodruff: History of His Life and Labors*, 308).

THOMAS BULLOCK (1816–1885) was part of the first pioneer company who came to the Salt Lake Valley. He was elected as clerk of that camp.
ca. 1840

As the pioneers neared the Salt Lake Valley, many fell ill with Rocky Mountain Fever. Orson Pratt was sent ahead with twenty wagons to break the trail. Wilford had been ill with the fever, but when he began feeling better, he rigged a bed in his wagon to carry Brigham Young and Brother Rockwood. Of this momentous occasion, Wilford wrote:

> This, the 24th day of July, 1847, was an important day in the history of my life, and in the history of the Church of Jesus Christ of Latter-day Saints. . . .
>
> After a hard journey from Winter Quarters of more than one thousand miles through flats of the Platte River and plateaus of the Black Hills and Rocky Mountains and over the burning sands and eternal sage regions, willow swails and rocky regions, to gaze upon a valley of such vast extent surrounded with a perfect chain of everlasting mountains covered with eternal snow, with their innumerable peaks like pyramids towering toward heaven, presented at one view to us the grandest scenery and prospect that we could have obtained on earth (Cowley, *Wilford Woodruff: History of His Life and Labors*, 313).

Some of Wilford Woodruff's most significant contributions to the Church were his journals and records of Church history. He preserved much of what we know about the Prophets Joseph Smith and Brigham Young—especially the speeches and sermons they gave. As he grew older, he realized how important his writings were.

In the October 1883 semi-annual conference of the Church, Elder Woodruff was sustained as Church historian and general recorder. He held this position until he became President of the Church in 1887. Regarding his habit of journal keeping, he wrote: "Men should write down the things which God has made known to them. Whether things are important or not, often depends upon God's purposes; but the testimony of the goodness of God and the things He has wrought in the lives of men will always be important as a testimony" (Cowley, *Wilford Woodruff: History of His Life and Labors*, 423).

Orson Pratt (1811–1881), was sent ahead with twenty wagons to break the trail to the Salt Lake Valley. *ca. 1862–1872*

Orson Pratt (1811–1881), was sent ahead with twenty wagons to break the trail to the Salt Lake Valley. *ca. 1862–1872*

The First Presidency was not immediately reorganized when John Taylor died in July 1887. Wilford Woodruff, as President of the Twelve, presided over the Church, but persecution by Federal marshals kept the Church leaders in hiding.

However, President Woodruff did make a public appearance at the October conference following President Taylor's death. The audience greeted him with warm applause, and no attempt was made to arrest him. Following the meeting, however, he again went into hiding. Wilford spent much of his time hiding in St. George and surrounding towns. He was on constant alert for Federal marshals, but still enjoyed fishing and hunting until a neighbor recognized him one day as he went about disguised in a sunbonnet and Mother Hubbard dress.

A special office had been prepared in the St. George Temple for Elder Woodruff to conduct business. While working in the St. George Temple, he had a unique experience with the signers of the Declaration of Independence. He reported that these men came to him while he was in the temple.

> The spirits of the dead gathered around me, wanting to know why we did not redeem them. Said they, "You have had the use of the Endowment House for a number of years and yet nothing has ever been done for us. We laid the foun-

WORLD EVENTS

Although the Utah Territory was undergoing one of the most repressive periods in its history, the world was enjoying new enlightenment. In Paris, impressionist painters were at their peak. Gauguin had just settled in Tahiti, Toulouse-Lautrec had produced the first of his music-hall posters, and Van Gogh's first exhibition opened. In the area of medicine, rubber gloves were used in surgery for the first time.

WILFORD
WOODRUFF'S FIRST
PRESIDENCY
George Q. Cannon,
President Wilford
Woodruff, and
Joseph F. Smith.
*March 1, 1894 on
President Woodruff's
87th birthday.*

dation of the government you now enjoy and we never apostatized from it, but we remain true to it and were faithful to God." These were the signers of the Declaration of Independence and they waited on me for two days and two nights. I thought it very singular that not withstanding so much work had been done, and yet nothing had been done for them. The thought never entered my heart from the fact that I suppose that heretofore our minds were reaching after our more immediate friends and relatives. I straightway went into the baptismal font and called upon Brother McAllister to baptism me for the signers of the Declaration of Independence and fifty other eminent men. I then baptized him for every President of the United States, except three (L. G. Otten, and C. M. Caldwell, *Sacred Truths of the Doctrine and Covenants*, 1:15-16).

PRESIDENT WOODRUFF

At the April 1889 general conference, the First Presidency was finally reorganized. President Woodruff was sustained as Prophet of the Church, and George Q. Cannon and Joseph F. Smith were sustained as counselors. The new prophet wrote:

> This 7th day of April, 1889, is one of the most important days of my life, for I was made President of The Church of Jesus Christ of Latter-day

WILFORD WOODRUFF AND HIS WIFE, EMMA SMITH WOODRUFF (1838–1912). *ca. 1898*

Saints by the unanimous vote of ten thousand of them. The vote was first taken by quorums and then by the entire congregation as in the case of President John Taylor. This is the highest office ever conferred upon any man in the flesh. It came to me in the eighty-third year of my life. I pray God to protect me and give me power to magnify my calling to the end of my days. The Lord has watched over me until the present time (Cowley, *Wilford Woodruff: History of His Life and Labors*, 564–65).

Shortly after he was sustained, President Woodruff became concerned about the length of time that the Church had been without an official leader. After engaging in considerable thought and prayer, he instructed Lorenzo Snow, the new President of the Twelve, and the other Church leaders that a new First Presidency should be organized as soon as possible following a prophet's death.

THE MANIFESTO

President Woodruff's most pressing concern was the Edmunds Tucker Act, which had caused virtually all Church property to be confiscated, and resulted in the arrest and jailing of many members of the Church. During conference in

1890, President Woodruff announced that the Lord had instructed the Church to stop practicing polygamy. When he presented the Manifesto to the Church, he noted that, as in times past, the Lord had accepted the efforts of his people. His sermon was based on a revelation that Joseph Smith had received after the Saints had failed to build the city and temple that the Lord had commanded them to erect in Jackson County.

Doctrine and Covenants, Section 124, records:

> Verily, verily, I say unto you, that when I give a commandment to any of the sons of men to do a work unto my name, and those sons of men go with all their might and with all they have to perform that work, and cease not their diligence, and their enemies come upon them and hinder them from performing that work, behold, it behooveth me to require that work no more at the hands of those sons of men, but to accept of their offerings (D&C 124:49).

The Manifesto was read in general conference on October 5, 1890.

> I have arrived at a point in the history of my life as the President of the Church of Jesus Christ of Latter-day Saints where I am under the necessity of acting for the temporal salvation of the Church. The United States government has taken a stand and passed laws to destroy the Latter-day Saints on the subject of polygamy or patriarchal order of marriage; and after praying to the Lord and feeling inspired, I have issued the following proclamation which is sustained by my counselors and the Twelve Apostles.
>
> Inasmuch as laws have been enacted by congress forbidding plural marriages, which laws have been pronounced constitutional by the court of last resort, I hereby declare my intention to submit to those laws, and to use my influence with the members of the Church over which I preside to have them do likewise (Roberts, *A Comprehensive History of the Church*, 6:220-21).

NEWSPAPER ARTICLE DECLARING THE ACCEPTANCE OF THE MANIFESTO

Following the reading of the Manifesto, Lorenzo Snow stood and proposed that those present vote to sustain it.

> I move that, recognizing Wilford Woodruff as the president of the Church of Jesus Christ of Latter-day Saints, and the only man on the earth

LAYING THE CAPSTONE ON THE SALT LAKE TEMPLE Approximately 50,000 people were on the temple grounds for the ceremony. F. M. Lyman spoke, and donated $1,000 toward completing the temple so that the dedication could take place on April 6, 1893 (40 yrs from the laying of the corner stone). *April 6, 1892*

at the present time who holds the keys of the sealing ordinances, we consider him fully authorized by virtue of his position to issue the Manifesto which has been read in our hearing and which is dated September 24th, 1890, and that as a church in general conference assembled, we accept his declaration concerning plural marriage as authoritative and binding (Roberts, *A Comprehensive History of the Church*, 6:221-22).

Samuel Bateman was in the audience when the Manifesto was read. He and some of his friends who had suffered exile and imprisonment had been determined to vote against it, but they couldn't. It was as though a higher power caused them to vote to sustain President Woodruff in this matter, and they felt at peace when they had done it.

However, some members were disturbed by the Manifesto. President Woodruff addressed the issue in several stake conference talks. In a meeting in Logan, he said:

I have had some revelations of late, and very important ones to me, and I will tell you what the Lord has said to me. Let me bring your minds to what is termed the manifesto. . . . The Lord has told me to ask the Latter-day Saints a question, and He also told me that if they would listen to what I said to them and answer the question put to them, by the Spirit and power of God, they would all answer alike. . . . The question is this: Which is the wisest course for the Latter-day Saints to pursue—continue to attempt to practice plural marriage, with the laws of the nation against it and the opposition of 60 million people, and at the cost of the confiscation and loss of all the Temples, and the stopping of all the ordinances therein, both for the living and the dead, and the imprisonment of the First Presidency and Twelve and the heads of families . . . or after doing and suffering what we have through out adherence to this principle to cease the practice and submit to the law, and through doing so, leave the Prophets, Apostles and fathers at home, so that they can instruct the people and attend to the duties of the Church, and also leave the Temples in the hands of the Saints, so that they can attend to the ordinances of the Gospel, both for the living and for the dead?

The Lord showed me by vision and revelation exactly what would take place if we did not stop this practice. . . . This is the question I lay before the

APRIL 1892

C. R. SAVAGE Photo.

SALT LAKE TEMPLE
DEDICATION.
President Wilford
Woodruff dedicated
the temple. He
records in his journal
that nearly 3,000
people assembled in
the upper room for
the dedication.
Crowds filled the
streets for the
celebration.
April 6, 1893

Latter-day Saints. [You have to judge for yourselves, but I want to say this. I should have let all the temples go out of our hands, I should have gone to prison myself and let every other man go there had not the God of Heaven commanded me to do what I did do] (Joseph Fielding Smith, *The Life of Joseph F. Smith*, 297-98).

THE SALT LAKE TEMPLE

The Saints had been working on the Salt Lake Temple for forty years. The men who foresaw and planned the magnificent building had passed on, but their vision continued, and finally the temple was finished. On April 6, 1892, after music and a prayer, Don Carlos Young shouted, "The capstone is now ready to be laid!" (Roberts, *A Comprehensive History of the Church,* 6:232).

President Woodruff stepped to the front of the platform and said, "Attention, all ye House of Israel, and all ye nations of all earth. We will now lay the top stone of the Temple of our God, the foundation of which was laid and dedicated by the Prophet, Seer, and Revelator, Brigham Young" (Roberts, *A Comprehensive History of the Church,* 6:232). With 60,000 spectators looking on and cheering, President Woodruff pressed a button that swung the capstone into place.

One year later, in April of 1893, the temple was dedicated. In his journal, President Woodruff summarized this momentous day, "I attended the dedication of the Temple. The Spirit and power of God rested upon us. The spirit of prophecy and revelation was upon us, and the hearts of the people were melted and many things were unfolded to our understanding" (Cowley, *Wilford Woodruff: History of His Life and Labors,* 582).

Seventy-five thousand people attended thirty-one dedicatory services over a nineteen-day period. In the dedicatory address, President Woodruff promised, ". . . the power of the adversary should be broken, . . . that the enemy would have less power over the Saints and meet with greater failures in oppressing them . . . a renewed interest in the gospel message would be awakened throughout the world" (Cowley, *Wilford Woodruff: History of His Life and Labors*, 583).

THE FORTY-FIFTH STATE

Now that plural marriage no longer was being practiced, many of the objections to Utah becoming a state were eliminated. Finally, on July 7, 1894, President Grover Cleveland signed an act authorizing Utah to become a state. For the next year and a half, the state constitution was drafted and other preparations were made. The proclamation making Utah the forty-fifth state was signed on January 4, 1896, an occasion that gave much joy to President Woodruff. On that day President Woodruff said, "I feel thankful to God that I have lived to see Utah admitted into the family of states. It is an event that we have looked forward to for a generation" (Russell R. Rich, *Ensign to the Nations*, 435).

Governor Heber M. Wells, the first governor of the state of Utah, recommended that July of 1897 should be a time of celebration to commemorate the fiftieth anniversary of the Saints' arrival in the Salt Lake Valley.

PRESIDENT GROVER WILSON CLEVELAND became President of the United States in 1893. He signed an act authorizing Utah to become a state on July 7, 1894. The proclamation making Utah the forty-fifth state was signed a year and a half later, January 4, 1896.

SALT LAKE TEMPLE WITH THE STATEHOOD FLAG DRAPED OVER IT. Statehood Day was January 6, 1896. The Tabernacle was decorated in red, white, and blue, featuring a 128' X 150' flag on the ceiling. Parades, and other festivities marked the occasion. Robert T. Burton, then 75 years old, was the "Marshall of the Day." *1896*

All . . . surviving members of the pioneers of 1847 were to be special guests. . . . The celebration began on July 20 and ran through July 24. On the first day the Brigham Young monument . . . was unveiled and dedicated. The ceremonies were preceded by a parade of the pioneers, and each pioneer was given a solid gold medal upon which was engraved a picture of Brigham Young with a pioneer wagon on the left, an 1897 model locomotive on the right, a beehive on the top, and a pony express rider on the bottom. . . . Each succeeding day featured a different parade. . . . Saturday, July 24, was the parade of parades when all previous parades . . . entered into one gigantic spectacle. On Sunday, July 25, a memorial service in honor of all deceased pioneers was held in the tabernacle as a conclusion of the spectacle (Rich, *Ensign to the Nations*, 436–37).

When President Woodruff presided at the 1898 April conference he was 91 years old, and was growing feeble. He and his wife traveled to San Francisco in August to see if the change in climate could help his health. However, he passed away two weeks later. At his funeral, Elder Cannon said:

WORLD EVENTS

'E UTAH PIONEER JUBILEE

In the passing away of President Woodruff, a man has gone from our midst whose character was probably as angelical as that of any person who had ever lived upon the earth. . . .

He was of a sweet disposition and possessed a character so lovely as to draw unto him friends in every walk of life. . . . No jealousy lurked in his bosom. . . . In spite of his high and holy calling, he was unpretentious, unassuming, and his character and life were as transparent as glass (Cowley, *Wilford Woodruff: History of His Life and Labors*, 631- 32).

As the century drew to a close, the world was not at peace. Spain had declared war on the United States over the Cuban issue, and the Spanish American War had begun. In Europe, Pierre and Marie Curie had just discovered radium; and a new underground transportation system, the Metro, opened in Paris. In the literary world, Lewis Carroll, the author of *Alice in Wonderland*, died, and Ernest Hemingway was born. Henry James wrote a thrilling short story, *The Turn of the Screw*, and H. G. Wells broadcast his radio show, *The War of the Worlds*.

50 Yr Celebration of Pioneers entering Salt Lake Valley Photograph shows the survivors at this time of celebration. *July 24, 1897*

LORENZO

SNOW

Soldier for the Lord

When President Wilford Woodruff died, Lorenzo Snow was sustained as President of the Church. Lorenzo was born on April 3, 1814, in Ohio. He had four older sisters and two younger brothers, and was often left in charge of the family while his father was away from home on business. His sister, Eliza, reported that Lorenzo always performed his duties with punctuality and thoroughness. He was a good student, and was always interested in learning. He was admitted to Oberlin College, and on his way to school, he met David W. Patten, an elder in the Church. Of this chance meeting, Eliza wrote:

> On his way to Oberlin, my brother accidentally fell in company with David W. Patten, an incident to which he frequently refers as one of those seemingly trivial occurrences in human life which leave an indelible trace. . . . He [David Patten] possessed a mind of deep thought, and rich intelligence. In conversation with him, my brother was much impressed with the depth and beauty of the philosophical reasoning with which this inspired Elder seemed perfectly familiar. . . . From that time, a new field, with

LORENZO SNOW served as President from 1898–1901. *ca. 1898–1901*

a new train of reflections, was open to my brother's mind (Snow, *Biography and Family Record of Lorenzo Snow*, 4).

Lorenzo did not join the Church at once, however. He went on to distinguish himself at college. Meanwhile, Eliza heard the gospel and joined the Church along with her mother and sister. She commented:

> Having been thoroughly convinced of the authenticity of the Gospel in its purity as revealed through Joseph Smith, I was baptized on the fifth of April, 1835, and in the autumn of the same year, left my father's house and united my interest with the Latter-day Saints in Kirtland, Ohio.
>
> A short time before leaving Oberlin, [Lorenzo] wrote, asking me many questions concerning revealed religion. . . .
>
> I answered his questions, and knowing he intended crowning his studies with a thorough knowledge of Hebrew, invited him to come to Kirtland . . . as a school was soon to commence there (Snow, *Biography and Family Record of Lorenzo Snow*, 4-5).

Lorenzo came to Kirtland and learned Hebrew with the Prophet Joseph and others. He also learned more about the Church. When he attended a meeting where the Prophet Joseph's father was giving patriarchal blessings, Lorenzo was amazed to hear the Patriarch refer to peculiarities of the person receiving the blessing without knowing anything about the individual's history. After the meeting, Lorenzo was introduced to Father Smith for the first time, who told him that he would be baptized into the Church.

THE CHAGRIN RIVER, in Kirtland, Ohio, where Lorenzo Snow was baptized.

The Patriarch then told Lorenzo, "You will become as great as you can possibly wish, even as great as God and you cannot wish to be greater" (Snow, *Biography and Family Record of Lorenzo Snow*, 10).

A puzzled Lorenzo later wrote in his journal:

> The old gentleman's prediction, that I should ere long be baptized, was strange to me, for I had not cherished a thought of becoming a member of the "Mormon" Church; but when he uttered the last clause, I was confounded. . . .
>
> I looked at Father Smith and silently asked myself the question: Can that man be a deceiver? His every appearance answered in the negative. . . . The prediction that I should soon be baptized was fulfilled in two weeks from the time it was spoken, and in about four years from that time I was reminded of the foregoing prediction by a very wonderful revelation on the subject in which the principle, as well as the promise, was made clear to my understanding. . . .
>
> I was baptized by Elder John Boynton, then one of the Twelve Apostles, June, 1836, in Kirtland, Ohio. . . . I received

baptism and the ordinance of laying on of hands by one who professed to have divine authority; and, having thus yielded obedience to these ordinances, I was in constant expectation of the fulfillment of the promise of the reception of the Holy Ghost (Snow, *Biography and Family Record of Lorenzo Snow,* 7, 10).

However, the manifestation Lorenzo desired did not come immediately. About three weeks after his baptism, while studying, he realized that he did not have a knowledge of the truth of the work. He laid aside his books and wandered into the fields. He later wrote about the experience.

> An indescribable cloud of darkness seemed to envelop me. I had been accustomed, at the close of the day, to retire for secret prayer, to a grove a short distance from my lodgings, but at this time I felt no inclination to do so. The spirit of prayer had departed and the heavens seemed like brass over my head. At length, realizing that the usual time had come for secret prayer, I concluded I would not forgo my evening service, and, as a matter of formality, knelt as I was in the habit of doing.
>
> I had no sooner opened my lips in an effort to pray, than I heard a sound, just above my head like the rustling of silken robes, and immediately the Spirit of God descended upon me, completely enveloping my whole person, filling me, from the crown of my head to the soles of my feet, and O, the joy and happiness I felt. . . . I then received a perfect knowledge that God lives, that Jesus Christ is the Son of God, and of the restoration of the holy Priesthood, and the fullness of the Gospel. It was a complete baptism—a tangible immersion in the heavenly principle or element, the Holy Ghost; and even more and real and physical in effects upon every part of my system than the immersion by water. . . .
>
> That night, as I retired to rest, the same wonderful manifestations were repeated and continued to be for several successive nights (Snow, *Biography and Family Record of Lorenzo Snow,* 7-9).

Six months later, Lorenzo received his patriarchal blessing from Joseph Smith, Sr. At the age of twenty-two, Lorenzo had done nothing to indicate that he would reach the great heights suggested by his blessing. The Patriarch told Lorenzo:

> Thou hast a great work to perform in thy day and generation. Thou shalt have faith, even like that of the Brother of Jared. There shall not be a mightier man on earth than thou. The diseased shall send to thee their aprons and handkerchiefs, and by thy touch their owners shall be made whole. If expedient, the dead shall raise and come forth at thy bidding. They shalt have a long life. The vigor of thy mind shall not be abated and the vigor of thy body shall be preserved (Lorenzo Snow's patriarchal blessing, given by Patriarch Joseph Smith, Sr., 15 December 1836. "Selected Patriarchal Blessings," New Mormon Studies CD-ROM).

In the spring of 1837, Lorenzo set out on a mission to his home state of Ohio. He was on foot and alone. He wanted to travel without purse or scrip as the apostles had done in the days of Christ; however, this made him uncomfortable since he had always been in the habit of paying his way. At one of his meetings, he preached the gospel to his uncles, aunts, and schoolmates. Lorenzo was optimistic that many of them would be converted and desire baptism, but the reality was that his family thought he had been deceived, and very few of his classmates accepted the Gospel. However, Lorenzo had better luck at other meetings. He was somewhat timid about preaching, but trusted that the Lord would guide him. Before he left the area, he baptized his aunt, uncle, and several cousins. As he continued his mission, his success grew.

One night he had a dream that he was in danger of falling into the hands of a mob. The following evening, as he sat talking with friends, two well-dressed young men politely invited him to accompany them to a schoolhouse to preach to some people who were anxious to hear his message. Lorenzo wrote:

> After a little hesitation on my part, they began to urgently request my acceptance of their invitation, . . . and I told them that I could not comply with their wishes. When they were convinced that I was immovable, . . . they not only manifested disappointment, but were exceedingly angry.
> The next day I learned that they told the truth so far as a congregated audience waiting my appearance, . . . but the object was entirely different from that reported by the young men—it corresponded precisely with my dream (Snow, *Biography and Family Record of Lorenzo Snow*, 17).

In 1840, Lorenzo was preparing to go on his third mission in four years, and received a unique revelation that helped guide him through his life. As he was making his way east to catch a ship for his mission in Great Britain, he stopped in Illinois at the house of Elder Henry G. Sherwood. They were discussing the parable of the householder who hired servants and sent them to the fields at different hours of the day to labor in the vineyard. Lorenzo wrote that during the discussion:

> The Spirit of the Lord rested mightily upon me—the eyes of my understanding were opened, and I saw as clear as the sun at noonday, with wonder and astonishment, the path way of God and man. I formed the following couplet which expresses the revelation. As man now is, God once was: As God now is, man may be. I felt this to be a sacred communication, which I related to no one except my sister Eliza, until I reached England, when in a confidential private conversation with President Brigham Young . . . I related to him this extraordinary manifestation (Snow, *Biography and Family Record of Lorenzo Snow*, 46-47).

Brigham Young told Lorenzo that this was a private revelation, and that at the appropriate time it would be taught as doctrine by the Prophet of the Lord.

As instructed, Lorenzo did not tell anyone about the manifestation. Three years later, when he had returned from his mission, however, Lorenzo related the revelation to the Prophet Joseph. Joseph told Lorenzo, "Brother Snow, that is true gospel doctrine and it is a revelation from God to you"(Jack M. Lyon, *Best-Loved Stories of the LDS People*, 228).

In his patriarch blessing, Lorenzo was promised that he would have the gift of healing and raising people from the dead. Throughout his life, he had many opportunities to fulfill this promise.

One of these opportunities came after his mission to the British Isles, when he was appointed to take charge of 250 Saints who were sailing for America. The captain and crew of the ship were courteous and kind to the passengers, which helped ease the discomfort on board. The steward, a favorite of the passengers, became ill and soon became so sick that death seemed inevitable. The captain called the crew together and told them to go in one by one and pay their last respects to their friend. One of the Saints on board asked the captain if Elder Snow could give the dying man a blessing. The captain agreed, but when Lorenzo entered the cabin, he tearfully told him, "Mr. Snow, it's too late; he is expiring, he is breathing his last" (Snow, *Biography and Family Record of Lorenzo Snow*, 66).

JOHN WILLIAM FREDERICK VOLKER (1859–1932), sitting at left, is shown with a group of Dutch Saints on the deck of a ship coming to the United States. Volker served two missions to Holland, and translated the Book of Mormon and other Church documents into Dutch. *ca. 1885*

Elder Snow sat down beside the dying man and, after a few moments of silent prayer, laid his hands on the man's head and prayed that he be made whole. To the crew's joy and astonishment, the steward was soon walking around the ship, praising and glorifying God for his escape from death. The officers and sailors acknowledged the miraculous power of God and several of them were baptized when the ship docked in New Orleans.

Soon after arriving back in Nauvoo, Lorenzo left to campaign for Joseph's bid for the United States Presidency. While he was away, he received word that the Prophet and his brother Hyrum had been killed.

Lorenzo felt that he would devote his life to missionary work and never marry. His sister Eliza explains what changed his mind. "To devote his time, his talents, his all to the ministry was his all-absorbing desire. . . . he had cherished the idea that domestic responsibility would lessen his usefulness; and, until the law of Celestial Marriage was fully explained to him by the Prophet Joseph Smith, . . . he had not conceived the idea that marriage was one of the duties of . . . mortal life. (Snow, *Biography and Family Record of Lorenzo Snow*, 84).

In 1845, Lorenzo was sealed to two wives, Charlotte Squires and Mary Adaline Goddard, in the same ceremony in the Nauvoo Temple. Soon after, two other women, Sarah Ann Prichard and Harriet Amelia Squires, also became part of his family. Following the exodus from Nauvoo, Lorenzo presided over a group of Saints under the direction of President Brigham Young. In the spring of 1848, he and his family organized a company of twenty-five families and made the trip to the Salt Lake Valley. At this time, his fifth wife, Eleanor Houtz, was sealed to him. The entire company crossed the plains without serious accident or injury.

The following year, Lorenzo was called to fill a vacancy in the Quorum of the Twelve. Almost immediately, he was sent on a mission to Italy. He and his companion spent weeks and months with virtually no success. However, one morning, the three-year-old son of a couple the missionaries were staying with became seriously ill, and everyone thought the child was going to die. After retiring for the night, Elder Snow began to pray, asking the Lord to spare the child's life. However, the next morning, the little boy was even worse. When it seemed that the boy was going to die at any moment, the missionaries went to the mountains to pray. Elder Snow said:

After a little rest upon the mountain, aside from any likelihood of inter-
ruption, we called upon the Lord in solemn, earnest prayer, to spare the life
of the child. As I reflected on the course we wished to pursue, the claims that
we should soon advance to the world, I regarded this circumstance as one of

vast importance. I know not of any sacrifice which I can possibly make that I am not willing to offer, that the Lord might grant our request (Snow, *Biography and Family Record of Lorenzo Snow*, 129).

While on the mountain that day, the missionaries dedicated the land for the preaching of the gospel. When the missionaries returned to their lodgings, they took some consecrated oil, anointed the suffering child, and prayed for his recovery. A few hours later, the child was out of danger and was resting comfortably. After this event, the work in Italy began moving forward. Eliza, Lorenzo's sister, deeply affected by this turn of events, wrote:

> On the mountain in Italy, . . . on the same memorable day in which the Church of Jesus Christ of Latter-day Saints was there organized, Lorenzo, in the force of his spirit, aroused by intense interest in the work devolving upon him . . . and probably without realizing the weight of his covenant, told the Lord that he knew of no sacrifice he could possibly make he was not willing to offer, that the Lord might grant a request concerning the mission before him. When I received a copy of the report of the proceedings of the day, . . . I was deeply struck with the coincidence. Just at this time, as nearly as I could calculate by comparing dates and distances, the Lord removed, by the hand of death, from my brother's family circle, one of the loveliest women (Snow, *Biography and Family Record of Lorenzo Snow*, 233).

Lorenzo Snow

Lorenzo's wife, Charlotte, had died. As Lorenzo mourned her passing, he said:

> Arriving at my home in Salt Lake City, . . . the happiness of once again meeting my loved and loving family would have been full, but alas! there was a sad vacancy. . . . Charlotte, my dear wife, had been stricken down by death, and her beautiful form lay moldering in the silent tomb. Yet there was consolation in the thought that her pure spirit was mingling with holy beings above (Snow, *Biography and Family Record of Lorenzo Snow,* 232).

After returning to Salt Lake City, Lorenzo became involved in city government. Though limited in resources, he built his family a nice, two-story adobe home. His family was more than happy to move out of the leaking log cabin where they had lived since coming to the valley. Lorenzo was elected to the Territorial Legislature and was appointed as one of the regents of the newly formed University of Deseret. He also was kept busy speaking at conferences in nearby communities.

After a few years, he was called to preside over the Brigham City area. The First Presidency had been calling apostles to help settle outlying areas, and Lorenzo was instructed to select fifty families to accompany him. At the time, Brigham City was nothing more than an insect-infested fort; but Lorenzo encouraged the Saints to build homes, and soon a small town emerged.

Many of the Saints in Brigham City, however, lived in poverty; and something needed to be done to fill their temporal needs. Lorenzo devised a plan to help alleviate the suffering of the poor. He asked the members of the stake to fast two meals each month and to contribute the amount saved to a fund that would be used to help the poor. This was the first time that a regular day of fasting was established to aid the poor. Soon, other stakes followed the Brigham City Stake's example.

LAHAINA HARBOR, HAWAII, landview.

LAHAINA HARBOR, HAWAII, oceanview.

Site where Lorenzo Snow nearly drowned while on a mission in the Hawaiian Islands.

In 1864, Lorenzo was called to serve a mission in the Hawaiian Islands. When he and his companions arrived in Honolulu, they boarded a ship bound for Lahaina. When they reached the harbor, they boarded a small boat that was to take them to shore. One of the missionaries, W. W. Cluff, recorded what happened.

> The boat started for the shore. It contained some native passengers, and the boat's crew, who were also natives. The entrance to the harbor is a

very narrow passage between coral reefs, and when the sea is rough, it is very dangerous, on account of the breakers. . . . As we approached the reef it was evident to me that the surf was running higher than we anticipated. . . . A heavy swell struck the boat and carried us before it about fifty yards. When the swell passed it left us in a trough between two huge waves. It was too late to retrieve our error, and we must run our chances. When the second swell struck the boat, it raised the stern so high that the steersman's oar was out of the water, and he lost control of the boat. The last I remember of Brother Snow, was as the boat was going over. I saw him seize the upper edge of it with both hands; fearing the upper edge of the boat or the barrels might hit and injure me as the boat was going over, I plunged head foremost into the water. After swimming a short distance, I came to the surface without being strangled or injured. The boat was bottom upwards, and barrels, hats and umbrellas were floating in every direction. . . . About the same time, Brother Benson came up near me. . . . Brother Alma L. Smith came up on the opposite side of the boat.

Nothing yet had been seen of Brother Snow, although the natives had been swimming and diving in every direction in search of him. We were only about one-fourth of a mile from shore.

The people . . . manned the lifeboat and hurried to the scene. Brother Snow had not yet been discovered and anxiety was intense. Finally, one of the natives, in edging himself around the capsized boat, felt Brother Snow with his feet . . . and pulled him out from under the boat at least partly from under it. . . . As soon as we got him into the boat, we told the boatman to pull for the shore with all possible speed. His body was stiff and life apparently extinct. Brother A. L. Smith and I were sitting side by side. We laid Brother Snow across our laps and on the way to the shore we quietly administered to him and asked the Lord to spare his life, that he might return to his family and home. As we reached the shore we carried him a little way to some large, empty barrels and rolled him back and forth until we succeeded in getting the water he swallowed out of him. After working over him for some time without any indications of returning life, the bystanders said that nothing more could be done for him. But we did not feel like giving him up and still prayed and worked over him with an assurance that the Lord would hear and answer our prayers. Finally we were impressed to place our mouth over his and make an effort to inflate his lungs, alternately blowing in and drawing out the air, imitating as far as possible the natural process of breathing. This we persevered in until we succeeded in inflating his lungs. After a little, we perceived very faint indications of returning life. These grew more and more distinct until consciousness was fully restored (Smith, *The Life of Joseph F. Smith*, 212-15).

Lorenzo himself remembered little about the incident.

In an instant, our boat, with its contents, . . . was hurled into a gulf of briny waters and all was under this rolling, seething mountain wave. It took me by surprise. . . . I felt confident, however, there would be some way of escape; that the Lord would provide the means, for it was not possible that my life and mission were thus to terminate. This reliance on the Lord banished fear, and inspired me up to the last moment of consciousness. In such extreme cases of excitement, we seem to live hours in a minute, and a volume of thoughts crowd themselves into one single moment. . . .

I had been in the water only a few moments, until I lost consciousness. The first I knew afterwards, I was on shore, receiving the kind and tender attentions of my brethren. . . . I asked in a feeble whisper, What is the matter?" I immediately recognized the voice of Elder Cluff. . . . "You have been drowned; the boat upset in the surf." . . . Are you brethren all safe? . . . "Brother Snow, we're all safe" (Snow, *Biography and Family Record of Lorenzo Snow*, 279-81).

After returning from the Hawaiian Islands, Sister William Smith who knew of Lorenzo's patriarchal blessing, which stated that he had the ability to heal the sick, sent him a handkerchief to bless so that her husband could be made well. Lorenzo later wrote:

I took the handkerchief and a bottle of perfumery, and on retiring to my closet, I prayed, and then I consecrated the perfumery and sprinkled it on the handkerchief. I then again bowed before the Lord, and in earnest supplication besought Him to remember the promises He made through His servant, the Patriarch . . . and let the healing and life-inspiring virtues of His Holy Spirit be imparted to this handkerchief, . . . and from thence to Brother Smith when it shall be placed upon him, speedily restoring him to life, health and vigor (Snow, *Biography and Family Record of Lorenzo Snow*, 264-65).

THE MANTI TEMPLE, in Sanpete County, Utah. Elder Lorenzo Snow was called to dedicate the temple. This was during a period when Church leaders were in hiding from government authorities because of the polygamy issue. *ca. 1887*

When the handkerchief was placed over William Smith's face, he recovered almost instantaneously.

While the leaders of the Church were hiding from government authorities during the 1870s and 80s, Elder Snow was called to dedicate the Manti Temple. After the dedication, he returned to his home in Brigham City. In his house, a secret chamber had been built below the master bedroom that was accessible through a trap door. When the U.S. marshals learned that Elder Snow had returned to Brigham City, they went to his home with a warrant for his arrest. They searched the rooms, closets, pantry, and attic, but found nothing. As they were ready to leave, however, Lorenzo's faithful watchdog was seen sniffing around a grate in the home's foundation. With the dog's assistance, the marshals discovered the trap door, found the secret chamber, and arrested Elder Snow. He was convicted of the charges against him and was sent to prison. However, after eleven months in prison, the verdict in his case was overturned and he was released. Elder Snow, then President of the Counsel of the Twelve, was 86 when President Woodruff became ill. He prayed and pleaded that President Woodruff's life would be spared and that the great responsibility of Church leadership would not fall upon his shoulders. But when he received word that President Woodruff had died, he had a wonderful, comforting experience. Elder Snow took a train to Salt Lake City and went to the Temple to pray for the strength to fulfill his new calling. After finishing his prayer, he expected a reply or some manifestation from the Lord. There was nothing. He got up, walked through the Celestial Room and out into the large corridor. There, the Lord Jesus Christ appeared and told Lorenzo that he had been chosen to lead the Church. Lorenzo's granddaughter, Allie Young Pond, wrote:

ALICE ARMEDA SNOW YOUNG POND (1876–1943) was the granddaughter of Lorenzo Snow who was told of her grandfather's visitation from the Savior. *ca. 1901–1908*

One evening when I was visiting Grandpa Snow in his room in the Salt Lake Temple, I remained until the doorkeepers had gone and the night-watchman had not yet come in, so grandpa said he would take me to the main, front entrance and let me out that way. . . .

After we left his room and while we were still in the large corridor, leading into the Celestial Room, I was walking several steps ahead of grandpa when he stopped me, saying:

"Wait a moment, Allie, I want to tell you something. It was right here that the Lord Jesus Christ appeared to me at the time of the death of President Woodruff. He instructed me to go right ahead and reorganize the First Presidency of the Church at once and not wait as had been done after the death of the previous presidents, and that I was to succeed President Woodruff." . . . "He stood right here, about three feet above the floor. It looked as though He stood on a plate of solid gold."

Grandpa told me what a glorious personage the Savior is and described His hands, feet, countenance and beautiful, white robes, all of which were of such a glory of whiteness and brightness that he could hardly gaze upon Him.

Then grandpa came another step nearer me and put his right hand on my head and said:

"Now, Granddaughter, I want you to remember that this is the testimony of your grandfather, that he told you with his own lips that he actually saw the Savior here in the Temple and talked with Him face to face."

Then we went on and grandpa let me out the main, front door of the temple (*I Know That My Redeemer Lives*, 76).

FIRST TRAIN FROM
OGDEN TO SALT
LAKE CITY
1870

For the first time, the First Presidency was reorganized immediately upon the death of the previous president. When Lorenzo became President, the Church faced severe financial problems due to the Federal government's confiscation of Church property. Heber J. Grant said, "The Church was in a financial slough of despond, so to speak, almost financially bankrupt—its credit was hardly good for a thousand dollars without security" (*I Know That My Redeemer Lives*, 74).

Before his death, President Woodruff also had worried about the debt the Church faced. Two years before his death, he wrote, "The Presidency of the Church are so overwhelmed in financial matters, it seems as though we shall never live to get through with it unless the Lord opens the way in a miraculous manner. It looks as though we shall never pay our debts. I did not want to die until the church and myself as trustee-in-Trust, are out of debt" (Roberts, *A Comprehensive History of the Church*, 6:352).

Although President Woodruff did not live to see his wish fulfilled, President Snow continued working on the Church's pressing money problems. The Church issued bonds and sold some mining and railroad operations that had been losing money. But a permanent solution needed to be found. In the spring of 1899, President Snow received an impression that he should go to St. George and hold a special conference with the Saints. He did not know why the Lord wanted him to go, but St. George and the surrounding area was facing one of the worst droughts in their history.

Nephi Savage, a resident of St. George, related how dire the situation was. There had not been any rain in the area for several months, and streams and wells had dried up, leaving the people facing starvation. Also, the people had quit paying their tithing, saying that the government would only confiscate any donations made to the Church. This in turn, left the Church in desperate financial straits

When President Snow made the long dusty trip to St. George, he still did not know the main purpose of his visit. The people of St. George hoped for an answer to the drought problem. Following the opening exercises of the conference, President Snow arose and said:

My brethren and sisters, we are in your midst because the Lord directed me to come; but the purpose of our coming is not clearly known at the present, but this will be made known to me during our sojourn among you (Thomas C. Romney, *The Life of Lorenzo Snow*, 430).

President Snow's son, LeRoi, was serving as clerk and recorded what happened.

It was during one of these meetings that my father received the renewed revelation on tithing. I was sitting at a table reporting the proceeding, when all at once my father paused in his discourse. Complete stillness filled the room. When he commenced to speak again, his voice was strengthened and the inspiration of God seemed suddenly to come over him, as well as over the entire assembly.

"The word of the Lord to you is not anything new. It is simply this. The time has come now for every Latter-day Saint who calculates to be prepared for the future and to hold his feet strong upon a proper foundation, to do the will of the Lord and to pay his tithing in full. That is the word of the Lord to you, and it will be the word of the Lord to every settlement throughout the land of Zion. After I leave you and you get to thinking about this, you will see yourselves that the time has come when every man should stand up and pay his tithing in full. The Lord has blessed us and has had mercy upon us in the past, but there are times coming when the Lord requires us to stand up and do that which He has commanded, and not leave it any longer. What I say to you in this stake of Zion, I will say to every stake of Zion that has been organized" (Milton R. Hunter, *Will a Man Rob God?*, 55).

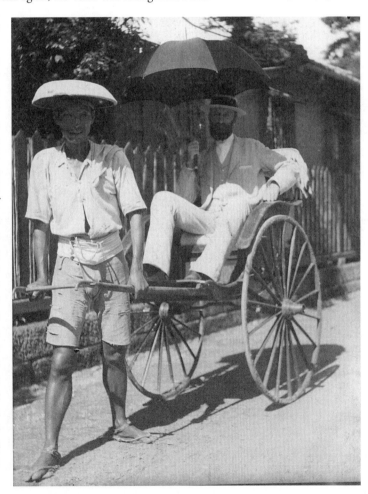

HEBER J. GRANT IN A RICKSHAW during his mission to Japan. *ca. 1902–1903*

True to his words, President Snow lost little time executing the Lord's plan. During his return trip to Salt Lake, he held special meetings and taught the members of the Church about tithing. He promised that great blessings would come from renewed obedience to this commandment. A year later, in 1900, President Snow reported that the Saints had paid twice the amount of tithing as in the previous two years. In less than eighteen months, the Church was well on its way to becoming free of debt. With the financial crisis solved, President Snow turned his attention to missionary work. The Church had grown to fifty stakes that were clustered in the Western United States, Canada, and Northern Mexico. Expanding the missionary program to the whole world, President Snow appointed Heber J. Grant to open a new mission in Japan. President Snow spoke to the Twelve and the Seventies concerning the worldwide missionary effort.

TITHING OFFICE BLOCK looking northeast from the intersection of Main and South Temple. View includes Lion house, and LDS University construction. The Joseph Smith Memorial Building now stands where the Tithing Building was located. *1901*

I want to say, here are the apostles and the seventies; their business is to warn the nations of the earth and prepare the world for the coming of the Savior. . . . Now we find ourselves in a compact, gathered condition, the church divided into stakes, and we come together from time to time. . . . It looks to me that our minds ought to extend somewhat, and we get out of the beaten track, and a little change to be made. For instance, we have started in this direction by sending Brother Grant over to Japan, but this is only a start. Things seem to be going on favorably with him; but whether he will accomplish much or not matters not in one sense; it is for the apostles to show to the Lord that they are his witnesses to all the nations, and that they are doing the best they can (Roberts, *A Comprehensive History of the Church*, 6:377).

When President Snow was eighty-eight, he caught a severe cold. The strain of trying to make himself heard during the October 1901 conference worsened his condition. After serving as President of the Church for only three years, he passed away quietly on October 10, 1901. Heber J. Grant said:

I know that Lorenzo Snow was a prophet of God. . . . Lorenzo Snow came to the Presidency of the Church when he was eighty-five years of age, and what he accomplished . . . was simply marvelous to contemplate.

He lifted the Church from the financial slough . . . this man, beyond the age of ability in the estimation of the world, this man who had not been engaged in financial affairs, who had been devoting his life for years to laboring in the temple, took hold of the finances of the Church of Christ under the inspiration of the living God, and in those three years changed everything, financially, from darkness to light (Heber J. Grant, *Gospel Standards*, 20).

WORLD EVENTS

The dawn of the twentieth century brought hints of the changes that would take place in the next one hundred years. The sounds of ragtime music filled the air in America. In Europe, Rachmaninoff performed his famed Piano Concerto No. 2. The first Mercedes car was produced, and telegraphic radio messages were sent across the Atlantic. Queen Victoria's lengthy reign came to an end, and U. S. President William McKinley was assassinated. Construction began on the Panama Canal, and J. P. Morgan organized the U. S. Steel Corporation.

In 1901, Church members mourned the death of President Lorenzo Snow, and Joseph F. Smith was ordained as the sixth President of the Church.

JOSEPH F. SMITH

A Mighty Man of God

In December 1837, an intelligent, well-educated young lady named Mary Fielding married Hyrum Smith. Hyrum's first wife, Jerusha Barden, had died while giving birth. Some people criticized Hyrum for marrying too soon after Jerusha's death, but he responded that, "It was not because I had less love or regard for Jerusha that I married so soon, but it was for the sake of my children" (Pearson H. Corbett, *Hyrum Smith, Patriarch*, 164).

A great love developed between Hyrum and his second wife, Mary. Several years before their marriage, Parley P. Pratt converted Mary and her brother and sister to the Church during his mission to Canada. Parley P. Pratt recorded:

> My first visit to the country was about nine miles from Toronto, among a settlement of farmers. . . . John Taylor accompanied me—this was before he was baptized—we rode on horseback. We called at a Mr. Joseph Fielding's, an acquaintance and friend of Mr. Taylor. This man had two sisters, young ladies, who seeing us coming ran from their house to one of the neighboring houses, lest they should give welcome, or give countenance to "Mormonism."
>
> Parley asked Joseph why his sisters had run away. "Ah why do they oppose Mormonism?"

JOSEPH F. SMITH served as President from 1901–1918.

"I don't know, but the name has such a contemptible sound; and, another thing, we do not want a new revelation or a new religion contrary to the Bible."

"Oh, if that's all we shall soon remove your prejudices. Come, call home your sisters. . . . we will take supper with you and all go over to meeting together" (*Autobiography of Parley P. Pratt,* 128).

Mary and her sister returned home, fixed supper, and accompanied their brother and Elder Pratt to the meeting. A few days later, all three were baptized. The Fieldings moved to Kirtland, and there, Mary met Hyrum Smith. When they were married, Mary became the stepmother of five children. She greeted the challenge with enthusiasm and resourcefulness—qualities that helped her cope with problems she faced later in life. Her husband, Hyrum, was a special man who occupied a unique place in the hearts of his family and the Church. The Prophet Joseph and his older brother Hyrum had a particularly special relationship. Joseph said of Hyrum:

> Brother Hyrum, what a faithful heart you have got; . . . O how many are the sorrows we have shared together. . . .
> I could pray in my heart that all my brethren were like unto my beloved brother Hyrum, who possesses the mildness of a lamb, and the integrity of a Job, and in short, the meekness and humility of Christ; and I love him with that love that is stronger than death (Smith, *The Life of Joseph F. Smith,* 39-40).

JERUSHA BARDEN SMITH (1805–1837), first wife of Hyrum Smith. She died in childbirth when 32 years old.

In November of 1838, when the leaders of the Church were arrested and jailed, Joseph F. Smith was born in Far West, Missouri. His birth came less than two weeks after his father had been taken from his family. Mary described these difficult days in a letter that she wrote to her brother, who was serving a mission in England.

> I have, to be sure, been called to drink deep of the bitter cup; but you know, my beloved brother, this makes the sweet the sweeter. . . .
> You have, I suppose, heard of the imprisonment of my dear husband, with his brother Joseph, Elder Rigdon, and others, who were kept from us nearly six months; and I suppose no one felt the painful effects of their confinement more than myself. . . . My husband was taken from me by an armed force, at a time that I needed the kindest care and attention of such a friend, instead of which, the care of a large family was suddenly and unexpectedly left upon myself and, in a few days after, my dear little Joseph F. was added to the number. Shortly after his birth I took a severe cold, which brought on chills and fever; this, together with the anxiety of mind I had to endure, threatened to bring me to the gates of death. I was . . . entirely unable to take

any care of either myself or child; but the Lord was merciful in so ordering things that my dear sister could be with me all the time. Her child was five months old when mine was born; so she had strength given her to nurse them both, so as to have them do well and grow fast (Smith, *The Life of Joseph F. Smith*, 144).

Later, Joseph F. Smith wrote about what happened during his father's absence. The mobs returned to the Smith home and ransacked it while Mary lay ill in her bed. Baby Joseph nearly smothered when some of the mob threw some bedding on top of him.

After Hyrum was released from prison, he moved his family to Nauvoo. He was called to be on the Nauvoo Temple building committee, and Mary started an organization among the women called the Sisters Penny Subscription, which helped pay for nails and glass for the temple. As money was collected, some of the coins were kept at the Smith home. One day, when Joseph F. was about five years old, he found several dollars of the temple fund in his father's desk. He innocently put the money in his pocket and went out to play—happily jingling the coins. To his great consternation, one of the neighbors grabbed him, took him to his mother and accused him of stealing the money. Although he was perfectly innocent, he resolved never to forget the fear he experienced in being called a thief and promised himself that nothing like that would happen again.

MARY FIELDING SMITH (1809–1852), second wife of Hyrum Smith. They were married shortly after Jerusha's death.

Joseph F. was less than six years old when his father was martyred in Carthage. The impact of that terrible event remained vivid throughout his life. Later, as President of the Church, Joseph F. walked the streets of Nauvoo. He stopped at the spot where he saw his father for the last time and said, "This is the exact spot where I stood when the brethren came riding up on their way to Carthage. Without getting off his horse, Father leaned over in his saddle and picked me up off the ground. He kissed me good-bye and put me down again and I saw him ride away" (Preston Nibley, *The Presidents of the Church*, 183).

Joseph F. also always remembered the night when he found out that his father and uncle had been killed. "I remember the night of the murder," he said, "when one of the brethren came from Carthage and knocked on our window after dark and called to my mother, 'Sister Smith, your husband has been killed'" (Nibley, *The Presidents of the Church*, 183).

His mother's screams and cries were etched deeply into the impressionable boy's memory. After Hyrum's death, Mary cared for her family; however, when the exodus from Nauvoo began, she was forced to leave the city, even though she was not fully prepared. She loaded her children and whatever belongings

JOSEPH FIELDING (1797–1863), brother of Mary Fielding Smith who accompanied her to the Salt Lake Valley.

they could carry into a flat boat and crossed the Mississippi River, where they camped under a tree and listened to the roar of guns in Nauvoo.

Mary sold some property, and bought wagons, teams of oxen, and supplies so she could move her family to Winter Quarters. Eight-year-old Joseph drove one of the ox teams.

As Mary was preparing to cross the plains, she and her brother took young Joseph with them on a trip to buy supplies. On the way, they camped near some men with a herd of cattle. The oxen were turned out to graze, but their neck-yokes were left on to keep them from being driven off with the cattle. However, the next morning, their best yoke of oxen was missing. Joseph and his uncle spent all morning searching for the missing animals, but they returned to the wagons tired and discouraged. Joseph recalled:

I was the first to return to our wagons, and as I approached I saw my mother kneeling down in prayer. I halted for a moment and then drew gently near enough to hear her pleading with the Lord not to suffer us to be left in this helpless condition, but to lead us to recover our lost team, that we might continue our travels in safety. When she arose from her knees I was standing nearby. The first expression I caught upon her precious face was a lovely smile. . . . A few moments later Uncle Joseph Fielding came to the camp. His first words were:

"Well, Mary, the cattle are gone." . . .

"Never mind; your breakfast has been waiting for hours, and now while you and Joseph are eating, I will just take a walk out and see if I can find the cattle."

"Why, Mary, what do you mean? We have been all over this country, all through the timber and through the herd of cattle, and our oxen are gone. . . . I believe they have been driven off, and it is useless for you to attempt to do such a thing as to hunt for them."

"Never mind me. . . . get your breakfast and I will see" (Smith, *The Life of Joseph F. Smith*, 131-33).

Before she was out of speaking distance, the man in charge of the herd of cattle rode up and called out, "Madam, I saw your oxen over in that direction this morning about daybreak" (Smith, *The Life of Joseph F. Smith*, 133).

She ignored him and headed toward a little stream. When she reached the stream, she turned and beckoned to her brother and son. Joseph wrote, "I was watching her every moment. . . I outran my uncle and came first to the spot where my mother stood. There I saw our oxen fastened to a clump of willows growing in the bottom of a deep gulch. . . . We were not long in releasing them from bondage and getting back to our camp . . . and we were soon on our way home, rejoicing" (Smith, *The Life of Joseph F. Smith*, 133).

This incident made a deep impression on Mary's young son. Later, he wrote, "It was one of the first practical and positive demonstrations of the efficacy of prayer I had ever witnessed. It made an indelible impression upon my mind, and has been a source of comfort, assurance and guidance to me throughout all of my life" (Smith, *The Life of Joseph F. Smith*, 133–34).

Mary Smith and her children spent nearly two years at Winter Quarters preparing to travel to Utah. Several other widowed women joined her group, and in the spring of 1848, Mary finally felt sufficiently prepared to make the trek. Nine-year-old Joseph was in charge of driving a team of oxen. Just as they were ready to leave Winter Quarters, the supervisor of their company visited their camp. When he saw how seemingly helpless they were, he advised them to remain in Winter Quarters another year.

> "If you start out in this manner, you will be a burden on the company the whole way and I will have to carry you along or leave you on the way."
>
> " . . . I will beat you to the valley and will ask no help from you, either."
>
> " . . . You can't get there without help, and the burden will be on me" (Smith, *The Life of Joseph F. Smith*, 147–49).

CROSSING THE PLAINS. The Saints prepared to leave Winter Quarters and travel to the Salt Lake Valley. *ca. 1865–1869*

Joseph was hurt by the treatment his mother received because he knew how hard she had worked to bring her family this far. He wrote, "She had trusted with the most implicit faith in God for deliverance from the jaws of death, for Winter Quarters was a most sickly place at that time . . ." (Smith, *The Life of Joseph F. Smith*, 147).

Mary Smith and her family finally started their trek across the plains. They had just crossed the Platte River when one of her oxen lay down and seemed to be dying. The company leader was angry about the delay. He said, "There, I told you you would have to be helped and that you would be a burden on the company" (Smith, *The Life of Joseph F. Smith*, 150-51).

But he was mistaken. Mary Smith asked her brother and a friend if they would administer to the ox just as they would a sick person. It was vital that the ox be restored to health. After the men blessed the animal, it immediately rose to its feet, and in a few moments, it was ready to be re-hitched to the wagon.

When the group finally reached the East Mountain, they glimpsed the Salt Lake Valley. The morning they were to travel down Emigration Canyon, Mary found that her oxen had wandered off. The captain ordered the others to hitch up their wagons and start down the trail. Mary and her family were left behind to search for their missing teams alone. However, just as the company was

PIONEERS ENTER THE SALT LAKE VALLEY *by Valoy Eaton* portrays the arrival of the first wagon train in Emigration Canyon, July 23, 1847. The lead company of pioneers traveled down Big Mountain Creek, took the steep trail to the top of Little Mountain, then descended to Emigration Canyon. *oil on canvas 1986*

ascending the last hill, a terrific thunderstorm crashed down on them. Their animals became terrified and had to be unhitched from the wagons. As the storm raged, the animals fled into a gully. As soon as the storm ended, Mary's oldest son rode up with her oxen. They hitched up their wagons and soon were on their way. Mary's brother Joseph asked, "Mary, what shall we do? Go on, or wait for the company to gather up their teams?"

"Joseph . . . they have not waited for us, and I see no necessity for us to wait for them" (Smith, *The Life of Joseph F. Smith*, 154-55).

Much to the chagrin of the company captain, Mary's little group passed by the main company and arrived in the valley that evening. The next morning, she gathered with others to welcome the rest of the company to the valley.

Just four years after arriving in Salt Lake City, Mary died. Thirteen-year-old Joseph was left an orphan. At age fifteen, he was called on a mission during the April 1854 general conference. He was sitting comfortably, enjoying the words of the First Presidency, when Brigham Young came to the pulpit. Joseph was shocked when President Young read the names of those called on missions, indicating that Joseph would go to the Pacific Isles.

Twenty other missionaries were also called to the Pacific Islands. They traveled by wagon train to California and then boarded a ship to Hawaii. When Joseph arrived, he was seriously ill with a fever; upon his recovery, he was assigned to labor in Kula on Maui. He became very discouraged and lacked self-confidence. However, one night he had a dream that helped him in his missionary labors.

LAIE, HAWAII
Many Hawaiian Saints were converted on the island of Oahu, and Laie, on the northern shore of the island, became the site of both the Polynesian Cultural Center and the Brigham Young University Hawaii campus.

> I dreamed that I was on a journey, and I was impressed that I ought to hurry—hurry with all my might for fear I might be too late. . . .I was only conscious of having just a little bundle. . . . I did not realize just what it was, when I was hurrying as fast as I could; but finally I came to a wonderful mansion. . . . As I passed towards it, as fast as I could, I saw a notice, "Bath." I

JOSEPH F. SMITH, son of Hyrum Smith and Mary Fielding. He served thirty-five years as an Apostle, and seventeen years as President of the Church.

turned aside quickly and went into the bath and washed myself clean. I opened up this little bundle that I had, and there was a pair of white, clean garments. . . . I put them on. Then I rushed to what appeared to be a great opening, or door. I knocked and the door opened, and the man who stood there was the Prophet Joseph Smith. He looked at me a little reprovingly, and the first word he said [was], "Joseph, you are late." Yet I took confidence and said, "Yes, but I am clean—I am clean!" He clasped my hand and drew me in. . . . I felt his hand just as tangible as I ever felt the hand of man. I knew him, and when I entered I saw my father, and Brigham, and Heber and Willard, and the other good men that I had known. . . .

When I awoke that morning I was a man, although only a boy. There was not anything in the world that I feared. I could meet any man or woman or child and look them in the face, feeling in my soul that I was a man every whit. That vision, that manifestation and witness that I enjoyed at the time has made me that I am, if I am anything that is good, or clean, or upright before the Lord, if there is anything good in me. That has helped me out in every trial and through every difficulty.

Now, I suppose that is only a dream? To me, it is a reality. . . . When I woke up I felt as if I had been lifted out of a slum, out of despair, out of the wretched condition that I was in; . . . I was not afraid of any white man nor of anyone else, and I have not been very much afraid of anybody else since that time. I know that that was a reality, to show me my duty, to teach me something, and to impress upon me something that I cannot forget. I hope it never can be banished from my mind (Smith, *The Life of Joseph F. Smith*, 445-47).

When Joseph turned sixteen, he was called to preside over the Island of Maui. After he became proficient in the Hawaiian language, he became a very successful missionary.

When he returned home to Utah, President Young greeted Joseph with great affection, and suggested that he join the men who were preparing to protect the valley from government troops. Joseph readily joined, and when it seemed that the city was about to be invaded by government forces, he helped with the evacuation of Salt Lake City, then stayed behind ready to set fire to the buildings if the soldiers tried anything.

After the soldiers passed through the city peacefully, Joseph helped his neighbors and relatives return to their homes. In the process, he became reacquainted with a cousin, Levira Smith, a charming sixteen-year-old who had grown up while he was away on his mission. Romance blossomed and, on April 5, 1859, they were married. The newlyweds had only one year together before Joseph was called on a mission to the British Isles.

On his way back east, Joseph and his companions stopped in Nauvoo. Although it had been sixteen years since his father had been martyred in Carthage, tender and painful memories came flooding back.

As he was leaving Nauvoo, Joseph met some rough characters who, for no apparent reason, were cursing Mormons. The profanities and the memories of his childhood filled Joseph with apprehension. When a Catholic priest asked him where he was from, he said:

> "Oh, from the West."
> "How far west?"
> "From the Rocky Mountains."
> "Are you 'Mormon' elders from Utah?"
> [Joseph was afraid for his life, and never before had he been so tempted to lie, but he replied:] "Yes, sir, we are 'Mormon' missionaries on our way to England" (Joseph F. Smith, *Gospel Doctrine*, 533).

The man then allowed them to go on their way.

Joseph F. Smith served his mission to Great Britain, and as soon as he returned home, he was called on another mission to the Hawaiian Islands. He was with Lorenzo Snow's group when Lorenzo almost drowned.

When the group was ready to transfer from their ship to a small boat that was to take them ashore, the waves were exceptionally high. Joseph F. refused to enter the small, unstable boat since he was well acquainted with the ocean and knew how foolish it was to attempt a landing. His older companions, feeling that he was being somewhat disobedient, left him on the ship and boarded the small boat. As the men were making their way to shore, the small boat overturned and only through a miracle was the life of Lorenzo Snow preserved. After this event, Lorenzo Snow declared that the Lord had revealed to him that Joseph F. Smith would someday be the Prophet.

When Joseph F. Smith turned twenty-six years old, he was ready to settle into a profession. However, for more than eleven years, he had been serving missions and had little experience in any trade. He started working in the Church

JULINA LAMBSON
SMITH (1849–1936),
second wife of Joseph
F. Smith. She was
George A. Smith's niece.
ca. 1890–1910

HISTORIAN'S OFFICE,
where Joseph F. Smith
worked was on South
Temple street. *ca. 1865*

historian's office under the direction of his cousin, George A. Smith. George taught Joseph F. the skills he needed and augmented Joseph's limited education. About this time, Brigham Young asked Joseph F. Smith to consider entering into polygamy. With the permission of his first wife, Joseph F. asked a niece of George A. Smith, Julina Lambson, to marry him.

Joseph F. later married four other wives, Sarah Ellen Richards, Edna Lambson, Alice Ann Kimball, and Mary Taylor Swartz. He had forty-three children of his own and adopted five others; he was a devoted father and husband. He said of his children:

> Oh! who can compare with or what is so precious and priceless as a loving mother! How God has blessed me with pure and loving wives and my children with darling, precious mamas! To be untrue to them in word or thought or deed, would be a crime of awful magnitude, either in myself or in my children. I would not for all this world willfully wrong one of them, nor cease to love them—for they love me and mine! And truer wives have never lived, nor more loving mothers, nor better women, according to their knowledge. Not only would they die for me but they live for me and my happiness, and they have been not only faithful to me but to my children and to God (Smith, *The Life of Joseph F. Smith*, 451).

The one great tragedy in Joseph F. Smith's otherwise happy family was the fact that his first wife, Levira, was never able to have children. She became despondent over her inability to conceive and, hoping to restore her health, left Utah and went to California. She later moved to St. Louis, Missouri, where she died on December 18, 1888.

Shortly after becoming a father, Joseph F. Smith was called to be an Apostle. On July 1, 1866, Joseph F. met with President Brigham Young and several of the Apostles in the upper room of the historian's office. Joseph was serving as a secretary of the council, and after the close of the prayer circle, President Young suddenly turned to his brethren and said, "Hold on, shall I do as I feel led? I always feel well to do as the Spirit constrains me. It is my mind to ordain Brother Joseph F. Smith to the Apostleship, and to be one of my counselors" (Smith, *The Life of Joseph F. Smith*, 226-27).

JOSEPH F. SMITH AND FAMILY
President Smith is seated center; Mary Shwartz, wife, is seated left; Edna Lambson, wife, is seated second from left; Julina Lambson, wife, is seated third from left; Sarah Richards, wife, is seated third from right; Alice Kimball, wife, is seated second from right; children and grandchildren. *1898*

Each member of the group was asked about his feelings in the matter, and all gave their approval. Joseph was ordained right then and there. However, President Young asked that the ordination not be made public until the 1867 October general conference.

Joseph moved to Provo and was elected to the Territorial House of Representatives. He resigned from this position when he was called to serve as President of the European Mission.

When he arrived in Liverpool, the overwhelming number of pubs in the town intrigued Joseph. He and an assistant counted forty-two pubs within a mile radius of mission headquarters. In the same area, there were only five churches.

While supervising the European area, he arranged transportation for many new converts who were emigrating to Utah to gather in the mountains of the West.

Joseph F. often saw humor in his life. During a bout with rheumatism that was aggravated by the fog and rain of a dreary autumn, he wrote, "Dirty days hath September, April, June, and November. From January up to May, the rain, it raineth every day. All the rest have 31 without a blessed gleam of sun."

On his thirty-sixth birthday, Joseph recorded in his diary:

JOSEPH F. SMITH
as a young man.

The day was cold, bleak and dreary, a fit and proper anniversary of the dark and trying day of my birth when my father and his brethren were confined in a dungeon for the Gospel's sake. . . . The bright sunshine of my soul has never thoroughly dispelled the darkening shadows cast upon it by the lowering gloom of that eventual period; yet the merciful hand of God and His kindliest providences have ever been extended visibly towards me, even from my childhood; and my days grow better and better, through humility and the pursuit of wisdom and happiness in the Kingdom of God. The objects of my life become more apparent as time advances and experience grows. Those objects being the proclamation of the Gospel, or the establishment of the Kingdom of God on the earth, the salvation of souls—and the most important of which to me is that of my family. The richest of all my earthly joys is in my precious children. Thank God! (Smith, *The Life of Joseph F. Smith*, 449).

Almost as soon as he returned from this mission, he was asked to return to England and serve again. This time he took one of his wives. However, they were in England only three months when President Brigham Young died.

After President Young's death, all of the Apostles were asked to return to Salt Lake City.

The Church entered a period of persecution because of the practice of polygamy, and most of the Apostles, including Joseph F. Smith, went into hiding. Joseph and his wife Julina went to Hawaii, where they stayed until the death of President John Taylor. When they briefly returned to Salt Lake City, Joseph was called to represent the Church in the eastern United States.

On October 17, 1901, just shortly after the death of Lorenzo Snow, Joseph F. Smith was set apart as President of the Church at a special general conference. When the action of the Quorum of the Twelve was ratified, President Smith commented about the order of the priesthood: "But there is one presiding President, and his two counselors are Presidents also. I propose that my counselors and fellow Presidents in the First Presidency shall share with me in the responsibility of every act which I shall perform in this capacity" (Smith, *The Life of Joseph F. Smith*, 322-23).

Three days after delivering this address, President Joseph F. Smith celebrated his 63rd birthday. He was at his height of mental and spiritual powers. He carried 185 pounds on a well-proportioned, 5-foot, 11-inch frame. His full

JOSEPH F. SMITH'S
FIRST PRESIDENCY
Anthon H. Lund
(1844–1921),
President Joseph F.
Smith, and John
Henry Smith
(1848–1911).
ca. 1910

beard and gray hair framed a strong face with steady brown eyes. President Smith was fond of music and sports. However, as far as sports went, he preferred to participate rather than watch. In later years, he took up golf and, although the game exasperated him at times, he became quite good. Charles Nibley recorded the following incident that occurred while he was playing golf with President Smith.

. . . We were up within about one hundred feet at the flag of the hole we were making for. A light stroke should have driven the ball nearer the flag, but the inclination to look as one tries to hit the ball got the best of him, and the consequence . . . was he topped the ball and it rolled only a couple of feet or so. He bent over for the next stoke, when he topped it again and it moved but a few feet further. The third time he went up to it and hit it a whack that sent it rolling one hundred feet beyond the flag. His son, Wesley, who was playing with us, called out, "Why papa, what did you do that for? You knew it would roll away down there in the ditch!" The President straightened up and said, with a smile, "Well, I was mad at it" (Smith, *Gospel Doctrine*, 520).

One of the most absorbing events during Joseph F. Smith's presidency concerned the hearings in Washington, D.C., about seating Utah Senator Reed Smoot, a member of the Twelve who was elected to the U.S. Senate. However, after the election, a flood of protests caused his election to be questioned. Finally, after two years of hearings, Reed Smoot was seated as the Senator from Utah. At the time, the Church was the target of widespread and harsh criticism due to the practice of polygamy. In the 1904 April general conference, Joseph F. Smith announced a worldwide manifesto concerning polygamy—reiterating the commandments contained in The Manifesto of 1890:

CHARLES WILSON NIBLEY (1849–1931), who played golf with President Smith.

UTAH SENATOR REED SMOOT (1862–1941), a member of the Quorum of the Twelve whose election to the U.S. Senate was questioned.

I hereby announce that all such marriages are prohibited, and if any officer or member of the Church shall assume to solemnize or enter into any such a marriage he will be deemed in transgression against the Church and will be liable to be dealt with, according to the rules and regulations thereof, and excommunicated therefrom (Smith, *The Life of Joseph F. Smith*, 374).

When the furor over polygamy died down and Church property was returned, the Church entered an era of comparative quiet. The auxiliaries, such as the Sunday School, the Primary, the Mutual Improvement Association, and the Relief Society, began to thrive. President Smith, worried that the auxiliaries might obscure the importance of the priesthood in the eyes of the young peo-

FIRST SEMINARY
BUILDING, GRANITE
HIGH SCHOOL
ca. 1912

ple, appointed a committee to study the issue and make recommendations. The committee recommended that the Church begin a correlation program where all of the auxiliaries would teach gospel doctrine.

President Smith also started several programs that are still part of the Church today. In 1912, the Granite Stake in Salt Lake City established a seminary program, and the school board granted the students permission to study Gospel subjects during the last two periods of the school day. This first seminary was quite formal and did not involve any social activities or class officers. However, the classes were popular, and the seminary program spread throughout the Church. Also at this time, the Church became the first charter member of the Boy Scouts of America. The third program that President Smith started was the family home evening. A loving father, President Smith enjoyed gathering his family around him at every opportunity. In 1915, the First Presidency issued this advice:

> We advise and urge the inauguration of a home evening throughout the Church, at which time Father and Mother may gather their boys and girls about them in the home and teach them the words of the Lord. This home

JOSEPH F. SMITH IN
LONDON, ENGLAND
Mission home on
Holly Road in
Liverpool, England.
Group portrait of
Joseph F. Smith with
wife Edna, and four
daughters; Charles
Dibley and two of
his daughters; Heber
J. Grant, his wife
Emily Grant, and
two of his daughters.
1906

evening should be devoted to prayer, singing hymns, songs, instrumental music, scripture reading, the family topics, and specific instructions on the principles of the Gospel and on the ethical problems of life. If the Saints obey this counsel, we promise that great blessings will result. Love at home and obedience to parents will increase, faith will be developed in the hearts of the youth of Israel, and they will gain power to combat the evil influences and temptations which beset them (*Messages of the First Presidency of the Church of Jesus Christ of Latter-day Saints*, 4:339).

President Smith was the first Prophet to visit Europe while serving as head of the Church. He made two trips to the continent, where he met with the Saints and encouraged the missionaries in a series of conferences. Returning from a trip abroad, his group crossed the United States by train. In the relative comfort of the train car, President Smith took a moment to reflect how things had changed, remembering how, in 1848, it had taken his

family four months to make a journey that now, by train, would take him less than three days.

As President Smith became older, his spiritual perceptions seemed to strengthen as his physical health declined. He spent the last several months of his life in meditation and prayer. During this time, he received an important vision. In the 1918 October conference, he told the Saints: "I have not lived alone these five months. I have dwelt in the spirit of prayer, of supplication, of faith and of determination, and I have had my communication with the Spirit of the Lord continuously . . ." (Smith, *The Life of Joseph F. Smith*, 466).

He then told the congregation about an experience he had had the night before. He had been sitting in his study in the Beehive House, reading the scriptures and preparing for conference. He said he was impressed as never before with the great themes of the Atonement, the Redemption, and the exaltation of mankind. He told the Saints:

> I opened the Bible and read the third and fourth chapters of the first epistle of Peter, and as I read, I was greatly impressed, more than I had ever been before. . . .
>
> As I pondered over these things which are written, the eyes of my understanding were opened, and the Spirit of the Lord rested upon me and I saw the hosts of the dead, both small and great. And there were gathered together in one place an innumerable company of the spirits of the just, who had been faithful in the testimony of Jesus while they lived in mortality. . . . All these had departed the mortal life firm in the hope of a glorious resurrection, through the grace of God the Father and His Only Begotten Son, Jesus Christ.
>
> I beheld they were filled with joy and gladness, and were rejoicing together because the day of their deliverance was at hand. . . .
>
> While this vast multitude waited and conversed, rejoicing in the hour of their deliverance from the chains of death, the Son of God appeared, declaring liberty to the captives who had been faithful (Smith, *The Life of Joseph F. Smith*, 467-68).

President Smith then went on to tell how Jesus organized a missionary force.

> And as I wondered, my eyes were opened, and my understanding quickened and I perceived that the Lord went not in person among the wicked and the disobedient who had rejected the truth, to teach them; But behold, from among the righteous, he organized his force, and appointed his messengers, clothed with power and authority, and commissioned them to go forth and carry the light of the gospel to them that were in darkness, even to all the spirits of men. And thus was the gospel preached to the dead (Smith, *The Life of Joseph F. Smith*, 468-69).

Following that conference, President Smith recorded this vision, and several weeks later his counselors and the Twelve Apostles accepted it as scripture.

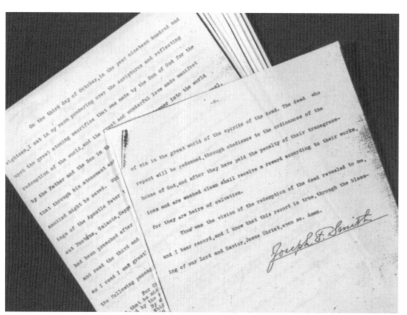

Nearly sixty years later, on April 3, 1976, the Vision of the Redemption of the Dead was formally accepted and authorized to be included as Section 138 in the Doctrine and Covenants.

On Sunday, November 17, 1918, President Smith suffered an attack of pleurisy, which quickly developed into pneumonia. He passed away two days later. At President Smith's graveside service, Heber J. Grant said:

TYPED COPY OF THE VISION of the Redemption of the Dead.

> No man that ever lived had a more powerful testimony of the Living God and of our Redeemer than Joseph F. Smith. From my earliest childhood days, he has thrilled my very being with the testimony that he has borne to all those with whom he had come in contact, bearing witness that he knew that God lives and that Jesus is the Christ, the Son of the Living God, the Redeemer of the world. The very spirit of inspiration that was with this man found lodgment in my heart and in the hearts of many others. I loved Joseph F. Smith as I never loved any other man that I have ever known. May God bless his memory (Nibley, *The Presidents of the Church*, 208-9).

In 1918, the country was in the grip of a deadly flu epidemic. In two years, twenty-two million people died from the illness. With thousands dying, public gatherings were canceled to control the spread of the disease. In Salt Lake City, there was no public funeral for President Joseph F. Smith because of the epidemic. Four days after the funeral, President Heber J. Grant was sustained and set apart as the seventh President of the Church.

WORLD EVENTS

As the twentieth century entered its teens, some of the optimism, excitement, and hope for the future had worn off. The world had fought a major war, aristocracies had fallen, and social unrest was on the rise. Ladies were bobbing their hair, and Mary Pickford became everyone's darling when she appeared in the film *The Little Princess*. Jazz became the new musical craze. Sigmund Freud published his *Introduction to Psychoanalysis*, and German Physicist Max Planck won the Nobel Prize for introducing the Quantum Theory. Daylight Savings Time was introduced in America, and regular airmail service was offered by the post office.

JOSEPH F. SMITH AND HIS WIFE, JULINA

HEBER J.

GRANT

Dynamo of Enthusiasm

In 1856, the Church underwent a reformation of sorts. Saints were asked to renew their baptismal covenants, put their families in order, cultivate their gardens, and care for their homes. Jedediah M. Grant, Heber's father, was one of the most ardent advocates of the reformation. He often held two or three meetings a night and was exhausted from overwork. He died eight days after his son, Heber, was born on November 22, 1856. Heber was given his father's nickname, Jeddie, as a middle name. When he was older, his mother asked him if he remembered an incident that happened in his childhood when Heber C. Kimball picked him up, sat him on a table and talked to him.

"Yes."

"Do you remember anything he said?"

"No, I only remember that he had the blackest eyes I ever looked into. I was frightened. That is all I can remember."

"He prophesied in the name of the Lord Jesus Christ that you would become an Apostle of the Lord Jesus Christ and become a greater man in the church than your own father, and your father, as you know, became one of the counselors to President Brigham Young."

My mother always told me, "Behave yourself, Heber, and someday you will be an apostle. If you do

HEBER J. GRANT served as President from 1918–1945.

not behave yourself, you will not be because we have, in a revelation recorded in the Doctrine and Covenants, the following statement: 'There is a law irrevocably decreed in Heaven before the foundation of the world upon which all blessings are predicated and when we obtain any blessing from God, it is by obedience to that law upon which it is predicated.'"

I said, "Mother, get it out of your head. I do not want to be an Apostle. I do not want to be a bishop. I do not want to be anything but a businessman. Just get it out of your head."

After I was called to be an Apostle, she said, "That is why I have told you to behave." (Bryant S. Hinckley, *Life of a Great Leader*, 26-27).

After his father died, Heber's mother became the dominant influence in his life. Some things were difficult for Heber, but he was determined to learn new skills, one of which involved learning to play baseball.

When I joined a baseball club, the boys of my own age and a little older played in the first nine; those younger than I played in the second, and those still younger in the third, and I played with them.

One of the reasons for this was that I could not throw the ball from one base to the other. Another reason was that I lacked physical strength to run or bat well. When I picked up a ball, the boys would generally shout: "Throw it here, sissy!"

So much fun was engendered on my account by my youthful companions that I solemnly vowed that I would play baseball in the nine that would win the championship in the Territory of Utah.

My mother was keeping boarders for a living, and I shined their boots until I saved a dollar which I invested in a baseball. I spent hours and hours throwing the ball at Bishop Edwin D. Woolley's barn, . . . Often my arm would ache so that I could scarcely go to sleep at night. But I kept on practicing and finally succeeded in getting into the second nine of our club. Subsequently I joined a better club, and eventually played in the nine that won the championship . . . [in] California, Colorado, and Wyoming. Having thus made good my promise to myself, I then retired from the baseball arena (Heber J. Grant, *Gospel Standards*, 343).

Heber's mother, Rachel Ridgeway Ivins Grant, was a marvelous woman who understood his desires to improve himself. Referring to his wonderful mother, Heber recalled,

. . . the one day we had at least a half dozen, if not more, buckets on the floor catching the rain that came from the roof. It was raining very heavily and Bishop Edwin D. Woolley came to the house and said:

"Why, Widow Grant, this will never do. I shall take some of the money from the fast offering and put a new roof on this house."

Heber Jeddy Grant was the son of Jedediah and Rachel Ridgeway Ivins Grant. He was an only child; his middle name was Jeddy after his dad. Nothing that he did came easy to him, but he worked very hard at making himself proficient in skills he desired to improve. It was customary to clothe both young boys and girls in dresses at this time. *ca. 1860*

"Oh, no, you won't. No relief money will ever put a roof on my house. I have sewing here. When I get through with this sewing that I'm doing now, I'll buy some shingles and patch the holes, and this house will take care of me until my son gets to be a man and builds a new one for me."

Bishop Woolley went away and said he was very sorry for Widow Grant and that if she waited for that boy to build a house, she would never have one, for he was the laziest boy in the whole Thirteenth Ward. He went on to tell how I wasted my time throwing a ball across the fence behind the house, hour after hour, day after day, week after week at his adobe barn. Thank the Lord for a mother . . . who realized that it is a remarkable and splendid thing to encourage a boy if he had ambitions along athletic lines (Grant, *Gospel Standards*, 344).

Heber seemed to know very early in his life that he wanted to be in business when he grew up. One day he was playing marbles with some boys when the bookkeeper from Wells Fargo Bank walked down the other side of the street. One of the boys remarked that he had heard that the man made one hundred and fifty dollars a month.

Heber figured to himself that, not counting Sundays, the man made six dollars a day. Then he figured that, at five cents a pair, he would have to polish 120 pairs of boots to make six dollars. At that moment, he resolved that someday he would be a bookkeeper in the Wells Fargo Bank. But a good bookkeeper needed to learn to write well. He decided that his first step in securing this job would be to become a good penman. At first, his penmanship was so poor that some of his friends said:

"That writing looks like hen tracks."

"No, it looks as if lightning had struck an ink bottle."

His friends' talk touched Heber's pride, and he said, "I'll some day be able to give you fellows lessons in penmanship" (Hinckley, *Life of a Great Leader*, 40).

Just as in baseball, Heber practiced his penmanship. He became so proficient that he was asked to write greeting cards, wedding cards, insurance policies, stock certificates, and legal documents. He later recorded: "I once made $20.00 on New Year's Day by writing forty dozen cards with . . . a man's name written in the corner. The next New Year's Day I made $37.50 in five hours. I wrote on fifty dozen cards the words "Happy New Year," and sold them and had to write more" (Hinckley, *Life of a Great Leader*, 40).

While still in his teens, Heber was offered three times his salary to go to San Francisco as a penman. Although he declined the offer, he later became a teacher of penmanship. George D. Piper wrote of Heber: "He was a teacher of penmanship and bookkeeping at the University of Deseret. I was a student and recall his going from seat to seat inspecting the work of pupils. His style became my model. Many sheets of paper were used up with his copy before me" (Hinckley, *Life of a Great Leader*, 40-41).

When he was fifteen, Heber was hired as a bookkeeper and policy clerk, but he wanted to learn more about business.

I wrote a very nice hand, and that was all that was needed to satisfactorily fill the position which I then had. Yet I was not fully satisfied but con-

THIRTEENTH WARD MEETINGHOUSE located at 143 East 200 South in Salt Lake City. Heber J. Grant and his mother lived in the thirteenth ward. Bishop Woolley once called Heber a lazy boy because he spent so much time practicing throwing a ball. *ca.1890*

tinued to dream and scribble when not otherwise occupied. . . . when not busy I volunteered to assist with the bank work and do anything and everything I could to employ my time, never thinking whether I was to be paid for it or not, but having only a desire to work and learn (Hinckley, *Life of a Great Leader*, 41-42).

When Heber was nineteen, he had so impressed the Wells Fargo agent that the company hired him, and he fulfilled one of his boyhood dreams.

Since his mother was a struggling widow, much of his childhood entertainment was homemade. When he wanted to see the performances in the Salt Lake Theater, he got a job carrying water to the people in the third gallery. Heber J. Grant also tried to learn to sing.

My mother tried to teach me when I was a small child to sing but failed because of my inability to carry a tune. Upon joining a singing class taught by Professor Charles J. Thomas, he tried and tried in vain to teach me when ten years of age to run the scale or carry a simple tune, and finally gave up in despair. He said that I could never, in this world, learn to sing. . . . Ever since this attempt, I have frequently tried to sing when riding alone many miles from anyone who might hear me, but on such occasions could never succeed in carrying the tune of one of our familiar hymns for a single verse, and quite frequently not for a single line (Grant, *Gospel Standards*, 351).

Heber wanted to sing so badly that he told one of his employees that he would gladly give two or three months of spare time if he could learn to sing even one or two hymns. The employee offered to teach him. The first hymn he tried to learn was "O My Father." After four or five days, he was able to sing the hymn with his instructor without any mistakes. After two weeks, he was able to sing it alone—although he was a little flat on the high notes. He kept working, and soon was able to sing about a half a dozen hymns. Finally, he decided to sing in public to encourage young people to learn to sing.

I attempted to sing "O My Father" in the big Tabernacle, hoping to give an object lesson to young people, and to encourage them to learn to sing. I

HEBER J. GRANT as
young man.

made a failure, getting off the key in nearly every verse, and instead of my effort encouraging the young people, I fear that it tended to discourage them (Grant, *Gospel Standards*, 353).

Once, when traveling with Apostles Rudger Clawson and J. Golden Kimball, Heber asked if they had any objections to his singing 100 hymns that day.

> They took it as joke and assured me that they would be delighted. We were on the way back from Holbrook to St. Johns, a distance of about sixty miles. After I had sung about forty tunes, they assured me that if I sang the remaining sixty, they would have nervous prostration. I paid no attention whatever to their appeal, but held them to their bargain and sang the full one hundred (Grant, *Gospel Standards*, 354).

Heber J. Grant's perseverance in learning to play baseball, succeeding in business, or learning to sing, gave rise to an adage that he often quoted: "That which we persist in doing becomes easier to do. Not that the nature of the thing has changed, but our power to do is increased" (Grant, *Gospel Standards*, 355).

WELLS FARGO OVERLAND STAGECOACH The Wells Fargo Company hired Heber when he was nineteen years old.

As a teenager, Heber's great ambition was to go to college, but his mother's finances were not sufficient for him to attend school. However, an unexpected opportunity presented itself when he met President George Q. Cannon, the Utah delegate to Congress, who asked young Heber:

"Would you like to go to the naval academy or to West Point?"

"I would."

"Which one?"

"The naval academy."

"All right. I will give you the appointment without competitive examination."

For the first time in my life I did not sleep well; I lay awake nearly all night long, rejoicing that the ambition of my life was to be fulfilled. I fell asleep just a little before daylight; my mother had to wake me. I said: "Mother, what a marvelous thing it is that I am to have an education as fine as that of any young man in all Utah." . . . I looked into her face. I saw that she had been weeping. I have heard of people who, when drowning, had their entire life pass before them in almost a few seconds. I saw myself an admiral in my mind's eye. I saw myself traveling all over the world in a ship away from my widowed mother. I laughed and put my arms around her, and kissed her and said: "Mother, I do not want a naval education. I am going to be a business man and shall enter an office right away and take care of you, and have you quit keeping boarders for a living."

She broke down and wept and said that she had not closed her eyes but had prayed all night that I would give up my life's ambition so that she would not be left alone (Grant, *Gospel Standards*, 349).

Heber declined his appointment to Annapolis and went to work. Even though he never had any more formal education, he used his spare time to read and improve his mind. Just prior to his twenty-first birthday, Heber married Lucy Stringham, a dark-haired girl with lovely eyes.

A few years later, on November 1, 1877, Heber was ordained a high priest and called to preside over the Tooele, Utah, Stake. This appointment came as a great surprise to Heber because he had never anticipated such a calling. Years later he wrote, "As a boy of seventeen I dreamed about my future life—what I was going to do until I became thirty-five years of age; planned it and worked for it. The moment I was called to go to Tooele I said good-by to all my plans" (Hinckley, *Life of a Great Leader*, 36).

Heber relinquished his business interests and moved to Tooele. Prior to his call, he had few opportunities to speak in public. At his first two speaking assignments in Tooele, he ran out of things to say after about five minutes. At a speaking engagement in Grantsville, he again ran out of ideas. He later wrote:

> I made as complete a fizzle, so to speak, of my talk as a mortal could make. I walked several miles away from that meetinghouse, out into the fields among the hay and straw stacks; and when I got far enough away so that I was sure nobody saw me, I knelt down behind one of those stacks, and I shed tears of humiliation. I asked God to forgive me for not remembering that men cannot preach the Gospel of the Lord Jesus Christ with power, with force, and with inspiration, only as they are blessed with power which comes from God. And I told Him there that if He would forgive me for my egotism—if He would forgive me for imagining that without His Spirit any man can proclaim the truth and find willing hearts to receive it—to the day of my death, I would endeavor to remember from whence the inspiration comes. I am grateful to say that during the forty years that have passed since then, I have never been humiliated as I was humiliated that day. And why? Because I have never stood upon my feet with an idea that a man could touch the hearts of his hearers, except that man shall possess the Spirit of the Living God, and thus be capable of bearing witness that this is the truth that you and I are engaged in (Nibley, *The Presidents of the Church*, 226-27).

LUCY STRINGHAM GRANT (1858–1893) Heber J. Grant's first wife. *ca. 1840*

Two years later, just before his twenty-sixth birthday, Heber J. Grant was called to be an Apostle. Following his call, he began to have doubts about his worthiness to serve in such a high office. However, while in Arizona on Church business in 1883, Heber had an experience that confirmed his call.

> While on the Navajo Indian Reservation with Brigham Young, Jr., and a number of others, . . .I was riding along with Lot Smith at the rear of that procession. Suddenly the road veered to the left almost straight, but there was a well-beaten path leading ahead. I said: "Stop, Lot, stop. Where does this trail lead? There are plenty of footmarks and plenty of horses' hoof marks here."
>
> "It leads to an immense gully just a short distance ahead, that is impossible to cross with a wagon." . . .

World War I ended, and the United States was set on reform; the Eighteenth Amendment, which established prohibition, was passed. Archeologists in Egypt opened King Tut's tomb. Radio was becoming popular, and general conference was broadcast for the first time.

DAVID O. MCKAY AND HUGH J. CANNON in Egypt during their world mission.

"I want to be all alone. Go ahead and follow the crowd." . . .

As I was riding along to meet them on the other side, I seemed to see and I seemed to hear, what to me is one of the most real things in all my life. [I seemed to see a council in heaven] and I seemed to hear the words that were spoken. I listened to the discussion with a great deal of interest. The First Presidency and the Quorum of the Twelve Apostles had not been able to agree on two men to fill the vacancies in the Quorum of the Twelve. . . . In the council, the Savior was present, my father was there, and the Prophet Joseph Smith was there. . . . It was given to me that the Prophet Joseph Smith and my father mentioned me and requested that I be called to that position. I sat there and wept for joy. It was given to me that I had done nothing to entitle me to that exalted position, except that I had lived a clean, sweet life. It was also given to me that that was all these men, the Prophet and my father, could do for me. From that day it depended upon me and upon me alone as to whether I made a success of my life or a failure (Grant, *Gospel Standards*, 195).

When Heber became an Apostle, he had not been involved in business for very long. However, he had gained a reputation for absolute integrity. After he received his call to the Twelve, he received a letter from a prominent businessman who was not a member of the Church.

> I never thought very much of the leaders of the Mormon people, in fact, I thought they were a very bright, keen, designing lot of fellows, getting rich from the tithes that they gathered from a lot of ignorant, superstitious, and over-zealous religious people. But now that you are one the fifteen men at the head of the Mormon Church, I apologize to the other fourteen. I know that if there were anything crooked in the management of the Mormon Church you would give it all away (Grant, *Gospel Standards,* 70).

Thirty-six years before he became President of the Church, Heber learned some valuable leadership lessons. One of them was a difficult lesson about forgiveness. A prominent man had been excommunicated from the Church. Several years later, when the man wanted to be rebaptized, President John Taylor referred the question to the Apostles and told them that the man could be rebaptized if they unanimously agreed. After some discussion, all of the Twelve, with the exception of Heber J. Grant, agreed that the man could rejoin the Church.

Later, when Elder Grant was in President Taylor's office, the President said:

> "Heber, I understand that eleven of the apostles have consented to the baptism of Brother So and So . . . and that you alone are standing out. How

will you feel when you get on the other side and you find that this man has pleaded for baptism and you find that you have perhaps kept him from entering in with those who have repented of their sins and received some reward?"

"President Taylor, I can look the Lord squarely in the eye if He asks me that question, and tell Him that I did that which I thought was for the best good of the kingdom." . . .

"Well, my boy, that is all right. Stay with your convictions; stay right with them."

"President Taylor . . . if you desire me to surrender the convictions of my heart, I will gladly do it. I will gladly vote for this man to come back. But while I live I never expect to consent if it is left to my judgment." . . .

"My boy, don't you vote for him as long as you live, while you hold those ideas. Stay right with them" (Grant, *Gospel Standards*, 260-61).

Heber went home to lunch. As he was waiting for his meal, he began to read the Doctrine and Covenants. When he opened the book, he read, "Wherefore I say unto you, that ye ought to forgive one another, for he that forgiveth not his brother, his trespass standeth condemned before the Lord. I the Lord will forgive whom I will forgive, but of you it is required to forgive all men"(D&C 64:9-10). Heber closed the book and decided that, "If the devil applies for baptism and claims that he has repented, I will baptize him." He returned to President Taylor's office and said:

"I have had a change of heart. One hour ago I said never while I live, did I expect to ever consent that Brother So and So should be baptized, but I have come to tell you he can be baptized, so far as I am concerned."

"My boy, the change is very sudden, very sudden. I want to ask you a question. How did you feel when you left here an hour ago? Did you feel like you wanted to hit that man right squarely between the eyes and knock him down?"

"That is just the way I felt."

"Yes, and how do you feel now?"

"Well, to tell you the truth, President Taylor, I hope the Lord will forgive the sinner."

"You feel very happy, don't you, in comparison? You had the spirit of anger, you had the spirit of bitterness in your heart toward that man, because of his sin and because of the disgrace he had brought upon the Church. And now you have the spirit of forgiveness and you really feel happy, don't you?"

"Yes, I do. I felt mean and hateful and now I feel happy."

President Taylor then asked if Heber knew why he had written a letter to turn the matter over to the Apostles. When Heber indicated that he didn't, President Taylor explained:

"Well, I wrote it just so you and some of the younger members of the Apostles would learn the lesson that forgiveness is an advance of justice where there is repentance; and that to have in your heart the spirit of forgiveness and to eliminate from your hearts the spirit of hatred and bitterness, brings peace and joy; that the gospel of Jesus Christ brings joy, peace and happiness to every soul that lives it and follows its teachings" (Grant, *Gospel Standards*, 260-62).

Heber enjoyed his assignments in the Church, but no matter how busy he was, he always had time for his family. His wife, Lucy, died on January 3, 1892. She was thirty-five years old, and left behind five daughters and a small son. On the death of his wife, Heber said:

About one hour before my wife died, I called my children into her room and told them that their mother was dying and for them to bid her good-bye. One of the little girls, about twelve years of age, said to me:

"Papa, I do not want my mamma to die. I have been with you in the hospital in San Francisco for six months; time and time again, when mamma was in distress you had administered to her and she has been relieved of her pain and quietly gone to sleep. I want you to lay hands upon my mamma and heal her."

I told my little girl that we all had to die sometime, and that I felt assured in my heart that her mother's time had arrived. She and the rest of the children left the room.

I then knelt down by the bed of my wife . . . and I told the Lord I acknowledged His hand in life, in death, in joy, in sorrow, in prosperity, or adversity. But I told the Lord that I lacked the strength to have my wife die and to have it affect the faith of my little children in the ordinances of the gospel of Jesus Christ; and I supplicated the Lord with all the strength that I possessed, that He would give to that little girl of mine a knowledge that it was His mind and His will that her mamma should die.

Lucy Grant passed away and Heber called the children into the room. His little son, Heber, who was about six years old, was weeping bitterly. His daughter took her brother in her arms and said:

"Do not weep, do not cry, Heber; since we went out of this room the voice of the Lord from heaven has said to me: 'In the death of your mamma the will of the Lord shall be done'" (Grant, *Gospel Standards*, 361).

A year or so later, Heber's young son contracted a hip disease. Heber had looked forward to the day when his son would go on a mission and spread the gospel, but it was not to be. Just before his son died, Heber dreamed that the boy's mother had come for her son. He dreamed that he struggled with her and succeeded in keeping the boy. However, during the struggle, Heber dreamed that he stumbled and fell on his son, further injuring his hip.

I dreamed that I fell upon his sore hip and the terrible cries of anguish of the child drove me nearly wild. I could not stand it, and I jumped up and ran out of the house so as not to hear his distress. I dreamed that after running out of the house I met Brother Joseph E. Taylor and told him of these things. He said:

JOSEPH EDWARD
TAYLOR (1830–1913)
ca. 1840

"Well, Heber, do you know what I'd do if my wife came for one of her children—I would not struggle for that child, I would not oppose her taking that child away. If a mother who had been faithful had passed beyond the veil, she would know of the suffering and the anguish her child may have to suffer. She would know whether that child might go through life as a cripple and whether it would be better or wiser for that child to be relieved from the torture of life. And when you stop to think, Brother Grant, that the mother of that boy went down into the shadow of death to give him life, she's the one who ought to have the right to take him or leave him."

I said, " I believe you are right, Brother Taylor, and if she comes again, she shall have the boy without any protest on my part."

After coming to that conclusion, I was waked by my brother, B. F. Grant, who was staying that night with us. He called me into the room and told me that my child was dying. . . .

I felt the presence of that boy's deceased mother. . . . But I sat by the deathbed of my little boy and saw him die, without shedding a tear. No power on earth could have given to me this peace. It was of God (Grant, *Gospel Standards*, 364-66).

Heber was also married to Hulda Augusta Winters, who had one child and to Emily Harris Wells who had five children.

This good man and these wonderful women lived the patriarchal order of marriage as only unselfish, and God-fearing people could do. These women, and all women like them, who subscribed to and lived this divine law belong to the elect of God . . . (Hinckley, *Life of a Great Leader*, 83).

When Utah became a state in 1896, Heber was considered to be a strong candidate for governor, but he decided not to run. He also turned down an opportunity to be the vice president of New York Life. Heber later said, "I missed a great opportunity, but I am not sorry" (Hinckley, *Life of a Great Leader*, 69).

Heber was a very generous man, but most of his acts of charity were not widely known. His secretary, Joseph Anderson, knew of his willingess to help others financially, and wrote:

President Grant was the most liberal and generous man with his personal means that I have ever known; in fact, I doubt if any have excelled him in this respect. He trusted me with his personal means, and with a record of his income and expenditures. He was a man who thoroughly enjoyed making money, but not for the purpose of accumulating it. His only desire was to have money that he might do good with it. On various occasions, he would come to me and ask how much money was in his bank account. Knowing the purpose for which he wished this money, I hesitated at times to give it to him without reminding him of certain expenditures he would have to meet in the near future. Invariably he would ask me to draw a check for the amount he

ALBERTA, CANADA
TEMPLE DEDICATION
The temple was dedi-
cated by President
Heber J. Grant.
August 26, 1923

THE JUVENILE
INSTRUCTOR AND THE
IMPROVEMENT ERA

desired, perhaps for $1,000 or $1500, telling me to make the check in favor
of some widow whose name he would give explaining that he wished to pay
off the mortgage on her home (Hinckley, *Life of a Great Leader*, 202-3).

President Grant served as President of the Church for twenty-seven years. He dedicated temples in Hawaii; Alberta, Canada; and Mesa, Arizona. During his administration, the Tabernacle Choir began regular weekly network radio broadcasts, and President Grant gave the message at the first broadcast. He helped the Church purchase historic sites, such as the Hill Cumorah and the Whitmer Farm in upstate New York, and encouraged and helped publish *The Improvement Era*.

✦✦

The Great Depression hurt many members of the Church. President Grant and his counselors realized that government welfare programs could not begin to take care of those in need and established a Church Welfare System. President Grant outlined the purpose of the Church's program.

> Our primary purpose was to set up, in so far as it might be possible, a system under which the curse of idleness would be done away with, the evils of a dole abolished, and independence, industry, thrift, and self-respect be once more established amongst our people. The aim of the Church is to help the people to help themselves. Work is to be re-enthroned as the ruling principle of the lives of our Church membership (Grant, *Gospel Standards*, 123).

SALT LAKE TABERNACLE CHOIR members on the porch and sidewalk in front of John Sharp's home at 409 First Ave. in Salt Lake City, Utah. They had come to serenade Bishop Sharp and his family on New Year's Day. Director Thomas Griggs, future director Evan Stephens, conductor Ebenezer Beasley (sitting in front with full beard) and William C. Dunbar (holding bagpipes) are among those pictured. *January 1, 1883*

During President Grant's administration, the Junior Sunday School was officially recognized as a part of the ward organization, and he saw that the Church would become a great power for good in the world.

As President Grant aged, he became quite ill and several times was not able to speak in conference. One of his last acts was to call two new Apostles to fill vacancies in the Quorum of the Twelve. The men he called were Spencer W. Kimball and Ezra Taft Benson.

Just before his death in May of 1945, President Grant called his secretary, Joseph Anderson, to his bedside, where he asked Joseph if he had ever been unkind to him. Joseph Anderson assured President Grant truthfully that he never had been. President Grant's reaction was one of gladness.

President Heber J. Grant died at age eighty-eight on May 14, 1945. At the time of his death, a newspaper reporter wrote:

Tall, slender, bearded, gray and grave, of striking appearance and patriarchal bearing, President Grant might have stepped forth from an illustrated page of the Old Testament. Had he lived in those far distant days he would

HEBER J. GRANT AND HIS WIFE, EMILY WELLS GRANT in St. Mark's Square in Venice, Italy. *1906*

WORLD EVENTS

The stock market crash of 1929 precipitated the Great Depression of the "dirty thirties" in the United States. Millions were unemployed, poverty was rampant, and the outlook was indeed bleak. Repercussions spread to Europe and contributed to Hitler's rise to power in Germany. Franklin D. Roosevelt's New Deal lent some relief to these dire economic straits; ironically, however, it was heavy World War II-related defense spending that stimulated a complete economic recovery.

have seemed and no doubt felt, at ease and at home in the tents of Abraham, Isaac, and Jacob.

He would have taken high rank among the potentates and prophets of olden times as a shrewd and sagacious director of temporal affairs, a rigid disciplinarian in spiritual matters. . . .

It would have required no great stretch of imagination to picture him leading the children of Israel through the wilderness, counseling with tribesmen of Canaan about their flocks and herds, hurling anathemas at idolators from the foot of Sinai, driving the chariot of Jehu toward Jezreel, swinging the sword of Gideon against the Midianites, smiting the walls of Jericho in righteous wrath, or marching at the head of a triumphant legion singing "Hosannas to the Highest" (Hinckley, *Life of a Great Leader*, 260-61).

President Grant died just six days after the war in Europe ended. He had stood at the head of the Church for twenty-seven years and was the only Prophet many of the members had ever known. Following his death, George Albert Smith became the new leader of the Church.

WORLD EVENTS

In 1945, the world was again at war. The Nobel Prize in medicine was presented to the discoverers of penicillin—a miracle drug that saved thousands of soldiers who had been wounded in the war. James Thurber was writing humorous stories, and the music of Rodgers and Hammerstein's *Carousel* was being hummed on the streets of New York. Rocky Marciano was named boxer of the year. World War II had been a long and terrifying struggle, but on May 8, 1945, Germany surrendered.

HEBER J. GRANT'S FIRST PRESIDENCY: Charles W. Penrose (1832–1925), President Heber J. Grant, and Anthon H. Lund (1844–1921) seated in the north boardroom of the Church Administration Building.

JOSEPH ANDERSON, secretary to President Grant.

GEORGE ALBERT
SMITH

An Enemy to No One

When President Smith became the eighth President of the Church in 1945, he recalled the tremendous changes he had seen in Salt Lake City since his boyhood.

> I have lived long enough to see practically everything we have had come into this valley myself, and I am not a hundred years old either. I saw the first water pipes that were laid here, the first paving, the first lighting of the city streets, the first irrigation systems put into operation, the first bicycle. . . . also the telephone, the airplane, the radio, the railroad across the country. . . . My own grandfather was one of the men, with his associates, who built the Central Pacific Railroad from the west to where the gold spike was driven (George Albert Smith, *George Albert Smith Collection* 5:11-12).

Even though George Albert's parents were not wealthy, he often commented on how grateful he was to be a member of their family, remembering their humble home across from Temple Square, and the love and happiness that prevailed there. George was an exuberant youth who enjoyed doing everything that boys his age did in Salt Lake City. He

GEORGE ALBERT SMITH served as President from 1945–1951.

swam, herded cows, rode horses, and picnicked. When a friend, Lewis Peck, got a newspaper route, George began sleeping with a string tied to his big toe. He would dangle the string out his window and waited for Lewis to tug on the other end and awaken him so he could go with his friend on his early-morning deliveries.

When George was a child, he became ill with typhoid. The doctor recommended three weeks of bed rest and a diet of coffee. George refused to drink the coffee. Since his father was away on a mission, his mother sent for their home teacher, Brother Hawks. George recorded: "He administered to me and blessed me that I might be healed. When the doctor came next morning I was playing outside with other children. He was surprised. He examined me and discovered that my fever had gone and that I seemed to be well" (*Teachings of George Albert Smith*, ed. Robert and Susan McIntosh, 1).

George was also something of a daredevil. One day, he had a sledding accident that nearly killed him. Richard R. Lyman tells:

> He was an unusually bold and daring youth. The steeper the hills and the smoother the ice that covered them, the greater the thrill . . . when coasting on his sled. The streets of Salt Lake City were then lighted with gas lamps, and he went to his grave with a long scar on the side of his forehead as the result of an encounter with an iron gas lamp post which all but cost him his life (President George Albert Smith, *The Pioneer*, July, 1951).

When he was sixteen years old, George became a popular entertainer. He had taught himself to play the banjo, guitar, and harmonica, and developed into an accomplished performer. He could send his audiences into hysterics simply by dressing in a bold, plaid suit that emphasized his homely, gangly appearance. Once on stage, he would sing:

> I'm not very handsome, I know that I'm not.
> I'm as ugly as sin and I ought to be shot.
> My mouth is a feature that can't be forgot,
> If you travel east, west, north or south.
> Shut it, shut it, don't open it quite so wide,
> Shut it, shut it, I don't want to get inside.
> (Susan Arrington Madsen, *The Lord Needed a Prophet*, 119).

GEORGE ALBERT SMITH as a child. *1874*

As he was growing up, George noticed a little girl named Lucy Woodruff who lived nearby with her grandparents. The only way he could think of to get her to notice him was to tease her and pull on her braids. Lucy thought he was bothersome, and often walked several blocks out of her way to avoid passing his house. Her grandmother, on the other hand, thought George was a wonderful boy and often pointed out to Lucy how kind he was to his mother and younger brothers and sisters.

TABERNACLE DISASTER AVERTED
A few years later, on a hot afternoon in July, George was sitting with Lucy in a hammock on his grandparents' porch. As the two were talking, they noticed a large paper hot air balloon, lit by a candle, floating overhead, heading straight for the Tabernacle.

The young couple watched as the balloon hit the Tabernacle roof. The candle ignited the paper in a rush of flames and started a fire.

GEORGE ALBERT SMITH AND BROTHERS. George is shown seated in the chair. He was the second of eleven children born to John Henry Smith and Sarah Farr. George was known for his fun-loving personality.

George told the watchman to call the fire department, then ran to Temple Square. The large wooden gates were locked, so George and several others broke the gate open, and everyone worked together to douse the flames. Luckily, the fire only burned a six-foot hole in the roof. In a few more minutes the whole building could have been destroyed.

George eventually learned how to get Lucy's attention without tormenting her, and on May 1, 1892, she consented to marry him. They were married by George's father in the Manti Temple on May 25, 1892. However, just before their wedding, George was called on a mission to the Southern States. One month after the ceremony, he left for the mission field. At his first mission conference, he wrote:

> It was out in the woods on a farm in Mississippi. We didn't have comfortable seats to sit on. The brethren had been permitted to cut down a few trees and lay the trunks of those trees across the stumps which were left. We balanced ourselves on these or else sat on the ground. Our meeting started right after breakfast time, and we didn't even think it was necessary to have anything more to eat, until evening. We stayed and enjoyed the blessing of the inspiration of the Almighty, and we certainly were blessed, notwithstanding the inconveniences and discomforts which surrounded us. At that time there was considerable hostility manifested in Mississippi and other states in the South, but we just felt as though we had walked into the presence of our Heavenly Father, and all fear and anxiety left (George Albert Smith, *Sharing the Gospel with Others*, 16).

On this occasion the missionaries were not bothered, but sometimes the elders had to face angry mobs. One evening the mission president, J. Golden Kimball, and five missionaries, including George, were staying with a member in a small log cabin. About midnight, they were awakened by terrible shouts of obscenities outside. It was a bright, moonlit night and they could see a large group of men pounding on the door. They ordered the Mormons to come out or they would shoot. President Kimball jumped up and started to dress. The men pounded on the doors and used filthy language, ordering the Mormons to come out, that they were going to shoot them.

LUCY EMILY WOODRUFF SMITH (1869–1937), wife of George Albert Smith. *ca. 1840*

EARLY MISSIONARIES *Back row:* (l to r) George Albert Smith, Alex Campbell, Will Ingham, Allie Smith *Front row:* Frank Beatie, Hugh Dougall

President Kimball asked me if I was going to get up and dress and I told him "No I was going to stay in bed, that I was sure the Lord would take care of us." In just a few minutes the room was filled with shots. Apparently the mobs had divided into four groups and they were shooting into the corners of the house. Splinters were flying over our heads in every direction. There were a few moments of quiet, then another volley of shots was fired and more splinters flew. I felt absolutely no terror. I was very calm as I lay there, experiencing one of the most humble events of my life; but I was sure that as long as I was preaching the word of God and following his teachings that the Lord would protect me. And he did (Leon R. Hartshorn, comp. *Classic Stories From the Lives of Our Prophets*, 241).

Another experience also taught George the importance of listening to the still small voice.

J. GOLDEN KIMBALL, President of the Southern States Mission.

Late one evening in a pitch-dark night, Elder Stout and I were traveling along a high precipice. . . . Our mode of travel of necessity was very halting. We walked almost with a shuffle, feeling each foot of ground as we advanced, with one hand extended toward the wall of the mountain. I left the wall of the mountain, which had acted as a guide and a steadying force. After I had taken a few steps away I felt impressed to stop immediately, that something was wrong. I called to Elder Stout and he answered me. The direction from which his voice came indicated I was on the wrong trail, so I backed up until I reached the wall of the mountain and again proceeded forward. . . . [While we were climbing a fence], my little suitcase popped open and the contents were scattered around. In the dark I felt around for them and was quite convinced I had recovered practically everything. We arrived safely at our destination about eleven o'clock at night. I soon discovered I had lost my comb and brush, and the next morning we returned to the scene of my accident. I recovered my property and while there my curiosity was stimulated to see what had happened the night before when I had lost my way in the dark. As missionaries, we wore hob-nails in the bottoms of our shoes to make them last longer, so that I could easily follow our tracks in the soft dirt. I retraced my steps to the point where my tracks left and wandered to the edge of a deep precipice. Just one more step and I would have fallen over into the river and been drowned. I felt very ill when I realized how close I had come to death. I was also very grateful to my Heavenly Father for protecting me (Hartshorn, *Classic Stories From the Lives of Our Prophets*, 242-43).

After George returned home from his mission, he and his father helped found the Republican Party in Utah. Shortly after this, President William McKinley appointed George to be the receiver of the United States Land Office and special disbursing agent for Utah. He joined the Society of the Sons of the American Revolution and was later elected national vice president of this organization. His political involvement and his later prominence as a Church leader gave him access to many important people, including nine Presidents of the United States. George became particularly close friends with Theodore Roosevelt after the two men met while Roosevelt was campaigning in Utah. George recorded:

GEORGE ALBERT SMITH WITH HELEN KELLER

I was in Washington for the day and went to pay my respects. I handed my card to his clerk and told him I only wanted the President to know I had called. As I was leaving the building, the secretary overtook me and said, "The President desires to see you." When I went into his private office, he extended both hands and greeted me warmly. I apologized for intruding on such a busy man and his reply was: "I am very glad to see you and I never want you to come to Washington while I'm President of the United States without coming to see me" (Glen R. Stubbs, "A Biography of George Albert Smith, 1870 to 1951," 165).

George had some indications that he was destined for prominence in Church leadership. As a fourteen-year-old boy, he received his patriarchal blessing under the hands of Zebedee Coltrin, which stated: "Thou are destined to become a mighty man before the Lord, for thou shalt become a mighty Apostle in the church and kingdom of God upon the earth, for none of thy father's family shall have more power with God than thou shalt have, for none shall exceed thee" (Hartshorn, *Classic Stories From the Lives of Our Prophets*, 232).

PRESIDENT THEODORE ROOSEVELT (1858–1919) IN SALT LAKE CITY. Roosevelt visited Utah May 19, 1903. He was the first U.S. President to speak in the Tabernacle, and to speak favorably of the Mormons. Theodore Roosevelt became good friends with George Albert Smith while campaigning in Utah. *1903*

Because of his responsibilities at work, George was not able to attend general conference on October 6, 1903. When he arrived home, he was overwhelmed by people who came to express their congratulations to him for having been sustained that afternoon as a member of the Quorum of the Twelve. He was both surprised and humbled, feeling neither capable nor worthy, but completely willing to do his duty to the best of his ability.

That October, President Joseph F. Smith ordained Elder Smith a high priest and an Apostle. George's father, John Henry Smith, told his son that he had been greatly honored by both the Lord and the Quorum of the Twelve, reminding him of his "heritage of Apostleship," and trusting him to honor it.

This was the only time in history of the Church that a father and son served simultaneously in the Quorum of the Twelve. George was very conscious of the fact that he had been named after his grandfather. After a severe illness, he was recovering in St. George and had a remarkable dream.

I lost consciousness of my surrounding and thought I had passed to the Other Side. I found myself standing with my back to a large and beautiful lake, facing a great forest of trees. There was no one in sight. . . . I realized, or seemed to realize, that I had finished my work in mortality and had gone home. . . . I began to explore, and soon I found a trail through the woods which seemed to have been used very little. . . . I followed this trail, and after I had walked for some time and had traveled a considerable distance through the forest, I saw a man coming towards me. I became aware that he was a very large man, and I hurried my steps to reach him, because I recognized him as my grandfather. . . . I remember how happy I was to see him coming. I had been given his name and had always been proud of it.

When Grandfather came within a few feet of me, he stopped. His stopping was an invitation for me to stop. Then . . . he looked at me very earnestly and said:

"I would like to know what you have done with my name."

Everything I had ever done passed before me as though it were a flying picture on a screen—everything I had done. . . . I smiled and looked at my grandfather and said: " I have never done anything with your name of which you need be ashamed."

He stepped forward and took me in his arms, and as he did so, I became conscious again of my earthly surroundings. My pillow was wet as though water had been poured on it—wet with tears of gratitude that I could answer unashamed (Smith, *Sharing the Gospel with Others*, 110-12).

Several years later, he spoke in general conference and referred to the dream and how it changed his life.

JOHN HENRY SMITH
(1848–1911)
ca. 1910

I have been in the valley of the shadow of death in recent years, so near the other side that I am sure that except for the special blessings of our Heavenly Father I could not have remained here. But never for one moment did that testimony, that my Heavenly Father has blessed me with, become dimmed. The nearer I went to the other side, the greater was my assurance that the gospel is true. Now that my life has been spared, I rejoice to testify that I know the gospel is true, and with all my soul I thank the Father of us all that He has revealed it to me (Smith, *Sharing the Gospel with Others*, 40).

As the Saints became interested in purchasing and preserving important Church historical buildings and sites, a group of men, including George Albert Smith and Joseph F. Smith, met with Mr. Pliny Sexton who owned the Hill Cumorah. Mr. Sexton and Elder George Albert Smith became good friends. In 1909, Elder Smith wrote a letter to Mr. Sexton.

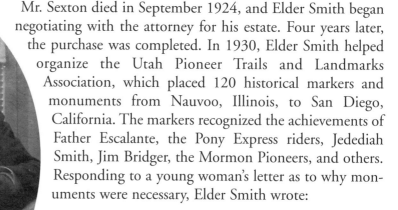

Mr. Sexton died in September 1924, and Elder Smith began negotiating with the attorney for his estate. Four years later, the purchase was completed. In 1930, Elder Smith helped organize the Utah Pioneer Trails and Landmarks Association, which placed 120 historical markers and monuments from Nauvoo, Illinois, to San Diego, California. The markers recognized the achievements of Father Escalante, the Pony Express riders, Jedediah Smith, Jim Bridger, the Mormon Pioneers, and others. Responding to a young woman's letter as to why monuments were necessary, Elder Smith wrote:

> It has been customary to build monuments to individuals that their memories might be retained. Great events have also been more permanently established in the minds of people by building monuments. In this part of the world there are many points of interest that are being forgotten and the people have felt that it was desirable to mark them in a substantial way so that those who follow will have their attention called to important events (Francis M. Gibbons, *George Albert Smith: Kind and Caring Christian, Prophet of God*, 139).

PLINY TITUS SEXTON (1839–1924) holding the proof sheets of the Book of Mormon.

Elder Smith also felt that the small marker used to represent where the first pioneers entered the Salt Lake Valley was a disgrace. He initiated plans for a new, larger monument, and Mahonri Young was commissioned for the project. Thirteen years later, on July 24, 1947—the 100th anniversary of the pioneers' arrival in the valley—the "This is the Place" monument was dedicated.

Elder Smith also encouraged the Saints to participate in the Scouting program. The Church adopted the Scouting program in 1912, just two years after it was introduced in America. When the Salt Lake Council was formed in 1919, George Albert Smith was chosen as a member of its executive board. In 1921, when he became the general superintendent of the Young Men's Mutual Improvement Association, he was given full responsibility for the LDS scouting program. In 1931, he was appointed to the executive board of the National Council, and suggested changes to strengthen and improve the program. For example, the National Council adapted the Church's program for older boys and created the Explorer Scout program.

Commenting on the subject of scouting, Elder Smith said, "There is nothing dearer to my heart than the welfare of the boys in our Church and in our neighborhood, and there is perhaps no other factor in our Mutual Improvement program which is being used more effectively for making fine manhood of boys than is this program of the Boy Scouts of America" (Gibbons, *George Albert Smith: Kind and Caring Christian, Prophet of God*, 112).

On May 21, 1945, in a meeting of the Quorum of the Twelve held in the Salt Lake Temple, George Albert Smith, who was seventy-five, was sustained and set apart as the President of the Church. President Smith was a kind and gentle man who enjoyed being outdoors. In his first editorial as editor of *The Improvement Era*, President Smith wrote:

> These many years as I have traveled up and down the world, I have come to know the faithful, devoted men and women of this Church. It has been my privilege

GEORGE ALBERT SMITH WITH FAMILY BY A PLANE (l to r) Lucy Woodruff Smith, George Albert Smith, Robert Murray Stewart, Jr. (first grandchild), Emily (mother of child, and daughter of George & Lucy), and Edith (daughter of George & Lucy).
GEORGE ALBERT SMITH'S FIRST PRESIDENCY with a group of men from Geneva Steel Company (David O. McKay, J. Reuben Clark on back row, left to right). *ca. 1949*

to partake of the spirit and hospitality of your homes, to feel the purpose of your lives, to sit with you in counsel—and it is my knowledge of you and your faithfulness, together with the sustaining hand of my Father in Heaven, that helps me to go on to meet any requirement and any service that may be expected of me in the days ahead (George Albert Smith, Editor's Page, *Improvement Era*, July 1945, 98).

President George Albert Smith led the Church through a difficult time in world history, and he was uniquely suited to help the world rebuild following the ravages of World War II. Patriarch Joseph F. Smith commented on the reorganization of the First Presidency.

It is frequently said that the Lord has raised up a particular man to perform a particular mission. . . . I wish that all the members of the Church could have witnessed the council meeting wherein the Presidency was reorganized. If ever there was a time when the Spirit of the Lord was indubitably manifest, it was on that occasion.

It is not for me to say what particular mission President George Albert Smith has ahead of him. This I do know, however, that at this particular time in the world's history, never was the need for love among brethren so desperately needed. . . . There is no man of my acquaintance who loves the human family, collectively and individually, more profoundly than does President George Albert Smith. Those two things coming in conjunction . . . at this time have for me at least, particular significance (*Conference Reports*, October 1945, 5).

GEORGE ALBERT SMITH WITH PRESIDENT HARRY TRUMAN. Truman was both touched and impressed by the humanitarian efforts of the Church following World War II.

SAINTS WITH
POTATOES to go to
Europe for foreign
aid after World
War II. 'Slide'
Cornelius Zappy
and Dutch Saints.

After the war, thousands of Saints in Europe were in desperate need of food, clothing, fuel, bedding, and shelter. Anticipating the end of the fighting, American Saints had sewn hundreds of quilts and blankets, and gathered boxes of food and clothing. However, much of Europe was still under military jurisdiction and it was difficult to get into some areas. President Smith went directly to President Harry Truman for authorization to help the needy. President Truman said:

"Well, what do you want to ship it over there for? Their money isn't any good."

I said, "We don't want their money."

He looked at me and asked: "You don't mean you are going to give it to them?"

I said: "Of course, we would give it to them. They are our brothers and sisters and are in distress. God has blessed us with a surplus, and we will be glad to send it if we can have the cooperation of the government."

He said: "You are on the right track," and added, "We will be glad to help you in any way we can. How long will it take you to get this ready?"

I said: "It's all ready. Mr. President, while the administration at Washington were advising the destroying of food, we were building elevators and filling them with grain, and increasing our flocks, and our herds, and now what we need is the cars and the ships in order to send considerable food, clothing and bedding to the people of Europe who are in distress. We have an organization in the Church that has over two thousand homemade quilts ready" (Lyon, et al., *Best-Loved Stories of the LDS People*, 425-26).

In 1951, President Smith was suffering from a rare skin and blood disease. On April 4, his eighty-first birthday, he was near death. His son, Albert, asked him if he had anything he wanted to say to his family.

"Yes," he replied simply, "I know that my Redeemer lives" (Merlo J. Pusey, *Builders of the Kingdom*, 358).

When President George Albert Smith passed away, thousands gathered for his funeral. Tributes poured in from world leaders. In an interview with *The Deseret News*, Elder Spencer W. Kimball said:

In 1951, the world was still recovering from the effects of war. The Berlin Blockade had ended, but a new conflict in Korea had broken out. Americans watched color television for the first time, and a heart-lung machine was invented that made heart operations possible. The Nobel Prize in chemistry went to two scientists who discovered plutonium. On Broadway, the hit musical of the season was *The King and I*, and at the cinema, crowds flocked to see *The African Queen* and *An American in Paris*.

> "Whenever I have thought of our beloved President, I have always felt that he was very, very near that kingdom [the kingdom of God].
>
> It seemed to me that every act, every thought of our President would indicate that with all his heart and soul he loved the Lord and he loved his fellowmen. Is there a mortal being who could have loved them more?" (*Conference Reports*, April 7, 1951, funeral services).

The Saints remembered their beloved President and Prophet for his stirring testimony.

> I have been buoyed up, and as it were, lifted out of myself and given power, not my own, to teach the glorious truths proclaimed by the Redeemer of the world. I have not seen Him face to face, but I have enjoyed the companionship of His Spirit and felt His presence in a way not to be mistaken. I know my Redeemer lives and gladly yield my humble efforts to establish His teachings" . . . (Smith, *Sharing the Gospel with Others*, 50).

DAVID O.
McKAY

"Every Member a Missionary"

Following the death of George Albert Smith, David O. McKay was sustained as the ninth President of the Church.

David O. McKay was born on September 8, 1873, at his parents' home in Eden, Utah. As David grew, physical characteristics that would become distinguishing features began to emerge. He inherited his thick wavy hair from his father, and had his mother's kind eyes. As a youngster, David was comforted by his strong parents. When he was alone, he relied on the things they had taught him. On one occasion, David became frightened in a severe storm and prayed for protection as his parents had taught him. As he prayed, there came into his mind the calming thought, "Don't be afraid, nothing will hurt you."

However, when David was seven years old, tragedy struck his family. His older sisters, Margaret and Ellena, died. Margaret died of rheumatic fever and Ellena developed a fatal case of pneumonia. The girls, who died within a week of each other, were buried in the same grave.

A year later, David's father was called on a mission. As his parents discussed the call, his father said, "It is impossible for me to go."

But his mother replied, "Of course you must accept; you need not worry about me. David O. and I will manage

things nicely" (Llewelyn R. McKay, *Home Memories of President David O. McKay*, 5-6).

Friends and relatives agreed that the mission call would be difficult for the McKays, but David's Uncle, John Grow, said, "Well, you may be right, and you may be wrong; but if Jennette has set her mind that you should answer the mission call, you might as well give in! I'll keep an eye on things and help out when I can" (McKay, *Home Memories of President David O. McKay*, 5–6).

When David McKay, Sr., left for his mission to Scotland, eight-year-old David O. started helping his mother with the farm. The neighbors pitched in and helped with planting and harvesting, and the family was blessed with two good years while David, Sr., served his mission. Young David learned many great lessons from his father. One day, David O. and his brother, Thomas, were helping their father cut hay. As they cut the hay, nine loads went to the family haystack and the tenth load was taken to the tithing office. The boys had finished cutting the ninth load in a low area of the field where the grass was poor, and were just about to start cutting the tenth load in the same place when their father called to them:

> "No, boys, drive over to the higher ground." He then directed them to an area with high-quality hay.
> One of the boys called back, "No, let us take the hay as it comes."
> "No, David, that is the tenth load, and the best is none too good for God" (David O. McKay, *Cherished Experiences*, 19).

DAVID O. MCKAY AND FAMILY
David is on his father's lap.

David's Patriarchal Blessing

Just a few weeks before his fourteenth birthday, David O. McKay received his patriarchal blessing. The patriarch's words outlined a life of devoted Church service and worldwide travel. The Church Patriarch, John Smith, conferred the blessing.

> Brother David Oman McKay, thou art in thy youth and need instruction, therefore, be taught of thy parents . . . that at an early day you may be prepared for a responsible position, for the eye of the Lord is upon thee. . . . The Lord has a work for thee to do, in which thou shall see much of the world, assist in gathering scattered Israel and also labor in the ministry. It shall be thy lot to sit in council with thy brethren and preside among the people and exhort the Saints to faithfulness (Jeannette McKay Morrell, *Highlights in the Life of President David O. McKay*, 26).

At the end of the blessing, Patriarch Smith placed his hands on David's shoulders and said, "My boy, you have something to do besides playing marbles."

UNIVERSITY OF UTAH FOOTBALL TEAM 1894 David O. McKay played right guard. *Back row (l to r):* Paul Kimball, David O. McKay, F. N. Poulson, Bernard Stewart, I. E. Wiley, and Theodore Nystrum. *Middle row:* Ernest Van Cott, Fred W. Reynolds, Alonzo E. Hyde, and Joseph W. Stringfellow. *Front row:* A. B. Sawyer, Fred J. Mays, Harry Kimball, Fred Earls, and Seth Thomas.

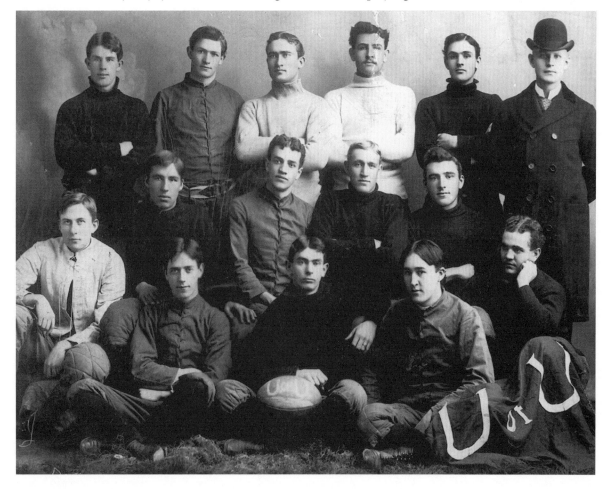

As David and his brother grew, they became a great help to their father on the farm. Their father had an unusual way of teaching the boys about responsibility. Each morning he would ask, "Boys, what is your plan for today?" (McKay, *Home Memories of President David O. McKay*, 7). He would then let the boys decide what tasks were the most important, and which needed to be done first.

At an early age, the boys felt that it really was a family farm. School was also important to the McKay family. David finished school in Huntsville and attended two years at Weber State Academy. He returned to Huntsville to teach, but wanted to continue his education. When his parents decided that the four oldest children should attend the University of Utah, the family made the trip to Salt Lake City together.

> My brother, my father, my sisters Jeanette and Annie, and I rolled over the sand ridge from Huntsville with horse and wagon, a cow in the trailer, with a sack of flour milled from wheat we had grown, with jars of fruit which mother had put up, going down to start our schooling at the university. We got as far as Farmington and had a chance to sell the cow, so we did this and took another one later. We were assured of bread, milk, and fruit. We rented a house and thus began our first year. The second year, we rented a house from Mrs. Riggs, the mother of my wife (McKay, *Home Memories of President David O. McKay*, 9).

DAVID O. MCKAY as a young man.

At school, David served as class president and was valedictorian. He played right guard on the football team, and remained interested in football throughout his life. He was loyal to his alma mater and, though he admitted having mixed feelings, always cheered for the University of Utah when they played against Brigham Young University.

A MISSION TO SCOTLAND

After graduation, David was called on a mission to the British Isles. When he arrived in the mission field, he became homesick for familiar surroundings. He wrote, "The dim light from the *blood like* sun, the long stretch of dismal looking warehouses, the strange faces on the dock, the queer looking cabs, together with the bustle and noise, all helped to make us aware of the painful fact that we were not *home*" (Francis M. Gibbons, *David O. McKay: Apostle to the World, Prophet of God*, 40).

David was assigned to Scotland. He had become discouraged by the many people who had rejected his message, but one evening, as he and his companion were walking back to their room, they passed an unfinished building that had something carved over the door. David went to see what it said.

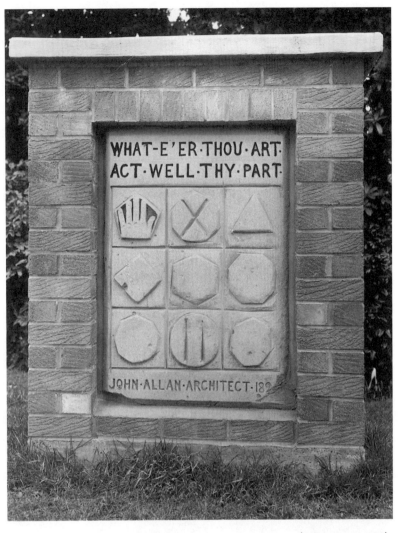

I was half way up the graveled walk when there came to my eyesight a striking motto as follows, carved in stone. "What E're Thou Art, Act Well Thy Part." I said to myself, or the Spirit within me, you are a member of the Church of Jesus Christ of Latter- day Saints. More than that, you are here as a representative of the Lord Jesus Christ. You accepted the responsibility as a representative of the Church. Then I thought what we had done that forenoon. We had been sightseeing; we had gained historical instruction and information, it is true, and I was thrilled with it. . . . However, that was not missionary work. . . . I accepted the message given to me on that stone, and from that moment we tried to do our part as missionaries in Scotland (Gibbons, *David O. McKay: Apostle to the World, Prophet of God*, 45).

"WHAT E'RE THOU ART, ACT WELL THY PART." Motto that inspired David O. McKay as a young missionary in Scotland.

After this experience, Elder McKay served with renewed fervor and resolve. Later, he was called to serve as the president of the Scottish Conference, which was part of the European Mission. Near the end of his mission, Elder McKay presided at a priesthood meeting that was attended by the two counselors of the European Mission Presidency. After a powerful meeting where the presence of heavenly beings was felt, President McMurrin, a counselor in the mission presidency, turned to Elder McKay and said, "Brother David, Satan hath desired you that he may sift you as wheat, but God is mindful of you. If you will keep

DAVID O. McKAY
AND HIS SISTER,
JEANNETTE McKAY

the faith, you will yet sit in the leading councils of the Church" (Gibbons, *David O. McKay: Apostle to the World, Prophet of God*, 14).

At the time, the young elder felt the statement was "more of a caution than a promise." He recorded, "At that moment, there flashed into my mind temptations that had beset my path, and I realized even better than President McMurrin, or any other man, how truly he had spoken" (Gibbons, *David O. McKay: Apostle to the World, Prophet of God*, 14).

ROMANCING EMMA RAY

When he returned from his mission, he renewed his acquaintance with Miss Emma Ray Riggs. Their first date had been his missionary farewell. When Emma found out that David was returning from his mission, she was visiting her cousins on Antelope Island out in the Great Salt Lake. Since the regular passenger boat would not get her to the mainland in time, she and her cousin, Bell, rigged up an old rowboat with a sail and managed to cross the lake in time to meet David when he arrived in Salt Lake City.

David's journal has as its first entry on 30 July, 1897:

> Went to Ogden to meet Mrs. White and Miss Riggs. They participated in the festivities and then in the evening took a ride over on South hills. Saw purple mts. at sunset. Very beautiful. . . . Went strolling with Ray. Told each other secrets. A memorable night! (David Lawrence McKay, *My Father David O. McKay*, 2).

In telling the story later, Emma would add, "We held hands all the way home" (McKay, *My Father David O. McKay*, 2).

David began teaching at Weber State Academy in Ogden. When Emma Ray graduated, she began teaching at another school in the city. Because their schools were on opposite sides of a park, they frequently met among the trees. It was at this park that he asked her to marry him.

She asked, "Are you sure I'm the right one?" He replied that she was (McKay, *My Father David O. McKay*, 6).

They were married on January 2, 1901. The following year, David became the principal of Weber Academy. It was a difficult job. One of his biggest concerns was finding the money to add a classroom and a laboratory to the school. At this time, he also was asked to help prepare lessons for a new Church program—adult Sunday School class.

CALLED AS AN APOSTLE

During the 1906 April conference, David received a telephone call asking him to come to the office of the Quorum of the Twelve. When he entered the office of the President of the Quorum, Elder Francis M. Lyman said:

"So, you're David O. McKay.

"Yes, sir."

"Well, David O. McKay, the Lord wants you to be a member of the Quorum of the Twelve Apostles.

David was speechless.

"Well, haven't you anything to say?"

David finally spoke: "Sir, I am neither worthy nor able to receive such a call."

"Not worthy! Not worthy! What have you been doing?"

When David explained that he had done nothing to make him unworthy, and that he was merely expressing his feelings of inadequacy, President Lyman asked:

"Well, then, don't you have faith that the Lord can make you able?"

"Well, yes, sir, I have that faith."

"Very well, then. Don't say anything about this until your name is presented in conference this afternoon" (McKay, *My Father David O. McKay*, 39).

When the names of the Twelve were presented for a sustaining vote, Emma Ray burst into tears. Somewhere behind them, someone said, "There's one of them. See his wife is crying" (McKay, *My Father David O. McKay*, 39).

Elder David O. McKay was a great favorite among the youth. He was often asked to officiate at temple sealings and was a popular speaker.

Following World War I, President Grant asked Elder McKay to visit Church members throughout the world. He was to observe how the wards and branches operated, and to strengthen and instruct the local leaders.

In December of 1920, Elder McKay and his traveling companion, Hugh J. Cannon, were given special blessings of health and protection prior to their departure. Elder Cannon especially was blessed that he would not be bothered by seasickness, an affliction that had caused him great distress in the past. The two men set sail for Yokohama on December 7, 1920. As they got to know each other, Elder Cannon wrote of Elder McKay, "It was discovered that his personality is built largely upon the fact that he is tremendously and righteously human. Anything other than perfect frankness is abhorrent to his honest soul."

Then, elated by his freedom from seasickness, Elder Cannon wrote:

> Brother McKay, being the leader of this tour, maintained his supremacy in the matter of sea-sickness as in all other things. He does nothing by halves, but treats every subject exhaustively, going to the very bottom of it, and this occasion was no exception. Sea-sickness is undertaken with the same vigorous energy

which he displays in running for a train (Gibbons, *David O. McKay: Apostle to the World, Prophet of God*, 102–3).

Elder McKay, suffering from the rough winter seas, wrote that "Brother Cannon jumped out of bed as bright and pert as a ten-year-old boy. He could steady himself as though he were anchored. With no apparent difficulty, he dressed himself and even shaved, an operation, which though ordinarily simple enough, seemed to me under the circumstances almost marvelous."

Looking at David's face, Elder Cannon advised, "If you aren't feeling well, I suggest that you don't look in this mirror" (McKay, *Home Memories of President David O. McKay*, 40).

The pair visited the small number of Saints in Japan, and then traveled through Korea to China. President Grant had commissioned Elder McKay to dedicate the land of China to missionary work, if he felt the Spirit move him to do so. Elders McKay and Cannon traveled to Peking, and were distressed by the somber, gloomy, oppressive nature of the city. On Sunday morning, however, they awoke with a different feeling. They walked to the Forbidden City and there, within a peaceful grove of cypress trees, they had the impression they sought. Elder Cannon later wrote:

DAVID O. McKAY AND HUGH JENNE CANNON (1870–1931) IN HAWAII Following World War II, President Grant asked these two elders to visit Church members throughout the world to observe how the wards and branches were operating, and to strengthen and instruct local leaders. *Front row: (l to r)* David Kalani, Virginia Budd, E. Wesley Smith (Hawaiian Mission President) *Back row:* David O. McKay, Hugh J. Cannon, and Moses M. Kekua *Taken above Akaka Falls near Hilo, Hawaii. February 10, 1921*

> A hallowed and reverential feeling was upon [us]. It was one of those occasions which at rare times comes to mortals when they are surrounded by a Presence so sacred that human words would be disturbing (Unpublished manuscript of world tour, Church Archives, 5–6).

On that morning, in that grove, Elder McKay dedicated the land of China for missionary work.

Their travels later took them to New Zealand, Australia, Singapore, Bombay, Syria, Egypt, Israel, Italy, Switzerland, and finally England. Although the world tour was a fascinating experience, David, at times, wanted to be home.

> I'm really homesick this morning. . . . I've thought almost continuously about the folks at home . . . the kiddies playing on the lawn, Mamma and LouJean on the summer porch, and Llewelyn on his way to the Dry Hollow farm. . . . I imagine him coming home happy because he had caught four fish. June is the most delightful month of the year in Ogden Valley (McKay, *Home Memories of President David O. McKay*, 75).

However, great spiritual experiences made the discomfort and inconvenience of travel worthwhile. While approaching Samoa, Elder McKay had an amazing dream.

DAVID O. MCKAY
AND HUGH J.
CANNON

> I . . . beheld in vision something infinitely sublime. In the distance, I beheld a beautiful white city. Though far away, yet I seemed to realize that trees with luscious fruit, shrubbery with gorgeously-tinted leaves, and flowers in perfect bloom abounded everywhere . . . I then saw a great concourse of people approaching the city. . . . Instantly my attention seemed centered upon their Leader, and though I could see only the profile of his features and his body, I recognized him at once as my Savior! The tint and radiance of his countenance were glorious to behold! There was a peace about him which seemed sublime—it was Divine!
>
> The city I understood was his. It was the City Eternal; and the people following him were to abide there in peace and eternal happiness.
>
> But who were they?
>
> As if the Savior read my thoughts, he answered by pointing to a semicircle that then appeared above them, and on which were written in gold words:
>
> These Are They Who Have Overcome The World—Who Have Truly Been Born Again. When I awoke, it was breaking day over Apia Harbor (McKay, *Cherished Experiences*, 101-2).

When he returned from his world tour of the Church, Elder McKay wrote, "I have an entirely different viewpoint of these countries now. . . . I realize the responsibility of this Church to proclaim the gospel is world-wide" (David O. McKay, *Gospel Ideals*, 583-84).

Almost immediately upon his return from his world tour, Elder McKay and his family were called to preside over the European Mission. While serving as mission president, Elder McKay began using a phrase that became his watch cry: "Every member a missionary."

When George Albert Smith became President of the Church, he gave President McKay responsibility over the new Church Welfare System. President McKay said of this new program: "We have in the Church one of the best systems in the world of aiding one another—the fast offerings. Our young people should be taught [it] from their youth; our older people should practice it and set a proper example" (Francis M. Gibbons, *Harold B. Lee: Man of Vision, Prophet of God*, 126-27).

President George Albert Smith also asked President McKay to head the 1947 celebration that marked the one hundredth anniversary of the pioneers' entrance into the Salt Lake Valley. The celebration included an amazing array of pageants, tours, projects, and events that helped the Saints remember this significant historical event. During this centennial year, the Church received nationwide attention. The Salt Lake Chamber of Commerce said:

1947 WAGON TRAIN REENACTMENT Spencer and Camilla Kimball watching the Centennial Trek caravan from on top of Independence Rock, Wyoming. *July 1947*

> Nearly every major magazine in the country has told the story of our history and achievements. Newspapers everywhere have done likewise. Hours of radio network time have been devoted to Brigham Young and his followers, and to the things being done here today to memorialize their achievements.
>
> Utah has gained much from her centennial. Our greatest rewards, however, will come through the years as we practice what has passed before our eyes this year in one grand panorama (Morrell, *Highlights in the Life of President David O. McKay*, 95).

A *Deseret News* editorial said:

> To President David O. McKay and the Centennial Commission . . . and to a host of others too numerous to mention, the people of Utah owe a vote of deep appreciation for the planning and management of the thousands of special Centennial events. The good that has come to Utah and the West as a result of their planning and leadership is difficult to estimate (Morrell, *Highlights in the Life of President David O. McKay*, 95).

CALLED AS A PROPHET

On April 9, 1951, forty-five years to the day after he was ordained an Apostle, David Oman McKay was sustained as the ninth Prophet, Seer, and Revelator of the Church. Following his sustaining in the Tabernacle during general conference, President McKay told the congregation:

DAVID O. MCKAY'S
FIRST PRESIDENCY
J. Reuben Clark, Jr.
(1871–1961),
President David O.
McKay, and Henry
Dinwoodey Moyle
(1889–1963).
ca. 1959

And now to the members of the Church. We all need your help, your faith and prayers, not your adverse criticism, but your help. You can do that in prayer if you cannot reach us in person. The potency of these prayers throughout the Church came to me yesterday when I received a letter from a neighbor in my old home town. He was milking his cows when the word came over the radio which he had in his barn that President Smith had passed.

He sensed what that would mean to his former fellow-townsman, and he left his barn and went to the house and told his wife. Immediately they called their little children, and there in that humble home, suspending their activities, they knelt down as a family and offered prayer. The significance of that prayer I leave for you to understand. Multiply that by a hundred thousand, two hundred thousand, half a million homes, and see the power in the unity and prayers, and the sustaining influence in the body of the Church.

Today you have by your vote placed upon us the greatest responsibility, as well as the greatest honor that lies within your power to bestow as members of The Church of Jesus Christ of Latter-day Saints. . . . May the spirit of this session remain in your hearts. May it be felt throughout the uttermost parts of the earth, wherever there is a branch in all the world, that that spirit might be a unifying power in increasing the testimony of the divinity of this work, that it may grow in its influence for good in the establishment of peace throughout the world (Morrell, *Highlights in the Life of President David O. McKay*, 105).

In 1954, President McKay authorized the Mormon Tabernacle Choir to make its first European tour. When the choir arrived at their first stop in Scotland, they were greeted by the Lord Provost of Glasgow who said:

As far as I know, this is the greatest invasion of Mormons in Scotland. . . . Many years ago I was associated with a man who was a member of your church (President McKay) and that was at a time when there was much criticism of your church, but I felt that any religion which had principles which could produce a man of such integrity must be grossly misrepresented. I care not what a man's theological beliefs may be, but I consider how that man feels toward his neighbor (J. Spencer Cornwall, *A Century of Singing: The Salt Lake Mormon Tabernacle Choir*, 113-14).

Time magazine reported that the choir created good feelings everywhere they went. During this European tour, the choir also sang at the dedication of the Swiss Temple.

When President McKay was serving as European Mission President, he was asked if the missionaries should continue to encourage the members to leave their native countries and go to Utah. He responded, "No, it is important that the branches be built up, and members should remain and work toward that end. Someday we shall have temples built for them which will be accessible to all, so that the desired temple work can be done without uprooting families from their homelands" (McKay, *Home Memories of President David O. McKay*, 33).

President McKay had seen the Swiss Temple in a vision and discussed the plans with the Church architect. The initial sketches of the new temple included some changes. When President McKay was shown the drawings, he said, "Brother Anderson, that is not the temple that you and I saw together." The plans were changed back to the original concept, and in September 1955, the Swiss Temple was dedicated.

DAVID O. MCKAY WITH ARTIST'S REN- DITION OF THE SWISS TEMPLE

President McKay left a lasting impression on nearly everyone he met. His demeanor and appearance, his kind face and wavy, white hair impressed people that he was indeed a Prophet of God. One of his special friends was Cecil B. DeMille, a moviemaker famed for historical epics. Salt Lake City was chosen for the world premier showing of the movie *The Ten Commandments*. Mr. DeMille felt that if the LDS people approved of the movie it would be a success. He also wanted to meet his friend David O. McKay again. "There is a man, a real man of God in our own time. There are men whose very presence warms the heart. President McKay is one of them. He has understanding, he has the true

spirit of Christ. He is a great pioneer of God (John J. Stewart, *Remembering the McKays*, 39).

When Cecil B. DeMille was presented with an honorary doctorate degree at Brigham Young University, he turned to President McKay and said, "David McKay, almost thou persuadest me to be a Mormon" (*BYU Speeches of the Year*, 31 May 1957, 3).

EMMA RAY MCKAY, DIRECTOR CECIL B. DEMILLE, ACTOR CHARLTON HESTON, AND DAVID O. MCKAY during filming of the epic movie, *The Ten Commandments*.

Others were similarly impressed. Arriving in New York City from an overseas journey, President McKay was greeted by newspaper reporters. A photographer took some pictures of the Prophet and returned to his office to develop the film. He stayed in the darkroom for over two hours, and when he came out, he had a tremendous stack of photographs.

His boss chided, "What in the world are you wasting time and all those photographic supplies for?"

The photographer replied that he would gladly pay for the supplies he had used and that they could dock his wages for the extra time he spent because he wanted the extra pictures of President McKay for his own. He said, "When I was a little boy, my mother used to read to me out of the Old Testament, and I have wondered all my life what a prophet of God must really look like. Well, today I found one" (Hartshorn, *Classic Stories From the Lives of Our Prophets*, 299-300).

In his closing remarks during the April 1959 general conference, President McKay recalled the challenges he had faced as the mission president in Great Britain in 1923. He then introduced the Church to a theme that he had used in Europe.

> Every member a missionary! You may bring your mother into the Church, or it may be your father; perhaps your fellow companion in the workshop. Somebody will hear the good message of the truth through you. And that is the message today (*Conference Report*, April 6, 1959).

President David O. McKay truly was a Prophet for a worldwide Church. During the nineteen years he was in presiding councils, great strides were made in taking the gospel to the ends of the earth. General conference began to be broadcast on television, and priesthood meetings and monthly Sunday evening firesides were carried via telephone to hundreds of chapels. A language-training institute was opened for missionaries who had been called to non-English-speaking missions, and the home teaching program was introduced. Monday night family home evening was also implemented. President McKay traveled extensively to all areas of the earth. The Church was growing so rapidly that the position of regional representative was created. New missions were opened in Italy and Spain. Members were encouraged to complete their four-generation family group sheets, and the Church built massive granite vaults to store genealogical records.

But in spite of the great success the Church was having, President McKay realized that the family unit was the most important organization of the Church. In a talk given during the 1964 April conference, he said:

> No other success can compensate for failure in the home. The poorest shack in which love prevails over united family is of greater value to God and

future humanity than any other riches. In such a home, God can work miracles. . . . Pure hearts in a pure home are always in whispering distance of heaven (*Conference Report* April 1964, 5).

President McKay had great love for his family. He and his wife were married 69 years and were almost always seen together holding hands. They had seven children—five sons and two daughters. Of his wife, he said:

> Willingly and ably she has carried the responsibility of the household. Uncomplainingly she has economized when our means have been limited. Always prompt with meals, she has never said an unpleasant word or even shown a frown when I have kept her waiting, sometimes for hours. . . .
>
> Under all conditions and circumstances, she has been the perfect lady. Her education has enabled her to be a true helpmate; her congeniality and interest in my work, a pleasing companion; her charm and unselfishness, a lifelong sweetheart; her unbounded patience and intelligent insight to childhood, a most devoted mother;—these and many other virtues combined with her loyalty and self-sacrificing devotion to her husband, impel me to crown her the sweetest, most helpful, most inspiring sweetheart and wife that ever inspired a man to noble endeavor (McKay, *Home Memories of President David O. McKay*, 192-93).

DAVID O. MCKAY RIDING HIS HORSE, SONNY BOY

On one occasion, a newspaper reporter interviewed President McKay. Towards the close of the interview, [the reporter] said he would like to know if President McKay had ever seen the Savior.

President McKay answered that he had not, but that he had heard his voice, many times, and that he had felt his presence and his influence. . . .

Then he told how some evidences were stronger even than that of sight, and recalled the occasion when the Savior appeared to his disciples . . . [he said to Thomas]: "Because thou hast seen me, thou hast believed: blessed are they that have not seen, and yet have believed" (John 20:29). President McKay then smiled and said, "That is quite a testimony I have given you. I do not know when I have given this before" (*I Know That My Redeemer Lives*, 138). The reporter left the President's office with tears in his eyes.

Shortly before his ninetieth birthday, President McKay had an accident that marked the beginning of a long series of health problems. He and his son, Llewelyn, had gone to Huntsville to ride horses. As the saddle blanket was placed on President McKay's favorite horse, the animal became frightened and bolted. President McKay said, "I was knocked down and pulled along the ground for about a block. However, he stopped and I was not hurt. We finally saddled him and he was his usual self and I had a very good ride on him which I enjoyed thoroughly."

Two months later he arrived home from work exhausted. His exhaustion was alarming to his family, and President McKay acknowledged that he needed to take better care of himself—he worked long hours, and often went without food.

During the last year or two of his life, President McKay was confined to a wheelchair but he still met with the other brethren to discuss and review Church operations. However, on January 18, 1970, he died in his apartment at the Hotel Utah at the age of ninety-seven.

The members of the Church felt a profound loss at the Prophet's death. During his presidency, the Church had tripled in size from one to three million members. President McKay had traveled nearly a million miles, and had visited Europe, South Africa, South America, New Zealand, Australia, and the Pacific Islands. The number of full-time missionaries had grown from 2,000 to 12,000; over 4,000 chapels and buildings were constructed; and eight temples were built or announced.

At President McKay's funeral, his successor, President Joseph Fielding Smith, said:

I thank God for the life and ministry of this great spirit who came here to preside in Israel. He did his work well and has just returned clean and perfected to the realm of light and joyous reunion (Gibbons, *David O. McKay: Apostle to the World, Prophet of God*, 423).

David O. McKay served as an Apostle for sixty-three years, nine months, and nine days—longer than any other Apostle had ever served.

WORLD EVENTS

In 1970, the world had entered the space age. Astronauts had walked on the moon, and men were able to see deeper into space with a newly completed 150-inch reflecting telescope at Kit Peak Observatory in Tucson, Arizona. One of the most popular songs in the United States was "Rain Drops Keep Falling on My Head," from the movie *Butch Cassidy and the Sundance Kid*. In sports, Joe Frazier became the heavyweight-boxing champion, Margaret Smith Court won the grand slam of women's tennis, and Billy Casper won the master's in golf. In the arts, Aleksandr Solzhenitsyn was given the Nobel Prize for literature, and a new playwrite named Neil Simon had a hit on Broadway.

David O. McKay

JOSEPH FIELDING

SMITH

Faithful and True to His Sacred Heritage

After President McKay's death, Joseph Fielding Smith became the tenth President of the Church. He carried the name of his father who served as sixth President of the Church, and his great-uncle, Joseph Smith, Jr. Sustained as Prophet at the age of ninety-three, Joseph Fielding Smith was an amazing link to the past.

Born July 19, 1876, in Salt Lake City, Joseph Fielding Smith was the first son of Joseph F. Smith and Julina Lambson Smith. Joseph Fielding was taught to honor his name, and a remarkable bond grew between the boy and his father.

In 1884, when little Joseph Fielding was just five years old, federal judges and marshals were persecuting the Mormons due to polygamy. His father was forced into hiding and spent several years in the Hawaiian Islands. Joseph Fielding's mother went with his father to Hawaii, but he and his older sisters stayed behind in Salt Lake City. He later recalled the times when marshals searched their home for his father.

> We lived a very peaceful and happy family,
> except when we became troubled and I became
> frightened by deputy marshals. In those early days,

JOSEPH FIELDING SMITH served as President from 1970–1972.

Ephraim George Holding, Temple Electrician, atop the northeast finial of the Salt Lake Temple. Ephraim emigrated from England to Utah in 1853. *1893*

they were always seeking to bring trouble upon the authorities of the Church, and because of those conditions, my father was sent away when I was a youth. . . . both father and mother were in the [Hawaiian] Islands for a number of years (Francis M. Gibbons, *Joseph Fielding Smith: Gospel Scholar, Prophet of God,* 14).

Joseph's Aunt Sarah also describes the fear that haunted the family: "Julina's five older children were left with Edna and me. This was known as the underground time. We had to watch the children constantly and keep ourselves out of society. We were under a strain all the time and we had to keep alert for fear deputies were sneaking about, trying to find Joseph" (Joseph Fielding Smith and John Stewart, *The Life of Joseph Fielding Smith,* 42).

As a member of a large family whose finances were limited, Joseph Fielding spent a lot of time helping with farm and household chores. One of his earliest memories was an accident he had while helping on the farm.

I had an unfortunate thing happen to me one time when I fell and broke a leg. That was not my fault. My brother and I were coming in with a load of hay. It was the last load, and we did not want to go back again. We built up what was really two loads. When we went in with what was to be [our] tithing load, I was swept off the top because there was a bar across the gate, and I fell and broke a leg (Joseph Fielding Smith, *Seek Ye Earnestly,* 48).

Joseph was ten years old when his parents returned from the Hawaiian Islands. He began helping his mother, serving as her buggy driver while she attended to duties as a midwife. Many times he was awakened at odd hours and told to hitch up Old Meg and drive his mother to the home of someone who needed her services. Joseph then had to wait with the horse until she was ready to go home. "Sometimes I nearly froze to death," he said. "I marveled that so many babies were born in the middle of the night, especially on cold winter nights. I fervently wished that mothers might time things a little better" (Smith and Stewart, *The Life of Joseph Fielding Smith*, 53).

Joseph Fielding was a good student, but he liked to study the gospel the best. He said, "I was born with a testimony of the gospel. . . . I do not remember a time when I did not have full confidence in the mission of the Prophet Joseph Smith and in the teachings and guidance of my parents" (Smith and Stewart, *The Life of Joseph Fielding Smith*, 55–56).

By the time Joseph was ten, he had read the Book of Mormon twice. His brothers remember him hurrying through his chores, and even leaving a baseball game early to have more time to read the scriptures. In 1893, when Joseph Fielding was seventeen, the Salt Lake Temple was completed and ready for dedication. Throughout his entire childhood, Joseph had watched the construction of the building. It had seemed incredibly slow to him. He said, "I used to wonder whether I would ever live long enough to see the temple completed" (Smith and Stewart, *The Life of Joseph Fielding Smith*, 62).

That same year, President Woodruff invited his counselors and some members of their families to accompany him to the World's Fair in Chicago. Joseph Fielding was one the children chosen to make the trip.

SALT LAKE TEMPLE ANNEX view before landscaping was done. This is the entrance used for access to the temple; connected by an underground tunnel. *ca. 1893*

I had the privilege of sitting in the state room or the room that was given to President Woodruff, and listened to his counsel and advice. Of course, I was just a youngster, and in the company with his son and one of his daughters, and someone else. . . . . We went out on the platform . . . to eat watermelons so we could throw the pieces away, and when we came in we got a

scolding. We were told that if that train had gone with speed around a curve we could have been swept off, which was absolutely true, and I remember that very keenly. And so we got scolded by President Woodruff (Gibbons, *Joseph Fielding Smith: Gospel Scholar, Prophet of God*, 63).

Joseph Fielding also remembers Lorenzo Snow.

> I was not too well acquainted with President Lorenzo Snow. He was a rather austere man. I was in his presence a great number of times, however. But, let me say to you, so far as integrity is concerned, and faithfulness and loyalty to the Church, these brethren who have gone on ahead of us were loyal and true to the Gospel of Jesus Christ. There was not one of them that would not have laid down his life if it had been necessary. They loved the truth (Smith and Stewart, *The Life of Joseph Fielding Smith*, 63-64).

JOSEPH FIELDING'S PATRIARCHAL BLESSING

When he was twenty, Joseph Fielding received his patriarchal blessing from John Smith, the Church Patriarch.

JOSEPH FIELDING SMITH as a young man. He was ordained as an Apostle at the age of thirty-three, and became President of the Church at the age of 93.

> It is thy privilege to live to a good old age [and] the will of the Lord that you should become a mighty man in Israel. It shall be thy duty to sit in counsel with thy brethren and to preside among the people. It shall be thy duty to travel much at home and abroad, by land and water, laboring in the ministry. . . . Hold up thy head, lift up thy voice without fear or favor, as the spirit of the Lord shall direct. . . . His spirit shall direct thy mind and give the word and sentiment that thou shalt confound the wisdom of the wicked and set at naught the counsels of the unjust (Gibbons, *Joseph Fielding Smith: Gospel Scholar, Prophet of God*, 49).

As a young man, Joseph Fielding worked in the wholesale grocery department in the basement of ZCMI. The hours were long, and the pay was low.

> I worked like a work horse all day long and was tired out when night came, carrying sacks of flour and sacks of sugar and hams and bacons on my back. I weighed 150 pounds, but I thought nothing of picking up a 200-pound sack, and putting it on my shoulders. I was a very foolish fellow, because ever since that time, my shoulders have been just a little out of kilter. The right one got a little more "treatment" than the left (Smith and Sewart, *The Life of Joseph Fielding Smith*, 65).

But jobs were hard to come by and the entire family needed help financially.

COURTSHIP

About this time, Joseph became interested in Louie Shurtliff, who was staying with the Smiths while she attended the University of Utah. She was slightly taller than Joseph, and about a month older. They found that they had a lot in common, and the fact that they lived in the same house helped their love bloom. During summer breaks, she returned to her parents' home in Ogden. Joseph was lonely, and trains were expensive. On one occasion, he rode a bicycle 100 miles round trip to see her. After she graduated from the university, Louie moved back to Ogden to help her father in his store and do some teaching. Joseph decided he couldn't live without her, and requested that she be his eternal companion.

> When she finished and graduated from her school, I did not permit her to go home and stay there, but I persuaded her to change her place of residence, and on the 26th day of April, 1898, we went to the Salt Lake Temple and were married for time and all eternity by my father, President Joseph F. Smith (Smith and Stewart, *The Life of Joseph Fielding Smith*, 75).

The young couple moved in with Joseph's mother, and he continued to work at ZCMI. The following year, Joseph Fielding received a mission call from President Lorenzo Snow to serve in the British Mission. Louie returned to Ogden to stay with her family and teach school while Joseph was away. Joseph was feeling very homesick, and when he arrived at the mission home, the door was locked and no one was there. As he waited, a group of neighborhood children gathered and began to heckle him. They chanted, "Chase me, girls, to Salt Lake City, where the Mormons have no pity" (Gibbons, *Joseph Fielding Smith: Gospel Scholar, Prophet of God*, 70).

EMILY LOUIS SHURTLIFF SMITH (1876–1908), first wife of Joseph Fielding Smith. She died from uncontrolled vomiting due to pregnancy.

MISSION TO BRITAIN

Joseph began his missionary labors on June 6, about which he wrote:

> This has been a very important day in my short life. I came from my home less than a month ago for the purpose of preaching the gospel of our Lord. . . . I have been out tracting today and delivered 25 tracts. It is the first of this kind of work that I ever tried to do and it did not come to me very easy. It was the first time I ever stood on a street to preach the gospel of

Christ. I bore my testimony to the world for the first time today, but will be able to do so better. With the help of the Lord I shall do His will as I was called to do (Gibbons, *Joseph Fielding Smith: Gospel Scholar, Prophet of God*, 73).

Joseph had a difficult mission. Although he worked hard, he performed only one baptism. Hecklers often broke up the missionaries' street meetings by pelting the elders with rocks, mud, or garbage. In Derby, Joseph was Elder Steven W. Walker, who was nine years his senior. Elder Walker is reported to have written home observing that his new companion was "very young, [and] a little green, but he will leave his mark upon the world" (Gibbons, *Joseph Fielding Smith: Gospel Scholar, Prophet of God*, 80).

His wife's letters from home helped encourage the young missionary.

LOUIE SHURTLIFF SMITH WRITING a letter.

My own precious Joseph, I do love you so much that I could not possibly tell you because it grows greater with each day that comes. . . . But I know that you love duty far more than you do pleasure and so I have so much love and trust that I feel as though you are about as near being a perfect young man as could be. . . . There are a great many things to write about, but somehow I like best to write "I love you." I sometimes think I could write it over a thousand times and still wish to write it again. . . . I am afraid if I did, you would soon be ready to scold me, but it is written in every word I write and in every stroke I make. Bless you, my own precious husband, is my prayer always. I am ever your loving wife, Louie (Gibbons, *Joseph Fielding Smith: Gospel Scholar, Prophet of God*, 95).

Joseph faithfully answered his wife's letters, and told her of his hopes.

My Beloved Wife, Another week has passed and I am that much nearer to you. . . . I am trying to learn something while I am here. Since I left Nottingham I have put my time in to study and I feel that I can hardly find a minute when I do not feel that I ought to be preparing my mind with useful knowledge. I feel that when I come home . . . more will be expected of me than I am capable of as it generally is with returned missionaries. They are . . . supposed to have learned all that the Bible contains or else they have neglected their duties. But it must not be expected of me for I am rather dull of comprehension. I have tried all day to learn a passage of scripture and have not got it yet. But I am determined to learn it before I am through (Gibbons, *Joseph Fielding Smith: Gospel Scholar, Prophet of God*, 83).

When Joseph returned from his mission, he and Louie began planning for their future together. Joseph looked for employment, and was offered a position with a temptingly large salary, but since he would be working with people whose reputation was questionable, his father advised him to look for a job among worthy associates. He said, "My son, the best company is none too good for you" (Gibbons, *Joseph Fielding Smith: Gospel Scholar, Prophet of God*, 106).

After rejecting the job offer, Joseph Fielding wrote a poem about his father's advice:

> By faith I walk on earth's broad plain,
> With hope forever in my breast;
> If valiant to the end, I'll gain
> A glorious mansion with the blest.
> O Father, lead me by the hand,
> Protect me from the wicked here,
> And give me power that I may stand
> Entrenched in truth, to me made clear.
> The best is not too good for me
> That heaven holds within its hand,
> O may I falter not but see
> The kingdom come o'er all the land.
> (Joseph F. McConkie, *True and Faithful: The Life Story of Joseph F. Smith*, 27).

CHURCH HISTORIAN

He later accepted a position in the Church historian's office. After five years in the office, he was appointed assistant Church historian. While serving in the historian's office, he wrote the book *Essentials of Church History*. He also wrote a regular feature in the Church magazine called *Answers to Gospel Questions*. These articles were later compiled into a series of books by the same name. As a historian, Joseph Fielding Smith was aware of his responsibilities, and had a keen sense of the importance of recording truth unsullied by his personal prejudices.

On March 30, 1908, Joseph's beloved wife, Louie, died from uncontrolled vomiting due to pregnancy. Louie left behind two daughters, Josephine and Julina, ages five and two. This was a lonely, hard time for Joseph. He closed his house and moved in with his parents so

GEORGINA ETHEL REYNOLDS SMITH, second wife of Joseph Fielding Smith.

JOSEPH FIELDING SMITH WITH HIS FATHER, JOSEPH F. SMITH

At the time of the photograph, Joseph Fielding Smith was an Apostle, and Joseph F. Smith was the Prophet. *May 2, 1914*

that his daughters could be cared for properly. His father counseled him to remarry, and Joseph prayerfully started seeking a new companion. After a time, he met and later married Georgina Ethel Reynolds. When Joseph Fielding was called to be an apostle, his sister, Edith, recorded:

> I remember Mother telling us that in 1910 father came home from his temple council meeting and seemed very worried. When asked what was troubling him, he said that Joseph had been chosen as one of the Twelve. He said the brethren had unanimously selected him and he said now he, as the president, would be severely criticized having his son made an apostle. Mother told him not to worry one minute as to what people might say. She knew the Lord had chosen him and said she knew he would be a credit to his calling (Smith and Stewart, *The Life of Joseph Fielding Smith*, 174-75).

APOSTLE OF GOD

Joseph Fielding was unprepared for the announcement during that April conference. He said, "I never expected to be called into the Council of the Twelve because my brother Hyrum had been called into that council before . . . and so having a brother in the council I never expected anything of that kind would come to me" (Smith and Stewart, *The Life of Joseph Fielding Smith*, 175).

Walking into the Tabernacle, he met Ben E. Rich, president of the Southern States Mission, who put his arm around Joseph and said:

> "Tell me, Brother Smith, are you going to take your place upon the stand as one of the Council of the Twelve today?"
>
> Joseph said, "Brother Rich, I have a brother in that council. There is no reason for you or anybody to think that I would be called into that council. I'm not looking for it or anything of that kind."
>
> As they walked through the tabernacle doors, the usher bantered with Joseph. "Well, Joseph, who's the new apostle to be?"
>
> "I don't know," Joseph answered, "but it won't be you and it won't be me!"
>
> Joseph took his seat and prepared to take notes. As the list of Apostles was being read, suddenly it occurred to him that his name might be the one read as the new member of the Twelve. When he heard his name read, he said, "I was so startled and dumbfound I could hardly speak" (Smith and Stewart, *The Life of Joseph Fielding Smith*, 175–76).

As Joseph later made his way through the throng of well-wishers, he hoped that no one would arrive home before him to

BEN ERASTUS RICH (1855–1933) President of the Southern States Mission; had an intuition that Joseph Fielding would be made an Apostle. *ca. 1879*

inform his wife and children. As he entered the house, he said, "I guess we'll have to sell the cow. I haven't time to take care of it anymore" (Smith and Stewart, *The Life of Joseph Fielding Smith*, 176).

Joseph Fielding recorded in his journal:

> The reading of my own name as an apostle . . . came to me, as to the entire assembly, as a most sudden and to me unexpected shock, and left me in complete bewilderment from which I have not in days recovered. I feel extremely weak and pray to my heavenly Father for strength and guidance in my great responsibility that I shall not falter nor fail to perform all that is required of me (Smith and Stewart, *The Life of Joseph Fielding Smith*, 177-78).

Congratulations poured in from friends and acquaintances. Apostle Reed Smoot, who was serving as a senator in Washington, D.C., sent a telegram, "God bless you in your apostleship. Be true and loyal to your leader" (Smith and Stewart, *The Life of Joseph Fielding Smith*, 178).

At the time of his call, Elder Smith was the moving force behind the Genealogical Society of Utah. When the Society began publishing a magazine, his daughter was under quarantine, sick with the scarlet fever. Joseph prepared the magazine's first issue, treated it with an antiseptic, and placed it in a box by his gate. From there, it was taken to the printers.

As a new Apostle, Elder Smith became accustomed to visiting stakes and attending conferences. Elder McKay often accompanied Joseph to these conferences. Joseph wrote about those days.

> In the early days . . . the brethren used to go out on assignments two by two. Often President McKay and I went together. We would travel as far as we could by train and then the local brethren would meet us with a white top or a wagon. Sometimes we continued on horses or mules or by ox team. Many times we slept out under the stars or in such houses or cabins as were available (Smith and Stewart, *The Life of Joseph Fielding Smith*, 184).

Joseph disciplined his children with love. When one of them misbehaved, Joseph would have a talk with the child, place his hand on a shoulder and softly say, "I do wish my kiddies would be good" (Gibbons, *Joseph Fielding Smith: Gospel Scholar, Prophet of God*, 227).

In response to a biographer's request, his wife, Ethel, once wrote:

> You ask me to tell you of the man I know. I have often thought when he is gone people will say, "He is a very good man, sincere, orthodox, etc." They will speak of him as the public knows him. But the man they have in mind is very different from the man I know. The man I know is a kind, loving husband and father whose greatest ambition in life is to make his family happy,

entirely forgetful of self in his efforts to do this. He is the man that lulls to
sleep the fretful child, who tells bedtime stories to the little ones, who is never
too tired or too busy to sit up late at night or to get up early in the morning
to help the older children solve perplexing school problems. . . .

The man I know is most gentle, and if he feels that he has been unjust
to anyone the distance is never too far for him to go and, with loving words
or kind deeds, erase the hurt. He welcomes gladly the young people to his
home and is never happier than when discussing with them the topics of the
day—sports or whatever interests them most. He enjoys a good story and is
quick to see the humor of a situation, to laugh and to be laughed at, always
willing to join in any wholesome activity.

The man I know is unselfish, uncomplaining, considerate, thoughtful,
sympathetic, doing everything within his power to make life a supreme joy
for his loved ones. That is the man I know (Smith and Stewart, *The Life of
Joseph Fielding Smith*, 247-48).

Joseph's children loved to walk to the railway station to see their father off
and welcome him home from his conference assignments. The family also had
a tradition of morning and evening prayer. Each morning before breakfast, and
each evening before dinner was served, the family would kneel around the table
and pray together, each taking their turn when called upon. One of the children
recalls, "It scared me every time I heard Dad pray that the purpose of the Lord
'would speedily come to pass'" (McConkie, *True and Faithful: The Life Story of
Joseph F. Smith*, 88).

When he was not on assignment, Elder Smith continued his writing. He published dozens of books and taught himself to type and prepare his own manuscripts. He called his typing method, the scripture system—"seek and ye shall find." He wrote primarily in the early morning and evening hours, but with a lot of children in the house, writing was not easy. He humorously dedicated one of his books, "To my children, without whose help this book could have been written in half the time" (Smith and Stewart, *The Life of Joseph Fielding Smith*, 6).

Joseph also enjoyed writing poetry, but he was hesitant to let anyone know. In a letter to his wife, he wrote:

> When I sent you that letter with the poetry, I told you not to show it, and if you didn't like it to burn it and you answered . . . and expressed the hope that I would try to write something again. You don't know how much good it did me to have you answer me in that way. I have written a great deal on doctrinal lines, and my writings have been published from time to time over my name. I have a confession to make to you now. I have written "poems," a *few* times before, and some of them have been published, but not with *my name attached* and no one knows it, except the editor of the paper, and I don't know if he even knows that they were mine. Some I have written, while on the train alone, to pass away the time, and they have been only for my own amusement, and afterwards I have destroyed them (Smith and Stewart, *The Life of Joseph Fielding Smith*, 190-91).

BRUCE REDD MCKONKIE (1915–1985) endorsed the gospel scholarship of Joseph Fielding Smith.

Elder Smith also became known as a scriptorian. His love of scripture reading, which started when he was a child, remained with him throughout his life and influenced his writing and speaking. He once said, "I never did learn to deliver a discourse without referring to the scriptures." (Gibbons, *Joseph Fielding Smith: Gospel Scholar, Prophet of God*, 49).

Elder Bruce R. McConkie, who edited President Smith's three-volume *Doctrines of Salvation*, said:

> Joseph Fielding Smith is the leading gospel scholar and the greatest doctrinal teacher of this generation. Few men in this dispensation have approached him in gospel knowledge or surpassed him in spiritual insight. His is the faith and the knowledge of his father, President Joseph F. Smith, and his grandfather, the Patriarch Hyrum Smith (Bruce R. McConkie, *Doctrines of Salvation: Sermons and Writings of Joseph Fielding Smith*, 1:v).

On August 26, 1937, Joseph's beloved wife, Ethel, died of a cerebral hemorrhage. One of his wife's last requests was to

JOSEPH FIELDING SMITH AND JESSIE EVANS SMITH, third wife of Joseph Fielding Smith.

have the famed Tabernacle Choir soloist, Jessie Evans, sing at her funeral. Jessie sang at the funeral, and offered to help in any way she could. She was a jovial person with an extroverted personality who had never been married. After a great deal of thought, Elder Smith wrote her a letter of proposal. He went to her home and told her that he had a special historical document that he wanted her to see. Jessie accepted, and on April 12, 1938, President Heber J. Grant married them in the Salt Lake Temple. Following the ceremony, President Grant said:

> "Now, Joseph, kiss your wife."
>
> President Smith said, "He said it like he meant it and I have been doing it ever since." About her marriage, Jessie Evans Smith said, "It couldn't be nicer. There's never been a cross word."
>
> Joseph responded, "Well, I don't know any cross words. I can't use them if I don't know them. Sister Smith is very helpful to me. She is such a happy,

pleasant person. We enjoy each other and often spend time studying together" (Smith and Stewart, *The Life of Joseph Fielding Smith*, 13-14).

A little more than a year later, in 1939, Elder and Sister Smith toured the European Missions. It was a dangerous and sad assignment. War was spreading, and missionaries were being called home. Concerning the Saints in Germany, Elder Smith wrote, "Some of them are as faithful as any that can be found in any land. . . . I have felt very keenly that I would, if I had the power, pick them up in one body . . . and transplant them somewhere in Zion" (Smith and Stewart, *The Life of Joseph Fielding Smith*, 282).

Elder Smith was also concerned about European genealogical records. Shortly after World War II started, the Church's efforts to obtain microfilm copies of vital records from Denmark were disrupted. England also refused the Church access to its vital records. Although Elder Smith was concerned about the safety of these records, he felt that after the war, the records would still be available. His feelings were summed up in his statement, "The Lord will look after his own" (Hartshorn, *Classic Stories From the Lives of Our Prophets*, 321). Following the war, literally millions of names were microfilmed, and numerous records were preserved.

Elder Smith had a direct way of looking at the gospel. He applied gospel principles to his own life and encouraged others to do the same. Once, a young convert asked him, "Shall I remain in Salt Lake City or go east to study?"

Joseph replied, "It doesn't make one bit of difference where you live, as long as you keep the commandments of the Lord" (Bruce R. McConkie, "Joseph Fielding Smith: Apostle, Prophet, Father in Israel," *Ensign*, Aug, 1972, 24-28). Outwardly, Elder Smith seemed reserved, but close acquaintances knew of his keen sense of humor and appreciation for adventure. One day, a visitor came to his office, but the secretary said he was not in. The visitor related:

> I remember my surprise one day when I called at his office. . . . His secretary . . . said, "Step to the window here and maybe you can see him." . . .
>
> All I could see was a jet streaking through the sky. Its trail of white vapor clearly marked some steep climbs, loops, dives, rolls and turns. . . .
>
> "You mean he's in that plane?" I asked.
>
> "Oh, yes. . . . He's very fond of flying—says it relaxes him. A friend in the National Guard calls him up and says, 'How about relaxing?' And up they go." . . .
>
> Well, I could not resist driving to the airport to be there when he landed. As the two-place T-Bird roared down the runway to a stop, from the rear cockpit climbed [President Smith], then about eighty, smiling broadly.
>
> "That was wonderful. That's just about as close to heaven as I can get just now" (Smith and Stewart, *The Life of Joseph Fielding Smith*, 1-2).

PROPHET OF GOD

Joseph Fielding Smith served as a member of the Quorum of the Twelve for sixty years. Following President McKay's death, Joseph Fielding Smith became the tenth President of the Church. He was ninety-three when he was sustained as President of the Church on April 6, 1970, at which time he humbly expressed his gratitude for the blessings of the Lord upon himself, his family, the members of the Church, and all the inhabitants of the world.

APOSTLE JOSEPH FIELDING SMITH "RELAX-ING" IN THE COCKPIT OF A FIGHTER JET. Joseph was very interested in flying, and took his first flight in a fighter jet on June 9, 1954. (l to r) Colonel Alma G. Winn, Joseph Fielding Smith, and General Maxwell E. Rich. *1954*

One of the greatest moments of President Smith's administration was the first all-British conference. This was the first time that all of the British Saints had gathered together to see and hear a Prophet of God in person. It was a thrilling and memorable occasion. President Smith enjoyed the experience, and continued to travel as much as his health would allow.

A year after his call, his beloved Jessie passed away. Her death was a severe blow and caused his health to begin to decline. On Sunday, July 2, 1972, President Smith attended sacrament meeting, then came home and listened to his granddaughter read from the scriptures. He ate supper, sat in his favorite chair and talked with his daughter, Amelia. At 9:20 in the evening, Amelia left the room for a moment. When she returned, she found her father unconscious. He died a short time later, without struggle or apparent pain.

Following his funeral, Harold B. Lee wrote a letter to President Smith's children:

> From the first time I heard your father, when, as a young boy I sat in the old opera house at Preston, Idaho, and heard one of the youngest apostles bear his testimony, and to preach doctrinal sermons, I have leaned upon and listened to his counsel and interpretations of the gospel principles, . . . knowing, as I have been told many times by him, that he was tutored by his father Joseph F. Smith. I have realized that through his father and his forebears generally, of the generations that have passed, he had the constant guiding inspiration from Joseph Smith, Sr. through Hyrum Smith and his father Joseph F. Smith, and to him personally. We who are the recipients of that kind of inspiration are now humbly grateful and I personally, that I can now dip into the treasure house of what he has left us and there be more certain than I otherwise could be in the responsibilities which now are mine (Smith and Stewart, *The Life of Joseph Fielding Smith*, 383).

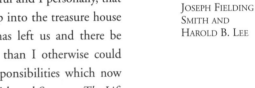

JOSEPH FIELDING SMITH AND HAROLD B. LEE

Elder Spencer W. Kimball commented on President Smith's kindness and solicitude: "Many times we have said that since the Twelve will be judges of Israel, any of us would be happy to fall into his hands for his judgment would be kind, merciful, just and holy" (McConkie, "Joseph Fielding Smith: Apostle, Prophet, Father in Israel," *Ensign*, Aug 1972, 24–28).

HAROLD B. LEE

Serving God and His Fellow Men

In Salt Lake City, when President Joseph Fielding Smith passed away, Harold B. Lee became the eleventh President of the Church. President Lee, at age seventy-three, brought renewed vigor to the office.

HIS EARLY YEARS

He was born in Clifton, Idaho, on March 28, 1899, and was the second child of Samuel and Louisa Lee. He later wrote what he had been told about his birth. "At the time of my birth, my Father was away from home working on a canal and the weather was very stormy. It was necessary to send Bert Henderson with the news of the pending birth. There seems to have been some disappointment when I arrived, Mother having hoped for a girl" (L. Brent Goates, *Harold B. Lee, Prophet and Seer*, 31).

Harold's older brother, Perry, described his younger brother as a child:

> Harold had beautiful, heavy, wavy brown hair, and Mother, I think somewhat disappointed that her firstlings were not girls, took full advantage of his crowning glory to train his hair into dangling ringlets

HAROLD B. LEE served as President from 1972–1973.

that reached below his shoulders. The neighbor ladies would exclaim him "a beautiful picture" in his Lord Fauntleroy ruffles and lace-trimmed sleeves, but no boy could tolerate such a travesty to manhood, nor did he, for too long.

We arrived at the small school every day dressed in knee pants with white starched cuffs folded back over the coat sleeves and white sailor-collars draped down over the shoulders. And those ringlets were carefully combed and painstakingly curled, dangling down our backs for all the world to see and pull—and scoff.

When Harold arrived at school, still with his mass of beautiful hair, it may have been the first time he went into training for the hard knocks of life to come. Suffice [it] to record that those curls caused more skinned knuckles and black eyes than either politics or religion. Finally, he had had enough. I remember now how our mother wept when he purloined a pair of scissors and literally "sawed" off one of the frontal danglers, spoiling the whole effect, which made it necessary to delete the remainder, a welcomed relief (Goates, *Harold B. Lee, Prophet and Seer*).

As a farm boy, Harold's work included feeding and caring for the animals and garden. During this time he learned a significant lesson about following the promptings of the spirit:

. . . As a young boy I was out on a farm . . . playing about . . . when I saw over the fence in the neighbor's yard some broken-down buildings with the sheds caving in. . . . I imagined . . . that might be a castle I should explore, so I went over to the fence and started to climb through. Then I heard a voice as distinctly as you are hearing mine: "Harold, don't go over there." I looked in every direction to see where the speaker was. I wondered if it was my father, but he couldn't see me; he was way up at the other end of the field. There was no one in sight. I realized that someone was warning me of an unseen danger—whether there was nest of rattlesnakes, or whether the rotting timbers would fall on me and crush me, I don't know. But from that time on, I accepted without question . . . that there are processes not known to man by which we can hear voices from the unseen world, by which we can have brought to us visions of eternity (*Stories from the General Authorities*, Mar. 1973, 12).

His life was also preserved on another occasion:

There was a severe thunderstorm raging near the mountains where our home was located. Our family [was] seated in the kitchen before an open door, watching the great display of nature's fireworks. A flash of chain lightning followed by an immediate loud clap of thunder indicated that the lightning had struck very close. I was playing back and forth in the doorway when suddenly and without warning, my mother gave me a vigorous push that sent me sprawling backwards out of the doorway. At that instant, a bolt of lightning came down the chimney of the kitchen stove, out through the kitchen's open doorway, and split a huge gash from top to bottom in a large tree immediately in front of the house. If it had not been for Mother's intuitive action, and if I remained in the door opening, I wouldn't be writing this story today (Leonard J. Arrington & Susan Arrington Madsen, *Mothers of the Prophets*, 172).

Harold's mother worried about her children when they were away from home. Perry, Harold's older brother, recalled how their mother kept track of her children:

Our mother had a system all her own in keeping her brood in line and under surveillance. She always saw to it that we went to our parties and various interests outside the home, two by two, secure in the knowledge that when we returned, she was bound to get the whole story—from the mouths of two witnesses (Goates, *Harold B. Lee, Prophet and Seer*, 27).

Harold and his brother also enjoyed music. Perry told how their musical interests developed.

Our father surprised us one day as we were convalescing from a bout with scarlet fever by bringing into our sickroom two shining instruments—a baritone horn for Harold and a cornet for me. That cured the fever in jig time, but I'm afraid the raucous sounds that came from those shiny horns in the learning process gave our parents many a headache (Goates, *Harold B. Lee, Prophet and Seer*, 46).

HAROLD B. LEE as a young man.

Harold played in the school military band and in the Preston Town Band. He also played his favorite sport—basketball. He became a reporter for the school paper and was on the debate team. He enjoyed his fellow classmates and participated in school pranks.

In the graduating class, there were but five girls and 25 boys; a great bunch of fellows. On the night of Founders' Day, we climbed to the top of the flag pole over the Academy and nailed our class colors, and then each in turn climbed to the flag and kissed the colors. After singing and giving class yells we retired to our rooms, and awoke in the morning to discover that during the night our colors were taken down by the junior class. A grand fight followed which was finally stopped by officers (Goates, *Harold B. Lee, Prophet and Seer*, 48).

LOVE OF TEACHING

When Harold was seventeen, he attended the Albion State Normal School at Albion, Idaho, to train to become a teacher. When he passed his examinations, he accepted a teaching position at the Silver Star School near Weston, Idaho. At the one-room school, he taught about twenty-five students who ranged from first to eighth grade.

So conscientious was I that I would count the youngsters on the grounds, and if they were all there, I would ring the bell, although it was many times not much after 8:30 a.m. Almost nightly I placed my school problems before the Lord, and although I never worried so much over a work, the Lord never deserted me and I learned some of the most valuable lessons of self-mastery of my life (Goates, *Harold B. Lee, Prophet and Seer*, 51).

SPARREL HUFF AND HAROLD B. LEE were debate partners in high school.

His older brother, Perry, wrote about his brother's first job, "His lone first grader, Vasal by name, was either his greatest problem or his prize pupil, for I heard his name muttered often in his nighttime dreams as he visited home on weekends" (Goates, *Harold B. Lee, Prophet and Seer*, 51).

The following year, Harold became the principal at the school in Oxford, Idaho. In addition to his duties as principal, he taught classes, organized the Oxford Athletic Club, and played the trombone in a dance band. When he was twenty-one, he was called to serve a mission in the Western States. He arrived at mission headquarters in Denver on November 10, 1920.

A MISSION TO THE WESTERN STATES

After his first day of door-to-door tracting in Denver, Harold recorded, "The first lady we met shut the door in our faces while we were trying to tell her our message. We had eight gospel conversations, one lady promised to attend our church, and only two refused our literature" (Goates, *Harold B. Lee, Prophet and Seer*, 61).

Early in his mission, Elder Lee was called upon to perform a blessing. This was the first time he had performed this priesthood ordinance, and he was nervous. He said, "When I began to anoint the girl I forgot the whole prayer and made a mess of things. While we were going home Elder Woodbury asked me if I would get sore at him if he told me something. Reassured, he said, 'For Pete's sake don't ever do it like that.' I'll never forget that lesson" (Goates, *Harold B. Lee, Prophet and Seer*, 61).

Elder Lee had been in the mission field just nine months when he was called to be the president of the Denver conference.

> Only nine short months since I arrived in Denver, and when I think back on all the wonderful experiences that have been mine in that time, I feel as though it had been but a dream, but I thank the Lord continually. The crying necessities of today wake me up to the fact that I must be working always if God is to accomplish anything through me (Francis M. Gibbons, *Harold B. Lee: Man of Vision, Prophet of God*, 56).

Presiding over a conference in those days meant being the presiding authority over all the missionaries, branch presidents, and Saints in a geographical area. During his mission, Harold B. Lee met a special person—his future wife.

FERN TANNER LEE AND HAROLD B. LEE

> Fern L. Tanner arrived in Denver just two weeks before I did, and I met her on her birthday, Nov. 14, 1920, three days after I arrived. From that day, her influence became a power in my life. Little did I dream that some day she would become my wife and the mother of my children. She was transferred to the Pueblo Conference, and we corresponded during the entire time she labored there. She later returned to the mission office in Denver to work a short period before her release (Goates, *Harold B. Lee, Prophet and Seer*, 76).

MARRIAGE AND PARENTHOOD

Fern and Harold continued to correspond after they had returned home from their missions, and soon they were engaged.

> On November 14, 1923, I was married to Fern L. Tanner in the Salt Lake Temple. . . . Never doubting our

ability to get ahead together, we put our full trust in each other and moved into our first home.

The first year of our married life was a glorious honeymoon in which we made preparations for our first baby. Despite the fact that we carefully followed the instructions of Dr. A. C. Callister, Fern came near losing her life from a serious hemorrhage when our baby [Maurine] was born.

Within fifteen months our second baby came. Fern had been in constant labor pain for sixty hours before Helen was born on November 25th, 1925. With her birth we saw the beginning of a sweet companionship of close sisters that developed with each year of their lives (Goates, *Harold B. Lee, Prophet and Seer*, 84).

CHURCH SERVICE

A few years later, at the age of thirty-one, Harold B. Lee was called to serve as the stake president of the Pioneer Stake. The country was experiencing a great economic depression, and President Lee was concerned about the welfare of those in his stake. In order to help the needy, President Lee organized a Stake Welfare Program that later became a model for the entire Church.

An employment committee in each ward . . . kept in touch with the available male and female workers. . . . Workers from all wards were assigned to farm and industrial projects, which were organized from Provo on the south to Layton on the north.

Workers were told that for their services the stake would undertake to see that food and fuel and shelter for themselves and their families would be provided fully. Hundreds of tons of produce soon began to roll in—peaches, tomatoes, fruits, vegetables and meats. Relief Society women were organized and two canning machines were purchased for their own use. . . .

After supplying our families and stocking our storehouse, we were able to sell considerable surplus to outside people.

The storehouse was known as the Pioneer Stake Bishop's Storehouse (Goates, *Harold B. Lee, Prophet and Seer*, 94-95).

The first Christmas after Harold had been made a stake president, he learned a great lesson.

He found a family nearby who had no Christmas gifts because their father was out of work. President Lee felt very sad about this. That night he knelt down and prayed to his Heavenly Father: "God grant that I will never let another year pass but that I, as a leader, will truly know my people. I will know their needs, I will be conscious of those who most need my leadership, and I will help them" (Madsen, *The Lord Needed a Prophet*, 179-80).

Steward over Church Welfare

In 1935, President Lee was called to the office of the First Presidency and asked by President Grant to take charge of a Church-wide welfare program. Harold was stunned and humbled by the calling.

> My humble place in this [welfare] program was described. I left there about noontime. I drove up to the head of City Creek Canyon. I got out, after I had driven as far as I could, and I walked up through the trees. I sought my Heavenly Father. As I sat down to pore over this matter, wondering about an organization to be perfected to carry [on] this work, I received a testimony, on that beautiful spring afternoon, that God had already revealed the greatest organization that ever could be given to mankind and that all that was needed now was that the organization be set to work and the temporal welfare of the Latter-day Saints would be safeguarded (General Conference Address, April 6, 1941).

Harold B. Lee did his best, and made quite an impression on others. Marion G. Romney remembered the first time they met. He said, "I ran across a back lot at lunchtime to a neighboring grocery store. The operator, a Brother Tanner, introduced me to his brother-in-law, Harold B. Lee. He was dressed in striped coveralls. He reached out his right [hand] to shake mine. Captivated by his magnetic presence, I felt I had found a friend" (Marion G. Romney, "In the Shadow of the Almighty," *Ensign*, Feb. 1974, 95-96).

Elder Lee Called as an Apostle

That same year, the Presiding Bishopric of the Church started a new membership record system that included a master record located in a central location. During April conference, the First Presidency announced a new position of Assistant to the Twelve.

In 1941, the United States once again faced the possibility of war. President Roosevelt signed the Selective Service Act. Then on December 7, the Japanese bombed Pearl Harbor, plunging the United States into war with Japan, and subsequently with Germany and Italy. In Europe, Nazi troops invaded Soviet Russia. And in the world of entertainment and the arts, Orson Welles's film, *Citizen Kane*, premiered.

Elder Reed Smoot had died, leaving a vacancy in the Quorum of the Twelve, and Harold B. Lee was called to fill the vacancy. He was forty-two years old, and twenty years younger than any other man in the quorum. Elder Lee wrote:

> When the call to the apostleship came, it was on a Saturday night of general conference. I was called to the front of the Tabernacle to meet the President of the Church and I walked into the general authorities room and found him crying. He put his hands on my shoulders and told me that I had been named to be a member of the Council of the Twelve. I said to him, "Oh, President, do you think I am worthy of that?"

As quick as a flash he said, "If I didn't think so, my boy, you wouldn't be called" (Goates, *Harold B. Lee, Prophet and Seer*, 158).

Then I spent a night I shall never forget. There was no sleep that night. All my life seemed to be coming before me as in a panorama. I could have told you every person who had any ill will toward me. I could have told you every person against whom I had any ill will, and the feeling came that before I was worthy to accept that call as an Apostle of the Lord Jesus Christ, I had to love and forgive every soul that walked the earth (*Teachings of the Prophet, Harold B. Lee*, Ch. 28).

Following conference, President Steven L. Richards approached Elder Lee. "Brother Lee," he said, "next Sunday is Easter, and we have decided to ask you to give the Sunday night radio talk, the Easter talk, on the resurrection of the Lord. You understand now, of course, that as a member of the Council of the Twelve, you are to be one of the special witness[es] of the life and mission of the Savior and of that great event" (*The Heavens Are Open*, 1992 Sperry Symposium, 103).

Elder Lee was profoundly touched and made special preparations for the talk.

. . . I locked myself in one of the rooms over in the Church Office building, and took out the Bible. I read in the four Gospels, particular[ly] the scriptures pertaining to the death, crucifixion and resurrecting of the Lord. And as I read, I suddenly became aware that something strange was happening. It wasn't just a story I was reading, for it seemed as though the events I was reading about were very real, as though I were actually living those experiences. On Sunday night I delivered my humble message and said and now, I, one of the least of the apostles here on the earth today, bear you witness that I, too, know with all my soul that Jesus is the Savior of the world and that He lived and died and was resurrected for us (*The Heavens Are Open*, 1992 Sperry Symposium,103).

Everyone who knew Harold B. Lee knew that he had a great understanding of the scriptures. His daughter, Helen, said that she and her sister Maurine grew up studying the scriptures with their father.

Whenever we had a question as we prepared for a two-and-a half-minute talk we were to give, or whenever anything was discussed around the table requiring an answer, we'd ask, "What about this, Dad? What do you think?" He would reply, "Get out your scriptures, girls, and let's see what the Lord says about it." He would get his book, too, and have us turn to the right scripture and we'd read together what we needed to know (Goates, *Harold B Lee, Prophet and Seer*, Ch. 9).

Elder Lee also helped his daughters overcome the insecurities and awkwardness of adolescence.

> In our awkward, adolescent years he would tell us often that he was so proud of his beautiful, charming daughters. Well, I knew I was anything but beautiful and charming. My hair was "Dutch" cut, I wore horn-rimmed glasses which I hated, I was pudgy and overweight and even had to wear corrective shoes. Yet, I reasoned, if Daddy thought I was beautiful, I must try very hard to be what he thought I was, because I just couldn't disappoint him. So every night in my prayers I asked God to help me become what my daddy thought I was already (Goates, *Harold B. Lee, Prophet and Seer*, 119).

Elder Lee vigorously began his assignment as a member of the Quorum of the Twelve. He traveled extensively and visited missions throughout the world. In a talk given at conference just two years after his call as an Apostle, he told about what he had learned.

HAROLD B. LEE WITH SPENCER W. KIMBALL These men were particularly close friends. When Elder Kimball had surgery to remove cancer from his vocal chords, Elder Lee was by his side.

When a decision has been reached by the presiding councils of the Church and a majority of these councils have decided on a certain policy, and there then develops a minority vote contrary to that majority decision, one may know with a surety that that minority voice is not speaking the will of the Lord. I tremble when I think of that statement. I am greatly concerned when I now sit in one of the presiding councils of the Church and remember that in days gone by, some have fallen by the way because they went out in contradiction of the majority decision of that body. . . . Should there be those, even though in high places, who may come among us who are not speaking the policy of the Church as declared by the men whom we sustain as prophets of the living God, the Church may know that those who thus speak are not speaking the mind of the Lord and the voice of the Lord and the power of God unto salvation (Hartshorn, *Classic Stories From the Lives of Our Prophets*, 342).

Elder Lee was particularly close to Spencer W. Kimball. When Elder Kimball had surgery to remove cancer from his vocal cords, Elder Lee was by his side. He accompanied Elder Kimball when the crucial decision about the surgery was made, and told the doctor, "This patient of yours is no ordinary man" (Goates, *Harold B. Lee, Prophet and Seer*, 301).

Elder and Sister Lee stayed with the Kimballs during and after surgery to make sure things went as smoothly as possible. The surgery was successful and, as they had hoped, Elder Kimball was left with a changed, but usable, voice.

Elder Lee continued his work on the Welfare Program of the Church, and helped make it a vital growing program. He was also asked by President McKay to help lead the correlation program, which was designed to help the auxiliaries work together more effectively under the leadership of the priesthood.

Harold B. Lee's life was visited with tragedy, however, when his wife, Fern, passed away on September 24, 1962 after a series of small strokes. Her daughter, Helen, had once talked with her about someone in their ward who had remarried following his wife's death. Helen had been shocked:

FERN LUCINDA TANNER LEE (1895–1962), first wife of Harold B. Lee, died after a series of small strokes.

"I think that's just terrible! I think that's being so disrespectful to his first wife. He must not have loved her very much!"

My mother then turned quietly to me and said: "Oh, my dear, you don't understand what it is to love someone. If I were to go before Daddy and I think that we will have to face that probability, I could never rest until I knew that your father was happily married again. I just couldn't bear to think of him being alone."

I replied, "Mother, how can you say that? Don't you love him enough so that you just couldn't stand to see another woman taking care of him and living with him?"

"It's because I *do* love him so much that I *can* think of it, and that's what I want for him. I cannot bear the thoughts of him being alone and lonesome and not having his needs cared for by someone who loves him as I do. I would want him to remarry, and I mean soon, after I go, so that he will not be lonely—don't you see?" (Goates, *Harold B. Lee, Prophet and Seer*, 138-39).

HAROLD B. LEE
WITH HIS SECOND
WIFE, FREDA JOAN
JENSEN LEE

Following Fern's death, Elder Lee became reacquainted with Freda Joan Jensen. When the two began contemplating marriage, Elder Lee sought the feelings of his children and shared his marriage plans with President McKay and two other intimate friends in the Quorum of the Twelve. He wrote:

After the Sunday concluding session of June MIA Conference I told Marian Romney of my plans to be married Monday. He was very emotional. Henry Moyle came and asked if he could be at the marriage. I asked if he would like to be a witness. With emotion, he replied, "Would you permit me to?" Marion Romney asked also. I told them if President McKay would perform the marriage ceremony and they two would be witnesses, it would be perfect (Goates, *Harold B. Lee, Prophet and Seer*, 360).

Just three years later, his beloved daughter, Maurine, died leaving a family of small children. Elder Lee was crushed. He said, "My heart is broken as I contemplate the passing of my darling "Sunshine" and the great need that Ernie and her little family of [four children]" (Gibbons, *Harold B. Lee: Man of Vision, Prophet of God*, 404).

In a conference address, Elder Lee spoke about his daughter's death:

Many times I personally have wondered at the Master's cry of anguish in the Garden of Gethsemane. . . . As I advance in years, I begin to understand in some small measure how the Master must have felt. In the loneliness of a distant hotel room, 2,500 miles away, you, too, may one day cry out from the depths of your soul, as was my experience: Oh dear God, don't let her die; I need her; her family needs her.

Neither the Master's prayer nor my prayer was answered. The purpose of that personal suffering may only be explained in what the Lord said through the Apostle Paul:

"Though he were a Son, yet learned he obedience by the things which he suffered" (*I Know That My Redeemer Lives*, 168).

On July 2, 1972, after spending a day in meetings, President Joseph Fielding Smith died quietly at his home. Elder Harold B. Lee's daughter, Helen, was with her father when he received a phone call informing him of the Prophet's death.

I'll never forget the look on his face. He kept repeating, "Oh, no. No. Oh, no." (Apparently Douglas Smith was rehearsing the details of his father's, President Smith's, passing.) He covered the phone receiver and looked as though all the cares in the world had suddenly settled upon him. He said to us, so gravely, "President Smith is gone." He finished his conversation with Douglas but was visibly shaken.

I had never seen him look so weak and so completely at a loss. . . . It was only a moment, however, until he straightened up, squared his shoulders, and began to take charge (Goates, *Harold B. Lee, Prophet and Seer*, Ch. 26).

FIRST GENERAL CONFERENCE ADDRESS AS PROPHET

In the October 1972 general conference, President Lee told the Saints that he had recently read a statement by Joseph Smith where he compared himself

to a great rough stone rolling down from a high mountain that was smoothed by the bumps along the way.

HAROLD B. LEE'S
FIRST PRESIDENCY
N. Eldon Tanner,
President Harold B.
Lee, and Marion G.
Romney.

These thoughts now running through my mind begin to give greater meaning to some of the experiences in my life, things that have happened which have been difficult for me to understand. At times it seemed as though I too was like a rough stone rolling down from a high mountainside, being buffeted and polished, I suppose, by experiences, that I too might overcome and become a polished shaft in the quiver of the Almighty (Harold B. Lee, *Stand Ye in Holy Places,* 170).

As President Lee concluded the conference, he testified that Christ stood at the head of the Church.

> There has come to me, in these last few days a deepening and reassuring faith. I can't leave this conference without saying to you that I have a conviction that the Master hasn't been absent from us on these occasions. This is his Church. Where else would he rather be than right here at the headquarters of his Church? He isn't an absentee master; he's concerned about us. He wants us to follow where he leads. I know that he is a living reality, as is our Heavenly Father (*Conference Report*, October 1972, 133).

President Lee led the Church for only 18 months. During his presidency, he presided at the first area conferences held in Mexico, and in Munich, Germany. He also was the first President of the Church to visit Israel.

His love for everyone was always apparent. At the area conference in Mexico, he told the Saints:

> Now I want to tell you a little sacred experience I had following the call to be the President of the Church. On the early morning thereafter with my wife I kneeled in humble prayer, and suddenly it seemed as though my mind and heart went out to over three million people in all the world. I seemed

HAROLD B. LEE PRESIDING OVER FIRST AREA CONFERENCE IN MEXICO

to have a love for every one of them, no matter where they lived nor what their color was, whether they were rich or poor, whether they were humble or great, or educated or not. Suddenly I felt as though they all belonged to me, as though they were all my own brothers and sisters (*Teachings of the Prophet, Harold B. Lee*, Ch. 28).

Barbara B. Smith, who was then serving as general president of the Relief Society, recorded after speaking with President Lee:

One evening as I conversed with President Harold B. Lee, I said to him, "President Lee, you seem different someway tonight." He smiled and said, "You know what it is, don't you." I shook my head and said that I really didn't know. Then he shared with me this remarkable experience, saying:

"After I became the President of the Church, I thought a great deal about what the Lord wanted me to do. One night, while I was sleeping, President McKay came to me in a dream. He pointed his finger and looked at me with those piercing eyes of his as only President McKay could do, and he said, 'If you would serve the Lord, you must love and serve his children. I awakened with a compelling desire to learn all I could about love that I might serve the Lord. . . .

After I had read everything the scriptures had to say about love, I began to put into practice all that I had gleaned from my study. That's what you can feel. It is my new-found ability to truly love and serve his children."

I watched President Lee even more closely that night and noted that not one person who came to the table to shake his hand left without receiving a special word of encouragement or an extra question that indicated the concern of the Prophet. No one went away without seeing his smile or hearing his words of love (Barbara B. Smith, "Love Is Life," *New Era*, Feb. 1986, 44-45).

HEALTH PROBLEMS

However, President Lee was plagued with blood clots in his lungs. On Fast Sunday, the first week of November 1973, President Lee stood and spoke briefly in his home ward. This would be the last time they would hear from him. "By way of testimony I want you to know that I know that God lives, that Jesus is the Christ and our Redeemer, and he is at the head of this Church; I am not. I *know* that he operates in all the affairs of this Church and I say this by way of testimony that you may know that I know he lives (Goates, *Harold B. Lee, Prophet and Seer*, 564).

On Christmas Day, 1973, President Lee was feeling weak and ill. He attended a family gathering and enjoyed the holiday. The following day, he was rushed to the hospital and, in spite of the doctors' best efforts, passed away. Russell M. Nelson recorded his reaction to the news of President Lee's death and a special dream he had regarding why President Lee was taken.

I learned about his passing while I was home playing games with the children, still full of the festive spirit remaining from Christmas the day before. . . . Shocked and struck with grief, I had an overpowering urge to leave home and go at once to the LDS Hospital. As I rushed there to the side of President Kimball, I quietly mourned for the loss of this giant in the kingdom, my beloved and esteemed friend, President Harold B. Lee.

Since the passing of President Lee, I had had two very special dreams involving him. In dream there were two vivid messages: First, that if President Lee had gone on living, a very severe affliction would have developed in his body, which if allowed to progress, would have given him great pain, suffering and incapacity. The medical details of this were dreadful and distressing. He said his sudden death in December of 1973 was brought about as an act of love and mercy, for the Lord wished to spare him and the Church the misery that otherwise would have ensued. His second message was that the revelations received and the actions subsequently taken by President Kimball were the very same as would have been received and performed by President Lee had he remained as the Prophet. President Lee exclaimed that the Lord gives His will to His living prophet regardless of who the prophet is at the time, for the Lord indeed is directing His Church (Russell M. Nelson, *From Heart to Heart*, 159-60).

RUSSELL MARION NELSON (1924–) had a special dream about why President Lee died.

Tributes and messages of sympathy poured in to the Church and to President Lee's family. One of the first to pay his respects was Elder Spencer W. Kimball.

President Harold B. Lee and I have been associated in the Council of the Twelve from 1943 until he was called into the First Presidency by President Joseph Fielding Smith in 1970. Even before that time we had established a friendship. He was my ideal. He had a tremendous understanding of the doctrines of the restored gospel of Jesus Christ, and of the organization and functioning of the Church.

President Lee was a great friend of the down-trodden and sorrowing. While he was an outstanding administrator and tireless worker, frequently he found time to visit the sick and those heavy of heart. When President Lee prayed, he really talked with his Heavenly Father.

He truly measured up as a prophet of God in every way—in leadership, perception, activity, and in his responses. He was a man of superior courage. Many times I have seen him stand alone for a principle. He would give his unshakable witness of the divinity of the restored gospel without hesitation, to the mighty of the earth as well as to the lowly.

President Lee stood tall as a leader among men, both within and without the Church (Goates, *Harold B. Lee, Prophet and Seer*, 585).

A NEW PROPHET IS SUSTAINED

A shocked Church received word that their Prophet of only eighteen months had died. On December 30, 1973, Spencer W. Kimball, President of the Quorum of the Twelve, was set apart as the twelfth President of the Church.

WORLD EVENTS

In 1973, East and West Germany were both admitted to the United Nations. Fierce fighting surrounded the beginning of the Arab-Israeli Yom Kippur War, and a cease-fire was finally effected in October. Pablo Picasso, considered by some to be the world's greatest artist, died at the age of ninety-one. And in the world of sports, George Foreman became the heavyweight boxing champion of the world.

SPENCER W. KIMBALL

"Lengthen Your Stride"

Spencer Woolley Kimball was born in Salt Lake City on March 28, 1895. He was the sixth child of Olive and Andrew Kimball and the grandson of Heber C. Kimball. As a small boy, when Spencer was asked if he had a middle name, he would answer "Woolley." The other children laughed at his name, so he began introducing himself simply as Spencer Kimball.

When Spencer was three years old, his family moved to the Gila Valley of Arizona when his father was called there as the new stake president. A call to Arizona was like a call to another country, and friends and relatives bid tearful good-byes. After four days of traveling, the Kimball family arrived in Thatcher, Arizona. When they arrived, the wind was blowing so hard that no one could hear the group of singers that had gathered to welcome their new stake president. The Kimballs moved into a three-room adobe house. Andrew expanded the living quarters with a tent, but one night, in a stiff wind, part of the tent collapsed, and Spencer, who was then five years old, rolled out of bed onto the ground.

[The family] were awakened by his pitiful cry, as it frightened him to fall onto the ground in the night. He came walking around to the tent door. We had a

SPENCER W. KIMBALL served as President from 1973–1985.

good laugh over it next morning but he did not think it funny while he was passing through the tent (Edward L. Kimball and Andrew E. Kimball, Jr., *Spencer W. Kimball, Twelfth President of The Church of Jesus Christ of Latter-day Saints*, 21).

The family had little cash, but it was entirely normal to wear hand-me-downs, homemade clothing, and patched trousers in their new hometown. Spencer later said, "We didn't know we were poor. We thought we were living pretty well" (Kimball and Kimball, *Spencer W. Kimball, Twelfth President of The Church of Jesus Christ of Latter-day Saints*, 23).

Young Spencer learned many valuable lessons from his parents. In the summer when Spencer was five, his father gave him and Alice a patch of planted potatoes. When Spencer had dug them with a garden fork and Alice had cleaned them, off they went with a box of potatoes in Spencer's red wagon. The potatoes sold. Spencer and Alice returned home jubilant. Andrew listened to them count their money, then said: "That's capital. Now what will you do with the money?"

The children answered: ice cream, candy and Christmas presents. Andrew gently said: "Now, you haven't forgotten the bishop have you? The Lord has been kind to us. We planted and cultivated and harvested, but the earth is the Lord's. He sent the moisture and the sunshine. One-tenth we always give back to the Lord for his part"

"Pa made no requirement," remembered Spencer, "he merely explained it so convincingly that we felt it an honor and privilege to pay tithing" (Kimball and Kimball, *Spencer W. Kimball, Twelfth President of The Church of Jesus Christ of Latter-day Saints*, 23).

⋇

Spencer loved Primary, and he found that by attending Primary he could also get out of helping with chores. One day he was stomping down hay that his older brothers were pitching onto a wagon. They were teasing him by pitching the hay on top of him and laughing as he struggled. Suddenly, Spencer heard the Primary bell.

SPENCER W. KIMBALL AND BROTHERS IN A HAY WAGON. Spencer is in the center, with his brothers Gordon and Delbert.

> "I've got to go to Primary."
> "You're not going to Primary."
> "If Pa were here he'd let me go to Primary."
> "Well, Pa is not here, and this one time you're not going to Primary."

Spencer recalled:

> Gordon was seven years older than I was and Del was five. They were much larger. I was just a little boy. They kept throwing the hay up and it all piled in the center of the wagon. They said, "What's the matter with you up there?"
>
> There was no sound. They looked off across the field and I was halfway to the meetinghouse. I've always gotten lots of credit from people for being a very good Primary boy (Kimball and Kimball, *Spencer W. Kimball, Twelfth President of The Church of Jesus Christ of Latter-day Saints*, 38).

However, when Spencer was seven, he nearly drowned at a community picnic. He recalled:

Father is such a good swimmer. How I wish I could swim like he does. All over the great pond he moves easily and seemingly without effort. Now he comes for me, his little boy. I am on his back with my arms around his neck so tightly that he must constantly warn me. The water is deep and I'm scared and I plead with him to take me back to the shallow water. At last we feel ground and I say "I'm alright now, Pa," and I see him turn and swim off toward deep water. I take a step toward shore and fall into a deep hole. Down, down, down! Water is filling my lungs. . . . I cannot scream! Why doesn't somebody get help? Will they never rescue me? Someone has now seen my predicament. Pa has heard their screams and is after me. I'm full of water and coughing, spitting, crying for a long time. I thought I was drowned (Kimball and Kimball, *Spencer W. Kimball, Twelfth President of The Church of Jesus Christ of Latter-day Saints*, 35).

Spencer loved and admired his father, and he even enjoyed doing chores when his father was there to help. Andrew saw something special in his son. One day while Spencer was busy milking one of the cows, his father stood in the doorway of the barn talking to a neighbor who had just delivered a load of pumpkins.

SPENCER W. KIMBALL AND CLARENCE NAYLOR as young boys. Clarence and Spencer were lifelong friends.

ANDREW KIMBALL (1858–1924), Spencer's father.

That boy, Spencer, is an exceptional boy. He always tried to mind me, whatever I asked him to do. I have dedicated him to be one of the mouthpieces of the Lord—the Lord willing. You will see him someday as a great leader. I have dedicated him to the service of God, and he will become a mighty man in the Church (Spencer W. Kimball, *Faith Precedes the Miracle*, xvi).

LOSS OF HIS MOTHER

One of the hardest times of Spencer's life was when his mother died. Spencer was just eleven years old, and his mother was pregnant with her twelfth child. She was sent to Salt Lake to be cared for, but miscarried and died from an infection. The children had no idea that their mother was in danger when they were called out of school.

"We ran home from school," Spencer recalled. "Dear Bishop Moody gathered the children around him.

"Your ma is dead," he said gently.

I ran from the house out into the backyard to be alone in my deluge of tears. Out of sight and sound, away from everybody I sobbed and sobbed . . . my eleven-year-old heart seemed to burst" (Kimball and Kimball, *Spencer W. Kimball, Twelfth President of the Church of Jesus Christ of Latter-day Saints*, 46).

When Spencer's father contemplated getting married again, each child was consulted individually. When they gave their approval, Andrew married Josephine Cluff.

A WELL-ROUNDED STUDENT

Spencer was a good student, had learned to play the piano, and was popular at parties. He loved sports, and attended Gila Academy where he played on the basketball team. One winter, their coach challenged the University of Arizona to a game. The University team agreed, and arrived in town, sure of their upcoming victory.

It is a great occasion. Many people came tonight who have never been before. Some of the townsmen say basketball is a girl's game but they came in large numbers tonight. Our court is not quite regulation. We are used to it, our opponents are not. I have special luck with my shots tonight and the ball goes through the hoop again and again and the game ends with our high school team the victors against the college team. I am the smallest one and the youngest on the team. I have piled up the most points through the efforts of the whole team protecting me and feeding the ball to me. I am on the shoulders of the big fellows of the Academy. They are parading me around the hall to my consternation and embarrassment. I like basketball. I would rather play this game than eat (Kimball and Kimball, *Spencer W. Kimball, Twelfth President of The Church of Jesus Christ of Latter-day Saints*, 65).

In his freshman year at Gila Academy, Spencer was elected to be the freshman class president. He was reelected each year. A classmate, Ella Lee, recalled his campaign strategy: "At the beginning of each school year, he would tell us how unwise it would be to change horses in the middle of the stream and how he had everything under control, and each year he was reelected president" (Kimball and Kimball, *Spencer W. Kimball, Twelfth President of The Church of Jesus Christ of Latter-day Saints*, 60).

Two events during Spencer's childhood made him examine his faith and actively work to improve his knowledge of the gospel. The first was a stake conference where Susa Young Gates, Brigham Young's daughter, spoke. She asked the large audience how many had read the Bible cover to cover. Although there were more than a thousand people in attendance, only five or six were able to raise their hands. Susa urged them to go home and begin. Spencer resolved to do as she had asked.

> At the conclusion of that sermon, [I] walked to my home a block away and climbed up in [my] little attic room in the top of the house and lighted a little coal oil lamp that was on the little table and [I] read the first chapter of Genesis. A year later, [I] closed the Bible, having read every chapter in the big and glorious book. [I] found that there were certain parts that were hard for a 14-year-old boy to understand. There were some pages that were not especially interesting to [me], but when [I] had read 66 books and the 1,189 chapters and 1,519 pages, [I] had a glowing satisfaction that [I] had made a goal and that [I] had achieved it (Kimball and Kimball, *Spencer W. Kimball, Twelfth President of The Church of Jesus Christ of Latter-day Saints*, 56).

The second experience came as a challenge, and struck Spencer like a bolt of lightning. A speaker said that for two generations the Church had stood strong with valiant people who had been persecuted for their beliefs. Spencer recalled:

> The first generation, fired with a new religion, developed a great enthusiasm for it. They were forced to huddle together for survival. The second generation came along, born to enthusiasm. They were born to men and women who had developed great faith. They inherited from their parents and soaked up from religious homes the stuff of which the faithful are made. They had full reservoirs of strength and faith upon which to draw. But wait till the third and fourth generation come along. The fire will have gone out, the devotion will have been diluted, the sacrifice will have been nullified. The world will have hovered over them and surrounded them and eroded them. The faith will have been expanded and the religious fervor leaked out. That day I realized that I was a member of the third generation. That day I clenched my growing fists, I gritted my teeth and made a firm commitment to myself that here was one third generation who would not fulfill that dire prediction (Kimball and Kimball, *Spencer W. Kimball, Twelfth President of The Church of Jesus Christ of Latter-day Saints*, 188-90).

A MISSION CALL

At Spencer's high school graduation, his father, as president of the school board, delivered an address. During his talk, he announced that Spencer would not be going to college in the fall. Instead, he told the crowd that Spencer would be serving in the Swiss-German Mission. Lela Udall, a classmate, recalled that she glanced at the unsuspecting Spencer. "I thought Spencer was going to pass out," she recalled.

For his part, Spencer noted: "Father informed me in these exercises before all the people that I was to be called on a mission. This took me by surprise for I had been planning to go to college" (Kimball and Kimball, *Spencer W. Kimball, Twelfth President of The Church of Jesus Christ of Latter-day Saints*, 68).

In spite of the shock, Spencer was pleased by the mission call. He had studied German and was anxious to put it to good use. However, when World War I spread over Europe, the missionaries were reassigned to safer areas. Spencer's call was changed to the Central States Mission, which was headquartered in Independence, Missouri. At first, Elder Kimball had some discouraging times, but he enjoyed his mission and was touched by the kindnesses of the people.

Once, while knocking on doors in St. Louis, he noticed a piano through a partially open door. As the woman was shutting the door in his face, he said:

SPENCER W. KIMBALL WITH HIS MISSION COMPANION Spencer is on the left.

"I see that you have a new piano."

"Yes, we just bought it," she replied with pride.

"It is a Kimball, isn't it? That's my name, also," he said as the door opened wider. "Would you like me to sing and play for you?"

"Surely, come in," she answered.

Walking to the piano he played and sang "O, My Father." This pleasant introduction led to many subsequent gospel conversations (Kimball and Kimball, *Spencer W. Kimball, Twelfth President of the Church of Jesus Christ of Latter-day Saints*, 79-80).

In 1917, the United States declared war on Germany in response to its unrestricted policy on submarine warfare. Popular songs of the day included "You're in the Army Now," and "Over There." Serious war-related food shortages plagued Europe. British Foreign Secretary, Arthur Balfour, issued a declaration calling for the establishment of a Jewish homeland in Palestine. And closer to home, Puerto Rico became an American territory.

CAMILLA

In January of 1917, Spencer returned from his mission. He enrolled at the University of Arizona, and that summer he noticed the new home economics teacher at Gila Academy, Camilla Eyring. Camilla later wrote about how they met and their first date.

One evening, soon after school began, when I had stayed at school for a faculty meeting and was standing on Thatcher's Main Street, waiting for a bus, a young man, Spencer Kimball, came along, going by bus to visit a friend. He introduced himself and we sat together in the bus and discussed Shakespeare and similar high-brow subjects. He walked home from the bus stop with me and asked if he might call sometime later, an indefinite date. A few days after the bus ride, he came calling. I had my hair up in curlers and was in a kimono getting ready to go to a dance with a date and few friends when here came Mr. Kimball. I was in a pickle. I had told him he could call, but no special time. I wanted to favor him and here I was in a dilemma. I visited with him out on the porch, thinking he might stay only a short time, but finally it became apparent that he had come to spend the evening. So I told him a crowd of us were going to a dance and I asked if he'd like to come along. He seemed delighted. So I rushed to get ready and when the car arrived, I went out to ask the first date if the new friend could go along. It was a really embarrassing situation (Caroline Eyring Miner and Edward L. Kimball, *Camilla*, 60).

So Spencer went to the dance with Camilla and her date, who was (understandably) upset and refused to dance with her all evening. When Spencer started attending BYU, the young couple wrote letters to keep in touch. In one of her first letters, Camilla included a picture of herself that Spencer trimmed and put inside his watch.

However, Spencer did not tell Camilla about one of his first experiences in Provo. He got off the train at Center Street and saw an impressive white building down at the end of the road. Without asking anyone, he started walking to what he thought was the BYU campus. As he got closer to the building, he was startled to see rather odd-looking men dressed in

CAMILLA EYRING KIMBALL as a young woman. Spencer was immediately attracted to Camilla when he saw her at Gila Academy.

CAMILLA EYRING
AND SPENCER W.
KIMBALL as a young
married couple.

drab clothes wandering around the grounds. Suddenly, he remembered that the state mental hospital was in Provo. Sheepishly, he picked up his suitcase and turned around.

Spencer left BYU when his draft board told him that he would have to leave with the next contingent from Safford, Arizona. He returned home and waited for his induction into the army. His life had been turned upside down, and he wanted it to return to normal. He did not know when or if he would be called up, so he and Camilla decided to get married on November 16, 1917. When the army contingent was filled, it looked like Spencer would not have to go after all. Then, the armistice was signed, and Spencer started looking for ways to support his family. During the day, he kept accounting books, and in the evenings he played the piano for two dance orchestras. When Spencer began working in a bank, he was careful and conscientious. He taught himself to type—a skill that came in handy later in life when he was unable to dictate messages due to his voice difficulties. In 1922, Spencer's stepmother died, and two years later, his father passed away. Spencer had been very close to his father and was devastated by his death.

A Call from Salt Lake

In 1938, Spencer was called to serve as president of the Mount Graham Stake. In 1943, when the local paper did a survey to determine the most prominent man in Gila Valley, Spencer came out on top. Business was going well and he and Camilla had just moved into their dream house. But on July 8, 1943, a phone call from Salt Lake City changed their lives. Spencer described the events of that day.

JOSHUA RUBEN CLARK (1871–1961) called Spencer from Salt Lake to tell him he had been chosen to become an Apostle.

It was noon and I was just entering the house for my luncheon. . . . I had had many calls from Salt Lake City through the years. . . . I realized I had no unfinished business with Salt Lake City. I knew that there were two vacancies in the Quorum of the Twelve but I had given it little concern. . . . Much happened in that short second. I was upbraiding myself for permitting such a thought to enter my mind; I was proving to myself that was only an ambitious dream, unworthily presumptuous, and that it was impossible, when the clear, pleasant voice of President J. Reuben Clark came:

"Spencer, this is Brother Clark. Do you have a chair handy?"

"Yes, Brother Clark," I answered with a quivering voice.

His words came with strength and power unmistakable. "The brethren have just chosen you to fill one of the vacancies in the Quorum."

I heard the words ringing down into my unconsciousness, but it was unbelievable. "Oh, Brother Clark! Not me? You don't mean me? There must be some mistake. I surely couldn't have heard you right." This as I sank past the chair to the floor.

"Yes. The brethren feel that you are the man. How do you feel about it?"

"Oh, Brother Clark, It seems so impossible. I am so weak and small and limited and incapable. Of course, there could be only one answer to any call from the Brethren but—"

A complete panorama came before me of the little, mean, petty things I had done, of the little misunderstandings I had had with people in business and with people in the Church whose feelings I might have hurt. It seemed that every person that had ever been offended because of me stood before me to say, "How could *you* be an apostle of the Lord? You are not worthy. You are *insignificant*. You shouldn't accept this calling. You *can't* do it." I must have hesitated a long time for Brother Clark said,

"Are you there?"

Catching my breath I said, "Yes, Brother Clark, but you've taken my breath. I am all in a sweat."

"Well, it is rather warm up here, also" (Kimball and Kimball, *Spencer W. Kimball, Twelfth President of The Church of Jesus Christ of Latter-day Saints*, 188-90).

Spencer was in a state of shock. He berated himself for his past weaknesses, and felt unworthy. He desperately searched for assurance that the call had been made by inspiration and that he would be able to rise to the occasion. While visiting Colorado to see his oldest son, Spencer rose early and climbed the hills around town. That morning, he received the answer to his prayers.

There was one great desire, to get a testimony of my calling, to know that it was not human and inspired by ulterior motives, kindly as they might be. How I prayed! How I suffered! How I wept! How I struggled!

Was it a dream which came to me? I was weary and I think I went to sleep for a little. It seemed that in a dream I saw my grandfather and became conscious of the great work he had done. I cannot say that it was a vision, but I do know that with this new experience came a calm like the dying wind, the quieting wave after the storm is passed. . . . My tears were dry, my soul was at peace. A calm feeling of assurance came over me, doubt and questionings subdued. It was as though a great burden had been lifted. . . .

I went down the mountain, not down the steep difficult precipitous way, but down the other side which was easy and gradual. . . . I felt I knew my way, now, physically and spiritually and knew where I was going (Kimball and Kimball, *Spencer W. Kimball, Twelfth President of The Church of Jesus Christ of Latter-day Saints*, 195).

WORLD EVENTS

The year 1945 was marked by world-changing events: American planes dropped atomic bombs on Hiroshima and Nagasaki, prompting Japan's surrender; and Soviet troops liberated prisoners at Auschwitz concentration camp. Franklin D. Roosevelt died on April 12, during his fourth term in office, and Harry S. Truman became President of the United States. The United Nations organization was established with the objective of preventing another world war from occurring.

In 1945, President George Albert Smith called Elder Kimball to supervise the Navajo Zuni Mission. To Elder Kimball, the assignment fulfilled a promise made forty-two years earlier in his patriarchal blessing. In the blessing, he had been told that he would preach the gospel to many people, but especially the Lamanites. He worked hard, and earned the trust of the Native American Indians. Over the years, he fought for Indian rights and for aid that had been promised by the government. He also encouraged education and Church involvement.

In 1948, Elder Kimball started having trouble with his heart. He was working too hard and began having chest pains. After a heart attack, he spent some

SPENCER W. KIMBALL WITH NAVAJO CHILDREN. He had a special love and concern for the Lamanites, and was delighted with his call to supervise the Navajo Zuni Mission.

time recuperating in the solitude of Arizona on the Navajo Reservation. During this time, he and some companions camped in a tent trailer near the hogan of some friends.

One morning, he was found missing from camp. When he didn't return by midmorning, the others started searching for him. He was found several miles away lying under a pine tree with his Bible next to him. His friends' frightened voices aroused him, and when they asked if everything was all right, he responded, "Six years ago today, I was called to be an apostle of the Lord Jesus Christ. And I just wanted to spend the day with Him, whose witness I am" (Hartshorn, *Classic Stories from the Lives of Our Prophets*, 370).

Following his recuperation, Elder Kimball resumed his busy schedule, but the pains returned. He reduced his activities, but then started having problems with a persistent hoarseness. After visiting with doctors, he was diagnosed with cancer on one vocal cord. That night he wrote in his journal: "Cancer! Cancer of the throat would render me useless from now on for the Church. I have done so very little in these six short years—there's so much to do—it is a black outlook, indeed" (Kimball and Kimball, *Spencer W. Kimball, Twelfth President of The Church of Jesus Christ of Latter-day Saints*, 263).

When Elder Kimball was operated on, the doctors decided that he did not have cancer, only an infection that needed to be cauterized. While being wheeled back to his room following surgery, Elder Kimball, though only half conscious, heard the orderly angrily profane the Lord's name. Elder Kimball asked with a labored voice, "Please don't say that. I love Him more than anything in this world. Please." The orderly answered, "Oh, I shouldn't have said that. I'm sorry" (Gibbons, *Spencer W. Kimball: Resolute Disciple, Prophet of God*, 181).

When Elder Kimball recovered, he was asked by President McKay to tour the European missions. He threw himself into an exhausting schedule, often meeting with people eighteen hours a day. Again, his heart began to bother him. Then, in 1956, Elder Kimball's voice again became hoarse. While in New York, he met with a throat specialist and had a biopsy. "It was a sad day," he later wrote, "I entered the hospital with a voice and came out the next day without one" (Kimball and Kimball, *Spencer W. Kimball, Twelfth President of The Church of Jesus Christ of Latter-day Saints*, 302).

Apostle Kimball's recovery was painful, but he kept in touch by writing hundreds of letters. After his throat healed, he was advised not to overuse his voice. At his first speaking assignment, he found that with good equipment he could be heard quite well. He told the audience that while in New York, he had fallen among cutthroats and thieves who had slit his throat and stolen his voice. During all of his health troubles, Elder Kimball kept up with his assignments and counseled literally hundreds of people who were searching for the way back after falling into sin.

WORLD EVENTS

In 1956, Egypt's president Gamal Abdal Nasser nationalized the Suez Canal, precipitating the invasion of Egypt by Israel, Britain, and France; the United States opposed the invasion. Using military force, the Soviet Union quelled an anti-Communist rebellion in Hungary. In the United States, a young preacher named Martin Luther King organized a bus boycott in Montgomery, Alabama, bringing him into the national eye. Elvis Presley topped the music charts with "Love Me Tender," "Heartbreak Hotel," and "Hound Dog." And the fairytale wedding of actress Grace Kelly and Prince Rainier of Monaco captured the hearts and fancy of Americans and Europeans alike.

CAMILLA EYRING AND SPENCER W. KIMBALL ON STEPS OF A PLANE as they tour the European missions.

SPENCER W AND
CAMILLA. KIMBALL

Based on his counseling, Elder Kimball wrote two books that have had a profound effect on people's lives: *The Miracle of Forgiveness* and *Faith Precedes the
Miracle*. He and his wife also traveled widely on assignments, dedicating buildings, attending conferences and visiting missions. In 1972, Elder Kimball

underwent an operation to correct problems with his heart. His surgeon, Russell M. Nelson, who later become an apostle himself, wrote:

> As the skin incision was made, my resident exclaimed, "He doesn't bleed." From that very first maneuver until the last one, everything went as planned. There was not one broken stitch, not one instrument had fallen from the table, not one technical flaw had occurred in a series of thousands of intricate manipulations. I suppose my feelings at that time may have been like those of a concert pianist rendering a concerto without ever hitting a wrong note or a baseball player who had pitched a perfect game, no hits, no runs, no errors and no walks. For a long and difficult operation had been performed exactly in ordinance with a blessing involved by the power of the priesthood. But even more special than that, was the overpowering feeling that came upon me as we shocked his heart and it resumed its beating immediately with power and vigor. The Spirit told me that I had just operated upon a man who would become President of the Church. I knew that President Kimball was a prophet. I knew that he was an apostle. But now it was revealed to me that he would preside over the Church. This feeling was so strong that I could hardly contain myself as we performed the routine maneuvers to conclude the operation. Later on in the week as he convalesced, I shared this news with him and he and I both wept (Nelson, *From Heart to Heart*, 164-65).

SPENCER W. KIMBALL CONVALESCING from heart surgery on his back porch at 2028 Laird Drive, Salt Lake City.

Near the close of the year 1973, President Lee suddenly became ill and died. A shocked Elder Kimball announced:

> President Lee has gone. I never thought it could happen. I sincerely wanted it never to happen. I doubt if anyone in the Church has prayed harder and more consistently for a long life for President Lee than my Camilla and myself.
>
> I have not been ambitious. I am four years older than President Lee (to the exact day, March 28). I have expected that I would go long before he would go (Goates, *Harold B. Lee, Prophet and Seer*, 34).

A VIGOROUS PROPHET

In spite of numerous health problems, President Kimball presided over the Church for more than a decade. His administration was vigorous and far-reach-

SPENCER W.
KIMBALL WITH
COUNSELORS AND
QUORUM OF
TWELVE *Back row:*
James E. Faust,
Thomas S. Monson,
L Tom Perry, Bruce
R. McKonkie,
Marvin J. Ashton
Middle row: David
B. Haight, Boyd K.
Packer, Gordon B.
Hinckley, Howard
W. Hunter,
LeGrande Richards,
Mark E. Peterson
Front row: Ezra Taft
Benson, N. Eldon
Tanner, Spencer W.
Kimball, and
Marion G. Romney.
ca. 1978

ing. He encouraged Church members to lengthen their stride. Missionary work doubled—then doubled again. A new emphasis was placed on temple work, and many new temples were announced and built.

President Kimball despaired that his speech was low and raspy, but the members of the Church came to love the sound of his voice. At the conclusion of the October 6, 1974 conference, he said, "As this conference concludes, we bless you, and we bring to you the blessings of the Lord of heaven. Brethren and sisters, I know that this is the work of the Lord. You haven't come these long distances for nothing. It's to feed your souls. I know that the Lord lives" (*Conference Reports, Ensign*, Nov. 1974, 113).

At the press conference that accompanied the laying of the cornerstone of the Washington Temple, there were representatives from all the major newspapers and television stations in the country, as well as several foreign correspondents. Someone asked the question: "Why is the Mormon Church growing so rapidly?"

"Because the Church is true," President Kimball replied" (Dell Van Orden and J. Melan Heslop, with Lance E. Larsen, "A Prophet for All the World: Glimpses into the Life of Spencer W. Kimball," 49-51).

When asked about the urgency of his calling as the President of the Church, President Kimball answered:

"I've been to the Mount of Olives where Christ said to the Eleven who were with him, 'Go ye unto all of the world,' and I remember that there are 900 million people in one country who haven't heard the gospel. Until we've touched them all, I feel an urgency."

One of the most far-reaching and important events of Spencer W. Kimball's presidency occurred on June 9, 1978. On this day, the Church announced that all worthy male members of the Church could hold the priesthood. President Kimball had spent many hours in the temple praying and meditating on the issue, and called a special meeting of the Quorum of the Twelve to consider the matter. He later recorded:

> I offered the final prayer . . . and I told the Lord if it wasn't right, if He didn't want this change to come in the Church, that I would be true to it all the rest of my life and I'd fight the world against it if that's what He wanted. Then as we had this special prayer circle, I knew that the time had come. . . . But this revelation and an assurance came to me so clearly that there was no question about it (Quoted in *This People*, Summer 1988, 22).

President N. Eldon Tanner made the announcement in general conference.

> President Kimball has asked that I advise the conference that after he had received this revelation, which came to him after extended meditation and prayer in the sacred rooms of the holy temple, he presented it to his counselors, who accepted it and approved it. It was then presented to the Quorum of the Twelve Apostles, who unanimously approved it, and was subsequently presented to all other General Authorities, who likewise approved it unanimously (*Official Declaration 2*).

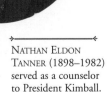

NATHAN ELDON TANNER (1898–1982) served as a counselor to President Kimball.

Many other significant events marked the administration of President Kimball. During the last four months of 1984, temples were dedicated in Australia, Taiwan, Texas, the Philippines, and Guatemala. New LDS editions of the Bible and Triple Combination, which integrated the Topical Guide, were printed, and a new hymnbook was published. In addition, a new genealogical library and a Church History and Art Museum were built.

In 1984, President Kimball's health began to deteriorate, and on November 5, 1985, a cold and cloudy day in Salt Lake City, he died due to complications of advanced age. Words of consolation poured in from world leaders. The President of the United States, Ronald Reagan said, "Spencer W. Kimball was a man whose love of God and country touched us all. . . . He made a significant and lasting contribution to this country by weaving tighter our moral fabric" ("Tributes and Messages of Appreciation," *Ensign*, Dec. 1985, 25).

When President Spencer W. Kimball died, the First Presidency of The Church of Jesus Christ of Latter-day Saints was dissolved, and leadership of the Church fell upon the Council of the Twelve Apostles. Eighty-six-year-old Ezra

Taft Benson, the senior Apostle, was ordained as the thirteenth President of the Church five days later. He personally mourned for his friend, Spencer W. Kimball. They had been set apart as apostles on the same day.

In 1985, Mikhail Gorbachev became the secretary of the Communist Party in the USSR; this led to an easing of the cold war. *Les Miserables,* the musical based on Victor Hugo's novel by the same name, premiered in London.

> With the passing of President Spencer W. Kimball, the Church and the world have lost a great and true servant of God. For more than forty years we have sat together in council meetings. I have lost a dear friend and brother.
>
> I know of no man who has more completely dedicated his time, talents, and interest to the work and ministry of our Lord. He has been a sterling example of love for his fellow men and our Lord, Jesus Christ.
>
> As a great Christian leader, deeply beloved by millions of our Father's children, he will be greatly missed by all of us.
>
> May God bless and keep ever alive the memory of his devoted life of faith and service ("Tributes and Messages of Appreciation," *Ensign,* Dec. 1985, 25).

President Benson had suffered from poor health and had not expected to live to become President of the Church. Following his ordination, he said:

> This is a day I have not anticipated. My wife, Flora, and I have prayed continually that President Kimball's days would be prolonged upon this earth and another miracle performed on his behalf. Now that the Lord has spoken, we will do our best, under his guiding direction, to move the work forward in the earth.
>
> We shall miss President Kimball so very much ("President Ezra Taft Benson Ordained Thirteenth President of the Church," *Ensign,* Dec. 1985, 5).

EZRA TAFT
BENSON

"Flood the Earth with the Book of Mormon"

President Benson was a descendant of pioneers. Some of his ancestors came to America from England in the 1600s. His great-grandfather, also named Ezra Taft Benson, met Joseph Smith and the Mormons in 1840, and was baptized soon after that. He served several missions, and was a member of the first pioneer company to enter Utah.

HIS GROWING-UP YEARS

President Benson's parents, George Benson Jr. and Sarah Dunkley, had a farm in Whitney, Idaho. Their oldest child, Ezra, was born August 4, 1899.

Ezra Taft Benson frequently spoke of the wonderful opportunity he had growing up in a loving, farm family. He often referred to two particular memories that had a great influence on him. The first was when his father was called on a mission. Ezra Taft, or "T" as his family called him, was just thirteen years old at the time.

WORLD EVENTS

At the time of Ezra Taft Benson's birth in 1899, William McKinley was President of the United States. Tolstoy, Ibsen, and Kipling were producing literary works, and Sibelius, Strauss, Bruckner, and Elgar were writing great music. Scientists made important discoveries related to radiation, and the first magnetic sound recordings were made.

EZRA TAFT BENSON served as President from 1985–1994.

We gathered around the old sofa in the living room, and Father told us about his mission call. Then Mother said, "We're proud to know that Father is considered worthy to go on a mission. We're crying a bit because it means two years of separation. You know your father and I have never been separated more than two nights at a time since our marriage. . . ."

While we missed him greatly during those years, and while his absence brought many challenges to our family, his acceptance proved to be a gift of charity. Father went on his mission, leaving Mother at home with seven children. . . . But there came into that home a spirit of missionary work that never left it. It was not without some sacrifice. Father had to sell our old dry farm in order to finance his mission. He had to move a married couple into part of our home to care for the row crops, and he left his sons and wife the responsibility for the hay land, the pasture land, and a small herd of dairy cows.

Father's letters were indeed a blessing to our family. To us children, they seemed to come from halfway around the world, but they were only from Springfield, Massachusetts; and Chicago, Illinois; and Cedar Rapids and Marshalltown, Iowa. Yes, there came into our home, as a result of Father's mission, a spirit of missionary work that never left it.

Later the family grew to eleven children—seven sons and four daughters. All seven sons filled missions, some of them two or three missions. Later, two daughters and their husbands filled full-time missions. The two other sisters, both widows . . . served as missionary companions in Birmingham, England.

It is a legacy that still continues to bless the Benson family even into the third and fourth generations ("Godly Characteristics of the Master," *Ensign*, Nov. 1986, 46-48).

As the oldest son, a great deal of the farming responsibility fell on "T" while his father was away. But Ezra grew to love farming. Another memory involved his mother:

I remember so well as a little boy, coming in from the field and approaching the old farm home in Whitney, Idaho. I could hear my mother singing, "Have I Done Any Good In the World Today?" . . . I can still see her in my mind's eye bending over the ironing board with newspapers on the floor, ironing long strips of white cloth, with beads of perspiration on her forehead. I asked her what she was doing. She said, "These are temple robes, my son. Your father and I are going to the temple at Logan."

Then she put the old flatiron on the stove, drew a chair close to mine, and told me about temple work and how important it was to be able to go to the temple and participate in the sacred ordinances performed there. She also expressed her fervent hope that someday her children and grandchildren would have the opportunity to enjoy those priceless blessings (Ezra Taft Benson, *The Teachings of Ezra Taft Benson*, 246).

These early experiences greatly influenced Ezra, and later, when he became President of the Church, missionary work and temple building were important themes of his presidency.

COLLEGE, COURTSHIP, AND CHURCH CALLINGS

In 1920, Ezra began attending Utah Agricultural College in Logan, Utah, where he met Flora Amussen. Their courtship lasted six years while they completed college and served missions—Ezra served in England, and Flora served in Hawaii. Following their marriage in the Salt Lake Temple, they moved to Ames, Iowa, where Ezra earned a graduate degree in agriculture. Then they returned to Idaho so Ezra could put his degree to good use. The couple had six children, and in 1939, they moved to Washington D.C. when Ezra was asked to serve as executive secretary of the National Council of Farm Cooperatives. While in Washington, D.C., he was called to be president of the Washington Stake.

When he visited Utah in 1943, he met with President Heber J. Grant and was called to be an Apostle.

EZRA TAFT BENSON
at age fourteen.

For several minutes [I] could say only, "Oh, President Grant, that can't be!" which I must have repeated several times before I was able to collect my thoughts enough to realize what had happened. . . . He held my hand for a long time as we both shed tears. . . . . [Although he was] feeble, his mind was clear and alert, and I was deeply impressed with his sweet, kindly, humble spirit as he seemed to look into my soul.

I felt so utterly weak and unworthy that his words of comfort and reassurance which followed were doubly appreciated. Among other things he stated, "The Lord has a way of magnifying men who are called to positions of leadership." When in my weakness I was able to state that I loved the Church, he said, "We know that, and the Lord wants men who will give everything for His work" (Sheri L. Dew, *Ezra Taft Benson, A Biography*, 174).

EZRA TAFT BENSON AND FAMILY (l to r) *Back row:* Barbara, Beverly, Mark, Reed, Bonnie, and Beth *Front row:* Ezra and Flora.

On October 7, 1943, Spencer W. Kimball and Ezra Taft Benson were sustained and ordained members of the Quorum of the Twelve by President Grant.

Elder Benson approached his new calling with enthusiasm and energy. He learned from the older brethren in the quorum, and when World War II ended, plans were made to reestablish contact with the Saints in Europe. Ezra Taft Benson was chosen to preside over the European Mission. However, due to the conditions in Europe, he traveled alone.

A "MISSION" TO WAR-TORN EUROPE

When he left Salt Lake City, on January 29, 1946, his wife, Flora, saw him off at the airport. She later recorded, "It was a peaceful feeling which came over me when I fondly kissed and said good-bye to my devoted and loving husband" (Dew, *Ezra Taft Benson,* 200).

Elder Benson was overwhelmed by the devastation of war, and often was frustrated by how difficult it was to travel to meet with the Saints. Although he was depressed by conditions in England, France, and Scandinavia, he was completely heartbroken by the state of affairs in Germany. His biographer, Sheri Dew recorded:

> In Karlsruhe, which was reduced to rubble . . . he climbed over the debris and hurried in the direction of faint strains of *Come, Come, Ye Saints* . . . inside a badly scarred building he found three hundred people. Most were dressed in rags; some were emaciated and in the advanced stages of starvation; and all were visibly shivering from the cold" (Dew, *Ezra Taft Benson,* 208).

EZRA TAFT BENSON PREPARING FOOD IN EUROPE WITH HIS WIFE, FLORA (Flora is on the far left, and Ezra is beside her.)

In 1952, Ernest Hemingway published *The Old Man and the Sea*. Dwight D. Eisenhower was elected president of the United States, with Richard M. Nixon as his vice president.

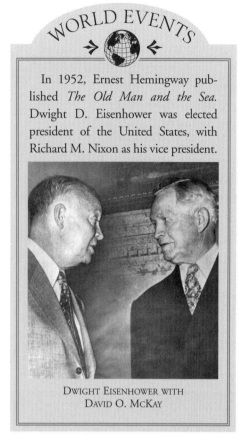

DWIGHT EISENHOWER WITH
DAVID O. MCKAY

Elder Benson recorded in his journal: "As we walked into the meeting every eye turned to us. I shall never forget the look in their faces as they beheld for the first time in [seven] years a representative of the General Authorities. It was not me, but the fact that a representative from Headquarters had arrived" (Dew, *Ezra Taft Benson*, 208).

Besides meeting with the Saints, Elder Benson distributed welfare supplies that the Church had collected. When the first shipment arrived in Berlin, Elder Benson and the acting mission president, Richard Ranglack, went to a warehouse that had been filled with the supplies. President Ranglack, overwhelmed to see so much food, medicine, and clothing, said, "Brother Benson, it is hard for me to believe that people who have never seen us could do so much for us" (Dew, *Ezra Taft Benson*, 219).

After serving in Europe for ten and a half months, Elder Benson returned home. He had traveled more than 60,000 miles, visited with countless members, reorganized missions, and distributed ninety-two boxcars full of welfare supplies. Ezra had been able to improve the lives of others, and he grew from the experience. As he was leaving, he said:

> I can truthfully say that never in all my experience have I appreciated more deeply a period of service in the Church. I have met Latter-day Saints in practically every country in Europe, under the most unusual conditions, in fact under every conceivable circumstance. I have met them in rags, huddled together, suffering from the cold, in bombed-out buildings, some of them in the last stages of starvation. I have been in their homes where they had no food, no furniture to speak of, none of the comforts of life, and yet they have been happy. I have heard them bear testimony to the divinity of this work, with tears streaming down their cheeks as they expressed their gratitude for their blessings, yet practically every material thing had been swept away from them—homes, all the comforts of life, and in some cases every member of their family through death. That is what a testimony will do. That is a most priceless possession—your testimony of the divinity of this work (Benson, *The Teachings of Ezra Taft Benson*, 365).

CALLED TO WASHINGTON

In 1952, Elder Benson received another call—Dwight D. Eisenhower, the newly elected president of the United States, asked him to serve as a member of his Cabinet as Secretary of Agriculture. With the encouragement of President David O. McKay and the other brethren, Elder Benson accepted the offer. Secretary Benson attacked the job with his usual vigor. He was outspoken and uncompromising on many issues, but he won respect—even from those who disagreed with him.

Many people in Washington viewed Mormons as a strange and isolated group of people. Elder Benson and his family helped dispel this myth, and won friends and respect for the Church.

While in Washington, the Benson family was featured on Edward R. Morrow's popular *Person-to-Person* television program. The Bensons were shown holding family home evening. The children performed musical numbers and gave talks, and the whole family sang "Love at Home." Near the end of the program, Mr. Morrow asked Flora Benson if she had any domestic help. She responded:

> No, we do not have a maid. We feel that we learn by doing. We prepare all of our own meals, and plan them. . . . We play together, sing together.

ELDER BENSON AS SECRETARY OF AGRICULTURE in President Dwight D. Eisenhower's cabinet, 1953–1961. *ca. 1953*

We're a very religious family. We have daily prayer—individual and together—because we feel that a family that prays together stays together. I feel that's true of a nation (Dew, *Ezra Taft Benson*, 298).

Morrow received more fan mail from this show than any of his other programs. Many people also wrote the Bensons telling them how much they had enjoyed the program. One letter stated: "Did you stop to realize that your television performance, seen by millions of people, was a stroke of missionary work of the first magnitude?"

EZRA TAFT BENSON served as an Apostle from 1943–1985.

However, Ezra Taft Benson's influence reached far beyond the borders of the United States. He traveled extensively in Europe, South America, the Orient, and the Soviet Union, studying and teaching about modern agricultural practices. When Nikita Khrushchev visited the United States, Secretary Benson took him to visit the Beltsville Agriculture Research Center and commented about government systems and their effect on agriculture: "Our farmers are *free*, efficient, creative and hard working . . ," he said. "Under our capitalistic free enterprise system they have developed an agriculture unequaled anywhere in the world" (Dew, *Ezra Taft Benson*, 338).

When President Eisenhower's second term ended, Secretary Benson returned to his role as Elder Benson. President McKay praised Elder Benson's contributions in general conference, stating that Elder Benson's work in the cabinet would have a positive influence in the nation, and would reflect credit on the Church.

In 1964, Elder Benson again was called to serve as mission president in Europe. This time his wife, Flora, accompanied him to a much more pleasant Europe. In 1966, he dedicated Italy for the preaching of the gospel. Later, as he became involved in the Church in Asia, he also dedicated Singapore and Indonesia.

PROPHET OF GOD

In spite of health problems—a broken hip, and heart troubles—after his ordination, President Benson was surprisingly full of vigor and strength. President Thomas S. Monson, second counselor in the First Presidency, explained:

President Benson grasps quickly matters which come to his attention. He doesn't need to consider an item at great length before he finds the inspi-

ration of the Lord directing him in a decision. With the expansive nature of the Church today, throughout the world, and with the multitude of matters that come before the First Presidency, this ability to cut through detail and get to the heart of the issue is vital to carrying out the administrative work of the Church (Dew, *Ezra Taft Benson*, 488).

President Benson vigorously shouldered his new responsibilities. At his first general conference in April, 1986, he boldly asserted the themes of his presidency:

> As I have sought direction from the Lord, I have had reaffirmed in my mind and heart the declaration of the Lord to "say nothing but repentance unto this generation." . . .
>
> We will be lengthening our stride in the future. To do so, we must first cleanse the inner vessel by awaking and arising, being morally clean, using the Book of Mormon in a manner so that God will lift the condemnation, and finally conquering pride by humbling ourselves ("Cleansing the Inner Vessel," *Ensign*, May 1986, 4, 7).

EZRA TAFT BENSON WITH COUNSELORS Ezra Taft Benson, President (at pulpit); Gordon B. Hinckley, First Counselor; Thomas S. Monson, Second Counselor. *Nov. 11, 1985 Press Conference*

President Benson closed the April 1986 general conference with a promise to the members of the Church: "I bless you with increased *understanding* of the Book of Mormon. I promise you that from this moment forward, if we will daily sup from its pages and abide by its precepts, God will pour out upon each child of Zion and the Church a blessing hitherto unknown" ("A Sacred Responsibility," *Ensign*, May 1986, 78).

During his presidency, he spoke forcefully to specific groups within the Church:

"The Lord wants every young man to serve a full-time mission. . . . What a sacred privilege—to serve the Lord full time for two years. . . . You can do nothing more important" ("To the Youth of the Noble Birthright," *Ensign*, May 1986, 44).

Give me a young woman who loves home and family, who reads and ponders the scriptures daily, who has a burning testimony . . . who is virtuous . . . who will not settle for less than a temple marriage, and I will give you a young woman who will perform miracles for the Lord now and throughout eternity ("To the Young Women of the Church," *Ensign*, Nov. 1986, 84).

There is no greater Church calling than that of a home teacher. There is no greater Church service rendered to our Heavenly Father's children than the service rendered by a humble, dedicated, committed home teacher ("To the Home Teachers of the Church," *Ensign*, May 1987, 50).

Mothers in Zion, your God-given roles are so vital to your own exaltation and to the salvation and exaltation of your family. A child needs a mother more than all the things money can buy. . . .

Teach your children the gospel in your home, at your own fireside. This is the most effective teaching that your children will ever receive. . . . Your children will remember your teachings forever. . . . Mothers, this kind of heavenly, motherly teaching takes time—lots of time. . . . This is your divine calling. . . .

I promise you the blessings of heaven and "all that [the] Father hath" as you magnify the noblest calling of all—a mother in Zion (Ezra Taft Benson, "To the Mothers in Zion." Address given at a Fireside for Parents 22 Feb. 1987. Published in pamphlet form by The Church of Jesus Christ of Latter-day Saints, 8-13).

Fathers, yours is an eternal calling. . . .
You must help create a home where the Spirit of the Lord can abide. . . .

Your homes should be havens of peace and joy for your family. . . .

May you always provide for the material needs of your family and, with your eternal companion at your side, may you fulfill your sacred responsibility to provide the spiritual leadership in your home ("To the Fathers in Israel," *Ensign*, Nov. 1987, 48-51).

God bless you single adult brethren of the Church. May your priorities be right.

. . . Honorable marriage is more important than wealth, position and status ("To the Single Adult Brethren of the Church," *Ensign*, May 1988, 51-53).

Single adult sisters throughout the Church, I want you to know of my deep love and appreciation for you. . . .

The sacred bonds of Church membership go far beyond marital status, age, or present circumstance. Your individual worth as a daughter of God transcends all ("To the Single Adult Sisters of the Church," *Ensign*, Nov. 1988, 96-97).

Dear children, our Heavenly Father sent you to the earth at this time because you are some of His most valiant children. He knew there would be much wickedness in the world today, and He knew you could be faithful and obedient. . . .

He expects your parents and leaders to teach you, to walk beside you, and to be shining examples to you so that you will know the way you should go. They must spend time with you and love you and pray *with* you and *for* you ("To the Children of the Church," *Ensign,* May 1989, 81-83).

God bless the elderly in the Church. I love you with all my heart. I am one of you.

You have so much to live for. May these golden years be your very best years as you fully live and love and serve. And God bless those who minister to your needs ("To the Elderly in the Church," *Ensign*, Nov. 1989, 4-8).

President Benson always bore a strong testimony of the Savior and of the divinity of the work. In a talk given at the close of the October 1988 conference, he said:

As a special witness of Jesus Christ, and as His humble servant, it is now my obligation and privilege, as the Spirit dictates, to bear pure testimony and witness to that which I know to be true. . . .

I testify that we are the spirit offspring of a loving God, our Heavenly Father. . . . I testify that throughout the ages God has spoken to His children through His prophets. . . .

I testify that during His mortal ministry Christ established His church upon the earth. . . .

I testify that God the Father and His Son, Jesus Christ, appeared to Joseph Smith in the spring of 1820. . . .

I testify that through the Book of Mormon God has provided for our day tangible evidence that Jesus is the Christ and that Joseph Smith is His prophet. . . .

I testify that America is a choice land. . . .

I testify that it is time for every man to set in order his own house both temporally and spiritually. . . .

I testify that not many years hence the earth will be cleansed. . . . Jesus the Christ will come again, this time in power and great glory to vanquish His foes and to rule and reign on the earth. . . .

I testify to you that a fulness of joy can only come through the atonement of Jesus Christ and by obedience ("I Testify," *Ensign*, Nov. 1988, 86-87).

Some of the subjects the First Presidency dealt with in the first years of President Benson's administration are summarized by his biographer, Sheri L. Dew:

Temples were dedicated in Korea, Peru, and Argentina; and the ground was broken for temples in Las Vegas and Portland. The missionary force surpassed 30,005 (March 1986); and while he was grateful for those who were serving, President Benson said there weren't nearly enough. President Monson organized the 1600th stake of the Church on June 22, 1986, in Toronto. The translation of the Book of Mormon into the seventieth language was completed. The First Presidency issued a statement opposing gambling. . . . They also announced a policy change authorizing the issuing of temple recommends to worthy members married to an unendowed spouse. . . .

At General Conference in October 1986, the First Presidency announced that all stake seventies quorums were to be discontinued, and that now all priesthood holders, not just the seventies, were responsible for teaching the gospel (Dew, *Ezra Taft Benson*, 488).

During Ezra Taft Benson's presidency, great political changes swept the world, and the Saints' prayers that the doors of the nations might be opened for the missionaries began to be answered. The *Ensign* magazine summarized:

Miraculously, the Iron Curtain in Eastern Europe began to part for the blessing of the people he had grown to love after World War II. In 1985 the Freiberg Temple, located in the German Democratic Republic, had been dedicated—a miracle in itself. . . . Then, in 1988, the Communist government . . . granted permission for missionaries to serve there and also for its young citizens to serve missions elsewhere.

By 1990, winds of political change were sweeping the world. Barriers between East and West began to dissolve.

> Marvel followed marvel as the Berlin Wall fell and East and West Germany were reunited. . . . In June 1991, the Tabernacle Choir made a historic concert tour through middle Europe and Russia. . . . During the following months, the U.S.S.R. was dissolved. Further, in the place of an Eastern Bloc dominated by authoritarian regime stood independent republics, most with elected leaders. President Benson lived to see a remarkable vindication of the principles he prized so highly ("President Ezra Taft Benson, A Sure Voice of Faith," *Ensign*, July 1994, 19).

THE FRIEBERG, GERMANY TEMPLE, was dedicated by President Gordon B. Hinckley on June 29 and 30, 1985. It is the only temple to have been built in a communist bloc nation. The Saints in the area sacrificed much in the way of material goods for this temple to become a reality.

This new freedom meant great missionary opportunities. New missions were organized, missionaries were called, and churches were built in Hungary, Poland, Czechoslovakia, Romania, Russia, and the Ukraine. Soon, Church service missionaries were allowed into Vietnam and Cambodia, and missionary training centers were built in Argentina and Brazil. Several African countries

THE MORMON TABERNACLE CHOIR 1991 in front of St. Basil's on Red Square, Moscow, Russia. This was the first time the choir had ever toured in Moscow and Leningrad (St. Petersburg). While there, the choir performed in the Bolshoi Theater, and recorded songs for a broadcast. It was at a dinner following the choir's performance that the announcement was given that Russia had given official recognition to The Church of Jesus Christ of Latter-day Saints. On this same tour, the choir performed in nine other European cities in France, Germany, Switzerland, Hungary, Austria, Czechoslovakia, and Poland.
June 24, 1991

opened their doors to missionaries, and the Church continued to grow. During the eight and a half years of President Benson's presidency, Church membership grew from nearly six million to nearly nine million. There were now 1,980 stakes and 295 missions. The number of temples increased from thirty-six to forty-five, and twelve more had been announced or were under construction.

An ambitious program to "flood the earth with the Book of Mormon" was begun. Members were encouraged to purchase copies and write their testimony in each one. These copies were then given to friends or sent to missionaries for distribution. In this way, thousands of copies of the Book of Mormon were sent all over the world.

During this time, some significant changes were made in the financial obligations of members. Ward budgets were discontinued, and the activities of wards and stakes began to be funded from tithing. This resulted in simpler activities and less stress on members' finances. A uniform donation for supporting missionaries was also adopted so that missionaries serving in expensive areas of the world were not unduly burdened.

In the 1989 April conference, President Benson gave one of his most powerful sermons—"Beware of Pride."

> God will have a humble people. Either we can choose to be humble or we can be compelled to be humble. . . .
>
> My dear brethren and sisters, we must prepare to redeem Zion. It was essentially the sin of pride that kept us from establishing Zion in the days of the Prophet Joseph Smith. . . .
>
> Pride is the great stumbling block to Zion. I repeat: Pride is the great stumbling block to Zion.
>
> We must cleanse the inner vessel by conquering pride. . . .
>
> We must yield "to the enticings of the Holy Spirit," put off the prideful "natural man," become "a saint through the atonement of Christ the Lord," and become "as a child, submissive, meek, humble. "
>
> . . . That we may do so and go on to fulfill our divine destiny is my fervent prayer in the name of Jesus Christ, amen ("Beware of Pride," *Ensign*, May 1989, 6-7).

This was one of the last times President Benson spoke to the general membership of the Church. During the next five years, his health deteriorated and he died on May 30, 1994. At his funeral, President Howard W. Hunter said:

> President Benson spoke lovingly and frequently of missionary work and temples and the responsibilities of the priesthood. He spoke of our pioneer heritage and the dangers of pride and the gifts of the Holy Spirit. But most of all he spoke of his beloved Book of Mormon.
>
> Will any generation, including those yet unborn, look back on the administration of President Ezra Taft Benson and not immediately think of his love for the Book of Mormon? Perhaps no President of the Church since the Prophet Joseph Smith himself has done more to teach the truths of the Book of Mormon, to make it a daily course of study for the entire membership of the Church, and to "flood the earth" with its distribution.
>
> At the very onset of his ministry as prophet, seer, and revelator, President Benson said unequivocally, "The Book of Mormon must be re-enthroned in the minds and hearts of our people. We must honor it by reading, by studying it, by taking its precepts into our lives and transforming them into lives required of the true followers of Christ." . . .
>
> Surely President Benson succeeded in a most remarkable way in the prophetic task that he enthusiastically undertook (Howard W. Hunter, "Ezra Taft Benson: A Strong and Mighty Man," *Ensign*, July 1994, 42).

President Benson's death marked the conclusion of a remarkable man's career. He had been a farmer, a government official, a Church leader, a husband, father, and grandfather, and finally, a Prophet. He promised members that:

> Men and women who turn their lives over to God will discover that He can make a lot more out of their lives than they can. He will deepen their joys, expand their vision, quicken their minds, strengthen their muscles, lift their spirits, multiply their blessings, increase their opportunities, comfort their souls, raise up friends, and pour out peace ("President Ezra Taft Benson, A Sure Voice of Faith," *Ensign*, July 1994, 19).

On June 5, 1994, Howard W. Hunter was ordained as the fourteenth President of The Church of Jesus Christ of Latter-day Saints in the Salt Lake Temple.

WORLD EVENTS

The year 1994 saw a major breakthrough in world politics as Israeli Prime Minister Yitzhak Rabin and Jordanian King Hussein signed a treaty that ended their countries' state of war. In addition, it was the year in which Yitzhak Rabin, Shimon Peres, and PLO leader Yasir Arafat were awarded the Nobel Peace Prize for the Middle East Peace Accord reached at Camp David in 1993. In the United States, the Justice Department charged CIA veteran Aldrich Ames with selling national security secrets to the USSR. Jacqueline Kennedy Onassis died after a long battle with lymphoma cancer. Scandal rocked the upcoming Winter Olympics as Tonya Harding instigated an assault on Nancy Kerrigan in an attempt to eliminate her from the figure skating competition. And in the entertainment world, Tom Hanks starred in the movie Forrest Gump, which won the Oscar for best picture of 1994.

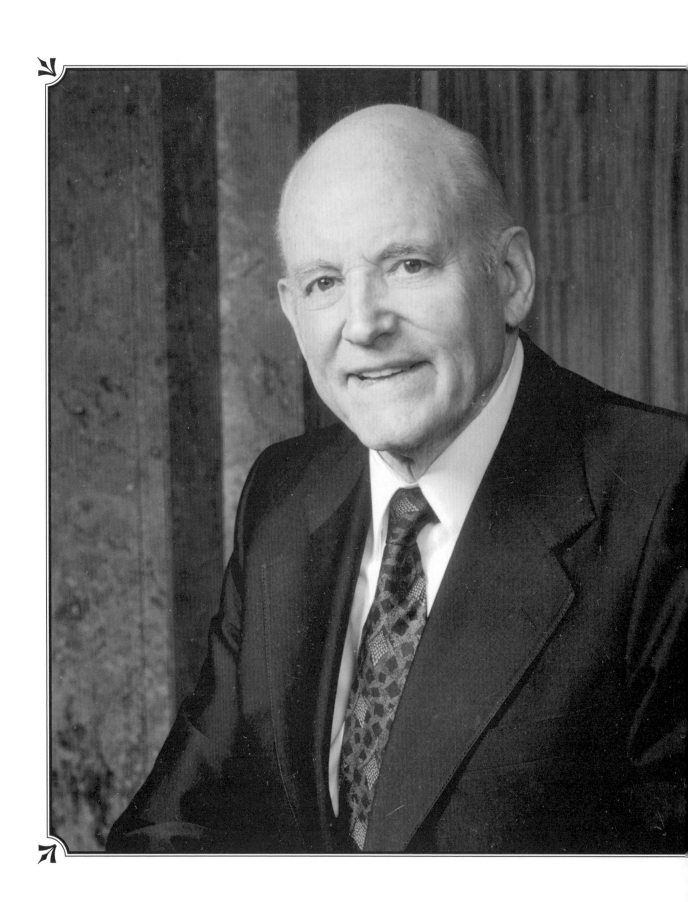

HOWARD W. HUNTER

Love, Hope, and Compassion

At 86 years of age, President Hunter had already had some close calls with death. Although he was frail, his soft voice carried a conviction and love that touched all who heard him speak. At a press conference the day after his ordination, he said:

> Our hearts have been very tender since the death of our friend and brother Ezra Taft Benson. We love him very much and will miss his company and sweet counsel. I have felt his loss in a particularly personal way in light of the new responsibility that has come to me since his passing. I have shed many tears and have sought my Father in Heaven in earnest prayer with a desire to be equal to the high and holy calling which is now mine.
>
> My greatest strength through these past hours and recent days has been my abiding testimony that this is the work of God and not men, that Jesus Christ is the authorized and living head of this Church and He leads it in word and deed. I pledge my life, my strength, and the full measure of my soul to serving Him fully. . . .

HOWARD WILLIAM HUNTER served as President from 1994–1995.

There are two invitations I would like to leave with the members of the Church. First of all, I would invite all members of the Church to live with ever more attention to the life and example of the Lord Jesus Christ, especially the love and hope and compassion He displayed.

I pray that we might treat each other with more kindness, more courtesy, more humility and patience and forgiveness. . . .

To those who have transgressed or been offended, we say, come back. To those who are hurt and struggling and afraid, we say, let us stand with you and dry your tears. To those who are confused and assailed by error on every side, we say, come to the God of all truth and the Church of continuing revelation. Come back. Stand with us. Carry on. Be believing. All is well, and all will be well. . . .

Secondly, . . . I also invite the members of the Church to establish the temple of the Lord as the great symbol of their membership and the supernal setting for their most sacred covenants ("President Howard W. Hunter, Fourteenth President of the Church," *Ensign*, July 1994, 4-5).

HOWARD WILLIAM HUNTER AT AGE TWO Howard was the son of Nellie Rasmussen and John W. Hunter. His father did not join the Church until Howard was nearly twenty years old. *1909*

FROM BOYHOOD TO MANHOOD

Howard W. Hunter was born on November 14, 1907, in Boise, Idaho. He was raised in a part-member family—his father did not join the Church until Howard was nearly twenty. His mother, however, instilled a great love of the gospel in her children.

Howard was an Eagle Scout and a very hard worker. Often, he had two or three part-time jobs while he attended school. He organized a dance band in high school, called Hunter's Croonaders. After graduation, the band got a job providing music for a two-month cruise on a passenger liner to the Orient. This experience exposed Howard to the joys and miseries of travel.

During the trip, he recorded: "Nearly every person on board is seasick. It was said that the captain is seasick for the first time in twenty-five years" (Eleanor Knowles, *Howard W. Hunter*, 49). Of his experience in the Orient, Howard wrote:

> Tokyo is a beautiful city and the people seem friendly. . . .
>
> People here dress differently, act differently, and are very curious about those of us who wear Western clothes and speak a different language. . . .
>
> In each port we have gone sightseeing and traveled about to see as much as we could knowing there is little possibility of returning to this part of the world again. The education has been worth what we have spent (Knowles, *Howard W. Hunter*, 50-55).

HUNTER'S CROONADERS
Howard W. Hunter with his dance band. Howard was offered a contract to provide a five-piece orchestra on on the passenger liner *S. S. President Jackson* for a cruise to the Orient. He selected four musicians to go with him. They played classical music at dinner, background music for movies, and provided appropriate melodies for ballroom dancing. Howard is in the center, holding the saxophone. He played alto and soprano saxophone, clarinet, trumpet, and drums.

A FAMILY AND A CAREER

AERIAL VIEW OF
TEMPLE SQUARE
looking east between
North and South
Temple streets, with
West Temple at the
bottom of the
photo, and State
street at the top.
"Salt Lake Airport"
appears on the roof
of the Tabernacle. In
the background is
the campus of
Latter-day Saint
college, the Bishop's
building, and Hotel
Utah. *1928*

In 1928 Howard traveled to California to visit friends and relatives. There, he got a job at a bank and continued to use his musical talents playing in orchestras. It was also there that he met Clara Jeffs. They dated casually at first and usually with other couples. However, by the spring of 1931, they made plans to marry in the Salt Lake Temple. Howard decided that playing in bands and orchestras was "not compatible with the lifestyle he envisioned with a wife and family, so he decided to give up professional music" (Knowles, *Howard W. Hunter*, 80).

Howard developed an interest in the law, and decided to go to night school. It was a rigorous routine trying to work days and go to school at night. Claire was supportive and encouraging, and their lives were further enriched by the birth of their first baby—Howard William Hunter, Jr., on March 20.

However, sorrow was on the horizon that summer. Little Billy became ill, and died shortly after surgery to correct an ulcerated diverticulum. In subsequent years, Howard and Claire became the parents of two more children— John Jacob Hunter, and Richard Allen Hunter. Howard completed Law School with high honors. He was admitted to the California bar on January 19, 1940, and started a private practice.

A Life Devoted to Serving the Lord

In August of that same year, he was called as the bishop of the new El Sereno Ward. His response was typically modest:

> I had always thought of a bishop as being an older man, and I asked how I could be the father of the ward at the young age of thirty-two. They said I would be the youngest bishop that had been called in Southern California to that time, but they knew I could be equal to the assignment. I expressed my appreciation for their confidence and told them I would do my best (Knowles, *Howard W. Hunter*, 94).

Bishop Hunter faced several challenges that became common as the Church grew throughout the world. The first was finding a place to meet—they rented some rooms from the local Masonic Lodge. Then they began to look for property and started raising funds to build a chapel. A ward member described one of the more interesting fund raising projects: "We were known throughout the Pasadena Stake as the ward with the 'onion project,' where members of the ward go each week, on day shifts and evening shifts, to a nearby pickle factory and trim onions as a ward project." . . . Howard added, "It was easy to tell in sacrament meeting if a person had been snipping onions" (Knowles, *Howard W. Hunter*, 97).

In 1950, Howard was called as president of the Pasadena Stake. As stake president, he encouraged the members to draw closer to the Savior and to love one another. Alicebeth Ashby, who served as Stake Young Women's president observed that "you felt appreciated and wanted and needed. He made people responsible when they received a calling, but if they needed his opinion or counsel, he was always there. We knew we had his complete support and interest" (Knowles, *Howard W. Hunter*, 137).

Howard W. Hunter and Clara May Jeffs Hunter (1902–1983). Clara was Howard's first wife. She died in 1983 after a long and debilitating illness.

CALLED AS AN APOSTLE

Nine years later, during the 1959 October conference, Howard W. Hunter was called to President David O. McKay's office and told that he was to be one of the Lord's special witnesses, and that he would be sustained as a member of the Council of the Twelve the following day. His biographer, Eleanor Knowles, recorded:

> Howard William Hunter became the seventy-fourth man in this dispensation to be ordained an apostle. . . .
>
> At fifty-one, Elder Hunter was only the third apostle born in the twentieth century, and the youngest member of the Twelve at the time of his call. . . .
>
> The average age of the twelve men in the quorum at that time was sixty-seven. . . .
>
> There were approximately 1.6 million Latter-day Saints in 290 stakes and 50 missions. . . .
>
> The inauguration of jet airplane service just ten months before his ordination and the development of satellite transmission of television and other communications media heralded a new age (Knowles, *Howard W. Hunter*, 148-50).

HOWARD W. HUNTER as a young Apostle. Howard was an Apostle from 1959 to 1994.

Elder Hunter remained in Los Angeles for several months after his call—transferring his law business to his partner and completing his service as stake president. He commuted to Salt Lake City each Wednesday evening to attend temple meetings with the First Presidency and the Twelve.

As an Apostle, he traveled extensively and held a great variety of assignments. He negotiated with government leaders, oversaw missions and temples, served as Church historian, and was President of the Genealogical Society.

He became interested in the New World Archaeological Foundation and made several trips to archaeological sites in Mexico, and Central and South America.

In 1965, Elder Hunter was made President and Chairman of the Board of the Polynesian Cultural Center in Hawaii. The struggling center seemed doomed to failure until the Church announced plans to build a new college in the little farm town of Laie. President McKay declared that Laie had the potential of becoming "a missionary factor, influencing not thousands, not tens of thousands, but millions of people who will come seeking to know what this town and its significance are" (Knowles, *Howard W. Hunter*, 205).

Elder Hunter caught the vision of these prophetic words and helped make them come true. When he was released in 1976, he recorded:

> This brings to a close the period of twelve years I have headed this enterprise. During this time we have converted from a substantial operating loss to a very profitable operation. Thousands of students from the South Pacific have been assisted in getting their education, most of whom would not have been able to leave their islands to go to school except for this assistance. The center has given large sums to the BYU-Hawaii campus, has become a major factor in building the image of the Church and promoting a missionary effort, has improved the community of Laie, and has become the most patronized tourist attraction in Hawaii (Knowles, *Howard W. Hunter*, 208-9).

In 1975, Elder Hunter was asked to travel to Mexico to divide and realign five stakes. He recorded:

> Our purpose was to reduce the size of the stakes, to better align them, to reduce travel of members, and also to provide for the rapid growth that is taking place in Mexico. It was the consensus that smaller stakes can be better trained, that leadership can be more effective, and the anticipated growth of about 1,000 members . . . will be better fellowshipped. . . .
>
> By eleven o'clock [in the evening] fifteen stake presidencies had been selected and called. . . . I doubt there has ever been such a mass organization in the Church, and we were tired by the time we got home (Knowles, *Howard W. Hunter*, 202).

After reporting to the brethren what he had done, he wrote: "I think the brethren were somewhat shocked, but I know time will prove that my decision was right" (Knowles, *Howard W. Hunter*, 203).

Less than two years later, several of those fifteen stakes were divided again due to the rapid growth of the Church in the area.

><

Elder Hunter also worked extensively in the Middle East. He visited nearly every Islamic nation in the world, and became friends with many heads of state and with government leaders. He also visited the Holy Land on many occasions.

In 1972 he received a special assignment. He later related, "Because I am going to the Holy Land next week, the First Presidency called me to their meeting this morning and asked if I would meet with the group leader [for the Church] in Jerusalem and with the mayor, if necessary, regarding a monument to the prayer of Orson Hyde in Jerusalem" (Knowles, *Howard W. Hunter*, 213).

In following years, Elder Hunter's negotiations resulted in the construction of the Orson Hyde Memorial Garden and the BYU-Jerusalem Center. He was widely praised for his skill in working with government leaders and citizens of Jerusalem. In 1989, when the BYU-Jerusalem Center was dedicated, Elder Hunter was President of the Quorum of the Twelve. He noted:

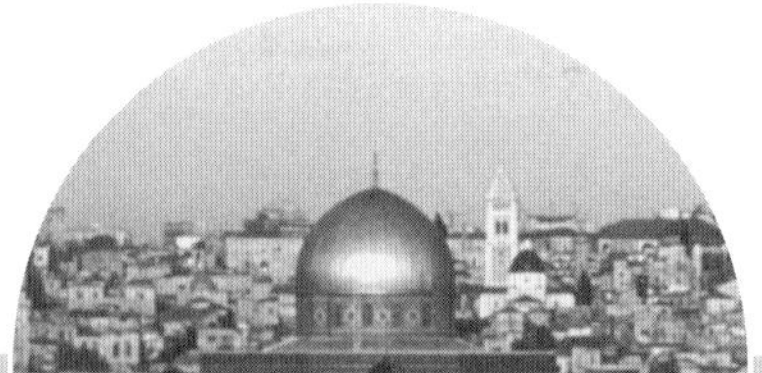

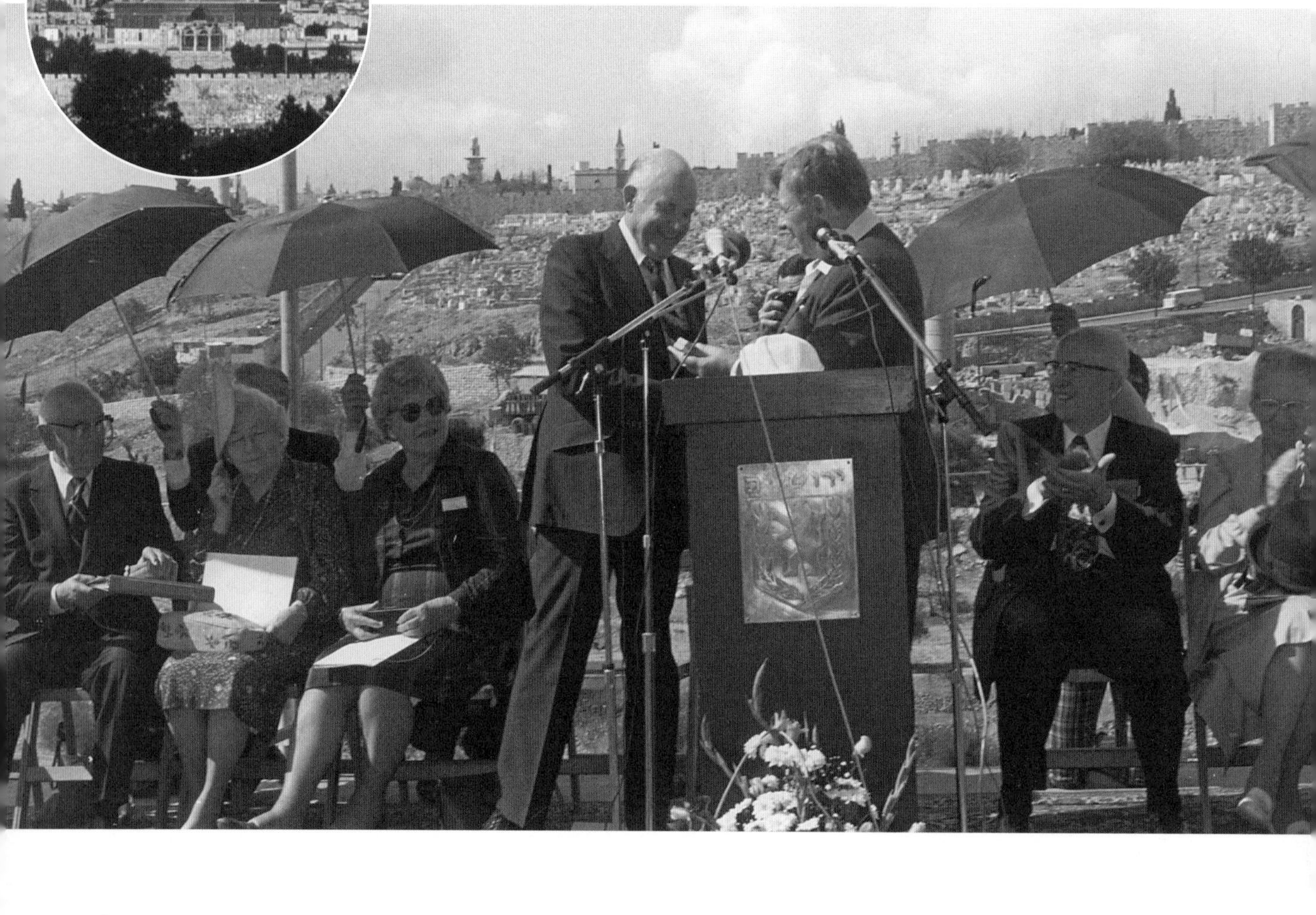

> [*Wednesday, May 19]* was a special day for the administration, faculty and students of the Jerusalem Center. Mayor Teddy Kollek of Jerusalem . . . paid an official visit to the center. He has been a good friend and has helped us in many ways since the beginning of the project. The securing of the land, approval of

JERUSALEM, ISRAEL

HOWARD W. HUNTER WITH MAYOR TEDDY KOLLECK (MAYOR OF JERUSALEM)

plans, and the endless problems of construction would have seemed impossible had it not been for his help and advice.

A large delegation greeted them as they arrived at the front gates at ten o'clock. President Holland escorted them through the domed gallery to the main auditorium. . . . All of the windows look down to the Old City. As they toured the building the mayor repeatedly said, "It is magnificent," and he said to President Holland, "I wasn't prepared to see such a magnificent building" (Knowles, *Howard W. Hunter*, 223–24).

In addition to his busy schedule of Church callings, Elder Hunter had to deal with his wife's failing health. For more than ten years, he tenderly cared for her as she became more and more helpless. After her death in 1983, Elder Faust said, "[The] tenderness which was evident in their communication was heartrending and touching. I have never seen such an example of devotion of a husband to his wife" ("President Howard W. Hunter," *Ensign*, April 1995, 15).

Elder Hunter also suffered from a number of health problems—a heart attack, coronary bypass surgery, bleeding ulcers, gallbladder surgery, and degenerative disks. Back problems eventually forced him into a wheelchair. In 1987, he spoke from his wheelchair:

> Forgive me if I remain seated while I present these few remarks. It is not by choice that I speak from a wheelchair. I notice that the rest of you seem to enjoy conference sitting down, so I will follow your example. . . .
>
> A line from Cervantes' great classic, *Don Quixote*, . . . has given me comfort over the years. In that masterpiece, we find the short but very important reminder that where one door closes, another opens. Doors close regularly in our lives, and some of those closings cause genuine pain and heartache. But I do believe that where one such door closes, another opens (and perhaps more than one), with hope and blessings in other areas of our lives that we might not have discovered otherwise. . . .

BYU Jerusalem Center Located on the Mount of Olives, adjacent to the Mount Scopus campus of Hebrew University, the Center consists of a branch chapel and housing and classrooms for the BYU Study Abroad Program. The official name is the Jerusalem Center for Near Eastern Studies—Brigham Young University.

Jeffrey Roy Holland (1940–), President of Brigham Young University, was present at the dedication of the Jerusalem Center in May, 1989.

World happenings in the year 1989 did not all reflect the joyous milestone achieved in the Church with the dedication of the BYU-Jerusalem Center. In the United States, U.S. savings and loan institutions were failing and losing billions of dollars, prompting new government controls.

This was also the year of an environmental disaster of staggering proportion—the *Exxon Valdeez* ran aground, polluting Alaskan waters with ten million gallons of oil. A continuing agitation for independence in the Soviet bloc heralded widespread political structural changes, the most significant of which was the dismantling of the Berlin Wall.

INIS STANTON HUNTER, second wife of President Hunter.

At various times in our lives, probably at repeated times in our lives, we do have to acknowledge that God knows what we do not know and sees what we do not see. . . .

If you have troubles at home with children who stray, if you suffer financial reverses and emotional strain that threaten your homes and your happiness, if you must face the loss of life or health, may peace be unto your soul ("The Opening and Closing of Doors," *Ensign*, Nov. 1987, 15).

Elder Hunter remarried in April of 1990, but preferred to keep his wedding plans relatively private and quiet, both with his family and the brethren. His biographer, Eleanor Knowles, explains it this way:

Near the end of the Twelve's meeting on Thursday, April 10, after all agenda items had been covered, President Hunter asked, "Does anyone have anything that is not on the agenda?" Having been forewarned privately that their president had something that he wanted to bring up if there was time at the end of their meeting, none of those present said anything. "Well then," he continued, "if no one else has anything to say, I thought I'd just let you know that I'm going to be married this afternoon."

One of the apostles who was there that day said, "My jaw went clear down to the floor, and everyone wondered if they had heard correctly. Then President Hunter, in his very modest way, explained, 'Inis Stanton is an old acquaintance from California. I've been visiting with her for some time, and I've decided to be married.' He explained that President Hinckley was going to marry them in the Salt Lake Temple and added, 'I've invited President Monson to be one of the witnesses and Inis's bishop will be the other one.' And then he told us that no one else was invited" (Knowles, *Howard W. Hunter,* 291-92).

PRESIDENT HUNTER'S MINISTRY AS PROPHET

On June 5, 1994, Elder Hunter became President of The Church of Jesus Christ of Latter-day Saints.

As if he knew his time was short, President Hunter began a vigorous ministry. He spoke via satellite to missionaries worldwide from the MTC in Provo. He participated in services at Nauvoo, Illinois, commemorating the 150th anniversary of the martyrdom of Joseph and Hyrum Smith. He traveled to Switzerland and Arizona. In October, 1994, he was sustained by the members of the Church in a solemn assembly as part of general conference. During this conference, he gave four talks. After he was sustained in the Saturday morning session, he said:

In assuming this responsibility, I acknowledge God's miraculous hand in my life. He has repeatedly spared my life and restored my strength, has repeatedly brought me back from the edge of eternity, and has allowed me to continue . . . for another season. I have wondered on occasion why my life has been spared. But now I have set that question aside and ask only for the faith and prayers of the members of the Church so we can work together, I laboring with you, to fulfill God's purposes in this season of our lives. . . .

It has been thirty-five years since I was sustained as a member of the Quorum of the Twelve. Those years have been rich in preparation. I have met the Saints and borne testimony in North and South America; in Europe and Eastern Europe; in Asia, Australia, and Africa; and in the islands of the sea. Many times have I been to the Holy Land and walked where Jesus walked. My walk is slower now, but my mind is clear, and my spirit is young.

PRESIDENT HOWARD W. HUNTER'S FIRST PRESIDENCY: Gordon B. Hinckley (First Counselor), President Howard W. Hunter, and Thomas S. Monson (Second Counselor) at a table in the Church Administration Building.

He reiterated his desire for the Saints to follow the example of the Savior in their lives and realize the importance of the temple, concluding:

> In the ordinances of the temple, the foundations of the eternal family are sealed in place. The Church has the responsibility—and the authority—to preserve and protect the family as the foundation of society. . . .
>
> A worried society now begins to see that the disintegration of the family brings upon the world the calamities foretold by the prophets. . . .
>
> As we become more removed from the lifestyle of the world, the Church becomes more the welcome refuge for hundreds of thousands who come each year. . . .
>
> I pledge my life, my strength, and the full measure of my soul to serving him. May we have ears to hear and hearts to feel, and the courage to follow ("Exceeding Great and Precious Promises," *Ensign*, Nov. 1994, 7-9).

Shortly after his ordination, his cancer, which had been in remission, returned. On March 3, 1995, President Hunter passed away. He was a hard-working, ambitious, warm, loving, quiet, thoughtful, wise man who had known sorrow and joy. During his presidency, Howard W. Hunter emphasized the Savior and temple work. Before his death, at the closing session of the October 1994 conference, President Hunter issued his final challenge to the Saints:

> We are at a time in the history of the world and the growth of the Church when we must think more of holy things and act more like the Savior

would expect his disciples to act. We should at every opportunity ask ourselves, "What would Jesus do?" and then act more courageously upon the answer. . . .

And now, my beloved brothers and sisters, through the power and authority of the priesthood in me and by virtue of the calling which I now hold, I invoke my blessing upon you. I bless you in your efforts to live a more Christlike life. I bless you with an increased desire to be worthy of a temple recommend and to attend the temple as frequently as circumstances allow. I bless you to receive the peace of our Heavenly Father in your homes and to be guided in teaching your families to follow the Master ("Follow the Son of God," *Ensign*, Nov. 1994, 87).

Elder Faust recounted how President Hunter's brief presidency had influenced Church members:

Perhaps the most remarkable occurrence during his short time as President of the Church has been that the members of the Church all over the world have become bonded to him in a special way as their prophet, seer, and revelator. They have seen in him the personification of the attributes of the Savior himself. . . .

Where did he acquire these Christlike qualities which he possessed so richly? No doubt they came as a gift from the eternities before he came to this world. . . .

These heavenly gifts and attributes were honed as he went time, time, and time again to Jerusalem in the Holy Land. . . . His desire to be where the Savior walked and taught seemed insatiable. . . .

Although humble, meek, and unassuming, he was also endowed with great intelligence and determination, always industrious, always working hard at a job trying to better himself. . . . Always charming, gracious, cordial, friendly, gentlemanly, kind, and sympathetic, he had a way of drawing people to him. There was a special magic in his personality. . . . He was at complete peace with himself. . . .

With all of you, I rejoice in the great blessing it has been to have lived at a time when he has been on the earth. We have learned so much from his life, his example, his influence, his love and his testimony ("Howard W. Hunter: Man of God," *Ensign*, April 1995, 26-28).

Following the death of President Hunter, Gordon B. Hinckley was ordained as the fifteenth President of the Church.

GORDON B. HINCKLEY

"Forget Yourself and Go to Work"

President Hinckley was born on June 23, 1910, in Salt Lake City, Utah. One of his ancestors had arrived in America on the Mayflower, and another, Thomas Hinckley, served as governor of the Plymouth Colony from 1681 to 1692.

After graduating from the University of Utah in 1932, Gordon's bishop asked him if he would be willing to serve a mission. The depression had made life difficult for nearly everyone, and when Elder Hinckley received his call to England, he was shocked. England was, at that time, the most expensive mission in the world and he had no idea how he would ever be able to afford to go. He wrote:

> We discovered that my mother, who had passed away, had established a small savings account to be available for this purpose. I had a savings account in a different place, but the bank in which I had mine had failed. . . . My father, a man of great faith and love, supplied the necessary means, with all of the family cooperating at a sacrifice. As I look back upon it, I see all of it as a miracle. Somehow the money was there every month ("The Question of a Mission," *Ensign*, May 1986, 40).

GORDON B. HINCKLEY was sustained as President in 1995.

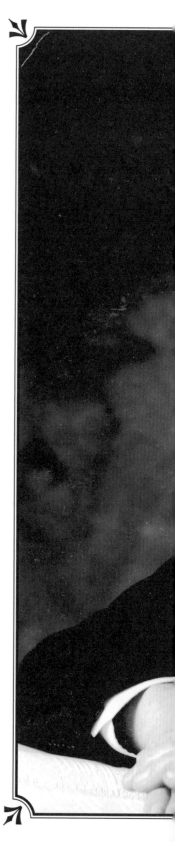

Like most missionaries, Elder Hinckley had trouble adjusting to missionary work:

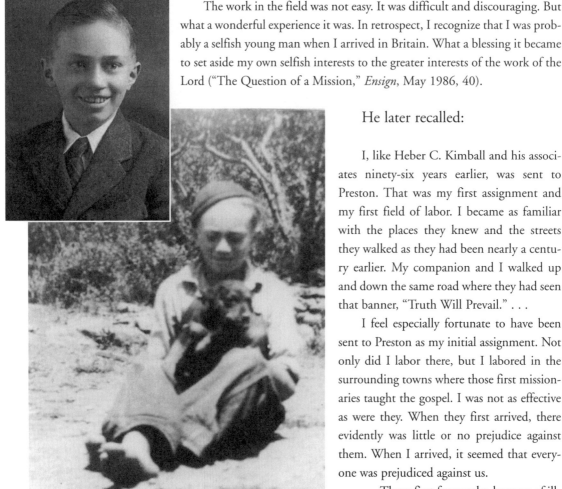

GORDON BITNER
HINCKLEY as a
young boy, and with
his dog.

The work in the field was not easy. It was difficult and discouraging. But what a wonderful experience it was. In retrospect, I recognize that I was probably a selfish young man when I arrived in Britain. What a blessing it became to set aside my own selfish interests to the greater interests of the work of the Lord ("The Question of a Mission," *Ensign*, May 1986, 40).

He later recalled:

I, like Heber C. Kimball and his associates ninety-six years earlier, was sent to Preston. That was my first assignment and my first field of labor. I became as familiar with the places they knew and the streets they walked as they had been nearly a century earlier. My companion and I walked up and down the same road where they had seen that banner, "Truth Will Prevail." . . .

I feel especially fortunate to have been sent to Preston as my initial assignment. Not only did I labor there, but I labored in the surrounding towns where those first missionaries taught the gospel. I was not as effective as were they. When they first arrived, there evidently was little or no prejudice against them. When I arrived, it seemed that everyone was prejudiced against us.

. . . Those first few weeks, because of illness and the opposition which we felt, I was discouraged. I wrote a letter home to my good father and said that I felt I was wasting my time and his money. He was my father and my stake president, and he was a wise and inspired man. He wrote a very short letter to me which said, "Dear Gordon, I have your recent letter. I have only one suggestion: forget yourself and go to work." Earlier that morning in our scripture class my companion and I had read these words of the Lord: "Whosoever will save his life shall lose it; but whosoever shall lose his life for my sake and the gospel's, the same shall save it" (Mark 8:35).

Those words of the Master, followed by my father's letter with his counsel to forget myself and go to work, went into my very being. With my father's letter in hand, I went into our bedroom in the house at 15 Wadham

Road, where we lived, and got on my knees and made a pledge with the Lord. I covenanted that I would try to forget myself and lose myself in His service.

That July day in 1933 was my day of decision. A new light came into my life and a new joy into my heart. The fog of England seemed to lift, and I saw the sunlight. I had a rich and wonderful mission experience, for which I shall ever be grateful ("Taking the Gospel to Britain: A Declaration of Vision, Faith, Courage, and Truth," *Ensign*, July 1987, 6-7).

After he returned from his mission in 1935, Gordon became the executive secretary of the Church Radio, Publicity, and Mission Literature Committee. After a long courtship, Gordon married Marjorie Pay on April 29, 1937, in the Salt Lake Temple. That same year, he also was called as a member of the Sunday School General Board. His every act, whether at home, in his Church callings, or at his place of employment has been characterized by a diligence and enthusiasm that has led to remarkable accomplishments. Throughout his life, he has served the Church—and by forgetting himself, he has gained the love and respect of those he has served.

ELDER GORDON B. HINCKLEY AND MISSIONARY COMPANION, Elder Armand S. Coulam (1914–1984). These young men served together in the British Mission. *ca. 1935*

In April, 1958, Elder Hinckley was called as an Assistant to the Twelve, while serving as president of the East Millcreek Stake. While filling this calling, he attended the dedications of both the London and New Zealand Temples. As supervisor of the Southern Far East and Northern Far East Missions, he traveled extensively in Asia, initiating missionary work and establishing a loving relationship with the Saints in that part of the world..

A CALL TO APOSTLESHIP

Three and a half years later, on September 30, 1961, Gordon B. Hinckley became a member of the Quorum of the Twelve Apostles. At that time, the Church had a membership of 1.8 million members in 345 stakes. As with all his other callings, Gordon was untiring in his service as a special witness of Jesus Christ. He traveled around the world with Marjorie, making stops in Asia, India, Israel, Greece, Germany, Belgium, and England; dedicated chapels and temples in various parts of the world; helped organize the Genesis Group for black Saints; and served as counselor during the presidencies of Spencer W.

Kimball, Ezra Taft Benson, and Howard W. Hunter.

"WE THANK THEE, O GOD, FOR A PROPHET"

After thirty-seven years as a special representative of Christ, Gordon B. Hinckley was sustained as President of the Church on April 1, 1995. In his first conference talk as President of the Church, he said, "I do not know why in His grand scheme one such as I would find a place. But having this mantle come upon me, I now rededicate whatever I have of strength or time or talent or life to the work of my Master in the service of my brethren and sisters" ("This Work Is Concerned with People," *Ensign*, May 1995, 51). He then continued:

We are becoming a great global society. But our interest and concern must always be with the individual. Every member of this Church is an individual man or woman, boy or girl. Our great responsibility is to see that each is "remembered and nourished by the good word of God" (Moroni 6:4), that each has opportunity for growth and expression and training in the work and ways of the Lord, that none lacks the necessities of life, that the needs of the poor are met, that each member shall have encouragement, training, and opportunity to move forward on the road of immortality and eternal life. This, I submit is the inspired genius of this the Lord's work. The organization can grow and multiply in numbers, as it surely will. This gospel must be carried to every nation, kindred, tongue, and people. There can never be in the foreseeable future a standing still or a failure to reach out, to move forward, to build, to enlarge Zion across the world ("This Work Is Concerned with People," *Ensign*, May 1995, 52-53).

After emphasizing the importance of each individual in the Church, President Hinckley expressed his love for the Saints:

I love the people of this Church, of all ages, of all races, and of many nations.

I love the children. . . .

I love the youth of the Church. . . .

I have tremendous respect for fathers and mothers who are nurturing their children in light and truth, who have prayer in their homes, who spare the rod and govern with love, who look upon their little ones as their most valued assets to be protected, trained, and blessed.

I love the elderly who have faced into the storms of life and who, regardless of the force of the tempest, have gone forward and kept the faith. . . .

Now, my brethren and sisters, in conclusion I wish to leave with you one thought which I hope you will never forget.

This Church does not belong to its President. Its head is the Lord Jesus Christ, whose name each of us has taken upon ourselves ("This Is the Work of the Master," *Ensign,* May 1995, 69-70).

WORLD EVENTS

The worst terrorist attack to ever occur on American soil was the bombing of the Murrah Federal building in Oklahoma City if 1995. It left 168 people dead, and a nation in deep mourning. In the Middle East, Israel, in accordance with the peace process, transferred control of the city of Bethlehem to Palestinian authorities. Just weeks later, Prime Minister Yitzhak Rabin was assassinated in Tel Aviv by Yigal Amir, a Jewish student who was angry at Rabin for giving Israel to the Arabs. In the world of sports, and on a happier note, the Atlanta Braves won their first World Series.

GORDON B. HINCKLEY speaks at Sesquicentennial Celebration *July 22, 1997*

In 1997, The Church of Jesus Christ of Latter-day Saints celebrated its susquicentennial of the Saints' arrival in the valley, starting with the reenactment of the Mormon Pioneer Trek—beginning near Winter Quarters, and culminating with a grand celebration in the Salt Lake Valley on July 22–24. President Hinckley was closely involved in the festivities and commemorations that included parades, concerts, and other gala events. He frequently expressed his love for the pioneers whose spiritual and physical hardiness created a legacy of faith for future generations of Church members.

✦

President Hinckley, often accompanied by his dear and faithful wife, Marjorie, has circled the globe, visiting and encouraging the Saints. While visiting members around the world, he became concerned about the inaccessibility of temples for many Saints in various regions of the world. In the October 1997 general conference, he announced that smaller temples would be located in "many areas of the Church that are remote, where the membership is small and not likely to grow very much in the near future." He continued:

Are those who live in these places to be denied forever the blessings of temple

ordinances? While visiting such an area a few months ago, we prayerfully pondered this question. The answer, we believe, came bright and clear.

We will construct small temples in some of these areas, buildings with all of the facilities to administer all of the ordinances. . . . They will be presided over, whenever possible, by local men called as temple presidents. . . . ("Some Thoughts on Temples, Retention of Converts, and Missionary Service," *Ensign*, Nov. 1997, 49).

CONFERENCE CENTER. Completed and dedicated in 2000, this new and magnificent hall seats 21,000 people.

GORDON B. HINCKLEY ANNOUNCING THE PROJECT of the construction of a new conference center. *October 1998*

Since that time, numerous temples have been built in diverse locations, affording hundreds of thousands of Saints the opportunity to enjoy the blessings of participating in holy ordinances for both the living and the dead.

The following year, in the October 1998 general conference, President Hinckley made another major announcement—a new meeting hall. He announced that the new building would seat 21,000—nearly three and a half times the capacity of the Tabernacle. President Hinckley continued, "I do not know if we will fill it, but I do know that we have spoken to much larger gatherings of Latter-day Saints."

In April, 2000, when the first conference was held in this new Conference Center, the building was filled to capacity for each of the five sessions. Over 370,000 requests were made for tickets. Although the organ had not been completed and some areas of the building had not been finished, the 105,000 members who were able to attend were touched by the beautiful music and powerful sermons.

Granite for the building was taken from the same quarry as the stone for the Salt Lake Temple. However, one part of the new building held particular significance for President Hinckley. In his first general conference address in the new building, he related the following story:

> I would like to tell you about another feature of this wonderful building. If I get a little personal and even a little sentimental, I hope you will forgive me.
>
> I love trees. When I was a boy we lived on a farm in the summer, a fruit farm.
>
> Every year at this season we planted trees. I think I have never missed a spring since I was married, except for two or three years when we were absent from the city, that I have not planted trees, at least one or two—fruit trees, shade trees, ornamental trees, and spruce, fir, and pine among the conifers. I love trees.

THE GRANITE QUARRY FOR THE CONSTRUCTION OF THE SALT LAKE TEMPLE is located in Little Cottonwood Canyon. This same quarry was used to obtain granite for the construction of the Conference Center. *ca. 1875*

Well, some thirty-six years ago I planted a black walnut. It was in a crowded area where it grew straight and tall to get the sunlight. A year ago, for some reason it died. But walnut is a precious furniture wood. I called Brother Ben Banks of the Seventy, who, before giving his full time to the Church, was in the business of hardwood lumber. He brought his two sons, one a bishop and the other recently released as a bishop and who now run the business, to look at the tree. From all they could tell it was solid, good, and beautiful wood. One of them suggested that it would make a pulpit for this hall. The idea excited me. The tree was cut down and then cut into two heavy logs.

The end product is beautiful. I wish all of you could examine it closely. It represents superb workmanship, and here I am speaking to you from the tree I grew in my backyard, where my children played and also grew ("To All the World in Testimony," *Ensign*, May 2000, 6).

CONFERENCE CENTER PULPIT made from the wood of a black walnut tree that President Hinckley planted thirty-six years prior to its being used for this pulpit.

The Conference Center was dedicated on Sunday, October 8, 2000, during the morning session of the general conference of the Church. Following the dedicatory prayer, President Hinckley led the congregation in the Hosanna Shout, a unique and thrilling experience both for those in attendance and the many thousands viewing or listening through other media.

President Hinckley dedicated the Palmyra, New York Temple on April 6, 2000. It was a significant event in several respects:

> The Palmyra dedication came on the date marking the 200th anniversary of the Savior's birth, and the new temple is within walking distance of the area where the Prophet Joseph Smith received the vision that heralded the restoration of the gospel. . . . almost 1.5 million people had the opportunity to participate via satellite broadcast. . . . President Hinckley made clear the significance of the place and the building . . . "I regard this temple as perhaps the most significant, in one respect, in the entire Church." . . .

[H]e bore powerful, repeated testimony that the Church organized by the Prophet Joseph Smith truly is the Church of Jesus Christ and that the vision reported by the young Joseph truly did take place in a nearby grove of trees (*Ensign*, May 2000, 107–8).

THE PALMYRA TEMPLE. President Hinckley said, *"I regard this temple as perhaps the most significant . . . in the entire Church."*

In June of 2000, President Hinckley participated in yet another "first" in Church history, dedicating four temples during the same trip. On June 11, he dedicated the Fukuoka Japan Temple; on June 15, he dedicated the Adelaide Australia Temple; on June 16, he dedicated the Melbourne Australia Temple; and on June 18, he dedicated the Suva Fiji Temple. "In addition to dedicating four temples in three nations, President Gordon B. Hinckley met with Church members and governmental leaders in Thailand, Australia, New Caledonia, and American Samoa during his trip across the Pacific in June." Commenting on this experience, President Hinckley said: "You can't look into the faces, light and dark and of all the many nationalities and many cultures and backgrounds, without having a tremendous emotional experience well up within you over what this work is accomplishing" (*Ensign*, Sept. 2000, 72–74). On October 1, 2000, the Boston Massachusettes Temple was dedicated, making it the one hundredth LDS temple in operation. Eleven more temples are presently under construction, and an additional ten temples have been announced.

A BIRTHDAY CELEBRATION

In honor of President Hinckley's ninetieth birthday, a glorious party was held June 23, 2000, in the new Conference Center in Salt Lake City.

> Every seat was filled. The Mormon Tabernacle Choir and Orchestra at Temple Square were in their places. Thousands of flowers bedecked the rostrum. House lights were turned low. The scene was complete when President Hinckley stepped into the spotlight at the podium, wearing a tuxedo adorned by colorful leis sent by Hawaiian, Tongan, and Samoan Saints (President Hinckley Celebrates 90th Birthday, *Ensign*, Sept. 2000, 75).

In his typically gracious and modest manner, President Hinckley declared the evening to be a "gift to the community" rather than an honor for himself.

As part of the gift, President Hinckley selected some of his favorite music for the program, including a repertoire of opera, hymns, folk, and contemporary pieces. . . . "You'll never hear anything better than that!" President Hinckley said in concluding the program, which had brought the house to its feet. . . .

Sister Gladys Knight then joined President Hinckley at the podium and led the audience in singing "Happy Birthday."

"Thank you," he said, becoming emotional when the 21,000 guests sang to him.

"It's worth living until 90 to have something like this" ("President Hinckley Celebrates 90th Birthday," *Ensign*, Sept. 2000, 75).

President Hinckley has been a gracious, caring, and dedicated servant of God. His energy is remarkable, and service has been the trademark of all stages and facets of his life—at home, in the community, and in his Church callings. He has a tremendous optimism about the future and a deep appreciation for the Saints. And combined with that optimism and appreciation is his expectation of excellence in the lives of the members of the Church:

Our membership in The Church of Jesus Christ of Latter-day Saints is a precious thing. It isn't a simple or ordinary thing; this is the Church and kingdom of God. This is the kingdom of God on earth. This is His work in which we are engaged, and there is no more important work in all the world than this work. It concerns the eternal salvation of the sons and daughters of God, those living, those who have lived upon the earth, and those who will yet live. No people have ever been charged with a greater, more inclusive mandate than have we, you and I. Our work, given to us by the Lord, encompasses all of mankind. We need to stand a little taller, be a little kinder, be a little better, each of us, than we have been (Houston, Texas, regional conference, priesthood leadership meeting, Sept. 19, 1998).

PRESIDENT HINCKLEY WITH GLADYS KNIGHT AT HIS 90TH BIRTHDAY CELEBRATION. Over 21,000 guests attended the gala held in the new Conference Center. Gladys Knight led the audience in singing *"Happy Birthday"* to President Hinckley.

CONCLUSION

And so from humble beginnings, The Church of Jesus Christ of Latter-day Saints—like the stone cut out of the mountain without hands—rolls forth. Led by the Savior, its destiny is clear. To a world groping in darkness, the Church stands as a beacon, lighting the way to an eternal association with our Heavenly Father and His Son, Jesus Christ.

Each Prophet in this, the Dispensation of the Fulness of Times, has been a faithful and devoted servant of God—each has filled a unique need and has served an honorable and divine mission.

The history of The Church of Jesus Christ of Latter-day Saints continues to unfold each day, and as President Hinckley has said, "The time has now come to turn about and face the future. This is a season of a thousand opportunities. It is ours to grasp and move forward" ("Look to the Future," *Ensign*, Nov. 1997, 67).

SALT LAKE CITY PANORAMA 1912

DOWNTOWN SALT LAKE CITY. View from the Conference Center looking southeast. The large spire on the left is the Conference Center; the Joseph Smith Memorial Building is to the left of the temple. The Church purchased Main street between Temple Square and the Joseph Smith Memorial Building for the purpose of making an underground parking facility and a beautiful garden area. *2000*

CREDITS
Photographs and Artwork

p. 63   Seneca Lake, New York, © Douglas L. Powell.

p. 64   *Joseph Smith Presides Over the Organization of the Church*, by William Whitaker, pastel on board, ©1970 Intellectual Reserve, Inc.

p. 69   Sidney Rigdon. Photograph courtesy of LDS Church Archives. A Fox and Symons copy of an original.

p. 70   Philo Dibble & Hanna Ann Debois Dibble, courtesy of LDS Church Archives.

p. 71   John Murdock (top), courtesy of LDS Church Archives.

p. 71   Orson Hyde (bottom), courtesy of LDS Church Archives. Photographer: Edward Martin.

p. 72   Edward Partridge, courtesy of LDS Church Archives.

p. 73   Frederick Granger Williams, courtesy of LDS Church Archives.

p. 74   *Enoch Preaching*, by Gary E. Smith, goache on illustration board, ©1975 Intellectual Reserve, Inc.

p. 75   Newell K. Whitney Store, courtesy of LDS Church Archives. Photographer: George Edward Anderson.

p. 76   Independence, Missouri, courtesy of LDS Church Archives. Photographer: George Edward Anderson.

p. 79   Girls in the weaving shed at Holehouse Mill, Blackburn. Courtesy Blackburn Museum and Art Gallery/G. Roland Whiteside.

p. 81   Martin Harris farmland, courtesy of LDS Church Archives. Photographer: George Edward Anderson.

p. 82   Lucy Mack Smith, courtesy of LDS Church Archives. Photograph of engraving: Charles William Carter. Engraved by Charles B. Hall.

p. 84   Valley road to Kirtland Temple, courtesy of LDS Church Archives. Photographer: George Edward Anderson.

p. 86   John Whitmer, courtesy of LDS Church Archives.

p. 90   William Wines Phelps, courtesy of LDS Church Archives. Photographer: Savage & Ottinger.

p. 93   Orson Pratt, courtesy of LDS Church Archives. Engraving: Frederick Piercy.

p. 94   John Johnson, courtesy of LDS Church Archives.

p. 95   *The Evening and the Morning Star*, ©1991 Intellectual Reserve, Inc.

p. 97   William E. McLellin, courtesy of LDS Church Archives.

p. 99   *A Prophet of God*, © Liz Lemon Swindle, pencil sketch, Repartee and Foundation Arts.

p. 100   *Joseph Smith Preaching*, by Mike Malm, oil on canvas, ©1997.

p. 101   John Johnson Farm, courtesy of LDS Church Archives.

p. 103   *Emma's Hymns*, © Liz Lemon Swindle, oil on canvas, Repartee and Foundation Arts.

p. 104   Brigham Young millstream, © Douglas L. Powell.

p. 105   Heber Chase Kimball, courtesy of LDS Church Archives.

p. 107   Brigham Young, courtesy of LDS Church Archives. Albumen print Marsena Cannon, ca. 1851–52. Photograph of print possibly by Charles B. Savage.

p. 108   First Hymnal, courtesy of the LDS Church Archives.

p. 109   War Revelation, © Don O. Thorpe.

p. 112   *Settling Missouri*, by C. C. A. Christensen, oil on canvas, ca. 1870, © Courtesy Brigham Young University Museum of Art. All rights reserved.

p. 117   Zebedee Coltrin, courtesy of LDS Church Archives.

p. 118   Vilate Kimball, photograph of LDS Church Archives. Engraved by H. B. Hall & Sons, ca. 1888.

p. 119   The School of the Prophets (both images), © Intellectual Reserve, Inc.

p. 123   Joseph Smith's plat map of the City of Zion, New Jerusalem, courtesy of LDS Church Archives.

p. 124   Kirtland Temple priesthood pulpits, courtesy Reorganized Church of Jesus Christ of Latter Day Saints, Library-Archives, Independence, Missouri.

p. 126   *Saving the Book of Commandments,* by Clark Kelley Price, oil on canvas, ©1987 Intellectual Reserve, Inc.

p. 126   Book of Commandments, © Intellectual Reserve, Inc.

p. 127   Daniel Dunklin, courtesy of Missouri Historical Society, St. Louis, Missouri.

p. 135   Partial map of Missouri, Illinois, and Arkansas territory by E. Brown and E. Barcroft, ca. 1827. Courtesy of Brigham Young University Harold B. Lee Library map collection.

p. 138   Wilford Woodruff, courtesy of LDS Church Archives.

p. 139   Zera Pulsipher, courtesy of LDS Church Archives.

p. 140   Lyman Wight, courtesy of LDS Church Archives.

p. 141   John Lowry, courtesy of LDS Church Archives.

p. 142   Andrew Jackson, as seen in James Parton's *Life of Andrew Jackson* (Boston and New York: Houghton, Mifflin and Company, 1887).

p. 144   Hyrum Smith, courtesy of LDS Church Archives. Photographer: Charles William Carter.

p. 145   Hyrum Smith's Kirtland home, courtesy of LDS Church Archives. Photographer: George Edward Anderson.

p. 146   Mary Ann Angel Young, photograph of daguerreotype courtesy of LDS Church Archives. Daguerreotype by Marsena Cannon, ca. 1853.

p. 148   *Zion's Camp Arrives in Missouri*, © Intellectual Reserve, Inc.

p. 154   *Abraham Lincoln*, by Dale Kilbourn, © Intellectual Reserve, Inc.

p. 168   Pearl of Great Price Facsimile No. 2 (from the Book of Abraham), *Times and Seasons*, vol. 3, no. 10, 15 March, 1842, 720.

p. 169   Sketch of papyrus found in Egyptian mummy coffin.

p. 170   Eliza Roxey Snow, courtesy of LDS Church Archives.

p. 174   Benjamin Franklin Johnson, courtesy of LDS Church Archives. Photographer: Edward Martin.

p. 175   Kirtland Temple, courtesy of LDS Church Archives. Photographer: George Edward Anderson.

p. 179   *Jesus Christ Appearing to Joseph Smith and Oliver Cowdery in the Kirtland Temple*, by Gary E. Smith, oil on canvas, ©1980. Intellectual Reserve, Inc.

p. 183   John Taylor, courtesy of LDS Church Archives.

p. 184   Lorenzo Snow, courtesy of LDS Church Archives.

p. 186   Erastus Snow (top), courtesy of LDS Church Archives.

p. 186   Kirtland Safety Society note, courtesy of LDS Church Archives.

p. 187   Willard Richards with wife, Jennetta, & son, Heber John. Photograph of daguerreotype courtesy LDS Church Archives. Daguerreotype by Lucian Foster, 1845.

p. 188   Cemetery near Kirtland Temple, courtesy of LDS Church Archives. Photographer: George Edward Anderson, 1907.

p. 189   President Martin Van Buren, courtesy of LDS Church Archives.

p. 197   William Clayton, courtesy of LDS Church Archives.

p. 198   Adam-ondhi-Ahman, courtesy of LDS Church Archives. Photographer: George Edward Anderson.

p. 201   Governor Lilburn Williams Boggs, courtesy of LDS Church Archives.

p. 204   Crooked River battleground, courtesy of LDS Church Archives. Photographer: George Edward Anderson.

p. 205   *Battle of Crooked River*, by C. C. A. Christensen, © Courtesy Brigham Young University Museum of Art. All rights reserved.

p. 206   Site of Haun's Mill, courtesy of LDS Church Archives. Photographer: George Edward Anderson.

p. 208   Amanda Barnes Smith, courtesy of LDS Church Archives.

p. 209   *Massacre of Mormons at Haun's Mill*, ca. 1900, © Intellectual Reserve, Inc.

p. 210   Amasa Lyman, courtesy of LDS Church Archives. Photographer: Charles William Carter.

GEORGE ALBERT SMITH

p. 430 George Albert Smith, courtesy of LDS Church Archives.

p. 432 Bicycle in front of Eagle Gate, courtesy of LDS Church Archives. Photographer: Charles William Carter.

p. 433 George Albert Smith, courtesy of LDS Church Archives. Photographer: Charles Roscoe Savage, 1874.

p. 434 George Albert Smith and brothers, © Intellectual Reserve, Inc.

p. 435 Lucy Emily Woodruff Smith (top), courtesy of LDS Church Archives.

p. 435 Early missionaries (bottom), courtesy of Special Collections, J. Willard Marriot Library, University of Utah. Used by permission.

p. 436 J. Golden Kimball, courtesy of LDS Church Archives.

p. 437 George Albert with Helen Keller, courtesy of LDS Church Archives.

p. 438 President Theodore Roosevelt in Salt Lake City (top), courtesy of LDS Church Archives.

p. 438 *New York Times* (bottom), courtesy of LDS Church Archives.

p. 439 John Henry Smith (Joseph F. Smith's First Presidency), courtesy of LDS Church Archives. Photographer: Charles William Symons.

p. 440 Pliny Titus Sexton, courtesy of LDS Church Archives.

p. 441 George Albert Smith with some family members standing by a plane (top), courtesy of Special Collections, J. Willard Marriot Library, University of Utah. Used by permission.

p. 441 George Albert Smith's First Presidency (bottom), courtesy of LDS Church Archives. Photographer: Clyde Anderson.

p. 442 George Albert Smith with President Harry Truman, courtesy of LDS Church Archives.

p. 444 Saints with potatoes, courtesy of LDS Church Archives.

DAVID O. McKAY

p. 447 David O. McKay, courtesy of LDS Church Archives.

p. 448 David O. McKay & family (both images), courtesy of LDS Church Archives.

p. 449 University of Utah football team, courtesy of LDS Church Archives.

p. 450 David O. McKay as young man, courtesy of LDS Church Archives.

p. 451 *What E're Thou Art, Act Well Thy Part*, courtesy of LDS Church Archives.

p. 452 David O. McKay and his sister, Jeannette McKay, © Intellectual Reserve, Inc.

p. 454 Emma Ray & David O. McKay, courtesy of LDS Church Archives.

p. 455 David O. McKay and Hugh Jenne Cannon in Hawaii, courtesy of LDS Church Archives.

p. 456 David O. McKay and Hugh J. Cannon, courtesy of LDS Church Archives.

p. 457 1947 Wagon Train Reenactment, courtesy of LDS Church Archives.

p. 458 David O. McKay's First Presidency, courtesy of LDS Church Archives. Photographer: Wallace McBride Barrus.

p. 459 Mormon Tabernacle Choir first European tour, © Intellectual Reserve, Inc.

p. 460 David O. McKay with artist's rendition of the Swiss Temple, courtesy of LDS Church Archives.

p. 461 Emma Ray McKay, Cecil B. DeMille, Charlton Heston, and David O. McKay, courtesy of LDS Church Archives.

p. 463 David O. McKay riding his horse, Sonny Boy, courtesy of LDS Church Archives.

p. 465 David O. McKay, courtesy of LDS Church Archives.

JOSEPH FIELDING SMITH

p. 466 Joseph Fielding Smith, courtesy of LDS Church Archives.

p. 468 Ephraim George Holding, courtesy of LDS Church Archives. Photographer: Mikkel A. Faldmo, 1893.

p. 469 Salt Lake Temple Annex, courtesy of LDS Church Archives. Photographer: Charles Roscoe Savage.

p. 470 Joseph Fielding Smith, courtesy of LDS Church Archives.

p. 471 Emily Louis Shurtliff Smith, courtesy of LDS Church Archives.

p. 472 Emily Shurtliff Smith writing, courtesy of LDS Church Archives.

p. 473 Georgina Ethel Reynolds Smith, courtesy of LDS Church Archives.

p. 474 Joseph Fielding Smith with his father, Joseph F. Smith, courtesy of LDS Church Archives.

p. 475 Ben Erastus Rich, courtesy of LDS Church Archives.

p. 477 Joseph Fielding Smith reading to Primary children, courtesy of LDS Church Archives.

p. 478 Bruce Redd McKonkie, courtesy of LDS Church Archives.

p. 479 Joseph Fielding Smith and Jessie Evans Smith, courtesy of LDS Church Archives.

p. 481 Apostle Joseph Fielding Smith "relaxing" in the cockpit of a fighter jet, courtesy of LDS Church Archives.

p. 482 Joseph Fielding Smith's First Presidency, courtesy of LDS Church Archives.

p. 483 Joseph Fielding Smith and Harold B. Lee (top), courtesy of LDS Church Archives.

p. 483 President Richard M. Nixon (bottom), courtesy of LDS Church Archives.

HAROLD B. LEE

p. 485 Harold B. Lee, courtesy of LDS Church Archives.

p. 486 Harold Bingham Lee as a young boy, courtesy of L. Brent Goates.

p. 487 Harold B. Lee as a young man, courtesy of L. Brent Goates.

p. 488 Sparrel Huff & Harold B. Lee, courtesy of L. Brent Goates.

p. 489 Fern Tanner Lee & Harold B. Lee, courtesy of L. Brent Goates.

p. 493 Harold B. Lee with family, courtesy of LDS Church Archives.

p. 494 Harold B. Lee with Spencer W. Kimball, courtesy of LDS Church Archives.

p. 495 Fern Lucinda Tanner Lee, courtesy of LDS Church Archives.

p. 496 Harold B. Lee with his second wife, Freda Joan Jensen Lee, courtesy of LDS Church Archives.

p. 498 Harold B. Lee's First Presidency, © Intellectual Reserve, Inc.

p. 499 Harold B. Lee presiding over first area General Conference in Mexico, © Intellectual Reserve, Inc.

p. 500 Barbara B. Smith, courtesy of LDS Church Archives.

p. 501 Russell Marion Nelson, courtesy of LDS Church Archives.

p. 503 Quorum of the Twelve Quartet, courtesy of LDS Church Archives.

SPENCER W. KIMBALL

p. 504 Spencer W. Kimball, courtesy of LDS Church Archives.

p. 506 Spencer W. Kimball's family, courtesy of LDS Church Archives.

p. 507 Spencer W. Kimball in hay wagon with brothers, Private Collection. Used by permission.

p. 508 Spencer W. Kimball and Clarence Naylor (top), Private Collection. Used by permission.

p. 508 Andrew Kimball (bottom), courtesy of LDS Church Archives.

Note: All images that are copyrighted by Intellectual Reserve, Inc. have been used by permission.

BIBLIOGRAPHY

Anderson, Karl Ricks. *Joseph Smith's Kirtland.* Salt Lake City: Deseret Book Co., 1996.

Anderson, Richard L. "The Impact of the First Preaching in Ohio." *Brigham Young University Studies,* vol. 11 (Summer 1971), 474-96.

Andrus, Hyrum L. *Doctrines of the Kingdom.* Salt Lake City: Bookcraft, 1973.

—, and Helen Mae Andrus. *They Knew the Prophet.* Salt Lake City: Deseret Book Co., 1999.

Arrington, Leonard J. *Brigham Young: American Moses.* Urbana and Chicago: University of Illinois Press, 1986.

—, and Susan Arrington Madsen. *Mothers of the Prophets.* Salt Lake City: Deseret Book Co., 1987.

Austin, Emily M. *Mormonism; or, Life Among the Mormons.* New York: AMS Press, 1971.

Backman, Milton V., Jr. *Eyewitness Accounts of the Restoration.* Orem, Utah: Grandin Book Co., 1983.

—. *The Heavens Resound: A History of the Latter-day Saints in Ohio, 1830-1838.* Salt Lake City: Deseret Book Co., 1983.

Barron, Howard H. *Orson Hyde: Missionary, Apostle, Colonizer.* Bountiful, Utah: Horizon, 1977.

Benson, Ezra Taft. "Beware of Pride," *Ensign,* May 1989, 6-7.

—. "Cleansing the Inner Vessel," *Ensign,* May 1986, 4-7.

—. "Godly Characteristics of the Master," *Ensign,* Nov. 1986, 46-48.

—. "I Testify," *Ensign,* Nov. 1988, 86-87.

—. "A Sacred Responsibility," *Ensign,* May 1986, 78.

—. *Teachings of Ezra Taft Benson.* Salt Lake City: Bookcraft, 1988.

—. "To the Children of the Church," *Ensign,* May 1989, 81-83.

—. "To the Elderly in the Church," *Ensign,* Nov. 1989, 4-8.

—. "To the Fathers in Israel," *Ensign,* Nov. 1987, 48-51.

—. "To the Home Teachers of the Church," *Ensign,* May 1987, 50.

—. "To the Mothers in Zion." Address given at a fireside for parents, 22 Feb. 1987. Published in pamphlet form by The Church of Jesus Christ of Latter-day Saints.

—. "To the Single Adult Brethren of the Church," *Ensign,* May 1988, 51-53.

—. "To the Single Adult Sisters of the Church," *Ensign,* Nov. 1988, 96-97.

—. "To the Young Women of the Church," *Ensign,* Nov. 1986, 84.

—. "To the Youth of the Noble Birthright," *Ensign,* May 1986, 44.

Black, Susan Easton. "The Evils of Rumor: Richmond, Missouri, 1836-1838," in *Regional Studies in LDS History: Missouri.* Eds. Arnold K. Garr and Clark V. Johnson. Provo, Utah: Department of Church History and Doctrine, Brigham Young University, 1994.

—, and Charles D. Tate, Jr., eds. *Joseph Smith, The Prophet, The Man.* Provo, Utah: Religious Studies Center, Brigham Young University, 1993.

Burnett, Peter H. *Recollections and Opinions of an Old Pioneer.* New York: D. Appleton & Co., 1880.

Burton, Alma P. "Karl G. Maeser, Mormon Educator." MS Thesis, Brigham Young University, 1950.

Cannon, George Q. Unpublished manuscript of world tour, Church Archives.

Card, Zina Young Williams. "Short Reminiscent Sketches of Karl G. Maeser." Unpublished typescript. Special Collections, Harold B. Lee Library, Brigham Young University.

Conference Reports. Salt Lake City: The Church of Jesus Christ of Latter-day Saints.

Cook, Lyndon. *The Revelations of the Prophet Joseph Smith.* Provo, Utah: Seventy's Mission Bookstore, 1981.

Corbett, Pearson H. *Hyrum Smith, Patriarch.* Salt Lake City: Deseret Book Co., 1963.

Cornwall, J. Spencer. *A Century of Singing: The Salt Lake Mormon Tabernacle Choir*. Salt Lake City: Deseret Book Co., 1958.

Cowley, Matthias F. *Wilford Woodruff: History of His Life and Labors*. Salt Lake City: Bookcraft, 1964.

Derr, Jill Mulvay, Janath Russell Cannon, and Maureen Ursenbach Beecher. *Women of Covenant: The Story of Relief Society*. Salt Lake City: Deseret Book Co., 1992.

Dew, Sheri L. *Ezra Taft Benson, A Biography*. Salt Lake City: Deseret Book Co., 1987.

Doxey, Roy W., comp. *Latter-day Prophets and the Doctrine and Covenants*. 5 vols. Salt Lake City: Deseret Book Co., 1978.

"Early Scenes in Church History." *Four Faith-Promoting Classics*. Book Eight of the Faith-Promoting Series. Salt Lake City, Juvenile Instructor Office, 1882.

Faust, James E. "Howard W. Hunter: Man of God," *Ensign*, April 1995, 26-28.

Fowles, John L. "Missouri and the Redemption of Zion: A Setting for Conflict," in *Regional Studies in LDS History: Missouri*. Eds. Arnold K. Garr and Clark V. Johnson. Provo, Utah: Department of Church History and Doctrine, Brigham Young University, 1994.

Gates, Susa Young, and Leah D. Widstoe. *Life Story of Brigham Young*. New York: The MacMillan Co., 1930.

Gibbons, Francis M. *David O. McKay: Apostle to the World, Prophet of God*. Salt Lake City: Deseret Book Co., 1986.

—. *Dynamic Disciples, Prophets of God*. Salt Lake City: Deseret Book Co., 1996.

—. *George Albert Smith: Kind and Caring Christian, Prophet of God*. Salt Lake City: Deseret Book Co., 1990.

—. *Harold B. Lee: Man of Vision, Prophet of God*. Salt Lake City: Deseret Book Co., 1993.

—. *John Taylor: Mormon Philosopher, Prophet of God*. Salt Lake City: Deseret Book Co., 1985.

—. *Joseph F. Smith: Patriarch and Preacher, Prophet of God*. Salt Lake City: Deseret Book Co., 1984.

—. *Joseph Fielding Smith: Gospel Scholar, Prophet of God*. Salt Lake City: Deseret Book Co., 1992.

—. *Spencer W. Kimball: Resolute Disciple, Prophet of God*. Salt Lake City: Deseret Book Co., 1995.

Goates, L. Brent. *Harold B. Lee, Prophet and Seer*. Salt Lake City: Bookcraft, 1985.

Godfrey, Kenneth W., Audrey M. Godfrey, and Jill Mulvay Derr. *Women's Voices: An Untold History of The Latter-day Saints, 1830-1900*. Salt Lake City: Deseret Book Co., 1982.

Grant, Heber J. *Gospel Standards,* Salt Lake City: Improvement Era, 1941.

Gunn, Stanley R. *Oliver Cowdery: Second Elder and Scribe*. Salt Lake City: Bookcraft, 1962.

Hafen, LeRoy R., and Ann W. Hafen. *Handcarts to Zion, 1856-1860*. Glendale, Calif.: Arthur H. Clark Co., 1960.

Hartshorn, Leon R., comp. *Classic Stories from the Lives of Our Prophets*. Salt Lake City: Deseret Book Co., 1975.

The Heavens Are Open: The 1992 Sperry Symposium on the Doctrine and Covenants and Church History. Salt Lake City: Deseret Book Co., 1993.

Hinckley, Bryant S. *Highlights in the Life of a Great Leader: Heber J. Grant*. Salt Lake City: Deseret Book Co., 1952.

Hinckley, Gordon B. "Look to the Future," *Ensign*, Nov. 1997, 67.

—. "The Question of a Mission," *Ensign*, May 1986, 40.

—. "Some Thoughts on Temples, Retention of Converts, and Missionary Service," *Ensign*, Nov. 1997, 49.

—. "Taking the Gospel to Britain: A Declaration of Vision, Faith, Courage, and Truth," *Ensign*, July 1987, 6-7.

—. "This Is the Work of the Master," *Ensign*, May 1995, 69-70.

—. "This Work Is Concerned with People," *Ensign*, May 1995, 51.

—. "To All the World in Testimony," *Ensign*, May 2000, 6.

"History of Orson Hyde [1805-1842]," *Millennial Star*, 26 (1864), 742-744.

Holbrook, Joseph. "History of Joseph Holbrook, 1806-1885," typescript, Special Collections, Harold B. Lee Library, Brigham Young University.

Holt, Reva Baker, ed. "A Brief Synopsis of the Life of John Murdock." Provo, Utah: Brigham Young University. 1965.

Hunter, Howard W. "Ezra Taft Benson: A Strong and Mighty Man," *Ensign*, July 1997, 42.

—. "Exceeding Great and Precious Promises," *Ensign*, Nov. 1994, 7-9.

—. "Follow the Son of God," *Ensign*, Nov. 1994, 87.

—. "The Opening and Closing of Doors," *Ensign*, Nov. 1987, 15.

Hunter, Milton R. *Will a Man Rob God?* Salt Lake City: Deseret Book Co., 1952.

Hymns of The Church of Jesus Christ of Latter-day Saints. Salt Lake City: The Church of Jesus Christ of Latter-day Saints, 1985.

I Know That My Redeemer Lives. Salt Lake City: Deseret Book Co., 1990.

Jackman, Levi. "A Short Sketch of the Life of Levi Jackman," typescript, Special Collections, Harold B. Lee Library, Brigham Young University.

Jaques, John. "Life and Labors of Sidney Rigdon," *Improvement Era,* vol. 3 (1899-1900).

Jessee, Dean C. "Joseph Knight's Recollection of Early Mormon History." *Brigham Young University Studies*, vol. 17 (Autumn 1976), 19-39.

—. *Letters of Brigham Young to His Sons*. Salt Lake City: Deseret Book Co. (with the Historical Department of The Church of Jesus Christ of Latter-day Saints), 1974.

—, ed. and comp. *The Personal Writings of Joseph Smith*. Salt Lake City: Deseret Book Co., 1984.

Journal of Discourses. 26 vols. Salt Lake City: Deseret Book Co., 1974.

Kimball, Edward L., and Andrew E. Kimball, Jr. *Spencer W. Kimball, Twelfth President of The Church of Jesus Christ of Latter-day Saints*. Salt Lake City: Bookcraft, 1977.

Kimball, Spencer W. *Faith Precedes the Miracle*. Salt Lake City: Deseret Book Co., 1977.

—. "Fundamental Principles to Ponder and Live," *Ensign*, Nov. 1978, 45-46.

—. *Teachings of Spencer W. Kimball*. Ed. Edward L. Kimball. Salt Lake City: Bookcraft, 1982.

Kimball, Stanley B. *Heber C. Kimball: Mormon Patriarch and Pioneer*. Urbana: University of Illinois Press, 1981.

Kirtland Council Minute Book. Ed. Fred C. Collier and William S. Harwell. Salt Lake City: Collier's Publishing, 1996.

Knowles, Eleanor. *Howard W. Hunter*. Salt Lake City: Deseret Book Co., 1994.

Laub, George. "Diary of George Laub," typescript, Special Collections, Harold B. Lee Library, Brigham Young University.

Lee, Harold B. *Stand Ye in Holy Places*. Salt Lake City: Deseret Book Co., 1976.

—. *Teachings of the Prophet Harold B. Lee*. Salt Lake City: Bookcraft, 1996.

Lyon, Jack M., Linda Ririe Gundry, and Jay A. Parry. *Best-Loved Stories of the LDS People*. Vol. 1. Salt Lake City: Deseret Book Co., 1997.

Madsen, Carol Cornwall. *In Their Own Words: Women and the Story of Nauvoo*. Salt Lake City: Deseret Book Co., 1994.

—. *Journey to Zion: Voices from the Mormon Trail*. Salt Lake City: Deseret Book Co., 1997.

Madsen, Susan Arrington. *The Lord Needed a Prophet*. Salt Lake City: Deseret Book Co., 1990.

Manuscript History of Brigham Young, 1804-1844, 46-47. Ed. Elden J. Watson. Salt Lake City: Smith Secretarial Service, 1968, 1971.

McConkie, Bruce R. "Joseph Fielding Smith: Apostle, Prophet, Father in Israel," *Ensign* (August 1972), 24-28.

—. *Doctrines of Salvation: Sermons and Writings of Joseph Fielding Smith*. 3 vols. Salt Lake City: Bookcraft, 1956.

McConkie, Joseph F. *True and Faithful: The Life Story of Joseph Fielding Smith*. Salt Lake City: Bookcraft, 1971.

McKay, David Lawrence. *My Father David O. McKay*. Salt Lake City: Deseret Book Co., 1989.

McKay, David O. *Cherished Experiences from the Writings of President David O. McKay*. Comp. Clare Middlemiss. Salt Lake City: Deseret Book Co., 1976.

—. *Gospel Ideals*. Salt Lake City: Improvement Era, 1953.

McKay, Llewelyn R. *Home Memories of President David O. McKay*. Salt Lake City: Deseret Book Co., 1956.

McLellin, William E. *The Journals of William E. McLellin, 1831-1836*. Eds. Jan Shipps and John W. Welch. Provo, Utah : BYU Studies, Brigham Young University; Urbana, Ill.: University of Illinois Press, 1994.

Messages of the First Presidency of the Church of Jesus Christ of Latter-day Saints, 1833-1964. 6 vols. Introduction, notes, and index by James R. Clark. Salt Lake City: Bookcraft, 1965.

Miner, Caroline Eyring, and Edward L. Kimball. *Camilla: A Biography of Camilla Eyring Kimball*. Salt Lake City: Deseret Book Co., 1980.

Morrell, Jeannette McKay. *Highlights in the Life of President David O. McKay*. Salt Lake City: Deseret Book Co., 1971.

Morris, Richard B., and Jeffrey B. Morris. *Encyclopedia of American History*. New York: Harper Collins Publishers, 1996.

Mulder, William, and A. Russell Mortensen. *Among the Mormons: Historic Accounts by Contemporary Observers*. Lincoln: University of Nebraska Press, 1958.

Municipal High Council Minutes of Winter Quarters, LDS Archives.

Nelson, Russell M. *From Heart to Heart: An Autobiography*. Salt Lake City: Nelson, 1979.

"Newel Knight's Journal," *Scraps of Biography*. Book Ten of the Faith-Promoting Series. Salt Lake City, Juvenile Instructor Office, 1882.

Nibley, Preston. *Brigham Young, The Man and His Work*. Salt Lake City: Deseret Book Co., 1937.

—. *President David O. McKay*. Salt Lake City: Deseret Book Co., 1951.

—. *The Presidents of the Church*. Salt Lake City: Deseret Book Co., 1977.

Nuttall, John. "Diary of John Nuttall," typescript, Special Collections, Harold B. Lee Library, Brigham Young University.

Otten, L. G., and C. M. Caldwell. *Sacred Truths of the Doctrine and Covenants*. Salt Lake City: Deseret Book Co., 1982.

Parkin, Max H. *Conflict at Kirtland*. Salt Lake City: M. H. Parkin, 1966.

Parry, Jay A., Jack M Lyon, and Linda Ririe Gundry. *Best-Loved Stories of the LDS People,* Vol. 1. Salt Lake City: Deseret Book Co., 1997.

Peterson, Janet, and LaRene Gaunt. *Elect Ladies*. Salt Lake City: Deseret Book Co., 1990.

Peterson, Lauritz G. "The Kirtland Temple," *Brigham Young University Studies,* vol. 12 (Summer 1972), 400-409.

Pratt, Orson. *An Interesting Account of Several Remarkable Visions and of the Late Discovery of Ancient American Records*. Provo, Utah: David C. Marten, 1975.

Pratt (Jr.), Parley P., ed. *Autobiography of Parley P. Pratt*. Salt Lake City: Deseret Book Co., 1985.

"President Ezra Taft Benson: A Sure Voice of Faith," *Ensign*, July, 1994, 19.

"President Howard W. Hunter: Fourteenth President of the Church," *Ensign*, July 1994, 4-5.

"President Howard W. Hunter: The Lord's 'Good and Faithful' Servant," *Ensign*, April 1995, 15.

Proctor, Scot Facer and Maurine Jensen Proctor. *The Revised and Enhanced History of Joseph Smith by His Mother.* Salt Lake City: Bookcraft, 1996.

Pusey, Merlo. *Builders of the Kingdom.* Provo, Utah: Brigham Young University Press, 1981.

"Religious Persecutions: Address to the Saints," given on 24 July 1885; printed in the *Deseret News*, 25 July 1885.

Reynolds, George, and Janne M. Sjodahl. *Commentary on the Book of Mormon.* 7 vols. Salt Lake City: Deseret Book Co., 1976.

Rich, Russell R. *Ensign to the Nations: a History of the LDS Church from 1846-1972.* Provo, Utah: Brigham Young University Publications, 1972.

Rigdon, John Wickliffe. "I Never Knew a Time When I Did Not Know Joseph Smith: A Son's Record of the Life and Testimony of Sidney Rigdon." Ed. Karl Keller. *Dialogue: A Journal of Mormon Thought* (Winter 1966), 15-42.

Roberts, B.H., ed. *History of the Church of Jesus Christ of Latter-day Saints.* 6 vols. Salt Lake City. The Church of Jesus Christ of Latter-day Saints, 1902).

—. *Life of John Taylor.* Salt Lake City: Bookcraft, 1963.

—. *Outlines of Ecclesiastic History.* Salt Lake City: Deseret Book Co., 1979.

Robinson, Ebenezer. "Items of Personal History of the Editor." *The Return.* Vols. 1-3. 1888–1890.

Romney, Marion G. "In the Shadow of the Almighty," *Ensign*, February 1974, 95-96.

Romney, Thomas C. *The Life of Lorenzo Snow.* Salt Lake City: Deseret Book Co., 1955.

—. *The Mormon Colonies in Mexico.* Salt Lake City: Deseret Book Co., 1938.

Smith, Barbara B. "Love Is Life," *New Era,* February 1986, 44-45.

Smith, Emma Hale. Patriarchal Blessing Book #1, LDS Archives.

Smith, Emma. "Last Testimony of Emma Smith," February, 1879, in possession of the archives of the Reorganized Church of Jesus Christ of Latter-day Saints, Independence, MO.

Smith, George A. "My Journal," *The Instructor* 81 (1946), 78, 95.

__. Memoirs of George A. Smith

Smith, George Albert. Editor's Page, *Improvement Era,* July 1945, 98.

—. George Albert Smith Collection, 5:11-12, LDS Archives.

__. *Sharing the Gospel with Others.* Comp. Preston Nibley. Salt Lake City: Deseret Book Co., 1948.

—. *Teachings of George Albert Smith.* Ed. Robert and Susan McIntosh. Salt Lake City: Bookcraft, 1996.

—. *The Pioneer,* July 1951.

Smith, Hyrum M. and Janne M. Sjodahl. *Doctrine and Covenants Commentary*, Salt Lake City: Deseret Book Co., 1923.

Smith, Joseph, Jr., *History of the Church.* Salt Lake City: Deseret Book Co., 1950.

Smith, Joseph F. *Gospel Doctrine.* Salt Lake City: Deseret Book Co., 1939.

Smith, Joseph Fielding. *Church History and Modern Revelation.* Salt Lake City: Council of the Twelve Apostles of The Church of Jesus Christ of Latter-day Saints, 1953.

—. *Essentials in Church History.* Salt Lake City: Deseret Book Co., 1950.

—, comp. *Life of Joseph F. Smith.* Salt Lake City: Deseret News Press, 1938.

—. *Seek Ye Earnestly.* Deseret Book Co., 1970.

Smith (Jr.), Joseph Fielding, and John J. Stewart. *The Life of Joseph Fielding Smith.* Salt Lake City: Deseret Book Co., 1972.

Smith, Lucy Mack. *History of Joseph Smith by His Mother.* Salt Lake City: Bookcraft, 1979.

Snow, Eliza R., *The Biography and Family Record of Lorenzo Snow.* Salt Lake City: Deseret News Co, 1884.

Snow, Lorenzo. "Selected Patriarchal Blessings," New Mormon Studies CD-ROM.

Spencer, Clarissa Young, with Mabel Harmer. *Brigham Young At Home.* Salt Lake City: Deseret Book Co., 1961.

St. George School of the Prophets, minutes, LDS Archives.

Stewart, John J. *Remembering the McKays.* Salt Lake City: Deseret Book Co., 1970

Stout, Wayne D. *Hosea Stout: Utah's Pioneer Statesman.* Salt Lake City: s.n., 1953.

Stubbs, Glen R. "Biography of the Prophet George Albert Smith, 1870-1951." Dissertation, Brigham Young University, Provo, Utah 1974.

Taylor, John. *Gospel Kingdom.* Ed. G. Homer Durham. Salt Lake City: Deseret Book Co., 1987.

Thorp, Joseph. *Early Days in the West.* Liberty, Missouri: Irving Gilmer, March 1924.

Tocqueville, Alexis de. *Democracy in America.* New York: Vintage Books, 1954.

"Tributes and Messages of Appreciation: Spencer W. Kimball," *Ensign,* Dec. 1985, 25.

Tullidge, Edward W. *The Life of Brigham Young; or, Utah and Her Founders.* New York: s.n., 1876.

—. *Women of Mormondom.* New York: Tullidge and Crandall, 1877.

Van Orden, Dell, and J. Melan Heslop, with Lance E. Larsen. "A Prophet for All the World: Glimpses into the Life of Spencer W. Kimball," *Brigham Young University Studies,* vol. 25 (Winter 1985), 49-57.

Van Wagoner, Richard S., and Steven C. Walker. *A Book of Mormons.* Salt Lake City: Signature Books, 1982.

Vogel, Dan, ed. *Early Mormon Documents.* Vols. 1-3. Salt Lake City, Utah: Signature Books, 1996.

Whitney, Orson F. *Life of Heber C. Kimball.* Salt Lake City: Bookcraft, 1945.

Widtsoe, John A., ed. *Discourses of Brigham Young.* Salt Lake City: Deseret Book Co., 1954.

Woodruff, Wilford. "Leaves from My Journal." In *Three Mormon Classics,* comp. Preston Nibley. Salt Lake City: Bookcraft, 1988.

Wilford Woodruff, Salt Lake 18th Ward Chapel. L. John Nuttall Papers, LDS Church Archives.

—. Wilford Woodruff Journal. LDS Archives.

INDEX

1880   1890   1900

1881 1882 1883 1884 1885 1886 1887 1888 1889   1891 1892 1893 1894 1895 1896 1897 1898 1899   1901 1902 1903 1904 1905 1906 1907 1908

CHURCH (1880–1909)

- John Taylor becomes 3rd Pres. of Church; Pearl of Great Price accepted as canon

- Assembly Hall dedicated; "Edmunds Act" toughens anti-polygamy laws; Relief Society opens Deseret Hospital

- First Maori branch organized in New Zealand; Thomas L. Kane dies (advocate for Mormon justice in Missouri and Nauvoo)

- Logan Temple dedicated; Judge Charles Zane convicts hundreds of polygamists; Utahns imprisoned for polygamy

- First LDS meetinghouse in Mexico (Colonia Juarez); 2,000 Mormon women protest federal abuse

- "Edmunds-Tucker Act" passed; Pres. John Taylor dies; Twelve assume leadership; Church property confiscated; U.S. gov. rents back to the Church some of its own property (including temple block)

- Pres. Taylor and others go into hiding to avoid anti-polygamy harassment; Idaho law prohibits Mormons from voting; "Statement of Grievances and Protest" presented to President Cleveland

- Manti Temple dedicated; Stakes instructed to establish academies; George Q. Cannon imprisoned for polygamy

- Wilford Woodruff becomes 4th Pres. of Church; first Relief Society conference

- Pres. Woodruff issues "the Manifesto" ending polygamy; religion classes created for elementary school students

- Relief Society becomes charter member of the National Council of Women

- Capstone placed on Salt Lake Temple

- Apr. 6 - Salt Lake Temple dedicated (40 yrs. after begun) Pres. Harrison grants amnesty to polygamists; Tabernacle Choir wins second prize at Chicago's World Fair; U. S. bill signed authorizing return of Church property (property returned 3 yrs. later)

- U.S. proclamation restores civil rights to polygamists; Geneological Society of Utah organized

- Mar. 28 - Spencer W. Kimball born

- Utah admitted as 45th state of the Union; fast day shifts from Thurs. to Sun.

- The Improvement Era begins publication; Jubilee anniversary of Pioneers of '47

- Youth encouraged to support America in Spanish-American War; Pres. Woodruff dies; Lorenzo Snow becomes 5th Pres. of Church

- Mar. 28 - Harold B. Lee born Pres. Snow reemphasizes law of tithing Aug. 4 - Ezra Taft Benson born

- Lorenzo Snow dies; Joseph F. Smith becomes 6th Pres. of C[hurch]

- Children's Friend published by the Primary

- Brigham Young Academy becomes Brigham Young University

- LDS Hospital opens in Salt [Lake] City; Joseph Smith Memoria[l] Cottage dedicated in Sharon

- Sunday School conducts first classes for adults

- Church purchases Smith farm in Manchester, NY; Nov. 14 - Howard W. Hunter born

- Bishop's tithing storehouse closed

- Weekly ward priesthood meetings commenced

- June 23 - Gordon B. Hinck[ley]

UNITED STATES (1880–1909)

- Thomas Edison invents lightbulb

- American Red Cross organized; James A. Garfield becomes 20th Pres. of U.S.; Garfield assassinated; Chester A. Arthur becomes 21st Pres. of U.S.; Billy the Kid killed; gunfight at the O.K. Corral

- American Baseball Association founded

- U.S. Civil Service System est.; Grover Cleveland becomes 22nd Pres. of U.S.

- World's first "skyscraper," Chicago

- John Fox introduces golf to America

- Statue of Liberty dedicated

- George Eastman introduces Kodak camera

- Benjamin Harrison becomes 23rd Pres. of U.S.

- Rubber gloves used in surgery for first time

- The clothing zipper invented; Sioux massacred at Wounded Knee

- First escalator patented; Sierra Club founded

- Hershey develops "milk chocolate bar"; Cole Porter born; Grover Cleveland becomes 24th Pres. of U.S.

- First moving picture public showing, New York City

- Alaska gold rush; William McKinley becomes 25th Pres. of U.S.

- First magnetic recording of sound; Henry Ford starts Detroit Automobile Co.

- SPANISH-AMERICAN WAR (July–December)

- Human speech transmitted by radio; hamburger invented in New Haven, CT

- J.P. Morgan organizes U.S. Steel Corp.; Pres. McKinley assassinated; Theodore Roosevelt becomes 26th Pres. of U.S.; Walt Disney born; ragtime jazz develops

- Wright brothers first flight at Kitty Hawk, N.C.

- Tyrannosaurus rex discovered, Montana; first teddy bear sold

- San Francisco earthq[uake] levels 490 city blocks

- Baden-Powel[l] Boy Scout m[ovement]

- Hen[ry] Mod[el]

- Helen Keller graduates from Radcliffe

WORLD (1880–1909)

- Cecil Rhodes founds diamond mining De Beers Corp.; Dostoyevsky publishes The Brothers Karamazov

- Jack the Ripper terrorizes London; Belgium hosts first beauty contest

- First underground railroad in London

- First Sherlock Holmes story published, A Story in Scarlet

- Adolf Hitler born; Eiffel Tower opens in Paris

- Karl Benz builds four-wheel motorized car

- Rudyard Kipling publishes The Jungle Book

- Marconi invents radio telegraphy; German physicist discovers x-rays

- First modern Olympics, Athens; Alfred Nobel dies, his will creates the Nobel Prize

- Jewish Zionist Congress meets in Switzerland; the electron is discovered

- Sigmund Freud publishes The Interpretation of Dreams; Paris Metro opens with art nouveau entrances by Hector Guimard

- BOXER REBELLION—China

- BOER WAR—South Africa

- Queen Victoria dies, Edward VII crowned; first electric typewriter, France; boxing legal sport in England

- Aswan Dam completed, Egypt; Beatrix Potter publishes Peter Rabbit; Monet paints Waterloo Bridge

- Jack London publishes Call of the Wild

- Puccini writes Madame Butterfly

- Bloody Sunday, Russia; Norw[ay] gains independence from Swe[den]

- Ghandi begins non-violent resistance in South Africa

- First cubist ex[hibit] paints Les De[moiselles]

- First [?] discov[ery]

1881 1882 1883 1884 1885 1886 1887 1888 1889   1891 1892 1893 1894 1895 1896 1897 1898 1899   1901 1902 1903 1904 1905 1906 1907 1908

1880   1890   1900

1940   1950   1960

1941 1942 1943 1944 1945 1946 1947 1948 1949   1951 1952 1953 1954 1955 1956 1957 1958 1959   1961 1962 1963 1964 1965 1966 1967 1968 19[69]

CHURCH (1940–1968)

- Assistants to the Twelve appointed; Ten millionth endowment for the dead performed

- USS Brigham Young launched

- USS Joseph Smith launched

- Pres. Grant dies; George Albert Smith becomes 8th Pres. of Church; Idaho Falls Temple dedicated

- Church sends aid to Europe

- Church membership reaches one million; Centennial celebration of Pioneers' arrival in Salt Lake Valley

- General conference telecasts begin

- Early Morning Seminary begins in southern California

- Pres. Smith dies; David O. McKay becomes 9th Pres. of Church

- Ezra Taft Benson becomes Secretary of Agriculture

- Church Indian Placement Program introduced

- Swiss Temple dedicated (first temple to use films)

- First student stake organized at Brigham Young University; Los Angeles Temple dedicated; Alvah Boggs, descendant of Governor Boggs, publicly bears testimony of the truthfulness of the Church

- New Zealand Temple dedicated; London Temple (England) dedicated

- Computers aid in providing names to temples; "Every Member a Missionary" program introduced

- First Spanish-speaking stake organized in Mexico City

- Film Windows of Heaven released

- Oakland Temple dedicated; Church pavilion opens at New York World's Fair

- Family Home Evening manuals published

- First South American Stake organized

- Lost Creek Dam completed in Utah

UNITED STATES (1940–1968)

- THE GREAT DEPRESSION

- Pentagon building completed

- Disney's Fantasia debuts

- Japan attacks Pearl Harbor; U.S. enters World War II; Orson Welles' Citizen Kane

- Internment of 110,000 Japanese Americans; Louis F. Fieser invents napalm

- Harry S. Truman becomes 33rd Pres. of U.S.; Atomic bombs dropped on Hiroshima & Nagasaki

- Dr. Benjamin Spock publishes The Commonsense Book of Baby and Child Care

- Henry Ford dies; Jackie Robinson joins Brooklyn Dodgers; CIA & Defense Department created

- Rodgers and Hammerstein's South Pacific opens

- U.S. enters Korean War; Peanuts comic strip premieres

- Color TV introduced in U.S.

- High Noon with Gary Cooper released

- Dwight Eisenhower becomes 34th Pres. of U.S.

- Ernest Hemingway receives Nobel Prize

- Atomic power first used; Disneyland opens

- Elvis Presley tops the charts with "Love Me Tender," "Hound Dog," and "Heartbreak Hotel"

- Dr. Seuss publishes The Cat in the Hat

- Alaska & Hawaii made states; Barbie doll released

- Alfred Hitchcock's Psyco releases

- NASA established

- John F. Kennedy becomes 35th Pres. of U.S.

- John Glenn orbits the earth; Marilyn Monroe dies; Pop Art is at a high

- JFK assassinated; Lydon B. Johnson becomes 36th Pres. of U.S.; Martin Luther King gives "I Have a Dream" speech

- U.S. actively enters Vietnam War

- Miniskirts come into fashion

- Mart[in]

- Ke[nt] University

- Rolling Stone [m]azine publish[ed]

WORLD (1940–1968)

- Florey develops penicillin as an antibiotic

- JAPANESE OCCUPATION OF KOREA

- WORLD WAR II (1939–1945)

- Fungus destroys rice crops outside Bombay, India—kills 1.6 million

- COLD WAR

- Juan Peron elected President of Argentina

- "D-Day"—Allied forces begin liberation of France with invasion of beaches of Normandy

- Dead Sea Scrolls found near Qumran

- State of Israel created in Middle East; Ghandi assassinated

- KOREAN WAR (ends in truce)

- Mt. Everest scaled by Hillary & Norgay; Joseph Stalin dies

- Fidel Castro launches revolution in Cuba; Egypt nationalizes Suez Canal

- Racial apartheid instituted, South Africa; NATO founded; Germany divided into east and west

- U.S.S.R. organizes Warsaw Pact

- U.S.S.R. launches first man-made satellite into space, Sputnik I; "killer bees" from Africa spread to Americas; Pasternak publishes Dr. Zhivago

- U.S.S.R. launches rocket with 2 monkeys on board

- VIETNAM WAR

- Berlin Wall built; Soviet Yuri Gagarin first man to orbit the earth; Bay of Pigs Invasion in Cuba ends in disaster

- Cuban Missile Crisis

- Beatles release "I Wanna Hold Your Hand"; China detonates atomic bomb

- France withdraws fro[m] [NATO?] dong begins Cultural [Revolution]

- SIX-DAY WAR

- Japa[n] stron[g]

1941 1942 1943 1944 1945 1946 1947 1948 1949   1951 1952 1953 1954 1955 1956 1957 1958 1959   1961 1962 1963 1964 1965 1966 1967 1968 19[69]

1940   1950   1960